A WHORE JUST LIKE THE REST

a WHORE JUST LIKE the REST

the **music writings** of
RICHARD MELTZER

DA CAPO PRESS

Library of Congress Cataloging-in-Publication Data
Meltzer, Richard
  A whore just like the rest : the music writings of Richard Meltzer.
    p. cm.
  Includes index.
  ISBN 0-306-80953-2 (pbk.)
    1. Rock music—History and criticism.   I. Title: Music writings of Richard Meltzer.
II. Title.

ML3534.M485 2000
781.66—dc21

cover design by Steven Cooley
text design by Jeff Williams
set in 11-point Janson Text by the Perseus Books Group

Published by Da Capo Press
A Member of the Perseus Books Group
http://www.dacapopress.com

2 3 4 5 6 7 8 9 10—03 02 01 00

CONTENTS

Genesis

Early

Less Early

Even Less

Prime Wallow

Quid Pro Quo

My Inane Career

Punk

Lester

Weddings, Breasts and Dirty Clothes

After

After That

Housekeys to the Kingdom

Whoring Again?

Curtains

To Greg Burk,
a true, true friend among the living,
and Claude Bessy,
the roaring, flaming son of some godless god,
now just another stiff

GENESIS

Grand Introduction

Depending on how you count these things (is a chapbook a *book*, for inst?), I've had between eight and twelve books published, but this is the first one that feels *mandated*. Mandatory—compelled—not by editors or a clamoring public but a screaming need to document my mess before it's too late.

I'm 54. I could live another 30 years, I could be gone in a minute. The way I'm feeling lately it looks closer to a minute. My stamina's so shot a day lasts like four hours. I wheeze and gasp walking to the nearest mailbox. Is my blood pressure (which no doc has checked in ten years) about to cancel my ticker or trigger a stroke? Are these troublesome 'rhoids possibly rectal cancer?

I'm fat, I drink too much. Simple hangovers now last two or even *three* days. In a bar the other week some woman guessed I was 44, but that's only because by some miracle I haven't turned grey yet. I feel grey, I feel old, I *am* old. This could be my last book.

Which leads to the question: How do I feel about "eternity," the "future"? I don't know how I feel about such biz—the notion of a "legacy." Leaving stuff for readers *after I'm dead*. Dunno what I think about *any* of that, that is I never spend time debating it w/ myself. I'm too fucking busy just stacking pieces I've done—picking, choosing, sequencing—while I'm still functional, something that seems RIGHT because, well, such things are *done*, and since it is my wont to neurotically fuss with old papers anyway, to stack 'em myself before somebody else does. 'Cause I don't trust anybody else to, okay?

Basically, tho, all things considered, this may not be the absolute BEST hand of old stuff I happen to hold. It is, however, the only one I'm currently empowered to play: the second or third most vital collection of recycled shit I could, if left to my own etc., probably put together right now. Rock remains topical, so what's an author to do? Part of me feels kind of ambivalent 'bout IT being, perhaps, the last meager slice of the pie for all you guys 'n' gals—Meltzerologists and non-'ologists alike—to chew and swallow. How long might we hafta live to see my 40-page golf rant of '87 collected between covers? My fabulous L.A. Riots piece of '92? My eating-out-of-garbage-cans opus of '74? The unforgettable "Pernod vs. Cinzano" (1969)?

When I moved to Portland three-four years ago, I was astounded to learn that while so many people knew my name, oh boy, they knew it almost solely for its association with the rockwrite game. Sheez. Not that my rockstuff wasn't hot shit—the *hottest* in shit—it's just that it'd been a while (like, oh, TWENTY YEARS) since I'd written about rock-roll in earnest, treated it as a *priority* subject matter, done so from urgencies more pressing than the begetting of minimal income. Talk about typecasting!

I felt a little like the Tombstone Kid, the protagonist of Edward D. Wood's *Crossroads Avenger*, his pilot for an unlikely series about an insurance investigator in the Old West. Incognito in brand new store-bought jeans, the Kid is finally unmasked by an old, wily Gabby Hayes type: "Say, ain't you that insurance feller?" Somehow my own jeans gave me away, and I had to admit that yes, shoot, I was indeed the once-famous rockwrite guy. What a "small" world, I thought—a bizarre fucking place in which such mega-dubious bullcrap might actually still play. What astounds me is not so much that people still wanna read *about* rock as that they might conceivably, of their own free will, have anything further to do with rock*writing*. Y'know, as tossed off by the harness bulls of professional rockscribble.

What daunts me more than a little about this book is the prospect of its re-typecasting me as such an animal. If truth be told, I would rather be known as just another jerk whose name rhymes with "seltzer" than exclusively, or even primarily, as an insurance, er, rock investigator. (Takes all kinds, eh?)

Oh, and if you're here because of the "MUSIC writings" teaser, don't go 'way—there's a carload, a truckload, of jazz, country, even classical in the pages that follow. But sure, yeah, lots o' rock, enough to choke a herd of wildebeest, and hey—really—I was only kidding. I'm *excited*. This stuff is seminal, people, it's superseminal!

Anyway, it's a long story. Let's get started, see what all the fuss is about. Let the legacy itself do some talkin' . . .

1
Rock-Crit Blood 'n' Guts (Part 1)

Well, for starters, I invented this shit. Rock writing. I was first. Well maybe not *literal* first, just one of the first two-three-four, probably the first to take the ball and actually *run* with the fucker; certainly the sole early manjack you're still reading now. Before Lester Bangs was, I am (and he's dead). Which, heck, I dangle as neither credit nor debit—just my way of saying hi.

Hi. I was always a fucking zealot. The giddiest smartass to hold the banner high. This is among *writers* we're talking; the rock-roll flag of whatever. (Something to do with the night.) We'd all be at this party, for inst, for the fabulozoolous Rolling Stones at some fussy French— or was it Italian?—New York eatery. After '72 at the Garden. There's this huge fountain, *indoors*, this incredible fountain—so who's gonna JUMP in the thing? I look around, I don't see no candidates, Mick's asleep face-down on a table. So it's gotta be me—*got* to, right? 'Cause if not, if the option's so clear and *nobody* does it, rock-roll as we um uh know it will um uh *perish*, y'know? . . . that sort of trip.

So I jump and they give me the boot, a big security jerk on each arm. And it wasn't only the *big* stuff I hadda flagwave at, like the Bitter End banned me for throwing banana peels and I think chicken bones at Dr. Hook and his band. The remnants of some crummy, yuggy press food; while they were up there, plodding through "Cover of *Rolling Stone*," at some Z-list press torture. Had I thought in advance I could have brought throwables of my own—dirty socks, a moldy sandwich from the fridge—but you get the idea: I once really, truly *gave a shit*; I cared religiously.

It even got to where—this religious biz—well I fucked three women who had lain with Jim. Morrison. The King of Rock-a-Roll. He was dead. They were in L.A. This is back when I was one big fool for moisture, twelve maybe thirteen years ago, when I sought it *constantly*, so you'd hafta figure the law of averages would dictate an *occasional* insertion where Jim had trod. But *three*, well, and they all said, "Yeah, I fucked him," just like that. So there was no mistaking, and no mistaking my motives—yeah, I sought it. That specifically. One of 'em, my favorite as things worked out, was even the one who drove him to Paris to die. To his flight.

So anyway I'd tell people, I was always a big talker, I'd tell them I fucked three and they'd say, "Christ—that's like fucking *him*." Wrong! Or that I was trying to worm my wiener into lingering tide-pools of his (possibly magical) demon seed—wrong again. No, really, bearing fully in mind that post-Beatles rock-roll godhead has really only computed, viably, as subject not object—as *I* rather than *Thou*—I would tell them (and mean it), "No—it's like *being* him!!"

But that's me. You probably wanna read about *them*. Okay, you get what you pay for—will David Johansen do? 'Cause I've got this good one, the Mercury Xmas party of '72 or '73. Mercury Records. New York '73, that's it, by which time if you had lunch with the publicist all they had for promo albs was Tom T. Hall and Johnny Rodriguez. Not much of a roster; Rod Stewart was long gone. Maybe also Uriah Heep. So anyway it's Xmas, Mercury's a joke and nobody comes, let's say twelve people, fifteen. I'm there, Nick Tosches is there, his wife, my girlfriend, and only because Warner Brothers didn't invite us to *their* posh fuckout a few choice avenoos to the east. Twelve-fifteen exclusive of staff (like this beefy mailroom gaga busting bottles and ripping down decor he'd originally been coerced to put up), and that includes not only the four of us but the only Mercury act to show— perchance to strut—those fabulous incredible New York Dolls. And their entourage of at most three.

Not much of an audience to strut at. But strut they do, and posture, preen, pout. This is, after all, their Big! Year!—they are not gonna waste it. An image fostered, an LP delivered, signed to a major, ready to burst out nationally, internationally—etc., etc., blah, blah, blah. The gaga, meantime, could care less, the publicist, the secretaries, me, Nick, our squeezes. We don't care. NOBODY CARES. If lesser execs had flown in from main-office Chicago they would (one surmises) not care either. A heavy dose of alienation—isn't that what these fine fellows sing about? Isn't it precisely what they, hey hey, *stand for*? Yeah but in context, that context being: starhood per se. Frustrated, their "press" having deserted them for rosier freebies, their major turning minor by the second, their 18-month "stranglehold" on local illusion loosening limp in the ether, they reach for the volume knob, shrieking their affectations a tad louder, and the Arthur Murray Book of Camp, cha-cha-ing 'em more deftly wall-to-wall.

Around & around they spin, but they never quite make it to the macaroni salad, a tight camera right to me and Nick, drunk. Not even half quite, actually, as starch would only wreak *havoc* with their belly lines, but also 'cause (obviously) we hate them and they hate us. Conspicuously. So you get this really amazing standoff: us the only writers, them the only band (hatred between). Like a force field. "Imagine guys *pretending* to be fags!" says Nick at one point, which pointwise seems hardly the issue. Listen—you may not believe it but this was *before* choreographed, telegraphed insincerity was the name of the rock-roll game; before, in any event, it was *compulsory*. Certainly not among its more bonafide, certified quasi-um-*underground* adherents 'n' practitioners. Had there, I'm asking now, '85, been a prior pack of so-called underfolk with as much *negative* existential oompah, who had been so thinly, merely, shoddily "about" things rock, who had tendered such aboutness (known today as "genericness") as so lame a claim of, yes, *innovation*? I mean what *weren't* they nonironically full of shit about? (The sex role stuff being but the cheapest, easiest drop in the pot.)

So anyway I'm standing by the macaroni salad, been there awhile, occasionally dipping my plastic fork into this big *vat* of the slop and up into my mouth, the communal vat nobody's challenged me for access to until suddenly . . . wait, I forgot to tell you how come I hate their guts. It's 'cause summer '72 at the Hotel Diplomat they were stupid enough to pull this ersatz generic-communal "Hey let's all get down" number and then when this poor sucker named Gary Pallens, a Bronx teenager who hung with this pack that later amoeba'ed into the Dictators, who themselves went on to at least do the whole ersatz generic thing *right*, or right enough (but that's a whole nuther etc.), anyway Gary took 'em literally, got up on stage to get down—and they beat the piss out of him.

So I'm at the macaroni, me and Nick but I'm the only one eating, when David Johansen blurts out, "Hey, don't eat it all—save some for meee!" Oh? So I fling him some elbows & mayo—this is *basic* mac salad, none of that "pasta" horseshit as had yet to appear on earth—the twelve or so feet between us. Aim: good, true, but the range is off.

Couple inches short, just missing Dollboy #1's spanking new red leather trousers, which lemme tell you are *beauts*. G-g-gorgeous. Really and truly, howev, leathers are far from absorbent (have worn some myself so I know); would NOT have been stained by the foodstuff. But what does he know from absorbent?—so he throws a shit fit. A classic series of jagged, angular, (perhaps) genuinely bemused oh-how-*could*-yous accompanied by invective, arm flails and general harumphing on the part of his cohorts. A mere twelve feet, maybe even eleven, and yet we stand firm, no threat apparent. As perfect a show of rock-roll sound/fury/harmless-from-the-gitgo as any Cyndi Lauper (for instance) would later, via video, bring to mainstream foreground as *product*.

Finally, to make a long story almost over, we're all outside in the cold, us on the north side of 57th St., Dolls on the south throwing snowballs. Lots, many; at us. Again we stand firm, cheek-turning Christians like you wouldn't *believe*—or at least a pair of "toughies." Our dames, meanwhile, unhip to the true cheese of the "assault" (or dreading, by now, *our* role in so bum a charade), cuss us out and back their heels to a storefront. Minutes go by, lots, many. Fifteen? About fifteen, a quarter fucking hour, and not one frozen *fart* hurled by these New Age beat boys has hit anything but trashcans, light poles, buses or taxis. Not us—true—and we're not even dodging or ducking. Which can get mighty boring, even tough guys (drunk) get bored, we're bored and hoping these gobblers, these turkeys, these jerks who will ultimately pull no more weight than to make the world safe for Motley Crue, whose sole function of note during their collective professional tenure will be as Malcolm McLaren's first test barrel of monkeys, we're bored and hoping these peckers give up soon 'cause we ain't quitting first. No way, then a cop comes along and they scatter like hamsters in the night. And I go home, contemplate sleep, feel like I've just witnessed the planet's latest giant step in Dying.

Yes, I always took it so personal, so serious, so world-cultural, didn't even *use* words like "culture," not then, but still I had a *feeling*. Right, whoops, ME again—Gay Talese I am not. It's hard just to be an observer. New Journalism sure takes a heap o' lying, y'know to lie yourself a story—just a story—by lying yourself *out* of it. It can be done, I've done it; lemme try and lie you one now. Stephen Stills. The Sting of his time: self-satisfied whitebread (or cardboard). Montreal, August '74. I was there but I'm not in it. His wife is, tho.

Veronique Sanson, this French person, French Europe not French Canada, they were married at the time. Both're in town for a show, hers, a superstar import chantoozy; marriage means travel (for stars). It also means, if you're Stephen, both parties parlez in English—tout le temps. It's his rule, he's got bigger bucks, not to mention a bigger duck, er, dick—and at the school he attended, i.e., the *old* one, a man's dick was still his castle. She wants French, does she, well she'll just hafta phone her ma. Months & months of which—the pressure builds—and here they are in (pronounce it right) Kaybek. French being kind of SPOKE here, it is inevitable the dam will break. As her contracted backup, the Ville Emard Blues Band, the 17-piece (no lie) "Grateful Dead of Quebec," tends like her to regard English as its back-burner tongue, 'tain't a minute before she's Frenching like a Frenchman, linguistically speaking. After which hubby—shaking, quaking, fire in his eye—stomps over to bass player Bill Gagnon, grabs his shirt, tells him (loud enough for the Province to hear): "Don't you ever speak in French to *my wife* again!!!"

Loads o' laughs—that's part one. The Sting of his time was real far out. He then goes and hires, no that's the punchline, he's seen *everywhere* at showtime, backstage, onstage, in the wings . . . anywhere where French and the missus run the risk of *extra*professionally intersecting. Singing it, fine, 's one of those occupational givens. Unfortunate perhaps, and since we're on the Good side of the Atlantic maybe a tad *shameful*, but the locals, many thousand turned-on happyfolk, are actually *buying* this shit—mother-tonguish ooh la la l'amour—so chalk one up to philology. Or something; anyway he'll survive. Meantime he's nervous and hovering. You can't look left, right or take a pee without noticing the creep in his Cleveland Browns (22) jersey like off the cover of the *Stills* LP. Finally it's over, the set, the show, there's a party. At which appear not one but *two* Stephen Stillses!! Like he'd hired some guy, or enlisted, a lookalike/dressalike so FOUR EYES could do double the spywork of two! What a dork! (They are no longer hitched.)

So okay, done: a fine tale in which "I" do not appear. Challenges are such a groove, I could prob'ly do it another four-five times, easy, between now and the final curtain, but who fucking needs it—am I right? Besides, and don't laugh, this is true, once upon a time rockwriters *were* rock-rollers; there was no distinction. Well, distinctions yeah like between high and low—I wasn't James Brown and neither was Pigpen—but not between them and us. Not per se, not so's you could notice in any way *they* insisted on pushing, certainly not at the dawn of things, Summer of Love and thereabouts.

Heck, these guys *welcomed* us, or at rock-bottom least the novelty of our parallel mission, the mere fact (dig it) of rock-generated Prose. Imagine, WRITING about rock! They dug it, really, so like first night at Monterey Marty Balin says to me and Sandy Pearlman, *Crawdaddy* jerkjoes who have ventured West solely for IT, that universe-manifesting festival (Pop) which they fucked the film up of *royally*, he says, "What, guys, you have no place to crash? Well by all means cop your z's on the carpeted floor of J. Airplane's motor lodge suite, availing yourselves of our righteous soft drinks and reefer, and please of course rap with us long into the a.m. re all things hip, hep, karmic, and cosmic," or equivalent co-conspiratorial twaddle. Or like '68, after signing and partying with Columbia—marinated octopus and mushroom caps—Big Brother & the Holding Co. bass person Peter Albin, a name lost in the ooze so gosh but you're not as impressed as you should be, invited several Crawdads to catch *The Graduate* with him—in lieu of MEMBERS of his v. own BAND. Hey, look, at the *very* very least we were never as totally, abjectly Outside o' stuff as the beats were to bop, the music *they* interloped, and once at a party J*i*m*i H*e*n*d*r*i*x actually came up, SHOOK MY HAND, and conspiratorially asked, "You were *stoned* when you wrote that [first U.S. Hendrix rant], right?"—which is more than Wardell Gray, let alone George Shearing, ever asked Kerouac.

Us/Them as brothers/sisters in flesh, flash, &tc.; pardon my wistful b.s. How long, tho (in *any* possible world), can such biz *reasonably* expect to endure? All it took in this case, y'know to lower the boom, was the Something we ostensibly conspired at never for godsake Happening At All; this made all too clear ("Death of Rock" historians please note!) by the obvious fact, no later than early '69, of the whole incredible shebang—in its *entirety!*—having gone to Product like so much terminal meat. With megabuck dice at last rolling *generally*, not just for Beatles and Stones, "publicity" departments grew in size, stature and malfeasance at companies great and small, not so much to directly generate sales (the domain, more properly of "promotion" and "marketing") as to placate the overpriced talent—*look ma, my album reviewed!*—and forcefeed fans a see-Spot-run of unfolding corporate b.m. Necessitating us writefolk trash, if we wanted in at all, to abdicate our Responsibility, that of *being* rock & roll, and accede toot sweet to our first official "duty," that of SHILLING for the bastards by keeping the urgency down, by (like nice li'l ladies & gents) re-viewing, pre-viewing, inter-viewing—in a word, writing *about.* Instead of *from,* from the fount of primal unity, from being the shit (in its purest form) 'stead of standing apart and (by accident) *seeing* it.

To stay in we hadda get Out.

That much was clear. Not that there weren't incentives—and who among us has not been a whore? Records . . . tickets . . . travel . . . ten billion horrible parties. The everpopular *look ma, me in print.* In mags that by now were actually read. Some writers, and this always amazed me, even got off *groupie-ing* the merchandise, just sitting in a room running a tape—oh boy—while some wheezer spoke. Me, I always hated interviews. I was willing to transcribe *their* words 'n' thoughts when they were willing to transcribe mine. They became such coddled schmucks, always crying to be serviced. Writers existed solely to write-about-them. Or even just, well like I was at Island Records, L.A., mid-'72; Jim Capaldi's there, ex-drummer of Traffic. We're introduced, he hears I write, and the first thing he says is "Get me some tea." Get your own tea, fuckface! (And try writing your own reviews.)

So okay, no more shillyshally: *I'm* in the rest of these yarns. You couldn't get me out with a crowbar. Enough of this rockocentric, starocentric bullticky. (Unless it wants to write itself.) Time for two more, me in the center, or let's say I'm half, of each. Which means *they're* half—and could be writin'—but they won't. Tales of the cancer of starhood—it's a blight, it's a killer. Lou Reed, Patti Smith.

First Lou. Originally we met spring '67 at The Dom, this Warhol-operated pit on St. Marks where Nico was doing three sets a night (backed by the 17-year-old Jackson Browne), but the story starts later, '70, '71. At this Lisa Robinson thing, one of these enormous parties she used to throw, Lou and I are talking and I tell him hey—remember?—we've met before; we'd sat around The Dom, talked music. I'd told him I liked "Black Angel's Death Song"; wow, he'd said, it's his favorite (first V.U. album) cut. Then he'd said listen, here's what's *really* great, his top guitar licks of the moment—George Harrison just before the *fake* ending of "Strawberry Fields" and Jim McGuinn's last nine-ten notes on the album version of "Why." None of which he remembers in '70, '71. Better tho, not in current retrospect (tho plenty okay *then*), he says: "*Wow* that's nice"—prior contact, prior vibes—"'cause y'know you're my favorite writer." Well, gee.

Which gets to be my *role* with him, with Lisa, with Lisa *and* him. I get an invite to another of her whatsems, I arrive and it turns out there's no party but an "intimate gathering"—me, Lisa and her husband Richard, Lou and his soon-to-be first wife, I think her name was

Betty. I look around, I'm not sure what gives, so Lisa pulls me aside, informs me I'm Lou's entertainment. "He really respects you." Uh, great. What gives is Richard's itching to produce the guy—a feather for his wighat, considering all he's done is Hackamore Brick and the Flamin' Groovies. Lou meanwhile is contemplating a "comeback," he's cooling out, working as a bookkeeper or something, writing songs at his parents' house following a so-called *breakdown*, the one you can still hear in progress on *The Velvet Underground Live at Max's*. Exhaustion, collapse; the rock-roll beast. Rightly he's wary, but thinks he could *maybe* return as a solo act.

At an opportune moment Richard hands him an acoustic guitar. He plays, sings rudimentary versions of "Walk on the Wild Side" and that other one, whatever the title, with "They're taking her children away." Invited, I sing harmony. Lisa videotapes, presumably for posterity, and after songs, jokes. Lou goes first, this is still being taped, tells one you've prob'ly heard about two guys out on the town, they try and they try but they can't get laid. They're desperate, it's getting late and they'll settle for anything; I've heard this a thousand times and as he's working it down to the punch line—i.e., they spot a big fat janitor sweeping up, he's got large *nostrils* so they each poke in a prong and pump, they come and the guy sez . . .—I've decided by then to spill the ending. Partly, I guess, to show I'm hip (*Hey Lou, I know it too!*), mainly tho 'cause *everyone* knows the fugger, even if usually the fatty's a woman, tho for bizness reasons (cultural insecurity?) Richard and Lisa are playing it dumb. "So the guy sez 'Do either of you boys have a venereal disease?'"—a rather *polite* telling, usually it's the syph or the clap—"They say 'No' and the guy goes . . . "—and *I* inhale deeply, that's the ending, and Louie is pissed.

The Robinsons too, like maybe I've killed the golden goose but no, was just a faux pas!—'s the Modern Age, and as Cole Porter said, *anything goes*—so he signs with RCA with Richard producing. I'm not forgiven, tho, when eventually I review it, the one called simply *Lou Reed*, and I don't spout whatever the party line was supposed to be. Can't remember what it was I said, those were the days I did 15 reviews a week without even listening, I'd look at covers (if that much) and that was plenty, but I *did* listen to this one, listened and liked it— but no party line so fuck me. At actual Lisa parties, those I was still welcome at (having by then picked up a rep as "Rock's Bad Boy"), Lou started avoiding me, branding it an act of "hostility" every time I tried to dialogue him as a non-deferential equal. Like I'd suggest, playfully, "You and Betty should sing Mamas and Papas harmonies on such and such," and he'd shoot back, "*God* you're hostile; you're telling me it isn't perfect as it is?" or "Whudda *you* know?—you're no musician."

Time marches on, it's '73 or '4 and we ain't spoke for a while when this interview appears in *Zoo World*, Fort Lauderdale's very own, and now very defunct, *Rolling Stone*, wherein Lou accuses me of (this is precious) PLAGIARISM. I've done some lyrics for Blue Oyster Cult, a couple LPs were out by then, maybe three songs're mine, and it seems to him I couldn't've writ diddleyrot—not a wonderful rock and ROLL lyric!!—without having sat at *his* feet, basked in his omnipoetic brilliance. Dunno, I've looked thru the Reed Omnibook (both then and now) and all I can *imagine* having stole from this paranoid lunatic is the word "autograph" from the Velvets' "New Age": "'Can I have your autograph?' he said to the fat blonde actress." In the Cult's "Stairway to the Stars" there's the line "You can have my autograph"—so I guess I must've also stole "can" and "have." Shame on me!

Things continued to deteriorate (Lester Bangs, for inst, told me about this Detroit show where Lou tells him, "Meltzer is number one, Lester you're number two, Pearlman is number three—I hate *all your guts*") 'til finally it's Thanksgiving '76, I'm living in L.A. and Lou's in town on a gig. Just to make contact—hey, it's *been* a while (and maybe I miss his lunacy)—I tell Arista okay, I'll do an interview. Thanksgiving night. So I'm eating my turkey, my stuffing, my cran— . . . r-r-ring goes the phone and it's Arista. Some publicist, Lou's canceled, he wants *nothing to do with me*. Fine, fine; he wantsa bear grudges, I can bear 'em too. I will not listen to groove zero by this asshole again (and I ain't).

Tho maybe you've gathered I don't listen anyway. To rock-roll anything anymore. (Basically I don't.)

Okay, Patti Smith. No room left? Aww. Hate to pull an Arabian Nights, but she'll hafta wait 'til next time. See ya!

(And you can call me Gramps.)

2

Days of Rockwrite Past
(excerpt)

Back in the spring of '64 I was a sophomore philosophy major at the State University of N.Y. at Stony Brook ('s on Long Island), a school only in its second year as well, so they were still rather tolerant—professors with oddball agendas were getting away with it and ditto for similarly inclined grade-chasers. I had this Modern Painting class with Allan Kaprow, the originator of the Environment and the Happening; Sandy Pearlman (later to produce Blue Oyster Cult and the Clash) was also enrolled. One night me and Sandy were doing a paper on the relationship between Fauvism and Futurism (the "bridge" was supposed to be German Expressionism), and we'd already exhausted too many hours talking it out, yielding nothing worth staying up and actually writing, when Sandy says, "I think the real bridge is surf music."

Ha ha, we get a few yucks out of that and head for our respective cells to grind out some Nodoz-assisted standard academic drivel on aspects of color and space in blah blah blah. Not that we lacked the, uh, *courage* to hand in something laced with rock-roll refs, it just seemed too *silly*. (Had to be some *reason* no bonafide scholar had messed with it before!)

Nonetheless, such crypto-scholarly baloney became more automatic in our subsequent "dialogues," aided and abetted by Kaprow lectures on Dada which made it clear that silly and serious were, if not one and the same, at least a snap to collapse, superimpose into a single concept—or handle as a continuum—along with some other dandy pairings like high/low, sophisticated/primitive, relevant/irrelevant, attractive/unattractive, awesome/trivial, original/derivative, real/fake, constructive/destructive, successful/unsuccessful, perfect/flawed, precious/worthless, sacred/profane, etc./etc.

One Sunday afternoon the Sandman and I were guests on the Legs Forbes Show over WUSB, with a range of no further than the campus parking lot. Lou Christie's "Two Faces Have I" was spinning when Forbes, trying to add a touch of whatever to the banal proceedings, asked us to analyze the lyrics. We were about to launch a rant on the obvious hetero/homo dichotomy in the tune when in walked the station manager, an upstate square-and-a-half named W. Ward Clark (a/k/a "The Hick"), who'd already threatened to cancel my own (jazz) show for on-air use of the word "orgasm." So without breaking stride we flew into a take on the two faces instead being FORM and CONTENT.

Hey, it was all interchangeable, even then!

3

Foreword to the Reprint of
The Aesthetics of Rock

Aside from happening to be my own first book, this here whatsis was/is, without much question, the first "serious rock book" ever written (though hardly the first one published), an achievement which I must confess has yet to make me sick. In rereading it now, however, 16 years after it ultimately appeared, I can readily see why certain people might question my motives in sanctioning, at this point in my so-called career, its less-than-inevitable *re*appearance.

There are whole enormous sections of text that seem so subarticulate (inarticulate?) that it would take a guided tour (or a supplemental voice-over cassette) to clarify, or even hint at, what I might conceivably have been trying to "express" in the first place. I use the single word "art," for instance, to unassistedly denote/connote everything from "art history" to "the art experience" to "the art scene" to "artists and their ilk" to "works of art" to "the art-making process" to "artifice" to "the creative impulse" to I don't know, lots of this, that and the other. I overuse (misuse?) such terms as "trivial," "tragic," "repulsive," "chaos," "boredom," "authenticity," and "good/evil" 'til they just lie there dead and pasty like last week's pasta fazool.

Then, likewise, there are passages, paragraphs so druggardly opaque, arcane, abstruse that no authorly assistance—I know my limits!—is at this stage even hypothetically feasible.

It could be argued, furthermore, that my "scholarship" is basically up my butt. As often as not I'll quote Schopenhauer or Heraclitus and then claim Dicky Lee did "Laurie," forget Hank Ballard did a version of "The Twist," and assert—with no probable cause—that Pete Antell's "Night Time" is about vehicular death.

But what *really* should embarrass me is all the misplaced idealism, all these gushing superlatives—"Rock is, after all, the first great in-context/out-of-context revealed religion other than the two-person love unit"; "Rock is the brute actualization where all earlier art is potential"; "Rock is the only possible future for philosophy and art"—for a form, a medium, which in the interim has given us little more than shitpissdoodooweewee w/ and w/out flies.

Lucky for me I don't embarrass e-z. In the course of my reread I've maybe occasionally *winced* a bit, but, hey, I can take it. I can even take it when this jerk, Michael Corcoran, writes in the 8/15/86 issue of the *Austin Chronicle*: "Meltzer's book, *Aesthetics of Rock*, overshadows both the Hitler Diaries and Clifford Irving's Howard Hughes biography in the annals of literary hoaxes. It's been said that if you have an infinite number of monkeys pecking away at an infinite number of typewriters for an infinite amount of time, eventually one of them would write *Hamlet*. It would take about 50 monkeys a couple of years to write *Aesthetics of Rock*." As if he knows what it's like to be a monkey!

First of all, *A. of R.* is hardly a "book" at all—more like a box of very broken (and very greasy) automotive parts. At all stages of its construction I fancied myself as more a visual artist than either a scholar or writer, and insofar as the thing even *contains* writing it's best viewed as simply a typeset *object* ("document") from BEFORE I LEARNED HOW TO WRITE. Now that I'm an international big cheese of the printed page, threading the language needle far and wide, and commanding in the process a whopping four figures (sometimes five!) in annual income, I am in fact *tickled*—you should be too—to face the evidence that I once upon a time mismatched subjects, predicates, *floundered* in the land of commas, and misspelled "cacophony" not once but twice in a single work. Mea culpa, mea culpa: I, monkey, can sure as hell dig it!

But as to the damn thing being a "hoax," geez, this fughead can't just be talking style, wordsmanly credential, degree of professionalism—he must be talking content. What the book "is." So what is it?

Well, as long as you're asking, *The Aesthetics of Rock* [get your felt-tip marker] is the nearly verbatim transcript of my first three years, 1965–68, of beating my head against various walls, personal and systematic, in an unguided, utterly ingenuous, unrestrainedly passionate attempt to make even *provisional* mega-sense out of something, far as I can tell even today, no one previous had particularly cared to "explore," verbally, much more than the frigging surface of: rock rock rock (and ROLL). Of which I was—gosh—a frigging, unwashed "disciple."

At each phase of my whacked-out journey I relied heavily, but not exclusively, on those tools, utensils, chalkboard paradigms proffered by the given moment's life-hand as dealt. In May of '65, for inst, a junior philosophy major (and art minor) at the State U. of New York at Stony Brook, I took an incomplete in something called Philosophy of Literary Form for the express purpose of taking my merry time with a term paper purportedly "about" rock and roll. While not my first stab at a "rock paper"—I'd already gotten A's for comparing Marcus Aurelius with the Beatles (two pages) and tossing off "The Concept of the Synonym in the Dave Clark Five" (three or four)—this one seemed like more than mere calisthenic, and I girded my loins accordingly. I huffed, puffed, read Nietzsche's *Birth of Tragedy*, saw the Beatles at Shea Stadium, revisited both sides of every scratchy 45 (and 78) I still possessed, and some months later turned in 156 pages enigmatically entitled "A Sequel: Tomorrow's Not Today." Topheavy with references to tragedy, comedy, and the proto-"performance art" shtick of my painting teacher, Allan Kaprow, the stack o' pulp got me not only an A+++ but the instructorly scribble—totally unexpected—"Should be published."

So I show it to this sociology prof who claims he'd gotten Grove Press to publish *City of Night*, he takes 'em a xerox, and six months later they say *thanks but no thanks.*

Meantime—fall '66—I'm a grad student at Yale. To beat the draft, sure, but also to "extend the text of philosophy" by dosing it silly with rock and roll. I'm on this mission, see—my undergrad instructors have *perhaps* overencouraged me—so hellbent 'n' stoked I run full throttle, blind, into an ivy-covered wall. I do rock papers, *great* ones, better than last time, for courses with names like Laws of Nature, Being and Becoming in Greek Philosophy, and The Ethical Given in Kant's Second Critique, and for so doing I am KICKED OUT TOOT SWEET ON MY ROCK-ROLL CABOOSE. (A *sensitive* missionary, I cry a river.)

So now, lucky me, I'm out of academia, no way I'll ever be the McLuhan of Rock, and meanwhile a pair of fortuitous whatsems transpire to keep me merrily, zealously a-writin'. First, from out of the blue, there's this quasi-highbrow rock mag, *Crawdaddy!*, which while I was at Yale had already excerpted (and renamed "The Aesthetics of Rock") 20 or so pages from my original undergrad manuscript and which, more importantly, bore the earmarks of being an actual ongoing forum for the promulgation of a "rock consciousness." A far cry from *Song Hits, Hit Parader* and their pulp-teen hype-sheet ilk, *Craw-*

daddy! was the first community of highfalutin "rock writers" per se, and through the spring of '68, when editor/publisher/zealot-in-chief Paul Williams and I had a terminal falling out over who can remember what, they printed virtually everything I gave them.

So I wrote a *lot.* I'd get up in the morning, smoke some dope, put on an LP, enter its, uh, *universe,* take profuse notes, play another album, jump from cut to cut, make the weirdest of plausible connections (no professors—wheeee!—to monitor the hidebound topicality of my thoughts anymore), more notes, more records, occasional meals and masturbation, more more, then hop in the car and drive to Boston for Jefferson Airplane—or Asbury Park for the Doors—and home to write it up on my sister's diet pills.

Still, continuing to regard myself as ostensibly a visualist (and confirming the i.d. by producing, at this nexus, such dandy *objets* as stillborn kittens in jello), I didn't particularly consider myself a "writer" at all: It was more like I simply *had no choice but to get it all down.* The far-as-the-eye-could-see (and -heart-could-feel) (and -mind-could-think) total gestalt of fortuitous whatsem #2, i.e., the emerging rock-correlated real-world *something* that by spring '67 had become one big fat undeniable Public Fact. Ten million new bands, a billion new tunes, a trillion nascent visions and revisions, a growing handful of viable drugs, a sense of *infinite* cultural possibility. When I'd started writing this crap there weren't even all-oldies stations, f'r chrissakes; now there were Jim Morrison, Arthur Lee, Jimi Hendrix.

With *articles* and *pieces* as my units of expression, I spent my time getting it down. For every *Crawdaddy!* piece ("Ah! Ontology," a treatise on "heaven rock"; the self-explanatory "What a Goddam Great Second Cream Album"; the first Hendrix feature in America), there were countless scribblings/typings intended "for no one." This was probably the only time in my writerly life where I kept anything tantamount to a notebook, and the constancy and fidelity of the exercise were, as I remember things, a continual source of general near euphoria. (Of course, the continuing saga of my book—additional rejections by Macmillan, Dutton, Prentice-Hall, New American Library, and six-seven others—I recall with a twinge of grief, so recollections of work-related euphoria may just be so much wish-related b.s.)

Finally, in a pre-spring month of '68, I forget which, somebody went for more than the article, the piece. My old buddy and colleague (high school, college, *Crawdad*) Sandy Pearlman showed a xerox of you-know-what to artist/publisher Dick Higgins, out at Stony Brook for some sort of joint installation with Allan Kaprow and Nam June

Paik, and after not too lengthy a self-conference he took it, bought it, agreed to have his Something Else Press publish the mutha. He gave me like six months to alter it, fatten it, do what I pretty much felt like, but the title—here he stood firm—had to be the arch-artso *Aesthetics of Rock*. Okay, fine, I can live with that . . . and I rose to the task of making the whole mess into a BOOK.

To the bitter end, I'm sure I continued churning out my daily quota of brand new text, tentatively adding it to the jumble of papers already covering the floor, but basically what I did was edit, truncate, order, reorder, mix 'n' match—composition, recomposition *ad infinitum*. Rereading the finished product, I notice very little re*writing* was apparently done—bridges were built, footnotes added, but miles of original text were left untouched—and imagine my major editing cues must've come from *Bike Boy* and *Nude Restaurant*, Warhol films from that time frame which I fucking *adored* . . . and in which footage used equaled total footage shot. Too much of my well-intentioned, yet subintelligible, undergrad hokum, for example, was run unaltered for me to guess that my gameplan could have been other than to let stand—for all bookspan eternity—pages I'd (simply) grown attached to. (How *else* to explain the retention of crude, earlier gropes at terminology—calling a vocal a "solo" or "lead," or a mono recording "single-tracked"—which had already been superseded by both conventional jargon and common cognizance?)

In addition to oh, I'd say 75 pages of unmessed-with college-boy mss., the *Aesthetics* which eventually saw the light of print contains huge chunks chipped from *Crawdaddy!* features, a review of Hendrix's second album rejected by the *New York Times*, a quasi-solicited "think piece" on jazz and rock rejected by *Down Beat*, scraps from the Yale fiasco, and even two pages (linking the Cowsills and the Rolling Stones!) from *Soft Dull*, an attempted first novel I took pleasure in feeding to a Manhattan incinerator in 1972.

I turned the thing in somewhere like mid-October, this is still '68, and it took them something like a year and a half to get it out. What took them so long was getting permission from all these music publishers to reprint lyrics; I'd quoted a ton. Something Else was this small artso company, they'd put out limited-edition concrete poetry anthologies and Claes Oldenburg, Merce Cunningham notebooks— no way could they afford to *pay* for reprint rights. So they had to bargain. For Beatle rights, they dispatched a signed copy of *Sweethearts*, by the Press's Emmett Williams, to Linda McCartney for Valentine's Day. (The Something Else-Beatle Connection—this is true!—had been established when John Cage, compiling an anthology of musical notations, assigned his former colleague Yoko Ono, in London for a gallery opening, the chore of obtaining a Beatle manuscript. She considered her options and finally chose JOHN as the Beatle to invite to the show . . .) How they got the Stones I'm not really sure. Dylan they couldn't get. Through hatchet man Albert Grossman he demanded $7500 per extended lyric; "Like a Rolling Stone," "Positively Fourth Street," et al—and virtually all text deriving from their quotation—had to be deleted from the book.

Also to go was the Appendix. Printing costs being what they were, a designated Epilogue was allowable, hey, but an Epilogue *and* an Appendix—don't be silly. So 30-40 pages went, including, if I remember correctly, treatises on Traffic, Pink Floyd, post-Monterey Otis Redding, and Quicksilver Messenger Service, a comparison of the second Vanilla Fudge album with, no kidding, John Coltrane's *A Love Supreme*, and a "sexual phenomenology" (let's see, the boything goes in the . . .) of "Norwegian Wood." I kept no carbons, I never asked for the pages back, so let's assume they're g-gone for g-good.

But the book—The Book!!—comes out, the 13th or 15th hardcover on the subject, only 2–5 years out of date, and on the basis of having authored it (though few will in fact buy, read, or give off object signs of "understanding" it) I'm sort of a minor celebrity through the summer, fall, winter of 1970. I'm invited to parties, I can get a table at Max's (should I give such a fuck), I'm placed on prime mailing lists, and—hoo hah—I join the ranks of the marginally employed when *Rolling Stone* and *Creem*, post-*Crawdad* biggies whose combined lifetimes at this point barely equal the time I've spent myself sussing out this Thing-called-rock (but to whom, until now, I've been an outsider, an egghead, a bum), suddenly open their pages (and checkbooks) to me.

Etc.

Etc.

Time passes.

During which the Thing became many people's, and a handful of corporations', mega-livelihood, one for which I could scarcely even feign affection. Fortunately, in the years since finishing *Aesthetics*, I'd acquired the wherewithal to occasionally string together sentences which clearly, unequivocally *said something*—something any simpleton could neither misread nor deny. And what I'd say (about most bands, band members, albums, tunes, "trends") was invariably a cross between *Screw this, screw that* and *Hey, it all died in '68 (anyway)!* Because it certainly wasn't very "alive" by '73, '74.

By then my pathetic insistence on keeping the (pre-megabuck) rock-roll "faith" had rendered me persona non grata with most mags, record companies, whomever. Operating under the premise that pranks 'n' antics were the basic, irreducible nub of any "true" rock experience, and that if *I* didn't commit 'em with ongoing frequency no one else would (so g'bye to all THAT), I'd do things like throw rubber snakes at publicists, dance on tabletops at press parties, review (harshly) albums I'd obviously never listened to (or concerts I'd never attended), reverse the word sequence of a text to make it read backwards (or delete, for no particular reason, every fourth word) . . . so by '74 it was pretty much g'bye for *me*. And I've never looked back.

No, that's not true, I look back all the time. But further back than the wretched early '70s. Every time I come home drunk and weepy-eyed from some horrible party where kids half my age, and with triple the energy, sit around a room—there's *always* such a room—doing nothing (not even talk!) but watch rock vids by who could care whom, I run for the headphones, pull out all these records from a time when the music was more concerned with *sound* than image, more about *risk* than fashion, more involved in the *dialectics* of profit than the 'fore-the-fact fact of it, more a touchstone of genuwine *liberation*, by gum, than crowd control for the post-puberty (under-40?) masses . . . I reach, as for a lifeline, for the records described in this book.

Hey, I didn't even *think* things like "liberation" back then. The goddam cup was so *massively* runneth'ing over—what has elsewhere been referred to as "an embarrassment of riches"—that it hardly seemed NECESSARY to define its shape, measure its perimeter, scratch & sniff its biosphere, sociologize its tide patterns, or mop and save its spillage. What seemed like the chore at hand was to dive headlong into an ever-enlarging Sea of Possibility and micromap, between stroke and breath, the vast infrastructure of *all* that it was remotely possible for the damn thing to *already be* . . . no fanciful speculation of "futures" on this swimtrip!

So when I slip out of my trunks, dry myself off, and declare (on p. 333) that "Hey Jude" exhibits a certain hefty quota of "osmotic tongue pressure," you'd better believe that not only am *I* on to something, but the something is shining—blazing!—in the cellular microblahblah of the rock-roll show & tell of I dunno, whatever month that was. That the osmotic tongue pressure of "Hey Jude" and related show'ems may have subsequently thrown in all possible towels is not the issue: Osmotic Tongue Pressure *was*, and was pretty all reet!—even if just as a lamebrain cellular pipedream. Actual futures have a way of disappointing, and the problem with rock is not so much that its future has always been NOW; it's just that its last viable now was pretty much THEN.

Food for thought . . . food for hope. Once upon a time you could be *nourished* by that shit: calories, nutrients, interest, surprise . . . oral mammal urgency. What's there to hope for, to "imagine as possible," today? That Bruce Springsteen and Michael Jackson aren't *literally* the Monkees? That David Byrne isn't Stephen Sondheim? That "We Are the World" isn't "God Bless America" as sung by the DAR? That heavy metal, that last bastion of sonic integrity, is really more than "closet classical music," a digital hoke-up of Wagner, Beethoven, Mussorgsky? Actually I don't mind heavy metal; I just never listen to it.

Except when I'm drunk and weepy-eyed, or at someone else's house, all I listen to anymore is jazz. (And a little dub music.) Rock, when it's totally, gloriously *on*, can go from A to Z—no sweat—*instantaneously*. Cock an ear to "Yes It Is" (Beatles), "Gotta Get Away" (Stones), "When the Music's Over" (Doors), "Here Comes the Night" (Them), "I See You" (Byrds), "The Red Telephone" (Love), "One of Us Must Know" (Dylan). Today, whatever I hear has trouble doing a credible A. Jazz can at least always be counted on for a good solid A, and usually B, C, D as well. (Dub: A, sometimes also B.)

Anyway, fuggit, here's this book. A good book, maybe even a great book, in any event the most excruciatingly "inside IT" book (as opposed to an "on the bus with *purveyors* of IT" book) you will ever meet. Why, at this late date, would a writingperson, sane or un-, choose to go even *halfway* inside the fugger? So this is it. I don't mind having written it, thanks for buying (or stealing) the reprint—thank you, thank you . . . now read everything *else* I've written (it's a whole lot better than this).

Introduction

Let's go chronological for a while.

The '60s. Before they were over they had at least begun.

I was 22, making flagrant demands on the Universe, which in those days the Universe would occasionally buckle to. As some guy later said of my writing back then, it "reversed the usual manner of validating the music," and of me: "instead of trying to enshrine it in the sacred Western canon, he made the tradition of Kant and Schopenhauer meet 'Surfin' Bird' on the Trashmen's own epistemological terms." Hey, you bet.

At the same time, it was pretty much the end, or the beginning of the end, of my overreliance on philosophic namedrop, make that *mere* philosophic namedrop. (Word of the hour: "mere." I had great fun with "mere.") If there's still a hefty residue of that slop, it's counterbalanced favorably by a stiff dose of druggggggs.

It was also a period for which I later got branded as having been more mind than heart: a bum rap if ever there was one. For one thing, this hadda be the highwater moment of rock's *own* assertion of mind in the proceedings, the highnoon where *its* heart, again beating on all chambers, was finally able to storm and *exploit* the goddam mindbank (ideation, structure, quirk, motive intelligence)—which in retrospect STILL seems a big leap forward.

The *musical* adjunct of which was an Apollonian upswing without pre-rock or non-rock taint, well, not *too* much taint (fuck off, "Eleanor Rigby"), or serious loss of Dionysian moxie (eat shit, "Yesterday"). In the hands of major players (Beatles, more or less; Dylan; for a while, the Stones) (Kinks; Byrds; Love; Doors; Velvets) rock's Apollonian tendencies were more often than not, for the time being, right on: an Apollo from within. (Today's Apollonians, by comparison, are not so much "mind"-driven as simply wussed out and flabby.)

Besides, the trip was more '60s-specific than even that, with more of a, well, not quite a hippie flavor—"consciousness" would prob'ly have been the buzz word.

And wasn't "psychedelic" defined as *mind manifesting*? So gimme a break on this mind shit, alright?

NOTE: Contrary to what Bob Roberts, 'scuse me, Bill Clinton (who during his *first term* as prez had already debased and falsified the cultural record) would have you believe, the '60s DID happen, and where they happened most conspicuously was in the music. Something so ACTUAL it could not be wished away, not by anyone, not by any millionsworth of anyones, rock-roll (circa '65–'67) was as f'r real a factor *writ large*—for real *in practice*, official *by acclamation*—as the 24-hour clock that all countries adhere to, by which they in cahoots *operate* . . . believe it.

4

Pythagoras the Cave Painter

This is the Hendrix whatsis alluded to a couple times already. Byron Coley once called it the greatest record review ever written, and who am I to argue? As Jimi surmised, I smoked a lot of reefer to write the thing—one sitting, and better yet: one draft (like virtually all my writing until about 1974).

New questions. New questions? Really? Old philosophers, played out even then, novel even now. But just hear, hear, and listen to the beginning *before* you conceptualize the possibilities for the question "Now that you know who you are, what do you want to be?" actually to be a question as opposed to an even-though-you-know-what-you-know-I-know-that-I'm-ready-to-leave. Gargle with mercury but if you don't know what's coming off you'll never realize that "Third Stone from the Sun" is the *D.C.* comics version of the Silver Surfer on an asphalt trip: that is, you sure as hell have to be arrogant even if you don't particularly groove on ego trips.

Many are the means of allegorically expanding it all and summing it all up. Remember Plato's myth of the cave bit? SEE THE SUN FREE! And Nietzsche: groove on murkiness and Dostoyevski's vaginal pit extensions thereof. And more or at least a few, to name a few. But what happens when everybody has seen the sun and wallowed in the shit? That doesn't mean hey *Time* and *Newsweek* have written up the hippies even though John Cannaday still doesn't understand Rembrandt or Andrew Wyeth. Or Genet is welcome in *Family Circle* and *Family Circle* is welcome in your own home so what do you do now, now that Janis Ian has taken STP and avoids Clearasil. But: Well you just gotta be better in your all-encompassing bit and think and know that better is worth something and worthiness isn't a drag and that infinite regresses are okay. Enter: Jimi Hendrix, standing on his head and knowing what that means too.

Afterthought is a different slightly different story. Inches can be miles if you want them to be, and the ground between the Beatles and the Stones is far greater than that between Jan van Eyck and Hoagy Carmichael, the development from "Dandy" to "Que Vida" is awesomely greater than that bridging the gap between Hans Memling and Marcel Duchamp. Irony is ironically important, and ironically these proportions hold ground anyway. The Byrds *sing* "Eight Miles High"; the Beatles, Stones, Doors and Jimi Hendrix *are* far more than eight miles high, and, with the way up and way down being one and the same, they cover a lot of space, traversing it without moving. Still one place to go. Lastly through a hogshead of real fire. But come up the years, too, perhaps. Perhaps.

Okay, let's work on a logic of ascent/descent that's more fun and less fun than Fitch proofs or Nelson Goodman or even the famous Aristotle. Man like we can be so high that the high is irrelevant and so systematic that system crumbles so we might as well be structurally ready and readily structural so we can guarantee a good time for all total awareness freaks. Of course A and not-A. Of course, of course. Although she feels as though she's in a play, she is anyway. I can pick your face out from the front or behind. It really doesn't matter, if I'm wrong I'm right. And some people like to talk anyway, like Paul McCartney in *The True Story of the Beatles*: "John propositioned me. He told me that he thought the group could do nicely and anyway it was a lot of fun. He didn't talk about the possibility of turning professional. It was me, I think, who realized that skiffle could easily lead to some useful pocket money so that we'd be able to date the girls and maybe get a few clothes for ourselves. Remember, though, we were very young . . . " (a peculiar quotation for a paragraph on logic). Enter: Jimi Hendrix, pre-literate, post-articulate, proto-logical, bi-lingual (at least English and American), plurisignative. His major logical connective:

(A *pubic hair* B)

All you've got to work with at any time is your bank of memories and the state of the world as it is under all sorts of internal and external interactions and things like that. "I Don't Live Today." Okay. Right. Present progressive time sense goes out, future-oriented past and past progressive come in. Jump from speaker to speaker, alternate sounds and silences, you're finally conscious of all the implications of musical spatio-temporality. Fine. Spade rock was three years ago or now or the year of the iron sheep? So? It's also in "Fire."

Law of identity fanaticism? Marvel comics too hung up on the avoidability of the identity of indiscernibles; D.C. knows that if you live on the planet Xzgronl#m you can tell your kid at the ninth meal of the 67.3-hour Xzgronl#mian day that here on our planet Xzgronl#m we eat purple potatoes and groove on bizarre tautologies. Jimi Hendrix grooves on the earth's "strange beautiful crescent green" with its "majestic silver seas" and "mysterious mountains" which he wishes to "see close." And somewhere guitars hum like bumble bees.

All this and deja-vu transcendence too.

Double-standard science-fiction rock too. Byrds have to be uninsulatedly "open" but not if they really knew that openness means inevitable openness to insulation. Paul McCartney suggests merely fixing a hole in Dave Crosby's jewel forest closet, and Jimi Hendrix wonders if maybe this chick's made of gold or something and asks her quite politely, man there are still some standard preciousness metaphors man.

Cage and Stockhausen might not really wanna play tennis with Rauschenberg but Jimi Hendrix wouldn't mind eating Marianne Faithful.

Are unknown tongues (units of change, awe, mere awe, taxonomic urgency) still possible? Sure, but they might just be about as significant as bottle caps. Bottle caps might be significant however too. The world is music but what is music but what is the world too. And monism pluralism monism pluralism too too. One of the alltime great *traditional* unknown tongues occurs early in "Third Stone from the Sun" at the first eruption of the theme played at a random speed which just might be 45 or 33 rpm I guess. But that's not the point about the Hendrix tongue relevance board of directors (get your mind together, there are a whole bunch of you) that should be made to relate to post-Beach Boys ethnomusicology in general. For, along with Schopenhauer, we know that music is the metaphysical equivalent of all the nitty gritty power of nature, but along with Johnny and

Brian and Jimi we know that music is also like the *World Book Encyclopedia* article on Brazil. Obviously Heraclitus contains Anaxagoras, but crystallization out of flux in music or in subway-car stability assertions might also be a different scene too. "Waterfall, don't ever change your ways" in "May This Be Love" is not only perfect Anaxagoreanism in a nutshell but even the perpendicularization of Heraclitus' river. The anti-tongue fadeout of "Foxey Lady" is the death of a guitar string. Best quotation tongue on the album: the Who-like beginning of "Love or Confusion." But how 'bout the beginning of "Hey Joe," a quasi-transitional passage which would be an awesome internal musical thingamajig in any Airplane context? That's nice too. And the first "Are you experienced?" is without doubt *the* definitive jack-in-the-box tongue. Morrison says, "Everybody loves my baby," right there in the middle of "Break On Through," right there conspicuously out of place. Lennon tells you in his book at the movies that he'd love to turn you on, right there where grass smells like World War II English newscasts. But Jimi Hendrix puts the question in the question slot, oh but where did the question slot come from and how did it get there?

"And the wind cries Mary" and "The Wind Cries Mary" sounds old, in a manner which peculiarly makes the whole album sound old for a while, not old as archaic or old like good-time music but old like a few years old. But just for a while, whatever a while is. And it's essentially appropriate that this actual real world introspective psychological time thing has the ring of "Queen Jane" by that groovy old temporally aware Dylan guy. Oh yeah, but on the other hand "May This Be Love" is reminiscent of great American Indian hits of the past as performed by the Crests. It could easily have been a hit as a direct followup to Johnny Preston's "Running Bear" or as a release within six months before or after the Beach Boys' "Ten Little Indians" or as the track before "Tomorrow Never Knows." Anyway, a grandiose *specific* past-oriented temporal tidbit. Open your mouth and you are referential, play a guitar and you are trans-referentially a reference guitar scientist too. Fall asleep and you are lying on an archetype. Hear "move over Rover and let Jimi take over" (in "Fire") and you might just believe you've heard a brand new big dog-little dog variation. "Manic Depression" is a post-*label salvation* song. "Manic depression is frustratin' mess": labeled content already old hat and no longer solution; neat tension between former label as subject and latter as enunciated experiential predicate. Byrds vs. Yardbirds in "Purple Haze" shows you that any polarity is usable, any dualism is okay for two minutes or so. And "not stoned, but beautiful" is an excellent spur-of-the-moment neo-eternal I-don't-want-to-tell-you-this-so-I'll-tell-you-that readymade dualism. "*That's* what I'm talkin' about, now dig *this*" (in "Fire") was ironically written on the same soil as all that Russell-Moore constipation!

Music-noise pleasure/displeasure conditioning is a funny thing. By changing my seat at a Jefferson Airplane performance in Boston a few months ago I discovered that all guitar sounds, down to the merest of guitar sounds, sounded okay from behind the guitar, on the same side of it as the musician. Now I can listen to Jorma on record as if I were in his guitar position. Jimi Hendrix presents a multi-faceted problem with his guitar pluckin', one so vast that it ceases to be a problem as such on the same plane as mere irritations like the sociology of knowledge or medium-message stuff and it merits whole new conceptual schemata replete with matching jargon shoelaces. Like Roland Kirk. Like Jasper Johns. Hendrix's spatial relationship to his guitar transcends any standard finite batch of prepositions. It even requires a few new sexual position-process metaphors, like sychronized cunnilinguo-copulation, since he's obviously capable of playing notes with his teeth while outdoing the whole Bo Diddley-John Lee Hooker mild-mannered exhibitionism with his crotch.

In the case of listening to a standard guitarist on record, the actual audience-artist spatial relationship is epistemologically irrelevant, and aesthetically relevant only in a rather limited setup. Required is a mental picture of the guy facing you and occasionally moving around; in conjunction with this you visually change the situation and sit behind him or turn the stage around, or you put yourself right in his shoes. This requires a tunnel view of space with enlargement-contraction due to imagined distance and 180-degree reversals. Or you can give yourself an *a priori* behind-while-in-front-of sort of compressed tunnel space. But the ambiguity of the actual spatial relationship between you as a person positioned all over the place in the world and such items as the guitar cat at the moment of recording and the hi-fi speakers as apparently flat in front of (as the case just as well might be) you while you're listening x hours later is never much of a concern, simply because it is never much of a concern. Most people, even psychotics obsessed with 180-degree guitar reversals, simply couldn't care less about getting additionally hung up with the problem of determining (or being gripped by the impossibility of ever, ever determining) their *actual* spatial relationship to this guy far over the mountains years and years ago who happened to have recorded the original raunchy version of the tune they happen to be humming while they're facing east, right now (or is it north by northwest and some time other than now, since the *en soi* and *pour soi* just can't get together). Just think about this: Jimi Hendrix makes this new realm of aesthetic psychosis tenable, not only tenable but groovy. You can *care* about it because his space is not tunnel space but PAISLEY SPACE. Not just a cylinder of relevance or a cone of relevances extended to a sphere of relevance, but a *paisley*, metaphorically wondrous and elusive enough to be even more all-encompassing without the "of relevance" attached. Implicitly, the record-listening experience has *always* been far more complex than the in-person experience. The Beatles always knew that. Reversed fadeouts and multitracking even scared some San Franciscans into a preference for live performances. Now Jimi Hendrix has thrown it all into everybody's faces, even the faces of those who have not heard him live or on record and those who never will and those who are frogs.

5

What a Goddam Great
Second Cream Album

And here's what I figure must be my first review of an album I didn't ex-actly love—*appreciating it for* being bad, *or not-good. Probably a sign that "A" bands of the late '60s (post-Beatles/Stones/Dylan) were already having a tough time getting over the hump of even a* second *LP. I never really cared for Clapton—too English Protestant church music-y. Geez I set impossible standards (but it didn't yet bum me out).*

Also, clearly, I'm avoiding all efforts to actually write. *Y'know, behave writerly—string words together for optimum or even semi-optimum clarity, comeliness or any of that—because I viewed such concerns as not only for squares but, well, pre-rock. (That one of rock's FUNCTIONS was to sweep such preoccupations from the table. Forever.) No backslide for this kid!*

Anti-writing? Reads like a cross between Burroughs, Beckett, and an un-copy-edited English-as-a-2nd-language textbook.

Still, it was probably among the first 10–20 or so rock reviews (as such) ever writ, as distinct from, say, jazz reviews in Downbeat, *and it's gotta be at least "4.2 months ahead of time," easy.*

(What a precocious little fuck.)

Mere uniqueness.[1]

Cute little vocals on one end, and top-flight instrumental extravaganzas on the other, slammed together through some sort of DONO-VAN-ZAPPA AVOIDANCE PRINCIPLE too, just a little too elusive to put the finger on.[2]

Not an ounce of eschatological viscera.[3]

With Cream, got to start with the NON-BUMMER GRID OF ANALYSIS: there are no true primary bummers, just non-bummers and non-non-bummers.

Ginger drumming like crossing very early Ringo with football marching band, and that's no bummer altogether.[4] Ginger Baker is basically *pre*-Ringo, if you can imagine both of them in the archaeological scene.[5]

"SWLABR": lots of Trini Lopez vocal by Jack Bruce. Sums up all that is or could be post-Balin. He accomplishes for a male vocalist in "We're Going Wrong" what anything by Janis Joplin would do for a female, or something in that direction anyway.[6]

Only Duane Eddy or Bo Diddley could do a Dizzy Gillespie on guitar and Eric Clapton is—let's see, he's not either A or B, he's C: Clapton. So he *can't* be doin' the Diz. But he is doin' _____.

Waste is rest, and it's restful not embarrassing here, and it implies lack of education to the waste-labelers, a gimmick borrowed from jazz.

"Mother's Lament" suggests the Phil Spector studio intrusion on one of the early Righteous Brothers albums even more than it suggests "Naked If I Want To" or any other bell-ringers of that ilk.[7] Once upon a time while it was playing Memphis Sam donated the comment: "'Strange Brew' is nice."

Cream goes for words about seven years old and 4.2 months ahead of time, implicating themselves in simultaneous necrophilia and prenatalophilia more obviously than do most with this combination as a necessity. "Got this thing, got to keep it sharp"[8] reminiscent of "Gettin' yer fork in the meat."[9] Words either folky or Fuggy, so narrowly miss the NON-NON-NON-NON-NON-BUMMER rap.

"Dance the Night Away" comes on like "Two Faces Have I" when that was fashionable and McGuinn when he was fashionable[10] plus an open window with snow mussin' around out there. No it doesn't.

But this is mystery-book puberty, not physiological puberty, and one of those prostate massages advertised in the *L.A. Free Press* would likely do a lot of harm to Cream.[11]

Thus I highly recommend *Disraeli Gears* (Atco 33-232).[12] Even more highly than the Strawberry Alarm Clock.

But hold on if you have to. That sure isn't enough data to make anybody go out into the cold to buy the album.[13] So here's more, okay? Sure.

Not even mere uniqueness, that is not even unique.

"Outside Woman Blues" is the[14]

"Sunshine of Your Love," right down to Clapton's "Blue Moon" reference pumicelike guitar plunkin', is hard-core RUBBER BAND MUSIC.[15]

"This tree is ugly and it wants to die" is part of the visual-literary bulk of the cover Zappa designed for *Absolutely Free.* He kept it visual-literary cause trees might just eat it as far as he was concerned or at least the concept of an ugly tree hit him only aesthetically or maybe it was all part of some nonspecific Polack joke new-content thing.[16] Cream's "World of Pain" not only is tree-pitying but it is *musical* as well.[17]

"Tales of Brave Ulysses" is the remaining unmentioned track.[18]

Notes

1. And, cause it's English, part of the English programmatic uniqueness scene, a stopover on the ENGLISH PROGRAMMATIC UNIQUENESS TRAIL, and nothing could be finer.

2. So you have either unobvious Smiley Beach Boys and first-album Buckley or you have Bee Gees when they sound like soggy shredded wheat, which is sure o-kay.

3. But typewriters don't have any either, and typewriters are fine.

4. And man, look, there's the DRUMMER BUMMER: really listen to Ringo's "What Goes On" and then listen to Ginger's "Blue Condition" and who knows what will bubble through? Anyway you got this drummer boy in each accompanying his own mere vocal, and why bother saying it's not a bummer just cause it's a standard non-bummer guy with lots of apparent *ad hominem* pressure? Cause you wanna deal with it as *good?* Man that's a drag. Why ignore the GRAND BUMMER just cause either bummers don't seem like moves anymore, or they're too much of a move and you don't wanna do the old Aristotelian piss-on-Plato move? 'Cept now you can deal with the NON-NON-BUMMER. Man you can be sure the innovative and non-mis-understanding BUMMER MOVE is approaching fast, but regrettably not as fast as moves are getting played out. And some day soon Eric Burdon may accept the reemergence of Bobby Vee.

5. In the archaeology cosmic framework, there is a basic BUMMER NEUTRAL-ITY. So you can say all sorts of value-laden stuff about it, like it's good or bad, but with Cream here it doesn't matter before the fact rather than the other way, the way the Kinks pull it off.

6. Ask yourself tonight: What is *vocal* summation?

7. Whadda we do with all this "suggests" and "sounds like" stuff? Get it?: even when BUMMER OBSCURITY snaps out history as inadvertent unavoidable reference to obscurity has become tiresome even though it has.

8. In "Take It Back."

9. You useta hear it everywhere.

10. Nice manifestation of the fact that the Byrds played out the whole Byrds thing on their own, destroying an entire prior eternity which can only return as a NON-

NON-NON-BUMMER MOVE.

11. Although N.S.U. will for all time signify the bike, here there's a hint of NON-SPECIFIC URETHRITIS.

12. All in all, the best and possibly less than the best record to play in the distance while you're smoking it up in the bathroom and you walk out and everybody figures you took a shit or masturbated or something cause you took so long. Cream takes its time too.

13. And what the fuck is the function of the art critic if not precisely to get people to buy records?

14. Very finest oo-hoo, just the very best.

15. If you have a cold, go on: call it the RUBBER BUBBER, go ahead.

16. Well at the very least he didn't mind exposing to ridicule and laughter the poor wretched death-oriented repulsive TREE.

17. Well, maybe Zappa didn't wanna *sing* about it, maybe he really felt bad for the tree and ya know he jus' was bitterly satirizin' tree-hate and insensitivity to tree-sufferin' and yeah that's it, he just couldn't get it up to sing about the whole morbid business. Let's hope that's it and listen to Cream anyway.

18. One of my favorite albums, the others being

6

R. Meltzer Interviewed
by A. Warhol

In the name of greater (albeit synthetic) coherency, this specimen uses simu-
lated speech to sputter out its arcane concept-spew.

Editor Williams refused to let me state that Andy Warhol had inter-
viewed me (some years before Andy in fact did *interviews), insisting such a*
claim would be "putting on" Crawdaddy's *audience, nor would he accept the*
compromise "A. Warhol," and it wasn't until the piece was reprinted in The
Age of Rock 2 *(1970) that the full original title was restored.*

Just before the end, at the urging of my colleague Pearlman, there's a cru-
cial mention of the band he managed, Soft White Underbelly, the v. first in-
stance of my being cajoled/suckered/dragged into shamelessly hyping these
bozos . . . no, in '68 they weren't bozos yet. (See my review of On Your Feet
or on Your Knees, *p. 357.)*

A. A, well-a, ya know, oh you wanna know all about the tongue,
   huh?
Q. How big is it?
A. Imperceptibly tiny one could . . . say. . . .
Q. Is it hot in the summer?
A. Only when it sucks pus-pimps.
Q. Why not upside down, or more directly in fact?
A. I want to tell you all about the UNKNOWN TONGUE.
Q. In fifty-two cogently reversible words, what is an unknown
   tongue?
A. The basic unknown tongue is, if you care, you know you can
   sort of fit it out through all four levels of Plato's divided line,
   you know all those levels. It's increment of change, increment

of awe, increment of mere awe, parenthetical awe, objectified awe or any of that, and lastly, increment of taxonomic urgency, you know like you just gotta label it *tongue*. You know: *there's* a tongue or there *was* a tongue right there. Oh it's a musical transition jargon thing.

Q. How about the need for further analysis and delineation of the paradoxical unknown?

A. Oh balls, the whole analysis of music bit is sort of use a pack of words to tack onto a pack of sounds juxtaposed with a pack of words. Every creep who ever bothered with that sort of crap didn't really groove enough on how silly, in the good sense, the whole operation has to be. How do you *talk* about music, anyway, particularly when. . . . It's also a matter of temporality and analysis, that scene you know. Like Aristotle, the original pumper, did that whole thing with his *Poetics*, you know, give you a hunk of quasi-decent explicit categories that make it so that you alter the way you see drama forever, like you see it as Aristotelian sculpture drama which is a groove but it drags too. So you take the concept of the rock track: it's short, it's not a long tedious grinding thing-in-front-of-you that you not only gotta pay attention to to keep up with but where labels sort of burden your whole temporal thing with the expectation bummer cause they're so easy to stick on legitimately. But you can piss on Sophocles anyway.

Q. Wha?

A. Why I'll be glad to tell you. What I'm sort of dragging my way into is that rock is the best-worst suited for being verbally dissected cause it doesn't matter, and at the same time rock analysis, not any of that Richard Goldstein asswipe or any of that, can be validly insipid and harmless-harmful enough to be irrelevant to rock transition *as* music. Epistemologically it's nice too cause you can repeat the record quick and see if you spotted a genuine tongue if that matters and it don't matter if you scratch the record unless it matters. . . .

Q. How does all of this affect your personal life?

A. Oh, aardvark tits! I guess I'm like an Arab in a burnoose standing almost near a telephone pole watching a swarm of red efts go by . . . anyway, historically, tongue jargon goes back to fall '63 when me and Memphis Sam were readin' this *Time* magazine article on Ray Charles and it said something about Southern gospel experts saying that he speaks the unknown tongue so we decided to find it. So in the Newport recording of I Got a Woman he starts off with something like "Oh sometimes, sometimes I get a little worried, oh but I just wanna tell you it's all right" then he does "be . . ." and takes his time breaking into "cause." The whole band comes in with ". . . cause I got a woman." Well that fragmentation of "because" is *the* definitive primal tongue.

Q. Just to be mundane, can't any musical genre whatsoever have the unknown tongue?

A. Sure, but the thing about rock is that it's really aware of the tongue as mere gimmick and mere structure and the use of any structure as ultimately mere gimmick, readymade or otherwise. With Country Joe, you've got recognition of the mere fact of music, all music. With the Beach Boys in Pet Sounds and the other one, you've got the mere fact of a specific *other* music, Beach Boys classical rock-classical form. The Beatles' move, the big Beatle move in those days, initially, was the explosion of total tongue consciousness.

Q. Well, why is there a tongue here as opposed to there?

A. You stupid or something? There isn't. It's all a matter of audience attention and that sort of thing. Like once I did a tongue demonstration for some guys and I put on I Feel Like Homemade Shit by the Fugs and everybody ignored the standard tongue points I was dealing with, they were just listening for the word "shit" behind all the gobble-gobble. As a moment of forced awareness the shit-point was a tongue.

Q. Are there any other tongues besides *unknown* tongues?

A. You know there are. Scads of em. Implicit tongues are self-explanatory. Meta-tongue is nice. The term is pseudo-philosophical and hence self-playing out . . . a jargon that gets into self-bummer territory before the stuff it's describing and it can't help precipitate playing out the stuff. Listen to that George song on Beatles VI, You Like Me Too Much, there's this part where they're building toward the tongue . . . that's something ya gotta clarify, what does it mean to *expect* the tongue; it's real post-surprise stuff or surprise-composition stuff, sort of just the thing in rock particularly after all that Ornette Coleman-John Coltrane goodies, you know rock irony and transcendental mere regularity . . . oh yeah, the meta-tongue. Well they go into "It's nice when you believe me, . . . if you leave me" and you sorta expect a drum-tongue by Ringo cause it's working that way, but Ringo pulls out and gets subtle as they go on into "I will follow you and bring you back where you belong." They do it twice, it's nice. There's the aquatic tongue transition into the big band in Yellow Submarine, in fact the whole song bobs up and down like the waves of the *standard* aquatic tongue. You can handle the entire Sgt. Pepper album as a meta-aquatic tongue field, I'll tell you about tongue fields right now. Oh I forgot to talk about the meta thing altogether. It's when you have a *different* level of surprise, okay?

Q. Okay, how about tongue fields?

A. Tongue fields are present most generally as entire tracks with constant tongue transition. Tim Hardin stuff, just because you say so, so that they're not mere folk trash, use every note as tongue transition, even the fretting. Incidentally, you could take it as mere external folk trash qua tongue too. The Kinks are masters of the quotation tongue field, you know like transitions of reference abrupt and potent enough to do it; listen to Where Have All the Good Times Gone. Tongue pressure is something else again, it's this setup with transition not merely within a single tongue field, but transition through tongue levels themselves, often with plenty of warning. To this day, Doctor Robert by the Beatles is still the only pure example of tongue pressure, although the break in Donovan's Epistle to Dippy has some degenerate tongue pressure. But tongue pressure is something like the anti-tongue too. The Association and Paul Revere and the Raiders are big anti-tongue groups. With the anti-tongue there's tension as to how that which obviously must be inevitably resolved musically will actually be resolved, it's like sticking overly obvious tongue indicators in your face so the multilevel thing can't be more than merely structural. But then again, tongue as mere structure is sort of the whole pre-rock musical scene anyway. And the Association is great at the irrelevance tongue, where you catch all the levels but many of them are too subterranean to matter except as setups for the ground and a little bit of flight, like with Looking Glass, one of their great masterpieces. Pandora's Golden Heebie Jeebies is nothing short of an anti-tongue pressure field.

Q. What else, oh and why haven't you mentioned the Stones yet?

A. Ah, the Stones have always been apart from standard tongue orthodoxy, and that's swell. Oh yeah, except for their Can I Get a Witness with the break-reentry thing around "... yeah, yeah ... up early in the morning." But they regularly use stuff like the Jagger Crescendo Principle instead of the strict tongue, so they get into second-orifice tongues by hitting you with tongues which appear such that the appearance itself is tonguelike, right? But I wouldn't call the Stones a post-tongue group, they're basically pre-tongue.

Q. Who's post-tongue?

A. The Doors, Love, stuff like that. With Morrison, you've got verbal and vocal freakouts and explosions working at an intensity so different from the moves in the tongue structure of the instrumental thing that it hits too thick to be just a tongue, the tongue is overshadowed. But sometimes there's this overshadow hitting in fusion with a traditional tongue motif anyway. Love uses tongues which are irrelevant merely as tongues cause they have series of entire tongue universes standing around too big for the detail to matter in kind; Arthur Lee's tongues are not straight reference tongues but actually tongues by reference, reference to specifics, reference to the very fact of music as absurd. The San Francisco rock scene is a scene of tongue avoidance if anything; it's sort of an attempt to work out a rock with a pre-rock tongue structure but without a tongue acceptance principle, like check out Morning Dew by the Dead, the tongues don't hit as hard as the hardest part of a song would imply by rock implication. That's sort of the opposite of what the Byrds do with Dylan's stuff. They take The Times They Are A-Changin and give it a time sense that Dylan wasn't up to yet, time as musical time jam-packed with tongues, the nitty-gritty of all temporal perception by the way, and the Byrds leave out that self-conscious dissertation on the metaphysics of time that Dylan had in his last stanza.

Q. Any more types of tongues, and can tongues involve merely words?

A. Oh yeah, words. The best example of the verbal tongue is the opening of Eight Miles High, the transition covered by "Eight miles high ... and when you touch down," and that's enough, even though it's musically reinforced anyway. Other kinds of tongues, well this interview is dull as dirt so I'll just

give you one more: the beef tongue. Obviously, that's a real
fat one. The first eruption of the theme in Jimi Hendrix's
Third Stone from the Sun is a beef tongue.

Q. More.

A. Um, the real masters of the tongue as a conceptual totality are
the Beatles, they cover the whole spectrum, they even use
tongues where other groups have attempted to show the impossibility of tongue interest. Take 2000 Light Years from
Home, it's Baby You're a Rich Man without tongues and not
far enough afield from the tongue universe to be beyond the
tongue. Now if they did it as a move out of the tongue universe along with all other universes, getting progressively further away . . . but it's nice and homey that they don't and
ironic as a chair to see the Stones homey. The great Beatle
tongue chestnut is the beginning of If I Fell: they go from
John Lennon saying "If I fell in love with you would you
promise to be true and help me understand cause I've been in
love before" and all that to the body of the song by a really
spiffy Ringo drum roll that you can even *see* in Hard Day's
Night. Love uses Michael Stuart for the same kind of drum
stuff in Red Telephone. Beatles, well. . . . Moby Grape's first
album is as wide a tongue move as the Beatles and they even
compress about three or four albums worth of tongue maneu-
vers into one. Another thing the Grape understands is that
part of the original basic rock move is the short track. It's easier to take a short track and pack it pumice-full with goodies
than a long one, and then the long one takes on too much of
the temporal-ordeal drama aura. But some rock guys have
been able to carry the move into that.

Q. Who, for instance?

A. Well, Dylan of Blonde on Blonde works out everything into
the muzak-tongue field, where periodic musical relief does
the trick in the long horse, like in Memphis Blues Again.

Q. Why do you call it muzak?

A. Well, in muzak the focal point is tedious smooth sound
strained to minimal interpretability and you gotta pull the
notes out of it to make it the song you know it is and you
wanna hear. You know. Dylan is a muzak master structurally,
and the Left Banke carries it all the way back by somehow
putting the whole thing back into the short track, accompanied by enough great non-essential-but-always-there-anyway

muzak components to break through to hard-core muzak pressure because they don't and can't break through.

Q. Got any analogies to elucidate this whole tongue thing? I still think you chew the root.

A. Okay, take the scenes in Hard Day's Night where the boys escape all the time by running away from the pack pursuing them and then, upon realizing there's no way out, they do it by going right back in the same direction they came from. Or you could take a photo of the earth and the moon and fold it in half and punch a hole in it and unfold it and stand in wonder. Good enough?

Q. What's next in the tongue framework, what's gonna happen?

A. It seemed as if you'd need a cunnilingual receptacle principle for the tongue, but there's the diz instead, the diz for all who don't know yet being the cleft of the penis. . . . No it isn't.

Q. Got anything concrete?

A. We got concrete diz clefts and everything else. Anyway there's a whole bundle of tongue transcendence and tongue played-outness too of course, tongues can become carpentry too. What do you think Bike Boy is? Or the Soft White Underbelly? Or The Fool on the Hill? Or Surfer Bird, the oh so awesome Surfer Bird? Screw the necessity of regularity elaboration and distortion, and get with it with the non-move. That Stones newie, what's the name of it . . . oh Satanic Majesties, well that's the groovy totally inadequate break-the-spell-of-Beatlistic-tongue-enforcement that failed. The Underbelly won't fail, isn't failing, will never fail. You don't know what it's like. You know, music as avocado, but avocado as turquoise cardboard dead cat run over by ivory toe. Okay, here it is in a nutshell: 1. crystallization in flux, fill in or at least do something with empty-full spatio-temporal infinitesima in putty; 2. form as field, field as form, _____ as _____, tusk as brutal face, brutal face as nasty vortex, nasty vortex as umbrella treatment scheme, but, all in all, umbrella treatment scheme as field qua field qua form. I'm sick of talking, 'bye fans.

Q. Another question. . . .

A. Another answer.

7

Liner Note to
The Super Super Blues Band

*I was up at the office, alone, when a call came in from Chess Records—would anybody at the mag care to review a forthcoming release? I scored bigggg: $25. First bucks I earned writing (*Crawdad *didn't pay, except for what you could steal out of subscription envelopes—we wrote for the so-called honor of it). It's possible I might've spoke to an actual Chess—Marshall? Not one of the old guys. He didn't know what he was getting into.*

Too many collaborations of musical giants turn out to be bummers where either the forces nullify each other, or only the mere fact of collaboration, and not the end product, is what matters. This collaboration is no bummer. It is, in fact, *the* paradigm meeting of titans on record. Description adds little to the event, but it is hard to resist throwing in your own critical gravy when men are throwing in so much of their own art. So here is perhaps the most awesome case of men really getting their teeth into each other's viscera, each other's cliches.

Muddy, Bo and Wolf stay out of each other's way, step all over each other, laugh at and with each other. They intimidate each other, shrug off and ignore each other, groove on and with each other. Equal moves from all directions come out of all this pressure, further insuring the same total nibbling at the entire cosmic scene—where everything is relevant because everything is visible and nothing is relevant because visibility is nothing and nothing is everything. Everything appears as hint because nothing is there, and there are no hints because everything is there. And the blues is all. And Muddy, Bo and Wolf are the blues. They are even the Nietzschean multiple divinity at the very least.

8

Recent Reinstantiations of Flea-Flop in the Mustard Tusk Scene

It might've been Dick Higgins who hooked me up with Gilbert Chase, an "eminent musicologist" guest-editing an issue of some arts journal put out by the University of Wisconsin. He walked slow, had trouble with stairs, seemed about 80, but years later, when I looked it up, it turned out he'd only been 63. Over dinner at a joint recommended by the Village Voice, *a sheet not then interested in my services, he asked me what rock albs to get and spoke of bouncing the baby Pete Seeger on his knee. Matching his birthdate with Pete's makes him 13 when Pete was born, so who knows? Big-cheese scholars can toss the shit too.*

The work he scored from me is ominously dense (or is it sparse?), a "difficult" "experimental" text mingling "abstract" and "mundane," an alternately rigorous and casual gobbledygook. Don't sweat it, but if you've read Absalom! Absalom! *you can certainly get through enough to tell your grandchildren. Dunno if I'd try myself—not without a pickax or a chisel—but what the hey: it's a document!*

('S likely I took Hawaiian woodrose seeds during the paragraphs on Moby Grape '69. *Otherwise, drug-free.)*

Bartok and Schoenberg were non-non-navigational archaeologists but they couldn't/can't withstand a gander at (real reliable masters-of-the-craft) Van Morrison or Moby Grape: Robert Plant and David Clayton-Thomas and whoever was the singer for the Knickerbockers and the actual (a surprise-if-you-want) (*actual*'s a surprise) empirical ____ of the conceptually-necessitated-but-long-unawaited non-non-

non-non-renunciation of the *vocal* quality-trash continuum (and quality-trash fusion and confusion, fusion-confusion fusion, fusion-confusion confusion), an art-for-art-sake mere structural pie easy-as-pie if
you're an audience person (it's non-non-palatable for you Jack and
you Jill and just for you too: post-Anything is post-Everything, pre-
post-post-pre-pre-post-pre-pre-pre-etc is ____-__-____-____-__-__
too of course: actual concrete collapse of your analogical framework
(any one you can think of, including the collapse framework,
George's-guitar-as-the-focal-point-if-nothing-else-too
framework,   ) and mine too). But that's near enough to barking
up the wrong tree to be something else entirely, so a couple of grains
of tentatively temporary temporally relevant focus-grit: 1. massive
potential suspension-of-valuational-disturbance-of-the-actual-meat-
experience in the midst of any and all actual meat experiences except
in any and all specific that-ones and vice versa and neither and both
and never: total heavy ad hoc (utterly insulated (and all other spots on
the insulation continuum)) spontaneity (plus-minus systematic infer-
ence and no); 2. ad hominem pressure, as massive as anywhere else
anywhere ever, and capable of being located and relocated anywhere
anywhere at all: like the Kinks're a groove so THEREFORE this
song by the Kinks is great even when it's not (if such a conceptual
stumbling block is conceivable: good-bad, art-non-art, this-that, all a
big lump of the total content of the total experience; experiential
rumblings for the systematic artifacthood of mere experiencedness/
experiencingness and tarpaper and . . . . . .); 3. thus the big utter hierarchy move (which includes the big monistic mushroom and the plu-
ralistic thing too) and 4. well the move move of course (afterthought
pressure or 5. afterthought pressure (and, obviously, the
beginning/end of all history/geography: it's all gone, it's all back, it's
all all, it's all even in the neat-as-a-pin total-clarity-as-applied-to-all-
that kernel, like oldies-but-goodies forever even then and across all
somehow-there's-been-a-content-change content changes involving
the very range of palatability etc)); 6.   7.   8.   9.   (you fill
'em in yourself: go ahead it's YOUR GROCERY LIST) 10.   11.

   Which (which? the grocery list reference) brings to mind Dylan
(and thus non-Dylan-by-way-of-being-post-Dylan-by-way-of-being-
still-around-after-his-motorcycle-accident (the great merely actual/
empirical anywhere actualization of the clearly inevitable in one form
or another *after*-the-fact (hence one more mere indication of the collapse of a priori-a posteriori distinctions both a priori and a posteriori

as you'd expect))) yeah Dylan one of whose grocery lists took up an entire side of an album, giving the illusion of 20-minutehood while just hanging around for 11 minutes or so and it's on a record which everybody owns and everybody scratches (giving rise to art:destruction analogies and of course there's the whole infinite ephemeral scene and money-spent-as-dissipation analogy-all-its-own too and so many similar scenes like buying it for the cover and the cover falls apart even sooner than the record (but now they stick cellophane over it) but with less impact cause there's still all the time-dissipated-but-over-a-much-*longer*-time potency of image while the record's getting scratched and so there's even more interference with (the status of) sound).

Which leads us to sound it's sound it's music, finally the big move form (often chewed and swallowed by guys like Duchamp and Babe Ruth and Al Kaprow and Muhammad Ali and J. Christ and Ozzard Dobbs) has been intersected with the famous publicly-acknowledged-as-magic move move form (music and stuff like that) just for the heck of it (just for the hell of it). Sometimes you get the senseless-masochism-of-reconstructing-it-all of Zappa or Eric Burdon or David Peel, sometimes the nothing-like-it-it's-easy-as-a-tadpole-and-I-sure-know-even-if-you-don't ease and grace of Ricky Nelson or infinite wisdom incarnate of the everlasting Trashmen (Surfer Bird). Or the. And. And Dylan's let's-take-a-move-move-break-right-now on John Wesley Harding and the effortless way people lay off infinite Dylan plagiarism opportunities while he's gone (well there was Who's Been Sleeping Here? but that's an exception and exceptions should be made as often as often, look what that would've done to prolong the Lovin Spoonful's career which might have mattered) but wait til he's back (and just mentioning now the whole bit about super-duper-plagiarism moves and move moves and afterthought and all: follow the Kinks thru Party Line to the Stones' Connection and everything else and stuff). And the internal-external definitive general repetition scene. And, speaking specifically, unchanged Paul Jones *readymades* in Something Happened to Me Yesterday.

And OH YEAH can't forget to mention the whole actual big fat source of something's form-content: the whole soul udder, which itself is big (enormous) on let's-not-even-bother-to-call-it-plagiarism-anymore and specific form-content specification with no rest at all and of course the whole great big (biggest) unity-of-form-and-content-in-as-many-places-as-you'd-care-to-look scene, leading to the whole merely-the-greatest-artist-of-all-time-and-that's-all abyss later perfected to oblivion by the Beatles (but there's, but that's, if-ya-want, in context), take heed of rock as the supercontextualizer of any everything you can name. And other sources (hick music, Redi-Whip cans, Indian garbage) could have served just as well (except people worry about their gonads a lot). In addition, transcendence of politics (the Dylan specific once made it clear) to the point of, of, of fun.

And, as we all know, transcendence-etc of meaning, meaning itself, even meaning as mustard: here's where continuum-pressure-rather-than-polarity is just about biggest, and the always-underhanded-any-way-postulation-of-credibility-as-a-variable becomes merely a variable like everything else (like would YOU drink to the salt of the earth? maybe you would: but you can still groove on the song: absolute valuational splits in a rock unit are possible, each totally vali-dating/invalidating all other possible-actual parts (the next-to-the-last note of Ticket to Ride can do it for you, so can Ringo's hair next week: heaviest dose of out-of-context sludge ever to be found any-where, and sure it's the heaviest useful and most useful dose too and height-and-weight and stuff like that is rich in immediate self-nega-tion-cross-negation/self-affirmation-cross-affirmation)).

Like-it-or-you-don't has varied (or hasn't) pretty much over the last ten yrs and for some big easily discernible irrelevant big reason 1956 is taken as a reference point or 1955 and things like that. Elvis Pres-ley, the mere father of modern mere charisma, only partially (mini-mally in fact) filled in those great expected satisfaction points/holes before slipping into some conventional unpalatability hole or other, etc. That's Elvis and his Hound Dog was originally a Big Mama Thornton song and he did it more vulgar by virtue of trying and not even having to try and the fact that *she* could just as easily have been a postulated vulgarity constant if you wanted or needed her as that even if she wasn't but she was anyway no, and anyway he was the birth of wow-in-wow's-clothing-and-but-what's-all-this-wow-man as far as he went and that goes while she was already working out of a quality-defined relevance-determined traditional art/culture/folkydoke/etc scene full of hierarchies and just the best at it well that's where she was or something so he had to without realizing or foreseeing it build a whole new scene that'd always been around. And that was the point.

Just think about how that famous fool (Leonard Bernstein), always the big promulgator of scenes he has no inkling of the true import of, gets knocked on the seat of his ass by a sudden mere handful of Beatle songs and sees the universe in Janis Ian. Well he's an *external* fool. Now look at how everybody, particularly everybody in this recent wave from England, has been caught up in the Vanilla Fudge fool's-product (naught but organ overkill although Country Joe and Doors already had alternative organ scenes) and has shown off the transcen- dence-of-foolhood metaphor concretion just by stepping on the right-wrong specific archetype bundle rather than _____. Led Zep- pelin's really something, huh?

And Eric Clapton, and the Yardbirds. Never an ounce of eschato- logical viscera, but enough specific-and-discernible noise and noise- quality to corner the market and generate a scad of easy plagiarism designations (like: "That's a Clapton cop" just cause there's wahwah- etc and it's not Jimi Hendrix or Tommy James). Nice. If everything's a more-or-less obvious spike-in-the-wood, here's an exercise for you: where's the next Miss Amanda Jones if it's not Chuck Berry? (wrong question but answer it anyway).

And have you traveled very far: far as the eye can see—and that's pure conceptuality man, like looking out on an unbounded Atlantic and picturing it as unbounded yet finite-as-hell like Lake Superior (that's what kind of job it is, not what *it* is): 8 miles high and when you touch down and it's chopped into units that still make quite a pile: I can't reach you + I can't see feel or hear from you (while also a billion ages past you, a million yrs behind ya too) and conceptuality of unit- hood or anything else is in the way (in the way of what? who knows, but you get the spatial metaphor in there for laughs and you can go anywhere you want, even musically reinforced and things like that: magic or mud or both or neither and the science-fiction of dull trash: Hendrix for one, Spyder Turner for another, Dr. Byrds & Mr. Hyde for another, Beach Boys for another, Arthur Lee for another, Mick for another, Fabian for another, the Poni-Tails for another, Eric Burdon for another, Chad & Jeremy for another, systematic clarity for an- other, etc).

Put on your thinking caps, are there any rock songs about spar- rows? You're darn tootin' there are, it's Pandora's Golden Heebie Jee- bies by the Association (what a song) and John Kay of Steppenwolf used to be in the Sparrow (were you?).

Question (to Ernie Graham of Eire Apparent): Are the Stones re- garded as gods and all that in England? Answer (by Ernie Graham of Eire Apparent): Yeah they're up there.

Q: What about the Zombies?

A: They're highly regarded musically.

Q: How about the Kinks and the Yardbirds?
A: Nobody listens to them anymore.
Q: How about the Searchers?
A: No.
Q: The D.C. Five?
A: As I hear they were pretty good on stage but I never saw them.
(So you get lots of geographic dispersion of public-world stuff, as well as lots of geography in lots of mere concept: bet ya a quarter rock's got the biggest load (all-time) of public-world breakdowns of the whole unitary sludge simultaneous with nearly undisturbed totality accompaniment etc. Numbers on the top 40 used to be okay too. FM radio really missed the point when they ended up with all that verbal torpor between tracks anyway, numbers are a better excuse for being dull and temporarily taxonomically irrelevant.)

The Waste Track (is what Looking Glass and stuff of that ilk is on the Association's Renaissance album) is not a rock exclusive but a *great* rock exclusive. In other art scenes you gotta wait til guys get senile or too young (or only occasionally) in order to see some wholesome throwaways.

Uses of the super-plethora: disperse monistic-&-or-pluralistic-but-spread-out-pretty-well interest in a big bulk (excite via *mere* plethora) AND dump so much on everybody that sorting it all out is a drag (the One's fun but the All's too tall): hit the famous All-One in terms of the playedoutness scene (the fire that burns out rapidly and whose flash is its mere flash (ephemeral etc), Fauvism as a 2-yr virus, Wayne Fontana & the Mindbenders forever for at least a minute; and it's short/long enough to be structurally ready to be boring as soon as poss., sometimes even before it excites and sometimes after, you know . . .). The whole very idea of Country Joe & the Fish took about six months to die.

And Monterey (Monterey Pop Festival '67) was the accumulation/release of it all (in terms of all (at least *nominally* all) the empirical prerequisites) at the moment of the youth of youth (not its maturity) when drugs were almost something new and Sgt. Pepper had just come out and the Beatles seemed to be there hidden inside stagehands and Paul McCartney masks and Brian Jones was really there dressed in alien freak attire when that was big and still on the horizon (things in rock are always already full-scale on any convenient horizon: triumph of raunch epistemology): well Eric Burdon was falling all over the place on an Owsley Flying Saucer (1000 micrograms of lucy in the sky) singing about San Franciscan nights (which he claimed were warm sometimes) and doing an electric violin version of Paint It Black and preceding Simon & Garfunkel on a dismal first night there (featuring Mr. Consistency, Johnny Rivers, who was thankin' everybody after each but not after the introduction to each (after *his* type of before)): LOTS OF HITTING THE NAIL ON THE HEAD WITHOUT EVEN TRYING, all on the one great big occasion for the whole thing as one big flash; and what is Eric's post-entropic comment on you know what, it was Down in Monterey (ha ha). Down in Monterey: (ancient) Greece is a drag no matter how you swing it, but not (ha) as geography (but no geologic (*heavy* geographic) interchangeability between the two scenes): oh phaw. Mark Twain's a hard scene to crack these days unless you're a foreigner.

Okay take a peek at the Grape's Moby Grape '69 album (oh man). Notice (for instance) that you've got the lackadaisical Beatles (white album) freakout: 1957 all over again (that scene in a nutshell carving) BUT just check out the difference in general approach. Beatles work out the generalized ALL by looking out from a ONE so heavy and effective that archaeology comes on too too strong so you're stuck with things like pretense (which is a gas) and cuteness (which can be pretty awesome too) in the context of Beatles (some context etc). So many canaries who are still waddling around the quality-credibility-authenticity-etc scene figure they're faced with a bummer and can't handle that very easily, maybe even just dump it right away without thinking for a second (although, as we know, bummers are just non-non-bummers all the while) and things like that . . . and so what. . . . The Grape (on another hand, THE other hand in fact) grab hold of Beatle-reformulated forms (which might seem like form-as-flash-as-form-as-flash-as- -as- and who knows the final component) and by doing a masterpiece type lazy job pull off a flashy version of form-resisting-*un*lazy-formulation-as-flash-as-form as mere form (read that any way you want, What's to Choose is a Grape goody: the Hey Jude cosmology-and-logic contained within Penny Lane and Me & My Monkey: and if it begins to turn into a swamp (a seductive swamp, even swamps beyond the Byrds' Younger Than Yesterday) well there's Going Nowhere's Who readymade (wow just like the one in Birthday where Townshend swings his arm around and turns a circle into a straight line long enough to make the big musical geometry move utterly explicit) to stomp it up to infinity so it's an instant explosion of polar cosmology (not polar cosmos but polar cosmology) (well take the case that Memphis Sam's trying to make about how the Byrds and maybe the Who have comprehended the FORM MODULE with which all readymades can be used to do ANY-THING at all: well the GRAPE, armed with NOTHING BUT a few scattered readymades which might just as well be the same to the unaided ear, armed with nothing but that and (aha) the CONTENT MODULE plus a little vocal oblivion and easy instrumental easy-listening torpor, well they pull off the biggest of all simultaneous Beatle (note those George Harrison boss licks at the end of the Grape's Captain Nemo) readymade usage plethoras and in-terms-of-everything-else equivalent Beatle parallel universal constructions (Arthur Lee once tried it but variety was too noticeable with him as he got along in years): reference to the whole thing by way of refer-ence to the whole thing and to the biggest of the big public reference points, the big oblique easy repetition-plagiarism MOVE MOVE conscious of itself within a mainstream for mere consciousness and within the traditional/conventional without in order to be beyond the point where they'll (who?) notice that your stuff is obviously su-per-explanatory (Traffic tried that once but only for five minutes, and the Grape's been tag-along approaching this point all along, now they've hit it and they're past it; what about the Stones, what about Dylan?: they've been hitting it too but only sporadically cause they've got the FLASH MODULE down pretty good so they haven't needed to resort to non-muzak structural resorts; but the Grape: form as form, form as function, function as fun, , , ,))). (Jazz comes in somewhere around there, Charlie Parker of 1946-7-8 cracked it, so did Eric Dolphy, Ornette Coleman, Albert Ayler, Monk too, Cecil Taylor probably, Jaki Byard, Pithecanthropus Erec-tus, Charlie Haden, but not Coltrane unless the Vanilla Fudge and Deep Purple too (so of course). . . .)

Grape and post-soul comes out in Ooh Mama Ooh. Ray Charles was the biggest lightning bolt ever until a merely alien form weighed so heavily that he became mechanical in his flash production (starting late in the Atlantic early Genius era and becoming utterly obvious by the time of the country-western stuff). Otis Redding finally arrived at no-longer-dynamic opposition to any-and-all form (soul music as the least adequate soul form, hence best crucible for soul freakout but in-evitably too familiar to be alien anymore so if you conquer it and transcend even Ray Charles-defined soul butter you're nothing but the most wholesome artist yet flashed around and the form has little to do with the flash) (listen to Otis' version of The Glory of Love) but there really wasn't an indication of total post-form vision at the be-ginning (it would've got in the way in retrospect—and empirically, if it *always* does, that's just a basic traditional qual-oriented mere-form-oriented remnant (of an older age) getting in the way (of the *transcen-dence* of creativity and other elderly buzzards: and leads to stagnation-before-the-fact, which is (it happens luckily to be the case) still in-context in the rock eggplant: even the victims of older Art Scenes that have made pretenses at rock and bummered out are in there kicking: even Donovan)). Ooh Mama Ooh (shamalama booma-lama mama-wawa dippity dom without laughter, following the Hey Grandma riff which follows a fakeout soul or bluesy or something guitar intro): the Everly Brothers (no not as sound or anything like that, just as some big metaphor or something) without the scars of culturally advanced country boyhood or the marines or doojy qua scars, all this before the fact, all form played out, all form alien, all form salvageable, specific forms taken together can do such and such a job, easy to handle right from the start and no formal specifics can get enough in the way to crucially interfere with anything (even in-evitably) (and nothing's crucial anyway), and this initial before-the-fact laying of groundwork is so simple and easy (and presupposition-oriented) that intensity and youthful exuberance are never cut into by the weight of any specific specific. Yeah, if you think music's abstruse try to figure why anybody tries to figure out post-musical music (what?), no not exactly but rock requires the smallest amount of literature and (lo and behold) it's got the most (and it does the least direct damage-wreaked-by-criticism-upon-art, least upon the stuff itself but since you're still stuck with occasional old-timers doing it an occasional mere artist will get trapped: Clapton convinced by Jon Landau (a remnant of Downbeat Aristotelian drudgery) that Cream was a drag and his guitar stuff was drag-full of clichés (parts of this are hard to believe)). Rock can without really trying (but when it tries wow) do the more powerful more potent more exciting more flashy less boring more/less anything (and vice versa) version of the old-time stuff, just as you'd expect.

As far as drugs and rock go I figure DET will be pretty big eventu-ally—but don't ask me why (listen to Ask Me Why on the Beatles' VeeJay album, then There's a Place, Please Please Me, I'll Get You, Thank You Girl (the Beatles were once a big harp band), Dear Pru-dence).

Underground status for that which was previously ineligible for un-dergroundhood, all thru the totally visible discrepancy between fame and fortune: Van Dyke Parks et al. And discrepancy between fame-fortune and extra-fame-fortune *relevance* is big too, once in a while it's with somebody who persists having hits all over the place but never in any designated place etc: Bee Gees? Used to be that way with the Four Seasons? Most stuff is too peripheral to official peripheral categories to be other than peripheral (to x or to peripherality). The Hollies, Blues Magoos, early Cream, Wind in the Willows, Graffiti, Influence, Spirit, Autosalvage, 1910 Fruit Gum Company, Fugs, early Richie Havens, future Richie Havens, Jefferson Airplane, Mamas & Papas, Phil Ochs, Stone Pillow, MC5, Ten Years After, Blues Project with John-John McDuffy, Dennis Johnston and the Beach Boys, Brute Force, Mad River, Red Krayola, Vagrants, Box Tops before the second thing came out, Martha & the Vandellas, Percy Sledge, C.C. & the Chasers, Taming Power of the Great, Blue Cheer. And in some easily graspable public-world stump categories, of course, are the Trashmen, the Grateful Dead, the D.C. 5, Pink Floyd, the Move, Righteous Brothers, the Cyrkle, Grapefruit, and your 11 favorite groups including the Chambers Brothers.

Jack Sprat could eat no fat.

LESS EARLY

Introduction

So OK, enough of THAT. No more angels-on-the-head-of-a-45, no mo' one-size-fits-all-horseshit categories, or if not none, a damn sight less, and far less vehemence 'bout shoring up the *occasional* dumb category with so many otherwise-unrelated whatsems, so much extraneous esoterica. While I remained a stickler for finding the absolute connection between things not connected, I now sought to keep the particulars *concrete*. Often just as rambling, as all *over* the fucking place, as within and without the interstices of flaming you-name-it, I began to focus more on details of surface, of the moment, and became "free-associative" in a real-time at-the-typewriter sort of way. Almost overnight, the work of writing became quite like play, delivering the reader (one suspects) a greater payload of *fun*.

At the same time I was freeing up the writing style—finding my "voice"—I discovered ironically that I had less interest in using it to express anything substantive on the subject of rock. With publication of *The Aesthetics of Rock* finally imminent, I felt I'd said it, said it all—mission accomplished—and saw no reason to repeat myself. Say it once, why say it again? . . . although who was I kidding? You've probably noticed by now how much I repeat myself, y'know *anyway*. (But that's how I saw it.)

For a while I didn't write about rock at all, except to occasionally drop a reference into this TV column I was doing, under the pseudonym Borneo Jimmy, for a Boston biweekly called *Fusion*. A typical paragraph: "You know what ad is really *heavy*? The, uh, the, the (Everly Brothers anti-speed ad) Midas Muffler commercial is boring and hasn't been changed since Dewey (Everly Brothers anti-speed ad) was prez. Um, um, the Preparation H (Everly Brothers anti-speed ad) commercial is (Everly Brothers anti-speed ad) informative but ultimately dullll. That famous (Everly Brothers anti-speed ad) commercial for blades with the French-Canadian (Everly Brothers anti-speed ad) logger is fine but fine ain't heavy. The (Everly Brothers anti-speed ad) Everly (Everly Brothers anti-speed ad) Brothers (Everly Brothers anti-speed ad) anti- (Everly Brothers anti-speed ad) speed (Everly Brothers anti-speed ad) ad (Everly Brothers anti-speed ad) is heavy. One of the Evs (can U tell them apart?) has a shoulder length 'mop top' (Everly Brothers anti-speed ad). That's all for the Everly Brothers anti-speed ad."

Still and all, with the frigging book at last a fact, it dawned on me that the content of *Aesthetics* was *old*, and that for the accomplishment, not to mention the mission, to be *worth much* I might hafta go and apply its "principles" to some new stuff, come up with a whole new set of *examples*. At odd moments I'd ponder: *Shit, do I wanna do it? Do I really wanna do it?*—then bang, as '69 gave way to '70, all these mags started calling me.

In addition to *Fusion* I heard from *Rock, Changes, Creem,* and a resurrected, reconstituted *Crawdaddy,* each of them offering 10 bucks and up for rock reviews, features, filler. Whether rockmags as such or counterculture sheets with music sections, they were kept afloat by record advertising and required massive infusions of rock-texted slop to demonstrate their ongoing devotion to the rock-roll cause. The oldest of the bunch and richest, though in many ways least, *Rolling Stone* had once turned down my offer of a boxing piece, but after running TWO reviews of *Aesthetics* (one pro, one con) they now welcomed me. They paid, I don't remember, 25 bucks or even 30 for a 350-word record review. Fat City.

So here I was, writing this hogwash again, and if there wurn't no new *things* to spout about rock 'n' roll, I would have to scare up some new *approaches*—p.o.v.'s, techniques, modes of jabber—critical "attitudes"—to at least give me a few hot variations on theme, y'know? So I tried a buncha variants on for size, from deadpan to slapstick, devout to irreverent, sleek to sloppy. Since writing conventional disc/concert/artist copy—what they more or less expected—didn't appeal to me in the slightest, my mischief at the typer often led to editorial friction.

Mischief! A tame word and a tame concept but heck—I'd only just begun.

That's right: I aspired in my rockwrite to the SPIRIT of rock, whatever in hell that was, and (improbably enough) was the only person then doing so. Which made me both cockier and more willful. *Somebody* had to get things right.

Mischief the equivalent of rock itself.

9

Remember When:
The *Other* Sixties

For its end-of-the-'60s "Pop Decade" issue Fusion asked me for a definitive, comprehensive roundup of '60s rock. Sounds formidable, no?—and more than a little tiresome—so I pulled a fast one and gave 'em the early '60s— what I vaguely remembered of it.

From "Recent Reinstantiations" to this seems a move from bogue (did he say rogue?) scholarship to no scholarship . . . one of my earliest "grocery list" articles. Rereading it now, I wonder: was I pretending—assuming—speculating the '70s would be the '50s?

Not talking good, not talking bad, I'm talking hits, okay? Not early, not late, not middle, the whole Sixties.

Oh. No time for whole? Then just early. (The part nobody cares about.)

WEST OF THE WALL, Toni Fisher's follow-up to THE BIG HURT (the beginning of underwater rock), couldn't've been any earlier than 1960, it's a sure bet it was a 60's record and the other one couldn't be earlier than 59 but maybe they were both 61 (no later than 62 at the latest). JOHNNY JINGO (Hayley Mills before Mick Jagger looked like her) was around 60-61, impossible for it to be earlier. SMOKEY PLACES is hard core spring 62 by the Corsairs. THE NIGHT HAS A THOUSAND EYES was winter 62 but his earlier hit STAYIN IN was more like 60–61 or 62 (Bobby Vee). SAILOR or SEAMAN or SEEMANN was some German chick (Lorelei or Medusa or somebody) probably in 61. I LOVE YOU SO by somebody and I LOVE YOU (I-I-I love you-oo-oo-oo-oo) by somebody else were 60-61 or 59 at the earliest and they were both summer but maybe not the same one. RUNAROUND (not RUNAROUND

GIRL) which sounded like something else that's hard to remember was summer 61. RUNAROUND SUE was Dion after he left the Belmonts but LONELY TEENAGER was even earlier mere Dion and it was around the very dawn of 60 and the Belmonts' first by themselves (I NEED SOMEONE) was not long after that but Dion & the Belmonts' DON'T PITY ME was definitely 58-59 so that's not 60's. And the Del-Satins did something around then too and Mike Phillips says they backed up Dion. Later Skyliners stuff (IT HAPPENED TODAY?) might just make 60, no, probably 59. LAVENDER BLUE was done by whoever did it whenever he did it, 59–60 (the rock version). Frankie Avalon was starting to wane and all he had was WHY in 59-going-on-60 but there was also BOBBY SOX TO STOCKINGS which was either before or after it. Neil Sedaka's BREAKING UP IS HARD TO DO was 61-62 dynamite and Jerry Butler's MAKE IT EASY ON YOURSELF (they say that breaking up is so very hard to do) was right there too, more like 61 actually, and Neil Sedaka had CAROL (I am but a fool) around 59 and there was lots in between (CALENDAR GIRL). BELIEVE ME was the last big Royal Teens hit (Al Kooper was there they say) and it couldn't have been earlier than very late 59. CRY BABY made it in 63, that's much later, that's Garnett Mimms. SUGAR SHACK (Jimmy Gilmer of Fireballs fame) was then too. Aiming back for 60 itself: MISSION BELL by Donnie Brooks *might* be 61 and *probably* was but it *could* be 60 and along with it I'M A YOGI by the Ivy Three and the Safaris' IMAGE OF A GIRL which might be as late as 62 but here's a sure shot for 60: ALLEY OOP by some group or other and also the Hollywood Argyles. GOOD TIMIN too by whoever did HANDYMAN (not the Del Shannon version): prelude to Lou Christie. Close to that for some reason were the Marv Johnson smashes YOU GOT WHAT IT TAKES FOR ME and YOU GOTTA CLIMB TWO MOUNTAINS (or something like that). Oh yeah it was Jimmy Jones. The Ventures made the big move no later than 61 with WALK DON'T RUN followed by the red hot PERFIDIA. Duane Eddy had shot his wad by 59-60-61 or whenever it was with stuff like the nifty wad-shooter FORTY MILES OF BAD ROAD and I think he also did PEPE and BECAUSE THEY'RE YOUNG after that and even later he added female voices (the Rebelettes) in fall 62 and isolation to albums for 5-6-7 years before coming back with the THERE IS A MOUNTAIN single. Paul Anka was still around, hitting with PUT YOUR HEAD ON MY SHOULDER in 62 and some bossa nova reference (ESSO BESSO?) in 62. But the big big bossa nova dam breakers were FLY

ME TO THE MOON (Joe Harnell) and BLAME IT ON THE
BOSSA NOVA (Eydie Gorme, which led to Steve Lawrence's big
breakthru, GO AWAY LITTLE GIRL) not forgetting muzak champ
Stan Getz with DESAFINADO, all 62 for sure, drifting into 63.
Bobby Rydell was either still around or just getting started, WE
GOT LOVE (by the numbers) and SWINGIN SCHOOL in 59-60-
61-62 (no earlier or later). The Four Coins (SHANGRI-LA, A BRO-
KEN PROMISE) didn't come close to the 60's, they were more like
57-58 and Peter Tripp (who stayed awake for 201 hours and died of
payola) liked them. But the Four Preps were and MORE MONEY
FOR YOU AND ME (first we take the Fleetwoods, a mighty nice
bunch of kids) even contained a mention of the Four Freshmen (61).
Same summer was I LIKE IT LIKE THAT (Chris Kenner) and
MOTHER-IN-LAW (Ernie K-Doe) was either then or 62, or 60.
RAMA LAMA DING DONG (the Edsels) was a real heavy back
then (60?) (61?) (62?), heavier or not than RAINDROPS by what's his
name in 62, 61. I'LL TRY SOMETHING NEW sounded like the
same landscape and was 62 for sure by the Miracles (as they were
known then) and it had one of the great fadeout lyrics of all time then
or now (if at first I don't succeed try again is what I'll do, always trying something new, always trying something that's new-ew-ew). SIL-
VER THREADS AND GOLDEN NEEDLES was a rouser in 62
and if Dusty Springfield wasn't in the Springfields then greater coin-
cidences have never occurred. AHAB THE ARAB (was that Ray
Stevens?) was summer 62 (novelty songs were always biggest in the
summer) and PLEASE MR. CUSTER (was that Ray Stevens?) was
summer 61. Brook Benton couldn't have been that late so figure
THANK YOU PRETTY BABY for summer 59-60. Same for Jan &
Dean's first biggie BABY TALK. BIMBOMBEY was Jimmie
Rodgers' last gasp around borderline 59-60 or 58-59. Pat Boone's
TWIXT 12 AND 20 was twixt something or other around the same
time as BECAUSE THEY'RE YOUNG (Dick Clark was still kicking). Hmm, the Everly Brothers were steady hard core hit makers until WALK RIGHT BACK and CATHY'S CLOWN, probably in that
order (ask someone), 59-60-61 or so. The Duprees foreshadowed
Steve Miller's first album with gems like YOU BELONG TO ME
(summer 61, *that's* for sure). And Gene Chandler recorded and became (for all practical purposes) the one and only DUKE OF EARL
some year around then. And another famous Gene, Gene McDaniels,
got his own ball rolling before 62 or 61 and just rolled them off: A
HUNDRED LBS OF CLAY, TOWER OF STRENGTH, CHIP

CHIP, POINT OF NO RETURN, flopping with SPANISH LACE (fall-winter 62) and ceasing to exist until he got slick enough for DownBeat. By that time HE'S A REBEL (follow-up to earlier-62 UPTOWN by the Crystals) and I WILL FOLLOW HIM by Little Peggy March had already arrived. And speaking of Phil Spector, his TO KNOW HIM IS TO LOVE HIM (when he was a teenager, by the Teddy Bears) was way earlier, 58-59 on a label with a feather on it. And one of those other guys, Barry Mann (of Cynthia Weill), did WHO PUT THE BOMP (in the bompa bompa bomp) some summer or other, most likely 61. And Johnny Mathis, the least of whose achievements was teaching Arthur Lee how to sing, had hits on both sides of the 59-60 line: SMALL WORLD in summer 59 and WHAT WILL MY MARY SAY in fall 62. The latter of which was when Bobby Boris Pickett did MONSTER MASH and Ricky Nelson did: not LONESOME TOWN (59-60) or TRAVELIN MAN (61 or 2) but TEENAGE IDOL. So was HEY PAULA by Paul & Paula who set the stage for Sonny & Cher's basic one-hit move way back then (fall 62). REVEILLE ROCK (Johnny & the Hurricanes) too. And TELSTAR (the Tornadoes) a year later. And THE LONELY BULL, Herb Alpert's one shot hit, that previous year. And SPANISH HARLEM (spring 62?) which was more horn prelude to Herb Alpert than late Ben E. King. But not the same for Ben E's DON'T PLAY IT NO MORE and I WHO HAVE NOTHING, the latter 63 (and on a Murray the K live album) and the former who knows when. THE STROLL (most likely the last hit for the Diamonds) and its re-discovered precursor Chuck Willis's C.C. RIDER may seem modern as hell but my guess is they're no more recent than 58 (stretch it to 59 at your own risk). And, goddam mother, how could I have overlooked THE TWIST so long? Twice a hit, in 61 and 61 (or 60 and 61), and then he came back with LET'S TWIST AGAIN and there was THE PONY too and additional multilingual versions of THE TWIST (about the same time, once it was all big) and he did THE POPEYE and he finally dwindled to doing THE FREDDY (where'd he get *that* one from? From Freddy & the Dreamers, summer 65, and who was *he*? Chubby Checker) but in the meantime he did SLOW TWISTIN with Dee Dee Sharp (61?) who also did GRAVY (FOR MY MASHED POTATOES) and GONNA GET ON MY PONY AND RIDE (62). Yeah and the great Joey Dee's never-to-be-forgotten PEPPERMINT TWIST and some time after that a real heavy non-twist number, something like WHAT HAVE I GOT TO CALL MY OWN (unless that was Trini Lopez's heavy post-first-album non-hit, and don't forget *his* first album, summer 63) or WHAT'S MY LIFE ALL ABOUT (I don't think that was it). And don't you forget that even Danny & the Juniors made it back and into the 60's with their twist smash TWISTIN U.S.A. And SURFIN U.S.A. wasn't even the Beach Boys' first and their first smash SURFIN SAFARI (62) wasn't even brink of the sixties, it was more like brink of the early middle sixties (in date) and brink of the actual middle sixties (in spirit), big things were promised for them from their first plethora (62-going-on-63). Popping into prominence at exactly the same time were those awesome Four Seasons starting with just a girl, SHERRY (summer 62), moving on to falsetto-intensified perverse accusation, BIG GIRLS DON'T CRY (fall 62), and then the sky was the limit. Roy Orbison too, he was around then too and RUNNIN SCARED (61 maybe) was his first harbinger of opera to come, or was CRYING first (or was ONLY THE LONELY operatic enough already)? And the great Brenda Lee then too, she was 15 years old in Life magazine with the voice of someone 3 times her age and she did SWEET NOTHINS (59-60-61) and IT STARTED ALL OVER AGAIN with somebody better than Harry James. And last but not least: Timi Yuro, another class of 60-61, whose best was something that ended with it's just startin for you. Doris Day made her 60's comeback with LOVER COME BACK and that was the last was seen of her (62). Then there was Jim Reeves' BURNING BRIDGES way back in 1960 AD. And of course TALL OAK TREE by some guy named Burnette, Johnny (59-60-61). And, glad you reminded me, SUM-MERTIME SUMMERTIME by the Jamies which was another smash twice-hit about two years apart in either 58 & 60 or 59 & 61. BARBARA-ANN (original) was enormous too, by the Regents, 61st year of the century approximately, excluding 1900. Little Eva scorched the needle too, first exploding with LOCOMOTION in summer 62 and then rocketing back the very next year with Big Dee Irwin on SWINGIN ON A STAR (one moonbeam, two moonbeam). I may be mistaken but it could be the same summer that Inez Foxx and somebody else, maybe even another Foxx, chortled thru MOCK-INGBIRD. Hey yeah and Bob B. Soxx and Johnny Thunder were around that nexus, and one of them did ZIP A DEE DOO DAH and one of them did HERE WE GO LOOP DE LOOP: who can touch it nowadays? And they don't make songs nowadays like Gene Pitney's TOWN WITHOUT PITY, spring 62. RUNAWAY (Del Shannon, spring 62) by itself would be too good to mention, but there's HATS OFF TO LARRY too. And they don't make shittt these days to com-

pete with the subversive swill of PP&M's first small one, you must remember LEMON TREE (nineteen hundred sixty-two). VENUS IN
BLUE JEANS was Jimmy Clanton's second best hit if he's the one
who did it and it was one of those years. So was Johnny Tillotson's
POETRY IN MOTION. SHEILA was something else again and it
launched Tommy Roe via the Buddy Holly readymade in the fall of
62, by which time the Crickets were backing up the well known
Bobby Vee. And Chubby Checker was clicking once again with
LIMBO ROCK round about then, as were the Marvelettes, following
up the fantastic success of PLAYBOY (196X), PLEASE MR. POST-
MAN (196Y) and TWISTIN POSTMAN (196Z but did *they* do it?)
with BEECHWOOD 4-5-7-8-9. And there'll never be another like
the Sensations' sizzler LET ME IN, and it's a full 7½ years since then
already. Almost ditto for Rosey & the Originals on ANGEL BABY
an extra year beyond that. PRETTY LITTLE ANGEL EYES (summer 61) was not without its rewards either. The immortal Curtis Lee
did it. Elvis (Presley) was still around but all he was kicking was a
football if he had one; his last universal prominence was getting
awarded record of the year (ONE NIGHT) and singer of the year
(himself) from Dick Clark while he was in the army, 1959, or maybe
as far back as 58; in the following decade he was not without his hits,
most notable being WOODEN HEART (in the summer sun of 60 or
61 and in German) and RETURN TO SENDER (no such person,
no such zone, fall 62). And Kenny Ball made it big too: MIDNIGHT
IN MOSCOW (60-59). And don't belittle CALCUTTA by you-
name-it bandleader Lawrence Welk during the months of 61. Which
was followed a few months later by Lonnie Donegan's live performance of DOES YOUR CHEWING GUM LOSE ITS FLAVOR?
While we're on that track, why not spin Little Stevie Wonder's FIN-
GERTIPS PART 2 right now? And while you're on your way don't
miss Ray Charles's final official total fame-and-fortune sellout content shift, I CAN'T STOP LOVING YOU. The Mystics were always in the thick of things, first with HUSHABYE (59), next
BLUEBIRDS OVER THE WHITE CLIFFS OF DOVER (60 or
61) and the stylistic change was incredible. And CONEY ISLAND
BABY (by the Excellents) and BABY BLUE (by) were in a class by
themselves altho years apart or the same week (either way) in the rol-
licking early 60's. Right, and there was Jimmy Soul's two versions of
UGLY WOMAN (cooks meals on time/she'll always give you peace
of mind; cooks meals on gas/she'll always give you a piece of ass) in
the famous 1963 or 2, no it was 3. Three to four years before that the

Kingston Trio, a bunch of real pros, were still winging (and more)
with chart busters like MTA; only two or three years later they were
down to their last meager nibble on the pulse of singles-buying North
America, something called ONE MORE TOWN or something like
that. Watch out cause here come the Contours (watch me now) with
DO YOU LOVE ME? no later than October 62 and, within two
years before that, the subtle intensive spuds of Ferlin Husky's ON
THE WINGS OF A SNOW WHITE DOVE. And THEME
FROM A SUMMER PLACE by you know who. And then in fall-
winter 63 along came Lenny Welch (SINCE I FELL FOR YOU) and
those remarkable Trashmen (SURFIN BIRD) summed it all up, and
you know what happened next. (And I forgot Bobby Vinton and the
Tymes but not SAVE THE LAST DANCE FOR ME or WHAT'S
YOUR NAME? or SO FINE or HE'S SO FINE or BEYOND THE
SEA or Acker Bilk or RUN TO HIM or TELL LAURA I LOVE
HER or PALISADES PARK or the Dixie Cups or MY
BOYFRIEND'S BACK or the Singing Nun or the Essex or EASIER
SAID THAN DONE or TELL ME WHY (the Belmonts, not the
original) or I WISH THAT WE WERE MARRIED or MR. IN BE-
TWEEN or MOMMY AND DADDY WERE TWISTIN or.)

10

Fan Clubs from
Here to Dubuque!

*Or here's an idea. When it looks like there's nothing left to say about what
rock is, why not fill pages talking about what it isn't?*

Membership in the KEITH RELF FAN CLUB can be had for a
quarter plus self-addressed stamped envelope. Your membership kit
will include Keith's photo, a drawing of his likeness by a well-known
artist, a laminated membership card and the monthly *Keith Relf Forever* newsletter for a year. Write: Magnice Putnam, 670 East Oak,
Clinton, Iowa 52732. Don't delay! . . . . Alice Yarbrough, 192 Beach
96th Street, Rockaway Beach, New York 11694, is getting the ball
rolling on the first ERSEL HICKEY FAN CLUB in years. It's nice to
know that Ersel is still remembered and Alice would enjoy hearing
from others interested in his cause. She's ready and willing to accept
all suggestions, so why not drop her a line?. . . . Getting rave notices
across the fan club circuit is the special disc issued by the Scranton
chapter of the CYRKLE FAN CLUB. Those in the "know" insist
"Eggnog Breather" is one hell of a recording. Black market prices
have risen sky-hi to say the least, a crime and a shame when you can
get it for a mere $3.75 (cash, check or money order) direct from
Cyrkle Fan Club Record Offer, P.O. Box CFC, Scranton, Pa. 18515.
Allow three to four weeks for delivery.
  SPOOKY TOOTH FAN CLUB co-prexies, Pete Pihos and
Franklin Kazin, are planning a benefit for their favorite band, who
didn't quite set the world on fire during their most recent U.S. tour.
The date: August 15, Griffith Park, Los Angeles. Admission will be
free, but contributions are welcome and several hats will be passed
around. Already inked to appear are It's a Beautiful Day, the Group

Image, Lee Michaels, Sandra Dee and Buddy Miles. All proceeds will go directly to the Spooky Tooth Survival Fund. A worthy cause and while you're at it, why not join the club itself? Send $1.50 to Box 181, Watertown, Mass. 02172. . . . Only one hit to their credit, yet the CHAIRMEN OF THE BOARD FAN CLUB boasts a membership total of 7648 at the latest count. On the roster are such notables as William Burroughs, Nick Gravenites, Mikis Theodorakis and Tracy Nelson (who, incidentally, has *three* new clubs on the books—more on that later). Although membership is free, there is no card or certificate. Instead you get something money can't buy: a sense of belonging. Write Kent Smythe for details: 666 Market Square, Houston, Tex. 77001.

Alberta Popwell is pleased to announce that BADGERS FOR THE BUTTERFLY, of which she is executive president, will soon be presenting for sale a number of items belonging to Iron Butterfly. Prices range from 98 cents, which will bring you a napkin used by two members of the Butterfly and their tour manager, to a whopping 75 smackers (that's *dollars*, Sam!) for a garter worn as a lark by Doug Ingle while in the Boy Scouts. The 4-page catalogue is free, simply send SASE to Iron Butterfly Sales, P.O. Box 1970, Ten Friction, Wis. 53545. . . . In case you've hesitated in joining the JIVE FIVE FAN CLUB, rest assured you're not alone. *No one* apparently felt like digging in their pocket for the $9.50 required for a two-color club card and boating privileges at the group's private dock, so club originator Turk Jurgenson has come up with a new offer sure to persuade a few "comparison shoppers" out there. For only one dollar the same privileges can now be yours, and a Jive Five letter opener will be thrown in at no extra charge. Address all orders to Jive Five Productions, Dept. R, 1542 Western Ave., Dearborn, Mich. 48121. . . . It's smashing news to learn there's finally a BLODWYN PIG FAN CLUB right here in the States, made possible through the efforts of Onar Frangione, the well-respected Denver blues archivist. If you'd like to help out in formulating club policy, mail your comments to him at 800 Stoneman Sq., Denver, Colo. 80202.

Janet Fenstermacher of Freehold, New Jersey, has become the 1000th person to join the CHRIS WOOD FAN CLUB. Since Chris, as you may recall, has always been concerned with his weight, founder Georgette Harper (65 Oak Terrace, Smithers, Ind. 46142) has made a habit of keeping tabs on the total weight of her organization. When you join it is requested you supply your weight to the nearest half-pound, and that you keep the club posted on any changes of five or more pounds. This is just for the records, and will be kept in the strictest confidence (Miss Harper would not divulge Miss Fensterma-cher's poundage, despite my prodding). Initial fee is 75 cents, dues only 50 cents a year thereafter. . . . Both Morrisons, Van and Jim, are represented by the BOTH MORRISONS FAN CLUB, whose appli-cation for chartership has just been approved. Carl Lee Bonds promises this will be a great one and he could be right. If you'd like to find out for yourself, or if you just like to join all the clubs, send 50 cents in coin to 8 Allstate Lane, Carondelet, La. 70131.

We all know what a lummox Frankie Lymon was to mess with hard drugs like henry and charlie, after all they took his life. But there's no denying he sure could sing. Dom DeMarco, the Florida exterminator known to his friends as "The Bug Plugger," has sought to honor the voice and the man behind it with his FRANKIE LYMON GONE BUT NOT FORGOT CLUB. Membership is 35 cents plus proof from a doctor that you have never taken drugs (you can pick up the form at any health agency), for which you will receive photocopies of Frankie's report cards from his school days, an autographed sem-blance of Frankie with his parents, also with his famous group, the Teenagers. That's Dom DeMarco, 4500 S. Clement Pkwy., Miami, Fla. 33504. . . . The rumor spread in this column that Antoinette Mu-lada of the TYRANNOSAURUS REX FAN CLUB goes down like a bunny has resulted in a number of nasty letters from enraged fans. Says Jerry Stallwank of Farmingdale, Long Island, "Yeah sure, but you didn't warn us about her seven brothers. I now have a broken rib and need four hundred dollars in denture work!" Okay, be fore-warned, she does have seven bros. and they are all big bruisers, but as Tyrannosaurus Rex themselves maintain, she is well worth it. If you have the resourcefulness, perhaps you can arrange something cozy and *safe*. Drop her a note (or pay a visit) at 704 Plymouth View Drive, Mastic Beach, N.Y. 11951.

Though the Easybeats have long since split their separate ways their loyal supporters remain steadfast as ever. As proof positive, maybe you saw the pix from the wild and wooly Easybeats Please Come Home In One Piece party in Devonport, Tasmania. The gen-darmes were called to restore the peace when countless multitudes stormed the fences. A picture postcard commemorating the event is in production, and orders are being taken. Cost is reasonable: 45 cents per card (measuring 16" × 12"), $3.00 a dozen (a tremendous saving) and $20.00 a gross. Send cash only to EASYBEATS FAN CLUB INTERNATIONAL, Postal Card Division, 49 Barton Shelby

Pl., Melbourne, Australia. Having seen the card myself I must admit it is not the usual postal oddity. You'll want to share it with friends so I advise buying in bulk—don't waste your bread on only one (or even 12). . . .Not accepting mail orders but easily reachable by vehicle is the EDISON LIGHTHOUSE FAN CLUB at 19 Ash Street, Cambridge, Massachusetts, a stone's throw from the Bosstown metropolitan area. All are welcome to drop in and gaze through the club's extensive library and collection between the hours of 10 A.M. to 7:30 P.M., 353 days a year (closed the first Wednesday of every month). Tickets by donation only (recommended ante: two bucks—no checks please) to defray costs of cleaning and laundering the many band uniforms and codpieces on display.

Achieving remarkable results in the face of obstacles that would give pause to ordinary fans, Horst Freihofer of Cheshireville, Vermont, has worked wonders with his startling new club procedures. The Freihofer motto: membership should not only be free to all but *unsolicited.* Horst simply ships cards, buttons and gift boxes to everyone in the phone books of Vermont and New Hampshire. The expense, as you might well expect, has been monumental. He's had to "suck up" to rich folks in the Cheshireville area and often must "kiss ass"—so to speak—in the process. So far raising nearly $110,000, he has funneled every red cent into the club, relying also on his personal income ($95 take-home) from grueling work at the local alabaster quarry. If you live in the bi-state area and have not yet received membership notification, be patient, as he is still without an assistant to help expedite the arduous mailings. The club? Pardon me, it's the DANNY KALB APPRECIATION SOCIETY. . . . Recuperating from the explosion and fire that ravaged their meeting hall (arson suspected), remaining survivors of the GUESS WHO FAN AND BEER CLUB may temporarily be reached c/o Box 175, Mister Roberts, Manitoba.

Did you know that Dusty Springfield was a regular on the British *Hopalong Cassidy* series as a young teen? Well, it's true. Just one of the many things you may learn (if you don't know them already) from the Dusty Springfield fact sheet which comes handsomely displayed in the sturdy plastic tote case you'll get *free* when you sign up for two years' membership in the DUSTY SPRINGFIELD FAN CLUB, all for the low, low price of $1.15—wow! Address all correspondence to: Arty Kuscle, 69 St. Genevieve Crescent, Altoona, Pa. 16603. . . . Fran Schtaichz, a true veteran of the fan club "wars" (asst. prez of the JOHN FRED AND THE PLAYBOYS FAN CLUB and former picnic director of the UNIT FOUR PLUS TWO F.C.), has taken off on her own with a PHIL OCHS/SMALL FACES FAN CLUB. Fed up with all the "ignorant, illiterate fans" she's had to deal with in her various capacities with other clubs, this time she says membership will be open to college graduates only. Whoa!—no!—I do not approve! Until July 1st Fran can be reached at 975 Fort Ustananga Blvd., Port Huron, New York (zip code not available). I urge sending her a piece of our collective mind in favor of equal entry for fans of all educational schoolings. If we stick together we can work this out, possibly even get the members' fee lowered (a bit steep at $8) and start a trend toward economic and social reform in the great arena of fandom worldwide.

Joining "under protest" may also be the way to go with Bill Lueck's brand new MICK AVORY FAN CLUB. A weekend guitarist of some repute, Bill (1405 N. Shalimar Ave., Chicago, Ill. 60615) believes he has the right chord for scoring with the seasoned fanning public. On the flip-side of each and every male clubber's ID is inscribed the phone number of a different Chicago cutie—so when you're in town you won't be lonely. Sounds fine, Bill, but let me ask you one thing. What about all the rockin' chicks who feel like honoring the Kinks' fine drummer but would *also* like to enjoy full privileges of membership? Surely, you'll agree, they would *not* favor cold sheets (any more than us guys) when visiting the Windy City! And what about our many citizens and fans living the "gay" life? As both a club columnist and member in good standing of too many clubs to count, I feel strongly that change *must come* with the changing times and suggest that all prospective joiners tell Mr. Lueck where they stand, *regardless of sexual proclivity,* when sending their 65 cents (stamp or coin) to join his otherwise outstanding outfit. Phone numbers for all (or for none!) must be the byword, and I'm certain he'll give in if—and only if—the majority of joiners lay it on the line.

11

The Terror Beyond Death

I've never been too keen on the dogma of barbed-wire boundaries between nonfiction and fiction, and rock journalism is where I hit my first full stride as a novice fictioneer. The rock beast itself has always been a dandy *generatrix of alternate universes big and small.*

Here's an alternate Altamont, as recounted by "Swedish sociologist Lar Tusb" (pinch-hitting for Borneo Jimmy) in a quickie exploitation paperback edited by Jon Eisen. Editors are prob'ly the last people you should expect to help you maintain a ruse, and Eisen beat my story like a dirty rug, shaking from it any and all Scandinavian dialect jokes—hey, it was ripe with 'em.

Joe Cocker Live, *by the way, does exist, altho I filmed it, not Lar, that is I found it in the garbage and titled it. Four minutes (8mm, silent) of crewcut whiteboys at summer camp, circa '58, it actually got rented once, by a girls' school in Pennsylvania—a good title will sell anything. I don't think Joe (or the Guess Who, for that matter) played Altamont, but y'never know.*

"There's a whole new way of living, Pepsi helps supply the drive" says a popular soda pop ad. And it may be telling the truth. Certainly there were a number of folks drinking large quantities of Coke, Pepsi and Seven-up up at Altamont on that fateful day, and many of them did get a nice size lift from it. But for every bottle of Coke there were fifty people with a bottle of wine and many more with LSD, amphetamines and downs pulsing through their veins. All part of that whole new way of living, but the proportion has changed: suddenly beer, booze and wine have taken the forefront, you'd think it was Prohibition & Repeal time all over again!

Some people are going to say it's just a matter of alcohol in the wrong hands. That's all well and good and true, but whose wrong hands do they mean? Can they mean the Angels? They might mean them and in so doing forget about incidents of violence that were going on all afternoon, all morning, and the night before, even in spots where a Hell's Angel never showed his face during the entire festival if you can call it that. It was more than one act so they called it a festival. It was free so they called it a festival. There were lots of people so they called it a festival. But it was actually no more than the Stones and lots of preliminary time-killers.

As early as 9 AM a gas leak had developed in the stove being used at one concession stand. People lining up for hotdogs had to put up with it as smell and potential danger alike. A group of tripped out thirteen year olds were running about fantasizing the eventual explosion that (fortunately or unfortunately) never occurred. One of the boys carried a huge lit stick and he was taunting a passerby or two; probably fewer than one percent of those who noticed the gas were burdened by any noticeable fears. Yet there were some who were quite open about it, particularly a girl of about seventeen or eighteen who muttered "We're all gonna get blown up, put out that flame, it once happened in my apartment" to no avail. But the country isn't the city, so there was no space limited enough to build up enough pressure for any big boom. Urban science is a drag that just one day in the country can extricate you from, many discovered.

Dogs were everywhere. "It's reigning cats and dogs" exclaimed one would-be punster. But there weren't that many cats actually. Just as the born/died/injured percentages always have a habit of working things out statistically at these events, rabid dogs have a statistical chance of showing up proud and strong too. There was at least one at Altamont, a German shepherd with no tag who bit at least one person, and who knows how many other dogs. There are probably people back home in Palo Alto with dogs beginning to foam at the mouth, or maybe not, since most dogs get inoculated these days. But most isn't all, so there might just be a few folks here and there howling with incurable hydrophobia right now, or shuddering at the prospect of all those really great shots in the belly, or wherever they stick it.

Wolverines are close relatives of the badger (whose hair they used to use to make shaving brushes), but for fierceness among North American mammals they stand miles ahead of the famous Grizzly, who can do no better than number two despite more deaths inflicted in the record books. But the wolverine finally etched itself upon the memory of people at Altamont, as Jim Tomio, his tired body parked just outside the woods, awoke with a shock to find a wolverine gnawing at his ankle. His foot and ankle had to be amputated, that was inevitable, but the quick thinking of his girlfriend, Betty Kahn, who awoke with a flourish to beat the animal away with an acoustic guitar (funny how people still bring folk instruments to rock concerts, funny how useful one of them has finally become), saved him from more serious disaster. It wasn't that others were afraid to act sooner, it's just that nobody gave any thought to such a nice looking hunk of animal joining the crowd. It's like that kid in the clean-up-the-cities ad who can't tell a rat from a cat. Maybe all these cats and broads who do the nature thing ought to put in some preparation in nature *study*. They do it for yoga and natural foods, don't they?

But one thing they were more than prepared for was traffic, and that doesn't mean the rock group. It means the cars, the buses, the trucks, you know—the *vehicles*. Within a furlong from the spot where my own automobile was parked (you couldn't even call it stalled or stuck or immobile, it was *parked*, resigned to its spot on the road, the middle lane of California 93), you could see every conceivable malady and misery for the overworked sets of wheels unfolding before your very eyes like a textbook—overheated cooling systems, busted clutches, oil leaks, worn out treads, crushed and abandoned hubcaps, unjugged carburetors, fuel line trouble, charred chrome, out of gas, seats soaked with human perspiration, paint smelling of rust, shattered windshields, starter buttons that had had their day. Right next to my sleeping '56 Chevy was the corpse of a late '40's Studebaker with a message inscribed on its side as I watched: "You want it? It's yours," a car hunter's dream come true! But there were no takers, or at least nobody who felt like holding down the fort against further takers. By the time traffic started flowing again after it was all over, no one's claim had yet been registered by the removal of the inscription, done in lipstick—if it hasn't been towed away by now it's yours! I'm pretty sure he left the registration inside for you, so no man alive will be able to doubt your ownership.

Sgt. Jack Berry, a highway patrolman from Oxnard all the way downstate, volunteered for traffic control because he wished to be helpful in keeping things moving. Once things stopped to a complete halt it didn't bother him much at all. "You'd think I'd be kind of frustrated by this scene all around. But for years I've been imagining what this would look like if everything just stopped for miles, daydreaming about it. I always thought it was sinful to chop down all the trees and mountains, just to build highways so people could drive on them to parks and fishing trips and all, when originally it was all one big park so you didn't have to travel to get there . . . but now, uh, just look at it all. It's really a beautiful sight to see, nothing moving except the people themselves, and it's just like the cars are part of nature too, or art, like in a museum. It's beautiful, really, and I sure hope the people don't distort this in the press because it really shows us what travel is all about. These kids are hiking over there to the rock and roll, the music, but I can't really understand why they don't just stay here and have a party around the cars. And there's probably gonna be a lot of thefts from the cars so I wouldn't leave mine unattended if I was them." Hats off to a fuzz-face and mixed metaphors galore, there were many like him at Altamont, although most of the law enforcement officials were—let's fact it—just plain *dull.*

You could, without difficulty, say the same about the majority of the bikers in attendance. Angels are Angels. They can't be beat, they're swell, they're interesting, they have the gusto, they know how to live and they're all poets at heart. But those are the Angels—and the Angels are far from the whole show as far as bikers at the fairground were concerned. Once the Angels had camped down near the bandstand and on the stage itself, many of the second, third, fourth and fifth-raters stayed away, some due to friendly harassment but most of them just punks. One such pack of would-be outlaws was a group identified by colors labeling them the Conjars, Portland (Me.), a name that must have more significance in their own home town and thereabouts. Their bikes were Suzukis and Kawasakis, their boots were suede numbers out of some weird hunting movie, their uniforms were leather (!) and their leather wasn't more than a month old. Yet they were out to look tough, a job made more difficult by the insistent laughter that greeted them every step of the way.

Okay, picture this: several football players and their girls hit the immediate area, down for the affair from Colorado State or whatever C.S.U. might happen to be. They wore their numbers, bright blue on canary yellow. The biggest (6'5" or so and about 250 lbs.) was proud of his number 69 (ha ha), identifying him as a guard on the squad. He wore that black stuff under his eyes that they use to cut down the glare during tough-nosed game action. He was raring to go! His buddies acknowledged him as a leader and he made constant demands to them like "Wine, Jim!" and "Hey man, let's find us a spot, mother." Okay, during an unguarded moment a Conjar bozo noticed himself one great heck of a nice broad. Too bad for him she belonged to number 35 (running back?), who could hardly stand up and was stooping over to pick up his Pagan Pink Ripple (the cap was lost and he was struggling to prevent heavy leakage). He finally sat down with a shrug and turned around to see his sweetie not really minding Mr. Conjar's grasp at all! Too much for him to take: "That's my old lady you stiff!" and the entire football wrecking crew was gang tackling the poor hungry cretin, adrenaline pumping all over the place, all their soused, stewed, smashed, potted, mindless energy directed toward one single goal, leaving Bozo in a pile of his own blood and bones. Success was theirs too, as not one Conjar brother made the least attempt to intervene (some bikers!) other than a few well-chosen descriptive words, but to no avail. But they *did* carry him to the medic, even though it was more than half a mile in the distance. No small feat considering the density of the throng.

Violence didn't inflict the only disappointment of the day. Sometimes it was just the old famous deprivation. A Sacramento youth who wished to remain anonymous stated it this way: "You think I came here to see the Rolling Stones? The Stones are *guys* and I'm sure not after no guys, you dig?" Unfortunately, he didn't get what he *was* after and why travel for what you can just as easily not get at home?

A not unlarge number of rock bands who figured *anybody* could play found out they were wrong. The Long Island Drug Division supposedly took off in their truck from New York Town on Tuesday and made it to Altamont just as the first act began. They presented themselves. The stage manager just laughed up his sleeve at them, claimed the schedule was packed already, and that it would've made a difference if they had only arrived sooner. One such group *did* arrive earlier, Crisp Apple from Reno. Same result—not a chance, you should have had your manager contact us forty-eight hours ago. But Tom Stith, bass man for Crisp Apple, was as philosophical as he could be throughout and after the encounter: "You know, I came here to have a good time and I wanted to help others have a good time by playing and putting on our show. But it's like the biggest gig we've ever had was bars in Carson City, so you can't expect this if you don't have a rep. But you also guess that the whole crowd is just waiting for the Stones, so it wouldn't make that much difference who went on first, you know what I mean? They told us they weren't set up but that was about two hours ago, and they haven't added anything since that time, look for yourself. It's really a nice spectacle."

Monterey had a light show, Woodstock had a light show. But Altamont was planned for daylight hours, hence no light show. But not everybody was betting it would be over before nightfall, so some fool with no official go-ahead invited stand-by light show people to wait in the wings just in case. David Flooke, the important East Coast light show personage from way back, didn't really believe it would come off (from past experience), but showed up nonetheless, ready and willing to be mildly disappointed. But when he walked up to stage creep Ned Butcher and got a who-the-hell-are-you routine, he understandably blew his top! He threw a box of slides at the worthless moron and if both parties hadn't been held back by others catching the vibes there would have been a real mess. Dave's wife Dale was livid with rage and kicked the idiot in the leg, so the Flooke team got in last licks, an impressive triumph.

George Waldeck wasn't as lucky. A father of two, he was merely attempting to get near enough to Rock Scully to get some autographs for the kids. But his overture was aggressive and a certain security character (who wasn't an Angel) interpreted it as an attack. He lifted the gentleman by the seat of his pants and passed him along a loosely knit chain of goons until, as witness Gary Ypremian substantiates, "He was so humiliated by them that he just walked away, more like *staggered*, just as bad as being *evicted*."

There's no way of determining exactly who the animals involved were, but revenge after the fact is fruitless in any event. Clearly they weren't in the pay of concert organizers and just as obviously they were not part of the Angels entourage either, they were just some clods who wanted some free authority, just waiting for any opportunity to shove their weight around with impunity; whoever gave them the authority should be shot, but that's another matter. But what does count is the matter of de facto eviction. At Woodstock the masses thought you needed a ticket to get in, and when they discovered you didn't it was all joy and glee and nobody fought over seats and nobody worried about getting kicked out. At Altamont, on the other hand, everybody already knew the score and nobody doubted they'd get in. The problem arose when everybody realized that jockeying for good seats was a competitive project, and that holding position was a grace-of-God matter. An ordeal to be sure, but undoubtedly there have been worse in the history of mankind (e.g. the Crusades, several gold rushes, the Oklahoma land rush of 1837).

It was usually subtle and merely implicit, but it got out of hand more than once. The most extreme outbreak occurred while the Guess Who surged into their hit "No Time Left For You." They had just finished "These Eyes" and were beginning to connect with the audience and gain their respect. There were no more dues to pay.

They reminded many of the early Beatles, the sound, the arrogance, the bestial voltage, the Liverpool basement murkiness under full sky. Nobody doubted there was something happening, the buzz was there. Eleven or twelve jokers caught the spark and charged forward, stomping on faces, legs, shoulders, backs and laps, catching most victims totally unaware but generating furor more than injury. "Look, I'm flyin' on Bacardis and speed. I'll admit I'm the kind of guy who naturally likes to beat butts, so some cat gives me a rough time of it while I'm tryin' to get near the music and I'm just gonna do him in, that's where it's at."

Joe Cocker wowed them too, knocking them dead in their tracks with his hilarious blindman antics which you had to strain your eyes to see, it was well worth the effort almost everyone would agree. This may seem like a plug, but I've put together a small film of the man himself entitled *Joe Cocker Live* (available through the Film-makers' Cooperative, 175 Lexington Avenue, New York, N.Y. 10016). It's not half bad as a document of the kind of stuff Joe displayed that afternoon in California that so impressed every man, woman and child on hand. I'll have to admit that he outdid the Stones (you would too if you were him). As a sign of how effective Joe was, during the last third of his performance two groovy flipped out teenage fans were just sitting there digging each other, one boy, one girl. Both were very stoned on heaven knows what. Both were smoking cigars! And both were doing something almost unconventional with their stogeys: they were burning deep scars into each other's facial flesh. Sounds good but it looked barely palatable to ladies and gents in the nearby shrubbery. Jake Scalzo ("Just horrible, God it was just horrible") finally grabbed the remaining butts from the couple and extinguished them immediately before summoning medical assistance. But Peter Katz disagreed: "Look, maybe *you're* here for music and *I'm* here for music, but what if some kids just want to spend their time differently. Even if it's burning holes in each other. Maybe they're going steady and it's a sign of affection, endearment. They do it in the jungles of New Zealand, and who's to argue with primitive man?" Nobody's knocking natural living, it's just that—

Even after the Stones were finished and most people were home in bed there were still parties going on. The Bellport Country Club was the scene of a gay glamorous party as members of the Bellport Chamber of Commerce gathered for their annual dinner-dance, not fully disconnected from the doings at Altamont. (Many were there and even more had offspring who made the scene.) Among those who cut the caper were Mr. James Lenox, Mr. William Florio, Dr. Woo Sik Kih and Miss May Hittner. Things were going great when, lo and behold, some bikers who hadn't yet had enough (none of them were Angels) and their friends busted things up long into the night, damage estimated at more than $140. A number of rapes were committed and several tears were shed, yet no arrests were made as the gang made a clean get-away. Nor was any connection made connecting them with the day of music. Nor was cause-and-effect necessary, everybody got the point without it, just as in the days of Alan Freed shows at the Brooklyn Paramount. The glory of rock und roll is BACK!

12

A Very Important Person

I did go to Woodstock, however, which even at the time felt very ersatz, ad hoc, and by all means after-the-fact. Bygone, y'dig? Yet it was only the beginning of such mega-shit, which even Altamont four months later did nothing to slow the momentum of.

Day one of Woodstock was pass-the-trash day, a time to satisfy various booking agents, record companies, entrepreneurial factions. Contrary to popular belief, Richie Havens did not open the festival. That honor fell to the Swami Satchadananda, whose interminable "set" (leading mantras, lauding the crowd's spirituality) was greeted with cries of "Fuck you—where's the music?," then Richie came on. "Isn't this groovy?" was his greeting and allegation, his epitome of the moment and its "vibe," and after him a band called Sweetwater hohummed the throngs, followed by Bert Sommer, blander than current memory has access to, wearing a dress (tho some might call it a kaftan), during whose set my companions and I, who had been there two days already (taking in the vibes like any other rubes), walked out.

Not everybody who got to Woodstock stayed the whole time, that's a fact not even a gambling man would try to refute: yes a sizable portion, maybe as high as .0003%, took a powder during day #1 of the big fandango, it's a fact which means it's true! You wanna know who left the first day? Well I'll tell you: there was Pearlman, there was Abrams, there was Shelly, there was Roni, there was me. By leaving the first day I don't mean I came back the next or the one after that, no that's not what I mean and it would be a lie to say it so I won't even hint it. What I did was never come back!

Now an entomologist such as myself treasures every moment out in the wilds with the hymenoptera. So it would take more than a crowbar to separate me from my wasps, which there were lots of at Woodstock: mud daubers, green pelicrees, whole hordes of em! What pried me away from the bugs was a human worse than six scumbags full of arsenic named Bert Sommer. That was his name and maybe it still is. If so then he's got an album out now which is his and nobody else's, since the name's on the cover, the inside and the record label itself. All three. I'm speaking of *Inside Bert Sommer*, Eleuthera Records number ELS3600.

Okay so here's what you can do: you can listen to it, you can not listen to it. Which will it be? First there's the first. If you do that then you'll need to have a puke bucket real handy, particularly if the smell of upchuck is something you don't want lingering around on the floor! Next there's the second. Second is the much better bet.

But then what if you hear it by accident while you're chugging down the street and somebody somewhere who got a free copy (cause who would buy it?) is giving it the test of the needle? If that happens you might well overhear it so don't be unprepared. What should you do in such case? You could try to faint, even if ya haven't done it before: unconsciousness beats nausea! You could also hum loudly or sing some tunes to cover it over so you won't have to hear it. If you have a friend along have him or her join in: two voices are louder than one. That way even if it's not more sound it's more volume! You'll drown it out like a silver thumb-bit!

At Woodstock nobody had a mike in their pocket so Bert's vocalities came out number one while he was up on stage, nobody even came in second except the helicopters, they came in second but he was first! His album is first TOO: first rate elephant shit!

What's the worst thing on the disc? They're *all* the worst! But if you like numbers the 1st worst is "Friends." The 2nd worst is "On the Other Side." The 3rd worst is "Smile." The 4th worst is "Here Is the Timeless Life." The 5th worst is "Mama, if You're Able." Tied for 6th worst is "It's a Beautiful Day" and "We're All in the Same Band." There is no 7th worst because the tie eliminates that. The 8th worst is "Uncle Charlie." The 9th worst is "Eleuthera." The 10th worst is "America." The 11th worst is "Zip Zap Melody." The 12th worst is "I've Got to Try." The 13th worst is "The Grand Pianist." This includes words, music, and singing. The ratings may change on a second hearing but hearing it again would be like letting the rattler bite you again so you can watch and count the rattles! Snakes are *bad business* if they hurt you or a loved one and albums are no different.

If you get the album for a birthday or Christmas see if they'll take it back!

He was in *Hair* which explains why so many cast members quit!

Also: his voice is not very good.

Yet: he is undeniably the finest WITH the sound o' the voice since Norman Greenbaum, who is in turn the most excellent since Domenico Modugno. Thus: this man is quite important in the world of music!

13

Marty Balin: Artist as Madman

One guy who played both Altamont and Woodstock was Marty Balin, who around that time was still kind of a friend and drinking buddy, so I felt entitled to say all sorts of stupid things about him. I don't remember how much of this is actually him, in fact—'cause some of it is me.

I'll readily cop to the source of all the exclamation points: Muhammad Ali—my original influence as a writer.

Wheaties now has larger flakes but there are no larger flakes than Marty Balin. When he played the Unicorn in '67 he went out and bought himself a dead butterfly! Cost him ten bucks! He once traded jackets with Gary Blackman and he traded Gary a peacoat for an old army coat or something; it turned out to be not a peacoat (not a real peacoat) but a peacoat with wooden buttons! He thought it was real! Once a loyal fan named Michael gave him a present of a rare edition of Marcel Proust and he said thank you! He was overwhelmed! He often spends his hours at the old pinball machine, baseball's his favorite and he never loses! Once he was in the same elevator with Josh White Sr. and he didn't recognize him! Far out!

Holy Hannah, the man's insane. His name used to be Marty Buchwald, he changed it! He's an avant garde painter! He uses aluminum foil, string, paint, and composition in his works! And he signs them all Buchwald! His real self! He once went to a sandwich place on Paul Williams' recommendation! And when the sandwich was worthless he said "Paul this is the worst sandwich I've ever eaten"! He said that "Today" was a parody on Andy Williams, not the real thing! When he was a teenager he was in a teen band called the Town Criers, they used to play at parties around the pool! That was his early musical experience! And when he first put together the original Airplane he AUDITIONED people for it! By the hundreds! In this day and age!

You might even say he's goofy. He fired Skip Spence because Skip never showed up for practice! He fired Signe because she was interested in hick life first, her family second and the Airplane third! He wanted to cancel the Airplane's Levi ad because of the Levi strike and his father was a big union man! He once had a roommate named Cliff! He never went to college! He's an Ohio boy, from Canton or Columbus!

You might even call him crackers. He used to drive an old Volkswagen microbus! He considers Ruth Ann Friedman (who wrote "Windy") a real nice girl! He was once feasted to a roast beef dinner at which he met Les of the Soft White Underbelly, who offered him a ride; he turned him down! He spent some time in L.A. where he once had a wife and child! In the summer of '67 he said hello to a Lotus dealer and mechanic in Sausalito! He claimed Aretha Franklin was singing R-E-S-P-S-T-P in "Respect"! Social consciousness for fellow musicians: he once refused to play at some Catholic school in California when the priest wouldn't pay the Buffalo Springfield (they were late)! The guy told Marty okay and then Marty played and then the check bounced! At the party following his first Stony Brook appearance he looked the most disgusted! When the Left Banke went on the turntable he paid no attention! During his Cafe au Go Go days he ate exclusively at the Tin Angel, went through the entire menu and said it was all bad! But he didn't mind the chicken as much!

The man is a kook. His favorite reading matter is *Réalités*! When he was in Boston he wanted to know what Harvard looked like! He's flown United Airlines many times! But Jefferson remains his favorite! He liked Quicksilver because Nick Gravenites was working with them! He liked Dino Valenti! He liked Cream very early in the game! He mentioned Zap Comics every chance he got! He liked Michael McClure and knew him personally! He liked the Gentle Soul but he didn't know Pamela Polland! He liked their song "Song For Three"! Is he a gull or is he not?! His favorite store in Sausalito is a Finnish shawl store!

Not only that but he's a dope fiend as well. He's taken a lot of trips! The lyrics of his songs deal with drugs! He told Gary Blackman he never had an ego loss! Gary told him that if that's the case well then he never took a trip! Marty once announced to the audience that Owsley the famous sound engineer was in the crowd! He met Paul McCartney in 1967 and played with him for a while! In return Paul let him hear a tape! The Town Criers played Vegas and Tahoe too! He rode to the Boston Armory with a motorcycle escort! He still has a copy of Kandinsky's "On The Spiritual In Art" that he borrowed a long time ago! He once did some acting! He had a pet turtle but not anymore! He told Sandy Pearlman that if he ever started a new band he'd make Sandy his singer! He told everybody that if they needed a place to stay on the coast his place was available!

Also, don't count him out as a nut. He doesn't drink or smoke! He once used grease in his hair! He played so well once that some kid thought he was the maraca man (not the singer) of the band! He can handle a bass too! Sometimes real well! A long time ago he wore buttons on his chest! Before he ever played out east he visited the Barge on a promotional tour! He got in for free without having to play! I bet he had a good time too! He thought Jim Morrison was just another Jagger imitator! What a description! Now he lives in a big house!

In fact you might say he's as wacky as a dodo. After all, didn't he buy a new watch?!! He even spent a few days at the Zen Center! He once had a dream about being rich and look at him now! As a youngster he excelled in archery, football, baseball AND basketball! He had himself a great time! But physical fitness was his first love! He enjoys travel but he likes to stay in one place too! He prefers the bohemian way of life to the straight and narrow! He often performs with two maracas, one on each side of the protruding mike! Freud would have a field day with that! When he cuts nose hair he does it safely, risking no infection! He numbers Jack Casady and Bill Laudner among his friends and associates! He never wanted to be an only child! As a young kid he once got into a fight and went home screaming that a playmate had ripped his ear loose! Turned out to be a piece of candy dangling from his ear! He was extremely fond of sweets! He believes strongly in peace! He's kissed more than one New Jersey brunette! On the lips! His favorite sandwich is a roast beef sandwich! He likes as little gristle as possible!

If no one's ever called him a raving maniac let it be said right now. He doesn't like to hunt with a shotgun but if he did he'd rather go for polar bears! Unlike most San Franciscans, he wears a full complement of underwear! It's a quarter to ten and he's still not asleep in bed! He's out carousing! What a wild guy! He's even been on boats! His hobby is reading! He is approximately 27 or 28 years of age! And yet he believes in astrology and the zodiac! For $7.95 he could have himself an electro-plating kit! Yet he's never purchased one! He played defensive cornerback for the football team and never made an interception! In the early days he used to guard Grace from the male fans! You couldn't get near her if you tried, unless you became Marty's friend! No, he

was never in the armed forces! It broke his heart to get rid of Skip
Spence! He's the most conservatively dressed man in the group! He's
the nicest guy you'd ever want to meet! As a professional animator he
has worked with Harvey Toombs and Gordon Zahler! He records for
RCA! Not only that but he is emotionally volatile! He disliked the
haircut he got about 3 years ago on the east coast! He likes his eggs
scrambled, he prefers warm weather to cold weather, but he doesn't
dislike the snow!

More than slightly crazy is what he is, crrrazy man! He and his
band once had a gig in the land of Dixie! Some of them were arrested
and the rest were permanently marred by the experience! When
Marty first met Paul Kantner he said "Paul I like your face, can you
play a guitar?" and Paul answered no and Marty took him anyway! He
has sung "Another Side Of This Life" more times than "Happy
Birthday To You"! That's a lot of times! He was fully clothed for his
first appearance in Portland! Another time in another town it was
summer, so he took off his shirt! Yet on the Smothers Brothers he
made himself so inconspicuous that they concentrated mostly on
Grace (he's schizoid)! On stage he once left the mike open for anyone
who wished to say or sing anything at all to do just that! He used to
lean back with the mike stand—but not anymore! At least not as
much—he's gotten a little older! He'd like to be as successful as the
Beatles! Few, however, take such psychotic longings seriously!

Now I'm not saying Marty ought to be locked up in a loony bin or
hospitalized in a sanatorium for his own good and everybody else's,
that's for the doctors to decide. But although I am not qualified as a
headshrinker I would hazard to say the facts indicate Marty is off his
rocker. He considers Yorkville in Toronto two years behind America
but a fine little hippy community just the same! Going even further
off the deep end, he has stated that Luke and the Apostles were an excellent band! It's a long time since his favorite writer was Albert Ca-
mus, but not long enough! Get this: he once abandoned stage and let
Tim Buckley replace him! He's frequently been in the same city (at
the same time) with Fathead Newman yet he's never bothered to look
him up! When Tim Jurgens wanted to be recognized so he could get
in free, who did it but Marty! His "Plastic Fantastic Lover" deals with
perversity! In "3/5 Of A Mile In Ten Seconds" it's FREAKS! Marty's
no freak, but he sure is weird! Take, for example, his preoccupation
with music and singing! Or what happened to "Pooneil" from the
drawing board to the recording booth to the mixing room! He wears

a ring and it isn't a diamond! Nor is it a wedding band! His favorite studio pianist is Nicky Hopkins!

This may all be well and good, but madness and intelligence are not mutually exclusive, they're different mental faculties. So Marty is no lamebrain, he's actually sharp as a whip! And in many cases being out of your skull can be correlated with uncanny capabilities of the mind. In this case it is Marty's extraordinary prophetic power: three springs ago he was already talking about Brian leaving the Stones to do a soundtrack! His creative enormity goes hand in hand with the wigged out, flipped out side of his personality, and rumor has it that he is being groomed for the emcee post of next year's Miss Globe pageant! Marty's amazing all right!

14

Getting It On and Taking It Off: Iggy and the Stooges

For years I thought this was a crummy, discontinuous little nothin', but only because the most recent version I'd seen was the reprint in Jon Eisen's Twenty-Minute Fandangos and Forever Changes, *bowdlerized—with an ax—to the point of incoherence. Hey, it turns out 's a good'un: a document of my "rediscovery" of the power of rock & roll—better than politics, drugs or sex (it sez here)—something you could (and conceivably still can) feel on any given night—but, oh!, the long haul . . .*

Written under some mundane head like "The Stooges at Ungano's," it began my stint as author of Screw's *biweekly "Rock and Raunch" column. Of all the papers I wrote rockstuff for, with the possible exception of* Rolling Stone, Screw *gave me the least leeway to, how you say, create. Everything had to have a sexual angle, however slight, and a glut of bombast bordering on cute—puns and alliteration and everything telegraphed. A column on Elvis thus became "Jailhouse Cock"; one on Linda McCartney, who as Linda Eastman had all but defined groupiedom, was renamed "Paul's Pussy."*

When, after a couple of years of this, I asked editor-publisher Al Goldstein for a raise, from $30 to $35, he immediately fired me: "If I have to choose between paying writers and lawyers"—legal authorities were on his ass— "I'll take lawyers."

Rock and roll is better than politics; it's better than drugs; and it's better than sex. What? Yes, that's right; but if you ever wanna jerk off to music, rock and roll is what you need. You need it? You got it! The Stooges. If you're in high school, stay there, 'cause if you're not you'll wanna get there where the action is. If Judy Garland had lived to see the Stooges she'd be back there too. There's a lot of blowing, eating and fucking and rock and roll has made it possible.

At Ungano's a week back, Scott Kempner and his pals and gals were down from Bronx High School of Science to catch the action from the front row. There was danger in those seats; there was always the chance of having an organ picked at in the shuffle. But if Niagara Falls was rock and roll they'd by lying under it, and me too. And the Stooges had an even better trick up their sleeves than a famous waterfall and that was Iggy, who had no sleeves. Instead he had no SHIRT, and ripped dungarees with red underpants. His gloves didn't stay on long either, he had some clawing and slapping to do.

For clawing purposes you need nails, so gloves won't do, even if the nails are as long as a cat's. Iggy's aren't; for him to draw blood from his face it's gotta be nail right on flesh. If he had pimples—protrusions are easier to get your hands on—it would be a heck of a lot easier for him, but his teenage complexion has gone away. So he's gotta pick and rip and he does it real good. If you wanna dig a hole in skin it can't be neat unless you're a mosquito and Iggy is not. But when face-digging is involved he keeps his excavations *small*; that way there is room for the future. There's talk he's gonna do some dueling scars and sandpaper scrapings and that sounds like a good idea. His blood is hot and it would flow fast and red and bigger scabs would mean easier picking for next time.

But it's gotta be more violent than that, which means lots of slapping. By Newton's Third Law it hurts his hand as much as himself and symmetry is the nature of his act anyway. He jumps on you, you gotta give him something in return. If you don't, you're a punk and a lazy artistic scavenger, even a vampire. After all Iggy even uses his body as the sounding surface for percussion just so you can hear the music more clearly. He's sacrificing his pud for your ears and mind, so you better reciprocate or you'll go to your death someday knowing you didn't have it in you to be a rock and roll star.

Ever since the adoption of a no-booze policy at Ungano's the place has become Snacktown, USA. Things are on a more solid basis than ever right now with Dinkees Bimi on the menu. Being less edible than Old London taco chips, Dinkees are used as throw material when great stage groups like the Canon Taxi need a nudge off stage. Yet nobody threw any at Iggy and this despite the fact that Ig himself dumped a can of the stuff into sax man Steve Mackay's instrument. The only thing anybody did at all was Patti Smith sitting on Ig's face as he lay on his back bluesing à la John Lee Hooker.

Steve learned his tenor honking from Adrian Rollini so he's murder on reeds. The key to good playing is teeth, tongue, lips and lungs.

Even a turtle has those ingredients but old Mr. Hardshell never came close in the rock and roll roundup. Nor was he as nice a guy as Steve Mackay. The fans at Ungano's demanded rock and roll and he served it up, no questions asked. He didn't have to know for what purpose or how loud, he just played it and played it right. Not only was it right but it was tight. So was the rest of the band.

Roy Larsen plays a mean set of tubs. Where rock and boogying intersect is in the vicinity of the drum head. Rock means beat and beat means drums, boogy means friction and friction means rubbing and rubbing means rhythm and rhythm means beating . . . beating on a drum. There's all sorts, snare, tomtom, bass, cymbal and cowbell, but Roy leans heavily towards the bass. After all, it's the best thumping. And that's what the Stooges do best.

Another kind of bass, the one with strings, is manned by Jim Bogo. He plays it like a man. If he was a girl his tits would get in the way of the strap, but that'll never happen so he can keep his shirt on and keep his style and stance intact. He's like Bill Wyman and Bill's a charter member of the Rolling Stones and the Stones have always had a lot to do with what raunch is all about. On "Doctor Robert" he sounds a lot like Doug Yule and that means Velvet country. But mostly it's just that good ol' bone vibrating erotic geology.

Tim Hardin—not *the* Tim Hardin—gives it all direction on ax. And that direction is erection, meat erection and music erection. Iggy had one, and two layers of crotch garment couldn't disguise it. Another part of him that was hard was his muscles and he flexed them voluntarily between shaking his ass and giving the combined finger and peace sign with both hands. Another thing he did was lie down and snarl and growl but he once almost smiled. That was when he was introducing the next selection ("For our next selection . . . ") and it really grabbed everybody's funny bone by the leg and didn't let go until he launched into "1970" which was the hit of the show, ax-wise.

But those are only their noms de plume, or in this case their noms de musique. Respectively, their birth certificates read Scott Asheton on drums, Zeke Zettner on bass (but he's no relation to Si) and Ron Asheton on lead guitar (he is a relation to Scott, in fact they're brothers). Steve and Ig are fortunate enough to have great names to begin with.

But my business is not so much musique as it is plume, so I've gotta proceed with caution. For every rock there's a criticism and for every raunch there's an epistemology. So raunch-wise, epistemologically speaking, my criticism of them is this: they dress real well, they have one shirt that's pink with a shrunken head design, they have another that says Cocaine using the Coca-Cola logo, they have a lot of good shoes and some good boots. They're what music is all about, going back even further than the first pair of blue suede shoes. And now that hair's come to be taken for granted, Iggy's just spent 20 hours in front of a mirror, scissors in hand, again risking all with rock and roll in mind. In addition he smokes Senator Club extra mild cigars (made in Holland where rock is king) and they taste like peroxide. Some people use it to bleach their hair, but not him—he's authentic all the way. He learned the big beat from pounding on his tinker toys when he was just a youngster. THAT'S THE ONLY TRAINING YOU CAN GET FOR A LIFETIME OF ROCK AND ROLL, which makes the Stooges the only guys who know what they're doing, including King Crimson.

15

More than Just a Whopping Good Picture

Lag time: another variable to play with.

Reviewing a finished cut of Performance *two months before it hit local screens meant it would be that long before anyone found out I made it up, re-plotted and recast the film, added new dialogue. As opposed to imagining something I'd neither seen nor heard, here I re-imagined the seen/heard—not really fiction, in this context, as much as misinformation (one of my favorite journalistic riffs). Lar Tusb's report from Altamont, by comparison, I hadn't expected anyone to believe, could not've imagined anyone dumb enough to be misinformed by.*

Denise Quigley I didn't have to imagine; she was someone who that summer I didn't have sex with, but who volunteered me a peek at her butt, accompanied by a fantastic line that would show up 25 years later, slightly changed, in my novel The Night (Alone) *(p. 116). Hey, Den', y'still out there?*

Performance is the best one around since *The Spy Who Came In From The Cold* even though there were no actors as good as Richard Burton. They weren't *as good*, they were *better*! James Fox was better than John Ireland, Michael Crawford, Neil Louison, Bob Mathias and John Davidson. Mick was better than Billy Fury, Joe D'Allessandro, Peter Noone, Nancy Sinatra, Bobby Vee, Francis X. Bushman and Abel Fernandez, and it is clear that he has learned the thespian trade from as formidable a teacher as George Harrison. Anita Pallenberg is better than Barbara Stanwyck, Grace Kelly, George Kennedy, Tippi Hedrin, Pamela Tiffin, Hoagy Carmichael, Raymond St. Jacques and Mamie Van Doren. Michele Breton, a Frenchy, is not as good as the rest but still she is better than most other people you can name, including Diane McBain, Chill Wills, Mona Jacobson, the late Monty Wooley, Richard Carlson, Sarah Bernhardt and Kathy Horvath, all better than average and usually good. Just a notch below their vast talent was a cameo by Bob Somma as Tony Farrell, a good part played by a good man.

Which brings things up to characters and story, both of which were good. James Fox played Chas Chandler. He kills a man and runs away. He ends up in Mick's basement and before too long he's on a camping trip out in the back yard with one of the 2 birds Mick lives with, Michele Breton as Linda Marzocco. They lie back to back in full nakedness when he decides to feel her up. She says that feels good and he keeps it up. Finally she says "I've never made love to someone I didn't know before but you can be the first one." But he falls asleep and so does she.

Meanwhile Mick as Turner is intoxicated on liquor and the lovely presence of Anita Pallenberg as Denise Quigley. Anita in real life of course lives with another Stone, Keith Richard. Even though they are not married they are the proud parents of a healthy 5-year-old male bastard. Maybe it was written into her contract that she could remain faithful to Keith because that's exactly the way it happened. Mick and her are lolling around and he's getting some soul kisses off her and some tit. They're sitting on the stairwell and he pulls her over down the stairs and by the time they've hit bottom she has unloosed her brassiere. His hands reach under her sweater and fondle her knobs to his heart's content and her nipples harden real quick, this fact confirmed by the dialogue ("Are they hard?" "Yes.") and several zooms in by the camera. Next he wants to know if he can make her and says it in so many words: "Let's go where it's a bit softer and lie down." She turns him down but adds "Though I won't do any fucking I'll show you my ass" and she does, lowering her trousers so the entire buttocks is visible. Then she shakes it and Turner grabs at it but to no avail as she is a strong woman and gets her pants back on before he can register much of a complaint. Next he tries more kisses and feels but that doesn't work either. In his disgruntled state he'll say anything and he does: "Well, let's just lie down next to each other." Again he is turned down. But don't count your chickens before they're hatched because before the night is through he has gotten it from the other dame, who happens to have dark hair like himself.

Then comes the big scene where Chas is discovered as a man with whip scars on his back (the reason they were back to back is so she couldn't see) and he lies about it being from a car accident. He didn't

look like a driver so lying gets him nowhere. The girls use their imagination and improve on his back condition by means of medicine and
bandages. Next he wants a photograph for a fake passport so he tells
them it's for his "new image" but that's a lie. He claims to be a juggler
and a show biz crony of the previous tenant who has moved out ow-
ing 41 pounds. Totaled all together including advances and deposit
against breakage it comes to over one hundred pounds and he pays it.
Who would pay it for such a throwaway apartment? So they know
he's full of shit and since he's got 2/3 of a magic mushroom down his
gullet they decide to make a fun time out of him.

   The invitation to experiment with Chas' image seems to Turner su-
pernaturally opportune. It is now apparent that he and Denise know
what, if not who, Chas really is, and they, for their part, intend to *use
him*. For in Turner's eyes, his lodger has assumed the proportions of a
demonic figure, personifying the magnetism of violence that Turner
knows was the core, or the cutting edge, of his own power as a performer. The reason for his present predicament—his creative impo-
tence—becomes clearer. At the height of his success, he had become
aware of anomalous extensions of his art that led towards inchoate violence. He learned that the atavistic rituals of the performance with
which he captured and manipulated his gigantic audience were capable of generating demonic forces beyond his control. After all he had,
as the little girl in the picture once said, "2 number ones, 4 number
twos, 2 number threes and a number four."

   But all this rigmarole goes down the drain when Mick puts on his
leather jacket and hair grease. In fact he looks like a combination between Don Knotts, Andy Bobroff and Ed Sullivan and also the
Swedish Angel (not the French Angel, Maurice Tillet) which is a far
cry from how he looks when his hair hangs over his face when there's
no grease in it. Another time in the picture there's grease and even
though there's no leather this time it's the height of the picture. He's
sitting behind a desk and since there's no desk in the apartment it has
to be in the office of Chas' boss and he has Chas' boss' seat and Chas'
boss isn't there. In other words he *is* Chas' boss which means he's a
mighty important person in Chas' life so Chas listens intently to
Mick's message. And the message is message *music* the likes of which
hasn't been heard since Barry McGuire. The guys in the office take
off their clothes while he's singing and they do because he asks them
to. No he doesn't actually ask but he does tell them that he wants
their *love* and they know what that means. A few of them cooperate
but Chas does not take it off, therefore he is out of place and that is

accentuated by his wig which they've put on his head to change his image. He doesn't look good but it's better than before.

Soon he calls up Somma and says he has the photo. Somma says we'll be over at 9:30 but *which* 9:30, AM or PM? That's when they come to get him and do they ever get him! About 9 or 10 gangsters and they mean him no good. Therefore he can't go to America (where *he* wanted) and he can't go to Persia (where Linda wanted) but he must instead go to death. But before that he has intercourse with Linda and doesn't really mind dying although the moment is not really right. He'd rather take a bath or shower first because his combined drug and sexual experiences have left him muggy and covered with dirt and he knows he has at least another 3 hours to live. They might as well be comfortable ones but they don't let him.

They do let him say goodbye to his friends, which include not only Mick but both women. Mick now reads to him from his forthcoming novel and it's not half bad, only it was written not by the real-life Mick but script-writers. In it are details of the original hash people, the ones who used to assassinate everybody. It seems they were told that even if they died they would go to heaven so it didn't matter whether they died or not. That's a good idea, so everybody in the room knows what it's all about to die, but nobody except Mick knows that Chas is going there himself. Chas doesn't know that anybody knows until Mick says "I do" and then Chas shoots him through the head.

What happens to his head is the greatest adventure in cinematic art since *Potemkin*. The bullet from Chas' pistol pierces the head and goes all the way through and it does not seem like a film-maker's gimmick, that's how real it seems. You get to see the entire tunnel made by the trajectory of lead through skull and the way it looks is reminiscent of the thing at the beginning of all Looney Toons with the concentric circles of red and the blue in the distance like at the end of a tunnel. And at the end of this particular one is the sky and the top of a building. Psychedelic! But also hard to believe, like how could it have been filmed without actually drilling the hole in Mr. Jagger's head? Could it have been a double? Perhaps, because the top of his head is all you saw and what he said could of been said from off stage. Still it's a trick of the camera that's hard to do, they'd have to use a telephoto lens to get the rooftop and then they would've lost all the clarity of the head wound. Somehow they did it and hats off to them! Unit manager Kevin Kavanagh to be exact. The picture ends with cars going into the hills, one of them containing someone who is supposed to be Chas but who looks like Mick.

Yes it was a good movie and it deserved its X rating, although it might've been an R and no one would have complained. Yet it was not merely a dirty movie in the ordinary sense even though there was some footage out of a real live stag film that included ass whipping. If it had been black and white just like the stag film and like *Hard Day's Night*—so similar to *Performance* that you could call them brothers—it might have been even dirtier because color takes your mind off fingering (a major reason why people do it with the lights off) and black and white does not. But it was in the field of *weirdness* that it really got off the ground, so far that it was the far farthest picture in the decade and a half since the release of *Twenty Thousand Leagues Under The Sea*. The weirdest guy in that one was not a guy but the giant squid and in this one it's a guy: James Fox or Johnny Shannon (Harry Flowers). When actors can do that it's always spectacular and often a work of art. In this case it's both. And when it's rock and roll too it's worth seeing twice and bringing along a bottle of beer.

16

John McLaughlin and the Song of Songs

I hated interviews, and didn't wanna talk to John McLaughlin nohow, but this gladhand schmuck named Kenny, see, who worked for Alan Douglas, whose company had just released McLaughlin's Devotion *LP, got me into Max's to see Alice Cooper, whose own company I didn't yet have access to, and I think he even bought me a meal and some beers—or signed a tab for them.*

This was back when Alice spit spitballs and used a Dutch door as a stage prop—very silly—as silly as McLaughlin was austere . . . stern . . . dour. One solemn geek.

Q: How come you cut your hair?
A: I was asked to by my guru, and uh, and uh it was nothing for me to do it. In fact I like it.
Q: It's better for the summer.
A: Yeah right. Last year it really itched, on my neck. And the problem then was I've got long hair, you've got short hair. It's bad, it's got nothing to do with anything . . . all it's got to do with is separation. It means I'm hip, and you're not. I don't even think about hair anymore.
Q: Even when you see it?
A: I don't even think of it when I *see* it. Before I used to comb it and brush it, ah isn't it beautiful, ah the shine . . . but that's all right.
Q: How about the beard?
A: Well that came off on the first day of spring. That came off just from my, from an inward feeling. It was getting too warm. It's good in winter, you have cold winters here.

Q: Did you play soccer?

A: Yeah.

Q: Well?

A: No, not well.

Q: That's like a really alien thing here, they're trying to introduce it but it's all foreigners, it's hard to get into, it's like
thinking about jazz in England and being American, because
English jazz seems like Tubby Hayes, stuff like that, Johnny
Dankworth. . . .

A: Well it *was* probably in the eyes of America, but in the eyes of
Europe, English jazz is more implied by John Stevens and
Evan Parker, people you've never heard of, Chris McGregor,
who are something else entirely.

Q: Like from the Bonzo Dogs and people like that you get the
idea that jazz in England is all comedy. . . .

A: No, no, that's not true, no, you can get that idea but it's mis-
leading. There are some valid things going on in England, in
fact the whole of Europe is in the process of getting together
and spreading out, as the result of the coming together.

Q: Jazz in the U.S. seems to have, since the mid-60's, stylistically,
it got as far as it could go so it became a matter of picking
where you wanted to play along the map. . . .

A: Oh no, you see jazz for me wasn't so much, it *was* the music
but it was *more* the people y'know and the development of
their consciousness and their spirituality, and uh because jazz
embodies the finest principles of music, which are namely improvisation, rhythm and melody. And so you can call *any* music that's improvised, that has rhythm and melody jazz. Jazz is
just a label to stick on so you can refer to it as that.

Q: The official jazz *scene*, y'know what's *labeled* jazz, has been
perceived to be very introspective rather than audience conscious. . . .

A: Well before you can go on stage and just *be*, I mean that's the
whole point about it, but before you reach it the whole thing
about it is you can't force me, I don't want to go on there and
indulge myself, it doesn't offer me anything, it doesn't offer
anything to anybody else. The person must be essentially introspective, must be an essential facet, everyone is introspective to a degree but a musician, especially one who improvises,
must develop this aspect, this facet of his personality just like
his outward aspect is developed when he plays out. But he
can't, he must have one, he must have the other, and there's

the balance between the two.

Q: American jazz in recent years has become more a commodity which people will *buy*, it seems as if it's been organizing the cliches and styles of past years, the ones that were obvious things that people would want. . . .

A: Well that's why I say that it's more the people. There weren't many people, and there aren't many people. . . .

Q: It's almost like you're asking from jazz more than you're asking from rock, you're asking a very different kind of, rock people are being asked very little. . . .

A: But as long as they ask, really. Because the music, people come to the music because they need something and people play music because *they* need something, and the audience and the performer mutually fulfill each other. And their respective degree of asking, everybody's different, everybody probably comes for different reasons consciously but subconsciously they come for the same reason.

Q: But you can separate the kind of performers who are showmen from those who aren't. Like Thelonious Monk, he wears a different hat every time he plays, he does a dance while the other guys are soloing. It's not so much that he's showbiz but that part of what he's doing has performance *aspects*. How conscious are you that what you're doing is something to be seen as well as heard?

A: Well, it's, you're always, everyone who goes on stage and plays an instrument is aware that people are watching. From the moment you ever start playing. I mean in school you're aware of it. In fact you don't even have to play an instrument to go up in front of people and know that people are watching you, that's the whole point. People wanna watch, they wanna see. They wanna hear, they wanna feel. But it's just varying degrees. That starts from 3 or 4 people, 5 or 6, a thousand, ten thousand, it's just varying degrees.

Q: But how much are you conscious of communicating on the visual level too, the way you move, do you think about anything like that at all?

A: No. It's unnecessary. Maybe some do, but it's not important to anyone who's sincere. Sincere about his music.

Q: I don't mean it like the difference between musician and star but a musician and somebody who's a musician plus something else.

A: What else can he be? What else can he be other than a musician? Someone who plays an instrument, he can be nothing but a musician. In the final analysis and from the very beginning that's all he'll *ever* be relative to what goes on in his conscious mind.

Q: Why is it that people who are musicians are exclusively musicians, that that's more of their life than somebody who's a writer is also other things?

A: You can't say a writer's not his way of life. A writer observes people, and he feels, and he writes about them.

Q: True, but is the way you sit musical, or the way you put a watchband on, do you feel it that way?

A: No I don't feel it that way except that music is in the very depths of my being, just like it's in the very depths of *your* being. That's why everyone loves music, because music unites everyone, and it eliminates separateness.

Q: How is music more basic than other things?

A: Because as you say, it just *is*, it's fundamental.

Q: Is it something you can talk about?

A: Because it's the sum of God's things through every one of us. Your soul sings its *song*. Roni is it? (Looking at Roni Hoffman across the room.) Your soul's singing your song, right now. Whether you're aware of it or not doesn't really matter, because in reality you're singing your song, all the time. And all a musician is, is someone who becomes aware of this and compels to bring it out into reality.

Q: But when you get to something like the relationship between music and *talent*, in other words like how you can move your fingers on the strings. . . .

A: What's talent?

Q: Just some marginally superior ability, than somebody else.

A: For talent you can substitute consciousness, it's degree of consciousness.

Q: But how about when it gets to having better control of your fingers than someone else, when it gets to that kind of level?

Q: The only reason anyone has better control of his fingers than anyone else is because he *hears* it more clearly in his heart and from there into his imagination, into his head and out into his hands.

Q: But don't you ever hear things you can't play?

A: Of course, of course, of course. Every musician can always hear more, you can never get to the end, can you?

Q: But the fact that there are those who can play better what they hear. . . .

A: Don't you see, you can *never* reach the end, never. You can be the greatest virtuoso and there's always more to play.

Q: What about being closer to what you hear than others who are also musicians?

A: Well the thing is you see, in the final analysis who is the realer musician, and who really plays? I can go into my own personal experience, which is this, that someone else—other than me—is the real player, and when I step away and let him take over then I'm just a witness.

Q: Say you hear somebody else playing the same instrument you play, don't you ever think of better and worse, you know, that somebody is not technically as good as you or technically better?

A: Why should I, why do I think that?

Q: I'm not talking about judgment of it but mere technique, control of the instrument. Where does it fit in that x can play better than y, in the scheme of things? What's the actual *relevance* of talent?

A: All I can say about that is people, some people, are closer to themselves than other people are. As closely as you are to yourself, closely you are to God and therefore the more lucid, and the more powerful and stronger and true will be your music.

Q: I mean just simple physical ability, the accident of being born with more coordination than someone else.

A: Well most people are born differently. If you believe in reincarnation as I do, then that answers all, some of us have been musicians *before*.

Q: We're all musicians.

A: We are all musicians. Well there's really only one musician and that's God and he sings through us.

Q: In terms of specifics, what musicians specifically do you think of as really *embodying* the whole story more than others? In this incarnation.

A: Well, the band I play with, all of them, that's Tony Williams, Jack Bruce, Larry Young, they embody something that's very special. Of course people like Fabris Khan. I'm not thinking of people who have died. There's a man called Dagar, who used to teach in Connecticut. He's tremendous to say the least.

Q: What do you think of Mayall, both looking back and in terms of what he's done since?

A: I can't really comment on that, I haven't the faintest idea what he's doing. I used to dig what he did.

Q: Was it ever like you were a relative youngster and he was doing things, I don't really know the history of the English blues scene. . . .

A: I never felt that. The only people I've felt that with, like kind of youngster and father, were Coltrane, Miles Davis, some Indian musicians, Pamilul Gosh, Guayub Khan, Ali Akbar Khan, Shankar too. These people were masters. Oh there was one man, Dick Heckstall-Smith, who was a giant, a giant. He plays incredibly well.

Q: Were R&B and blues a really important source of things?

A: The most.

Q: Why is it that a group like, say, the Rolling Stones with their particular blend of the blues made it big over the years whereas John Mayall did not with *his* particular blend from out of a very similar pool of what's happened?

A: You're asking me questions I'm not able to answer.

Q: I mean you're aiming for the music of the spheres but how much is what you do influenced by your idea of what is topical, what is in vogue? You're trying to get the truth to people but you wanna get it in terms of what *they* wanna hear at the same time.

A: It's like when you want to speak to someone in a foreign country you have to learn their language, and speak to them soulfully and eloquently so you can express your feeling. But when we're playing we're not telling anyone a message, all we're doing is expressing the truth of our own being.

Q: But your beings have been focused by what you have individually chosen from what you've *heard* over the years.

A: But you have two things. You hear something and you're inspired. From what you hear, it's like connection between the music of the inner world and the music of the outer world, it makes a connection in *you*. And now if music exists in the inner world and in the outer world the most important thing for any musician is to get the music of the inner world into the outer world. Anyone can play, no not anyone, but go and listen to any tenor player in town to know whether Trane lives.

Q: At the same time you can find out whether Dolphy lives or seven other people. But what are the actual things *you* have heard which you would agree are a big part of what you're doing? Like people who were part of your background and were so important and truthful to you that you're *still* interested in what they've done.

A: Well to give you a synopsis of my musical education, my first influence was Muddy Waters, Big Bill Broonzy was the first, then Muddy Waters, and Leadbelly. Then, but before this, I'd been playing, from seven I was listening to classical music. I was subject to classical music and after three years began acquiring a taste for it because there was so much of it in the music of my family. So around that time I started learning piano and playing classical piano, and I took up guitar and immediately I heard Big Bill Broonzy and Muddy Waters and Leadbelly. And these people just really told me where it was at.

Q: As guitarists?

A: No, just you know, as feeling.

Q: Did you wanna sing when you heard them?

A: No. Then I heard, well actually I did want to sing but I wanted to play more. I sing now, I write music and Eve writes the lyrics and we sing together, and also we sing the poetry of our guru, sublime poetry. But when I am playing with the group I am a guitar player, first and last, just a guitar player.

Q: When you heard Muddy Waters, it was predominantly what he was through his guitar . . .

A: Oh tremendous, I couldn't believe what he was doing. Robert Johnson, Fred McDowell, all those people. But then I heard flamenco music from classical Spanish, it really took me over and I started playing like that. Then I heard Django Reinhardt and that was another tremendous influence. All these people had so much gravity, so much savvy over me, I'd go from one thing to another, and this was all guitar. Then I heard electric guitar, Tal Farlow, and then electric guitar was it, the end of the world. From Tal Farlow I went to Miles Davis, Coltrane, Cannonball Adderley and all of that.

Q: What is it like hearing people play horns and being a guitar player?

A: It doesn't matter to me what instrument they play. It doesn't matter at all, I don't even think of it, what interests me is to feel them in their inwardly, just feel their being in their world. How they phrase it differently, that's just an outer manifestation, but the actual instrument is immaterial. The actual technicalities of it don't interest me one iota.

Q: But doesn't it have anything to do with the type of solo you play, not having to breathe, or how long it can be?

A: I don't even think of it in terms of a solo. When I'm soloing the whole point about it is I'm playing with other people and we're communicating, without words, communicating on a different plane, communicating deep feelings. And I'm not saying I'm soloing, I'm playing with everybody else on stage, it's not soloing, it's just a difference in conception. With Tony Williams nobody's soloing or everybody's soloing, it depends on your frame of mind.

Q: Does it ever occur to you to play, not in harmony or against somebody else, but *independently* of, just fly off in a direction where nothing equivalent is happening with anything else that's going on?

A: It's all relative, it's always directly relative, it may sound like it's got no bearing on what anyone else is doing at all . . .

Q: But I mean do you ever *intend* to have no bearing?

A: I've been through that, playing free music, in Europe. Nobody knew what we were gonna play at any time. We'd just go on the stand and start playing. And then you get into all kinds of things, you're bound to, especially if there's no rhythm. Then you're just into color, sound texture, contrast.

Q: But you'd *prefer* not doing that.

A: The joy for me is when you become one with someone else, not only with someone else, when you become one with several people. But just if you become one with one person is a joy, a joy, you cannot describe. You know when you make love, if union occurs, you cannot describe it, can you? It's the same with music, when two souls unite, it's on all levels. And music is no less physical, just different. Sound is physical but not just physical, it's much more.

Q: The last song of a long set, everybody's very tired, it's a different kind of physical relationship . . .

A: If you're very tired sometimes you just cannot make it. I've been at a stage where I, my fingers have not been able to make it, just from lack of strength.

Q: But is it that a group which is tired will meet each other on a different plane . . .

A: No, the music just sounds bad.

Q: . . . or that they're trying for music on a plane that they can't make? Do you ever play intentionally tired with everybody else playing that way?

A: Good heavens no!

Q: It seems like you could meet each other *as* tired people rather than aiming for a thing that you can no longer do because you're tired.

A: No, no, never, definitely not! (laughter) Definitely not, because you know what you're capable of.

Q: If the audience is tired too . . .

A: Then it's up to us to wake them up, just inspire them, lift them, that's our job.

Q: So one deep spiritual state you're trying to avoid is tiredness, lethargy.

A: It's not that I'm trying to avoid it. Music should be beyond it and it is, only sometimes, if you played four one-hour sets a night six nights a week in stifling fumes, beer, no air, sometimes the last set might sound tired. But there and again, at the end of the third set you might feel exhausted and you go out for the fourth set and you *overcome* your tiredness, because the spirit comes down and energizes you, totally. Not only spiritually, intellectually, emotionally but physically too.

Q: The Grateful Dead played over the weekend, they played from midnight to 6 AM every night and at the end the audience was just as tired as the band. And Jerry Garcia came out smiling, grateful for an encore and the chance to keep playing and he played real strong. But the audience was so tolerant they probably would've been just as happy with a tired finale. It's almost like what they were was bedtime music, playing the last things you hear before you go to sleep.

A: Well, what can I say about that? You cannot expect people to stay up all night and not be tired, doing something that is a very high experience.

Q: But you also have all this low energy music, like you lie in bed and turn on your clock radio to hear fifteen more minutes of music, that'll turn off after you're asleep or maybe you're not.

And you turn it low, the music is soothing, it's almost like, why wouldn't it be proper for a live band to put everybody to sleep, play music which would just soothe them to sleep?

A: Why not? Very good idea, very good idea. Except people have to get out of the place. If you could stay there, great!

17

Better Dead than Bed

Now ain't this a coincidence—a piece that begins where the last one left off. I got into the whatsit, the last of a week's worth of "Midnight with the Dead" shows at the Fillmore East, by giving Jerry Garcia a copy of The Aesthetics of Rock. *When I showed him his picture, he said, "Oboy, I'll show it to my mom," and handed me a pair of tickets.*

The A. of R.: which if you ain't read, i.e., don't own, well, do—buy the damn thing. The reprint's on Da Capo, and if it sells enough to get another printing I'll get to correct some more typos—I spot a few every time I look.

A lot of groups play until 2, but they're always tucked into bed by 5:30. Not the Dead. They're still going at it at 6, which is when TV is already back on again. It's a great time to play, not just before bedtime, but *during*. Instead of sleeping and dreaming, you see the Dead.

Which is better? Depends on what kind of dreams you have, but the music in them's seldom as good. Dreaming is free; but the Dead is free most of the time, and you can't take a tape recorder to dreamland—and if there's already one there, you can't bring it back. So the Dead's the best of both worlds, you can have your cake and eat it too.

Sounds swell, huh? Well, the Dead not only have swell ideas but they make them *happen*. So they got all their strings and gongs together and took up at the Fillmore East for five days of midnite-to-six each 'n' every night. When they're finished they're tired like a dying mule, but they come out for more, grinning and smiling and thanking the life out of you for being so nice as to invite them back.

When they're finished they hit the hay with their cuties and you hit the hay with yours. Or maybe a party all nite long, but no, because nite's already disappeared behind the horizon and who ever heard of a morning party? If anybody had one it would be the Dead, they could have fun morning, noon or nite and probably do.

Max's didn't keep 'em from having a good time at their party in the afternoon, even though the food was a *throwaway*. This is some Dead they got there.

They start real quick and casual with their Acoustic Dead set first and what a start! Starts are followed by what comes next and song number two was even better. And not just better than the first *song*, but also better than a Clint Eastwood movie. And not just the soundtrack, the whole goddam movie.

It was exciting, it was cowboy, it was great words, it was great Garcia vocal, it was great tune, it was in great color (first good light show in FOUR YEARS). It was great. All the ingredients that make up a great western. Lines about the "mail," then get away from the sheriff "or I'll spend my life in jail." That's not all the words, there were more but the rest weren't better. Including something about the Texas border from one side or the other.

That's adventure when adventure wasn't boring business, but the real thing you had to *work at* to get in on. Like the difference between Daniel Boone and Davy Crockett—both of them were great but there *was* a difference. A Dead adventure is real adventure, whatever that means, because it ain't boring and it ain't business. By definition they're you know what, plus they're more exciting than heroin addiction anyway. When you burn the candle from both ends you can't be beat.

The second set was the New Riders of the Purple Sage which had Garcia playing his pedal steel like Alvino Rey on theremin. Some guy in the audience said he never liked Hawaiian music before and he was right. Marmaduke was the one using his pipes on this set; Garcia never opened his mouth and he was allowed to sit rather than stand.

They played all these favorites that the Byrds could've done, such as "Honky Tonk Women" and they played "The Weight" the second it was requested, no waiting at all. Even at their worst, they sounded like the Byrds at their *best*, they were never more than a lamb's tail away from McGuinn's creepos. If you're that good without even trying then you're very good and chances are you can be even better. And they were.

Set number three was the one the frenzied crowd was *rehearsing* for during the first two. The Fillmore stage people even had a Grateful Dead sign in neon to start things off. They started off with "Casey Jones" and what better way to get going with two drummers on stage (Bill and Micky) than a railroad number since they sound like a chugging choochoo chuggin' down the track.

Trains run on fuel and so does a band but a band does not live by fuel alone. Instruments are needed and you have to be able to *play* them. The Dead have the best of both, well, I'm not an expert on axes so I can't testify at all on that, but I will say they definitely got the best of the latter. Who plays better bass than Phil? Does Andrew Winter? No. Does Jack Bruce? No. Does Jimmy Blanton? No. Does Duck Dunn? No. Does Richard Robinson? Not since Dick hung up his bass. Does Sam (the Man) Taylor? No. Therefore Phil's the best, the proof is in the pudding, you have to hear him and when you do your ears will not lie.

Same thing for Bob Weir. Who's better: him or Allen Lanier? Him. Him or David Crosby? Him. Him or John McLaughlin? Him. Same for Garcia. He's better than Dave Davies, Don Roeser, Barry Melton or you or me. But he doesn't put it on so thick you go running home and take out your Mitchell Torok how to play guitar album (seven lessons, one for every day of the week but you'd need a lot of weeks to play as good as him, maybe too many). He's gentle about it and he just leads you to the apex without chopping your head off at all.

Instant recognition was the order of the day for every last number but the first instant hip hip hooray was "Morning Dew" which everybody knew from way back. The ending was no disappointment, as he launched into playing the banjo on his geetar. That's no mean feat and it's also once in a lifetime if that often. Real, real good. And it was melodic too and not just any melody, but "Morning Dew" as a matter of fact. The notes were all there, so were the chords.

Sooner or later they were doing "Dark Star." It took them over a minute to get to the first recognizable sequence of notes so you knew it was that but they finally got there and it was a real humdinger. The only bummer was that the light show's scumeroos inserted a photo of the astronauts and who in his right mind associates astronauts with space? The Dead did about 15 minutes of space music and that's a tough act to follow.

But then they did what sounded for all intents and purposes like the electric version of the music from the anti-cigarette ad that has Eddie Bracken in it. In the ad it's only subliminal, but the Dead play it big as a mountain. Not the Alps, but a friendly little mountain big enough not to be a hill. And you know what? That *wasn't* what song it was, it was the intro to their version of "Good Lovin'."

That called for Pigpen's first big appearance of the night. He made more than 20 small appearances before then, but none of them amounted to more than hitting a tambourine on one beat and then hitting the air for another two. He didn't do any maraca work but he sat at the organ every chance and sometimes played for as long as thirty seconds or more. Now he was singing and moving as only his new skinny frame can do. Side to side and back and forth, all the unconventional things you're *not* supposed to do as written down in the book.

When his vocal came to a close he put the mike back atop its stand and said a word or two about doing it. They were good words and he stepped aside and before too long both drummers were soloing together, tapping and thumping around the world for 20 minutes. Once in a while somebody'd do something out of the ordinary like an extra beat or some topnotch syncopation here and there. There was always a response, half the duo was always pickin' up on the half that was gettin' it goin', but both were always playing except the time between one contact of wood and skin and the next. But a rest is still part of the music so even during silence there's something happening and tonight was no exception.

The rest of the gang slowly but surely joined in, never abruptly enough to make it other than credible every step of the trip, but still a bigger step than you have feet. Finally everybody was playing and Pigpen was standing around waiting to do something so he did. He grabbed the mike and he belted out the rest of the scorching old favorite and everybody else stepped up to a mike and threw in their worthwhile vocal background when needed. It was better than the Rascals and not just the way the Stones are better than the Rascals, but the way God is better than an apartment house.

The hours ticked off and before you knew it they were doing "Uncle John's Band"—even better than on the album. Live is better than album, but live is never better than Dead, because nothing's better than Dead and Dead always outdoes itself. The playing was right out of Brian's mandolin solo on "Sitting on a Fence" and—as usual—it crossed over the fence and reached to infinity which the eye can see so how come there's less good stuff like this around nowadays?

How come indeed. The Velvet Underground playing today is a walking nostalgia factory. So is the Dead: they conjure up the whole three-plus years ago when Haight Street was not only the best place in the world but the best place in the entire Bay area. But where the Velvets aren't as good as *their* three-plus years ago (that's the way it goes) the Dead are the best San Francisco (if it still exists) has ever been.

Rock and roll once settled down in that little coast town but it wasn't for long and now the town is more famous for its Monterey Jack Burgers but why no Dead Burgers or Dead Tacos? Because the Dead have hit the road and if you miss them in New York one night you might just see them a month later 'cause they're always back. If they stayed on the coast nobody'd be able to hear them on the other coast or in from either coast or *real* far in.

If you see them from coast to coast (and border to border) it'll put you back a pretty penny unless you walk and get in free but whatever the price it's worth a damn sight more. An apothecary shop couldn't sell you a better item for your well-being—unless of course they have a record rack with the Dead's latest and greatest.

18

D for the Dead

And sure enough, not too many months later . . .

And D is for Dead and the Dead were dead as a doornail. And D is for Danny Fields and he's the one who first gave them the D, they were bound to get one sooner or later and it was bound to be fitting when you consider them and the fourth letter of the alphabet having been stablemates all along. But who would've expected it to be at their triumphal first nite at Manhattan Center in New York, the Dead's honorary home? Not me, I didn't expect it, neither did *Creem*'s own Dave Marsh, who was on hand at the close of his tour of New York. But D is what they got, not an F, not a D-, not a D+, but a D on the nose.

Howard Stein the promoter sold 1000 more tickets than there was standing room for, 6000 instead of 5000. Stand was what was supposed to be good about it, standing meaning dancing and it was called a Marathon Dance anyway and the Dead are well known marathon musicians so it looked pretty good. And it started at 8 and as things looked it seemed destined to continue until 2. And since an estimate of 2 with the Dead usually means 4 it was gonna be an 8-hr. show. But it was over by 1:20, totaling out a playing time of only 5:20, the skimpiest they've done in 6 yrs.

But time is just time, playing and singing are a different matter. They don't have Micky Hart anymore and they didn't have him at Manhattan Center. Micky Hart's not that essential unless you want them to have two drummers and the only reason they needed two drummers was they sounded better that way. Sometimes sound is important, the only time it's not is when you're taking a piss and even then if there was no sound you'd have to take a look to make sure you were really pissing. And the sound at Manhattan Center was so bad the audience was able to overwhelm the band without really trying.

And it wasn't even yelling like at a Stones concert but just a lot of clapping of the old palms and fingers. Like a jazz event with tons of respect for all the musicianship. But the clapping was so unrelated to the beat that it was like a constant haze of insect noise interfering with the beat of the band. And the beat of the band wasn't too outasite even when the crowd shut up their hands, the drum was so underamplified that you might've mistaken them for the pre-electric Dylan.

Or the Kingston Trio. Like their "Truckin'" is nothing if not the Kingston Trio version of "Dancin' in the Streets," never one of their best but at least one of their ones. This wasn't one of their ones, it wasn't them. But it was. It was them and they had to take the rap for their own swill. Like doing "Me and Bobby McGhee" with Bob Weir letting his hair down à la Janis. But not just any Janis, it was the Janis of long ago in the vicinity of Monterey. He bellowed a lot and it got a big response but *anything* would have got a big response.

'Cause the audience was that way. And they were made up of lots of 15 yr. olds and greasers but the more passive of both. Guys were walking around selling downs and offering a free hit of clean water from downstairs in the bathroom. Things were so crowded there was no movement except during intermission and during intermission a whole pack of people from the front muscled their way up to the john and the water fountain and the 50c soda concession but even then it was hard to move in either direction (there were only two, up front or towards the back) whenever the guys walking one way ran into guys walking the other way. But walking isn't what it was and it sure wasn't truckin' either. It was bulling and bulldozing and elbows were the best weapon but even with an elbow and six pals pushin' behind you it was still difficult getting even 2/3 of the way up to the front so you could hear something for god's sake.

And what was there to hear? New Riders? It was to hear but what was there to hear *in* it? Music? Yeah but so what. People's music? Yeah but so what? Wasn't high energy or even 3/4 energy so why bother unless you just couldn't move? And then when the Dead proper got up there it became a matter of patience. You hadda have the patience and a prayer that they'd get good after another 3–4 songs but things started dragging.

They did about 42 songs that even Lisa Robinson didn't know the name of and Garcia was busy looking at his feet thru his Toby Mamis beard. Lesh had his shortest hair ever and he was busy hiding behind Bill the drummer most of the time. The only time he came out front was when he had to sing. Did I say sing? I mean when they opened their mouths and screeched their famous harmonies and then finally they went into "Saint Stephen," people were waiting and time was a-wasting so they finally did it.

But they didn't do it just yet. Before that they had Pigpen do Otis' immortal "Too Hot to Handle" in his finest soul-man finery. He's never been this skinny and his acne has all but disappeared and the little girlies up on the edge of the stage were knocked out by his excellence. They would of been knocked prone but there was no room. Well, anyway, he's in a class by himself except for two other people, Mae West and Stepin Fetchit. Mae's famous you'll remember for being a woman impersonating a woman and Stepin likewise for being Afroid and impersonating Afroidness. Pig is a punk impersonating a punk and since he's a punk he's the punkiest of the trio and since he's the punkiest he's number three out of the three (one is the highest). His head moves and tambourine improvisations alone would be enough to earn him that honor but the band he's in helps too.

They're ALL PUNKS when you get down to it and at dance-o-thons all you can possibly do is *get down* even though there's no room. "Kick Out the Jams" was never more relevant, not even enough room to get down to *getting* down so all you could do was either be patient or suffer or get into a fight and there were no fights (not one). That's the plot, if everybody's on acid and smoking joints all you need is not enough room for anybody to breathe and everything'll work out all right. That's what happened, the proof is unquestionable so it must be true.

So they're all punks when you get down to it and here's why: well whenever they tried their hat at R&B it was laden with *too much tolerance* for diverse shit in the strummin' and the pickin'. Garcia played his axe like a second drum but when it wasn't a drum it was a lute or a mandolin and it wasn't even à la Ry Cooder, just Al Caiola or Tony Mottola or Chet Atkins. And there wasn't no organ or keyboard of any kind because they won't entrust that to Pigpen anymore so why do they keep the slob? Tolerance for Pigpen is okay but not tolerance for guys who don't know that R&B means *discretion and rigidity*. What do these guys think they're doing, they weren't even wearing tie-dyeds?

And before they did "Saint Stephen" they did an intro that nobody even knew was an intro, they just thought it was one more patience-challenging goddam motherfuckin' ballad. It was the ballad that that Okie was singing in *Grapes of Wrath* (the movie not the book because if it was the book nobody'd know where they got it from) about "I ain't gonna be treated this-a way." They were doing that for minutes and minutes and finally they plopped the whole thing right into "Saint Stephen" and not a second to lose. If they had waited nobody coulda cared anymore.

That doesn't mean *nobody* coulda cared because at Woodstock there were at all times at least 40,000 people cheering their condoms off for whoever was up there at the time, even the Swami and even Sweetwater or Bert Sommer. But there wouldn't have been cheering where I was standing because all around me were impatient people whose patience was tiring. So they finally did "Saint Stephen" and they got to the part where they plunge into the big thing in the middle from off the *Live Dead* album and it was a good plunge and also the first *real* plunge of the nite. But plunge they did even though the energy dissipated 20 seconds later and THEY DIDN'T PLAY AN ENCORE. First time they didn't play an encore since they got booed off the stage in merry old England the time they went on before Mungo Jerry. And they didn't play an encore *of their own choosing.*

Which means they CHOSE not to do an encore. Which means they were aware of a thing or two such as the fact that they were playing bad. And more than once the reason they were playing bad was by choice too. You could tell because they'd get something going and then drop it. Was it that they hated New York? No, because they don't have any hate in their hearts as the lyrics of "Uncle John's Band" will attest ("There's no time to hate, barely time to wait"). So here's the lowdown on their awful heinous performance before six thousand screaming applauding wild maniacs of the Woodstock Nation (also known as Alia Nation): INTENTIONAL BUMMER.

They did an intentional bummer because there was nothing left for them to do because they had already (previously) played good quality music for all their hearts and souls were worth, they had gone beyond music to the living ozone of the pancreas and even beyond that, they had forged their way beside many a tunesmith of the freaking cosmos and much, much more. So they had to throw down their shields and live up to their reps as *gurus.* Gurus often do things like shock their followers by obliterating expectations, it apparently teaches detachment. Detachment is even more important than getting laid so that's exactly what they did. But nobody was shocked. So it all fit.

Next time Central Park can't be got for a Be-In maybe they'll get Manhattan Center, an additional 3000 could have been housed with little or no difficulty. But if there's entertainment you oughta bring some stilts. If you wanna see anything. Tall people had such an advantage that their advantage made them elitists. But since it's congenital (being tall) they can in no way be held responsible before a revolutionary tribunal. And the Dead better get smart and play on a stage that's just as crowded, who are they to get all that space to themselves?

And after they get rid of Pigpen and make him their personal valet or keeper of the picks and strings they'll just be a 4-man band. So what they oughta do then is change their name to the Beatles, to the best of my knowledge the name has never been patented.

19

Cactus: *One Way or Another*

It was rarely anything like fun working for Rolling Stone. *Not the writing, not the aftermath.*

If the previous piece was finished in 25 minutes—automatic writing at its most efficient and fruitful—this one probably took a month to complete, what with the additional work I had to do. Review editor Jon Landau, a stickler for such crap, didn't think I'd mentioned enough specific cuts and sent it back to me. Grrr—and these were the days I didn't even like to proofread *my single drafts—but I did as requested . . . and where did that get me?*

Kicked off the Atlantic Records mailing list.

Writing for the Stone, *you were out there quite naked, by which I don't mean you were encouraged to write nakedly, 'cause even if you did, by the time they were through with you, x many times through the sifter, you came out sounding stilted . . . starched. What you were was* exposed*—unprotected—record companies were sure to read you—and Atlantic did me, and didn't care for my comments on their latest shithook "supergroup."*

Albums were an important perk—you could sell 'em. Well, not every one that came in; aside from what you might be reviewing, you might occasionally feel the need to keep abreast of current bullshit—y'know, "research." During this period I probably listened to more diverse music than I had for a while, if only because it was free. (I wouldn't've bought two percent of this shit on my own.) Free and salable, but if you broke the shrinkwrap, the value of a promo LP slipped from a dollar to 35 cents—so you weren't inclined to indiscriminately break the wrap. (Concert tickets were something else. Although you could get face value from kids outside shows, you ran the risk of bumping into company creeps, and even if not caught doin' *it, you could be stuck having to go inside and see the show—one you didn't wanna see in the first place.)*

So anyway, it was a real slap, punishment with a message, for a company to cut you off—not don't do it again *but* you're gone here, g'bye—now don't do it ELSEWHERE. *The real lesson? When it came to reviewing acts signed to majors, honesty was a fairly moronic policy. For the record, I somehow (miraculously) got reinstated by Atlantic, only to be booted for keeps, a year later, for a swim at an indoor press party (as alluded to some pages ago).*

WARNING to would-be toilers in these gamy waters: don't let yourself be seduced by such trinkets—they're a habit worse than crack (almost as vile as watching TV).

Time was when Atlantic was the real trailblazer in album cover art (remember Hank Crawford's *Soul Clinic?*) but this one, *sheesh!* The album and its package reek of death: it was recorded at the Electric Lady Studio and Jim McCarty has a bottle of Southern Comfort in his front pocket. A bit too obvious if they wanted to be obvious. So chances are it's just the way things *are* with them and the music doesn't budge an inch from this reality.

It starts with Dick Penniman's "Long Tall Sally." Are they the American Juicy Lucy or just Rod Stewart singing with Cream? Well, anyway it's the clearest enunciation of those dandy old lyrics yet. Then a "let's give 'em a little fun" followed by enough guitar shit to make you realize right off the bat that it could be second Fudge album revisited. "Rockout, Whatever You Feel Like" keeps the pressure high with a message as fresh today as it must've been when such pioneers as the Chambers Brothers rattled off something like it four years ago or so: "I know some of you people like to dance and I know some of you people just like to roll and rock and roll and rock and roll . . ." There's a touch of "move over Rover" later on and Cactus has finally tipped its hand: their talent is in disguising their source or at least *delaying* overt hints as long as possible, but not *too* long. No patience.

So finally by only the third cut, "Rock N' Roll Children," complete with Buckingham riffs and Steve Miller and "Wind Cries Mary," you know that this is a dumbass way to do a rock revival. Halfass, actually. Show-offy *interpretations* of what's supposed to be old. And when the old Fudge stuff pops up it's a reference to something far deader than 1956. Poets will tell you there's nothing as dead as the *recent* past. But the whole Cactus concept reeks of enough poetry already, so . . .

"Children" ends with a series of fake endings and fadeouts and fadeins and such, you'd think it was the second Buffalo Springfield album or the return of Shadow Morton.

The rock-as-sex message gets whipped across in "Big Mama Boogie—Parts 1 & 2": "I like to rock and I like to roll, most of all I like to ball." The voice is Van Morrison until the fateful moment when John Lee Hooker is forced into the picture. "I'm from Deetroit where the boogie was born, I been boogying since '51," then something about John Lee himself, poor John Lee. "Woman she got my child" rhymes with "drives me wild" and if they weren't black (ha ha *ha*) I'd swear they were singing about the days before pills or something!

Chuck Willis' "Feel So Bad" is a slow Led Zeppelin change of pace and then the chorus comes in and so does the Robbie Krieger, proof that tame and derivative guitar can be OK. Not one unfamiliar lick. It's true that you can't help stepping on lots of prior stuff, but taken with the rest of their approach there's a note of *intent* and a consistency overload. In other words they're a *together* band so who needs 'em?

"Song for Aries" begins like Traffic, odd how they're always using somebody else's calling card to introduce their own (in this case wahwah plus heavy-handed tom tom or whatever). It's a nice move, I'll give them credit for that. Finally it's some "She's So Heavy": the Fudge always admired the Beatles and it was far more substantial and subliminal an influence than with more-obvious-about-it groups. Their Long Island copy band roots must've had something to do with it. There's even the sudden nothing ending of "Heavy," just paying a debt to their tutors I guess.

"Hometown Bust" has the "She's So Heavy" *vocal, really* heavy stuff, then it's more like Country Joe singin' up a storm as he's so capable of doing. There's some old Dead/C.J. Fish organ-sounding stuff on guitar, suddenly a harp, then another fabulous San Francisco geetar line. Showing Cactus to be just as arbitrary in their musical transitions as the Bee Gees and Led Zep, two other fine Atlantic outfits.

Finally the final cut, "One Way . . . Or Another." Well, it's been one way so far, maybe now another? Nope. Now that none of their playing or messaging is any longer viable within the rock *mainstream* it's just gotta be a matter of flexing their muscles for a pack of blind people or maybe they're just simple guys. Or they're four salesmen to the teen set à la such third-raters of days gone by as Terry Stafford or the Astronauts or the Swinging Barbarians. All good of course, but good because they were bad. Exclusively.

Is Cactus gonna admit they're bad? I doubt it. So unless you're gonna marry Carmine Appice or something like that, *don't be deceived by inferior merchandise.* Unless you wanna be. It's all in the spirit of rock and roll so it's OK with me.

20

Who'll Be the Next in Line?

Meanwhile they'd been dropping like flies—some actual superstars—and a deathsploitation quickie, edited by Fusion's *Robert Somma, invited me aboard. Liza Williams, head of publicity for Capitol Records, complained that my contribution was "offensive, repellent, repulsive and totally without redeeming social anything." What, she questioned, had been my objective, "to outsleez [sic] Jonathan Swift and William Burroughs?" But she didn't cut me off the Capitol list—whew—even though one of the dead'uns whose graves I'd danced on, Jimi Hendrix, had an LP in the Capitol catalog* (Band of Gypsys), *and when I convinced her it had just been a naughty, naughty rockwriterly CALISTHENIC, we became good friends. (Still are.)*

Since he also had a piece in the book, it's possible my line about Lou Reed "going ga-ga" caught his attention, setting the stage for my critique of his next record terminating that *friendship. Or not im*possible.

If the ending doesn't compute, or sticks out like a weird thumb, it's 'cuz I planned it as half non sequitur, half "ass rapping" in its own right. Or two-thirds, one-third. You know what you can do with some plans.

When Jeremy Bentham said that death was but a whip across the face of life he was some big dummy. Not only that, it was a lot of hogwash too: DEATH IS JUST A LOT OF ROTTEN, PUTRID, ROTTING, STINKING FLESH and only the bones and the teeth are left when it's over and all you can do with them is put them in a museum or an anthropology class. Also there's no life in it at all except the stuff that's still alive and hasn't died yet, stuff like *cells* and cells aren't people even though they're the building blocks of you and me and life itself.

The pen can be mightier than the teeth and when it's a letter about death it's nearly always a sad, sad, sad one as in the case of this fine one right here to *Circus* magazine:

October 15, 1970
Dear Circus:

OPEN LETTER
to
JANIS JOPLIN

Janis, you'll never know how much we'll miss you, because you never really knew how much we loved you. We bought your albums, we screamed at your concerts but that wasn't enough, was it? We know you had a hard, rough life but you were reaching your peak man, success doesn't come easy ya know! We know it's tough for a chick on the road alone but who said you had to work your life away just trying to entertain us. Just because you were Janis, that's why we loved you. We thought you were tough, but by using smack you proved you were weak too. But it did prove a point to all of us, it proved that you were only human like everyone else. You had problems too, but you had to neglect them because of us. We built you up to be superhuman and you had to follow that course according to script. We'll love you more than ever now, because we took you for granted before when you were alive. Your flame will never burn out Janis. But hell we're gonna miss you bad.

God, Rest her soul.
Peace
an unhappy
chick from Boston

An excellent letter indeed and ditto for the sentiment expressed. It was sent via air mail which is always the best way to send letters about the newly departed. First time I saw my father read without his mouth I was six years old and I didn't get the point at all. Maybe Janis isn't reading with her lips wherever she is and if you're less than six (or maybe it's younger now due to the generation gap) you won't understand either if you see her doing it, but since you can't see her doing it everything's okay.

Another thing about this letter is that while the unhappy chick might've worn black up in Beantown there's no way of us knowing unless she sends a photo and that's expensive. Letters are cheaper and they convey the message far better than customs like black veils and crying into a handkerchief. She didn't leave her address so there's nowhere to send the letter to when she herself kicks the bucket which will probably be before the second half of the twenty-first century judging from her apparent youth. One thing she wasn't youthful about was her sophistication in talking about the smack, a euphemism for both junk and for nookie. So the chick caught hold of the awesome ambivalence of it all in relation to the greatest J.J. since J.J. Johnson, the only major triple-J in the world of music during this century.

But it took a double-J to supply the topper for the other two single-J's, Jimi and Jones. There's a heck of a lot of J's left around and any one of them could be next. Jim Morrison. Mick Jagger. Johnny Winter, who even *worried* over it with Patti Smith, Janis's favorite N.Y.C. confidant. Good thing McGuinn isn't Jim anymore, but John McLaughlin, Jimmy Gilmer, Joe Bouchard, Jack Casady, Jerry Garcia and Jake of Jake & the Family Jewels (Miles Aronowitz is in the group so maybe his daddy Al's obit for Jake is already all writ up) are still in a heap of trouble although Jerry's probably in less because he's very careful not to die and he might even be GRATEFUL to be DEAD (hey maybe he's dead already and we don't know and he's not talking). All these fellas oughta get their monikers traded in real quick even if it means—as with McGuinn—a Subud guru, which could mean a lifetime of meditation, discipline and prayer. McLaughlin is already ready for it, he even cut his curly locks on guru command. But just the same it might suddenly turn into R or P (or height, weight, girth, diet or cigareets) so there's no real clues into the eternal contumescence, the only recourse is neverending prayer and consultation with Saint Augustine. Especially his chapter in the *Confessions* all about time, it can aid and abet and comfort like nothing this side of a papaya cocktail.

As an instance of something other than J, R *or* P (or any of the others for that matter) is Bobby Fuller, whose Bobby Fuller Four recorded and released the hit single "I Fought the Law." Bobby died of depression with the world and the record business, that was one of the causes of his untimely death four years ago, the big one was the carbon monoxide he pumped into his lungs out of his car, a car bought with the sweat of his brow and musical genius. Bobby's one of the very few *known* and *substantiated* suicides in rock and roll (Johnny Ace?), they shoulda brought in the suicide prevention squad and then followed up the rescue by loving kindness to keep him from trying again.

His death was a very interesting one, on the other hand Janis's was the most boring of the week. Had it been any other week the story would have been different but good timing pays off. Jimi could have picked a better week too and even a better year, like two years earlier would have been just right, that way it would've been promise as yet unfulfilled (unless you agree with me that it was no promise at all and just fulfillment right from the beginning but that would be controversial and that's the last thing on my mind) instead of mellow performer losing a few future decades of mellowness. But few, many, that's just man's time, God's time is a different kit and kaboodle if there ever was one!

In this tough-nosed land of ours the requirement for a postage stamp is death, that is you have to die (for five years) to get on one, you don't have to die to use one however. They oughta go ahead and make up Jimi-Janis-etc. commemoratives even if it's illegitimate mailwise. They could be used in postage due mailings and attempts to fool the stupid old post office into thinking it's good postage. They could also be good death seals for death letters and condolences, no postal clerk's gonna interfere with it if he knows something as grave as the grave is involved.

Elvis oughta die real soon. He deserves it both because he's no good no more (so he deserves to die like a dirty dog) and because he's still okay or at least used to be (so he deserves a better peace than all the cretins squawking at him saying he's no damn good). He could die in his pool (Brian set the precedent and he likes swimming even more than Brian and is less fat so it's easier to drown because fat is lighter than water). He could get killed in a fight with his wife due to sticking the noodle into young starlets. He could trip on his kid's toys and break his thigh and then complications could set in which unattended could mean certain death. He could die of a heart attack after losing a sudden death playoff in the Elvis Presley Open due to being surprised because it was fixed for him to win. Whatever way he dies hopefully it'll be soon.

Johnny Cash oughta die soon too, same for Country Joe, The Oxpetals (so they can tell us what it's like up in the sky or *down below*), Buddy Miles, Joe's even a likely candidate with his first (last) (or middle depending on which it is) name. Johnny's been in with some pretty fast company for all these fifteen big years as number four or number five behind Elvis, Jerry Lee Lewis, the late great Eddie Cochran, Gene Vincent and Carl Perkins, one of whom has already bought a farm and the other of whom are all extremely old. John has always (recently) been everybody's favorite proof that country music is more than Boots Randolph, nobody needs the crutch anymore so it's no loss if he's offed by a speeding locomotive. Eddie's demise was automotive but he was not at the wheel so it was not the result of a steering wheel through the gizzard. Neither was the famous Otis behind his wheel when he landed, or more correctly *crash*-landed, in that bog where his very own life was snuffed away by impact with the terra firma. Why don't these characters like to pilot their own vehicles, it would be much safer in the long run due to a higher level of consciousness in their cranium and higher awareness.

Then there's the unreported deaths of Dylan and Lou Reed, both of them dead TO THIS WORLD but for very different reasons. Bob's just a stiff, pure and simple, he's been that way since the mishap with the bike. Louis is on account of going ga-ga in relation to space and time and making funny hand movements and threatening to buy a knife: in other words he's left *this* world for *another*, he's looking good so it's likely it's real good where he is. Bobbo's in New York recording with Mr. Paul McCartney so where he is isn't so good but it's the first recording between two officially or unofficially dead guys on record. So it's about time for some of the *fake deaths* which have been reported to be revealed just like Paulie had the integrity to do.

So which of them is really not dead and just waiting for the moment to get resurrected? Is it any of the J boys and girl? Well some people saw the corpses and they looked pretty still and quiet but maybe that was good acting. Even if a fly was on their nose they didn't move a muscle. One of them's COMING BACK next week while Jethro Tull is playing at Ungano's. If whoever it is is COMPLETELY alive it'll be some surprise, also if he or she is only partially alive. If there's a dead limb that smells awful or a dead hand that can't play or a dead head that's real dumb it'll be the biggest thing since Dracula. But the *is* is not the *ought* so IT MAY NEVER HAPPEN and probably not much of a chance with these particular stiffs-as-the-case-may-be.

Another thing is what did they get buried with? With Brian a good guess would be his bottle of pop. Most likely Al Wilson took his amazing wax collection. Jimi, and this is only speculation, took his spoons along to the Elysian Fields Motel, he was packed and ready to go. Little doubt Janis was buried with a Phillies Cheroot up her kitchen. Once again it's a matter of whether it really happened or just really *oughta* of happened so those were the guesses for the really happened.

There's more evidence for the oughta of happened and for Janis it was undigested food or tampon or both. For James it was gold teeth and unused sperm. For Al it was a compass and a Bowie knife to help him find his way around his permanent resting place. And for Brian it just had to be the three pounds of grass, four packs of papers and who knows how many watches given to him by Howard Klein six blocks away from Salvation three years ago which he never used.

All this proves is that rock people are a bunch of amateur punks when it comes to exiting the planet. Compare them to the kitty cat that Pearlman hit in his car in Chinatown, the cat just writhed and ran away and will someday be dead. Bruce Angelman may have died in a car wreck two years ago, nobody knows for sure but they do know one thing: IT WOULD HAVE BEEN BETTER FOR HIM IF HE HAD. They're not sure if he's still living or dead but they all agree on one thing: WHAT'S THE DIFFERENCE? He stood outside the Anderson Theatre in the cold winter of 1967–68 when Neil Louison wouldn't let him in to see The Soft White Underbelly, Jim Kweskin and Country Joe, he had lost his teeth not too long before and he was crying on 5000 micrograms and it was fuckin cold outside, Jim!

Jim Gurley's wife was one of the potential dead muffins at Monterey who took advantage of her potential to the fullest. Jimbo left her because she was shooting speed and not long afterwards she OD'd. That leaves only me, John Dowd, Hurricane Nancy, Gary Blackman, Ellen Sander, Pearlman, Wendy, and that's all who I know for sure who were there and are still around and the number could get smaller every day. If it does and I'm still one of the ones left to do the counting it's not gonna bother me at all cause if your number's up it's up and there's nothing you can do about it. If it isn't up you can get hit with a steel piano and it won't kill you.

There are very few critters walking the face of the earth who don't know of somebody whose light has gone out. For instance I know of two grandparents. Bill Hartack knows of Solitude the horse who had to be shot for broken legs and sold to the glue factory after only three furlongs of the Wood Memorial. Edie Adams had Ernie Kovacs. Van Morrison had the hooker who was the star of "T.B. Sheets." Spanky & Our Gang had somebody somewhere along the line. Buddy Holly, Richie Valens and the Big Bopper were all motherless even before the time of their own dissociation with life. Otis's mom is still living but she won't be for more than forty years, then there'll be nobody but archaeologists to weep for him. Which would you rather have die first, the other fellow or you? Think about it, it may someday be your choice and you'll have to decide.

Which is easier, being sick or being dead? Eartha Kitt was asked and she said dead. Della Reese was asked and she said sick. Neither one has been dead but both have been sick, so only Della *knows* what she likes, Eartha's only guessing. She won't miss the water till the well runs dry. If she dies of thirst it'll hit the nail right on the head, especially if she's sick along the way.

Which brings up a really great (so great it's just *great*!) idea of what to do with departed rock stars is ACTUALLY USE THE BLOOD FOR SACRAMENTAL PURPOSES!!! Drink it, bathe in it, drink it some more. Plus drink the wine on top of it, there's no reason to leave it out just because there's real blood handy. The blood of Al Wilson's always-bloody nose, or the blood of Janis's menstrual faucet. Which would have been hard in the latter case if she didn't happen to be bleeding at the time she breathed her last breath. So she should have, with fans' encouragement of course, saved it up month by month, using a funnel so as not to spill any on the floor where all it would do is dry up. But in the case of males such donations would require the actual donation of blood from a vein, not exactly the sort of thing just any man will do, even a generous one. You know the number of bonafide rock and roll stars who donated their precious blood during the Lake Tahoe blood shortage of several months ago? Zero. That's how many gave to a worthy cause. But say the cause wasn't worthy. Maybe they'd be more likely to get rid of the red stuff if it was just for the sake of aesthetics. The situation would be helped if not only fans but musicians were part of the demand for the stuff. Instead of plagiarism there'd be liquid cannibalism, and if the blood type was right there'd be more than a little SHOOTING of the stuff.

THAT'S WHAT SHOULD BE DONE: a blood fund for living stars to belong to (it could be casual, it wouldn't have to be organized, it could be backstage and they could have blood type identification kits to make it easier). But would cannibalism of the blood ever be *vampirism*? Not unless it was from the neck. Maybe it could be decided that it wouldn't have to be *directly* from the neck of the person, that it could be just from a *bottle* that got blood from the neck out of a tube. But every once in a while there'd be a live show on stage where they could do the real thing with actual blood being sucked from the jugular of Iggy Pop or Tracy Nelson. Of course a law would have to be passed so it wouldn't be a felony if someone's life expired during the ceremony since it doesn't nearly deserve such harsh penalties. But it can be done! And must be. It's the only way death can be put in proper perspective within the confines of rock and roll. Those confines are enormous so it would in effect mean WITHIN THE CONFINES OF THE WHOLE WIDE WORLD! Death would count again and that would be good. Real good.

There wouldn't be any more of this ass rapping about Jimi's death on the cover of the *San Francisco Chronicle*, there'd instead be room for some honest and true concern about the deaths of *all the righteous brothers and sisters in the struggle for freedom*. Don't they count as much as these frivolous entertainers? Isn't this death stuff proof positive of the ultimate rip-off of the REVOLUTION by rock and roll, huh?

21

Section Deleted from the Published Version of "Who'll Be the Next in Line?"

What 'zines were good for then is precisely what they're good for now—for publishing what more mainstream publishers won't.

Without consulting me, Somma cut this—three and a half paragraphs that more than clarify what the essay had arguably been "about": rock fandom's (not to mentions rock's) ever-burgeoning cannibalism or whatev. Insert this chunk between the first and second 'graphs of the preceding. (It seems so necessary it's a wonder anyone—Liza included—found the fugger readable without it.)

Brian, Jimi, Janis and Al are therefore all dead animals and there are a number of talented dead animal sculptors in the world so how come they didn't give up their carcasses to art? The best way to do a dead animal sculpture is dead animal in Jello. You take the animal or any piece thereof and dump it into a large container or mold. Then you brew up the Jello one or more packages at a time. You start it from the bottom and let it harden so you can cement the dead thing to the bottom and it doesn't float up to the top. If it floats to the top some will be sticking out the top of the hardened Jello and smell something awful and get covered with filthy, horrible mold. Now that kind of mold is just fine if it's the Jello itself that gets moldy up on top. Which happens almost every time if you keep it in the fridge for upwards of a couple years and there's no reason why you won't. So it's a damn good idea for it to be the Jello and not the animal that gets moldy and diseased. Jello-derived disease is better than corpse-derived disease so it's always preferable. On top of that the Jello will preserve the animal if the animal is completely covered. The Jello it-self will eventually die but for Jello death only means getting unsolid, that is, liquid. Therefore if the piece of horse-flesh is anchored down (as with sinkers & fishing gear) it would be insured a resting place for nigh on to forever.

Janis has already been burned to oblivion so she can't get cut up for Jello but her nipples would sure have been great appetizers in celery flavor Jello on the Thanksgiving table—or Christmas for that matter, or one for each solemn occasion. It would have been yum-yum-yummy in the taste department too if proper refrigeration were sup-plied for preservation. Warm refrigerators just won't do tho the cold night might be perfect. But it's all in the realm of fantasy now with her ashes surrendered to the wind and waves out in California way.

People in the United Kingdom have a recipe for hare that calls for the hare to hang on a hook and when it has decomposed enough to fall thru the hook and onto the floor or table or pot as the case may be it's time to eat! In other words even the already putrefied meat is mighty good so Jimi still might make a good meal altho Brian could be a few years past his prime. Al Wilson'd probably be fit for cooking now, wait I forgot they put that embalming fluid in them! That would not only be bad *tasting* but it might be poisonous enough to kill. You'll end up joining them in kingdom come after their entrails join yours in all the digestive juice. Hmm, is there such a thing in this wide world as suicidal cannibalism? There is some brain disease they get from eating certain kinds of human brains, no it might be *general* body disease but it comes from brains. Even if there's no formalde-hyde in the brains of Jimi and Al it would be a good idea to steer your fork *clear* of them.

I had a close call with death of my own so I know. It was a fever of 104 combined with visions of my eyes being in Morristown New Jer-sey so the psychological side of the great cutting edge is less fun than the food side of it. If you listen to the Dead's "Black Peter" you'll pucker up to a nifty picture of dying like a dog and whenever you die there's always weather around. You die in weather and your body's got its own weather and temperature, also you're in this life before you're not and your body *has* life before it don't: but you don't die *in food* (even though your body's about to *be* food for either the worms or the fires of cremation) unless that's the way you die and so far in rock it's never happened.

Paper is sometimes food although its nutritional value is question-able but it can be used just as easily for writing letters on.

22

The Doors: *L.A. Woman*

Next fly to drop was Jim's, er, Jim. Morrison. This review appeared only a couple months before he croaked.

One thing to bear in mind is how unlikely it was to get an assignment reviewing an alb you really wanted, you'd just take pot luck; this is one of the few choice acts I got to cover in the early days, especially for a major sheet.

Besides being "heavy" in their early days the Doors were funny too. Funnier than a fish. Who can forget those great Morrison ad libs like the one he once did during a lull in "Gloria" ("Little girl how old are you, little girl what school do you go to, little girl suck my cock")? He was an earnest drinker, which of course helped. Now he's drinking more than ever, hence some additional *basis* for all the laughs. And since heaviness has been kicked in the ass of late all the kickers owe it to themselves to sit down with this one. There isn't one serious cut on the entire album.

Just consider the extent to which Jimbo's snake and lizard obsessions contributed to the wanton slaughter of zillions of members of the reptile population for the sake of boots and belts. His influence on that and other fashion trends has to be considerable, an absurd fact considering how the man himself has been literally abandoned by the hippos of rock fandom during his darkest hours. Well now he's taking no chances about being taken seriously or with "universal" import. In fact he's not even writing his own snake lyrics anymore. Instead there's John Lee Hooker's "Crawling King Snake," a whopper of a readymade and proof positive that he and his boys are still listening to the roots, even after the death of Al Wilson (don't forget that Canned Heat was once L.A.'s number one comedy band). On it Morrison demonstrates his grasp of all the vocal chicanery only hinted at in flashes on "Love Street." Which means he's finally found complete security in caution-to-the-winds Hollywood lemonade singing, the mid-point between bubble gum and singing an Oscar nomination at the 1972 Academy Awards.

And what's more Jim's backup band has finally reduced its approach to one of ping-ponging the essential free-as-air spirit the man's been toying with ever since be abandoned Bertolt Brecht for Mel Torme. In other words the Doors have never been more *together*, more like the Beach Boys, more like Love (the band they originally played second fiddle to at the Whiskey or the Troubador or wherever it was). So when Morrison sets the tone with lines like "Why did you throw the jack of hearts away?" in "Hyacinth House," it's Manzarek, Robbie and Densmore keeping the second-to-second ridiculousness going with merry-go-round tirades of mere pleasantness straight out of Derek and the Dominoes, and even some pseudo-classical fancy stepping for good measure. In terms of what they're after here the Doors as a band never falter and there isn't one bummer cut on the album—obviously a first for them.

It's also the first time since "The End" and "When the Music's Over" that they've been able to pull off anything interesting in the way of long cuts. There are two of them here, "L.A. Woman" (with maybe the best Chuck Berry riffs since the Stones and a hell of a lot more Sixties/Seventies American flavor) and "Riders on the Storm" (signaling a return to Del Shannon from whence the Doors' mysteriosohood was largely derived to begin with), both of them minor monsters. And I'll be a monkey's unc if "The WASP (Texas Radio & The Big Beat)" doesn't showcase Morrison's finest command of spoken jive to date, far superior to "Horse Latitudes," a demon of timing at least the equal of George Burns in his prime.

You can kick me for saying this (I don't mind): this is *the Doors' greatest album* (including their first) and *the best album so far this year.* A landmark worthy of dancing in the streets.

23

The Rolling Stones: *Sticky Fingers*

Apropos of my remark about assignments, sometimes you hadda take the bull by the horns. Presuming the Stone*'s readership—i.e., "the world"—urgently needed to hear thus and such re the Decline And Fall of the group for whom that paper was named, I surprised 'em with this unsolicited gem, one of those damn-fool things young people sometimes do, licked my ensuing wounds, then dispatched it to 'zinesville . . . good riddance. It has the feel of rock-talk like I got into at parties back then—surge to a headful of rock adrenaline, taste the beast in my mouth and blather away, and somebody would say, "Why don't you write that?" and if I took notes on a napkin, or remembered any of it in the morning, maybe I would.*

Is Dylan still good? You tell me, I ain't gonna tell you. Tell me: RIGHT FUCKIN NOW!!

That's how easy it is to talk about this one (one what?). (Like what the fuckin goddam shit is the reason for *interest* in this one: tell me right the hell *now*.)

Is this one good? a) yes b) no c) 1492 d) I wish I knew e) "Knowledge is the insanity of enlightened fools"—Rudyard Kipling f) 3 of the above.

How about tonite, babe? Well how about it? C'mon: HOW ABOUT IT!!!

So it's not: "What's the answer?" hence "What's the question?" It's: question becomes exclamation. And question becomes mere doubt: *"I don't know."*

Reviews are answer records. Even when they're not self-conscious they are (self-conscious). Name one that isn't. "And if we close all our eyes together then we will see where we all come from." Huh?

So what's all the fuss? After all you don't find folks waiting for reviews of the, uh, the latest, the latest Wilkinson bonded shaving system. Nor do you find them *waiting* for the shave they give. This album ain't even *FUNKTIONAL*. (Will it guarantee that you get laid?) (Will anything?) (Yes, a knife pointed at the neck.) (But some people are invulnerable even to that.)

How many people have done this album before? Ans.: 16-plus (Santana, Byrds, Al Kooper, CSNY, BST, Beatles, Doors, Bukka White, J.C. Tremblay, Hoyt Axton, Dionne Warwick, Rachel Gallagher, Beach Boys, Tubby Hayes, Dave Brubeck, Stones) (are all Stones albums identical?).

Try something new this time: don't learn any of the words or even the titles. Just don't (after all you don't have to). But that don't mean you ain't gonna let *memory* enter the picture: cut after "Wild Horses" = walk right back to me this minute, bring your love to me don't send it, I'm so lonesome every day.

Second cut, side two: has there ever been a worse Stones cut? Worse Otis cut? Last note is GOOD, Jim.

It's only love and that is all (I've got nasty habits) why should I feel the way I do (I take tea at three): *Rubber Soul* as in *condom*? Cut before "You Got To Move" is so ripe with "Day Tripper" you can pick it off the branches without impairing the growth of the roots. (How many times is the word "nigger" used or implied on the album?)

Second cut, side one: I'm comin down off amphetamine and I'm in jail cause I killed a queen. L.A. is more wanton than the Stones ever were. How come Terry Melcher never produced them? Beer drinking's *necessary* with this cut.

"Wild Horses" doesn't include Keith's red T-shirt from *Gimme Shelter*. Could it? Would it? (Gram Parsons once walked into the Troubador and was mistaken for Graham Nash.)

Stones are the *least* together band that ever was. 'S what's good about them. Is it singing that separates the men from the boys? Is it playing? Are the Stones men? Boys?

Hitler lives, Hitler was the first Nixon. Buddah (or somebody) was the first Jesus Christ. Jagger was the first Morrison. Is first best? Better? Some people *still* think Jagger is better than Morrison. 'Tis a pity, the poor dummies. Well at least Mick *plays an instrument* other than harp this time. Mick J. that is. Sometimes it's even the two Micks playing and who's playing lead? Mick T. unless miracles have been waged in Anglo-America (doubtful). If the Stones are going to refrain from being *together* they need Morrison or David Crosby or Mick(ey) Dolenz, they need to get rid of the last vestige of Stonehood (they couldn't be the old Stones anymore if they stood on their heads), their lamer-than-ever singing duck. Keith could get along very well (musically) without him. The world could get along very well without me (you) too, and vice versa. There's a cut aboard ship called "Moonlight Mile." Don't tell me you've already forgotten "Moonlight Drive."

This album was tested on bad equipment and good bourbon and it was plain awful. Then it was given a second chance—aren't they all?—on good equipment and bad ale and it was plain ordinary but listenable. Listenable equals better than bad equals ____ equals ____ equals GREAT. Great album, particularly the Rocky Raccoon cut and the Motown-Bee Gees cut (the last on the second side).

This is no 3-sided masterpiece.

This is no 4-sided boat ride down the Maguire.

This is no 2-sided reason to move back from the suburbs. But it *almost* is. The food in the city's always better and there's more movies and more *albums*. And a lot less reasons to sing except for your supper. There's creation and there's listening—one has eight letters and one has nine.

The Stooges got rid of Steve Mackay the great and exciting saxophone genius for reasons of irrelevance. The Stones *hired* a great and exciting sax bozo for reasons of irrelevance.

Side two, cut two sounds like "Don't Sleep in the Subways." It sounds even more like "I've Been Loving You Too Long." No way to discredit them for that preference. (Where there's a will there's a way.) (Going my way?)

"Sister Morphine" ("Rocky Raccoon") is a Neil Young OD and why shouldn't it be? Which is the better death song, "Sister Morphine" or "Black Peter" by the Dead? Which is the better cowboy song, "Friend of the Devil" (Dead) or "Wild Horses"? Is any of it better than beating your meat?

Are you happy to be alive?

"Dead Flowers": "Taking bets on Kentucky Derby Day." Well N.Y. State now has off-track coverage of the Derby. So when's there gonna be some off-track *groupies* for the fans to sink their chops into?

The Stones keep a pretty close tab on certain groups. Fourth cut on side one it's the Velvets (Lou Reed was always the *real* M. Jagger). All you gotta do is read the title and then you'll get the subtle Little Richard joke ("—Knockin—") coupled with a couple of vocal inflections: what a superduper exciting wonderful JOKE (thanks Mick, Mick, Keith, Billy, Charles).

The camouflage is gone and this group is shit but name a band that's older. Duke Ellington? Count Basie? They've changed their personnel too much. Stones are at least 3/5 the same. Remarkable. Music is forever.

I JUST REALIZED IT: "Moonlight Mile" is the Dead!! There were clues galore and it took me this long to get it straight! I'm a dummy I guess.

Without "Brown Sugar" there'd be no excuse for this album.

Cut after "Brown Sugar" SUCKS. Fellatio may be pleasurable but this ain't that good.

Lew Alcindor counts for more. He really does.

Such painfully nostalgic music, you'd think it was Los Indios Taba-jaros: the old Stones no longer exist (are dead) (forever) (forget them).

Last part of "Can You Hear Me Knockin": are you kidding? The Stones playing (not just Santana but also) Cream?????????

"Moonlight Mile" = "Odessa" (Bee Gees). Equals it. No shit. Equivalent. "Head full of snow": Stones have always had a knack for arcane doperisms.

"Hear Me Knockin" is their greatest since "Complicated" or something like that.

Jim Jackson's "I Heard the Voice of a Porkchop" (Blues Classics 5) tops a lot of this stuff. Listen to it, it's good.

Beatles always gave relevance to other groups, though their biggest attempt to do so failed—their white album. The Stones never really did but this is *their* white album and it's got fewer decent cuts. Two or three.

24

Creedence Clearwater Revival: *Pendulum*

I repeat . . . you repeat. And rock repeats itself more than any of us ever *could.*

I was never too nuts about Creedence. For all their flashy-splashy rock-roll "energy," I thought they were kind of a half-assed throwback to the fifties, or maybe completely assed, but too ostentatious about it, too shake-your-booty without full payoff. They just weren't the whole fifties thing, *yet they had little inkling of sixties ramalama either: what the sixties had in fact* added to the world. *Proof, more than anything—oldies package tours to the contrary—that the fifties could never, would never happ'n again. (If Creedence couldn't, who* could?)

You you you kinda kinda kinda get get get the the the impression pression pression that that that Creedence Creedence Creedence Clearwater water water keeps keeps keeps doing doing doing the the the same same same thing thing thing over over over and and and over over over again again again. Too too too bad bad bad their their their first first first single single single was was was Suzy Suzy Suzy Q Q Q, too too too bad bad bad because because because it it it was was was itself itself itself an an an attempted tempted tempted imitation tation tation of of of early early early Stones Stones Stones plus plus plus some some some new new new stolen stolen stolen guitar guitar guitar riffs riffs riffs. That that that way way way they they they gave gave gave people people people the the the wrong wrong wrong impression pression pression when when when their their their next next next single single single was was was different different different. That that that way way way it it it took took took until until until around around around two two two or or or three three three more

more more singles singles singles before before before people people people realized realized realized that that that all all all they'd they'd they'd be be be doing doing doing from from from then then then on on on would would would be be be echoes echoes echoes of of of Proud Proud Proud Mary Mary Mary.

Well well now now they've they've got got this this brand brand new new idea idea that that it's it's time time to to stop stop the the echo echo. Well well they're they're wrong wrong because because the the camouflage mouflage isn't isn't so so good good. It's it's still still the the same same old old (good good) shit shit but but pendulums dulums only only move move this this way way and and then then that that way way. Just just two two ways ways. Just just two two. Rather rather than than more more. No no *reverberation ration* therefore therefore. And and who who needs needs rock rock and and roll roll that that isn't isn't an an echo echo anyway nyway?

Well this whole thing sounds pretty fake to me. "Chameleon" is different from "Molina," which is different from "It's Just a Thought," which is different from "(Wish I Could) Hideaway," which is different from "Pagan Baby," which is different from "Sailor's Lament," which is different from "Have You Ever Seen the Rain," which is different from "Rude Awakening No. 2," which is different from "Hey Tonight." Or was it they were *supposed* to be different? Shit, I'm losing track of what's supposed to be the story, or is it that I'm stupid? All I know is that if they're gonna start doing weird stuff two-three years after weird stuff got crossed off the list, and if they're gonna take that weird stuff and start duplicating *that* from here on in THEY'RE GONNA TURN INTO A BUCKET OF SHIT. And they won't even have an easy time of it either. So there.

EVEN LESS

Introduction

Well, enough of the subterfuge. Of maintaining in print, or pretending at all, that anything was still "going on." Have I said a'ready that "it" ended, at least began going WRONG, somewhere in late '67, at the latest '68? Have I said it twice?

Well let's hear it again: rock's freaking promise RENEGED ON . . . the twin coins of a once-grand realm, its now and forever units of relevance, etched in stone (pun intended?) as PRODUCT and HYPE . . . too many bands, signed to too many labels, recording too many records with inordinate budgets, resulting simply in everything sounding like shiiiiiiit—an overprocessed, denatured, demographically provident sop for tin ears. That's for starters.

Hype was our writers' end of the bargain. For our subsubsistence wage we were expected to feign credulity, manufacture public compliance, and in any case not spill the beans. I was a spiller, it's what I was *there* for, and looking back it amazes me how few of my contempos copped to the fact that their big-little rockworld was going to hell. It often felt a bit lonely, and pats on the back from occasional confreres for doing *their* dirtywork—*Way t' go!*—didn't assuage my feeling of isolation. At times it was like being the lone mocker in a room full of newsfolks cheerleading Reagan's buttfuck of Grenada (or Bush's rape of Panama).

Mid '71 through '73 was a prolific period for me; at what I was paid, it had to be. In '72 I stacked carbons of everything I wrote that got published (unpublished was another pile). At year's end I counted and found I'd averaged six pages a day, seven days a week—for jus' what was published—about 20 times as fast as I write today. Not that the written word was the sum total of my criticism. There were bands I felt strongly about, one way or 'nother, that I never reviewed—"symbolic acts" were more direct and usually sufficient. At an Eagles showcase, pre-first LP, I yelled, "You guys suck!!" while banging my fists on the edge of the stage (an action which didn't halt their march to world domination). I released live roaches at a Melanie show. Even my ignoring a band could be LOUD. I would storm out of rooms, buildings even, to avoid hearing *Who's Next* or Leon Russell.

Also in '72, I had another book out, one which took a "post-rock" tack that most reviewers chose to interpret ironically, insisting that by post-rock I really meant *rock*, or *advanced* rock or something—like how could anyone be willfully past it? (Boy, did I have news for them.) People who knew of *The Aesthetics*, or had actually read it but had no idea what I was getting at, found *Gulcher* an easy read—like falling off a log—even if this time they didn't *believe* what I was getting at.

TWO BOOKS, gee—the welcome mat was still basically out—but 'twasn't long before my grope for the ur-spirit of rock, or post-rock, or whatever the fuck, undercut all that, eviscerating my credibility—the *opposite* of what I mighta guessed.

There are times when I just don't know dick.

25

The Byrds: *Byrdmaniax*

"R. Meltzer's reviews are always the same. They never tell me anything I want to know about the album, and he always writes about things he more or less has contempt for. That's one sorry, useless cat." So read a letter run by Rolling Stone *smack in the middle of page three—the first thing your eye would light on when you opened the paper—the week this wake-the-town-and-tell-the-people humdinger also appeared.*

The letters that mags print, coupled with those they don't, especially at high-circulation mags that always receive a ton of correspondence, can sometimes *tell you how they feel about certain of their hierarchically less cozy contributors. (In the two years I wrote for the* Stone *I must've sent 'em a dozen pseudonymous raves about my own pieces—none ran—so I* know *they did get some.) "Controversy" is one thing; scapegoating a stooge is another.*

I'm probably just "being paranoid," but could they thus possibly have, uh, meant to blunt the impact of, the reception for, my bleak assessment of the state of recording arts & etc., circa last half of '71? (Does a bear shit in the woods?)

What a boring dead group. But then again aren't they *all?* Right, that puts it all in a different perspective. Increments of pus. Anything un-festering is a bonus. Two halfway decent cuts makes an album a winner, maybe even one.

The cover features death masks of the Byrds. But the eyes are closed and lots of stiffs have their eyes open. When you're alive and having your face cast you have to watch out for the eyes. So it looks like things have returned to the pre-fanatical days before the plaster casting of cocks, George Segal is a big cheese again and mere faces are worthy of consideration. Jeez; you'd think it was 1964 again and this was a Billy J. Kramer album with an exceptional cover. But it's only another Byrds bummer and the Byrds have never picked any bones about bummer covers, it hasn't been an abrupt descent, they've always just kind of accepted one after another. What a great bunch of mock stoics they are and always have been.

"Glory, Glory," written by the same person who dreamed up "Jesus Is Just Alright," is just loaded with George Harrison doing "My Sweet Lord." McGuinn used to do Dylan and George did some Dylan on his triple album and now it's McGuinn doing George. Ain't rock brotherhood grand?

"Pale Blue" is more of the same. The Byrds were always the number one more-of-the-same band in the land, now the thing that they're all the same as ain't the same old thing it used to be the same as, it's a different story. "I Trust" starts ominously and there are stretches where the same-as that it's the same as is the old one. There's even a couple moments of vocal hanky panky where you wonder whether Roger's been catching up on his Iggy and his Lou Reed now that there's no longer any need for him to teach Dylan how to sing rock and roll. He actually did that once so don't forget now that the tarpits have swallowed all.

"Tunnel of Love" is a much better than average Delaney & Bonnie cut by Skip Battin with not-out-of-place sax and chorus and organ stuff. It's good. "Citizen Kane" is also by Battin but it's a horse of a different color; it's that Eric Burdon flip side called something like "Good Times." It and "I Wanna Grow Up to Be a Politician," which follows, have the kind of words the Byrds always showed signs of degenerating into, namby pamby innocuous mickey mouse with latent-blatant political content. Or maybe they're just mocking out David Crosby, there's really no way of telling.

Battin's "Absolute Happiness" is downright pretty and if he displayed a little more mustard in his vocals he'd pass for Freddy Cannon. So I guess that must be where he got the "Tunnel of Love" thing from. Gene Parsons' "Green Apple Quick Step" is just that, something better left for the Nitty Gritty Dirt Band. "My Destiny" has Clarence White doing McGuinn doing Merle Haggard but even that's only in spots.

"Kathleen's Song" is as good as "Bells of Rhymney" and "Get to You" transposed into "Backstreet Girl" terms, in other words it's the second or third decent cut on the album. "Jamaica Say You Will" is by

Jackson Browne, so there's no way it could be *that* bad. It's sung as faithful to the current Jackson style as Nico did with Jackson '67.

If the Ginny given thanks to in the credits happens to be Ginny Ganahl then let me take this opportunity to say, thanks Ginny, for that swell time in L.A.

26

Connie Francis: *Grandes Exitos del Cine de los Años 60*

This one I was expected *to dislike, dump on, throw tomatoes at, as if the artist presented an especially fat target, fatter than any slew of vaunted mainstream with-its, and as if I particularly relished or needed them fat, so when I not only didn't dump but took things seriously, at least as seriously as the Dadaists took the bad art of* their *day, Jon Landau, who'd assigned it, for chrissakes, it wasn't my idea, and who could tell that no rewrite, no series of rewrites, would alter my review to his satisfaction, refused to run it in the* Stone. *So I gave it to* Fusion.
  Landau: who called himself the King, as in "Have you got a stick of gum for the King?" and you'd look around the room for George V or Faisal or Curtis before realizing he meant himself; whose own musical tastes were so rigid and narrow that one day in the mirror he saw eyes which, yes, wept for Carole King and was so unnerved he had to tell his shrink (and later Lisa Robinson, who fortunately told everybody*); who, only treading water at the* Stone *until a SCORE floated by, would eventually leave to invent (or was it reinvent?) Springsteen as a vendible commodity, but not before using the* Stone *to set the table, making him the first rockwriter to parlay wretched opportunism into wretched affluence . . . give the man a nuclear cigar.*

"Strangers in the Night" ("No Puedo Olvidar") starts things off on this latest and greatest of Connie's foreign-language escapades (it's in Spanish if you haven't figured that out yet). *Very* goddam good strings before her voice even enters, like the kind you don't mind backing up Ray Charles, only *occasionally* though. There's a touch of "Thunderball" or "Goldfinger" or one of them somewhere in the orchestration. Orcastration? No, now what is it people have against strings? Well there are two kinds, parent music (show, classical, 101 Strings) and slick playboy stuff; people who are neither parents nor playboys are always dumping on those who are, I guess. Kokomo's solution to the problem of strings was to insert a helping of piano-roll anonymity, keep it hackishly otherworldly; Benny Golson and Larry Wilcox's solution (they're the guys who do it on this one) is Connie Francis. She's better than Dionne Warwick doing "You'll Never Get to Heaven."

"Call Me Irresponsible" ("Eres") starts like *something else*, there's musical trickery afoot and an unknown tongue for you when you realize what song it really is (unless you know Spanish you just have to play it by ear). A few seconds later there's a Joni James-type attenuation of a passage into a squeal. She gets slightly Hebraic in her lilts and whatchamacallits, but anybody who's ever had trouble learning a high school language will understand, pronunciation is never easy. If you don't know from nothin about languages or any of that, here's an analogy for you: it's like learning to fake black music! You know, it's gonna occasionally come out pretty damn lame but after all nobody's a perfect polyglot.

Things got strange for me during "Ya Te Hablaran De Mi" (from *Inside Daisy Clover*) because I had no idea what song it was. It was just abstract muzak, not familiar like a department store version of "Santa Claus Is Coming to Town." Non-referential muzak (barber shops usually have that kind, supermarkets generally have the other). At one point it sounds like ——, oops, lost it. Well it was something very hip and funky! Both it and what it sounded like. But I can't tell you at *what* point, I don't know the lingo. But I can point out the Roy Orbison/Italian r&r ending, it's right at the end.

"The Second Time Around" is changed around slightly to compensate for the change to "El Segundo Amor." Connie seems to have some difficulty in turning off her mind to the way she knew it to be in the past. One kind of muzak interfering with another, it was abstract even for her, a good object lesson for jazz jooks like Archie Shepp. The ending sounds English this time, she just couldn't hold it back, *something* had to be the same as in the original.

"Lara's Theme" ("Sueño De Amor") starts off flamenco or Italian-restaurant on guitar, but it's subtle, it's kept modest, there's no attempt to force or direct anything. There's no attempt to make it anything but "Lara's Theme" as everybody knows and loves it (I bet YOU like it too). So there's *all* the expected inflections: hence it translates well and is truly international.

If Astrud Gilberto can do "The Shadow of Your Smile" in English then Connie can do it in Spanish ("La Sombra De Tu Sonrisa"), but then again Astrud used to do the translating between hubby João and Stan Getz. Even though the problem of translating a song involves *musical* translation as well, it's the language problem that predominates since who can even sing his or her *own* language decently, musically? So it's the words and how they're to be pronounced that dominate.

Connie really flows (fffflllloooowwwwssss) (f—l—o—w—s) through "Fue Nuestro Amor" ("Wives and Lovers"). Spanish seems to free it from both the meaning and jaggedness that it's stuck with in English, it sounds like a good early Bossa Nova. Nice string and horn interlude. Benny Golson is responsible. But there's this part beginning with "los dos . . ." where the language structure is still conducive to vocal awkwardness. And Connie gets a little out of breath near the end due to flowing so much, so English would seem like a wind-saver with natural rests.

In "La Buena Vida" ("The Good Life," the finest version of which is by Betty Carter on an old Atco disc) her voice falters in one spot and the arrangement reinforces it. It's a shit arrangement I guess, because she wasn't shown up any other time, I guess that's the only way you can judge. It's lazy but always halfway out of bed, good idea, but she's too *night*-tired rather than morning-tired. An awful sax ending puts it to sleep anyway, making the time of day irrelevant.

FINALLY: "Where the Boys Are" ("Donde Hay Chicos")! It starts a beat later than in the original, otherwise it's exactly the same (except the middle section where it's slowed down somewhat). It's (naturally) the most Italian-sounding track, it lapses into total nostalgia, she spills all the beans: oops, so *that* was the point of the album after all! (One more time of "Where the Boys Are.")

The last cut, "Olvidemos El Mañana" (from *The Yellow Rolls Royce*) sounds *Russian* in spots, otherwise it's utterly ordinary, even as an abstract muzak piece, an *obvious* last cut. The most obvious last cut since "Mr. Moonlight" and "Everybody's Tryin To Be My Baby" on *Beatles 65*.

27

Commander Cody and His Lost Planet Airmen: *Lost in the Ozone*

So here's where the gig ended. Dig the irony: an album I wasn't required to dislike, or like—one way or the other—but didn't even dislike; liked. It was accepted and it ran—uncut, unchanged. And still it got me canned. Good story.

Nick Tosches and I were at a press party for the album, the band; plenty of whiskey. I remember coconut ice cream. The Commander played and we had so much fun we agreed to each review the thing. As to why *we had fun, well, it wasn't rock, not really, it was* something else. *Country music, even pseudo-country, even what amounted to basically a* rock *send-up of country, seemed for the moment an antidote to most things rock, a possible way out of the rock morass. Nick was so buzzed he took the first mental step down a path that would lead inexorably to the writing of* Country—*still the definitive overview of cowpoop music—and* Hellfire, *one of the great music bios of the last 200 years. I would write my share of country pieces too. But before any of that we decided to both review the Commander—under each other's byline.*

I secured the Fusion *assignment, which he then wrote in my name; he pulled off likewise with* Rolling Stone, *and I wrote that one in his. When Landau somehow found out, he was furious. For our little bitty "gag," our flaunting of low-level "kicks," our breach of I dunno, whatever it was a breach of, he booted us both—his two best reviewers.*

All told, I was done with this sorry, useless publication in less than two years. People I run into still hit me with "Ooh, didn't you write for Rolling Stone?" *"Yeah," I say, "but at least I've had the smarts never to stick my pecker in a garbage disposal."*

Finally!

Jesus H. Christamighty this sleazo-honkoid album's been overdue! Years and years and years of qual-oriented country hooting, it seemed

like it would never end. All that *music*, all those punks going on thinking and acting like country had something to *do with* music. Quality and
music, and cornhuskers from Jersey City pursuing *long lost goldmines in
the dew*: Commander Cody where were you when we needed you?

As everybody and his Uncle Bozo should have known all along
country's nothing but Homer & Jethro with or without the camouflage, it's the world's longest standing comedy routine and it's all the
same even when it's not. Santana's just a country band in principle
with some geographical distortion thrown in for disguise, with the utter ignorance of their primary audience being all that's needed to prevent the laughter. But they're still too alien to their true roots to circle
in on anything cosmic or even ozonic. Commander Cody hits the nail
right on the head.

Webster's Seventh New Collegiate Dictionary defines ozone as: 1)
an allotropic triatomic form of oxygen that is normally a faintly blue
irritating gas with a characteristic pungent odor, is generated usu. in
dilute form by a silent electric discharge in ordinary oxygen or air, and
is used esp. in disinfection and deodorization and in oxidation and
bleaching; 2) pure and refreshing air. Well, both these definitions'll do
for these jackasses. Like what's more/less irritating than pure air (and
thus in turn more/less eminently *functional*)? And what's better/worse
than utter trash? And if "Beat Me Daddy Eight to the Bar" isn't trash
then my name is Vivian Stanshall. And if these boys aren't the American Bonzos then "Back to Tennessee" isn't the best glue song ever
executed.

But the one major disadvantage in ever recording groups of this ilk
also comes through all too clear from first cut to last: studio electronics can't help but *improve the sound* and in so doing remove the last
vestige of gratuitous *funk* (is there another word to describe?) from
the whole professionally amateur whatchamacallit, rendering it all
just another competent Flying Burrito Brethren with better lyrics.
And there's no way the uninformed listener's gonna know just from
listening that sometime lead singer Billy C.'s stage routine consists of
him wandering around with an acoustic guitar round his neck without
doing *anything with it* save for "strumming" an occasional unmiked,
inaudible, irrelevant chord or two whenever the spirit hits him. How
is anyone to know whether he's doing it here on "Daddy's Gonna
Treat You Right" or "Lost in the Ozone"? In other words: it's what
they're not doing that's just as crucial/uncrucial as what they are doing and there's no way you're about to know just exactly what they're
not doing by use of ears alone.

A hopeful sign for next time: now that Bobby Black's replaced the virtuoso West Virginia Creeper on pedal steel (the latter handles those chores on this disc) the next CC & the LPA vinyl event is likely to be a step in the right direction, *downhill*.

28

Marc Benno: *Minnows*

. . . And back to not *listening; to no way out but custom-designing one.* *"Fantasy," anyone?*
But let's begin non*fantasy—a classic case of building a review from the* little you know—*hmm, says here he played rhythm guitar on* L.A. Woman—*and there's always simply the names of the cuts (quick!: can't sell it till you've written them down)* . . . then *let 'er rip.*
Was he actually some kind of Christian?—a snippet of topical "data" saved for the end—or did I make that up too? At this point I couldn't even GUESS.

He played rhythm guitar on the last Doors album that had all four of them, he was even noticeable once in a while and he's noticeable here. And he's always excellent. He's excellent on "Franny." He's excellent on "Put a Little." He's excellent and in fact *excellent* on "Love in My Soul." He's very excellent on "Stone Cottage." He's excellent plus on "Speak Your Mind." He's mighty excellent on "Back Down Home." He's excellent and a half on "Good Times," not the same as "Good Times, Bad Times" by either the Stones or Led Zeppelin. He's tops in excellence on "Baby I Love You." He's excellent on "Baby Like You." He's even excellent on "Don't Let the Sun Go Down." In other words, *Minnows* is top drawer excellent from first note to last.

But it's also a perfect example of a novel that never should have been made into a play, let alone a musical. The music does not improve the book, *Cold Minnows* by Suzanne Poteau: how could anything improve it? It's the greatest book of all time according to Bobby Abrams and altho I haven't read it myself his word is generally to be taken as gospel. It seems the book's about an orphan youth lost in the sway of postwar turmoil in Budapest after the war. As if that war wasn't enough he gets into a private war with his only friend, an elderly plumber harrowed by all the busted pipes created by the bombings. Eventually the boy murders the old man with a chair handle just to get the old geezer's fish for himself. But he quickly learns that you can't get away with killing a plumber cause the plumbing in the house goes bad right away and the fish die, hence the title of the book. That's where the book begins and the kid takes the guilt with him wherever he goes, including Marineland of the Pacific where a girl he is dating insists he bring her. First fish he sees drives him to the brink of insanity and he decides to call off the engagement. Hence, heartache is his destiny.

Good enough idea for the printed page yeah, but the musical idiom is something else entirely. The story just doesn't hold together from song to song, especially with Marc in the role of Janos the youth. He's blustery when he should be cautious and spontaneous when he should be crackling. In other words: he's a ham! No fish in him except sometimes baked ham tastes fishy and there's times here when he's baked all right!

But these objections are just trivial and immaterial and they in no way prevent this album from being—among other things—the most Christian album in more than a decade, apparently Marc takes his Jesus seriously!

29

Steve & Eydie at
the Palsy Telethon

Sometimes it's easier not making anything up.
   Catch it on a telethon, for inst, and music will just about review itself.
   WARNING: offensiveness in high gear! (Gearing up for the offensiveness wars.)

That's cerebral, there's more than one kind. Jay Lee had the kind that just paralyzes half your face so it's hard to talk and you drool a lot and it was only temporary and he doesn't have it anymore. But even while he had it he was still able to go up to Clive Davis and sell Columbia Tom & Sharon and sell himself as a producer too. Now he's a rich man and the palsy he had didn't prevent it. On the other hand cerebral palsy is never your palsy walsy, it's mean and disgusting and it fucks up babies and they're sometimes born with it. When they are they can't walk a straight line and they can't stand up. Why do they call it cerebral if it's the legs and voice that're shot to shit? Maybe because you have to *think* about it.

   And Steve Lawrence and Eydie Gorme made sure that every living man, woman and children would have it on *their* minds because it could happen to them and theirs at some future time. But here was the paradox: while Steve and Eydie were singing everybody's mind was on musical *enjoyment* and besides it's FREE, you didn't have to PAY to see it, paying was just like a tip (HEY WHY DON'T READERS SEND WRITERS TIPS IF THEY LIKE THEIR STUFF, writers as a group are harshly underpaid). The other paradox was: paradox = two doctors (get it?). Eydie sang without lipsynch except when she did her newest hit which she didn't know the words for, something like "It Was the Best Time." It was the 20th Anniversary

Celebrity Parade for Cerebral Palsy, does that mean it's only existed 20 yrs? Abbreviation for it is CP, if Corinne Calvet had it it would be CCCP, yes they have it even there! "Can't Buy Me Love" was real good by Steve & Eydie when they went out in the audience just like Iggy and the folks there got even more intimidated than with Iggy cause they hadda give em their money: maybe Iggy's in the wrong biz, maybe he oughta be in POP! They did the wrong chords of the song too, just like Elektra recording artists the Wild Thing used to do with the same song at Steve Paul's The Scene a number of happy yrs ago.

At 3 AM it stood at $145,623, no it wasn't the CP victims who were standing and it couldn't be that high because no CPer has ever been richer than 10 dollars at a time: that's what the *total* was from the benefactors. And Steverino sang "3 O'clock in the Morning" to celebrate a moment in history that would never occur again no matter how long you wait. BUT suddenly the phones stopped ringing so Dennis James who used to do the Corn Flakes ads on the old *What's My Line* but didn't get rehired when it moved to NYC local TV, so Dennis James said PLEASE START THEM RINGING AGAIN. And they did. I myself called up a bogus amount of 65 dollars in the name of Johnny Winter and they read it over the air, so you can subtract that from the announced total if you want accuracy.

A Spanish dancer reminiscent of Jose Greco but other than him got up and danced the old Spanish Jig and his band had 2 guitarists and a hand clapper. Jose Madrid was his name from the Chateau Madrid which is in this nation, no his name was Jose Molina (no relation to Moline and Molette or any other various and sundry Molinet). A man with almost the same initials, Morty Gunty was the announcer on that one and his coverage was thus: "When the guys are singing, it sounds like high holy days in Peru. I'm not kidding, it sounds like Rushashunna." The fuckin yid!

Dennis James and the girls at the phone were unable to *watch* any television while they were on camera except for the monitor—and the monitor doesn't have any dials on it. But the greatest service performed by the show's performers was that the show was on all nite, it wasn't off even for station identification and that never happens except for special events like death of DeGaulle, which you can give or take, er, I mean take or leave. But all you could do with CP was watch or not watch, give to or not give to, the logic was hardfast.

Then just before channel 2 went off there was a CP ad on channel 2 to go along with the CP Telethon on channel 9: they were the only remaining channels (television channels, not the English) still on and *both, both, both* of them had some CP coverage or other. But at least the telethon was mixing entertainment with salesmanship and the other wasn't. It was but not the kind you pay to see, it was repulsive and disgusting and they showed a film of a CP baby having a slow hard time of it. On the other hand the telethon was doing it live and the time wasn't so hard.

But you didn't get to see that until the next morning because 3 AM is a little too late past bedtime even for CPs so they hadda be brought out in the morning. It *was* the morning but I mean the *late* morning. So they brought out about twelve of em, both sexes and that musta been one sixteenth of the country's CP population. Well they were instructed to walk over to Steve while he was singing "Bei Mir Bist Du Schoen," no that was the Barry Sisters. Steve was singin "For Once in My Life" and this piano stylist was backin him up and you couldn't see the cat's face because his back was to the camera but he was damn good! Steve was sittin at the piano bench with him, it wasn't a stool and it had four legs and Steve was facin the camera. He had his *face* facing the camera, that is his feet and back were facing somewhere else. So Eydie told a lovely little CP girl with braces on her legs to walk over and give hubby a big smooch, she didn't mind because she knew Steve wasn't gonna think about fuckin the young little beauty. And Eydie was standin right behind her so if she fell Eydie'd be right there to catch her so her injuries wouldn't be complicated any more than necessary. BUT Eydie was even more helpful than that: whenever it looked like little girlie-pie didn't wanna do it she'd pick her up and carry her a few feet just to keep her interested. It was very impressive. And very safe too, safety and aesthetics were forever wed.

Is a wedding worth $200? If so maybe everybody who got married shoulda dedicated 200 to the telethon. If not, then not. But it was worth the *investigation* on their part and they didn't do it.

One thing they did do was arrange with ABC to let em do the space shit off ABC: yeah *that* shit was on the same time, too bad cause the telethon was getting to be the last refuge from the space launch as all the other channels were pickin it up. But one thing ABC wouldn't let em do was get the actual coverage *piped in*, all they let em have was a tube with it on in front of their camera: A TUBE WITHIN A tube, another telethon first! As it occurred Dennis James told everybody to count down with him but the station manager or somebody said not until it reaches ten, what a fuckin killjoy!

But that's only if there *was* joy, indications were there wasn't. But Dennis was a juggernaut of reverence all down the line: "God bless them and God speed." But before that he said "Weather must've cleared over Kennedy" altho which Kennedy did he mean? Ted, Bob, Jack, Ethel, Jackie, Ari, Eunice or Ari? Or was it Kennedy Airport, Kennedy Stadium in DC or Kennedy Avenue? But after God speed he said "Oh my aching back" which is a prime good example of how useful long, long shows can be. If the show hadn't been on for 19 hrs he never would've been tired. If he had never been tired he wouldn't of gotten so casual. Casual enuff to say "Oh my aches and pains." God bless him!

Then there was the analogy about the rocketship going up up and away, away up high in the sky and so was everybody involved in the broadcast *high on love* for the wonderful children who were giving their time and bodies to the cause. The cause was good or they wouldn't have raked in a whopping $1,042,779 as of just after coming back from the space. Then Louie Armstrong came on and smiled for a while and then he played with the Steve Lawrence orchestra and they were real good in backing up the aging genius of skat-de-dat. What else happened on the show? Not a fuckin thing except it ended.

One man conspicuous by his absence was Roy Rogers and Dale Evans. They knew the bite of tragedy and yet they were too tied up in their own personal problems to show up on the show. You'll remember no doubt that they adopted FIVE kids (Jesus Piss!) and two of em died. And the one child Dale and him got by natural means of sperm and ova was born a retard. One of the likeliest reasons they didn't show was they were busy with their 12 wonderful grandkids at their ranchhouse in Apple Valley, Calif. What, they've abandoned Texas and Oklahoma?! Yes and Dale's also busy on her 11th book, the first was an international best seller based on the life and times of that retard she had. But in between it's been nothing but sadness and dishearteningness as NINE in a row were non-bestsellers.

30

The Full Jerry Vale Treatment

WHAT? you ask—this *was enough to piss Lou Reed off?*
(Don't complain if you've read some of this before.)

Lou Reed is a man of his name. He *reads* a lot. Lita Eliscu once gave him a book and he read it; he reads his ass off. In his pursuit of the printed page he's come across many a Raymond Chandler book. They have good covers and since he's not blind he came around to liking them a lot. Albums have covers too so when Lou finally got to do his long awaited solo album he called on Mr. Tom Adams to do him a cover. Tom's the guy who did those Ray covers and now he's done a Lou cover too. It's got at least two different species of bird on it, maybe even as many as four. One of the birds appears to have no wings but he sure can walk, could be he's a distant relative to the kiwi, New Zealand's national bird.

But it would take an ornithologist to identify the others, all he could even tell you himself is they have wings. Strange birds. Could be hummingbirds because they appear to be humming. They're hovering around humming at bouquets of flowers in the name of Lou Reed. The flowers are hovering too, all by their lonesome, hovering over an ocean erupting on the kiwi who's walking the city streets right next to a jewel that's inside a jewel-encrusted jewel case. A lot of wealth is about to go down the drain and a kiwi's cousin too . . .

But does it pass the judge-a-book-by-the-cover test? YES! You know why? 'Cause I played it for my parrot—Perry the Parrot—he's a small parrot, not a big one but he's no parakeet either. And he fuckin' *liked* it, he liked it enough to sing along and the only word he knows is "perry." And the song he was singing along with was: that's right, "Ocean"!! Birds and oceans so the album passes with flying colors.

Which means it's one of the greatest albums ever put together and even the words are good.

And why shouldn't they be? After all words are the tools of the poet and if Lou's no poet then George Washington never crossed the Delaware. Proof positive that Lou is that poet is if you've ever read *Fusion* mag you've no doubt seen Lou's POEMS printed on those pages from time to time. One time was that time when they gave him a double-page spread with a photo of blue skies over New England as the illustration. Another time was that time when he got the lower righthand corner. Once it was the whole lefthand side of the furthest-over column. Poets get to move around the page a lot (a lot faster than novelists if you ask me) and nobody knows this better than Lou. He's even moved around the pages of time.

Like take one of his lyrics from off of *Lou Reed* (RCA LSP-4701), for example "I was talkin' to Ed who'd been reported dead by mutual friends" from "Wild Child" on side two. What year does that line remind you of? Yes, of course it's 1967. That was the year that lyrics were really getting far fuckin' *out*, man. They were really headed for hell and gone but something happened to gum up the works, psyche-delic. Psychedelic lyrics entered the pitcher and things got real silly overboard sort of pseudo-weird. Instead of being solid outasite far out. It was just so much *flimsy shit*. Well Lou is still doing what was intended to be done back in ninety hundred sixty-seven and he's doing it well. Well? I mean he's doing it fine, *real* fine in fact.

And he's never one of these shit-pretty poetry cats either, like lots of singer-songwriters I could mention but I'll spare their families the embarrassment and leave them nameless. What's his secret for avoiding worthless pretty swill or the excesses of poetry per se? Well it's on account of he always liked Ogden Nash. Liked him? He *worshiped* him. Now as every mother knows it was Ogden who laid the groundwork for such later duds as Allen Ginsberg, people who actually *took poetry seriously*!!! Lou does no such thing, he uses his verse just for a laugh, and what a laugh: "Life isn't what it seems, I'm forever driftin' into dreams, such a sad affair, to always be driftin' into air." Ha ha ha, that's a funny one.

But not half as funny as the joke he once told at Lisa Robinson's house. Sandpaper up your funny bone 'cause here it is. These two guys come into town lookin' for some action and they gravitate to Greenwich Village but they can't find any action *anywhere*. This goes on for some time until they come across an elderly derelict sitting outside the Hotel Earle who agrees to let them insert their puds in his very large nostrils. They get their jollies in this manner to the point of ejaculation. Upon removal the derelict sez "Do either of you gents have a social disease?" "No," they shake their heads to indicate a negative answer. No sooner said than he inhales briskly with each nostril! Jesus that's a good one!

Now the Lisa whose house that was at is not (repeat *not*) the same Lisa who's in "Lisa Says" on side one. A different Lisa altogether—but not totally out of the picture either. No sir or ma'am as the case may be. No 'cause Lisa's the spouse of Richard Robinson who co-produced the album with Lou himself. The whole gang was there in the U.K. to cut it and they ran up a pretty fair hotel bill! Yeah well but music is worth any price you can think of, whether it be a dollar forty-six or $9,652,409.22.

Especially when the music is better than the Stones and this album is. Everybody who's ever heard Lou croon a tune has known deep down they've been witnessing THE REAL JAGGER. Everybody. 'Cause it's true, Lou does more acrobatics with his vocal apparatus than Mr. Mick has thought of doing in years. Mick's a classicist, one of those old stuffed shirts who parade their wares via the Hi-Tone Route, professional product, that sort of thing. He'd never think of swallowing a razor blade for the sake of a song. He's never gonna take no chances anymore 'cause he's got a distinguishable *style* and he ain't gonna sacrifice that for nothin'. But Lou ain't no chicken, if he's gonna record at all he's gonna take the big risk.

Just think of all he's risking on "I Can't Stand It," the opening cut on side one. He's risking life and limb and he may not get social security if they don't wanna give it to him 'cause now they got grounds for withholding it on the grounds of he's a risk-taker. Like why would anybody hire Susan Comstock to sing back-up vocal? Such a move has a limited audience at best and if the wrong people are listening there's bound to be a fight or a riot. But wait—it isn't even Susan Comstock!! It's somebody named Helene Francois, this Reed maniac has gone out and hired an untried amateur! What a cad! My hat's off to him! Crazy, man, crazy! Far fuckin' outafuckinsite!

"Why am I so shy?" asks Lou toward the end of "Lisa Says" but he does not answer. I don't know the answer, do you? He's asking Lisa but all she does is *say*, she does not answer. But she sure says real cool-ass stuff like "Honey if you stick your tongue in my ear . . . "

Also Lou is the REAL RAY DAVIES, if you don't believe me take a gander with your ears at "Berlin" which closes out side one. Close enough to Ray to be made an honorary third Davies Brother along

with Ray and Dave. Yet he does not cloud the issue with a bogus
English accent like Ray does whenever he sings about faraway places
and decadence you can cut with an olive knife. Lou gives it the full
Jerry Vale treatment, something Ray wouldn't touch with a ten-foot
pole.

(In case the name Lou Reed doesn't strike the appropriate chord inside your skull here's a clue: VELVET UNDERGROUND! Holy
cow! Yeah man, he sang with 'em and wrote all their stuff and he's the
guy who had that great crack-up the last night they played Max's and
it's all down on tape with him saying spaced out *things* between songs
and it's supposed to be coming out soon and it's about *time* but it's not
out yet and this one is . . .)

31

John & John (The Two Johns)

And what have we here . . . *anti-limey? anti-Yoko? anti-John?—and he used to be my fave—what's the world coming to? Anti-Paul too, but that's given. (The Brit Invasion was one thing; the Brit Occupation was another.)*

But Yoko: Yoko. Yoko was as out of place in '70s rock as let's say Maria Callas if somebody'd convinced her *to "cross over," and not over to show tunes, I mean covers of Led Zeppelin and Rod Stewart. She was as stone goofy a rock presence as Wild Man Fischer, twice as superfluous, and about a fortieth as "provocative." (Strictly from Interlopersville.)*

Question: Was I still friendly with Creem *editor (and future Landau co-conspirator) Dave Marsh? Gee. One's own ancient past can be a pisser.*

Would any sane person think that "Oh Yoko" is as good as "Dear Prudence" from whence it came? No. Would any insane person think ditto? No. The only people who would are the total DUDS, there are lots of duds in the world. Some of them have puds and some do not.

And speaking of Mrs. Lennon—otherwise known as Ms. Ono—she preys upon duds even more than him, her move is to make use of the complete ignorance of most duds and non-duds alike concerning the history of art. Nobody knows the history of it beyond the big names, nobody knows who Yves Klein was, some people do but not most. So she goes and does this show that includes nothing, a show of non-works with the catch being "of course there are works but you gotta use your imagination." Well, I'll be dipped in shit but Yves Klein went and did that around fifteen years ago, maybe it was thirteen but it was around then. And when he did it it had a context, like Rauschenberg was doing blank canvases so why not a blank show? Yoko wants to come off as new as tomorrow but she's about as up to date as Walter Keane, I mean what is all this *art* shit, particularly when it's just more of the same played out whatsis, and when she does

her actual (salable) objets d'art they're even neater than the ones
Duchamp used to do and neatness was his weakest point. So fuck her.

And John does and he eats her too. Does he like the taste? Of
course! But even limey fusspot John Stuart Mill used to dip his
tongue in the honey pot once in a while and even Bert Russell. And
come to think of it there ain't really that much difference between *any
of the following* limeys: J.S. Mill, B. Russell, T.S. Eliot, George Eliot,
Alec Guinness, Peter Sellers, David Hume, John Locke, John
Lennon, etc. Nigel Bruce and George Sanders are better than the
whole pack of them.

These days John's still good at what he's always been good at, alienating affections. If you go back to *Hard Day's Night* there's this business about Paul's grand-dad alienating affections and breaching
promises, well John's doing the former now and he's done it before.
For instance: John Sinclair of the Motor City used to really get on
well with Dave Marsh and now he doesn't even speak to him from his
cell. Dave didn't get invited to the recent big John Sinclair press conference. The reason? John S. had been discovered by John L. and
John L. even wrote a song for him so now he's buddies with John L.
and not Dave M. There's nobody better for giving you a taste of stars
in your eyes than good old Johnny Lennon.

But there's no way John could ever be as bad as Paul.

32

The J. Geils Band:
The Morning After

I beat Peter Wolf at checkers, beat him easy . . . mind if I brag?

Peter Wolf is a lousy checker player. He's worse that me. He's worse than you. You can beat him. I can beat him. He takes out his board. Carries it everywhere. Made of ivory. Got his name on it in gold. Brand new checkers. He can't win. Got to lose. If you leave the room he'll move the pieces. But he still won't win. No way. You can't lose. If it's him you're playing. I can't lose. If it's him I'm playing.

So let's see. There's ten songs on this album by him and his boys. You can't do an entire game in ten moves so that's out. Can't do one move per person per cut. That's out. Um. Gotta be something you can do with an album besides play and enjoy it. All the cuts are good so let's see. Um. Uh. Here's one. A new game for every cut. Most pieces left wins. At the end of each cut. Two boards are needed. Somebody has to set up a new one while the old one's being played on. Let Magic Dick do it. Can you use the album cover for the second board? Yes. But you must draw all the boxes on it first. Or it gets confusing. You won't know where to move anything to.

"I Don't Need You No More." Only 2:35. So it's gonna be a fast one but not that fast. It only takes two seconds to make a move. But you can take as long as you want. Within reason. Wolf loses no matter what.

"Whammer Jammer." One second shorter. 2:34. Wolf ain't even on it. Magic Dick is. The game's being played on the board he set up. Wolf loses again.

"So Sharp." A little longer. Time to stretch out and use some checker strategy. 3:09 is a long time. But not long enough for Wolf. Another loss for him.

"The Usual Place." Down a bit to 2:44. Faster moves cause it's on the album cover board. Cellophane. Less friction than ivory. Friction won't help Wolf. His loss. Your win.

"Gotta Have Your Love." A real long one. But don't get cocky. Four in a row doesn't mean shit. Just concentrate on every move and you got it. It's 4:32 but it might be over in 4 minutes flat. But take your time and it's five in a row for you.

Take your piss break before side two. So you come back to an unfucked board.

"Looking for a Love." 3:45. More than the average for side one. You win again.

"Gonna Find Me a New Love." 3:23. If it's getting monotonous just beating Wolf why not listen to his songs of love and laughter? Good idea but don't feel sorry for him.

"Cry One More Time." 3:21. Can you notice the two-second difference between the last one and this? See if you can. You can win with your eyes closed by now.

"Floyd's Hotel." 3:08. It's a sprint. You can make it if you try.

"It Ain't What You Do (It's How You Do It!)." There's every reason for Wolf to be crazy baby by now. He's reeling more than he's rocking. Longer than hell this time. 5:12. Let him win. It's only fair. Let him win. He gave you a record. Okay. It's 9-1 in your favor. You're happy. He's happy cause he won the last one. Everybody's happy. Good.

33

Arthur Miller:
Hanging Out and Settling Down

Perks other than the aforementioned.

If you're a record reviewer and you don't have a mailbox the size of a refrigerator you know damn well that every morning about 10 there's gonna be a ringing sound and it won't be your alarm cause reviewers don't have to get up in the morning so they don't have alarm clocks. The ring-a-ding's at the door cause the mailman has to let you know he's got records for you and it's either get out of bed or they go back to the post office and that's an eight-block walk. So if you live on the sixth floor it's hurry into your pants and rush down all those stairs and if you're lucky he's one of those mailmen who saves all your mail for you in one pile instead of putting the small items in the box.

Okay so you get upstairs again and get back into bed with your mail and your clothes and it's beating time: TIME FOR SOME PUD PULLING! What else can you do at 10 in the morning? So if you're lucky there's a press release somewhere in with all the records, an 8¹/₂ X 11 rectangle to whiz off on. You can always jack off in the sheets but then you gotta wash. So it sure must've been a SHOCKER for all those reviewers in reviewland to receive their Arthur Miller album without *one shred of excess matter* in the package: nothing but a record!

Well so there has to be something else about this record to make it worthy of a listen, something. After all Columbia doesn't just sign up anybody off the street. The first something is the fact that this ain't the original Arthur Miller, the one who used to pop his tart in Marilyn's toaster. He wrote more bad plays than even Shakespeare. Shakespeare was awful and he looked like an artichoke. Arthur Miller (thank god he didn't write *Death of a Salesman*) looks like a pear. If you put him in a juicer you'd get pear nectar and nothing beats that when thirst hits you about throat high.

Second something is he's not the Arthur known as Godfrey. That Arthur bought his books on bridge from Patti Smith at Scribner's Books on 5th Ave. and 48th St. He's the guy who used to be Arthur Godfrey & All The Little Godfreys. Well this Arthur is Arthur Miller & All The Little Millers and thank the lord above he *isn't* Arthur Godfrey. That Arthur's last major appearance on record was—coincidentally—a Columbia disc of a few years ago, the second Moby Grape album. But like I said this is a different Arthur.

Third something is he isn't Arthur Garfunkel. You might think now that that Arthur doesn't have a Paul Simon to fall back on he might get desperate and change his name to something simple like, say, Miller. He might. But he hasn't. No, he's just living in Connecticut somewhere.

SO GIVE IT A LISTEN, IT'S A GREAT ALBUM!

34

A Fatal Jerkoff on the Moon

Speaking of jerkoffs . . .
(Oh, by the way: this had to be the first write-up anywhere for Robert
Mapplethorpe—before he was really doing photos. Rejected by Zygote,
which soon folded anyway, it ended up six months later in Gulcher.*)*

There was this party for Robert Mapplethorpe at the Chelsea and
there was a shopping cart full of cans of Budweiser rolling around and
guys were starting to snap em open. Plus they would drink em. Well
then somebody dumped an ounce of boo on the table and cats and
kitties got their kicks that way and the beering halted. Well then Todd
Rundgren lit a match. He stuck the match down there with the ounce
and he was still holding it so's he could get a good fire going without
the light going out. There weren't too many matches left. Well no
sooner had the ounce fire gotten off the ground than the area was
mobbed with grass fans opposed to the blaze. And it wasn't cause they
were Smokey the Bear types, it was cause if there was gonna be a fire
they wanted it inside a joint. Jesus the world sure has a mile of weird
creatures with even weirder preferences! And they were all lined up
around the forest fire even though it wasn't a forest. Some people
used to call it a forest when it was just seeds and stems—mostly
stems—because that's the way it looked. This wasn't even a forest, it
looked a lot more like lawn mower cuttings shredded up even more.
Some people like it like that but Todd saw thru their dumb game and
he was having the most fun at the party. There was even a joint made
up of a dollar bill with the stuff rolled up in it, if the stuff was gonna
get smoked it would have to be under unusual circumstances or over
Todd's dead body. And he wasn't gonna die for anybody. In fact it was
a whole lot like that one where Mr. Natural tries to throw the TV set
out the window and everybody stops him. He got stopped dead com-

pletely and he had to leave but not Todd. Todd prevailed and prevail he did.

But when he was a kid he used to get beat up on by this meany named Bruce. So when he grew to being older he never liked people named Bruce but he liked me anyway even though Bruce was my middle name. Which means he's sure a good guy. Did I say he was a good guy? I mean he was a good guy. He used to be a real short guy when he was a kid and usually guys who are real short grow up to be perverts so they can take it out on the world. Not Todd. He grew up to be unshort, he just willed it and he grew some extra inches and they added up to feet. Funny because when you're producing Jesse Winchester and others of that ilk they let you sit down so it doesn't matter how tall you are. And since Todd's done that sort of thing he's been allowed the privilege of the chair more than once. But you can't sit down all the time or your legs would never unbend. And you need good legs for rock and roll or even just walking down the street.

Such as the streets of Great Neck. That's where he lived when he was with the Nazz and the main drag there is called Middle Neck Road. Most of the cheap food there is in supermarkets but for gourmets there's this place called Kuck's. Not Kucks as in the name of that guy Johnny Kucks who used to pitch for the Yankees in the World Series but Kuck's. As in Mr. Kuck. Well this guy Kuck was a Mormon by trade and he used to go to his store at around 4:30 AM in order to get the jump on his competitors. Wait a minute, he wasn't a Mormon, he was a Christian Scientist but he went to the Christian Science Convention when it was in Salt Lake City where all the Mormons live their polygamous lives or die trying. Kuck used to shove that ugly Christian Science *reading matter* in people's faces. That may be okay and well and good in the waiting room of the Poughkeepsie railroad depot but it ain't exactly fun when food's on your mind. Nothing beats food and Kuck knew that food and fun were worth bucks in his pocket. So he used to charge 59 cents for a can of potato sticks that other places charged 17 cents for and he always got it because rich dippos would pay it rather than rub up against minorities in the supermarket. On Halloween the local kids still throw eggs at Kuck but they buy the eggs elsewhere. He always follows people (meaning kids) all around the store to make sure they don't steal anything. Such as the cheese-covered almonds which are good and you should try them but don't buy them at Kuck's. They're about a dollar there. Andy Winters of the late Soft White Underbelly once bought them but it was somebody else's money so it was okay. They were the other band in town. The Nazz was the other one. Todd was in it and you know what else he used to call Kuck's? He used to call Kuck's *Kooks* as in Kookie lend me your comb. Pretty good, huh? But it didn't lessen the situation foodwise.

For instance the only hamburger meat in the place was patties, not meat. Patties are mostly soy bean crud. They cook up quick because they're so thin and the Soft White Underbelly preferred them but not the Nazz. Todd never ate them but he likes the name Patti anyway, particularly when it's attached to the name Smith. He likes Patti Smith a whole lot and she was at the Robert Mapplethorpe party too. Robert's art stuff was good too, real good in fact and one of the things had a long bent male mutton dagger with the balls hanging over a sharp edge. Geez that must hurt! And there was some poon stuff too with paint over it sprayed on thru some sort of grid like the ones they use for spaghetti. There wasn't any spaghetti there at the Chelsea and there weren't even any pretzels, just beer. Kuck's used to be the favorite beer buying spot for late-nite drinking after the other places closed for both the Nazz and the Underbelly included.

What else about Todd? Well the only other thing about him is his music and where he lives. He lives in L.A. in Nicholas Canyon or someplace like that. Ask any stranger on the street in Hollywood where Nicholas Canyon is—or even Watts for that matter—and they won't know. Because L.A. is all spread out. And so is his house. It's spread out and he has two refrigerators full of Dos Equis at all times, just in case somebody wants to start a party. The way L.A. is spread out is kind of like the way Long Island is spread out and after all Great Neck is a member of Long Island. So you need a car to get around but Todd doesn't need one. Todd gets around just as easy with no car in his garage.

But that's not where he was born. He was born in Upper Darby, Pennsylvania. But that's not where he was born either, he lived there but he was born somewhere else but where he was born is a mystery. Nobody knows where he was born including myself. Or if they do they're not talking. Well Upper Darby is where he lived and it's near Philadelphia, home of Frankie Avalon and Smokin Joe Frazier and Fabian Forte and Dick Clark. Todd's never been invited to the *Dick Clark Show* even though he's got a city in common with the stupid goon. Something like that once happened to Bobby Vinton. Bobby's originally from Canonsburg, Pa. It's a suburb of Pittsburgh and Perry Como grew to fruition there too and Bobby's dad was once the leading bandleader in the greater Pittsburgh area. Yet Perry never let

Bobby on his show despite all the million sellers and the musical excellence. Well so the Bobby Vinton Fan Club put their two cents in the next time Perry arrived at the airport. They had these signs that read "Bobby Vinton, the greatest singer in the world" and was Perry ever embarrassed! Yet today Bob and Perry are living right near each other again on—of all places—Long Island! What a small world.

Well so it's obvious Todd could get all his fans together and do the same thing next time Dick Clark lands at L.A. International and they can have signs urging Dick to take Todd back to Philly with him for the Saturday afternoon show from coast to coast. Dick's watched as much in L.A. as anywhere else and the folks in Todd's new home town would sure enjoy seeing him perform live via satellite or however they do it from East to West. But Todd isn't that way at all so don't you go ahead and do it if you're one of his fans. Todd just wouldn't wanna see dumb Dick treated so bad, he's a damn nice guy. Todd is, Dick isn't but blessed are the creeps.

And as far as the music goes there's this bird named Brownie who's either a sparrow or a finch and he lives indoors because he was found weak and unable to fly very far. He was flying into a revolving door at a Horn & Hardart and somebody almost stepped on him but a young lady picked him up and brought him home and now takes care of him. She feeds him hamburger meat in thin strips like worms and he eats it up. He likes fruit cocktail too and enjoys hearing his chirps played back on a tape recorder. And his taste in music is pretty good too. His little keeper used to leave the radio on to keep him company when she was away and it was always on a muzak station like WPAT or WRFM and then she tried WPLJ and Brownie preferred the muzak to that. But finally Brownie discovered "Wailing Wall" on Todd's *The Ballad of Todd Rundgren* album and now he'll listen to nothing else. Whenever it's on he'll stop whatever he's doing and he concentrates fully on both the words and the music and the singing and the playing. And it's followed by "The Range War" which reminds his pet-mistress of Carole King so she likes it a whole lot. So her and Brownie have a whole lotta fun with those two cuts and they play them incessantly whenever they get the chance. And I kinda like the cut after those two, "Chain Letter," so the three of us get along just fine.

(By the way "Wailing Wall" may seem like a yiddle song but it's not even though that's what the title seems like.)

Other than music and living he's got hobbies too, foremost of which is reupholstering sofas in original designs. "It's an awful lot of fun. Of course I get attached to some of them occasionally and twice I've kept them instead of selling them or giving them away. But they never get to know you or respond to you when you call their name or any of that." I asked him if raising fabrics from the fabric store shelf to the best couches in town had anything to do with producing luminaries like the Band which he does whenever Robbie Robertson isn't in the mood. He said no.

As a result he's one of the top five itinerant hotdoggers based in other than New York. The others are Tom Nolan, Dave Newberger, Charley Payne (hey Charley give me a ring or drop me a line care of Straight Arrow or if you know him tell him to do it) and Howie Klein. No three of them have ever been at the same place at the same time and only two of them are in the recording business, Todd and Tom. Todd's contributions are well known and documented but not Tom's. Tom did some yelling during the mastering of the Woodstock version of Sly doing "Higher" and his voice is on the album yelling "higher" along with the rest of them. Only one of the five is affiliated in any way with Albert Grossman and that's Todd. He's also the only one who was ever in the Nazz. They did this great song called "Open My Eyes" or something like that and all of Long Island was singing it for a while. Kathy Streem who's now John Wilcock's secretary was just a teen then and she used to hang around outside the Nazz homestead because she couldn't figure out how to get inside. But she's got a good figure, a very good one in fact. Maybe Todd would have given her a tumble if he had looked out the window at the right time.

Since that time three Nazz albums and two Todd albums have graced the pantry. The first Todd one is called *Runt* cause that's what he calls himself because it rhymes with Rundgren or at least the first syllable. *Gren* is a lot like Grin and they have a good album out too but he's not on it. He hasn't done a bad album yet. Will he ever? God only knows but chances are he never will. Who says? Me.

Is he in it for the money? No he's in it for love. Is he moving to England real soon? Yes.

35

Afterword to
the Reprint of *Gulcher*

For all intents and purposes, Gulcher *was my last piece of work published by* Rolling Stone *(on its short-lived Straight Arrow imprint). When Citadel reissued it in 1990 they couldn't get Elvis Costello (their bright idea) or Jacques Derrida (mine) to write an intro and instead reprinted Lester Bangs's 1972 review of the book for* Coast. *For the outro I wrote the following, heading it "More About This Dizzy Book"—I'm nothing if not self-effacing.*

A couple more things should be said about the context in which most of the dizzyness was conceived:

For better and worse, however narrow/broad you wanna draw the demo-graph, rock-roll was/is—and clearly was then*—a music earmarked for KIDS, and one of its bottom-line burdens was thus to arm kids against their parents and, at a real trench-warfare level, their teachers. As a rockwriter (or hell: postrock-writer) it seemed* my *burden as well: to interpose myself in there somewhere, to offer a pattern of disobedience and with it (perchance) a system for transcending schoolteach authority, its culture, its spell: to, in the most basic fashion, get in there and muck it up so that kids, if they followed my example, did* my *homework, ha, would never again be COERCED into unsplitting their infinitives, knowing which president fought Sonny Liston, or accepting ANY school-hands as dealt, any classroom/textbook paradigms of anything. (Though I use the kindergarten model, obviously this entails the whole damn K through 12.) Hey, I'd been liberated, time to pass it on.*

I also sensed that the only sure way to avoid counterculture cliché (and with it the cloying sense that "we'd" failed) was to go beneath *its curve, to use rock—or yes: the most primitive lingering stink of its "spirit"—as an es-cape hatch down out of it, so that rock's ultimate (only?) ongoing usefulness would be for it to be and become, in a word, PUNK. Was I a prophet or what?*

A couple months ago, filling out my Citadel author questionnaire, in response to "Please write 75 to 100 words on the book's theme, intent and underlying concept," like a good little boy I scribbled the following:

When I first wrote the damn thing, in the summer-fall (I believe) of '71, rock criticism, while still in its infancy, had already become as big a whore, a cripple, a mocker of truths both emotional and factual, as any marketplace-tied "critical" genre that had come before. My own program ("mission") *as* a rockwriter, one scrupulously ignored or avoided by virtually all others, was to systematically disassemble—*deconstruct*, ha, as it were—the monster/mess I'd played such a passionate role in helping create in the first place (and which, 1990, is still with us, more loathsome than ever, with us unfortunately *forever*). With this book I focused my deconstructive rage and rigor on not only rock-critical thought and behavior but on various related (and unrelated) genres of etcetera ("countercultural" and otherwise), and in the process managed to pull off (luck into??) a landmark of Ameripostmodernist ya ya ya. Propelled by *classic* torrents of "automatic critical prose," its most enduring subtext is the screaming need for punk-rock, for *a* punk-rock (well before the fact).

What horseshit, right? But that was before I'd actually read the fucker, reread it, for the first time in 18-19 years. Having just right now done so, jeez, I can't begin to tell you how AMAZED I was, am, by the goddam *ferocity* of the "deconstruction"—demolition's more like it. The kitchen sink, dad: destroy all discourse! Song, singer, singin'—all down in flames. Coherence, even euphony, tension/release, cadence, have no place, certainly no "privileged" place, in this prose. "Sounds good," "reads good"—a pair of quaint, disposable bourgeois notions (disposed with).

Some of it reads so clunky I just wanna kick it. Line after line of "intentional bad writing" (believe me) that isn't even *good* bad writing, it's just bad. Too many *and*'s, *so*'s, *even*'s, *the*'s, *that*'s, *too*'s, extraneous whatsems only there because they *were* extraneous: someone, evidently, was looking to *fill pages* or something. All these ridiculous exclamation points—gee how *bombastic*. The expression "beat his ass" 93 times. Reading this trash now, meticulous frigging professional that I've become, I feel like the final Flying Wallenda, whatever his name was, on his final ropewalk over that plaza, the time the wind blew him off. Still holding his pole, halfway down he clutched it to his chest, the final reflexive act, and here I go wincing, kicking and (just as reflexively) writing this pointless afterword . . . nothing of import I can do to break *my* fall either. (I still use no net.) How can I let them reprint this shit?

Then I remember—thank fuck for something—that what it was about was KINDERGARTEN. Kindergarten, y'know, preschool, as sacred writerly First Principle: everybody, I contended (and still contend), should go play with mud for a while, fishtank slime, at least blocks. Stack 'em, knock 'em over (piss on 'em). Splash paint on teacher's pantsuit. Throw spitballs. Every growed-up writeperson, every so-called creative jackjill (of whatever persuasion), really *should* get that "basic"—or why bother?—am I right? Well, I can't think of too many fellow writers, "Counterculture Era," who actually went and did it—Nick Tosches and a handful of fanziners; S. Clay Wilson and Rory Hayes if you count comix—which in all fortuity has left *Gulcher* as our sole surviving bulk record of what this sort of number (made print) might even have looked like. Truly *infantile* (the Fount of It All) it probably ain't, but you can't have everything. (Usually you can't have anything.) Likewise, my bull-in-a-china-shop antics seem at times too bull-lame, bull-immature, bull-leisurely, stopping short of total devastation, or even bona fide *devastation*—remember, this was play, not work.

And *what* play, christ, what joy! THIS, if anything, is what I right this sec feel mega-nostalgia for, far more than for rocknroll, which in any event had been dead, gone, g'bye long before *Rolling Stone* deigned to found (and briefly fund) Straight Arrow. (Lester to the contrary, this *is* a post-rock book, I wouldn't shit you.) Boy oh *boy* do I wish I could still write this way, one draft with malice, mangling syntax, mixing metaphors, sprinting down the page and not caring beans whether pages/filled were "good pages" or "bad pages," caring even less whether in the process I'd actually "said anything" (if it ain't said in real time, real *writer* time, what could it possibly mean to say it?), least of all whether every damn syllable had been in place—this was *prose*, man (not poetry!), laid down like easy miles of asphalt. Which is not to say I *would* write this way, not at the expense of all sorts of grim, solemn, writenose-to-the-grindstone middle age claptrap, not unless, that is, you could turn it on/off like a faucet, which of course you can't (required—hey—is a full-life commitment to *total* play, total mischief), but it's nice, I guess, to know that I once wrote this way, that I once (at the grindstone) had "fun."

Fun, sure, Lester was right about that much—but "humanist"? "Interested in absolutely everything"? Sorry, dead guy, and sorry you never made it to middle age like I have, but the one key flavor you seem to have missed in *Gulcher* is its CONTEMPT. Contempt for, well, the cultural kitchen sink (and nearly all its plumbing). The goodtime Lester, especially early, had a blind spot for such biz, though we always buzzed a shared contempt for that canon of Alternate Fascism, the smarmy notion of "hip." If for *any reason* you suspect the book, through no fault of its own, of having picked up a crust of hip cooties like so many barnacles, please burn it, stab it, wipe your hind parts with it, or feed it to goats. Please!

PRIME WALLOW

Introduction

Which is where 1973 comes in. Geez.

So many ways to view this stuff . . .

A total-assault *Editor, take this.* If you're not trying your damnedest to "get away with something," why bother? (Why should rockstars get away with more?)

Intentional bad writing at its finest—but was it even really that *bad?* It felt good to think so then.

Worm in the apple. Juan Rodriguez labeled me Rock's Bad Boy. Some other wag called me The Patrick Henry of Rockwriting. How 'bout The JUDAS of Rockwriting?

Yet some called me a "people's rockwriter." I took no sass from *anybody* in the food chain, from musicians and record cos. to mag clowns and promo hacks. Biting the hand that fed me—at two low figures a pop. My head rolling from mastheads and mailing lists left and right.

Jackson Pollock, asked if his drip paintings imitated nature, replied, "I *am* nature." By '73 I *was* rock, to the point where I didn't need to *consult* it any longer, to witness directly what *it* was doing. There were bands I went out of my way never to listen to—Genesis, Yes, Foghat—just as later I would totally avoid R.E.M.—but in a way I didn't *even* not listen to 'em, or only *merely* didn't listen, never meeting them at the crossroad of *even once* listening for FAKE. Most of the shit "covered" in this section—whatever wasn't complete fantasy to begin with—was what I *actively*—officially—didn't listen to. Levels and degrees of not.

(For the record, I still danced in those days, usually drunk. People told me I was pretty good . . . I *rocked.*)

Some of these aren't even anti-reviews or non-reviews or anything from, of or in the critical domain so much as things-in-themselves. I was starting to feel my oats not so much as an artist, a maker of calculated "art works," but as *some* version of a creator, yup, a bloke just HAPPENING to use the printed page as his medium, his stage, his less-than-sacred surface, and I could/would no longer SUPPRESS my own strictly creative—as opposed to exegetic—tendencies. Dinky li'l rock assignments as massive occasions to get down and *author.*

Some of this ain't about anything as much as it's about NOTHING itself . . . while being nothing itself. Nothing about nothing.

Did I break on through to the other side, or simply show how rickety—flimsy—transparent—the whole scene and backdrop really were?

The beginnings of grownup sturm & drang. Of revulsion at my ridiculous youth slip slipping away w/ rock as an increasingly useless means to an end, a mode of hi-jinks or kulture that in no big way any longer engrossed me. Of being/feeling as *wasted* writing-it as any wasting 'emselves rocking-it.

A simultaneous deep and shallow wade in stagnant dishwater. Reading some of this now I get the feeling that I really *did* get my-t-close to the basic early-'70s rock molecule, micro, macro—closer, f'r sure, than any other fool dared attempt.

My rockwrite lowpoint? Highpoint? In any event, a *point*: the most utterly distinct juncture in my long and now weary journey as a writer "about" (or not about) anything—a tall float in my endless parade, a neon freak-flag in my endless night. "Quintessential Meltzer" the angels call it (but they're *way* behind in their reading), quintessential under-30 R.M. anyways.

The bulk of these items first appeared in *Zoo World*, a biweekly out of Florida bankrolled by that fraternal organization with roots in where was it, Sicily?, that according to some didn't exist. I wasn't aware of that end o' things until someone from the paper whose name I didn't know called to say he's in New York and would like to *see me.* We meet uptown in this palatial brownstone, a working fireplace, marble chessboard laid out with gold chessmen, a butler or something lurking about. Leisure-suited before there were leisure suits, the spitting image of Kenny Rogers, he smalltalks me for a minute, puts down his Chivas Regal and lights up a joint, passes it to me. Giving me time to exhale, he looks me in the eye and announces as grimly as they do in movies: "Now that our paths have crossed don't you *ever* cross us again."

The *us* part was clear but otherwise what gives? My writing was costing *Zoo World* ad money he says, though it was obvious to me I was just a fall guy. (Did record companies actually think more of this dowdy, typeface-ugly waste of newsprint, so hard-up for copy it never rejected anything—sliced & diced but never rejected—than of me?)

I'd better shape up, he tells me, and write more "upbeat" pieces—he'd never read me but company ad stiffs had called me a "downer." "Do you know," I ask, "how much I'm paid for this shit?"

"No, tell me."

"$12.50 a review."

"Oh really . . ." Nobody'd told him writers came so cheap. He agreed to let me no longer write for them, and not long thereafter the fraternal org (sensing no headway in the circulation war vs. *Rolling Stone*) pulled the plug. Eventually one of the editors drew a 6- or 7-figure salary in the hierarchy of Sony/Columbia. What a fucking world.

36

The Year of the Grapnel (excerpt)

There've been good years and bad years but years are just years. They're just a lotta days and a lotta months and when they're over everybody goes to sleep and there's plenty more years where that came from (years are boring). To rock & roll they're just ripples in the stream so wuzza buzza buzza . . .

37

Fraser & deBolt:
With Pleasure

Guess I'm taking a chance reviewin' this one without first checkin' in with the Zoo World higher-ups. If somebody already reviewed it no way they're gonna run a second one on it 'cause nobody ever heard of it so it don't merit two reviews. Actually I heard of it, I know they did another one already, maybe even two. A lot of people have heard of Fraser and deBolt. How many people is that? Many.

But not too many. Too many people haven't heard of them. But many have. Anthony Perkins for instance. He heard of 'em and went and wrote the liner notes for them, maybe even for free. If somebody like that likes you you're on Easy Street forever. Note the easy looks on their faces. They love life. They love to play beauty-ful music all the livelong day. They smile a lot and pose for black and white pho-tos. One of 'em even has the left shoulder of her dress hangin' off her shoulder in a sensuous manner as she holds her acoustic six-string with but two fingers of her left hand (strong fingers isn't even the word for it, she's a powerful southpaw). There seem to be at least thirty fans listening delightedly under the sunshiny sky.

But tell me this (and I'm not the only one who wants to know): WHERE'S THEIR AMPS? Nowhere, they don't have any.

Sorry, F & deB, *I'm not gonna listen to this one.* I wouldn't listen to eleven tracks of acoustic if they were by my own ma—and F & deB ain't even my kissin' cousins. Can you IMAGINE! I mean it's 1973 and this ain't even on Folkways or Broadside or Folky-Dokey. Where they been all these years?????

38

Ned

My personal favorite of all the zillion reviews I've ever written.

Asphalt is great. They slop it down mile after mile and it's all sizzles. Siz-z-z-z (it sizzles). Steam steaming off of it. Tho it can be walked on, sneakers should take care so as not to melt. Don't get runned over by a steamroller. Next day it's as cold as ice cream, solid as a beefcan. Tires will not burst.

Asphalt can be used to cover cobblestones. It can be taken home (if no one is lookin'). Asphalt should not be confused with, with, with, with . . . asbestos. Confuse them at your own risk. Insects will sometimes live in cement but never asphalt. Asphalt soup tastes like tar. Asphalt soap does not clean especially well. Asphalt dopes are QUITE dopey. They know nothing of asphalt (having never seen it); some live in Alaska. HAS A MAJOR ROCK GROUP EVER TOURED ALASKA? Tell us please and your name will be published in a future "ish" of Zoo World (a great honour). Asphalt collectors meet annually in Salt Lake City's oldest suburb, West Ovum.

A-S-P-H-A-L-T: spell it correctly. There was a group once called Canadian Assfault (they no longer exist). Names are important, for instance NED. Which stands for "No (asphalt) ever dreams"—a damnable lie. It's also John Mendelwhatsit's middle name and he's a very ugly man.

ALBUM SWAPPER'S CORNER: I will swap my Ned album for any of the following: the Charlie Parker album that has "Congo Blues" (actually it's a Red Norvo session), Charlie Parker album on the Charlie Parker label (MGM) with 6 takes of "Congo Blues," soundtrack from *Prince Valiant*, soundtrack from *The Fugitive Kind*, original English *Mr. Fantasy*, any Doors bootleg with "My Eyes Have

Seen You" from a live show, Italian pressing of *Aftermath*, Thelonious Monk on Prestige with "Nutty," *Gassers for Submarine Race Watchers*, any unscratched Yma Sumac EP or LP, the album the Mets made when they won the Series, anything by Bozidar Kunc, any twist album by Lester Lanin.

39

Barbara Mauritz: *Music Box*

Yes I wrote this, but in an obvious sense it sort of wrote itself, and you *could've written it too. (It's okay if you plagiarize it.)*

This is Van Johnson's favorite album. It's Horst Bucholtz's 2nd favorite album. It's Jeremy Steig's 3rd favorite album. It's Mamie Eisenhower's 4th favorite album. It's Lex Barker's 5th favorite album. It's Doug Sahm's 6th favorite album. It's Richard Neville's 7th favorite album. It's Sheila Jordan's 8th favorite album. It's Dr. Joyce Brothers' 9th favorite album. It's Mimi Fariña's 10th favorite album. It's Ray Heatherton's 11th favorite album. It's Lydia Lasky's 12th favorite album. It's Denny Greene's 13th favorite album. It's Penny Banner's 14th favorite album. It's Bruce Dern's 15th favorite album. It's Claudia Dreifus's 16th favorite album. It's Henry Hank's 17th favorite album. It's Mike Saunders' 18th favorite album. It's John Denver's 19th favorite album. It's Pete the Barber's 20th favorite album. It's Robert Penn Warren's 21st favorite album. It's Kate Taylor's 22nd favorite album. It's somebody who once fucked Kate Taylor's 23rd favorite album. It's Danny Mihm's 24th favorite album. It's Patti Johnson's 25th favorite album. It's Benita Hack's 26th favorite album. It's the bank robber in *Hot Pistol*'s 27th favorite album. It's Steve Ditlea's mother's 28th favorite album. It's Scott Asheton's 29th favorite album. It's Lefty Frizzell's 30th favorite album. It's *TV Guide*'s 31st favorite album. It's Anjanette Comer's 32nd favorite album. It's Dewey Martin's 33rd favorite album. It's John Agar's 34th favorite album. It's Marvin Hart's 35th favorite album. It's Sweetwater Clifton's 36th favorite album. It's Mrs. Jacob Javitz's 37th favorite album. It's Resa Harney's 38th favorite album. It's Mr. X's 39th favorite album. It's North Carolina's 40th favorite album. It's Chief Knockahoma's 41st favorite album. It's what's left of the Chad Mitchell Trio's 42nd favorite album.

It's Archie Shepp's 43rd favorite album. It's Flipper's 44th favorite album. It's Patty Duke Astin's 45th favorite album. It's Marc Bolan's 46th favorite album. It's the inventor of Chloraseptic's 47th favorite album. It's Frank Perdue's 48th favorite album. It's Texas Ruby's 49th favorite album. It's Nat Hentoff's 50th favorite album. It's Maryjane Geiger's 51st favorite album. It's Liz Taylor's 52nd favorite album. It's Les Baxter's 53rd favorite album. It's Andy Hebenton's 54th favorite album. It's "Maggie May's" 55th favorite album. It's Marlo Thomas's 56th favorite album. It's Angela Lansbury's 57th favorite album. It's Robert Morley's 58th favorite album. It's Stan Freberg's 59th favorite album. It's Princess Anne's 60th favorite album. It's Bernie Leadon's 61st favorite album. It's Linda McCartney's 62nd favorite album. It's Jack Eisen's 63rd favorite album. It's Bill Gawlik's 64th favorite album. It's Kurt von Meier's 65th favorite album. It's Lorna Luft's 66th favorite album. It's Red Ruffing's 67th favorite album. It's my 68th favorite album.

40

Ernest Tubb: *I've Got All the Heartaches I Can Handle*

Grelun Landon, Colonel Tom Parker's "man inside" RCA, stopped sending me RCA product on three separate occasions (and started again twice). This record was on MCA, so I was safe.

Me and Tom Nolan were up at Grelun Landon's office long about a while ago. He apologized profusely for wearing a tie. Casual guys like him don't usually wear em. On his mug was a smile, a smile which only tightened up his hatchmark wrinkles, a smile in honor of his new book *Golden Guitars*—the story of country music. Me and Tom thumbed thru the venerable gent's volume with great interest. Photos of the Beatles and the Rolling Stones—two examples of contemporaries indebted to c&w—dazzled our eyes. Thumb, thumb, thumb but where was Hank Williams? "Where is Hank Williams?" we asked the man as responsible as anyone else for Elvis's easy ride these past umpteen years at RCA. "He isn't in the book at all. He didn't write any of his own songs, Freddy Rose did. Oh well he scribbled ideas on napkins and scraps of paper and things like that, but it took Freddy to polish them up. And besides, he isn't even one of the top three performers in the history of country music, Roy Acuff, Lefty Frizzell and ERNEST TUBB."

Okay so the question remains, is Ernest Tubb any good at all?

You bet your bulb he is. At least for a geezer (nowadays modern with-it people don't call em "old geezers" anymore, just "geezers"). Cause this geezer's a good *bitter* geezer, not one of them mambi-pambs like Tennessee Ernie or Kate Smith. He's not a comic geezer either like Johnny Bond of "Here Come the Elephants" fame. Or a tired geezer like Maurice Chevalier. Or a dying geezer like Billie Holiday. Or a wised-out geezer like Leadbelly. Or a washed-up geezer like the Pelvis. Or a geezer's geezer like Moms Mabley. No, Ernest Tubb is—pure & simple—a bitter geezer and a damn good one at that.

Who else but a bitter geezer could make palatable something as unpalatable as yet another new SHEL SILVERSTEIN contribution? Cause that's what the title song is and you'd never know to listen to it. All the bogus pseudo-country hee-ha Shel's always tossing is ignored cause Ernest's mind is just on grouching it up. He's been p.o.'ed by virtually everything he's encountered on the road down life's highway and he'd just as soon have you get the hell out of his sight. And lyrics better just not assert themselves out of turn unless that's their function, to enhance his grimace and shrug.

Which brings it all down to "The Lord Knows I'm Drinking," a Bill Anderson tune. In it Ernest (as in "Ernest Hemingway" but he's better than him as the night to day) is sitting with bottle & broad and this other broad walks over and insults the three of em so Ernest tells her to go shove it, sister. Then he out-self-righteouses her by adding that at bottle's end he's gonna have himself a *better talk* with the goddam Lord than she's ever had. You ain't gonna catch Merle Haggard singing nasty stuff like that even to draft card burners. If he did you wouldn't catch yourself believing him cause young whippersnappers like him just ain't that mean while cutting wax (it's in their contract). And Ernest is meaner than Iggy Pop.

Reading between the lines (cause that's all country ever lets you do): this man is the *king* of the cussers no doubt.

41

Black Grass

I suspect Nick Tosches was in the room while I slapped this out.

Few jook jousers are "further out" than Phyllis Lindsey of Black Grass. She's no kin of Lindsey Nelson but she's got an 11-year-old boychild whom she has fondle her softness while she's singing "Come Across Your Bridge," written by Rev. P. Henderson. It's—natch— about *stupration*. But she's never sucked his dick. At least that's what she sez and her face looks incredibly honest. Backing her up are a buncha Okies.

And their off-beat lingo is really *off the wall*. In the lexicon of Black Grass "shoe" becomes "shor." "Not" becomes "nor." "Way" becomes "we're." When they write "we're" down it becomes "we'er" like on the liner notes which they wrote all by their self. Back to their spoken words however, "safe" becomes "cafe." "Right" becomes "thought." "Either" becomes "eithere." "Address" becomes "process." "Council" becomes "culture" which might present some difficulties when they want their mail to get to the Council on the Arts. "Possible" becomes "podsible" (these folks are sick!). "Went" becomes "when." "Hear" becomes "jear" with a j. And "peasant cooking" becomes "fascist cooking."

Speaking of the cooking included inside the sleeve (*inside the sleeve beside the record* but it doesn't scratch it cause it's smooth) is "A Guide to Good Eating," printed at their own expense. Fan's health is impor- tant to these zanies from the Sooner State. The typeface in this infor- mative booklet is a little hard on the eye-yi-yi but it will teach you a great deal about the world so by all means read it a few words at a time.

Read while you listen, that way you can kill 2 birds w/ 1 stone. Cause you've never heard such Tupelo Vomit in all your life. But you mighta guessed that yourself. Guessing is easy cause you take the b from Black and the g from Grass and you put em together and you got the Bee Gees: they're as bad as the Bee Gees! They're a 1,000 times worse. The Bee Gees used to do "Holiday," whadda *these* stupey-dupeys do? They do "Lock, Stock and Barrel." Never heard (i.e. "jeard") of that one. Can't be any good. If you never jeard of it it can't be any good.

And it's not—er—*nor*. It sounds even worse than it sounds. Sound that abounds. Arounds. Clowns! Funny musik! THAT'S A LIE, it's nor funny at all. Serious (you must take them seriously or they'll dig their nails into your back). "Sweeping through the City" is the most serious track ever committed to wax. It's grave. Puts you in yours. YOU DIE IF YOU HEAR THIS ALBUM!

42

Who Sez Noo Yuck
Ain't a Swingin' Burg!

Last laugh by the author on Mr. Reed. Ha ha . . . ha.

John Lennon continues to waste his time being a waste of time in N.Y.C. Any 9-year-old runaway from Arkansas in town for 6 hours is more hep to what's hap in the Big Ap than Johnny and his Mrs. after—how long is it?—3 years or so. Foko, whatsername, Joko's best friend is Jerry Rubin who is 4'9" (there oughta be a law). Rumor has it they will soon kick the 2 of them out and we the peoples of N. York say GOOD RIDDANCE LIMEY DOGS!

Those two Britishers stunk up the city with their beef & kidney pies for far (far far far) too long. Kippers for breakfast and kippers can *destroy* good food just by being anywhere near it. Like at the Xmas party Mercury threw in '72. Someone wrapped up the lobster chunks and the big shrimp and black olives in the same package as the kippers. Nothing was edible on account of proximity to the limey fish (smells like stuff a dying cat wouldn't eat out of a garbage can) but now we can breathe easier with the Lennon-Onos headed back to the United Kingdom where they belong.

New Yawk now finally belongs to its indigenous local talent instead of a pack of boring foreigners. And local is just the word cause you won't be findin it nowhere else. Damn good bands like the Dark Ages from Kew Gardens. Bill on guitar, Bob on drums, Dennis on guitar (they got TWO of em!) and Mac on bass. Expect nothing but good shit from the Dark Ages.

Ditto for Danny Merrill. A great attraction, Danny is truly "on the scene." His remarkable note bending and swing phrasing make for a flexible sound that musicians dig and would move any patron to praise. Per. Mgr. Bob Anglin—1094 Longfellow Ave., Bronx, N.Y. 10459—(212) 323-4029. Appearing nitely at the Kit Kat Korner, 253 W. 125 St. This man is boss. You will like him. Cookin with heat! The two of em, the Dark Ages and Danny Merrill, they're undeniably one and two, respectively, now that J & Y are takin the big boatride. But there's lots more hotte bands in the Apple playing that good ole hotte music and the Monady Funday Sextet is no exception. No indeedy as this righteous combo from Staten Island can really shake it down, down, down. Their big number is of course "Where Have All the Flowers Gone," a different song entirely from the one all the folkies used to do at hoots (this one's about I'm not tellin you what, you'll have to go see em yourself). They're Bob Iuliucci's all-time favor-it group.

Speaking of islands, Manhattan is one too, boasting a band quite a bit more authentique than Malo or El Chicano. Pazo is their name (East 19th Street). If you don't know your timbales from a tamale then Pazo is not for you. September 15 at the Mercer Arts Center—with a finale where they wave a chorizo in the air so bring one along and you can wave it too!

Another audience participation act worth a big fat look within the 5 boros is Snow White from Lexington Avenoo. They often request that members of the audience masturbate themselves during the soaring solos of 12-stringer Tony Proust. Many actually do and the object is to not actually stick your hand inside your knickers, you gotta do it just by rubbing through the crotch. If you open your fly or lift your skirt the bulls can lock you away but if you keep your apparel intact IT'S COMPLETELY LEGAL!!!

Yes rock & roll has come a long way—while health has declined. If you don't have your health you die. That's what happened to Kath E. Miller's dog Tara just the other day. It seems the bitch (Tara was a lady) used to belong to Kid Krazy-A-Z of Flycatchers Anonymous of Fordham Road. He gave it to her in exchange for a screw. She didn't take care of it. Consequently, it died. But Flycatchers are still going strong so *don't miss em.*

THE KRAUTS ARE COMING. Turning many a "head" in the Yorktown area are the Sick-Ass Muh-Fuhs, Friday & Saturday at the Berlin Bar. Their attire is outrageous and they may go far. But their lifestyle may dump them in an early pit cause they've been boining their candle at both ends (drinking!) (fighting!) (cussing!) (all hours of the nite!) (these guys are strange!). Two weeks ago they squatted on a plate of sweetbreads at the Cafe Colonial and the management 86'ed them so now they're at the B.B. How long they stay there is anybody's guess. But their art is flawless.

Same can be said for Dick "China Cat" Blum who didn't make it to the Stones concert on account of lying face down in a pool of puke. Too many sopors was the culprit. But Dick's in good spirits this wk. and he's gonna be singing for Tommy the Truck as soon—if not sooner—as the band of that name gets it together. First gig was a beer and whiskey blast at Jerry Leichtling's house where the personnel was: Dick on lead vocal, Andy Shernoff on rhythm guitar, Scott Kempner on lead guitar, Dave Udis on lead guitar until Scott told him to fucking quit it. Xcellent show they put on and a whole new concept in the making: no song lasts longer than 15 seconds, might as well stop playing once you get people to know what song it is, get it all over with so everybody can go home and watch *Burns & Allen*!

Word is the Group Image has been jamming nitely in the Williamsburgh section of Brooklyn. Jamming up traffic, that is!

Contrary to popular belief, Ramatam is not from Long Island City. They're from Tampa. Mrimnody's from L.I.C. Featuring Lydia Laske on vocals, Klooky Alexander on mellotron, "Sir" Carl Malden on lead guitar, Chas Ermp on rhythm, Back Knutson on bass, and Ali Myers on percussion. Strictly a copy band so far, they are noted for their personal renditions of "Jumpin Jack Flash," "Tommy," "Doctor My Eyes," "Heart and Soul" and "Lost in Space." They're real "George."

Sometimes the name sez it all. Jazz Me is a jazz-rock fusion unit par excellence and par for the course (of course). If you go for Ohnedaruth and Zoot you'll go apeshit over Jazz Me cause they're root patoot zoot for the noot (toot!). A&M has just inked them and their first elpee, *Cots for Sleeping Six Abreast*, is now in progress. Look for it come October.

Planning yet ANOTHER comeback is Lou Reed when & if he overcomes the miz'ry and grief the loss of his ma and pa has put him thru. They lost their lives in a vehicular death in Valley Forge, Pa., en route to relatives for Labor Day fun. How tragic.

The Better Business Brothers are Eric Waxman on keyboard and vocals, Sandy Brown on bass, and Howard Hoffman on tubs. Just a buncha rich hebes from Queens!

Who *sez* Noo Yuck ain't a swingin burg!

43

Poems in Neil's Suede Pocket

Though not the first recap of a concert I didn't attend, the first extensive *recap.*

Neil Young rhymes with real young. Neil Young, however, is 29 years old. At Carnegie Hall he sang "Old Kentucky Home" (original version written by Stephen Foster who got played by Don Ameche—Neil's favorite actor—in the movie). Anybody who sings "Old Kentucky Home" is r-e-a-l old (maybe he oughta change his name to Neil Gold and then he could sing "Heart of Gold" about himself).

But of course no one is more a master "of the" song. Few understand so well *the* art *of* incorporating divers *elements* into a smoothly operating *whole*. It is movement *itself* which fascinates James, er, *Neil*; his songs speak of how "Borneo, Georgia, is where the hot weasels abode/If half of their time were amusing/And the other half were it in choosing/Then in Borneo, Georgia, the losing would be in its toads." In other words it is disturbing, then, that we sometimes notice a predictability creeping into Neil's work. And predictability a la Carnegie sure ain't one half the treat that SCHNITZEL A LA CARNEGIE (around the corner at the Carnegie Tavern) is.

For instance, those Canadian clothes he wore. We know he's from New France but does he have to shove it down our throat *every time* we see him in person?

For instance, "Down by the River I Shot My Baby." Does he always have to switch to dulcimer for that song?

For instance, the pro-marijuana stance of "Refried Beans and Succotash" (a new one but the sentiment is old, old, old).

The list could go on and on and indeed it did. But the undeniable *presence* was still in evidence, it was NEIL YOUNG we were watching (me and all the other $12.50 customers—prices are outrageous!) and

we watched with tongues limply a-drooling: Neil Young does not
come to N.Y. every day! And what town is more Neil's than N.Y.?
Whenever he's in town he goes down to the Buffalo Roadhouse on
7th Avenue and Barrow Street (it's the bohemian in Neil that drives
him there). Next time he's here you'll know where to find him, go
down the Roadhouse and maybe he'll buy you a beer (he's a swell
guy). But don't mention his father. Mr. Young (Scott to his friends,
the author of *Face-Off*—the Canadian *Love Story*—to others) disowned Neil many years ago when he asked his pop for an AMP.

Three of the songs Neil performed at the Hall were specifically
dedicated to the extinction of his dad, "A Man Needs a Maid," "Are
You Ready for the Country?" and "Ohio." On "Ohio" his chin sagged
and his hands shook from sheer *je ne sais quoi* as the anger of a generation *echoed* from the rafters (Carnegie acoustics gotta go!).

Part two of this highly unorthodox concert consisted of Neil *dis-
missing his accompanists* and seating himself on a round-bottom backless stool. The spotlight shone down on his balding head as he
took—from his back pocket—a roll of *poems*. Yes it was poetry that
would dominate stage two of this evening of music. Patti Smith had
done it a week before and now Ontario's gift to North America was
about to read his verse amid scattered boos from the oafs in the auditorium. He opened with a piece entitled "Routine Rear Barrels":

> she insists
> it's imported swiss
> she & sis
> is imported swiss

The gang in row B did not take kindly to this moment in avant
garde history, greeting his effort with cries of "Sissy!" and "Go back
to T.S. Eliot!" But, thank the lord, most patrons reacted like ladies
and gentlemen. His finale *en verse* was a definite "up," and even the
diehard rock and rollers had to agree it was terrific:

> SIMPLE SUPPER and SO SUPPER so supper so
> SO SUPPER SO

A short intermission followed, during which time many youths
were seen guzzling their cheap bottles of scuppernong and muscatel
from paper bags. Time to get in the spirit! This *esprit de corps* pre-

vailed throughout the second half, and detractors were few and far between.

Walt Frazier of the New York Knicks, resplendent in a brilliant pink "mod" outfit, just made it to his seat in time for the opening chords of "Harvest." "I was almost there/At the top of the stairs/With her standing in the rain . . ." and a masterpiece of its genre it was, too. Followed in rapid succession by "Broken Arrow," "Tell Me Why," "Everybody Knows This Is Nowhere," and the pensive "Round and Round" from Neil's *Hawkeye* LP (Canadian Reprise). The entire concert, incidentally, was recorded, including the *ars poetica*. It will be released in the states in April.

Between tunes there was that old familiar Neil Young rap. "Wahl I juzz wan tell y'all shore luv sengin fer yew h'yar in Mads in Skwayer Gurdin." Wotta sense-o-humour!

Even after the fourth encore they would not let him leave. Exhausted to the point of near-collapse, he responded with a wearisome rendition of "After the Gold Rush." Let's face it, it was just plain *bad*. All those sour notes were no less sour due to Canadian sweat and toil.

It is said that Neil has in recent months experienced difficulty with his front teeth. It seems that one of his lower teeth was never corrected by orthodonture and consequently it jutted out just enough to make a minor mess of his two front uppers. They're constantly competing with one another for domination of his upper mouth: first one will stick out a bit, and then the other. It's apparently too late to do anything about it short of braces, and since Neil has nixed being a "metal mouth" he'll just have to grin and bear it.

Was *that* what wrecked his Carnegie debut?

44

Sutherland & Pavarotti: *Rigoletto*

WATCH ME NOW: taking "sides" with witless rock partisans "against" classical.
A fine example of my kneejerk negativity.

Classical music stinks (smells) (pukes on its mom's jabooty). So does that wimpy simpy version of it known as the Doody Blues. And so does that loud & monotonous form of it known as heavy metal (= loud & monotonous classical swill not wonderful R&R at all as claimed). The only thing worse than classical music is show music.

When they play classical muzak in the supermart it sounds just like show muzak so when the chips are down they're all the same (stink) (smell) (puke on their mom's jabooty). The only time classical muzak sounds good is in elevators in Ohio. Those elevators are stuffy & the muszaick is real fine.

Semi-classical is good cause it should only be semi (= one half) and never any more. Hemi-classical is o.k. too (also = $^1/_2$ classical). Ditto for demi-classical. Centi-classical (= .01 classical) is even better. Milli-classical (= .001 classical) is better still. And micro-classical (= .000001 classical) is even better than that. But sesqui-classical (1.5 X classical) is unbearably horrible and even more so for bi-classical (2X) and tri-classical (3X). Kilo-classical (1000X!) is gotta be the worst thing in the world.

This album is only classical-classical (mildly unbearably horrible) but they got the gall to press it in stereo-classical (2 ears both of em different) so that's a fate worse than death. The only thing on record worse than it is the soundtrash from *1776*. Which has words and if that wasn't bad enough *so does this one*. Words! Which means! The worst kind of classical ever invented! OPERA!!! Holy Christmas mommy, opera is even worse than spinach!

Whoever invented opera should be locked in a smokehouse with the smoking mullet. Person should be smoked but not out. Can't get out cause the door's locked from the outside and the key isn't in the lock so he can't shake it out and catch it on newspaper and pull it under the door like they do in the movies. Whoever invented opera (most likely an Italo-European) is now dead (justice is done).

The inventor of this one, let's see, who invented *Rigoletto?* Did Carmen invent it? Beethoven? Bach? Brahms? Gilbert & Sullivan? Aaron Copland? Charles Ives? Currier & Ives?

Heh heh heh, it's another Eye-talian after all, Verdi. Smoke *him* with the mullet. Croaked in 1901 so smoke his bones. Smoke his descendants too, smoke em out first so they show their face and then smoke em in.

And speaking of descenders could it be that Oscar-nominee Donald Sutherland is descended from this Sutherland person who "sings" on this one (quotes around it cause it ain't fair to dishonor the word since all opera "singers" "sing" like a goat)? Is she his granny? If so he sure must have a can of Lysol handy to de-scent the house whenever she comes for a visit (opera goats smell like ahh-ahh with flies on it). Pee yew!

45

Jim Ed Brown:
Bar-Rooms and Pop-a-Tops

But when somethin' was THIS GOOD, I would just come right out & say it, quickly, and hope the shorter word count didn't mean a cut in my twelve-fifty.

It's hard to be restrained about this elpee, after all it's got THE FINEST LINER NOTES OF ALL TIME (Ed Penney wrote 'em and he mentions Omar Khayyam!) and THE FLASHIEST UN-KNOWN TONGUE SINCE "CAN I GET A WITNESS?" ON THE FIRST STONES ALBUM ("Pop a top . . . again" which ain't even in the title song but in the similarly titled "Pop a Top" produced by Felton Jarvis and it's good as anything Hank Thompson ever did and this guy don't even look like an alcoholic and all he drinks in the song is beer anyway and imagine a bar that only has it in cans!), in fact all I can stop and say is man oh man oh man, holy Christ-o-Jesus, far far out, gosh oh gee, swear to god, puh-leeze please please forgive me for the shortness of this piece of rock crit but I just gotta read the notes again and spin this disc some more, wanna hear it 30-40 times before the sun comes up, thank you for your kindness and I'll give you a Jim Ed Brown album of your own for Xmas!

46

Sesame Street Live

When this ran, the first paragraph was cut. I was so proud of it, I kept the carbon, hoping to someday rescue it from oblivion.
  That day is now . . .

Columbia Records & TAPES has offered (& I have 'cepted!) the sum of $one million dollar$ American to revue this—and no strings are 'tached.
  Real nif-T package featuring not only photos but the nos. 1 THRU 10 in all the colors of the rainbow. Kids'll luv it, specially the ones who like to count. Counting is great, so is reading words. So is listening to educational music. It sure is swell being a kid being educated the teevee way. Sure as hell beats the classroom way.
  Speaking of which when I was 8 and in the 2nd grade they had this teacher of the beaux arts come in from the district or something and check us out for our artistic aptitude. She handed out one of those blank paper type things in tan or whatever color it was supposed to be (wasn't white) and scissors and glue. And pencils maybe. We were supposed to do *whatever we wanted* and then she was gonna evaluate it all and tell us whatever. Almost every kid in the class just kinda glued & pasted & drew & cut. Every kid except for me cause what I did was cut & draw & glue & paste & FOLD. I introduced the 3rd dimension with a treasure chest containing those ring kind of things that you make for Xmas trees and this was even the days of 3-D motion pitchers and *Treasure Island* and *Peter Pan* so I was a hot item that day, a real cre-8-tive little buster. Too bad there wasn't somebody around with a gun.
  Well anyway at least I know my 3-D and the 3-D on this package just don't work. Cause as you look at it the panel on the left folds from the center so the outside is stickin out further than the inside

when there's nothin there to prevent it due to the cardboard or whatever they're usin strugglin to unbend itself. There's an extension of
that piece of cardboard with the Sesame St. street sign printed on it.
It's stickin out towards the right and it's part of the same piece that's
poppin out on the outside so it gets bent by the poppin. Bends! Even
without wear & tear. And it ain't supposed to. Whatta dud package!

Which proves that teevee ain't really that much better than classroom as far as something-or-other or whatever-it-is goes. Neither
one ain't really built a better pablum in the last 15 years. Kids—however ridiculous they are—could be sold an empty bottle of mer-
thiolate and it ain't even as cool as their post-smallfry kin gettin
bill-of-goodsed by the R&R deejays. Rest of teevee, okay, but kid
tube action ain't worth its weight in electrons. The stupid stuff
they've had to put up with since *My Little Margie* reruns and *Lancelot
Link—Secret Chimp* went off the air is enough to make even kid-haters
feel sorry for the lousy brats. It's gettin worse all the time and meanwhile *Sesame Teeth* seems as solidly forever as Walter Cronkite. Plus
the tots gotta listen to *albums* of it?

There ain't one song on here that compares to the theme song from
Gilligan's Island.

But it could be worse. It could be DISNEY!

47

Genya Ravan:
They Love Me/They Love Me Not

How cooler can you get than using something (an outtake from Gulcher*?)*
as a joyful expression of something else?

The cover of this one looks like a Bazooka Joe cartoon. And Bazooka
Joe stinks!

Chester Morris is dead, even if he isn't dead he's dead. Wayne Morris is definitely dead, he's just plain dead. Gouvenor Morris is dead
too. So is Bill Morris (Bill Morris is dead!). And last but not least
Wesley Morris is deader than a puppy. Which sure was prophetic.

'Cause there never was a puppy in a Bazooka Joe strip and Wes wuz
the guy who drew it. Serves him right to be dead (Bazooka Joe never
was any good). 'Cause Bazooka Joe never was any good. Never as
good as Pud, that's for sure. Both of 'em came with gum but the gum
with Bazooka Joe was always better than Bazooka Joe itself and the
gum with Pud (Fleer) was never as good as Pud itself. Plus the Fleer
was always better than the Bazooka.

Plus the lettering on Bazooka Joe was always worthless. Plus they
never made use of the whole rectangle like with Pud 'cause of those stupid ads for worthless garbage like free baseball batting glove (ages 10-
14) for 375 Bazooka comics or 75 cents & 15 comics. Those x-tra 15 are
still 15 cents so it's 90 cents total which means it's a real cheapie baseball
batting glove and in other words it will fall apart after 13 at bats. So who
needs baseball batting glove ads interfering with the comics?

Plus the stories are (pee-yew!), they're just (ugh!), they're, they're
terrible. To read them is to puke like this one for instance: The guy
with the turtle neck over his mouth sez *"I've got some cold in my nose!"*
To which Joe replies *"There's someone who suffers more than you when he*

gets a stuffed nose!" Turtle Face then sez *"Yeah, who?"* The answer is wordless, it is just the silhouette of Joe pointing his finger towards the fatso elephant behind closed bars in the zoo or maybe it's a circus but anyway there's bars and the pachyderm has its trunk (i.e. nose) immersed in a bucket of water. The bucket is white and the elephant is grey and the thing about these small comics is the people and animals are almost as small as the dots and the turtle guy has these gesture marks all around his silhouette to show his astonishment. He is astonished. Wotta dumb strip!

Then there's this one where him and the turtleneck—this time the t.n. has a sailor hat on—are in the restaurant and there's a human fatso who is eating at the counter. Turtle sez to Joe: *"Since I'm working the lunch counter business has improved!"* Joe: *"Selling a lot of sandwiches?"* *"Nope—stomach pills!"* Yes the fatty's tummy is all messed up by the onslaught of greasy-spoonitis but let's ignore the humor for a second and go back to the first frame. In it there is a reference to *"the lunch counter business."* In other words it is not a restaurant at all but in actuality a lunch counter, perhaps at a small-town drug store or maybe the suburbs or Whelan's in New York City. In other words the location is ambiguous but the ripoff of Wimpy for the fat guy is not: the fat guy is ripped off from Wimpy.

But the wax on the comics is not ripped off from the bees. 'Cause it's paraffin not beeswax. Beeswax costs too much and if they used it they'd have to charge 2 cents. Do they charge two cents yet? Dunno, it's very likely, but if they used beeswax *then* they'd have had to charge 2 cents in 1955. Nobody had two cents in 1955.

Also, when was the last time you saw green in a Bazooka Joe? Never. Cause they never have green. Pink, yes, but no green and mostly just yellow and blue and red and black. Colors you wouldn't want your mother-in-law to be stuck with and they expect you to buy Bazooka Joe! Crazy!

But there's a lotta drama in Bazooka Joe 'cause when you open 'em up it's whether it's gonna be red on white or white on red at the top of the page where it sez *"Bazooka Joe and his Gang."* It could be either and it's never neither. Too bad, 'cause if it was neither then maybe it would be NO BAZOOKA JOE AT ALL (Bazooka Joe stinks)!

So it's lucky for Wesley M that Wesley M is long gone 'cause if he wasn't long gone he'd be soon to go and that's a lotta worries to carry on your shoulders in addition to having to draw Bazooka Joe every day or every 6 months or whenever it is. How often did Wesley Morris have to do it? Dunno, ask his widow if she isn't with the maggots herself.

And if you flip over the album to the rear cover you'll see that Genya looks pretty cadaverized herself (but her nipples and cigarette look pretty lively). Poor Genya, who is left to mourn *her*?

48

Johnny Rivers: *Blue Suede Shoes*

Smell any good releases lately?

"Picture yourself in a train in a station with plasticene porters with looking glass ties" sez the lyric of "Lucy in the Sky with Diamonds" (immortal). What's a looking glass tie? A tie with a looking glass on it (looking glass = mirror) so you can see your face in it while it's tied around somebody's neck such as your own. What's a plasticene porter? A porter made out of plasticene (that fake kind of modeling clay). Yeah, so what?

Well years and years have gone by and the whole *Sgt. Pepper* trip has been all but 4-got-10. So it is indeed a surprise (& a good one as a matter of fact) that UA would at this stage of the game decide to release an album that SMELLS LIKE PLASTICENE. And it does (the cover) (also the sleeve) (also the disc itself but maybe that's just due to its proximity to the sleeve cause it doesn't smell as plasticenelike as the cover or the sleeve). Is it in the ink?

But why doesn't it smell like a blue suede shoe? Or a searching? Or a so fine? Or a hang on sloopy? Or a feel a whole lot better? Or a solitary man? For instance.

Well what's a searching actually *smell* like? Like a scavenger hunt (smells bad). And what's a hang on sloopy smell like? Like a sloop john b (smells like a ship = an underwater smell = fish). And what's a feel a whole lot better smell like? Like the feeling of death (feels awful). And what's a solitary man smell like? Like a man who does not bathe.

And what's a blue suede shoe smell like? Like shoes. And how about the odor of a so fine? Sofe ine (= sofa iodine = medicinal furniture smell).

So it goes without saying that plasticene has them all beat in the nose department. It is an excellent smell that artists and non-artists alike can agree upon. So where do you get it? Well you can get it direct from the source, i.e., a hunk of plasticene. Plasticene is not cheap, you can buy it but it is not cheap. Once you have it all it is is plasticene. It won't model itself into the form of Johnny Rivers. WHEREAS *Blue Suede Shoes* by Johnny Rivers both smells like plasticene *and* resembles Johnny Rivers (great photo of his bare foot on the front cover with a pair of shoes under it if you lift it up).

Plus the fact that plasticene is silent (it makes no noise at all unless you throw it at a stack of dishes). DON'T BUY PLASTICENE when you can get something a whole lot better that smells just as good: namely you know what.

49

Denny Lile

Did Denny Lile possibly have a mustache? Is he the governor of New Jersey? Did he live to 23?

A personal pronoun beginning with a capital letter, followed by a transitive verb in the present indicative, followed by a preposition, followed by a possessive pronoun, followed by a common noun, followed by a conjunction, followed by a definite article, followed by an intransitive verb in the present indicative, followed by an adverb, followed by a conjunction, followed by a contraction consisting of a personal pronoun and an auxiliary verb in the present indicative, followed by a present participle, followed by an indefinite article, followed by an adjective, followed by a common noun, followed by a conjunction, followed by a possessive pronoun, followed by a common noun, followed by an auxiliary verb in the present indicative, followed by an adverb, followed by a past participle, followed by a preposition, followed by a definite article, followed by a common noun, followed by a comma, followed by a contraction consisting of a personal pronoun and an auxiliary verb in the present indicative, followed by an adverb, followed by a past participle, followed by a preposition, followed by a possessive pronoun, followed by a common noun, followed by a period. A contraction beginning with a capital letter and consisting of a personal pronoun and an auxiliary verb, followed by a preposition, followed by an indefinite article, followed by a conjunction, followed by a possessive pronoun, followed by a common noun, followed by an auxiliary verb in the present indicative, followed by an adjective, followed by a conjunction, followed by a contraction consisting of a personal pronoun and an auxiliary verb in the present indicative, followed by a present participle, followed by an adjective, followed by a common noun, followed by a preposition, followed by a definite article, followed by a common noun, followed by a definite article, followed by a common noun, followed by a period. Open quotation marks, followed by an intransitive verb in the present indicative beginning with a capital letter, followed by a preposition, followed by a definite article, followed by a common noun beginning with a capital letter, followed by a preposition, followed by a common noun beginning with a capital letter, followed by close quotation marks, followed by an auxiliary verb in the present indicative, followed by a present participle, followed by a period. An adverb beginning with a capital letter, followed by a personal pronoun, followed by a transitive verb in the present indicative, followed by an indefinite article, followed by a common noun, followed by a preposition, followed by a possessive pronoun, followed by a common noun, followed by a conjunction, followed by a contraction consisting of a personal pronoun and an auxiliary verb in the present indicative, followed by a present participle, followed by an indefinite pronoun, followed by a contraction consisting of an indefinite pronoun and an auxiliary verb in the present indicative, followed by a common noun, followed by a preposition, followed by an adjective, followed by a common noun, followed by a comma, followed by a conjunction, followed by a personal pronoun, followed by a transitive verb in the present indicative, followed by an adjective, followed by a common noun, followed by a preposition, followed by an adjective, followed by a common noun, followed by a contraction consisting of a personal pronoun and an auxiliary verb in the present indicative, followed by an adjective.

Maple Leaf Cowpoop Round-Up

Intended as filler 'n' frolic for the Jon Eisen country anthology See and Double You *(I ain't shittin' ya, that was the title), this bit of whimsy was one of 30 pieces Nick Tosches and I did under the misapprehension that Eisen was gonna play fair for a change and share the booty. To get around the standard disbursement of $25 per submission, a setup Nick and I, who'd been through this with Eisen before, considered exploitive, we were this time each to be paid to pseudonymously write a third of the book—Eisen would be doing the other third—for a third-share each of the total author pool. As it turned out the page count he gave us was actually for* half *a book each—while he wrote nothing for his third of the author bucks (plus his editor's advance)—a scenario remarkably similar to one, fictitious per se, on p. 152 of* The Night (Alone).

The collection never came out anyway. In 1987 the piece got recycled as the chapbook A Sitting Duck for Your Tender Loving Spiked Heal on My Scrotum—*ain't shittin' you on that one either.*

And what the heck is it? Two ongoing texts, each combining a series of press-kit bios for Canadian country acts. To read linearly, stay on either the parenthetical or non-parenthetical track—you'll be glad you did.

Diane (Like) Leigh (many) is (Canadian) no (entertainers,) stranger (Maurice) to (Bolyer) country (is) music. (a) For (Maritimer) five (from) years (Woodstock,) she (New) was (Brunswick.) featured (He) on (is) the (a) C.T.V. (highly) show (talented) "Country (entertainer) Music (on) Hall." (many) In (stringed) 1965, (instruments,) 66, (especially) 67, (the) 68 (banjo.) and (His) 69 (outstanding) she (abilities) was (with) voted (the) Top (banjo) Female (have) Country (won) Vocalist. (him) She (the) has (title) had (of) numerous (King) songs (Of) on (The) the (Banjo.) country (He) charts, (is) has (a) appeared (member) at (of) the (The) famed (Tommy) Gold (Hunter) Nugget (Show) in (where) Las (he) Vegas (is) and (often) the (called) famous (upon) "WWVA (for) Jamboree" (a) in (solo) Wheeling, (number) West (due) Virginia. (to) Her (viewers) latest (response.) release (Maurice) on (is) the (also) Quality (an) label, (outstanding) "Devil (exponent) To (of) Angel," (honky) is (tonk) quickly (piano.) climbing (Colin) the (Butler) charts (is) for (only) this (11) "Cinderella" (years) of (old) country (and) music. (shows) For (great) thirty (promise) years (as) Gordie (a) Tapp (country) has (music) been (star.) entertaining (He) country (started) fans (singing) all (at) across (age) Canada (5) and (in) the (Sudbury) U.S.A. (during) Star (a) of (matinee) several (with) of (Terry) his (Roberts.) own (He) Canadian (has) T.V. (appeared) shows, (all) he (across) is (Canada) now (and) a (in) star (parts) and (of) writer (the) for (U.S.,) the (receiving) very (strong) popular (audience) "Hee (response.) Haw" (He) show. (will) Comedian, (have) songwriter, (his) singer (first) and (LP) instrumentalist, (release) Gordie (on) is (the) Mr. (Paragon) Versatility (label) of (this) Country (May.) Music. (Give) A (a) personable, (listen) fun-loving (and) man, (you'll) Gordie (agree) has (that) established (Colin) himself (Butler) as (is) a (destined) top (to) performer (become) in (one) the (of) entertainment (Canada's) world. (brightest) Rodeo (country) recording (music) artist (stars.) June (Bud) Elkhard (Roberts) proudly (is) holds (the) the (man) title (with) of (the) Canada's (big) First (voice) Lady (from) Of (Moncton,) The (N.B.) Fiddle. (who) Her (has) ability (such) with (a) the (terrific) fiddle (way) has (with) won (truck-driver's) her (songs.) many (His) awards (first) and (big) admiration (hit) from (was) her ("Alcan) fellow (Run.") fiddlers. (Since) She (his) has (first) composed (L.P.) many (of) fiddle (the) tunes (same) that (name) can (he) be (has) heard (joined) on (the) her (fast-growing) three (ranks) LP's (of) on (the) the (hit-makers) Rodeo (on) label. (the) Truly (Boot) a (label.) lady (That) in (Bud's) every (rich,) sense (clear) of (voice) the (was) word, (made) June (for) is (recording) a (is) credit (in) to (full) Canadian (evidence) fiddling (on) and (his) the (latest) country (Boot) music (release,) scene. ("This) Shirley (is) Field (Bud) was (Roberts.") born (Brown-eyed) in (five) Armstrong, (foot) British (Norma) Columbia. (Gale) She (comes) has (from) two (Moncton,) albums (New) on (Brunswick.) the (At) Rodeo (the) label (age) with (of) the (20) first (she) one (moved) containing (to) six (Montreal) yodeling (where) songs. (she) In (began) 1948 (her) she (career) was (on) given (radio) the (and) title (T.V.) of (Johnny) "Canada's (Burke) Sweetheart." (also) She (hails) has (from) won (New) numerous (Brunswick.) awards (Both) for (Johnny) her (and) songwriting, (Norma) singing (currently) and (reside) yodeling. (in) Shirley (Toronto) and (and) her (are) husband (regular) Bill (members) French (of) have (the) just (Caribou) released (Club) their (TV) first (Show.) duet (Jimmy) l.p. (Arthur) on (Ordge) Vintage (is) label (a) #SCV–115 (country) entitled (singer) "Together." (from) Bill's (the) own (city) exceptional (of)

QUID PRO QUO

Introduction

Tradeoffs.

Through all my judashood, my mockery, my subversion, whatever you wanna call it, I never stopped writing articles in EXCHANGE for things. A shill when asked to be, not always but often enough, even sometimes when the asking was merely implied, I was as human as the next asshole, and occasionally as co-optable. We're talkin' *positive* treatments of rock-roll merchandise, or let's say non-negative—as non as someone like me could muster.

In New York during the first half of the '70s, when music money still flowed like water, the roster of inducements served up by record companies began with sustenance—meals!—a literal food tube/feed-bag extending down to the lowliest of writers. Press parties four-five nights a week (food plus open bar) took care of your dinner needs. If you felt ambitious, frequent lunches with publicity-department menials could be arranged over the phone. If you just sat and waited, since they couldn't tap their expense accounts without a writer in tow, these equally needy beings would inevitably contact *you*.

I rarely wrote after parties—they were at night, I drank more, by the time I got home I was done for the day. If it was still day, however, I invariably *felt* like writing.

What would happen, once every couple weeks after lunch with a publicist at some joint I couldn't afford, cocktails, dessert, the illusion of friendship, is I would get home, sit at the typer, play whatever record he/she gave me, the taste of the meal still on my chops, bourbon & soda in my veins, writing adrenaline at play (as ever). Hype, or something like it, would emerge very naturally, and it never seemed especially tainted—it was simply an extension of the lunchtime experience, an outgrowth of its *talkiness*, a mining of the moment like any normal afternoon sitting there writing whatever was hanging in the air: the most *obvious* jugular to tap. Killing two birds with one stone? No: to think of it consciously would've made it too tasklike a task. At its easiest, it was like digesting the experience and instantly *shitting it out* (speaking of food tubes).

Discharging debts.

As debt-makers go, tho, vittles w/ beverage paled beside TRAVEL: covering bands on the road. In exchange for coverage you got first-class flights, unlimited room service, new sights and scenery, and access to the same road kicks partaken by the bands themselves. Such trips became addictive, natch—a *way of life* even—and justifying yourself as a "road correspondent" at company expense, giving them their pound of hype as, well, you never knew—was it down payment on the *next* trip, or final installment on the last one ever?—proved one stress-filled, thankless chore.

It would be nice to think I hyped with a difference, that it was counterbalanced by effortless, unpremeditated anti-hype, that while I sometimes *thought* I was giving the bastards what they wanted I also *knew* I wasn't, that at the very least it was never delivered on the dotted lines of your average shameless jazzbos like Nat Hentoff and Ralph Gleason, and that in those pieces where I openly *admit* my tradeoffs, where the pieces at the same time *are* the tradeoff, I stand TOTALLY, WILLFULLY, AWKWARDLY NAKED, stripped of more cover than any "critic" you ever saw work the pike, but I could be fucking wrong.

All I know is that before looking this stuff over I thought most of it would make me wince. It doesn't.

51

A Ton of Texas Tuzz

Funny, but it never occurred to me to feel "indebted" over records—even those I converted to cash—records were stuff. So was coke. It was the, uh, intangibles that at times had price tags . . . like (say) the whores. (Guaranteed 100% nonfiction.)

Three and three is six, six and six is twelve, twelve and twelve is twenty-four and you know what? The Three Dog Night show at the Cotton Bowl was on July 24! So it was more than the quest of the buck, the franc or the ruble that brought me to Dallas on that lonely Saturday. You better believe it, it was the musical excellence of Three Dog Night that got me up at 6:30 and into a limo at 7 and into a plane by 9 and out of the plane by 10 or something (Texas time). And not just me, it was a lot more people than me who were willing to risk plane crash and injury and possibly death just to see the amazing and terrific Three Dog Night (that's the group we went to see).

But there was another group first. Buddy Miles. He's not exactly a group, he's more of a drummer but he has a group behind him so you could sort of call the whole *thing* a group. And you know what he SAID? He said "Hey how's about all y'all wanna go thru some fucking changes?" That's what he said and they all got up en masse and shouted Texas style. They were all young Texas hippies and their gal-friends and they were even more wholesome than the pack at Grand Funk at Shea. Their mom and dads must've been proud of the way they looked as they left for the show in dad's auto. They got there and sat down (they did not dance) and they only sat in half the stadium. They only filled them into half the Cotton Bowl and it's a good thing too: otherwise only *half* the people could have seen them play and Three Dog Night plays for *the people*. Well they don't actually play, their back-up band does the playing, but they sing for the people.

But they didn't get on until Buddy was finished and he didn't get on until Lobo was finished. Lobo: they used to be the ROYAL GUARDSMEN!!! And they're better than ever. And they could sure be heard easily from where me and the rest of the press were seated. We weren't exactly *in* our seats but in the press box where Howard Coswill gets to sit when he's doin' the games from up there. We got all the hot dogs we could swallow (plus free mustard) and free reign over the Doctor Pepper machine. If we wanted we could've let the machine spill it all out onto the cement but none of us did (but we could've and Texas wouldn't have minded one bit, they're real nice in the Lone Star State). Well the ads for the Doctor never tell you what it tastes like, they just tell you what it doesn't taste like: it tastes like cherry coke.

And speaking of cherry, sometimes it can be a proper noun. It can even be a name of a person (female) and often in Texas it is. But it's not the name of the Butter Queen, her name is Barbara (Barbara Cope). Old Miss Butter herself made it down for the concert but she didn't make it down for the fornication in the hotel the afternoon before. She was supposed to (Gary Stromberg of Gibson & Stromberg promised her to everybody but she never made it in time so he had to find a substitute). He didn't *have* to find a substitute—everybody could've fended for himself—but he's a naturally generous guy so he sent Cherry instead.

"Hi my name is Cherry" she said as she strode thru the door in her nifty grey outfit (2-piece plus underwear and shoes). "Let's take off our clothes" and so we did, both of us. Her tits were on the hard side or should I say firm. Yeah they were firm and there was a tan line around them like she must've been out in the Texas sun (150 degrees in the shade). And she had the tan around her puss region too and also her buttocks. *Nice* butt I might add. Well the first thing she did was take out the pillow from underneath the bedspread, it was under there and she decided to put it out on top of the spread. A woman's touch I guess. Well then I kind of reclined on my back with my head on the pillow and I tell you it didn't feel no different from when it was inside the bedspread but anyway she was sort of licking around my navel by then, to the left of it to be exact. Well in a matter of seconds it was my pud she was tonguin' and it felt kind of pleasurable as a matter of fact. Okay so at that moment she was facing me, she was sort of between my legs so I just kind of reached over for some leg (hers not mine) and pulled her over in my direction so as to get her on top of me. "Oh well if you want it that way that's swell" she said and it was her on top of me on top of the pillow on top of the bed on top of the rug on top of the 17th floor on top of the other floors on top of the planet earth.

Her clit was on the tasty side and it was like a couple of unrubbery rubber bands, maybe it was more like a string. It was mighty good eating and I plum forgot about what was goin' on down around my very own crotch of my own. It seems that after about 50 seconds— maybe it was more like 105 but it could also have been 28 (I was drunk as a skunk and I left my watch in New York)—my white sticky stuff was already somewhere in her gullet so she got up. No I think she let me chew on her damp for another few seconds. Well whatever it was. She then said "Are you married?" and I told her no. "You're not? Well you eat a good pussy so I figured you had to be married." Did you ever hear anything so sexist in your life: saying I had to be married to be good at licking puss whereas SHE could do a decent job of sucking dong tho out of wedlock! Geez but she had these great leopard panties that she was already putting back on because she had to visit the rest of the gang including Toby Mamis. She gave them all a ring (Gary must've given her all the numbers) but one by one they weren't in so I said "Hey babe how's about stickin' around here a little longer?" but she was a working broad so she would not.

And speaking of work and speaking of not, Chuck Negron (he's in Three Dog Night) had his work cut out for him as he would not allow the MDs to pump him full of pain killers. It seems he'd been in a car mishap along the way and his right arm was busted up pretty bad. But pain killers would've made him drowsy and drowsiness is the enemy of good performance so he didn't wanna give the kids any shoddiness, at least not in Texas. So he performed while in the throes of excruciating agony, just for the fans! A great man and my hat's off to him.

But it isn't a cowboy hat even though Texas is famous for them. Maybe it's just in Dallas but there weren't more than about 4 or 5 cowpoke hats during the entire weekend, including Chill Wills who was at the party the next day at the McClendon Ranch. But back to the show itself, it was on artificial turf. And there's this big bulge in the middle of the field, longitudinally speaking. That's so that drainage is possible but there wasn't anything to drain. Perfect weather for a perfect concert. If it had been raining the fireworks wouldn't have gone off and go off they did. Up, up into the sky and the whole place was lit up like Coney Island and the Fourth of July even though it was the 24th. They had this guy dressed up in a Jeremiah the Bullfrog outfit in honor of their song about same called "Joy to the World" (you know the one I mean) and if *he* didn't get laid that night it must've been because he didn't feel like taking off his frog suit and no frogs would have him. Because the ladies in the place seemed pretty anxious for some of his meat and they yelled and screamed every time he strode by.

The best song they did was "One Is the Loneliest Number" which was appropriate because there wasn't much in the way of one that night. There was this party back at the hotel after the show and in walked Cherry and she still remembered my name and I didn't even have to ask her, maybe she took a memory course from Joyce Brothers. Well anyway Cory of Three Dog Night (the other dog's name is Danny by the way) was getting offers left and right from all the little Texas honeys and the one he chose was not exactly the best of the bunch but, as they say in France, chacon a son gout. Anyway at about that time Bobbi Cowan was sort of lazing around the table near the entrance with her back entirely bare so it looked like a good thing to rub. And being a Venus in Taurus I rubbed what I saw and within minutes we were scurrying up to her room. The thing she was wearing had some tit sticking out that you could get at from both the front and the back and I tried the back. I guess that was the wrong way because I found myself *banned from her boudoir* before you could say Aurelio Rodriguez. So I retired to my own room to watch some color TV (good stuff was on) and enjoy the air conditioning before calling room service for some Chateauneuf-du-Pape and a dozen snails to go with my steak (hey do they slaughter steers in Texas or do you have to send them up to Chicago and then back again before you can eat it?) and then I discovered that the door which connected my room with a Vanguard Records lovely was unlocked. Well so I opened the door and in the darkness within I could just *smell* the action awaiting me— and I'll leave the rest to your imagination.

It sure was a dynamite weekend (those Three Dog Night folks sure know how to show an out-of-towner a good time) and the topper was the McClendon Ranch, known as Cielo which means sky. The sky was cloudy and it rained but then it cleared and sunstroke came with it. But before we got there we were on the road in the bus supplied by Three Dog Night and they had two little sweeties serving soft drinks. One of them had black hot pants with little yellow and red figurines and the other sweet petunia had the same thing in light blue but with a string on the side that you could pull in order to loose the pants for the purposes of, say, removing them or something. Several gentlemen aboard got their jollies by pulling and she giggled every time. *Texans* never gave her so much fun. And then at the ranch there was this tree house with the insides carved out and stairs leading up to the top and plastic birds all around and the sound of a real live jungle and a number of local 16-yr-olds didn't mind accompanying us gents up to the top where there was this room with cushions for the purpose of comfort. This one particular teeno laughed when somebody said how there oughta be a television up there and she said "Well don't you think there's better things to do up here than watch TV?" and so I let my hand do what it wanted and it found her thigh. She pushed it away and in so doing spilled Coca-Cola on the rocks on my trousers. I responded by emptying my Bud on her lap, those Texas CT's sure are somethin' else!

Then there was plenty of swimming and bourbon and horses and gin and copperheads in the woods and Chill Wills in person and scotch and soda and vodka collins and even some movies. One was something like "Girls in Cages" made in Latin America and the best scene was where the big fatso not only strangles the North American but strangles her underwater (he holds her head under and she dies). Also the uncut version of "King Kong" and two out of the three Dogs were actually there (no Chuck) and also the drummer and maybe a guitarist too. There was an entire room in honor of Arthur Godfrey and also one for "Big John" Wayne and also an enormous john that was connected to all the other rooms so you could just barge in on some defecating and urination any time you wanted. As I said before, three dog night's A GREAT BAND. Probably the greatest in the whole world.

52

Hot Tuna Is Hot Fuckin Shit

An actual press release, for which I never got paid, but after being flown to San Francisco for the unveiling of Grunt Records, plus a Mexican meal in Sausalito, a round of parties in Mill Valley, and sex (in a manner of speaking) with Diane G., head of publicity, it didn't seem appropriate to ask.

Sept. 28, 1971

You know what's a good thing to do with your cans of tuna? Open them. And once it's open the best thing to do is mail it to a friend. You don't have to pay postage, you can mail it postage due. Just put the guy's name on it and be sure to use the proper zip code but if you put down your return address it just might get mailed back so leave it off. If the grease and everything starts dripping out the mailman'll put the whole thing in a plastic bag to protect the other mail and it'll get a lot of individual attention. So there's no way it won't get thru. It's got a lot better chance of getting thru than a postage due envelope without grease, like a postage due envelope full of rat's hairs or a postage due envelope full of dry sand.

Of course it's better to give than receive but what's a body to do if he or her as the case may be *receives* some open tuna via the U.S. Mail? Heat it up of course. And turn on either the latest Hot Tuna album or the one before that and invite somebody up from the street to share both kinds of HOT TUNA with you and yours.

And after that, what? Um, uh, well let's see, yeah there's only one thing left and that's go see them live. See what, tunas swimming in the deep blue sea? No, you've already seen that. SO GO SEE HOT TUNA and you know what? THEY'RE GONNA BE IN NEW YORK. Go see Hot Tuna because Hot Tuna is hot shit, hot fuckin

fuckin hot fuckin shit and you really better oughta catch them cause they're great. They're really okay, y'know?

And the best month you could ever see them would have to be October cause then it'll be autumn in New York and that's a mighty good time. Well how fortunate can you get? Cause that's when they'll be playing TOWN HALL!!! OCTOBER 6 & 7. Wednesday nite and Thursday nite are the two greatest nights of the week so Jesus Christ this is gonna be the most goddam outasite gig in the history of Delaware!

53

White Duck

Lester Bangs might not've known how to say Thankyou, Mike, but I sure did.

MCA is the greatest record company in the business. If it isn't who is? Dunhill? Ampex? White Whale? Well anyway nobody throws better parties than MCA and nobody has better entertainment at those parties than ditto. MCA had this real cool blowout a while back in L.A. and the food was great (endives!) and they even had Ricky Nelson on Decca nite and Sonny & Cher on Kapp nite. They didn't have White Duck on Uni nite but they could have.

After Uni nite was over everybody kind of gravitated to Mike Sherman's room for a round of Suntory the imported Japanese whisky (it ain't bad). Lester Bangs was sticking to gin and scotch that nite but his words to MCA publicity ace Sherman were no less cogent. His eyes were closed and all other signs said he was asleep but he was still talking and here's what he told Mike: "Mike I wouldn't tell you this if you weren't such a nice guy but MCA covers are ugly."

Well Lester you may live in Walled Lake Michigan and I may live somewhere else but I'm sure we can agree on one thing: this new *White Duck* album cover is *not a bit ugly*. It's what you might call attractive. In fact it's the album cover of the year. If it isn't what is, *The Music People* on Columbia? It isn't that so it must be this. I mean look it's got a frog picnicking with a mole, she (the mole) is drinking wine and he (the frog) is just sitting there with *his* wine on a blanket taking his time. The guys in the band are on a white duck and one of em's petting a large snail. None of them are wearing white ducks as the pants used to be called but they do have garden tools. Also in the garden is a beetle (no not the rock and roll kind!) fishing and a fish just looking and a dragonfly buzzing and a bumblebee reading and a caterpillar with an army helmet.

A mighty good cover!

54

David Bowie: *Hunky Dory*

The only publicist who didn't on some level demand (or even solicit) a return on his generosity, the only major-label guy who in fact was generous, was Paul Nelson at Mercury Records. After a typical lunch he would walk you to the closet, "Take 40 records," that being the max he'd determined could be carried on foot to Sam Goody's—so cab fare wouldn't cut into your monetary score. He was so nice I felt bad I never wrote up any of his crummy acts, certainly not David Bowie, who had at least a couple of releases on that label.

After Bowie moved to RCA I had lunch with somebody whose name or face I can no longer place (male?), who strongarmed me into a review—"C'mon, David needs it." For years and years, every time I thought about having given D.B. a boost, I felt a deep sense of regret—how could I?—I've always hated him so (the man most responsible for the willy-nilly return to mass conformity under the aegis of hip: fashion, if you will), but perusing it now it seems no boost was given: what a load off my mind.

The first thing it looks like is that it's a Dory Previn album (I guess it would be her *third*, is that it?) but she don't look like that at all, her hair's different and she has those big eye-glasses. She don't look a bit like Lauren Bacall and neither does Bowie when you get down to it even if he's supposed to. In fact Paul Nelson accompanied David to Boston when he was on Mercury and he says David looked kind of like Dylan then and that's kind of what Dory Previn looks like now so who knows?

But he don't *sing* like a girl, even if the arrangements behind him are sometimes like the kind of stuff people like Shirley Bassey and Morgana King get to work with. Neil Young sings like Gladys Knight and Aretha and Carla Thomas but David Bowie sings like a John Lennonized Lou Reed with about a ton of additional United Kingdom afternoon tea thrown in. With that in mind the compositions come off like really drawn out versions of "Happiness Is a Warm Gun," there's more Beatles on the album than Kinks, a heck of a lot more. And why not draw them out, like what's the hurry? Like if albums are gonna compete with television as time killers/fillers . . . *Abbey Road* started it and *Hunky Dory* carries on even better than Chad & Jeremy's *Cabbages and Kings.*

And the songs are just damn good. Say you got "Kooks" playing, it's all about kooks and who's called them that since beatniks walked around with bongos and berets? Well anyway if you got that playing there's nothing gonna make you take it off unless you discover the Delfonics doing "Didn't I Blow Your Mind?" on channel 13, is it channel 13? Jeez, I never would have expected *them* to have anything that good on! Well by the time you're three-quarters thru the Delfonics you might just as well put Bowie back on and it's too bad if you took the needle off instead of just lowering the volume. One of the bothersome things about the songs on this album is you gotta listen to each one all the way through to get the picture cause he puts in different stuff along the way, so if you gotta start from the beginning again, well I don't know . . .

"Quicksand" is a great title for any song, I wrote one once with it IN the title so I oughta know ("What Is Quicksand?," The Stalk-Forrest Group, Elektra EKM-45693, but don't try to order it cause they only pressed 200 copies), and David Bowie's "Quicksand" is no exception.

What else? Well he's no Rod Stewart. But neither is Knuckles O'Toole.

So if I haven't said enough good stuff about this album yet I guess now's the time. Um. Let me see, well I guess you could say if this ain't the album of the year (you can even start the year around September, '71) then what is? *Hot Burrito? Smash Your Head Against the Wall? Happy Just to Be Like I Am?* John Mayall's *Memories?* James Moody's *Everything You Always Wanted to Know About Sax (and Flute)?* Clearly it's none of them so why look any further? This is it, *Humpty Dumpty* by David Bowie, whoops I mean *Hunky Dory.*

55

Kim Fowley Visits America (excerpts)

Kim Fowley, the self-proclaimed King of Pus, came in so far under budget on his I'm Bad *LP that Capitol Records feted him to a promotional tour—nine cities in nine days (none of them New York or L.A.). Liza Williams, who'd once deemed my writing repulsive, got Capitol to hire me to write a daily dispatch (subhead: "Not just another historic journey"). To keep expenses down, the only other members of the tour were Mars Bonfire (author of "Born to Be Wild"), Kim's guitarist, and Jeffrey Cheen, his producer.*

Most of my explicit sexuality was edited out and I shuffled some of it into Freeloader Frolics.

Dispatch #2: Washington, D.C.

Rain greeted the gang upon arrival in the Nation's Capital. Rain, rain go away, little Kimmy wants to play but the clouds kept pissing out their wet all day. But at least a Holiday Inn was on the agenda, the first of many scheduled for the trip. Holiday Inns are where for physicians and dentists call Hotel Operator for assistance. No one needed a sawbones or drill sergeant but it was nice to know they were there if needed. For churches check the directory in lobby but nobody needed God cause God can't do shit for a cold.

Kim had a cold that he caught in Atlanta from the air conditioner, didn't know how to turn it off so it froze his ass overnite (his resistance was not lowered by beating his meat cause he did not beat his meat). Testing his voice, he found it harsh and growly: o-right!!

Okay but not so hot were those nasty wrinkles in Kim's white suit, the kind of calamity that can cause all the rack hacks to gulp on their gin & tonic: get this pressed immediately!

The grooming continued and Mars went to work on his nails with a clipper. "Hey why don't you use a nail file?" asked Kim. "I prefer this clipper" rejoindered Mr. Bonfire. "Well I got a better clipper than that" Kim was then heard to say. This nail dispute did not go much further.

Points of interest: LIBRARY OF CONGRESS (1st bet. E. Cap. & Indep. Ave., S.E.); FOLGER SHAKESPEARE LIBRARY (2nd and E. Capitol Sts. Mon. thru Sat. 10 A.M. to 4 P.M.); NATIONAL ZOOLOGICAL PARK (Adams Mill & Ontario Pl. N.W. Mon. thru Sat. 9 A.M. to 6 P.M.—hey wait, was that *Ontario?*—even room in this country for Canada our neighbor to the north!). As time prohibited, *none of these amusing "points" were visited*, not even by the Canadian-born Mars, visiting the seat of government of his adopted nation for the first time ever.

So much for the TRIVIAL aspects of Kim's first hrs. in D.C., time for some MEAT. Okay so there's this party, see, just like the one in Atlanta. From the first it promised to be even better than same. A lot fewer rednecks and even some members of the *underground press* were in attendance, notably the gang from *Woodwing*, which ranks fourth behind *Rolling Stone*, *Changes* and *Zygote* among major rock mags. Tom Zito and the lovely Stephanie made their presence felt too.

Not so for the Swiller Bros., who sat along the sidelines with their MOMMY not doing shit. Kim had to help these poor unfortunates (KIM IS THE PEOPLE'S SINGER) so he wove them a tune, bringing a smile to their chuckle and mommy lit up like an Xmas tree on Halloween.

Also featured was the 2nd nitely beer chugging event in as many days. Yours truly was stuck representing the Fowley side of the biz and, as the nite before, a chub of ponderous proportions round the belly was chosen to represent the biz side of the biz. In Atlanta I got stuck having to drink a full can and the big-boy beat me going away, no more of that for me so this time Jeffrey was on the spot with only half a beer for me and a full one for the other fellow. Only trouble is it wasn't bottles, it was cans, no, the other way around: bottles rather than cans so everybody could *see* it was only half full but I won so big shit.

By the end of party time it was time for more, much fuckin more for cryin out loud. A beardo with a Rolling Stones tongue logo around his neck invited Kim & Co. to his radio show in Maryland. (Speaking of Maryland there's 2 places with *Mary* in em outskirting

D.C., Mary-land and Virgin-ia, fuckin *weird* ain't it?) What followed is this: you won't believe it.

Starts out Kim is being interviewed for the PEOPLE out in radioland to hear his unique and compelling story and he told it straight from the shoulder (JOHN SINCLAIR could not have done better): "My cock is a mile long and I'm alone tonite so why don't you cunts come on over." As Mars put it later there was a lot of restraint in that simple message from "4 Eyes" Fowley and yet this asshole objected due to *paranoia*.

2 versions exist as to what happened next. First there's the one that in walked the owner of the station who said "If you play any Kim Fowley it'll be the last thing you ever play." Second one is the D.J. only *claimed* that's what this hypothetical owner said, that in fact he made it all up as an excuse to not play Kim's smash album cause he never intended to in the first place. In any event these SONSOF-BITCHES deserve to have their nozzles made into glue AND ANY-BODY WHO LISTENS TO THEIR STATION IS A TOAD (A DEAD ONE).

Proof positive that Kim Fowley is a *people's singer* and without a doubt the Elvis of our generation. Also he's Marc Bolan and Mick Jagger too. Represented graphically this relationship can be shown as

KIM = ELVIS = KIM = BOLAN = KIM = JAGGER

Right on Kim!!! Power to the people!!!!

Dispatch #8: Meltzer Reflects.

Free association summary of the 1972 Kim Fowley promotional tour: Kim, Jim, Bim, Tim, Tiny Tim, Tiny Jim, Tiny Mim, Mim-nim, M'nim, Wiss, Tipp'n, Wutz, Huts, Sound-off 1-2, Hot Towns in Town, Wide Whales, Death, Caesar Salad, Caesar Swim, Jim, Bim, Him, Kim . . .

Aesthetico-commercial summary of the tour: Kim is a *superior performer*, superior to David Bowie, Elvis, Rod Stewart, David Cassidy, Lou Reed, Marc Bolan, Mick Jagger, Iggy, Burt Reynolds (somebody in Minneapolis said she wouldn't fuck Kim but she'd FUCK BURT REYNOLDS). He plays as good guitar as Jeff Beck without even using a guitar, just his mike feeding back. A genius, Einstein would say.

Weird Fowley habits: 1. will not drink a beer another mouth has touched (fear of germs); 2. will not walk out of an airplane first (someone else must do it); 3. two items at each meal (one of them a *tuna sandwich* despite the mercury warnings—the man's SUICIDAL!); 4. his suits—white and green velvet, respectively—must never have wrinkles (cleaning and pressing bills go sky-high); 5. when he calls his Calif. girlfriends who still live with mom and daddy he gets another girl to call them so he don't have to talk to mom or pops; 6. he shaves every day, rather than every other day; 7. etc.

In other words, he's nutz!

Special thanx to Jeffrey Cheen for all the vitamin C and that stuff he had that numbs your teeth when you stick it up your nose (funny stuff), Kim used to ask him for it just before showtime, he'd ask him for it by name but I can't remember the name, what's it called? Jeffrey also did the driving except a few times when Mars took over for a spell because of Jeff's arthritis. He also had a swell assortment of Neil Young tapes what wiled away many an hour.

And who can ever forget Kim's instructions to Mars during the heat of performance? "Mars . . . *Creedence.*" "Mars . . . *folk-rock.*" "Mars . . . *John Cage.*" "Stop . . ." Who can ever forget . . .

56

Freeloader Frolics

My most copious overview of the rock-trip trip—but is it an "exposé"? a con-
fession? celebration of excess? Well, okay, all of 'em, but even more a declara-
tion of discovery, of having finally got to where the reputed lingering rockroll
FUN was (now that it wasn't in the music): in roading, rowdying, wench-
ing, burning out the American night.

I didn't title this. I never felt like a freeloader (you work hard for this shit,
y'know?) but I did gloat, eh?—so ragingly innocent I didn't realize its publi-
cation would put the kibosh to the steady supply of future trips. (I didn't get
another for two-and-a-half years.)

Some elaborations/clarifications . . .

Ellen Willis: When I say I put my hand on her leg, it was more like her
knee (jus' "boasting" for the piece) and only a single brief touch, three fingers
(no pressure) for a second or less, as if to ask, "Sexual content, perhaps?"—
rather tame even by late-'90s neo-Victorian standards, but certainly in the
form of a question seeking an answer. Couldn't've been more non-harassingly
up front w/out getting vulgarly verbal—"Kissy poo? Fucky wucky?"—and
she answered, just as non-verbally, by immediately scramming.

Richard Robinson/Yale: He was there as a privileged blueblood undergrad-
uate; I was a struggling grad student (and got expelled).

Munich/Oktoberfest: Never got there, in fact the non-rock world-o-travel
closed up for me pretty quick too.

CURRENT THOUGHTS on gonadal rockthink, circa '73—Among
other things, sex was the prime element of rockrockrock and roll I/me/myself
did not throw back . . . From day one, rock's most salient show-&-tell had
been how to live in one's own skin; with this came the warrant to, that's
right, THINK WITH YOUR PECKER OR CUNNY—in life and in my
case also on paper . . . If rock itself was no longer an arch-expression of hot-
dang desire, there was no reason not to use a max-whoopee SIMULATION
of same (like everybody else did—professional or non) as backdrop/trigger to
your ritual night-wriggle, as I did for my own droll/preposterous/right-on
coming-of-age (25–35) male overkill number, the cheezier repercussions of
which I wouldn't actively rethink until punk-rock.

That some of the people discussed herein were "groupies" probably made them 2000% more appealing, and in carrying on with them (in 2 cases: falling in love) I felt I'd experienced exactly *what touring, roadbusting rockers did: my deepest penetration, yes, of the rockroll night. In the same way that I figured record people would find my candidness refreshing, I was sure sex partners would be PLEASED by my little tributes to them—homages!— payback for their having granted me* memorable *intimacy . . . what sick SILLY romantic art-think!*

(I.e.: none of 'em ever fucked me again.)

Last free trip I got off a record company was a trip to Philly where I didn't even get in the pants of M.T. the famous deejay's wife who I really did expect to get into like I did on the Kim Fowley tour of last June but this time it just didn't work out. They flew a whole lot of us to the City of Brotherly Love to see Alice Cooper and we got to take the Metroliner back to New York (oh boy!). They put us up in a Holiday Inn with enormous-size room numbers (mod-rin art!) and the first thing I did when I got to the room was call up Ellen Willis and invite her down for some Jack Daniel's but she had a headache but she came down anyway and I put my hand on her leg and she hasn't said a word to me since. (I don't have to use her initials 'cause I didn't get anything off her.)

Trips to Philly always stink anyway and this was no exception because Lisa Robinson and her hubby Dick were around. The two of them may be the biggest no-talent hustlers on the map but they get to go everywhere free all the time. *But?* Who am I kidding?! I ain't that naïve. I know it's *because* they're no-talent hustlers that they get to go everywhere for free, yeah. Well this time around we were all sitting down eating our free din-din at the sumptuous Holiday Inn banquet room when I decide to throw a bowl of sour cream at an Alice poster on the wall. Bullseye! Whadda these Robinson creeps then do but the Lisa one goes off to try to get me kicked out of Philly and sent home early (a freebie first!) by *telling on me* while the Richard one (in his freshly plastered short hair that Lisa decided he needed for that "now" look so prevalent in New York) sez to me "Richard, when're you gonna grow up?" I coulda said to him "Richard, when're you goin' back to Yale?" but talkin' to him woulda ruined Philly completely for me on top of not getting laid so I held my peace. Later on

I went out and went halvesies with Nick Tosches on a rubber girl's face that you stick your dick in the mouth of for only $12.95 so Philly turned out to be all reet daddy after all.

But when you get down to it trips useta be a fuckin' fuckin' *fuck* of a lot better. Like 3) San Francisco paid for by Grunt. That's 3) on the list of all of 'em, the whole list of all of 'em being 1) Aspen for the Nitty Gritty Dirt Band paid for by United Artists in '70; 2) Dallas for Three Dog Night paid for by somebody or other (including a tasty-puss hooker) in '71; 3) San Francisco paid for by Grunt in '71; 4) L.A. paid for by MCA in '72; 5) L.A. again in '72 paid for by Asylum or Atlantic or somebody to interview the ever-boring Jackson Browne; 6) the big nine-city Kim Fowley tour of '72 paid for by Capitol plus I even got a salary to write it up and they even rented me a typewriter but it broke; 7) L.A. again for the boffo Signpost party at Ciro's just when they were changing the name to whatever Ciro's is now; 8) India but rock and roll didn't pay for it, *Oui* did, '72.

Best of all was 4). MCA was having this big convention kind of thing with Sonny and Cher and Roger Williams and El Chicano and Conway Twitty playing for everybody three nites running and we were all poshed up at the Sheraton Universal and they gave us free rein over room service (!!!!!). There was this one meal where I had everybody over before going to the wrestling matches (27-man battle royal and Pete Senoff of Atlantic was paying!) and we called down for all sorts of prime rib and crabmeat and Blue Nun wine and it came to 55 bucks so we wrote down a $40 tip for the guy or maybe it was $45 (an even $100?). But that wasn't shit compared to Gary Kenton's three-day food tab of 220 bucks. I think he got to fuck L.W. on that trip too (something which I didn't get to do till trip No. 5).

Also some blond broad whose name is now totally forgot, me and her got to boogie on Alan Rinde of Columbia Records' living room floor while he was entertaining a honey of his own between the sheets of his very own bedchamber. Took me a while to get my fork in the meat and I even hadda show her how legit I was by finding an *Esquire* lying around with me as a member of the Heavy 89 right across from John Sinclair. I came too fast for her or something so she left in a huff and I got to sleep alone on the couch paid for by Al's swell Columbia salary.

Well anyway back in the beginning of when I useta take these trips I was real conscientious and I useta write tons of articles every time I got sent anywhere. For the Nitty Gritty Piss Band (free ski lessons included in the package) I wrote it up in 11 places including the TV column I had in *Fusion* ("Hot Flashes from Channel 106, Aspen,

Colo."). Whether they loved me for it or not I don't fuckin' know but after that it started getting less and less and it didn't seem to matter. The thing I wrote on the Grunt party for *Screw* never even got printed and big shit . . .

As I sit here writing this pap several roaches have been crawling across the keys reminding me that there were *no* roaches at the Jack Tar Hotel where we stayed for the Grunt booze-out. (Y'know what I did at the Grunt party? I went up to Charles Perry of *Rolling Stone* whom I had never had the pleasure of meeting before altho I knew him to be an asshole from afar and I spilled wine all over the food he'd been waiting in line for an hour and a half to get and both the wine in me and the wine on his chicken were paid for by Grunt!) But I did happen to come across an insect (arachnid?) or two as crablice from off the hot swampy poon of D.A. managed to stray onto the hairs attached to my scrod and accompany me back to N.Y.C. (Grunt did not pay for my crab medicine.)

But I didn't get crabs or any sort of VD at-tall from the Kim Fowley tour (Atlanta, Washington, Philadelphia, Boston, Cleveland, Detroit, Chicago, Minneapolis, Houston). Figured I'd come up with some sort of blight from bein' with a Fowley tour but I got to pop my cork in three cunnies without contracting so much as tuberculosis (which is curable). M.T., K.W., F.M., luv *them* all to this day still too.

K.W. was in the nation's cap but now she's livin' in L.A. so if you read this, K., I really fuckin' *enjoyed* lickin' your slit on the floor of that radio station before they kicked us out. I've just been thinkin' about the whole thing recently and it beats me why I didn't take my pepperoni out of my pants while we were in the car and you already had your panties off, you coulda sat on it in the back seat with Mars Bonfire sitting next to us, I can't for the life of me figure out why we didn't do it until we got back to the Holiday Inn. Beats me.

Capitol paid for K.W.'s gas (she had her own car which she drove later in the eve). Capitol paid for a lot of things on that trip (even a large bathroom dispenser comedy-type condom that me and Jeff Cheen gave Kim at the pizza place in Detroit as a gift from us to him). But they did not pay for the Dristan I hadda buy in Chicago after coming in F.M.'s snag and mouth for a total of eight times (if you don't believe me ask *her* how many and she'll tell you *eight*), my nose was stuffed that nite and breathing wasn't e-z and I hadda keep blowing my nostrils in the bedsheets much to F.M.'s chagrin.

Time's been marchin' on since then and Capitol won't even fly me to L.A. to interview Kim for *Interview* mag 'cause they think my name's been attached to his so nobody'll believe anything I say about him anymore (they won't believe an *interview*???). I gotta think up another way of getting to L.A. so I think I'm gonna write a letter to Marty Cerf at U.A. and ask him to fly me for whenever they have that big Move/E.L.O. bonanza that they're bound to have sooner or later. "Dear Marty, ran into Bill Roberts yesterday and we got to talking all about the Move. Gee it really got my juices flowing, after all they've been my favorite group ever since I heard their first elpee on Regal Zonophone which my sister mailed me from Europe but was never released in the U.S.A. You never heard it? I'll let you borrow my copy! Hey while we're on the subject how's about flying me out to that swell party you're throwing the boys? I bet it'll be *just as good* as the one you threw for the Legendary Masters series! Gee Marty, all I can say is please will ya huh? Your pal, Rich." That's what I'm gonna write. He likes me. He'll fly me. I'm sure he will.

'Cause I've got a special hankerin' for headin' out there 'cause I feel like meetin' this pen pal who I've only seen pitchers of so far but me and her have been correspondin' for some time so it's only right that I get to meet her in the flesh, right? Right.

So I could use a free ticket (747's with piano lounges are my favorite if anybody's listening). Dave "I-Hate-Capitalist-Ripoff-Record-Companies-And-I-Wouldn't-Accept-Shit-From-Them" Marsh gets free tickets every other day. Lester Bangs too, he's fuckin' been to England already! A few weeks ago he calls up and sez he's goin' to London again to see Alice Cooper this time but he's drunk y'see and he don't realize until he actually gets there that it's London, *Ontario*!!! Ho ho ho and well if you record people are gonna send Lester all over the world so he can give your bands write-ups in places like *Phonograph Record Magazine* and *The New Haven Rock Press* then you could at least send me to L.A. this once and I promise I'll write up whatever it is in: *Rock, Zoo World, The Drummer* (Philadelphia's *oldest* underground newsshit!), this mag, and maybe *The Real Paper.* That's all I write for anymore (coulda lied and said I write for *Sports Illustrated*) but use this article as a sample and you'll readily agree that I can write real good. Just remembered I still write for *Fusion* too and *Raunchy Rock* on Staten Island. Wouldn't mind getting flown to New Orleans too. Never been to Seattle either.

Once again it ain't rock but it's O.K. by which I mean that *Oui*'s gonna be sending me to the Oktoberfest with a "k" in Munich come October with a "c." (So if you record companies or publicity/promotion outfits wanna send me somewhere I hope you do it *before* October 'cause I got a lotta time to kill 'tween now and then.)

Another free thing I once got off a company was Paul Nelson of Mercury took me to the closed circuit of the Ali-Frazier fite (sat in the second row). Wasn't exactly a trip but I ain't knockin' it.

Travel really broadens your outlook.

57

Jimmy Spheeris:
The Original Tap Dancing Kid

Quid pro suck.

The vinyl produce of Jimmy Spheeris, brother of filmmaker Penelope Spheeris, was (what's the word? what's the word?) skunkshit. Even a juggernaut like Columbia Records, who had signed him why?—prob'ly so some other company wouldn't have him—couldn't give his albs away. He was so useless he wasn't even being negatively *reviewed.*

Jonathan Coffino, a "product manager" with the label who knew me from my connection to (ugh) Blue Öyster Cult and had heard I was, well, prolific, made me an offer. In exchange for three reviews in three rock sheets under three different names he would give me a hundred sealed Columbia elpees. Inotherwords—minus cab fare—a hundred bucks. It's a deal.

I used my own name on this humdinger, published in Zoo World. *For* Rock *(lauding the album's "European grandeur") I was Matt Damsker II. In* Phonograph Record Magazine *(praise for side one's "rock tribute to the first all-female exploration of Africa") I was Kentucky Sutton. Three good'uns.*

He refused to pay me.

(11:51) S'fear us. We fear anyone over 6 foot 6. Jimmy Spheeris's 6 feet 8 inches of skin, bones (11:52), muscle, organs, feet, legs, face and fingers. On his tippy toes he (11:53) is taller than a library (a sphere of the world in his hand). Cover from off a Polynesian decor—flowers (11:54) and sinuous leafs—for Mr. Hawaii a.k.a. James Spheeris of Matterhorn, New Jersey (11:55). Six foot eight of musicianship you can slice with a knife, spread thickly among grooves of shiny black (this ain't no Fantasy (11:56) elpee circa '58). When musicians meet they say "Pleased to meet you, sir, madam or junior." A musician addressing Jimmy asked "Please may I see your (11:57) playing hand?" Jimmy did just that. This disc is the result (11:58).

Blades of grass in shady groves of summer's golden sunrise o'er continents unknown to man, Jimmy sits (11:59) in azure groves of cold, cool, cool . . . cool waters of THERE'S SUN ACROSS HIS FACE!! Palm trees offer shade, palms that are (12:00) shady bear fruit. The fruits of musical labor are many and varied. No one knows this better than Felix. Felix was rich before (12:01) he met the Maharishi. His Indian trimmings fit loosely so production isn't painful (it's e-z for Felix). Not Felix Krull but Cavaliere (12:02). You remember him. Never made a bad one. No exception is this circular plane o' plastic called you know the name 'cause it's up at the top of the page (12:03). Felix has produced a winner and cuts is why.

"Beautiful News" (12:04) is the greatest cut of all time. "Original Tap Dancing Kid" is 2nd best. "Sweet Wahini Mama," dedicated to the island of Oahu, is numero three (12:05) (of all time). "Open Up" is the fourth most excellent (ever). A wow a minute, this album is unequaled, it's unparalleled, unprecedented (12:06), in all likelihood the finest ever made, produced, pressed or recorded. History will look kindly upon it in the many years to come (12:07) and historians of a music-o-logical stripe will proclaim: "Jim Spheeris's *Tap Dancer* or whatever it's called is perhaps the number one long-play record waxing in the long and honored annals (12:08) of recording."

This alb is very, very good. Wonderful alb. There's not a thing you can say about it. Other than good (12:09). When something is good you say so (am I right?) and this one is just that (I wouldn't say it if it wurn't (12:10) true): GOOD.

58

Meltzer's Lunch with Tanya

Another year, another burn?? Was it s'posed to be Coffino "making it up" to me? And/or me "getting back" at him? (I still can't get a read on it.)

Said he thought matching me with this year's product, Tanya Tucker, would make for interesting reading. *Right away I couldn't tell, was I just there as some kind of prop?—part of an office joke?—and what about* her? *Only reason I'd agreed in the first place was lunch at the 21 Club (I'd never been there), and that part fizzled immediately.*

Tanya actually thanked me when I ran into her two years later . . . jesus.

I will *take credit this time for hand-on-leg. (Why does anyone put up with me?)*

Jonathan Coffino of Columbia (he collects trains) set it up for me to go to lunch with the first lassie of country Miss Tanya Tucker (people from Vegas don't call themselves Miz). Hadda be chaperoned tho on account of my rep as Rock's Bad Boy (many uncalled for urinations and other impolitenesses in polite company). So Murray Krugman hadda go along and also Ed Naha from publicity but he was too busy with somethin else so just Murray and bearded Jonny her product manager were required and the ground rules were I was not to be left alone with her for even a second. But her male parent Bo (Ike silver dollar belt buckle) and her older sis Lacosta were not necessary, just the Columbia people (some folks just like to hog all the chaperone action themselves).

First choice of everyone was the world-renowned 21 Club down the block which was featured in Alfred Hitchcock's *Spellbound* of more than 20 years ago (before Tanya was born or conceived or her name even picked out). Actually it was only my choice cause the Columbos didn't wanna roll out *that* much of a red carpet for me just to get photos of me and Tanya together so they could send em to the *National*

Star and say it was me and her announcing our secret engagement which was (unbeknownst to me at the time) basically their sole purpose for inviting me up there and Tanya didn't know enough about NYC restaurants to even of heard of the 21 so the cafeteria downstairs was decided upon but when we got there it was too damn crowded. And outside was rain. So the CBSers decided it was cool to send down for sandwiches so it was upstairs again to check out the 2-page menu.

"Do you like pastrami Tanya?" axed Jonathan but no such luck cause of too much fat (on the meat). "Well we can just order it lean." Swell so they're about to phone down for Tanya's pastrami-corned beef combination plus a coke and "lots of coffee" (combo #3 for me and 3 beers) when somebody suddenly realizes Tanya's got another interview somewhere else in half an hour so they move to send a so-called "girl" down for it to save some time. But alas all such chattel have departed for a lunch of their own already (it's in their contract) so after a couple of harumphs on these bigwigs' part it's me and Murray (complained or it woulda been just me—there ostensibly as a goddam *interviewer* who they're supposed to wine and dine) runnin across 53rd St. to a different sandwich place where we gotta do some quick substitution to come up with edibles resembling those originally selected.

Real grizzly as hell pastramo for Tanya and I got myself (i.e. *selected* for myself cause Goddard Lieberson's bailiwick was still gonna foot the regrettably infinitesimal bill) a provolone and anchovy with pimento on rye and 3 Miller half-quarts. Meantime Murray hadda make sure I had all my questions thought out in advance cause he wanted to get the whole thing over with even tho it's HEAVEN to be near Little Miss Virgin (caught her press gig at the Bottom Line a couple nites before and hadda kiss her hand and profess erotic luv as she left in a taxi, me not Murray) who meanwhile was waitin patiently or nervously or whatever up on the 12th floor of the house that Clive built.

Okay so finally (whew) we're in this conference room with me in my double-breasted sportjack from my cousin Bruce who had no more use for it now that his only brother'd already been married and a tie that Andrew Winters the ex-bass player of the Soft White Underbelly gave me 4 years ago cause they weren't bein worn anymore (plus an almost-white shirt so the cutey wouldn't know I was a slob and for the 21 cause that's probably what they require) and her in her blue-green doggie-pattern blouse like you might give your 9-year-old granddaughter for her birthday and neater-than-a-pin light blue jeans and a pimple on her chin that makeup could not hide (adolescence creepin in). Hair was in slight disarray (hers cause mine was neatly combed tho wet). Halfway thru the provolone I axe question #1: "Have you ever seen the Doors or even listened to them?" Seemed reasonable enough cause those black satin pants she'd been poured into for the Bottom Line (stitching on the panties underneath was as *visible* as such undergarmentry ever is) in which to gyrate like a topless gogo gal or at least one with pasties bore a strong resemblance to those that Jim (may he r.i.p.) used to operate in. "Doors? What are *they*?" Okay, answer #1: Billy Sherrill or somebody is more responsible for her act than she is (coulda *guessed* that so nothing very earthshaking about hearing it from her but in any case from *observing* her up close it sure ain't a matter of her tapping into Morrisonry of her own accord—even by accident—cause away from the stage she ain't even as spicy as Brenda Lee). Offered her some of my beer but she rejected it on the grounds that she only quaffs Michelob. Yeah sure.

Noticed her gagging over her slices of bread and meat and took that as a good time to go into a half drunken rap about how the myth of country in NY was just a myth (nobody listens to it but me and Nick Tosches and we only listen on Thursdays), told her she might never make it in the Apple unless she cut a rocko or two in which case she'd become the new Lesley Gore overnite. Seemed undismayed about country's gloomy prospects (Coffino hadn't mentioned it to her so it couldn't really matter), never heard of Lesley but yes Billy was checking out new material for her that very moment down in Mason-Dixonland (goody). Jonathan offered up a query of his own at this point which from its pidginness (acted like she was a foreigner just outa the cradle) wasn't so easy to decipher but it had to do with groupies, like whether or not C&W has em too. (Really seemed to want to know if any of em of the *male* persuasion have penetrated her—cough cough—*veil of purity* but the words did not leave his lips and her juvenile id's reading grade was insufficient for her to read tween the lines—no way this jr. chanteuse was gonna know what "Would you lay with me in a field of stone?" could possibly mean.)

Turned out that yes she had once been surrounded by a group of teen boys and her only recourse was to kiss them all. "A wet one?" axed I. "No, on the cheek"—oh boy. (A tease? No, cause she's just too unaware to be one no matter what her inclination at this stage might be. Genuinely innocent? No, cause it's more like she's not too *bright*—like an intelligent 12-year-old at best—so that even if she's been hipped to the birds and bees it just ain't sunk in despite the nascent hormones makin their move.)

Interview was over with that one cause the photog had arrived, time for me and her to look each other in the orbs as had evidently been someone's plan from the very start. Sure didn't mind (got to put my hand on her leg) and neither did she (cooperative and unsnotty beyond belief, Shirley Temple could not've been any nicer and probably a whole lot worse). Her eyes were the kind you see on angelic preteen child stars in movies just before they kill the kid off for a touch of poignancy, plus a dash of Ohio bowling league mama thrown in (far cry from Loretta Lynn's). After the shooting I finished her sandwich.

59

Grapefruit Juice with Peter Ivers

Waxpaper was this upscale "tip sheet" Warner/Reprise Records mailed to reviewers every month in the hope they would listen to the month's releases once (at least) before selling them, if only because it was their so-called peers, fellow rockwriters (no publicists!), who reviewed/previewed everything. This was after they were already punching holes in covers, no more shrinkwrap; if you'd had to break the wrap, thus forfeiting value, there's no way ersatz "peer pressure" would've been enough to convince you to play anything. Payment for pieces was pretty good (on a par with what the Village Voice *was paying), as it was of course in direct exchange for literal nonironic ad copy, P.R., what else would you call it? (Very evil shit.)*

The day before I met up with Peter Ivers, the subject of my first Waxpaper *piece, my girlfriend left me, moved to Texas, and visiting him (one of the geekiest lizards on the planet) felt like a trip to hell. Maybe the least blue-collar rockguy who ever lived, he made David Byrne seem like Joe Hill, but I let him tell it* his *way . . .*

You could say I needed the money, or I *could say it, but that would be no excuse: hit me with a rotten tomato . . . please. (And to think Alan Freed took a fall for "payola.")*

Welcome to the real swell Laurel Canyon pad of Peter Ivers. Real swell but why're the windows sealed so tight on so hellishly hot a morn? "When they're open you realize how hot it is outside." Okay. No beer in the fridge tho ("I don't drink alcohol here") so grapefruit juice'll hafta do, fine but my host wantsa see if I can *finish it all* like it's one of those kiddie drink-races at suppertime and that thirsty I ain't, sorry Pete. Tells me he went to Harvard, majored in the classics, sez Catullus is every bit as all-goddam-reet as Brecht, even pronounces it Ca-TULL-us rather'n CAT-ul-lus like my hack humanities teach used to do, giving all he says in this regard the ring of *authority*. Notices the well-worn blue Pumas on my feet and a bell rings in his bean: just bought the exact same pair himself. Hasta prove it tho (is this man eccentric?) so he runs to the closet and brings em out: exact same. Proven beyond a shadow of a doubt so it's time to listen to Peter's new album, *Peter Ivers* (the follow-up to '75's *Terminal Love*), on Peter's reel to reel machine.

At ear-shattering volume. "One thing you'll notice is my lyrics are very direct and uncompromising." I sit and wait for evidence but before the issue comes up I notice the first 10–15 seconds of "I'm Sorry Alice" are *pure Alice Cooper.* "I'm glad you think so—something to pull the kids in." Speaking real loud into my ear cause of the volume. Very pleased that this time he's finally finally finally got himself a producer (Gary Wright) capable of giving him a commercial sound—and fuggin solid and thoroughly commercial it surely is. But not to the point of diminishing or obscuring the importance of his message, i.e. the fear of having made a miserable *fool* of himself the night before and being lucky to still be standing today and in a position to, yup, *apologize* (great exposition of vulnerability).

"In Pursuit of Treasure" starts ominous and Alice-like again but quickly it suggests to me an "In My Little Town" freed from all that Paul Simon cloy and preciousness. "I respect Simon's work but he's so concerned about being middle-class that it gets in the way of his clarity of expression. My stories are more working class." Indeed. "Eighteen and Dreaming" immediately strikes me as Springsteen without all the Fonzy-esque window dressing and, once again, Peter is pleased. Pleased that he just might stand a chance in the current nostalgia marketplace. Stands a chance and a half by golly.

Good horny sexstuff too, with an emphasis on the horny: "Peter," "Send Your Love Over," "Rock and Roll Embarrassment." Songs about hunger as writ and sung by a still-hungry sonofagun (hungry musically, hungry professionally, hungry sexually, *hungry*) instead of one of them simps who gotta consult the innermost recesses of their memory bank to summon up the proper pose of what my pal Nick Tosches calls "carnal oompah." Even gets behind his taperoom mike stand to lipsynch some of it in mime of the stage carriage he'd like to utilize someday soon in actual live circumstances (ain't taken any of his more recent *personas* directly to the people and would like to take that leap altho he *still has his doubts*: a true musical innocent). And hey: Carly Simon accompanies him on "Peter," putting him in the same boat as Mr. Jagger himself ("We get different mileage out of her tho, like in my case I *admit* I'm so vain").

Plays me this thing called "You Used To Be Stevie Wonder," a quite appropriate underlining of the fact that Peter considers himself "a totally unique harmonica player." Cause he really is. Laces every cut with a dose of his playing and in every instance the phrasing is what you might call saxophone-like ("I really get off on all the sweat and saliva"). A reference to classic bluesharp every now and then but essentially the guy's genuinely got himself a real landmark popharp style that's, y'know, almost without peer. Can't think of any analogues myself except maybe the Country Joe of '66–'68 when that gent's blowin was an integral part of the Fish's total ground-moving pop sound. "I never really listened to San Francisco music" but, funny, he even *looks* like a sawed-off version of vintage Joe McDonald right down to the khaki pants from when *that* biz was in vogue. Strange.

"Gilbert and Sylvia." Described by Peter as a song that if he heard it while drivin would pull off to the side of the road because, geez, how's a person to continue *functioning* with so devastatingly heavy a message ringing in his ear? Heavy. Hard times knockin a blue-collar couple right off the hayride and into the murk of mere survival. "I think that if I hadn't been sort of tongue-in-cheek with names like Gilbert and Sylvia it would've been too depressing to listen to at all." Maybe so, maybe so. In any event the guy's got himself a *system*.

End of record, some stuff for next time on the piano (including the answer song to all those surrender-to-the-universe whatsems, something called "Happy on the Grille"), more grapefruit squeezings, a very friendly yet biznesslike goodbye (guy sure does know his bizness) and I'm off into the blazing midday blaze . . .

60

Linear with Lotsa Guitar

Waxpaper . . . a year later . . . where I cease to kiss Warner artist ass. (So clap, dammit.)

Waiting in the waiting room at Bennett Glotzer's real classy well-upholstered office with carpeting up to your *nostrils* and BG himself's in the other room yellin somethin about NO POLYGRAPHS FOR US (yellin is the word cause he was yellin). He's Zappa's lawyer among other things and this studio where some of Frank's equipment got ripped off don't wanna take nobody's word for it without a lie detector. Several articles of the Bill of Rights are at stake and Glotz will have none of it (hats off to mr. civil liberty!).

Meanwhile Frankie's off in the back spinnin a pressing of some of the cuts from his new and latest forthcoming record and before he's done I get to catch the tail end of it. Lotta jamming and solos and guitar stuff and decent bass levels and things like that and lots of it's just plain *linear*, y'know not too many of them famous patented Zappa changes of musical direction, stoppin on a dime and 180 degrees and all of that (some but less'n you'd expect: just a lotta *playin*). The man himself is nattily attired in a dark blue v-neck shirt with one of those wing type collars and a narrow chain (silver) round his neck. Prefaded lightblue jeans with a slight flare and cut off at the ankle. No belt. Shirt's stickin out of his trousers. Brown shoes (*still* don't make it) with heely heels and lotsa fancy stitching. Sox with a brown & beige diamond pattern like your mom useta buy you in the 3rd grade and biznessmen wore in the '40s (*real* snappy!). The usual facial hair that everybody's familiar with (rest of the face is fresh shaved) and the strands on top're tied in back without too much hangin past the knot (been a hot summer).

Music stops a-playin and Zappo gets to talkin. The one thing that's
set is the title: "*Zoot*-Z-O-O-T—*Allures*—A-L-L-U-R-E-S," he hasta
spell it out exact cause us writers are known to sometimes get the
whole thing incorrect like once this pal of mine in Montreal got the
number of musicians in Mr. Z's troupe wrong in a review and Franco
called up the paper to complain. "I figure that anybody who can't
count who's standing on the stage probably wasn't there to review the
concert anyway, and since I know how you guys work that's probably
what happened. The Los Angeles *Times* did that to us twice when we
were first starting out. They sent somebody down to a couple of our
shows at the Shrine. The guy wrote that we had played this horrible
version of 'A Hard Day's Night' when in fact it was the first warmup
band—a group called Rain I think—that played that and the guy left
before we went on. We called the newspaper and mentioned it to em,
they said well yes the guy *had* left and didn't know what he was doin.
So I said send another guy down next time we're gonna play and they
did it again, y'know, same fuckup. So we got very annoyed and after
the second phone call the guy came and reviewed us at the Whiskey
when it was absolutely an *abysmal* show, everything was breaking,
wrong from the top to the bottom, and we got a *great* review. So that's
the way *that* industry works." Uh huh . . .

Okay, right, so what's the, uh, personnel on this new one gonna be?
"I'm playin guitar, keyboard, bass on some of the cuts, uh, drums is
Terry Bozio, there's a couple other bass players that're used, there's
Dave Parlatto and, uh, Patrick O'Hearn. There's other people doing
some background vocals." A departure for you in any noticeable way?
"It's a departure from *Bongo Fury* in that it's a studio album that definitely has more guitar playing on it than some other albums had. I
happen to like it very much, it's a well-produced studio album. I think
it shows the work." Took around three months to put together and it's
his own personal fave since *Lumpy Gravy*.

Subject matter on it? "Well, I can tell you the vocals that'll be in
there, there's one called 'Disco Boy' and there's another called 'Wonderful Wino,' there's one called 'The Torture Never Stops' and another one called 'Find Her Finer.'" The disco thing done in a disco
vein? "Actually it's sort of an anti-disco hit, it's done sort of bump-
kinized rather than disco." Aware of disco's existence then? "Oh yeah,
I *like* disco." I axe him about that biz of a few years back when he was
supposed to be listenin to all sorts of current popstuff just to check it
all out. "Yeah that was so when people ask you who's your favorite
group and what records you listen to I could have something to say

besides 'I don't listen to the radio'—which I still don't." Likes Queen these days tho and Gentle Giant.

Uh, ever think of directing yourself at a different audience? "There *isn't* any other audience, the only audience that matters is the one that's out there for the mainstream of, uh, pop music. Y'know, suppose I sit down and write a fantastic symphony, who's there to listen to it? Only the kids. I'm perfectly satisfied with the people who're listening now, I don't need to acquire an entourage of blue-haired ladies. That's all that's left over once you get into the classical branch. There's no reason why a kid who likes to bang his head on the edge of the stage cause he's so downed out he can't tell what he's doing shouldn't be able to enjoy things *other* than that, just a sidelight."

But was all that doggy wee-wee stuff of not too long ago an attempt to reach a *younger* crowd maybe? "No, I think that people of all ages can be appreciative of dog wee-wee and other forms of wee-wee and all sorts of physical byproducts. I think that it helps people to come to grips with the real world when they start thinking of those kind of byproducts. It's typical of these publications that they should be more interested in subjects like that than the rest of what's going on on my albums but if you wanna talk about wee-wee . . ." Uh, um, sorry sir, I was just . . . "The audiences at the concerts started to get younger not because of doggy wee-wee but because of, uh, we were getting radio exposure, on the AM." So you ain't actually *aiming* at the 11- and 12-year olds? "Gee I wish I could, they're pretty smart at that age." Okay that ought to do it—thank you, thank you, thank you Mr. Wazoo, I will not trouble Your Highness any longer, it's been swell!

MY INANE
CAREER

Introduction

Well here's your lucky day: I've decided to leave the lion's share of my *Voice* claptrap OUT.

Whut?!?!, you say? Isn't that the shit manymost people regard as the earliest evidence I'd finally gotten "serious"? Aren't there in fact gold stars alongside this garbage in my permanent record?

Um—that's certainly what you *hear*. I've never actually zine, excuse me, seen mine, but I tend to view such material as a BLIGHT upon that record (if one indeed exists).

Heresy!!!, you scream? Against the grain of standard freshman Meltzer Studies? Well, I tell you what—how 'bout we compromise? I'll just feed you fewer items from my FIRST *Village Voice* Period, as the delineation usually goes, consisting of all my music crap (for the *Voice* or otherwise) from August of '74, when I started writing for those pigs, until the heyday of Punk. (Punk Period *Voice* is another matter.)

Hey, I'm not saying this junk isn't "good"—it's veryveryvery good—but this is *my* guided tour, folks. On my tour the nose clips come OFF, and w/out clips lemme tell ya, this stuff smells like surrender: of my fire, my authority, my sense of the rightness of things *not* elevated to expedient culture-pedestals—talk about compromise! It most-all reads like I'm bucking for a career. (Did he say "yer ear"?)

Mannered . . . stilted . . . But let's back it up a notch. *Trying to get out.*

By spring-summer of '74 no more than half of what I wrote for publication was rockcrit. I did stories on things like chewing tobacco and porn films, wrestling. Some film reviews. I was midway through a 400-page sports rant, *The Outside Dope: A Fan's Eye View of Sport*, which as shitluck would have it never came out, but at this point I was still confident of getting out of rockcrit alive—and maybe soon.

The half that was rockcrit, meanwhile, felt like no more, no less than a lousy dead-end job, a hostile and farcical "position"—you'd've had to be a simp to call it a vocation. Of course I still threw my entire wad into it, utilized my full bag-o-tricks, but I'd certainly rather've deployed the tricks elsewhere. Running ever further out of original things to say—things I *wanted* to say—even *not*-about rock, just superimposed on its neutral cardboard face—I rued squandering what was left down at the same jive sweatshop, on the same old topical malarkey. My most lucrative employment, rockcrit or otherwise, was covering U.S. groups for a pair of slicks in Japan, but as everything hadda be super-easy to translate ("A. plays keyboards. B. is the bassist. Their songs are about cruelty"), it was also the most excruciating.

Then the fucking *Voice* called.

Ha. For seven years, going back to the Summer of Goddam Love, I'd been knock-knocking on their triple-bolted door, sounding out, chatting up, hitting on the likes of Robert Christgau and Richard Goldstein, whom between 'em I probably asked 30-40 times if I could possibly y'know FUCKING WRITE FOR THEM. Christgau especially I'd run into at press parties and I'd ask and he'd tell me, "You're not ready yet"—"Oh? So when will that be?"—"I'll let you know"— what a dogfucker.

Why I kept it up was, well, shit: three things. The *Voice* was hometown (so your friends might read you); pay was decent; it still seemed a "class venue," like the London Palladium in the old Lenny Bruce routine, though that's probably just how you feel when stodgy a-holes bar the door.

So after seven years, keeping it up just to keep it up, I get the call— door's open—and what the bleary hell do they want from me? Music crap.

Okay, do it—be a *pro*, goddammit—but in doing it . . . watch out. I didn't watch out.

The Occasion got the better of me.

Right off the bat, my writing got incrementally more mannered, more term-paper formal. Stiff? Stiff. (Everything but glib.) I repeated stylistic riffs not because that was the easy road, or 'cause I'd merely lost track, but because I wanted to be *known* for them, especially my manglings (and pseudo-manglings) of language. Whether the diminutive of *because*, for instance—or verb endings without the g— should have an apostrophe became an Important Expressive Issue. For the first time, I felt the need to grind my ax rather than simply wield it, stumping for pet propositions and themes, turning overnight into a standup ideologue . . . a fucking blowhard.

Reinforcing and compounding the travesty was the intimidating presence of Christgau at the other end of most assignments. For all his goofy cordiality, he was without doubt the most oppressive editor I've ever had, in the most piddling, petty, control-for-control-sake sorts of ways. As often as not, he demanded rewrites not because they were needed—textually, journalistically—but as stations of ritual abasement, meant to establish caste distinctions between editor and writer, to wring extraneous labor from momentarily idle hands. There were pieces where you had to fight for every word, to justify each word *use* as not only proper, "by the book," but palatable (to the nth) to *his* hambone sensibility, his hermetic aesthetic. Every premise not explicitly confirmed on paper had to be shown as confirm*able*, at least verbally, 'tween you and him (should Music Crit Court-in-the-Sky someday choose to take up the case).

After a while I sensed his specter eavesdropping on every syllable I wrote, considered, reconsidered or discarded, and lost all flow thinking up my defense for stuff before I was finished writing it. He would even pull stunts like peeling off those paper stick-ons people used (before computers) to type over a word or a line, peel it to see if he preferred what was underneath. I sometimes took the time to retype entire pages rather than endure the shit that might ensue if I left any such trails suggesting my own imperfection or indecision.

No matter how stilted and deformed my *Voice* writing got, I never managed to rise above secondary status. For the most part, Christgau treated *all* those he edited as secondary goods, though time and again I came as close as any to being sub-secondary: an untouchable. Which isn't to say he didn't in fact LIKE ME personally (strange duck that he was) and even to some extent professionally. It was just that when I stood within proximity of his precious tabloid—last bulwark of civilization as he wished to know it—the beacon light up on top couldn't help but reveal my sordid shadow i.d.: anti-intellectual trash! scum!— and a college graduate yet—akin to being a Commie or a junkie (or a rock and roller) in those dark, dark (oooh) Eisenhower '50s. Mutant riffraff, I was in the short run, long run, any run unfit for the roster of his "rockwriter establishment" . . . the odd man out of anything substantial in his editorial orbit . . . "the exception that proves the rule" (his ultimate put-down) on the wrong side of every controversy. Only in retrospect does my role become clear: as a vulgar exhibit in his proto-multiculture briefcase—proof before God and man of his infinite tolerance and patience. What a prig.

Richard Goldstein, on the other hand, who had once edited me at
Us, Bantam's paperback quarterly, regarded me (in my *Voice* incarnation) with even greater apprehension, ajudging me a dangerous "hip-
ster"—speaking of '50s riffraff—like some wild un-declawed gutter
beast. A mahoney from the gitgo, here was a guy who if you were playing word-association and said "Lowlife" he'd say "Frozen foods"—
he'd lived a sheltered life, see. (In '68 he told me he'd be *really* upset if
the Russians beat us to the moon—speaking of *us*.) I to him was *very*
lowlife, and he was too, too squeamish—which only made me lay it on
thicker. His forte as editor was to grumble about text but leave it completely alone, then slap a title on things that would make the mind
reel. A '77 feature of mine, "Arnold Schwarzenegger and the Mind-
Body Problem," thus became "This Hunk Is Not a Fruit" (before
Goldstein himself had left the closet). A mahoney and then some.

In my '88 essay collection, *L.A. Is the Capital of Kansas* (p. 2), I claim
shabby treatment by jerkingtons at the *Voice* as a third of the reason,
in the fall of '75, for my leaving New York, or more properly: that
these joiks were a third of what I *envisioned myself leaving*. I would now
put the ratio at no more than a fifth.

Blowhards, mahoneys, untouchables, dogfuckers, ducks . . . what a scene!

61

Elvis Exhumed! (excerpt)

There's no denying Christgau's approximate affection for me, some 30 years ago, nor his niggardly approbation. In a 1970 Village Voice *piece he called me "the Bob Cousy of the rock criticism game," as well as "a light-heavy-weight up-and-comer with some staying power and a lot of flashy moves," but that still didn't qualify me as "*Voice *material." What ultimately did, four years later, I now THEORIZE, was the publication of these four paragraphs (at the start of an Elvis concert preview) in a San Francisco biweekly two-three months before Mr. C finally pegged me as worthy to join the* Voice *fold.*

   In direct quotation I employ someone named "Robert Christgau" as a stand-in for myself, and my guess now is the real R.C. read it, didn't mind the ludicrous namedrop, or pick up on the ludicrousness, was in fact smugly flattered (believing it an homage), and figured hey, maybe Meltzer's time has come. If I hadn't written it—or if I'd used Ed McCormack's (or Tom Nolan's, or John Morthland's) name instead—maybe he'd NEVER have let me into his lousy paper, who knows? (When he gave me the call I didn't even make the connection, likely the piece had already slipped my mind—I did senseless name substitutions all the time.)

   But I wouldn't have used one of them, they had too much on the ball. I picked Christgau because he was the 3rd or 4th least rockin', least candid, and least colloquial writeperson I knew.

"Yeah I was this creepy little kid of eleven" sez a nostalgic Robert Christgau, slightly drunk (Chateauneuf-du-Pape 1969). "I was living in Rockaway and my parents never played anything but the original cast album of *Carousel* and the radio was never on except for weather in the morning, it was really shit. I didn't know what the fuck was comin' off, my favorite music was the theme from *Prince Valiant* starring Robert Wagner or somebody. I hated music, music was what they forced you to listen to in music appreciation class.

"Then it was the night before my first day in junior high. My family had moved and I didn't have any friends where we were living and I was 4-foot-7 with real ugly glasses and I was totally *lost*. Usually they would only let me stay up till about 8:00 the night before a schoolday but this time they let me stay up till 9:00, maybe I got out of the tub later than usual so I hadda be allowed to see *some* TV so maybe that was it. First time I ever saw Ed Sullivan and this guy named Elvis Presley was on, I never heard of him before. He was so fuckin' *amazing*. I had never seen anything remotely like it with the exception maybe of Kevin McCarthy at the end of *Invasion of the Body Snatchers*, he had the same madness in his eyes—it's the end of the world and there's almost this *glee* about it. With or without his hips moving Elvis's eyes said it all. He did 'Hound Dog' and 'Don't Be Cruel' and they had this big surrealist thing of a guitar up on the wall and he was just too much.

"It saved my life. He just, I mean like I was headed nowhere, all I wanted was to become a mad scientist and build some new kind of bomb or create monsters and he just saved my life, period. A few days later my mother was out buying a cha-cha record with a tango flip side cause she and my father went to dancing class at some elementary school and I went along to the store and insisted she let me get 'Hound Dog' and 'Don't Be Cruel' on the same single, I didn't even know they'd be together, the first 45 I ever bought. After that I played the radio all the time, checked out all the rock and roll stations I could find, discovered Fats Domino and Little Richard. 'Party Doll' was real big then. Gained complete control over sound in the house. And started picking out my own clothes instead of letting them buy it for me and stopped going to the barber and asking for a 'regular haircut' every time. Really changed my fuckin' life around . . ."

Thanks Bob, must've been tens of millions of kiddos like yourself from coast to coast and border to border, I oughta know cause I was one too. Why I remember each time Elvis was on Ed Sullivan (three big times in all) everybody in home room would go *nuts* reliving it the next morning. Usually we'd file in stoically with our hundred pounds of books ready for another day of torture but after an Elvis appearance there'd be a buzz that would continue way past the taking of attendance. The birth of revolutionary consciousness, more relevant to school-going city kids than *Blackboard Jungle*. The stupid teacher might even have seen the Pelvis herself the night before but most likely just missed the whole thing cause she really had no idea why on three apparently random Mondays there was all this commotion. Black kids, white kids, Puerto Ricans, *everybody* was uncontrollable, it was total anarchy.

62

Topical Bozo

My first Voice *piece. Does it read like I was nervous? I had less than 24 hours to deliver it, which would've been fine for* Zoo World—*I could've written* seven *reviews in that time—but the "monumentality" of the situation made me use every minute for just the one.*

For sure it's a two-drafter—at least—the beginning of an end which has proven grisly and endless (even this sentence *is multidraft)—two before turning it in, plus all the hoops Christgau ran me through after.*

Overwritten? You bet. But then again I was overprepared, or y'might say overrehearsed. The old shtick is laid on pretty thick—drumbeating all these cosmo-historical linkages—and old it is*, it* wasn't even *current b.s. I was showing off to my "new audience." There's something ungainly (ill-placed and -timed) about much of what I'm flaunting, which in a funny way reminds me of Glenn Gould, the young Bach speedster, assaying the Beethoven sonatas (at Columbia's behest, but mainly just to show he could), sacrificing speed and grace for bombast and not even pulling it off, slamming too many pistons into valves where they don't fucking fit. (For bombast, in my case, substitute* inflated relevance.*)*

But if we're gonna continue with the theory about Christgau and the Elvis piece, why if he was finally gonna use me did he wait two-three months? My guess: there wasn't much country coming through New York back then, and it was that long before the first country act hit town. He knew I listened to that shit, me, Tosches and not too many rockwritin' others, and assigning it to me (and not long afterwards, Nick) was an expedient way of getting that odious task taken care of. So it could be said his paper covered it all. That's my guess.

During his tenure as summer replacement for the Smothers Brothers back in '68 or thereabouts Glen Campbell one Sunday eve introduced a veritable unknown named Waylon Jennings to a national tv audience, introduced him as "an example of the new breed of country singers," seemingly a pack of amiable saps since (stated Glen) it also included series regular John Hartford, a known wimp. From his first moment on camera tho this Waylon person came off as anything but innocuous, especially with his hair standing firmly & shinily as without doubt the most *magnificent head thereof in the history of the biz*—going back even to the original pre-movies Elvis (true). Something more-than-one-dimensionally ornery about the gentleman too and in a mod-rin vein, kind of like Richard Harris in "This Sporting Life." (Mark this buzzard a definite prospect!)

Time marches on and here comes the Waylon Jennings of TODAY taking the stage at the Bottom Line, fame & fortune more or less assured and primal tough-motherness basically intact. He's definitely honed his act a bit and become more affable and less threatening but his utterly viable presence hasn't suffered an iota in the process, hoots of neo-cowpoop approval greeting his every word and gesture. As little in the way of posturing as you're likely to see meanwhile, and with so little of either the affected acridness of Willie Nelson or (on the other side of country's crypto-macho coin) the oh-so-sensitive papfulness of Kristofferson in evidence (except for a lyric or two and a man's gotta get 'em from somewhere!) it would seem that WJ now stands at the TOP of the topical bozo heap.

Startling however is the total change in the Texan's foliage, ordinary de rigueur hippie moptop a la Canned Heat '68 (accompanied by mustache-goatee combo a la ditto) having replaced those noble grease-sculpted locks of yore. Leather over blue pseudo-workshirt and plain black jeans (standard-issue country tinsel on the Campbell show). And a band that actually seems dedicated to collectivity, non-superficiality and *higher bass levels than country's ever seen* (just him and his acoustic on Campbell)! Hmm, looks suspiciously like he's gettin' his shit together via one hot non-sentimental journey several years backward far as the pop world at large is concerned, back to some official archetypal roots proclaimed as such by the late lamented San Francisco Rock Company, Inc., rallying his socio-musical totality at a starting point in yesteryear in a manner not so diff from those early-'60s limeys who took '50s r&r&b as their stack of first principles.

Interesting sidelight is Waylon just happened to *be there* participating in the '50s firsthand as one of Buddy Holly's Crickets and San Fran surely wasn't *prior* to his experience, merely (regrettably) foreign enough to it at the time for him to be going at it now with an earnestness unseen since either of Eric Burdon's first two crusades. Kind of thing in this day & age which could easily make you puke in any context other than hickmusic (Dion and Bobby Darin didn't get away with it for more than a minute) and not there either if the extra-musical imperatives of your move are too naked, too casual. Lucky for Waylon he's suddenly as credible as they come within either c&w or r&r (put him in the movies!), he's already a good candidate in both the Hank Williams and Jim Morrison apocalypse sweepstakes, lucky him. . . .

Blah blah blah and you know what? He stands a better chance of becoming the *Kerouac of the performing arts* than any of the hippie musicos ever managed!

Finale at the Bottom Line: the Allmans' "Midnight Rider"—Nashville '74 equivalent of Jose Feliciano doin "Light My Fire"!!!

63

Meltzer at the Met

My first Voice *piece for Goldstein, and he didn't even get me a ticket. I bluffed my way into standing room, rushed home after the first act and reverted to quick-write mode—it was due in two hours. 'S a total coincidence it's Verdi and so was my previous take on classical music—*Rigoletto, *for* Zoo World—*I'm sure at the time I didn't think anything of it.*

The following week, on the letters page, Leighton Kerner, the paper's regular classical guy, called me a "cockroach" and said, "The next time Meltzer gets that close to my music column, I'm reaching for the Flit gun." Which made me feel like a million bucks—job well done!—the brightest ray of sunshine in my first year at the Voice.

Everybody and his banker was there for opening night at the Met. A real Eyetalian opera by Verdi, "I Vespri Siciliani" (something about Sicily no doubt). Everybody but Jacqueline Fitzgerald Onassis but maybe she was busy soothing her ex-brother-in-law's brow (day Teddy decided he *wouldn't*). Plenty of other filthy richers tho, wearing their form-fitting rich people duds. Millions of unrented tuxes and bowties and this broad in a rhinestone (diamond?) backless sort of gown type thing w/matching head whatsit and custom-looking lashes out to here. Really looked alien and grotesque and all sorts of things like that but then again opera's always been a means for the gotrocks clan to go sublimely weirdo. Manic moneybagsers in pink ruffled (stuffed) shirts with their nutso Beethoven faces that they'd hafta rub off for tomorrow's board meeting or a polite afternoon on the yacht. No cleavage whatsoever (tres gauche apparently) and only one top hat (ditto). One male turtleneck on a mere upper middle-classer (Johnny Carson hasn't worn one in months).

Not much sign of any of the old shoemaker folk who used to line up for tickets three years in advance and end up on the $64,000 Question. Only individual of obvious papal descent in fact was this gent doin a mod imitation of Peter Falk playing Columbo. No cigar on his lip tho and the one I happened to be puffin on caused an old bejeweled seahag nearby to pull a real cornball *cough-cough* routine. Lotta ashtrays all around which musta been for put-out purposes only cause nobody was even smokin cigareets (don't wanna risk burning garments).

As far as famous creeps went it was hard to distinguish em from the rest of the unsurly mob, y'know like they don't wear nametags (expect you to identify em). Was that Paul O'Dwyer? Naw—no eyebrows. And how about that one, Richard Tucker? Saw him on Joe Franklin but that was last week so can't be sure it was him. One photog guy axed another who a certain couple was the former'd just snapped. Turned out to be Anna Moffo and Sarnoff. David Sarnoff? Dunno. Guy who identified em even supplied the snapper with an address and phone from his primordial bizness memory—so he could sell em a blowup for a good piece-o-change.

Sneaked inside past the thousand-foot Chagall and the mod-rin chandeliers like 3-D snowflakes and snatched me a spot in the standing room section. This geezer outside in a grey cowboy hat name of Monty had been sellin ducats at face value to those without but he got rather churlish when some joker asked for a standee ("Even standing room is at a premium, you're a damn kid and a dope and I won't put up with you, I'm 72 years old"—end of sentence) so I knew I'd hafta protect my footspace with my feet, certainly wasn't willing to with my life.

There was this dog of a short-lived Buddy Hackett series in 1956 (lasted about a month) where he loses some cultured gangster's ticket and saves his own life by convincing him the *real* opera fan doesn't mind standing, "he stands, that's where he sits." With that in mind I looked and listened around for some realies and overheard a mini-conversation about Cristina Deutekom the evening's prima donna. Was pleased as punch to hear "she starts a little shaky but once she gets warmed up no one can hit above C as well as she and Sutherland."

Curtain went up after the Star Spangled Banner (guy next to me sang along cause after all it is pretty fucking operatic) and Ms. Doodycum turned out to be just that, another shallow insipid variation on the whole Kate Smith-Joan Baez bellow scene (true). Nobody in my vicinity seemed all that inspired by her shrill swill or anybody else's for that matter and yet they refused to miss a note of it. Real pindrop conditions and somebody rattling keys was told "Stop rattling those keys" and another somebody really worked overtime slowing down a fart (also true). Topper of the first act was when those offenders in the audience who applauded at the *wrong time* quickly corrected their error in time to never do it again (millionaires and their ilk love rules even if they ain't their own and fall in line toot sweet).

Intermission and the first sound out of anybody was "Those costumes were awful" (thought so myself), followed by "No excitement" (said that already). Left (would've sooner if the exits hadn't been roped off: an effin fire hazard) wondering why the hell hoarders of wealth choose such worthless tedious dull dead crap for their entertainment pleasure, like why not just watch gold being mined? Some possible answers: 1. *operatic* noise is the most sanctioned form thereof and noise is something everybody likes an occasional dose of; 2. this stuff is downright *grave*, something they're only a step or two out of anyway; 3. the foreign language angle offers em a quicker trip to Europe (money's no object but time can't always be spared).

Do taxes support this dootz, even 1% of it?

64
Fear and Languor at
Lake Tahoe (excerpt)

My first Voice *article after moving to California was a 3500-word feature on Alice Cooper's one-nighter at the Sahara Tahoe, a trial balloon for contempo-rock at casinos (it flopped). Because of a snowstorm, my return got delayed half a day, which coupled with the fact that Christgau wouldn't sit on it a week (claiming it was a priority* news *piece) and the three hours I lost due to the time difference—do I complain too much?—forced me to stay up ALL NIGHT writing it, then phone it in word by word to some chump in New York who didn't even have time to read it back to me, resulting in my copy being BUTCHERED. Out of the whole mess as published, this paragraph is the only unit clump that reads like I might actually have written it (no manuscript version survives).*

Okay, so the show turns out to be (don't tell me you didn't guess!) bland with a very small b. That stupid cyclops that even on TV looked stupider than the cheaper incarnations of Godzilla. Dancing gargoyles with faces like James Brown, tophatted skeletons with canes for cocks, a stuffed fake broad who Alice drags across the stage by her fake-blond hair (same stage 's'matter of fact where Ali kayoed a live Bob Foster), coffins that don't look like coffins with hands coming out of em, Danny Kaye references galore, y'know world-of-theater type shit. No more impressive than "Romeo & Juliet" at Hofstra University. I mean like you'd at least *hafta* expect maybe a *pint* of blood or something red during "Only Women Bleed," right? Not a goddam *drop* tho in Aunt Alice's nightmare, wonder what Freud'd say about that.

65

Redd Foxx Gets off the Pot

Another year, another lounge act . . .
*A story an eyewitness told me: Goldstein didn't edit this, but when it came
out he found it revolting. Running 'round the office in search of Jamaica
Kincaid, in a frantic rush to keep her from reading it (believing as he did
that it would grievously offend and perhaps* destroy *her), he finally found
Jamaica, who before he could alert her asked, "Have you seen the Redd Foxx
review? It's the best piece the* Voice *has run on black culture by anyone besides me." Was he mortified!*

GOLDSTEIN: Usually people point to his Sgt. Pepper *review as the
moment he got his scarlet T, for turkey. He* panned *the record, dig, at precisely the instant when everybody was getting rather off on it. In recent
times, certain revisionists and cynics have not only forgiven him, but consider
him to have been* right—*what a joke. The piece that told* me *what a ninny
he was was his review of the second Doors album, in which he alleged that
the ONE THING we'd come to think when we thought Doors was strangely
absent from the pressing:* guitar. *Guitar? That's the one thing? And it's absent? Like what about "My Eyes Have Seen You"? "Love Me Two Times"?
And if "When the Music's Over" is a little guitar-skimpy, so, um, WHAT?
Pshaw . . .*

The great singer-comedian David Roter (who will someday get the
recognition he sure ain't gettin conducting church rap sessions on
contemporary dating etiquette) was once walkin down Bleecker St.
readin the NY Post and payin no attention to where he was goin
when he walked right into a head-high protruding air conditioner,
falling to the pavement in PAIN for his efforts. Across the street an
Afroamercian window washer cracked up and pointed at poor David
for all to see, prompting Davey to spontaneously *almost* come back

with "What're you laughin at? Your face is the color of shit!" He had the presence of mind to keep the great line to himself (*isn't* it a great line tho, huh?) but in any event that's gotta be one of the *very few* applications of the word *shit* (i.e. the resemblance its color bears to Afro-Am pigmentation) not brought into play by Redd Foxx on his current "You Gotta Wash Your Ass" live elpee, his first in 12 whole years.

Point is Lord knows Redd uses the word *nigger* thereon in enough of its proto–Amos 'n' Andy ramifications to certainly be *amenable* to such a usage of the old scatological standby, probably it's just escaped him so far and if he reads this review (Dear Atlantic publicity person: Show it to him!) next time he takes to the Apollo stage he'll have a newie to recite in righteous pursuit of the cosmic giggle. *Damn* biting in an honest Swiftian way on the subject of human ugliness including black (his comments on Shirley Chisholm's medusa mug ain't likely to get her to vote for him if he ever tosses his toup in the ring) (but he *does* admit that "Mrs. Roosevelt will always be #1 . . . champion . . . that's an *ugly* woman") but getting back to bowel droppings per se he's really got the subject covered. The fact that St. Bernards don't doo-doo, they *shit* . . . the epistemology of breaking wind versus poopin outright in terms of one has lumps and the other don't . . . an exposition of the etymological rootings of the word *funky* in Redd's St. Louis neck of the woods, namely the raunchy aroma of grandpa's long johns with "the nicotine stain in the back" . . . etc., etc.

Point is he's got this all reet old fashioned offensive mere dirty (as opposed to sexy or erotic) joke routine that's as funny as it gets and in that regard he beats poor scapegoat Lenny Bruce to—pardon the pun—SHIT: clearcut distinction between more-than-incidental prurient *art*-if-that's-the-word-you-want and mere references to same cause Redd's as tuned into systematic filth *as it ever gets* yet he's still as stodgy and Victorian about certain aspects of the whole whatsis as Bob Hope and maybe that's what it's all about anyway: arbitrariness. Basically he's still got a goddam silly notion of the hygiene-cum-aesthetics of it all, namely that an asshole's not the nicest place to plant your face. He thinks a cow's nothing but a "big snotty nose and dirty tits" yet is willing to "clean up the dirty tits." But in the title gag he's advising lovers to scrub their anus before bedtime cause if soixante-neuf's on the agenda "it ain't but a inch away." This in the face of remark upon remark about the veritable *necessity* of lickin that slit (to hecklers for inst at various stages of his monologue: "Rest your lips cause you got a busy night tonight"; "I hope you get lockjaw at the motel, *that'll* mess up your sex affair"): the man ain't never licked a female butthole! (Tastes rather like beef Redd and the texture sure beats sushi!) Crazy pops!

66
No Waylon, No Willie, No Goat

*Arguably my best country piece. For the time being, local L.A. music didn't
piss me off.*
   *Goat turned out to be David "Goat" Carson, hellion brother of screen-
writer Kit Carson and painter Neke Carson. After getting the write-up, he
pestered me for more f'r another four-five years. I've never been sure, but he
might've fucked my girlfriend Marsha.*

"We're *loaded* with perverts tonight," announces pot-bellied,
besweatered Harry Newman of KLAC, the spotlight accenting molelike nose growths like you sometimes see in paintings of obscure Italian nobles by long-dead, too-honest bozos with a brush. Another
weekly talent showcase at North Hollywood's Palomino Club is about
to unwind: all the pathos and bathos that Thursdays up Lankershim
way have been entailing for the past 17 years; beehives and bandanas
from Simi to San Dimas pouring their hearts and lungs out for the
$100.00 grand prize.

   Some slight interference tonight: simultaneous doings (and undo-
ings) across town at the Academy of Country Music Awards fandango
will be vying for relevance with the contestants' valiant, mournful
look-at-me. No big deal when Harry reveals that (1) he's failed to win
deejay of the year honors "for the seventh year in a row" and (2) Billy
(not *the*) Graham, fiddler tonight in the makeshift band required to
back up all the wide-eyed amateurs, has copped *bassplayer* of the annum kudos, but the proclamation that "Waylon Jennings will be here
after the awards with his lovely wife Willie Nelson" *just might be con-
strued* as willfully detracting from the urgency and poignancy of high-
school opener Laurie Canterman's brace-faced rendition of the Linda
Ronstadt version of the Everly Brothers' "When Will I Be Loved?"

Yes, Linda's gotta be the number one source this evening, with Karen Blair in her white-flowered Mama Cass sarong contributing "Love Has No Pride" and Jody Chelik in red and black (a Stendhal fan?) getting her 2 cents in with "You're No Good." But Ray Price is also drawn from (earringed Gino Vanelli lookalike Jamie Wayne with "Crazy Arms"), as are Jeannie Sealy (Joanne Alexander, her features as psychically maimed as one ever gets to see on a *nightclub stage*, eyebrows narrow, lips too cold to kiss ice cream, lending a dash of hard meaning to "Don't Touch Me"), Kris Kristofferson (balding, workgarbed Chuck Schaefer stalling through the final chorus of "Help Me Make It Through the Night" until Harry orders his hippie butt off stage *pronto*: "maximum of four minutes per act"), "Teenager in Love" (sloppy/slobby David Caleb, T-shirt sticking out from under his bland beige "business" shirt) and even "Abraham, Martin and John" (former winner Scott "T," Troy Donahue-like in the white three-piece leisure suit chances are he squandered his previous winnings on at C & R Clothiers, struggling to find his groove *a cappella*) . . .

Then of course there are those who'd rather *write their own* (just as crucial as *rolling* your own): Michael E. Strain (dull-sheened western shirt with an "I've had my troubles" tune the band can't follow nohow), Chuck Curtis from San Juan Capistrano (immaculate work duds; reverent lyric about Hawaii), Connie Birdwell (long skirt, flirty, eyes way too big for her face; a "town we were born in" item that falls on dead, deaf ears), Steve Shannon ("no stranger to the Palomino," your perennial loser, "Some Man Will Never Know," a title and everything: stoic with a soft center of stale, mushy cornflakes), etc., etc.—*many* etceteras.

And lest we forget our fine not-yet-employed country *comics*: Tiny Brooks ("three hundred pounds of rompin'-stompin' love"—more like three-fifty—her jokes what you might call, um, *racy*), Lee Coleman (black, "I'm a nigger impressionist," a George Wallace routine drawing hoots of "Three cheers for George!") and the "aptly named" L.A. Knockers (five "country sluts" in dancehall scanties, "I screwed more cowboys than I can count," Harry Newman becomes *unglued*) . . . yawn.

Talent, talent *galore* you'd have to admit. But nothing to *compare* with the awesome artistry of this gent Harry welcomes right after he's called attention to a post-awards Mel Tillis and Tom T. Hall entering the men's john together: cat name of *Goat*. Goat! Wild! Shades of Peter Wolf! The blues! In black! Scruffy beard! Boots to his knees! Grungy! Scuzzy! Out on the dance floor! "Gun at my side" inane lyrics! Crawls on the floorboards! Clucks like a chicken! Insults the band! Shoves his mike in audience mouths: "Testify!" Go go Goat!

Looks like a man a hundred bucks richer *for sure* but before the results are tabulated there's time for Messrs. Hall and Tillis to strut forth their *professional* variety of eternal country verity but funny 'cause Tom—seriousness ringing his cowlike phiz—*ain't really no better* than a good two-thirds of the amateurs (true). Steve Shannon for random instance could easily have outdone Thomas's unstirring, lacklustre "Clayton Delaney" with rolled up napkins up his snoot (I wouldn't lie to ya, Steve, keep up the blah blah etc.). Melvin though, his famed stutters and stammers working overtime, is simply *ace*: "I didn't expect to get up and sing—this is my *night out*. I've had too much to drink, I'm like Don Ameche." Spotting the bulbous Tiny Brooks down front: "I *like* you, who are you?" Tiny: "Moby Dick." Mel, quick with a *good'un*: "You're the only g-girl I know where I could run through two inches of hair and two inches of fat and run out of d-dick . . . is it okay to say 'dick'? There goes my image, baby!" Don't worry Mel, your image is safe with us patrons of the "Pal"!

Okay, down to six finalists and Goat is among them, lookin' good. Shouts of "Goat! Goat!"—lookin' better. Runner-up ($50) is named: David Gross (ponytail and straw hat, sang "I Can't Stop Loving You"), at least they're not denying Goat his full hunnert smackers. FIRST PRIZE: John (whuh?) Anderson (huh?), yoyo who did Waylon and Willie's "Good Hearted Woman" and reminded this word jockey *strongly* of the guy who used to sing for NRBQ (i.e., a goddam *pro!*). We wanna recount! At least an applause meter!

And—hey!—where're Waylon and Willie for cryin' out loud?!

Sheee . . . (gal's room has a Li'l Legs pantyhose dispenser though).

67

Excellent Panties in Nesmith's *The Prison*

THEN it pissed me.

If that's what you call 'em. Y'know 'cause they kinda stretched up past the butt and crotch to the belly and beyond—but for sure there was plenty-o-garment visible about the groin. In such provocative colors as black and grey (*real* good grey). Worn about the procreative area of Katherine Warner as Marie. Also about Carolyn Hauser as Janey's organ region as well, altho the first few times she got danced around by the skinnyboy she was paired with YOU DID NOT SEE MUCH. Guy didn't lift her high enough. Next time was okay tho, and the fine outline of her pudding was revealed.

Setting for all this clothed-privates excitement was opening night of ex-Monkee Michael Nesmith's *The Prison*. "Concert/Rock Ballet" read the program and indeed it was. A band of 6- and 4-stringers picked away at stage left amid potted flowers and ferns (nature in the raw) while Mikey narrated and dancers mimed the brazenly lysergic theme: liberation of the human whatsis from its self-imposed bonds. The mind reels to think that this same Mr. Nesmith once picked & sang for the most heinous anti-psychedelic out-of-sync-with-the-rest-of-'67 beat combo in all of phonus balonus L.A. As mentioned, the fleurs in pottery were real.

Anyway, Nesmo's narrating this thing about how, well, you're in this prison, see, but it's of your own devise (theme borrowed from the late Jim Morrison) and all you gotta do's step thru this hole, um, into the void. The void'll bother you for one whole night (soft soil underfoot) but by morning there's clover and purple skies and a cabin with Janey and her stringbean dancer as your guides. They guide you back to the original hoosegaw and tell you all y'gotta do's remember the walls are false (memory's the key). So the guy goes back (name's Jason, he wants some womanlove, which as fate has it this particular jail's just *lousy* with) and, sez Michael, "The thought at first gave him courage to resist the sense input he was getting" (*damn* good way of puttin' it) till eventually he forgets and starts seein' walls and bars again, his subsequent panic necessitating act number two . . .

Is it still intermission? No, it is not. The belly dancer is part of the show. As are the oud (oud?) and tabla players, one of each. They're playing, she's dancing and sweating, this goes on and on when on walks—could it be??—Jason in street clothes. The guy who played Jason has returned! To hassle the belly, oud, tabla AND the audience! A taste of PIRANDELLO and act the 2nd is underway . . .

Capsule summary of this amazing, incredible, outasite act: lots more dancing, picking, plants and narration. Lots more slips-o-tongue than first half too (gettin' more comfy and casual by the minute), but Mike's tongue work on the tricky w-h's—all the whys, wheres, whats, whens, whiches and whencefors—remained *solid*. Also real good: a film strip, *Cycles*, featuring forest fires, atomic nuclei, sky, skydivers, red, blue, yellow and white. And orange. Ultimate message: no space, no time—they don't "exist"—love is all.

Only two misgivings about the whole two and one-half hour *thing*. (1) Why no horses on stage? (2) Old "fogey" in act one moves his feet too fast for a fogey with a cane. But blame that on the foot coach—not on fogeyplayer Dan Orsborn or his feet.

TWO is not a bad number at all. Six or seven mighta been but two is just jake.

68

Delbert McClinton:
Genuine Cowhide

And one of my last *country pieces. Apparently, by the end of '76, I was as used up on country, on* reviewing *country, as I'd more than once been used up on rock. My impatience with myself over my inability to GET OUT is bubbling over, it's all over the stove. Like why am I still (s t i l l) (STILL) writing about* any *of this???*

The angst . . . the ennui . . . oof *(like a punch in the gut) . . . situation deteriorating FAST.*

What I wanna know is where the hell is Billy Swan's name on the cover? Don't see it *nowhere*. All I see is that from the looks-o-things somebody hasn't gotten his dogbone wet in a *year* of Sundays ('cepting maybe at shower-time or naked in a rainstorm or a beer mighta got spilt on him at a party) 'cause that there impression of a scumbag (YES, THAT'S WHAT ME AND MY PEOPLE USED TO CALL 'EM WAY BACK WHEN AND STILL DO 'cause in my numerous travels I have found that some folks actually call 'em weird stuff like "rubbers" and "condoms" and even "prophylactics" when in actuality they're just talkin' about everyday garden variety *scumbags*) on the outside of the wallet must've taken at least 10-11 months to work its way through the genuine cowhide if that's what it really is 'cause I've had one in my own wallet since last Xmas ("just in case"—haven't needed it yet tho, 'cause nowadays women have a system or two of their own so you don't even need a wallet to carry) so I oughta know (not sure if mine is cowhide tho, so I could be wrong).

Anyway, there's not a single dang mention of Billy Swan, who in actuality is really doin' all the singin', on the cover unless I am very much mistaken but, hmm, let's see, there's *lots*a names and everything on the sleeve—too many to sift thru for the likes of me (a very poor reader: I'VE ONLY READ 20-25 BOOKS IN MY ENTIRE LIFE THAT I DIDN'T HAFTA FOR EITHER SCHOOL OR RE-VIEWS) so in lieu of hurting my eyes I guess I ain't really got much of a case for the B. Swan claim, so I'll just retract it here and now and get down to reviewing this real good elpee of oldies or whatever they are that's without doubt the second best long player of the entire annum ('76, that is—y'never know when these things'll be getting printed up), second only to Cledus Maggard's *The White Knight* (Mercury).

Yeah, this album is real good (*real* good) but y'know, it ain't exactly gonna be the easiest thing in the world to tell ya all the whys-'n'-wherefores of exactly why the hell I should be makin' such an outrageous claim 'cause, well, I just went to the closet and counted up all the rec revs I've ever wrote and lemme tell ya, I ain't lyin' when I say that this is the 2384th album writeup I have been employed to script so, well, how the hell much do I got left to say about wax and music and even covers that I ain't said at least 932 times already if not 2383? Really hate to repeat myself so I'll just avoid the standard usual pap like "it sure beats heck outa South Side Johnny's attempt at same" (military metaphor), "contains a better version of 'Let the Good Times Roll' than Johnny & Edgar Winter" (mere comparison), "my real good pal Mr. Nick Tosches is real good pals with Mr. McClinton and I'll take his word for it" (nepotism) and "it sure does *rock out*" (pleasure principle) and just tell ya which cuts I like the best: all of 'em (*said* it was a good'un!).

All I wanna know is how come it's us overworked veterans of the write game who gotta keep plunkin' out these reviews and not the musicians themselves (a thankless lot) and what I also wanna know's in thanx for all we've done for 'em over the years so far when the heck're they gonna start at least doin' songs about *us* (a fair trade) if not a whole entire "concept" LP now and then (like f'rinstance *Billy Altman Is Cookin' Out, Daddy* by John Mayall or *Richard C. Walls: God's Gift to the State of Michigan* by Uriah Heep), just somethin' I'd like to *know*, y'know?

Note to ABC: that line about "second best in '76" may be quoted as much as you like ('cause it's true).

69

Dolphy Was Some "Weird" Cat

So why don't I write about something I really and truly CARE ABOUT,
care about enough that it's worth doing W/OUT irony? To bare my critical
soul probing something I love: wouldn't that be nice? Something which fur-
thermore, and better yet, could be addressed to a specific *readership, one I*
could get behind sharing my insights with, performing a righteous critical
service for . . . izzat possible?

Well, hmm, let's see . . . maybe some JAZZ. Which damnsure has been in
my blood, come to think of it, lurking in the wings since day one of this, uh,
musicwriterly undertaking, awaiting only an auspicious occasion. And
whaddaya know—ain't we lucky?—here's an Eric Dolphy reissue . . . great.
I bet this could work with—man oh man: PUNK-ROCK is happening! I
could pitch it to these kids a smidge younger than myself (I'm 32) who could
maybe use it as their entry point to jazz, which somehow 'til now they've
managed to miss. A common ground between jazz and punk, wow; who
could ask for anything more?

So I clear it with Christgau and write up this saxophone guy as close to be-
ing sacred as anyone in my own jazz temple; I deal with him sacredly, wor-
shipfully, ecstatically, *celebrating what I take to be his unique sonic bent.*
Editing the piece, Christgau busts my hump no more than usual, then after
it runs this pigfucker I've had no previous truck with lunges out of the
scenery, stomps up and down, screaming like I've just shit in Dolphy's tomb.

Hogs defer to bigger hogs—the natural oinking order—and Gary Giddins
was a bigger hog than Christgau and Goldstein put together. Christgau, for
one, kissed his royal Irish ass. From the cushy throne of his Voice *column,*
Weather Bird, *Giddins issued decrees proclaiming select musics and musi-*
cians *his jurisdiction, his jazzcritical fief. A testy swine who raised the roof*
when Ry Cooder dared to appropriate the word—the word!—"Jazz" as title
for an LP containing none, he slammed Round Midnight, *a mere fiction*
film, for being too cut-&-paste with jazz history, only to then
herald/hype/cheerlead a truly vile bio-pic, Bird, *as loathsome a begetter of*
outright LIES as The Benny Goodman Story *or that Cole Porter pic,*
Night and Day. *Producer/annotator of the Charlie Parker/*One Night in

Birdland *album, he's also the know-it-all who bought, and sold to the world,
Dan Morgenstern's mis-ID of Little Jimmy Scott as Chubby Newsome.*

*So anyway Giddins writes Christgau a three-page letter, single spaced,
LIVID with objections to my piece, things like "suggesting that they were after noise, he denies their intentionality and design as artists" (bullshit—I'm*
extolling *their i. and d.!) and "The reason his weird notes sound weird is
that they were used so judiciously" (sez fucking* who?*), concluding with the
remark that my jazz writing "has about as much thought and substance as
Rex Reed's, though the prose is jauntier." To which Christgau, who's thinking now he didn't bust my hump* enough *this time, adds his own two pages,
tut-tutting me with comments like "Nowhere in your piece do you say this is*
all *that Dolphy was doing. But you certainly imply something like that,
quite deliberately, with your tone" (please, would somebody* shoot *that
tone?).*

*Even Goldstein hadn't asked me to answer Leighton Kerner. Christgau,
however, insisted I respond to Giddins, point by bloody point, or never work
for his asswipe of a sheet again. Which I ended up doing because I, well—I
am a whore like the rest—deemed the* Voice *essential to my so-called career.*

*But hey. HEY! This was stuff I knew like the back of my hand; knew as
extensively in my way as Giddins (quite possibly) knew in his. In reaching
for the words, the sonic references, to adequately discuss MY knowing of Dolphy, most likely I was* overreaching*—is there any other way to reach? Kick
me if I got any of it "wrong." If we talk about art like polite little ladies and
gentlemen, one approved baby step at a time, we not only DEMEAN art—
by treating it like a bowl of cereal—but waste our allotted breath and time
and fluids. Better hamsters should enjoy such business than us.*

Anyway, YOU read it, you can be the judge . . .

Four-five years ago I was sitting in the Riviera with Murray Krugman
who wanted to know what Eric Dolphy sounded like, lotsa people
knew the name by then and he just wanted to know. So I tell him the
guy would make his appearance after like twunny-nine minutes of
Coltrane spewing out classic sheets of sound on soprano and just *jump
the hell in* with a couple minutes maybe of PARODY ON SWING
ERA CLICHES. I'm not finished but this eavesdropping limey
waiter we're stuck with leaps into the fucking conversation and tells
us "I've played with Elvin and lemme just tell you Dolphy was a genius." Refused to serve me my chiliburger.

Point is there's all these apparent PEJORATIVES that make self-appointed genius-watchers turn purple cause they're stuck thinking of the whole thing in terms of GOOD MUSIC & NOTHING BUT. These assflames've obviously never caught the import of rock-roll's biggest gift to mankind, the fact that it (as more-than-form) re-verses/collapses good/bad/etc. dichotomies/polarities *in its sleep.* Any-way Dolphy was a more-than-master who could see beyond all the conventional "good music" palaver and had the sense to go "slum-ming" (not a bad thing at all) in search of the raw materials for trans-musical advancement, and he had a fucking *cosmic* sense of humor to boot. He could dig playing Joseph Cotten to Coltrane's Orson Welles cause he knew that in many ways it was Cotten who made all those stoopid "art films" tick, y'know?

And like there's this Charlie Parker review a while back wherein the claim is made that Bird foreshadowed Ornette in that the former was "one of the first to recognize that jazz timbre would have to be recon-sidered, just as he was prescient in feeling the pinch of harmonic im-prisonment." Fucking EUPHEMISMS, daddy, cause what we're talking about here is the revolt into NOISE pure & simple, y'know the move to instrumental *sounds* that were not so fucking musical at all anymore because music per se could no longer contain either the human emotional RANGE or the human desire to transcend the in-strument as an embodiment of tedious fucking sonic RULES (imag-ined or otherwise). The Bird of the '50s played noise and Ornette played and still plays noise and Dolphy most assuredly played *noise.* I mean is the term that hard to take?

Anyway there's this new Dolphy reissue twofer, *Status* (Prestige), that's as good a way as any to demonstrate from scratch a lot of what Eric the unfearing-of-pejoratives was all about. First there's that god-dam WEIRD SOUND (cause it is) that permeates everything he ever did on both alto (take "Miss Ann" for example) and bass clarinet ("God Bless the Child"), the latter itself a harbinger of all WEIRD INSTRUMENTATION to come. Like while Ornette has always been plenty able to get more-than-strange EFFECTS out of his horn Eric's approach was to *start with* a sonic concept that'd always have that sort of aural impact, note-in note-out. In this regard Eric stands alone as an across-the-board "timbral" archetype for virtually every-thing that's happened jazzwise since his death. He was also a lot more playful with his sources than Ornette's ever been, a sort of one-man Mingus band with a total-recall jazz-nostalgic reference system fully internalized and just *dig* some of these sources, like *tell me* "The Way

You Look Tonight" isn't RIPE with angular ripoffs of the whole Zoot Sims-Stan Getz-Paul Desmond school of dumbass whiteness (at times it's so thick the only contemporary parody-on-whitey analogue would hafta be Richard Pryor).

Then you get stuff like the way be lets notes run into each other just to set up OBSTACLES FOR HIMSELF like on "Status Seeking" where he's evidently *in the market* for interference problems that Ornette or Bird—who ya gotta admit're his technical superiors rhythmically at least—would never need to encounter: more functionally adventuresome with his LIMITATIONS than you usually get to see, and without doubt on-the-edge "experimental" in the pejorative sense *Down Beat* useta use to put down anything "progressive."

"Laura": watch the way HE destroys a standard (anti-euphemism for uncovering its escape tunnel to the universal music-stream). Bird ("I'm in the Mood for Love") would fuck with the chord structure writ large. Ornette ("My Embraceable You") would just arrange it to sound harmonically ridiculous. Eric plays completely around it like it wasn't there and then reduces it all to a goddam PLAYING OF SCALES, something Braxton was later to elevate to the level of raw meat but Eric was there a decade-plus before.

And for diversion (ha!) there's his straight-ahead use of that throwaway piece of metal called the flute on stuff like "April Fool," I mean who the hell else but Roland Kirk before he was Rahsaan ever played it worth a damn? Prince Lasha maybe but that only makes three. Even the Blues Project ("Flute Thing") knew it was just a diversion, an ultra-"listenable" flavor of filler . . . The guy knew what he was doin!

70

Patti Smith: *Radio Ethiopia*

Back to rock and fucking roll . . . you mind? (Or: When in doubt, or in need of attention, try a barefaced play of the "celebrity" card.)

At the point I wrote this I knew Patti Smith six or seven years. The day after Jim Morrison died we sat around in our underwear drinking 151 rum, playing Morrison Hotel *and* L.A. Woman. *We were buddies. In '74, at a chaotic rock symposium in Buffalo, she declared, "Rock and roll is anything Richard Meltzer does"—it was nice to hear. I supported her and she supported me. Aspirations, ambitions (all that kinda shit). I'd always wanted to do her a bankable favor, but by the time of her second album she needed no favors, certainly not from me.*

Though I say here that Patti was "beyond punk by '74"—I'm talking musically—it would probably be frivolous to classify her today as having ever been punk, and even pre-punk is stretching it—she wasn't all that close to the cusp. She was far too avid about reciting rock proper's tired litany, hauling out its inventory—personalizing and invigorating it, sure, but primarily REITERATING it. "The rock and roll fan club meets here" could've been her band's motto, and she herself, onstage, ponied up to even the grimace of punk only 'cause (and when) it was suddenly in vogue, a fact of rock commerce, and application of the term was so merchandise-friendly as to render it taxonomically worthless. For all its come-as-you-are neo-primitivism, "punk-rock" as practiced by lots of groups ('74–'78), and certainly the Patti Smith Group, was as mere-rock an offering as anything by the Stones, Rod Stewart or Boston.

Musical pigeonholes aside, it was painful to see Patti—friend, person, mere citizen—transformed by celebrity to neutered nothingness, her reality bleached and blotted out, all those hallmarks of allure and quirk which gave her the shot to begin with. Rock and roll may BE meticulously choreographed insincerity, like that's what it is (for all else it might sometimes be), and Patti was that, perfectly. Never has one aspired to a state of rock and more perfectly achieved it (for all her rep as liberator of ten million riot grrrls). If you had to choose her signal achievement, you would not be off base in citing

271

her as one of the great BETRAYERS rock has known (see pages 185–188 of
Please Kill Me*).*
    Or maybe just a typical *betrayer. Or is the word simply "phony"?*
Y'know, it's funny. Once there was no rock and roll in anybody's
life, then there was, and it was nearly all there was. It filled up the
world as lived and was the shape you gave to events and used to frame
units of time and measure the durability of relationships; it was the
coding for everything from passion to purpose to fad to deed to au-
dacity to indifference. The world, once empty of it, then full.
    Today, even when emptied of actual content, of that cluster of gist
and substance which memory has resigned to the dumper, the fullness
lingers on, fully, emptily, too fully (and far too emptily) for anyone's
goddam good . . .

Back in July or August of nineteen hunnert sevendee Ronnie Finkel-
stein of *Circus* mag told me there was this dynamite broad working at
Scribner's Bookstore in NYC who was givin people free books all the
time and takin outa the register and one of the books she was givin
was my harder'n-hell-to-read (never read it myself) rockbook which
she was even reading. Told me she looked like Keith Richard so I
couldn't miss her. Had this dentist around the corner from the joint
so one cavity drilling afternoon I paid the honey a visit (she stole me
Ball Four and *Only the Ball Was White* and showed me the cover on
some New Directions paperback by Blaise Cendrars—*long* cigarette
ash danglin down—who I later appropriated as a pseudonym) and we
hit it off so good she wrote the date down in her notebook and we
useta celebrate the anniversary (can't remember the date myself cause
I'm only good at years & seasons) by havin bloody marys at the El
Quijote next door to the Chelsea. Never slipped her the pork—just
friends!—but she once gave me a pubic hair that I still got mounted
somewhere.
    Got to hear all these great stories that she ain't tellin anymore like
how the rats ate her birth certificate on the bad side of the tracks (in
Chicago) and how her aunt so-and-so once spent a hot nite with
Hank Williams in Chattanooga where she was then claimin she
(Patti) was born and how her real father was a Philadelphia gangster
and how her mother had an affair with racetrack announcer Fred Ca-
posella and how her "father-father" told her the fax-o-life by sayin

"The erect male penis is put into the female vagina and you only do that when you're in love" so when the first guy offered it to her she told him she didn't love him so he axed her if he could eat her and she said she'd hafta ask daddy who told her "Forget it" and how her brother (now a butcher) who looked like Paul Newman useta be a transvestite. Dylan never told Nat Hentoff a better batcha tall tales & true. Anyway so time marches and the annivs stopped getting celebrated and now she don't even return my calls and last time I talked to her in the flesh she was already turnin her attention somewhere else before I was halfway thru my second sentence but that's cool cause she's a star so she's *entitled* (really mean that—no foolin—only hurts the littlest littlebit).

Anyway so there really ain't no way I'm gonna be anything but thrilled to my shorthairs by a Patti LP and this one's no exception. Altho the last one was a bit less *grave* cause y'know her live show (still—when it's *on*—the best by a woe-man since Billie Holiday and best by either gonad group since Morrison's prime) has its moments of excruciating gravity but it's also got her laffing it up and spitting on the stage. Like the title cut's great and tense and all that but it could've extracted a *wee* bit more from the lesson of the Fugs' "Virgin Forest" (y'know like even the *first* experiment in self-conscious homogeneous length hadda yield its right-o-way to self-parody and stuff like that) cause like you can't do "Goin' Home"-"Sister Ray"-"The End" forever cause after a while it just kinda bristles with more than a splinter of, uh, *datedness per se.* Less Velvets in evidence than last time tho but in its stead you got Patti paying abundant vocal homage to currently faddish punkdom (wake of the Velvets anyway) which is okay for the *band* to indulge in but why waste your pipes straining for functionless punk *poses* that make you force your notes thru all sortsa dumb strainers like George Foreman tryin to punch in a straight line? Like this sweety was already vocally past punk forever by '74 (Buffalo State concert that spring she was down on her knees wailing the neo-blues—as only she's been able to wail em—for Patti Hearst and hitting lost chords without breakin a sweat) and by the winter of '75 she was so far ahead of all other femmesingers in the orchestration-of-it-all that almost anything with a sharp easy-croon feel for any kinda BIG MEAT sounded like it could very well be somethin Pat just *dashed off* (first 12 or so times I heard "Rhiannon" I thought it was her—FM stations in LA usually don't burden you with data like who did it). Singin on side one of this one sounds like too much needless *struggle.*

But that's mostly just nitpickin cause "Ain't It Strange" is an improvement on "Miracles" at its own game (great Chicken Hirsch drummin!) and "Pissing in a River" now gives her two entire weewee songs ("Piss Factory" on the Mer label was the other) altho maybe she oughta try *ending* her orgasm with urination some time (so far it's only been the beginning) and "Pumping" is as rewardingly hot & desperate as trash pulp sex circa '58 and "Distant Fingers" is "Third Stone from the Sun" as told by the stone (as well as a nifty play on Pearlman-Roeser's "ETI"—Allen Lanier's co-authorship presumably supplying the topical incestuous excess) so it's really a bonafide certified *good'un*, y'know?

Introduction

What appealed to me about punk-rock, *real* punk, the moment it finally GOT TO ME, was that it wasn't rock at all, it was something else. Vom (you can rest assured) is not where it got to me.

I'm not gonna structure these pages, shuffle the documents, to make it appear I was always on to what was happening. My earliest feeling about punk, before really hearing it, just *of* it, was aversion: aversion to but the latest marketplace wrinkle—ho hum—'specially when it seemed a sign, if anything, of rock-roll's health. Because I really did want rock to DIE.

In the end, it was no longer something else, but for a brief while it was—and I was *dazzled*. Once I realized punk took in all these vast disparate turfs from primitive chunka-chunka to the most bizarre and experimental, it was like being in love again. In love with, of all things, *culture*.

And what it didn't take in, the very *fact* that it didn't, was almost as appealing: the spectrum of all the actual market-rubbish (neither dying nor thriving) that had fed my aversion in the first place.

It sounded closer to avant-garde jazz or industrial clatter (kids throwing Tinker Toys at the wall?) than to rock, seemed concerned with the *primacy* of sound and expression, or let's say expressive*ness* (in the way art to Kant involved "purposiveness without purpose," we could maybe call it expressiveness minus the *necessity* of expression), and fiercely resisted market temptation ('cause it wasn't even *close* to what the market could use). For blazing, incandescent moments it oozed and spurted something *antithetical* to rock: it was honest. About its own pain, its own hunger, without candy coating, without vanity, without an *iota* of formulaic dissimulation. "Rock that is honest"— how more oxymoronic, by the mid-'70s, could you have got than that?

But as to what it intrinsically *was*—as opposed to things it was like and unlike—I didn't bother defining it then, and I won't try now.

Back then I was simply *absorbed* with it—living it, undergoing it—and today I jus' see it as a good old dog I once loved. Things you love you don't feel it too nec. to languagize. Rock as such, on the other hand, if only because I've spent so much time *over*applying wds. to it, I'd feel no qualms summing up right now as, well, *a ritual party music of the '50s and '60s lifted liberally from the blues.* That's it? Close enough.

Punk certainly had something to do with giving in to previously "unallowable" impulses (verboten for reasons political, mercantile, macro- and micro-cultural, certainly biological), dealing a bigger operational hand while effecting the breakdown of boundaries between artist and audience, an upping of the populist ante. *Something* to do with, yes, but still, it would be difficult, 20 years later, getting a rigorous enough read on the matter to satisfy my current standards of clarity and concision: too bad.

But so you know a little less vaguely where I stand, I guess I should at least let you know which BANDS I would recognize as punk, and which not. The short list. Re New York, my take is the opposite of that given by the compilers of *Please Kill Me*, who feel that punk ends with the Ramones and includes Blondie. Punk *begins* with the Ramones, certainly includes Lydia Lunch, James Chance, et al. (and some tho not all of Richard Hell), but excludes Blondie, Talking Heads, Mink DeVille and any band featuring Johnny Thunders. And the earlier shit—Dolls, my friends the Dictators, Television, and of course Ms. Smith—definitely not punk.

Of the Ohio people, Pere Ubu and the Cramps are punk, the Dead Boys are just loud and snotty rock 'n' roll. (Devo isn't even on the map.)

Jello Biafra? Barely.

England: the Pistols, the Clash and the Damned, obviously, and at least two generations of others, from Wire and the Fall to the Anti-Nowhere League, but not the Stranglers. Or Adam Ant. Or XTC. Elvis Costello—does *anyone* anymore consider him to 've been punk for half a minute?

Anything after, oh, 1983: nope. Doesn't matter if it's ostensibly punk—up the yinyang—'cause by then the moment had passed, the world which gave it rise had expired, the market was no longer resisted, and whatever it then was was no longer anything *remotely* else. It was part of the same damn, same old rock "thing."

71

Any Old Way You Lose It (excerpt)

By the time the Ramones were happening, I was gone from New York, so I missed them for a while, along with the rest of early N.Y. punk. Where the whole thing first winked at me, then unfolded its fullness, was L.A.

After a period of disbelief—like how could it be happening there?*—what was* there *turned out to be none too shabby.*

From mid-'77 through somewhere in '80 or possibly, on the outside, '81, L.A. (believe it 'cuz it's true!) was not only the hottest, hardest-core punk-rock venue in the U.S. but the second most vital such culture-seat in the world (behind the U.K.). With bands like the Germs, X, the Screamers, the Plugz, the Bags, the Weirdos, the Controllers, the Flesh Eaters, Black Flag, B-People, Black Randy & the Metrosquad, Fear, Nervous Gender, UXA, 45 Grave, Vox Pop, Monitor, Catholic Discipline and Gun Club, and a pair of swell mags, *Flip Side* and my all-time favorite rockmag, *Slash*, this shithole came as close to being a fertile musical oasis as any I've stumbled over.

Very little of which I bothered to write about. Aside from the fact that my rockwrite licks had already been worn to dysfunction, I was just too busy *experiencing* it all, gulping in the most atypical mass of fresh air I've encountered in this burg. I did, however, have an FM punk show, "Hepcats from Hell," on the local Pacifica station 'til they axed me for letting musicians use cusswords, and I even, for a total of eight horrible gigs, had a band of my own called Vom, for which—as "Mr. Vom"—I sang (and the less said about which the better).

In retrospect, what L.A. Punk *was* was a rock-roll stripped of nearly all glitz, pomp, bourgeois confectional gesture/intent. With hardly even passing obeisance to "professional standards" or conventions of rock-behavioral strut, it was raw, uneditedly human, unchoreographedly headstrong, yet neither macho nor wimp (which helped *me* for one—honest!—clean up my own lingering rock-sexist act). All told, it was arguably the most *specifically* anti-totalitarian U.S. rock-roll ever, and the one true Southern Cal "underground music" after Central Avenue bebop of the forties.

And the great shocker in all this, greater even than the mere fact of anything so substantial 'n' life-supporting actually *happening* in L.A., was its ultimate source. Basically this wasn't kids working factories, or on welfare, but the lawnstained, hot-tubbed progeny of "safe middle-class homes" in Endless Summerville. To which their basic measured response—bless 'em, may their tribe increase—was fuck!-this!-shit! in Beast Town, U.S.A. Way to go!

And it did go, it went. The whole thing lasted maybe three-four years, which I guess is a longish time in the general scheme of things, and then *poof*, it became the same old shit as everything else. As the rest of rock.

72

The Dregs of Alice Cooper (excerpt)

The Miamis? Did such a band really exist? Somewhere in '77, I was still out of the loop. I had Pistols 45s and that was it. My notion of punk was that it was a new subset of mainstream rock, a new round of fun & games (with a heavy element of cute). The Babys? The Shirts?

Yes I was out of it, but no more so than mainstream chameleon Alice Cooper. "We were really punk rock"—ah! the dreams dreamers dream!

RM: Whaddaya think of punk rock?

AC: Well, when we were up there in the early days with the eye makeup on we were basically saying, "If you don't like it, *leave.*" We were really punk rock, because we didn't have anything to lose.

RM: How 'bout punk rock today?

AC: I think it's neat, Johnny Rotten! That's *great!* Heh heh! But I always look at the rock industry, I always look at it as an enormous *menu.* I love to put on Burt Bacharach and then put the Stooges on, y'know, and then put Laura Nyro on and some of that, uh, electronic music. I think the more variety you've got in the business the better, I think punk rock is great. But I haven't heard any of the new groups . . .

RM: You haven't heard the Shirts or the Miamis?!

AC: Ha! I haven't really even heard the Ramones yet . . .

RM: The Babys . . .

AC: Y'know, *my* old band is gonna be called the Billion Dollar Babies, they all got back together, hey I think that's *neat* . . .

73

Electrocute Your Cock

*But the fun & games did appeal to me, plus the apparent ease (the freedom!)
of constituting a band from scratch. If I ever harbored a desire to perform,
this was my shot. Soon I'd be too old.*

I did most of the singing for Vom (as in vomit*) 'cause I wanted to, but also
because I couldn't do anything else. I didn't play an instrument, didn't know
chords, there was very little I could communicate to anyone else in the band of
a* musical *nature. Beyond "I don't like that break" or "Could you do it a little more like Beefheart?" there was nothing I could say or do to shape the
music to my liking. Somewhat perversely, I also felt that once a song was finally worked up, beat into shape, why play it again? It seemed an especially
bad idea to get it right in practice,* before *using it at an actual gig—like a
boxer overtraining, leaving his best licks in the gym. After not too many club
appearances, I was sure we'd already used up all our material, if only because
we knew how to perform it.*

A bigger problem was performance strategy. *At the Sex Pistols show in
San Francisco I was asked to emcee, and I went out and provoked the audience and they threw things at me and Bill Graham, who was promoting it,
chucked me out of the building—what a rush. From that I got a warped
sense of how it would (and should) always be. Confrontation seemed a good
variable to play with, but we took it too far. Further than we could handle it.
For our next show we got a big box of live crickets at a bait store, and when
the crowd tried storming the stage I released them—they looked like
roaches—and backed everybody up 10 feet. From there we moved to crayfish
and worms. At the Whiskey we wrapped barbed wire along the foot of the
stage so nobody could get at us, which only made 'em heave chairs up over it.
I ended up hitting some guy in the head with my mike stand, he'd been
pulling at the mike cord, and it* bothered me *how automatic it had been
(I'm lucky I didn't take his ear off), what ridiculous overkill it was. I didn't
have the heart for physical hostility.*

*There were other local punk bands, including some who likewise pushed
total-offensiveness buttons, who went for big intimidation, with a lot more*

*dignity than us, than me. (Even Fear had more dignity.) By the time I quit
I was feeling very foolish and old.*

    *It was pretty much a bust altho I do think I sang OK, and "Electrocute
Your Cock" was a* classic *lyric, a classic song.*

Electrocute your cock,
Electrocute your cock,
Lookin' for a handjob,
Stick it in a clock.

Lookin' for a job,
Lookin' for a job,
I'm so horny
I think I'd fuck a frog.

Cauterize your cunt,
Cauterize your cunt,
Every mutt in town
Loves a bleeding sump.

It's 2 a.m.
And I'm dying to cop.
I hope that the fingers . . .
That the fingers on my meat don't stop.

Lookin' for a hole,
Lookin' for a hole,
If I don't get some soon
I'll even fuck a bowl.

Circumcise your nose,
Circumcise your nose,
Every girl in town
Wants to fuck a garden hose.

All day long
I've looked for hands of love.
At this point, baby,
I'd settle for a baseball glove.

Lookin' for some snatch,
Lookin' for some snatch,
Syphilis is cool,
I'll take a scabby thatch.

Poke your sister's meat,
Poke your sister's meat,
Poke your best friend's wife,
Then do her for an eat.

Electrocute your pud,
Electrocute your pud,
Stick it in a socket
In the middle of a flood.

All night long
These bimbos tell me no.
Pretty soon, baby,
I'll whack off in some Ivory Snow.

Electrocute your cock,
Electrocute your cock,
Lookin' for a handjob,
Stick it in a clock.

74

Cocktails with Claude

More than anything else, what finally set me straight was reading Slash, *especially the rantings of its editor, Claude Bessy, a/k/a Kickboy Face—the greatest rockwriter you never heard of. In matters of punk vs. not-punk, I defer to Claude.*

In the original preface to this interview, conducted over a fifth of Jim Beam, I called him "a Lester Bangs for the '80s" and was tempted to call him simply "the real Lester Bangs." Though Lester was still alive (and the older and better friend), it woulda been hard not to admit that in some ways he'd already been superseded.

I'll never forget the sight, in fact, of Claude dumping a press copy of Lester's Blondie book the moment *it arrived in the mail—he wouldn't touch it long enough to* sell *it. (Nothing personal against Lester, but Blondie had to go . . .)*

Q: *Hey, let's start at the beginning. When and where were you born?*

A: Although I have no precise recollection, I was born in June of '45 on the French side of the English Channel. My father was released from German prison camp about a year before so obviously he didn't waste any time. The day war was declared his cavalry outfit was supposed to fight the German tanks on horseback with sabres. After about five days of running south as fast as they could all 1200 of them surrendered to six Germans in two tanks, but two lieutenants on white horses, part of the old French nobility, committed suicide. My mother was still in high school and she waited four years for him to get out of whatever potato farm in Germany. He said four years in prison was better than having to go through Stalingrad and all that shit that other people his age went through. I was the product of two definite pacifists.

Q: *When did you first become aware of rock and roll?*
A: I was about 14 or 15. I didn't have a record player, but my parents did, and they played a lot of opera and light classical music, Johann Strauss. I bought my first 45, "What'd I Say" by Ray Charles. After one spin my mother grabbed the fucking record and broke it on her knee, saying "I don't want to hear that savage music." I knew then that if this could send my tolerant parents—both of them were schoolteachers—into such a rage, it was definitely something that had to be explored.

Then I got into things like the English equivalent of the Ventures, the Shadows, all the French and English Elvis imitators like Eddie Mitchell and Cliff Richard, and I got into Dion, y'know, the whole stuff. I think my favorite cut when I was a kid was "Runaway" by Del Shannon, it obsessed me for about nine months.

Q: *How'd you end up in the States?*
A: Well I was in high school, I was a pretty good student but I was definitely parting from the normal way as far as taste is concerned. I was just reading a lot and being bored, and just from pure luck and bluffing I got to come here as a foreign exchange student in New Jersey for a year, a nice little taste of freedom. It was in the year of '63–'64, when Kennedy got done in and all that stuff, and I was having a great old time.

There were two factions in high school then, the collegiates—madras, people planning on going to Rutgers—and greasers—the Puerto Ricans, pointed shoes, purple shirts. I was definitely a lot closer to the greasers although I was supposed to follow a nice crowd. I was already into the guys listening to the Four Seasons—"Big Man in Town"—the New Beats, Dion—"The Wanderer"—and all that shit.

Q: *What came next?*
A: I tried a couple years of the Sorbonne, except I never showed up to classes. Also, a bunch of friends had stolen a bunch of movie equipment from the French army and I was kind of assistant to the assistant director of porno flicks. I did a terrible, terrible version of the soundtrack from *The Longest Day*— some French girl with an American hairnet just marching through with bombs exploding.

My first year of university was okay, I passed, second year I totally flunked. I was kicked out three months before the end of the year for being dead drunk in class one morning at nine o'clock, for being caught with a bottle of brandy and threatening a teacher. So it was either the French army or America. I'd used up everything France had to offer, I was already very bored with the French climate, French culture, everything.

Q: *Did you leave with any sense of the grandeur of French avant garde or any of that crap?*

A: No, I was fed on it but I never thought of it as some kind of monument. It was just something to use for your own personal means, an incredible pool of material from Rimbaud to Artaud. But France is actually one of the most conservative countries on earth, why do you think the word *bourgeois* is French? So I came back to New York, spent about three-four months there, and right when the whole psychedelic nonsense was starting—summer of '67—here I was, first time.

I left New York with five dollars, nobody told me where to go, and where do I arrive after three and a half weeks of hitchhiking and shit, I arrive right on Brooks Avenue in Venice! The Doors when I was here were the Doors of Perception, Love came a bit later, there were the Turtles . . .

Q: *Was music already your cultural backdrop then?*

A: No, I was just hopelessly, naively romantic. Music was a great soundtrack to the adventure of being that age and getting free of everything. The first time I took acid it was also the first time I saw the Airplane, and it became so hopelessly distorted I don't know if they were great or y'know. Anyway, after that '67 madness period, I lived about a year and a half in the Middle East.

Q: *Dealing hash?*

A: Well, trying to, getting busted for it, but mainly using it. I got stuck in Afghanistan for almost a year, so obviously I wasn't living on Perrier water. And it felt like just three weeks! I picked up a pretty nasty drug habit, methedrine, all you had to do in those days was go down to the pharmacy and ask for it, and they say yes, hydrochloride or sulfate? And they asked you if you needed the syringes to go along with it. So I made a habit of getting a room above a pharmacy whenever I stopped in.

Q: *Had you read William Burroughs before you did any of that.*

A: No, only recently. I discovered all I went through had literary connotations *afterwards*, when I would bump into a book or something and realize I just lived another cliché! I didn't feel like a cliché, except that it made it very hard to talk about it because everybody said oh no, not *that* story again. In the meantime I showed up for the French draft three years late and I told them I came as fast as I could. Before I knew it I was in a padded cell, I got put away in the civilian psychiatry ward because they said they didn't have the equipment to treat me. I was really in a methedrine world, and as far as the little army base in the middle of France was concerned it was the biggest case they'd seen.

Most problems in this part of town were people who drank too much cider and here I was with arms looking like Swiss cheese, they couldn't believe their luck. It said on the original diagnosis totally schizophrenic, probably dangerous, but those people don't want a really, really dangerous element in their midst. I pulled a whole number, said that I knew a way to find God, a shortcut, and they really started worrying. I've been thinking about it lately, if the same thing happened again I'm not sure if I'd wanna get out, I might wanna try to taste the horror. I've become so fucking obsessively antiliberal I know that one day that attitude is gonna drive me to extremes.

Q: *So how long have you been back in L.A. on a semi-permanent basis?*

A: I've been here seriously since about '70, with one year-and-a-half interruption in London. I'm definitely from Los Angeles, there's no doubt, it's closer to the heart of the beast. But I did spend about four or five years in this town being really on the other side. I was a busboy in every greasy spoon in Santa Monica, I worked the bumper cars on the pier, throw the ball in the basket, all the carnival shit. I've tasted having to compete with wetbacks to get a dishwashing job—you won't work for less than $2.50 an hour and this guy will work for $1.65. I didn't see any way out, this country made me bitter, which is one of the reasons I'm really grateful to it. I'm glad I went through all of that because it really gave some focus to my hate. I learned how to hate well, which is really good, so many people waste their hate on the wrong targets.

Q: *How did punk happen to enter your life?*

A: Well I wasn't listening to rock and roll in those days, with the exception of maybe John Cale, because nothing was fucking happening at all. I was just listening to reggae, which I'd discovered through my English girlfriend Philomena. I remem-

ber having 25 bucks and going to the record store and not being able to fucking spend it.

Then suddenly, incredibly, for the first time in my life,
there was this music in which my "political," my "sociological," my "aesthetic" outlook finally blended with my pleasure
and entertainment outlook. Before it had always been a dichotomy. I loved Rasta music but of course I never swallowed
that whole repatriation number. I did love a lot of the Beatles,
Rolling Stones, but I never swallowed, y'know, *get down*. And
I loved the blues and shit like that but I never felt like I was
down and out in Chicago, looking for my baby. For the first
time it all came together, my feelings towards society, towards
everything around me, and the *sound* of it. I didn't have to
pretend, suddenly it was the only way it could come out.

Q: *So when did you start writing?*

A: When I first came here in the late '60s there were some drugs
people were taking that left you no alternative but to either
write or endlessly doodle on a piece of paper. It was just totally self-oriented writing at first, pure mental doodles with
absolutely no value whatsoever. But it made me use the
words, especially since English wasn't my natural tongue. I
started fucking around, spending hours in the dictionary.
About a year and a half before *Slash* I started sending a few
weird things to various so-called alternative, underground
magazines, the kind of obscure things Bukowski and those
people used to write for, various Canadian outlets, poetry
mags, clique stuff. And I got rejected left and right, so I
quickly brought the whole silly project to an end, I just went
on being a waiter, a dishwasher. Until this *Slash* thing started,
which suddenly, out of the blue, was my first and last chance
to open my big mouth in a big way.

Q: *How'd the whole thing come to be?*

A: Well the guy who had the original idea, Steve Samiof, who
was more or less into graphics at the time, called me up one
day because he knew, vaguely, from a couple of conversations
at parties, that I did write a bit. He always wanted to do a little publication and he had read a couple of papers about the
punk explosion in England; he had heard a couple singles. So
he said let's start a paper, we'll just get into a couple of outrageous numbers, we might even get an ad from A&M, based

on pure luck, for some group they've got called Eddie and the Hotrods. So we got this one ad from A&M and another from I don't know where, which totally financed the first issue, which came out May Day, 1977. And by luck we ran into the Damned, who were doing their first concert here, for an interview in that issue.

For the first two or three issues we pretended there was an L.A. scene, when there was really nothing. But before we knew it the paper started interesting some kids, some bands started forming because of the paper, and before we knew it we had a scene to report on, it started snowballing. The media and the artist became very connected. We featured the Screamers on looks alone—we let them play the very first *Slash* concert before we had heard one note of their music— and it *worked*. Suddenly *Slash* was indispensable!

Q: *When did you realize that* Slash *was being perceived on a larger scale than just L.A.?*

A: I don't know, I guess it was about six or seven months ago. For quite a while we felt like we were screaming in the desert, we got such low-level feedback that we thought we were wasting our time. And then suddenly we got all these lame middle-of-the-road publications calling up all the time, wanting to know what the truth was. Like we were holding some secret and everybody wanted to pry us open like an oyster, to get the pearl.

Q: *How'd you come to start Catholic Discipline?*

A: I did it for personal reasons. Before I got too old I had to know what it felt like to be on the other side. You might also think there are things you would like to do that haven't been done but you give up on that naive concept very early, usually after gig number one, suddenly being on stage and coping with that PA and this musician and your pathetic lack of any kind of vocal talent. This is the only town where we could all look at each other—those people were my friends before they were in my band—and we knew in this town everything is possible, there's an opening for even the kind of shit we have vaguely in mind. Right now everybody's so confused with labels, so confused with what's hip, that no matter what off-the-wall, tinny, gigantic, pompous, humble sound you come up with you're gonna get a listen.

We have not that much of a bit of an intention to ever be a
serious band, to ever record, to ever get serious bookings or
whatever. We're doing it just for the fun of it, we've been can-
celing gigs more than we've been playing them. The second it
stops being fun and kind of crazy and adventurous it just *stops*.

75

The Throbless Noise of
Throbbing Gristle

After something of a lapse, I was writing for the Voice *again, using it (this
time around) to anoint myself as an out-of-town hepcat and beat gongs for
stuff Christgau and his circle knew nothing about. Wanting my first review
of punk* per se *to be suitably extreme, I chose a band I'd read about in* Slash
who seemed outré enough.

*As a result of the piece Genesis P. Orridge and I corresponded for a couple
years, and he and his band would've been my radio guests in May of '81,
only that was the week I got canned.*

*(Note use of the term "new wave." I hadn't yet purged myself of that
filthy media conceit.)*

Hi, me again. This time around I got this new wavish show on LA
FM. Between two and six a.m. every Saturday night/Sunday morn I
try to cram in as much borderline unlistenable as possible and I'm not
talkin' about Rickie Lee Jones. I'm talkin' *No New York.* Singles by
Half Japanese and Black Randy. Roscoe Mitchell and Sunny Murray.
Live tapes by the fabulous Nervous Gender (you never heard 'em but
lemme tell ya they're PAINFUL to listen to). Even "Piss Bust"—this
relentless half-hour of unbearably boring loops I put together in '67
on my v. first tape machine with 3-second hits of Jimi Hendrix ad infinitum.

Complaints do sometimes come in from among the hundred and
eleven or twelve faithful morons who regularly tune in to all this punishment, y'know like would I please take such & such OFF right now.
Other idiots wanna know what it all "means." Far and away the most
vehement, paranoid calls I've gotten either way have been in response

to a Brit foursome known as Throbbing Gristle and what I'm trying
to figure out is how come?

On a superficial earing of their four available discs (two UK-import
LPs, a French single, a Brit 45 soon to be released stateside by I.R.S.,
real swell titles you could look up) the cerebro-aural intimidation
seems to be simply that: superficial. Monotonous but only half-assed
synthesizer whitenoise; spastic "sci-fi" upchuck; workaday factory cacophony; barely audible production-camouflaged vocalizings on thematic grotesqueries like germ warfare and fistfuck rapes in the local
men's rm. It's reliable obnox-noise alright, clinically colored and all
that but basically just your standard unpalatable racket, big deal—
where's all the MENACE?

The weeks and months go by and finally the stuff is actually truly
making my own goddam bones ache, forcing me to put two and two
together or suffer the ambiguous consequences. Okay, I've put my
thinking cap on and it seems to me what this Throbbing Gristle business is all about is a music that's 1. totally non-apollonian and at the
same time 2. totally non-dionysian. Which when you get down to it is
really no mean feat. In reaction to the pop pap that's come before, the
new wave has always been anti-apollonian to a justifiable extreme; but
in reaction to ZZ Top, Foreigner, et al its anti-dionysian aspect has
mostly only revealed itself as de rigueur anti-dramatic desex
posturing—the BEAT (at least) has nearly always come through to
render it something diff. What Throbbing Gristle delivers is a nerve-
wracking limbo that is ABSOLUTELY NEITHER: no ethereal
chord-change sublimity for even an instant, no pound-it-out/scream-
it-out to at least occasionally rupture one's umbilical to functional
mundane blah blah blah. (The only moment of palpable R&R urgency in TG's entire corpus of recorded work—"Blood on the Floor"
on the *D.o.A.* album—is production-diluted and quickly faded to
boot.)

Which translates as a music "of the future" that's intentionally
anti-responsive to any of the so-called needs of the human nervous
system—including of course at one end the oh-so romantic *intellect*:
good-bye to everything from wimp-out to dig-it to enthralment and
back again. "Alienation-wish" is the only chord that's forcibly struck.
TG are the Velvets of a "new age" (had to happen), leaving even
Lou's old crew, who at their most dense/distended at least exhibited a
certain *pulse*, in the horrific wake of an abandonment of socio-sonic
"adventure" once and for all. Just as the new wave has aptly demon-
strated the formerly unrecognized *universality* of Dada kneejerk

hoop-dee-doo, Throbbing Gristle sturdily forecast a future (a *near* future) awash in the non-dance of terminal techno-neurosis. But, so uncompromisingly arch and anti are they that they even refuse to make a *fully realized* statement to that effect (hence the obvious half-assedhood)—the intellect inserts itself after all (but for how long?).

Whether they "mean it" or not is a moot point (Edward of Nervous Gender tells me he's met 'em and they don't seem suited for the role)—they've DONE IT's enough.

76

Late-Nite Chuckles with
the Child Molesters

So anyway, my show.

    My show was so loose, so freeform, it made the only other punk offering in town, Rodney Bingenheimer's, sound like top-40 radio.

    I always let strangers phone in and play along—drums, horns—with bands live in the studio. On one broadcast I hand-cranked the LP of a Beethoven symphony backwards. *To simulate a fading signal, I cut the volume on my own show and turned up a tape I'd made of something from a Mexican station—a violation of FCC rules. When Johnny Rotten came on to promote the first Public Image tour he made sure to say, "Hey, Mr. Deejay, what's that white powder on your face?" Somebody'd given me a hit of speed.*

    Stuff like that plus guests with names like Castration Squad and Hal Negro and the Satin-Tones didn't endear me to the station, nor did letting everybody curse all the time while failing to read the sensitive-language disclaimer . . . I didn't last forever.

    This aircheck is from a typical broadcast, Groundhog Day 1980, transcribed years later to accompany a piece Byron Coley was doing on South Pasadena's Child Molesters.

CM: one of the Child Molesters
MELTZER: Richard Meltzer
Caller: self-explanatory

record: Child Molesters' "Don't Worry Kyoko (mummy's only looking for her hand in the snow)"

CM: That was from about the second or third Child Molesters gig.

CM: Live at Chromos.

CM: Live at Chromos in Pasadena in 1977 with the pseudo-original line-up, which I wasn't a part of. So I'm not going to say anything else.

MELTZER: Here we've got a caller who's been holding for hours.

Caller: If this was ten years ago I'd almost swear that you'd be doing the same thing.

CM: Thank you.

Caller: It's good radio.

MELTZER: It's so good, that it's good.

CM: Thanks. Where's the girl?

Caller: She's behind the green door. You guys are doing a hell of a job.

CM: Are you watching TV?

Caller: I don't watch TV.

MELTZER: But this is the time that the good things are on. Okay, let's introduce the band.

CM: Over here, on your radio right, we have the Rev. Toad-Eater.

CM: I play modified melody maker.

CM: He writes real keen songs every three or four years.

MELTZER: Did you write "Hillside Strangler"?

CM: No. That was spontaneous. It wasn't a classic.

CM: Then we've got M.T. Lubotomy, not on guitar at the moment.

CM: Yeah, 'cause some asshole ripped my guitar off.

CM: He's got a Hagstrom. And if anybody sees a Fender Music Master bass floating around, it's mine and I want it back now.

MELTZER: Maybe the Fender Buddies . . .

CM: Yeah. Well I just play guitar and I try to play loud and get obnoxious and lose my cool.

CM: He broke the door at Hound Dog Studios.

CM: He kicked out the lights at the Rialto Theatre.

CM: He did it.

CM: And over here we have Spud Bub, who thought it was a good idea what he did. Spud plays real swell bass, but you can never hear him so maybe you should listen better next time we play. And we've got a real swell new guy—his name is Reichstag Burning and he plays drums with the band. I think he should say a few words on behalf of the group.

CM: A few words on behalf of the group.

CM: Oh well, that's an old joke.

CM: Speaking of old jokes, if we've got any young girls that are still awake now, why not call?

MELTZER: Okay. Some more CM on record.

CM: Wait a minute. This one was recorded at Hound Dog Studios and we broke the door.

MELTZER: And this is the cut where you stole the line from "Fortune Teller."

CM: So I've been told.

CM: Stolen Stones.

MELTZER: But "Fortune Teller" was not a Stones original anyway.

CM: These kids don't know that.

record: Child Molesters' "(i wanna see some) Wholesale Murder"; record: Weirdos' "Jungle Rock"

MELTZER: Okay. We had a request for that. We played it.

CM: Hope you're happy.

CM: Gave me a headache.

CM: Yeah. We'd like some phonecalls from girls.

CM: And I don't mean the kind that'll go one way or another.

CM: Regular girls.

MELTZER: You want basic hetero sluts?

CM: Right. Perfect terminology.

CM: Next girl who calls in gets all our phone numbers.

records: several

MELTZER: That was Frankie Avalon. These days people say he was a wimp, but I think he was the first incarnation of Lou Reed.

CM: That's no honor.

CM: You mean he slept with a transvestite too?

CM: Who was it that called up and told us to knock wood?

CM: If it's a girl . . .

MELTZER: It wasn't a girl.

CM: Well, it should be a girl who calls and says who the guy was.

MELTZER: We've got the b-side of the latest Child Molesters single.

CM: It's a pop song.
CM: This one I wrote.
CM: The proud songwriter.
CM: And I'm prouder of the other one that isn't out yet.
MELTZER: How soon is that due?
CM: After we save up enough money after we pay off our equipment.
MELTZER: How have the other two sold?
CM: Extremely . . .
CM: The first sold better because of its novelty, even though it was a rush job.
MELTZER: Even though it cost three bucks in a lotta places.
CM: Did it?
MELTZER: Yeah. It cost three bucks at Rhino. Three entire bucks.
CM: Well, we made 200 and we moved 'em so fast we had to make 200 more and they're gone. We made 200 of the other one and it took them a lot longer to go. They're pretty much gone now too.
CM: So here's some pop songs for all you girls. Wake up!
MELTZER: Would you settle for some Catholics?

record: Child Molesters' "I'm Gonna Punch You (in the face)"

CM: We're the mean-looking unknown band.
CM: In case anybody forgot—this is the Child Molesters, not acting like anybody new or exciting.
MELTZER: Just a traditional rock 'n' roll band.
CM: That's what we are, only we're just about the best.
CM: It's the only thing that makes us different.
CM: I'll fart to that. And you'd be wise to do the same.
CM: I'll knock.
MELTZER: Someone in this room played with Donna Fargo. Let's hear about that.
CM: Donna Fargo wears falsies.
MELTZER: Yeah?
CM: I had to wear a funny suit.
CM: Yeah? Well two of us in this room have played around in a band with Warner Willtrout. We were in the Seeds and we also played with Wild Man Fischer.

MELTZER: What was it like backing up Wild Man Fischer?

CM: What was it like backing up Larry?

CM: It was like—"Here's the next song. Let's play it." If you knew what the next song was, that was good. If you didn't, okay.

77

X-Tremely All Reet

Did I overstate this? I.e., were X "overrated"? In the long view, I'd hafta say the first two X albums were great, very great, and after that it was a question of finding a few cuts that still had as much fire and invention. Who can sustain anything for more than two albums?

In Waiting for the Sun, Barney Hoskyns misses the point when he tries to recruit ex-Germ Pat Smear in support of the claim that X were not, er, hard core enough . . . that others were harder. L.A. Punk was anything but monolithic. Until the Orange County cretins took over, it was not only an uncommonly diversified scene but one that functioned very much as a, yup, community. Bands of all punk stripes related to being in the shit together. Besides, an equal case could be made that X represented an advance beyond stage-one thrash-bang punk: a multiplication of interest, a continuation— in no way a diminution. (And the Doors weren't the Velvets either, y'know?)

Re Manzarek: a few months later in the men's room at the Whiskey, Ray walked in, took the next urinal, and let me know how pissed he was with my not-quite-putdown of his production. In retrospect, his production was fine.

My days as a prolific rockwrite buster are basically *over*, only got about 11 or 12 reviews left in me so's a damn good thing X has finally released an entire goddam LP, thus enabling me to take this space and use one of the 11 or 12 to tell all you Applers *what's really happening out here in L.A.*—which (*Los Angeles*) just happens to be the name of the alb, on the town's swellest indie, Slash Records (no tapes). What's NOT happening is such high-visibility "heart of the beast" disgustos as the Knack, the Pop and 20/20—bands whose SOLE REASON FOR EXISTENCE is to get signed *by whatever sell-out possible* (buncha corporate hooers). What IS going on is a still hot-to-trot neo-punk underground that has not surrendered one iota to the soul-devouring demands of new wave/nouveau pop, an underground the likes of which this piss-poor republic ain't seen since bebop (true). On a hardcore level this unlikely burg's just LOUSY with a good solid *many* of the most uncompromisingly inventive bands in the whole entire Western Hem: bands like Nervous Gender, Fear, Wall of Voodoo, the Germs, Bpeople, and Catholic Discipline.

And of course the best of the best (for want of a better term—don't wanna get gratuitously *grandiose* on ya), the crowning glory (altho they are far from monarchically inclined) of the whole dang lot: X. Christ, there're so many superlatives I could dump on you you'd never believe me, so I'll start e-z and just hit you with a couple HISTORICAL CLICHES y'might relate to: 1. Not since the heyday of those current dinosaurs who once were not, the Grateful Dead, has a "people's band" so single-handedly summed up the socio-musical oompah of a geo-cultural domain as does X for the clubs and alleyways of L.A. 2. Even more than your fave-rave Cramps, X just might *BE* THE DOORS, an across-the-board eerie FACT which goes well beyond such topical items as their choice of producer (Ray Manzarek, who also lends the mix an occasional keyboard tickle) and sole copy tune ("Soul Kitchen"), and even if they ain't they're at the *very least* a member of the Raymond Chandler/Jim Morrison/X triumvirate of wizards who have SPOKEN IN TONGUES WITH SO-CAL'S DEMONS OF THE NIGHT like nobody else (before or since).

Historical ref pts. aside (like f'rinstance "Sugarlight" is the GREATEST HEROIN SONG since "Heroin," and "Nausea" is the GREATEST EVOCATION of *that* perceptual dimension since Sartre coined the term), the foursome of John Doe, Exene, Billy Zoom and Don Bonebrake simply *can't be beat* when it comes to churning out no-holds-barred scenarios of joy and madness, hope and despair (cliches again but you get the point), with rhythmic clout and lost-chord changes to back 'em up like you WOULDN'T BELIEVE folks're capable of anymore. Good as vintage '50s/'60s tuneweavery if that's your meat. 'S definitely in that ballpark, with utterly novel musico-emotional transitions you'd swear you ANTICIPATED YOURSELF only 'cause you're pulling a Plato and "remembering from your immortal soul." No fat, none of the usual pompous TEASE that so often accompanies the contemporary search for the rock-roll IT: bared-to-the-bones mindblowers like "Johny Hit and Run Paulene" and "The Unheard Music" only come along once in a goddam ERA (a *plug*—which you probably ain't too used to seeing me do, so treat this miracle accordingly).

Lest you resist the notion howev of being suckered in by *mere hype* and you want some SPECIFICS OF THEIR SOUND before you'll work the bucks out of your pocket, all I gotta say's they're the nexus where all these farflung unexhausted founts of rock-roll hoop-dee-doo MEET without a trace of concession, without surrender from any quarter. Don't wanna spoil YOUR fun in discovering for yourself textures so simple/so complex that you can roll up the carpet or grab the headphones to delight your hammer, anvil & stirrup WITHOUT MISSING A BEAT but (don't tell me I don't play *fair*) I will give you a couple clues: 1. Hard punk (and I do mean *hard*) meets rockabilly (and don't cringe and think this is just more Ray Campi revivalism, no *way*); 2. Beneath a "deceptively seductive" surface lurks danger that will CUT YOUR SPLEEN if you give it a chance, tear at your HEART (the physical pumper of your system's mighty red). Something so *basic* about the whole thing that the eight-year-olds next door come to my window whenever I play it and meanwhile the sickest-ass pogoers in all 48 go apeshit with their finely honed heels, elbows 'n' beerbottles the second X strike a note. Other'n that I will say no more, I'll just let you "swim in mystery" (as Jimbo would say) until you've checked 'em out yourself.

Lyrics: X literally REWRITES THE LEXICON OF BIG-BEAT POETRY, leaving calculating pretenders like P. Smith and R. Hell in the dirt. Like there're images in "Sex and Dying in High Society" which make all those excruciatingly detailed sexual treacheries in umpteen million Stones songs seem like a grade-school catechism lesson, while meanwhile "The World's a Mess: It's in My Kiss" totally dismembers traditional R&R devil/angel symbology and gives it its long-awaited doomsday due.

While this is *far from* the ultimate X recording (they're a heck of a lot *harder* than Manzarek provides evidence of), 's enough for now from the MOST IMPORTANT BAND W/ EVEN *HALF* A COMMERCIAL CHANCE IN THE U.S.A. TODAY.

78

Two Poets in Search of an Eraser

And here's the harder *core . . . first L.A. generation, anyway.*

Can't remember if Marc Bolan in the pre-T. incarnation of Tyrannosaurus Rex used to include a lyric sheet but he wasn't singing in
English anyway, sounded more like Sanskrit or Bulgarian. You never
knew what the hell he was saying, but that just heightened the simpy
wimpy exoticism so you didn't really care if in fact you cared at all. In
any event, he was working outside—as opposed to through, around or
against—your basic Anglo-Am words-to-music tradition, so even if
his music had had more, uh, power to it, it still wouldn't've represented any sort of redefinition of or challenge to that big fat shitpile
of uncontested rock-roll convention.

It wasn't really until punk that systematic indecipherability and
things like that were approached with any across-the-board intent
(bands like the Buzzcocks, Eater, and the obvious 137 others) and it
wasn't until NOW, with the arrival of a couple of L.A. punk longplayers, *Germs (G.I.)* by the Germs and the Flesh Eaters' *No Questions
Asked,* that the project has achieved the status of bonafide-certified
historical landmarkhood. 'S been a long time coming but a pair of
goddam geniuses named Darby Crash (Germs) and Chris Desjardins
(F. Eaters) have finally lowered the boom, succeeding to an incredible
degree at putting the TNT to the whole fragile whatsis of musically
accompanied language per se—y'know like words as meaning &
sound, words as touchstones of human interactive blather, words as
reliable triggers of ritual auto-response, words as masks and icons
unto eternity, words as repositories of cornball rhythm & rhyme.

For starters, neither can be readily followed even *with* a lyric sheet
(both supply 'em), 's just no use, you'll get so lost you'll never catch up
or even know what song you're up to. Darby loses you by keeping

everything basically at one overwhelming speed (super-overdrive) and when he slows things down in a song like "Manimal" it's like he's got peanut butter in his mouth anyway; Chris leaves you twisting & turning in the frustrating face of irrational shifts of speed and direction. With Darby moments of sync between the rhythmic cadences of instruments and voice are pure laws-of-chance affairs; with Chris they're tensions to be relieved, intensified, or ignored at the artist's whim. To both, a snatch of lyric (large or small) can be made to fit *anywhere* in the musical fabric, either to create density-for-density's-sake or be snarlingly, conspicuously anti-linear—or just plain stick out like an awesome festering thumb. Even on the melodic front their vocals are as conventionally "inaccessible" as Ornette Coleman mighta seemed in his early days, and the last thing either of 'em's gonna do is give you enough syllabic clarity at crucial points to help you imagine their sixteenth notes doing anything as eminently disposable as, for instance, *rhyming*—a far cry indeed from "I wanna BEEE . . . anarCHEE"!

Out of the frying pan into the fi-yer, you descend to the printed sleeve and actually *read* what these jokers have to offer: "bad poetry" on the highest flame yet—by which I don't mean Bob Dylan over bar-b-q coals, I mean Teenage Jesus at the Inquisition stake. Verse as endless herky-jerk inscription on miles of toilet paper that're already overcrowded with real shit in perfect analog to a real-world between-the-lines so stultifying that machine-gun angular shit-rant is the only honest linguistic option. "I'll beat the plan/I'll become divine/Since I'm leading the damned/Oh yes hemorrhage in my hand," as the Flesh Eaters say. Nobody's more scathingly honest than Darby and Chris, who know in their bones that in a cultural U.S.A. gone berserk the language of reason and facticity is just a crock of merciless ruling-class hype, that classy straightforward poesy is just so much suburban formica. Backed against as nasty a wall as ever there's been, you're left with SELF-DESTRUCTING CLUMSY UNMUZZLED HEAD-BANG DOGGEREL as the only language that's truly hokum-free. Hence: "new languages" every cut that're ultimately no languages at all (who'd wanna *speak* 'em?), a fully realized BLABBERMOUTH LOCKJAW OF THE SOUL which you gotta admit is kinda neat.

79

Punk-Out 1980
Beats Heck on Love-In '67

Community? Anti-community? Optimism? Pessimism? Whatever.
Anyhow, here's everybody (give or take a few) in one place, giving me call to beam the message northward to San Fran. The anti-hippie wrath, so au courant *in those days, reads kinda stale, and it probably wouldn't have hurt to add beatnik to the hopper. Though this may sound jive, it seems clear today that the prevailing influence of beat "skipped a generation," that its begetting of hippie was ad hoc and in virtually all regards superficial, and that its tenor and substance have* far *less correlation with hippie than with punk (hey: it wasn't hedonism, it wasn't flowers, it was more, y'know, beat). Oh, and four months later Darby was dead.*

Three bowls of non-storebought macaroni salad featuring green peppers in EACH: one w/ small macaronis, one w/ small macs and black pepperCORNS, one w/ big macs and I ain't talkin' MEAT. Potato salad, sorta SOFT in most spots (bad spuds?), w/ mushroomy stuff and anonymous brownish *sludge* all the way thru it. Chips (look up brand) & dips. Tortilla chips & two bowlfuls of SALSA. Peanuts! Egg salad SANDWICHES, stacked in the clear plastic bag from the bread that MADE 'EM. Celery, cauliflower, carrot sticks, zucchini. White wine (Almaden), champagne (Korbel), rosé (Carlo Rossi), red (Mondavi). Clear plastic glasses that broke real e-z, not the styrofoam kind that are tough but give you cancer. Concealed by the 6-pack in bags behind backs & trees: beer (Olympia, Bud in both bottles & cans, Pabst BOCK). Concealed in pockets & sleeves: some tequila, some vodka, gin, Jack Daniel's. No soda pop: who needs it!

The occasion: Tomata du Plenty's birthday celebration at Wattle's Park which is hid all the way up top of Curson Ave. as it meets the

Hwd. Hills and is so empty except for invited guests that nobody musta known it EXISTED, one o' them million or so enclaves o' nature in the raw (i.e., not too many palms) that you'd hafta be an enclave expert t' know about.

Not that it was empty or anything NEAR, 'cause the guests were a good solid MANY: past, present and future SCREAMERS. Tomata, KK, Trudy, Tommy Gear and Paul WHATSISNAME, Claude and Philomena of SLASH MAG, Nervous GENDER's Edward (getting a divorce) and Girardo and that video guy who's always taping 'em but not today, Dix Denny of the WEIRDOS w/ *v.* short hair, fabulous PHRANC w/ her T. Kennedy button (expects t' be invited to the White House by Joan K. if T.K. is elected), Robert who used to be in the ZEROS, that small person Dee, DARBY CRASH LOOK-ALIKES galore, whatever their names are from CASTRATION Squad (in their full Castration SQUAD regalia), the ubiquitous James Valentine, BAG for all seasons even tho they gotta change the name Craig Lee, Jane who useta work at FREDERICK'S of Hollywood and has performance arted on *several occasions*, Bill Pope who's doing camera for the Screamers' "video DISC project," many wimmen with that popular greyish anti-complexion one of whom mighta been Lorna of the GERMS (didn't have binocs and she was at the other end of the PARK), that kid from the CIRCLE JERKS who used to be in Red Cross I think I mighta seen TOO, Bob Biggs of Slash RECORDS & Penelope of Slash FILMS w/ her hair black this time, Geza X w/ red hair & mustache, El Duce of the MENTORS w/ shirt open to the waist and his guitarist, MASQUE HONCHO Brendan Mullen, Hugo of Gang o' FOUR in town "on HOLIDAY," Gorilla Rose, whats-their-names from VINYL FETISH, Kent & Michelle Beyda, their friend Mark, UNINVITED POP CON-MAN KIM FOWLEY WHO DID NOT BELONG and his latest "discovery" (shag-cut creep in ostrich-skin *shoes*), and of course a *whole heckuva whole lot more*.

Gathering of the punk tribes y' might say which probably rings a few San Fr'cisco BELLS (and I don't mean bottoms). Lotta similarities to all that '60s SF crap—smiles & sunshine & FUNNY HAIR & such—but (here comes the MESSAGE of the piece) lotta dissims too, lot more than not and I ain't just talkin' no acid in the koolaid and no Angels bikin' around the blankets 'n' windchimes. I'm talkin' ways in which LA punk BEATS THE LIVING TAR out of SF psychedelia *on its own terms* and I don't even mean beating tar as in beating tar, I'm talking depth of genuwine *commitment*.

First of all LA punk's gotta be anti-estab *PER SE* (fuck the *pose* which in the '60s ultimately checked out as little more than goodbye mom & dad—which the first two months of conventional middle-class outatown COLLEGE woulda taken care of just as e-z). Only natural therefore that it'd PISS ON empty "turn on . . . drop out" sloganism and could give TWO SHITS about common-denom universality and the mere desperate trappings of token connectedness (like dope, frisbees, forced communal sharing and interpersonal rituals of one's own corny DEVISE). It's *truly* concerned with counterculturism (no surrender—while the most marginal of reorientations would prob'ly result in payoff in so despicably music-moneyed a town) 'stead of TREADING WATER waiting for a hipped-up pop mainstream that somehow this time might not *really* exploit and tear yer guts asunder. It's less escapist (nobody's spaced o-u-t or asking your sign), less forcibly exotic (no sitars), less concerned about making its goddam music 24 hours a day (no GUITARS), less ponderous in its exhibitionism (no tokedown contests) and—yes—A HEL-LUVA LOT LESS SEXIST (Tomata made the crummy tater salad himself, not some duly assigned brown-rice EARTH MAMA; nobody's trying to cop some "cosmic contact" with the nearest available GAM).

Most of all it respects its own privacy and thus at least contains the seeds of its own potential survival: it's UNDERGROUND AND PROUD OF IT, first real underground in the crassest of all possible burgs since bebop in the '40s. San Fran if you remember scattered all vestiges of *its* once almost viable underground to the GODDAM WIND by pulling the mock-egalitarian number of inviting the whole dang planet to COME AND GIT IT W/ DAISIES IN YOUR EAR, unflinchingly yielding its tribes' buffalo grounds to hordes of snot-faced casualties-in-the-making from Montpelier, New Hampshire who couldn't generate any tribal adventure on their own local turf *so fuck 'em* (the line SHOULDA BEEN—peace, love & communal b.s. NOTWITHSTANDING).

Fuck 'em is exactly the line this time around, LA's punk-derground wantsa *stay that way* and not out of any secret-society elitist trumpery. It just ain't promising (or even faintly suggesting) any bogus nirvanas, so even if dumb write-ups like THIS made the whole thing more "accessible" to the outside world it still wouldn't be a very *tempting* draw for even the most curious of suburban uninitiates. Plus in no way is it bold or stupid enough to offer cowering losers instant community-for-its-own-sake, 'cause like what's it even a community OF?

"Of-ness" maybe? Anti-of-ness is more like it 'cause except for a healthy handful of commonly shared attitudes & preferences that turn with the seasons THERE REALLY ISN'T ANY GLUE. Less sticky and less autocratic than hippiedom ever was and hence (I sorta think) FAR MORE HUMANISTIC—now how's *that* for irony!

Meanwhile up by the Bay whatever it was people were so locally precious about 13 years ago is so dead & done it don't merit more'n a semi-nostalgic *whimper* anymore. I mean folks still SMOKE IT and DRESS IT and some still even got braids that hang down to their ASS and all the standard visuo-cultural relicry that goes with that kind of pathetic INERTIA while what'd everybody's rampage to pop-sploitation really leave 'em with but a terminally warped sense of you-name-it that drugs alone couldn't have sprung on a cage fulla mice in a month of centuries. Like I got this call the other day from some-body managing a band with some silly name like the New Super-heroes or the New I forget whats featuring—are you ready for this?—Nick GRAVENITES and John CIPOLLINA (!!!). Sez they're down in LA looking to get booked into an "I-don't-care-if-you-call-it-punk-or-you-call-it-new-wave-or-you-call-it-whatever" type club and he's wondering if maybe *I* can get 'em into the Hong Kong or the 88 (where the hell'd he get my NAME???).

Picnic's been goin' on maybe an hour before I realize: whole park's on a 45-degree angle or at least a good THIRTY. 'S a real PROJECT walkin' down to the porta-john and on back UP. Inotherwords IT'S ALL DOWNHILL (unless you're really a masochist or your inner ear's kinda fucked). Geez how ironic 'cause like I once had a c-o-n-v-e-r-s-a-t-i-o-n with famous Frisco person JERRY GARCIA (what're columns GOOD FOR if you can't irrelevantly namedrop your cousin Charlene?) on this Hell's Angels boatride around Manhattan where it was so smoggy you couldn't see BOTH New York AND New Jersey at the same time and it sure looked like AIR WOULD SOON BE UNAVAILABLE f'r the lungs (this was '73 or '74). Seemed to him & me (we were talkin') like it was ALL DOWNHILL earthwise from THERE ON OUT; we "decided" (or I was so drunk I ranted it out and he "agreed") that DOWNHILL WAS BETTER, all y'hadda do was pull a Jack & Jill and ROLL W/ IT, letting gravity BE YOUR FEETS—'s e-z.

Okay so the ground's on this angle that evidently we've all been fighting with our skeletal unconscious W/OUT KNOWIN' IT f'r quite some time and I stop & muse on the metaphoric SITUATION.

This is just *me* thinkin'—doesn't gotta be communal or even involve
DIALOGUE this time around 'cause that simply AIN'T THE
SCENE—and here's what I think: I think scenewise at least (fuck the
WORLDWISE bit, 's for Ron Reagan, Nat Hentoff and Giorgio
Moroder to discuss on the DICK CAVETT SHOW) the angle *sez*
somethin' (hear it talkin'). Sez yeah 's all on the verge of beginning to
get steeper still and I ain't talkin' UPHILL AGAIN 'cause uphill's already been DONE, to wit: Germs're fallin' apart (Don Bolles replaced by Darby's "peg-boy" who cannot play Mary Had a Little
Lamb on *spoons*), Bags falling somewhere, Screamers 'emselves 've
seen BETTER DAYS (I mean what's WITH all this video DISC
shit?), Castration Squad ain't playing for three and a HALF wks., X is
headed for New York and deserved fame & FORTUNE and maybe
signing next time with Deutsche Grammophon, when was the last
time any of us even SAW a member of the Dickies? Telltale signs of
somethin' or MAYBE NOT, I don't see any signs, what signs you
talkin' about, where's the signs, I don't see 'em. GEEZ THE NEED
TO PUT A PUNCHLINE ON YER COLUMN can sure wreak
havoc with the goddam truth or the goddam poetry or the goddam
whatever else there is that isn't one or t'other 'cause hey the picnic
was swell so this final paragraph was just a RED HERRING 'cause
what the fuck *else* was I supposed to describe, the hairs comin' outa
people's NOSES?

80

Belsen Is No Longer a Gas

Then another shoe dropped . . .

I see you grab that SS patch
from out of daddy's SS drawer
TSOL is playing and you gotta be dressed just
right
words from Mein Kampf
scrawled on your leathers
iron cross
—original model—
dangling from chains as dumb as from the necks
at singles clubs or Hot Tub
Fever
well lemme tell ya (Jack)
it's time you updated the pose:
no more swastikas
you've made your point
f'r fucksure I've made it myself
but mommy & daddy
2,000,000,000 Republican geeks
and all the nuke-powered ships at sea
are no longer shocked
if in fact
in their heart of hearts
they ever really were
and boys in blue
who tug on Black Flag's cord at the drop of a
beer
chuckle at all the silly boys & girls

stirring the playpen.
this ain't the trenches no more
it's more like the pits.
let's look at Adam
that pathetic insect simp
two steps back from you
(which really ain't too far)
with that stupider than shit AMERICAN FLAG
on his belt
and low-level fascist antpoop
in all his songs—
time is ripe to take it two steps *ahead*
and challenge the fascist
in symbols that give him no yuks:
hammer & sickle daddy-o!
(wear it with pride)
and piss the living urine
out of bladders weak & strong.
yes I am a kike
a goddam yid
a hooknoser and all such shit
altho in certain lights I could pass for Italian
but fuck a *duck*
Hitler was a vegetarian who dug blue-eyed
South Bay
surfer boys
is *that* your idea of apocalypse now?
pardon the expression
but it's time to
GO FOR IT
go for the hammer
go for the sickle
you'll be glad you did.

81

A Hermit's Tale

And then it was DONE, or I was done.

Peter Laughner, the proto-punk from Cleveland who died in '77, wrote a review once where he pontificated 'bout experiencing music "live, in person, where your eyes and your groin and your undercover Sigmund Freud connections to the realistics of rock 'n' roll can all be engaged at once"—like wouldn't that be nice? Dunno 'bout you, but I've been to far more live shows that were stiffs (burns, even) than were rapturous; I tend to regard the "realistics," as manifest in concert, as low-yield crapshoots at best, and for years have preferred my ration-o-music at home, where you get a bouncer-free environment, control of volume and the sequence of tunes, wider choice of refreshments (at non-club prices), non-mandatory mammal contact, a place to crash without having to drive . . . things like that. The closest I ever came, on a regular basis, to the Laughner aberration was briefly in the '60s and, more crucially, during the peak years of L.A. punk, when I got fed, clothed and blowjobbed by the action at rock clubs, week in/week out, until suddenly I didn't anymore, and I'm quite sure I never will again.

Re: Central Avenue in the '40s. Sunset Strip in the '60s had too many major-label acts to be considered "underground," even if cops were beating on everybody nightly. (For the record: the LAPD, county sheriffs and whatnot are still bullying bands—mainstream bands—and their patrons in the late 1990s.)

For most of the 24 years I've now been writing I've been one stern critic of just about everything, godblessme, and it's only in fairly recent times, say the last seven-eight years, that I've actually turned enough corners *with* my writing that I finally almost don't mind reading my own stuff. No, I don't read it for "pleasure"—I'm not *that* big a narcissist—I read it to proofread it, and the fact that I can stand it as consistently as I do seems a minor miracle. As unswervingly hard as I tend to be on the best efforts, so-called, of all the hacks, superstars and scoundrels of various and sundry creative genres, I at times these days even rather *like* the words and whatnot I manage, somehow, to fill pages with, and certainly not 'cause I've grown any easier to please. Heck, I'm *merciless* with myself, I'm as tough on my ass as on anyone else's, and to get out from under my own savage lash has required work-ethic bullshit up the old wazoo, a commitment of time and effort that's necessitated my becoming a virtual hermit.

I hardly ever leave my apartment cum office, I hardly leave the hardback chair in front of my desk, so it's just as well there's nothing much "out there" to even marginally distract me from the task at hand. Day, night: not much. Would I rather see/hear Philip Glass at Royce Hall, for inst, than endlessly move/shift prepositional phrases up/down/around $8^1/_2$ X 11 rectangles of beige/white/yellow? Not in ten thousand lifetimes. Would I rather watch the Lakers vs. Utah than do thesaurus scans of synonyms for "prognostic," "acclimatize" and "contextual"? Not in *this* lifetime at least. (For instance.)

Once, though, within the time frame represented by the life of this sheet, just barely but what the hey, there *was* something I left my home for on a regular basis, something I cared for *passionately*, an actual Light which originated locally and lit the world, an undeniable Something which without compromise, without *option* of compromise, poked at (and often pierced) the heart and scrotum of many a so-called Beast, either universal or local: L.A. Punk. Before a genius named Darby Crash chose to sigh his last sigh, before the children of Orange County's finest brought their nazi legacy northward to the clubs of Hollywood and etc., before the nation's mightiest Music surrendered its sound (and integrity) in the studios of IRS Records, before the whole damn thing coalesced with rock-as-usual and that subset of local death twaddle—Melrose!—which today owns this paper by the shorthairs, L.A. Punk offered as decisive a break from prevailing death shit qua Culture as anything (on a nearly nightly basis) this town had seen since Central Avenue bebop in the '40s, and I attended its rites fervently, religiously, two-three-four nights a week.

The last show I willingly went to was in some black neighborhood around Inglewood: Black Flag (playing under an assumed name) and three Orange County bands whose identity you'd have to hypnotize me to recall with any certitude. The Adolescents? Dunno. TSOL? A union hall or something. Must've been '81. Midway through Black Flag, who had the good sense to go on first, bottles started flying—full bottles of Budweiser and Heineken (and what sort of weird rich a-hole throws 'em *before* they've been drunk?)—tables got smashed, chairs, windows. (Rock as usual.) After the cops closed the joint, the kids (who heroin addict Peter Townshend used to claim were alright) went out and trashed the ghetto, pissing and puking in doorways, hurling bottles through the windowglass of fried chicken stands, ripping wipers and antennas off old Buicks. Loathsome dogfood: fuck 'em. I never went back.

If I've been inside a rock club since, *any* kind of rock club, makeshift or mainstream, it's been either 'cause I've temporarily lost my marbles and agreed to open for some synth-pop band by reading poems or some such, or because someone I know has dragged me there. No more clublife equals no more nightlife, thankgod. Nightlife for me now is identical to daylife, and I suspect it will remain so. Thanks to L.A. offering nothing remotely better, I seek synonyms, move prepositions around and about, and of course bleed, sweat, cry and masturbate for the sake of literature. Thank you!

LESTER

Introduction

The next time I entered a rock joint after I stopped seeing punk was the night after the morning I heard that Lester Bangs was dead. I was maudlin and two-thirds drunk and when one of the guys I was drinking with took off for the Cathay de Grande I went along. Dream Syndicate were playing and though I knew two or three members I paid no attention, I just drank.

Kickboy may have been the real Lester, but Lester was the actual Lester, the one who had to live inside the poor boy's skin. I'm as ambivalent by now about Lester and the chore of praising him, *continuing* to praise him, as I am about any of the rest of this bizness. He was my friend the way few have been, but so much of the baggage of his life, his lives, reeks of the *hokiest* rockroll terminality. Even what parts of it didn't contribute to killing him flavored him, and the flavor is still there, indistinguishable from his own vivid stink.

And I find that stink and its purported significance *maddeningly* boring today. I would rather be Dan Quayle than be Lester having to smell the cliché on himself.

82

A Song for Lester
(You Can All Join In)

Between sets at the Cathay de Grande somebody asked me if I'd like to "read some poems," they'd give me a mike. I wrote and recited this and went back to my beer.

LET'S ALL SING!!!

1. I saw the Romilar and the damage done
   a little part of it in everyone

2. Music is your only friend
   dance on fire as shit intends

3. WO-WO-WO WELL HERE IT COMES:

   night of the living Lester
   night of the dead Lester
   on April 30, 1982
   Lester Bangs is
   DEEEEEAD!

83

Lester Recollected in Tranquility

When two editors at the Voice, *one of them Christgau, sat on this for over a year I yanked it away. By then Lester was* very *dead—too dead, one assumes, to play as their Death Chic poster boy.*

On December 14th, this *December 14th, Lester Conway Bangs, while probably not the greatest writer of his generation, arguably its most vital so far to die, would have been 36. Haunted and driven by demons, so-called, a cheerless many of whom/what/which—or their kindred ilk—he directly sought, found cum stumbled upon, or was inadvertently ensnared by on the demon picnic grounds of Rock and Roll, he never made it to 34.*
   Following the lead of a handful of babes in the rock-critical woods, one of which I'll admit (if sometimes reluctantly) to having been, Bangs at the dawn of the seventies played as prominent a role as anyone in both expanding the expressive boundaries of rockwriting as a form and giving it a voice that played the newer, more mannered and cautious, mass-market rockmags like Rolling Stone *and* Creem—*the latter of which he even edited for awhile— as on the dime as it had played the catch-as-catch-can, limited-edition fanzines whence it came. Though he also served as the burgeoning genre's* most *prolific* scribbler, *a mission he sustained with relative ease for the bulk of his days, it is to the man's lasting credit that he rarely delivered copy on anyone's dotted line. In fact, he probably "got away with more" in major-publication print than all his rockwrite brethren combined, conceivably (however) because it merely simplified matters to have a single Designated Outlaw, one entrusted with a* blanche *enough* carte—*and unmonitored options galore—to spike with "authenticity" a rock-media stew of bogus Freedom and ersatz Candor.*
   Retrospectively clichéd or not, there was *an existential purity to the sheer* commitment *evinced by Lester's prolonged wallow in (and about) the rock-and-roll Thing-in-itself. It was, in many ways, the critical headbang to end all*

317

critical headbangs; it would be hard to even imagine, for instance, a profes-sional art-film bozo, a jock-sniffing sports jerk, or a food-review lunatic more uninsulatedly gung-ho vis-à-vis x—either as primary experience or typewrite wankery. His patented shameless multi-page gush, coupled with an unswerv-ing advocacy of certain conspicuously over-the-top rock genera (Velvet Under-ground offshoots; Heavy Metal; Punk Rock), made him a must-read favorite with both cognoscenti and dipshits alike, and he came as close to encountering idolatry per se as any non-musician in R&R. A good deal of which—natch—could not help hitting the self-consciousness fan, but while a man's life was ulti-mately undone in the process ("I'm Lester—buy me a drink!"), the integrity of his art/craft was essentially unaffected. For, while he might have been a tad too glib-messianic those last couple years, he was by no stretch of things an oppor-tunist, never really giving a hoot for what in squaresville would be known as a career. (Or, perhaps, unlike his role model Kerouac, he simply didn't live long enough for that, too, to be strenuously tested.)

In any event: dead, cremated; literal ashes. California born (Escondido '48), bred (El Cajon, ages 9–23), and traveled (I first hung with him in San Francisco, last in L.A.), Lester bought the big one on the opposite coast—his final home, the fabled Apple—April 30/82, ostensibly from a hefty pull of darvon employed, in lieu of aspirin, to placate the flu.

Since his death, variously interpreted as a mile-radius teardrop's once-in-a-lifetime terminal burst, a joke and a half on both himself and his precious chosen whole damn Thing, and—by occasional uncouth louts—the final glo-rious triumph of his excess, the spectrum of Bangs-in-ongoing-print has dwindled from monochromatic/sparse to colorless/nonexistent. Of the two books in his name which appeared during his lifetime, quasi-coffeetable numbers on Blondie and Rod Stewart, neither a particularly representative Lestorian effort (or even particularly good: *the former admittedly hacked out "in two days on speed," and* looking *it, i.e., ad hoc and forced; the latter disowned as a clumsy, if innocent, foray into "writing as whoring"), both are either out of print—officially—or on the back burner of barely having ever been* in *same, at least as regards* this *coast, where I've yet to see either in bookstore one. Nor have two posthumous whatsems,* Rock Gomorrah, *co-written (early '82) with L.A.'s Michael Ochs, and a projected collection of unpublished fragments scrounged from Bangs's apartment a day or two after his death, gotten more than inches off the publishing ground—the former for reasons which if herein revealed would get me sued but good, the latter be-cause, in the words of editor Greil Marcus, "the stuff is less tractable than I thought at less than 5000 words or so."*

Also stalled, and/or abandoned (and/or nonspecific pipedreams to begin with): all known plans to reissue out-of-print Live Wire LP Jook Savages on the Brazos, *recorded, Austin, TX, Dec. '80, by Lester Bangs & the Delinquents, lyrics and vocals by guess who. In fact, the only* anything *by L. C. Bangs readily available where availables are sold is his liner copy for* The Fugs Greatest Hits Vol. I, *released by PVC/Adelphi some months after he'd croaked, for which he (or rather his atoms) later copped a Grammy nomination, and for which, reliable word has it, he never was paid.*

●   ●   ●

Well, I've been proven wrong; it hasn't been easy recollecting Lester in even *half* a toto in so much tranquility. Didn't seem like such a bad idea back when obits were appearing left & right and at least two-thirds of 'em smacked of revisionism at its well-intentioned worst; having ridden the range with the guy, having been as intimate with his daytime/nighttime revealed essence—I would bet my boots—as anyone in or out of various possible beds with him, I had fiery goddam galaxies to say in his behalf that were simply not being said, at least not in print by his designated peers; and, although my no longer living in New York couldn't help but delay my shot, remote and after-the-fact seemed like the ticket, y'know anyway, for some major necessary *re*-revision.

But here it is two, two and a half years gone & more, and whuddaya know if all the raw goddam pain (at the loss of, yes, a brother) and jagged fucking anger (at a waste of life, life-force, and relative inconsequentials like "talent" and "genius"), an unbeatable duo which for weeks, weeks, months gave the Lester totality so cosmic a shape, scale and intensity, have by their own inevitable burnout given way to the contemplation of standard-issue mere *data*, of the skeletal remains of a larger-than-life life which have come to make sense (or not) in too neat, too linear, a manner. Well—hey—fuggit: Even if grocery lists, chalk diagrams and hokey storytellin' are the forms ongoing life-as-life has imposed on the mission, there's still a heap of essential Lester *information* that could use, uh, exposure to printed-page light.

What too many write-biz intimates sought to do in the wake of his death was debunk the Lester Legend (solely) by reciting evidence that his bark was worse than his bite. While I'm sure he'd have "wanted it done" (i.e., have the saga-as-litany scraped of treacherous barnacles, or at least of *their* treacherous vogue), I can't imagine the projected post-life *intent* of such a wish as in any way entailing cosmetic overhaul, especially in the service of moral/experiential object lessonhood. Lester's day-to-day transaction with post-adolescent life-as-dealt was—let's be conservative—94% *anything but pretty*. If he'd have wanted his entire whatsis to serve up viable scenarios for intimates and non-intimates alike (gee, would the Pope *prefer* to be Catholic?), there's no way the deal'd come out even *provisionally* Lester-functional without interested non-intimates having retroactive access to as hefty an eyeful of the not-so-pretty—in all its hideous, non-Clearasiled blah blah blah—as intimates galore regularly managed to cop and, in their various per- sonal ways, have *already* learned from. To deglorify an earlier incarna- tion of shit (which the man himself was clearly hellbent on doing in his waning days on earth) you've got to at least speak its name—loudly!— for the whole entire planet: c'mon now, one & all. A solemn responsi- bility (I call it) which, credibly/incredibly, the smelly sumbitch's closest associates have, to this day, all but refused to consider.

To wit: For every time *anyone* saw the defanged, declawed Lester teddybear rear its cuddly li'l head (see obits 2, 3, 5 & 7) the man was *uncountable times* the asshole, the buffoon, the sodden tyrant; been those things myself—in semi-prior lifetimes—so I know. Back in '73, for inst, the soon-to-be-dead Lillian Roxon gushed shameless *love* for the s.o.b., in New York on *Creem* business, ordering up a Lester but- ton and leaving it in his hotel box; response to this purest of offerings was "What's that fat cunt *want* from me?" About a year later I get this call from Nick Tosches requesting that I please take Lester, who'd shown up at his door on acid, "off my hands"; took him to a party at John Wilcock's place, during which he verbally *brutalized* Wilcock's wife (in green fingernails) for being a "hooker," snapped at an affable Ed Sanders for being "the only alkie in the counter-culture," and had nothing more to say to Les Levine's Asian girlfriend (wife?) than "Yoko is a lousy gook"; further into the night, at Vincent's Clam Bar in Little Italy, he literally bellowed (more than twice), "There's a lotta fuckin' *wops* in this joint." And how can I forget the way he treated me and Nick, his closest approximate *friends* f'r crying out loud, as our wonderful editor while at *Creem*? He'd call us each up at 3 a.m. to ur- gently solicit various (rather specific) reams of pap, needed via Special D *toot sweet*; we'd climb outa bed, peck away bleary-eyed to whack out the closest possible takes on what he'd claimed he wanted, whereupon he'd reject 'em with a *vengeance* ("I won't print *beatnik shit*"), then run thoroughly like-minded somethings—under his own byline—with our words, usually verbatim, laced throughout. Just a few "examples," dunno if they sound like big stuff or small, in any event *typical Lester*, with plenty, plenty more where they came from—y'know times n- plus-many.

In spite of such anticommunal upchuck, or quite possibly *because* of it—post-adolescents of a post-summer-of-love feather & all that—I did have deep affection for the bastard during my final years in New York; he could really piss me off (and I, I'm assuming, him) but by-gones were always eventually ditto. In those days I generally shared his affection for The Edge, and might even 've *gone extreme* slightly ahead of him; in January '72, this is true, he actually dubbed *me* "the Neal Cassady of rock and roll." But by fall '75, when I split New York to at least *simulate* an escape from the Frantic and Hyper (and he subsequently arrived, ostensibly to *embrace* same), I was feeling the first stirrings of apprehension re my own prolonged massive intake of Edge Substances (emotional, cultural, but above all chemical) and was on the verge of an early series of attempts to, y'know, *cut down,* to maybe get off my collision course with all sorts of walls, both metaphoric and real. Lester, meantime, seemed on a rapid *upswing* in the intake dept.; what had so far served as mere horizon or frame for his trip, or at most been its semi-essential *fuel,* was now lunging head-long for the foreground of his life . . . or should we call it the *twin* foregrounds (life as Mythic Construct; life as physical/emotional/cultural Hard Mundane Reality).

Hey, the guy was beginning to *scare me.* Certainly as an advanced—or rapidly advancing—version of what I no longer wanted to be and could (possibly) imagine once again becoming, but more as this vivid, palpable spectre of specialized human decomp not just out there but *right* there: a pal & a buddy headed (willy nilly?) for the sewer. From late '75 immediately onward, on those unlikely occasions when separate coasts—underscored by far fewer rockwrite junkets—any longer allowed for it, I was usually unable to handle being in the same room with him, knowing I'd have to witness whole new increments of what could really no longer be passed off as anything but (gosh) misery and (dig it) horror. Where in the earlier '70s it was almost *cute*—once in a while—the way Lester would stumble into *classic* self-directed drunk jokes (like the time he called me from the Detroit airport to tell me he was headed for an Alice Cooper show in London, presumably England, only he'd drunkenly got it wrong and was on his way to London, Ontario), there was this half-week in '79, for inst, during which he hung out at Michael Ochs's house in Venice with no daily design but to get skid-row-calibre gone and stay there, that was just fucking *grim.* Looking as unhealthy as I'd ever seen him, basic shit-warmed-over with an ugly bump on his forehead (which he claimed he was "treating with Romilar"), he refused to eat without an Occasion.

When, one evening, Michael and I pretty much dragged him to a Mexican restaurant, he refused to actually step inside until he'd fortified himself with the cottons from six Benzedrex inhalers—the local pharmacist was out of Romilar—busted open on the sidewalk with a shoe. Washing down their remnants with a Dos Equis as his enchilada sat there staring at him, he quoted (or claimed he was quoting) Sid Vicious: "Food is boring."

So, inevitably, when Billy Altman rang me up from N.Y.C. early on a California morn, to let me hear it straight from a friend—"instead of from a creep"—my immediate response to no more Lester, steps ahead of all the pain & anger & whut, was *holy fucking shit, the fucker finally did it*; it'd been in the real-world cards for long-long times for Lester to cease to be. Though even on his gonest days he was no way a classic cornball suicide-romantic—heck, I don't really think he was all that clinically *suicidal* (big-sleep fantasies never overtly/covertly lured him, not even metaphorically, from the *darkest* sub-basement of his World of Dread; nor was Danger, though he often nonstop lived it, itself the merest tickle of a ripple of a *thrill* for him, a context before the fact)—he'd sure staged more corny, frightful dress rehearsals than Jim Jones plus Judy Garland (squared) for simply *ending up dead*.

Biggest of which *I* ever saw was January '81. I'm at Nick's place in New York, en route back to L.A. from Montreal, when who should pay a surprise *visite* but Mr. Bangs, cassette in hand. It's a tape of these tracks recorded during an Austin romp I'd heard about second or third hand (he'd planned to "live there forever," it was said, 'til a night in the local drunk tank—on top of who knows *what* else—totally changed his mind), and in the course of the next 12–15 hours he played it, for us and at us, *many times*. Also during this stretch, after boasting, rather proudly, that he no longer drank, he managed to ingest at least 36 cough-suppressant tablets (three 12-packs of Ornical—we weren't always watching) washed down with sizable slugs of bourbon, as there was nothing else but water to wash 'em down *with*.

All stages of this ordeal, in which Nick and I were little more than foils for surge upon surge of what we'd come to regard as typical Lestorian bathos, were hardly bearable in the state we were in (after far too many "nights with Lester," going back to the days when we even could dig it, we'd opted for a change to take this one *straight*), but the morning-after phase was literally one for the books. On the umpteenth playback of what was soon to hit the racks as the *Jook Savages* LP, Lester insisted that one particular vocal was pure Richard Hell (in Lester's cosmos an a priori *yay*); my dogtired no-big-deal of a response was it sounded existentially *neater* than that, more on the order of Tom Verlaine (a Lester nuh-nuh-*no*). Suddenly hair-trigger sensitive—in a *performance*-trigger vein—he tapdanced back with "Then I might as well go *sell shoes* in El Cajon." Next cut he compared himself to somebody (very contempo) else, prompting me to comment, for non-pejorative, sleep-denied better or worse, that his vocals (across the board; in general) had the same basic flavor as those on such country-western *parodies* as *Sanders' Truckstop* or the Statler Brothers' *Johnny Mack Brown High School* LP. Affecting grievous offense, as if any of this b.s. actually mattered (the Lester of '73/'74—in *any* chemical state—would merely 've giggled), he took things up a full notch of indignant/sarcastic: "Well I guess I'm just *no fucking good.*"

But he wouldn't stop playing the crap, not with every cut looming as a supercharged occasion for kneejerk call-and-response, a challenge for him to goad Nick and/or me into goading him, in turn, into mock-self-deprecatory one-liners *ad nauseum*—a dress rehearsal, as it were—his puke-stained sweater seemed appropriate—for his triumphant appearance on *Johnny Carson*, which he had no doubt the worldwide success of his Blondie book would imminently *require* . . . along with a shot of his mug, clean-shaven, on the cover of *People* (over which he whined "fear" of besmirched personal image).

Ultimately Nick and I, weary of further compliance in so shoddy an interpersonal number, old buddy or not (and/or old bud in particular), found ourselves laughing in his face; enough was enough, and the sight of this bumbling mammal going gaga for an audience of two-who-knew-better *was* kind of otherworldly amusing. The object of our yuks, however, took it as us laughing *with* him: Great Moments in Standup/Audience Rapport! Swollen with illusory (or whatever) whacked-out self, Lester then proceeded to announce his *program*: (1) to save Rock & Roll; (2) to become president (presumably of the U.S. of A.); (3) to move to England and in turn save *their* Rock & Roll. As mere dipshit goals, nos. 1 and 3 meant topically little to either of us—geez, we'd all but *buried* the Anglo-Am mainstream as even an idle, y'know, hobby or whatnot—but (2) hit us firmly, instantaneously, in the breastplate. Lester's neurons, no recent model of health to begin with, had made the short-circuit of Lester Bangs . . . [tenor saxophonist] Lester Young . . . [latter's nickname] Pres . . . Pres/U.S.A. per se!!!

Guffaw, guffaw—we guffawed—though I guess we could've gasped (or shuddered). Then: a *heavy silence*, as cosmic (or whatever) as it was awkward, filled presently by the man himself: "Hey! I'm gonna buy some *import albums*! I'll get a *whore* I know to lend me her charge card! Cab fare too!" And he was off; no amiable nudging, no "Get the fuck out of here" could take the place of timeless vinyl hunger. Gone at last—and we gave him (in all solemn, empirical, non-jive reckoning) *six months to live.*

But of course he fooled us, by (nearly) a whole damn calendar year. Surprise, surprise; but an even bigger surprise was the extent to which he managed to actually turn things around—well, *almost*—during that extra annum, especially during its, and his, final months. Not only was he still among the living, not only did he no longer seem conspicuously earmarked for premature exit—the Lester with whom I spent a rather refreshing week in February '82 gave every indication of having already gone beyond mere survival (as an issue) and appeared, astonishingly, to be *thriving on the theme.*

In L.A. following his mother's eventually fatal stroke and staying with his 56-year-old half-brother in Studio City, he accompanied me one night to a low-stakes poker game attended by members of the Blasters, the perfect setup, you'd figure, for Lester to revert to type. But no, he just minimally fun-&-games'ed it like anyone else—no lookin' for opportunities to "be Lester," no showing off for rock-roll peers either verbally or intakewise, no diving for the evening's jugular and letting 'er rip—and after two beers (!), without so much as a grimace, he declared he'd had enough. Post-game he engaged Phil Alvin in a lively musical dialogue, but at no point did fightin' words fill the air, or were axes even *poised* for grinding. The pair agreed to exchange tapes—a wholesome friendship in the making—and next day Lester *complained* (true, true) that *reefer had been smoked.*

As the week wore on in consistent, low-key fashion, I was struck by the fuckload of inner capacities the guy was perceptibly calling on, left, right and center, to extend his defiance of Death to the domain of just plain living, capacities I hadn't caught sensory evidence of—all previously told—for more than 11 minutes total. A far cry from anything as cheaply benign as, let's say, more frequent eruptions of "Lester washes the dishes" (see obit #4), what I got to witness was kind of on the order of a *whole new Lester,* one who'd finally found a non-lethal, functionally less jagged (though in no way "benign") rhythm for his life. Engaging him in tight quarters with more open-heartedness per se than I'm sure I'd ever mustered (sharing an Edge does not always make for brotherhood-by-*numbers,* let alone by pure, unedited *inclination*), I willingly submitted to his rap/rant and bought its tenor if not its verbatim transcript; by the time he returned to New York, his mother still hanging on, I'd seen and heard a New Lester series pilot that could credibly have played—prime time—on the Pro-Life Network.

For starters, he'd learned to slow down, to proceed apace through a given experience without easy reliance on everpopular on-off switches. He'd gotten far more selective about the company he kept, seeking out, for the first time in his known adult life, social interactions stressing soul-warming interpersonal *comfort* over thrash-trigger me-you *tribulation*. A good deal less insistent upon strapping each day to an emotional chopping block (as recalled, for inst, in that old chestnut of his, "I need to be *in love!*"), he'd begun to let his life embrace emotional *motifs* of greater duration and resiliency. And, as stuff like this fed back to his theoretic apparatus, even Lester's ideas (as stated) began to display an unexpected day-to-day congruity; no longer, it seemed, would he write an anti-racist *wowser* for the *Village Voice* in one breath and scream, "Fuckin' niggers!" at Village Oldies the next. Lester-as-flux had had its thoroughly engaging run, and for this to give way to a "maturer" unpredictability was not the worst of possible outcomes.

Even the drastic reduction in Lester's intake of physical poisons bore little trace of on-the-wagon-or-bust—y'know, as if any day, minute, second the tension of it all would cause him to snap right back with equal vengeance—particularly with its status as but part of a whole-body package that included both eating at regular intervals and a radical *olfactory* modification: He now took *baths*. (One afternoon in '74 Nick and I met Lester at some ritzy midtown hotel. Though he'd been in the room all of an hour, the smell was like a dog had died there, and been left to rot, weeks or months before. Consequently, we vetoed his offer to call down for drinks on *Creem*'s tab, suggesting, to his consternation, that any dump of a bar would be more, uh, whatever. *Many* of his heterosex liaisons had foundered on the rocks of precisely this issue.)

In terms of cultural orientation, no longer was he monomaniacally enslaved to rock & roll (-or-perish). For virtually the first time since the sixties he didn't *need*, burningly, brand new Big Beat LP's in his mail slot each (and every) day; the state of the Art, wobbling on a multi-year terminal gimp, no longer served as his external psychic barometer, his armband of first-person pride (or shame); having finally produced Music of his own, to severe personal specifications (regardless of the giggles it inspired in jerks like me), he no longer needed to *prove anything* with it or through it. Crucially, though some would probably like to deny it, he no longer saw Rock'em-Sock'em as a viable metaphor for his (or *any*, kindred or otherwise) state of being, viewing it as *the* all-too-easy—and ultimately, revoltingly, *unsatisfactory*—crystallization of (mega-numerous) blank and scattered lives. Lester's break with rock-roll mythos as his be-all/end-all of etc., which I have no doubt (had he lived) he'd've sooner rather than later made *official*, was as profound, and profoundly moving, as his break with the Myth of Lester. As one committed jackass who'd made the same painful transition—goodbye, Rock-Automated Self!—I knew how tough a bond the chronically intermingled personal/cultural can be to crack (and my heart went right out *to* him).

It also warmed my cockles, considering his record in the mere civility dept., to see him relate (graciously) to his half-brother's wife, this unaffectedly pretty 21-year-old rural Mexican the macho blusterer, a stuntman by trade, had recently acquired, maritally, while on location Down South. Though she knew purt near zero English, my first sight of her she was watching some random English-language crap, while hubby rested for a shoot of the *Fall Guy* series, on the tiny TV in her fussy suburban kitchen; materially cozy for the first time in her life, she seemed lonely, disoriented, far from home. Silent and solemn, she visibly stiffened—shyly? menially?—at the intrusion of Lester, my girlfriend Irene and me, only to be put at ease by Lester *introducing us*, without missing a beat, as, well, *friends of the family*. Like it mattered to him that she feel *like* family—and thus shared in all aspects of etc.—and for a moment the loneliness left her face; she smiled broadly, shook (or at least took) our hands, went back to her tube.

But what came off as so genuine when he was dealing with *his* family, *his* friends, kind of sputtered into the ether when he tried to branch it to the family of Man. Whenever he got to talkin' Hard Humanism, which had all the earmarks of being his preoccupation of (Rock-replacement) record, he'd make these broad, lecture-ish, relatively flavorless statements which often didn't wash. Never wholly credible 'cause once again he seemed to be *performing*—without booze/etc. but surely with a *script*—he'd say thus & such about human courage and folly that not only had an artificial ring, it tended to run in direct opposition to what had clearly been his experience. Even his word choice sounded stilted, alien, *not his own*; when he spoke of "women" he could easily have been reading straight from a column in *Cosmo*.

A lot of which suggested a Lester so hellbent on being a *good boy* once and for all that to merely work overtime cleaning up his own act was scarcely sufficient; he had to render a transpersonal commentary that made his good intentions "universal," even if the topical universality he'd taken an option on was simply the first he found it comfortable song-&-dancing a provisional connection to. There were moments when his bill of particulars made me uneasy, realizing that to intellectually *challenge* any of this would be like kicking mud on some kid's newest/truest pastime, 'specially when it was one so socially redeeming, so *non*-self-destructive, one which, for all intents and purposes, I basically shared with him anyway. What really *counted* was the miracle of Rock Tough Guy #1, after 15 years of rocknroll plug-in and little else, during which he'd come to thread *that* needle upside down (and asleep), to the point (even) of smugness, flipness, pomposity, out on a goddam limb over *something else*: a neophyte at last! (I could dig it.)

Anyway, finally, on the last night of Lester's stay—which worked out as our last time together, period—we did something we'd previously never found the appropriate nexus for: trading rants (in earnest) with blank tapes a-rolling. For something like five-six hours we went apeshit re such topics as: the sellouts & prejudices of mutual colleagues; novels and novelists; New York as (quite possibly) the coldest outpost on Emotional Earth; the usual standard rockish garbidge (plus some un- and some non-). We also hit on shrinks-we-have-known, with Lester's rap on this rooty-toot of a subject being *the* single one, from the four-and-a-half hours I've so far transcribed, which most tellingly nutshells the excruciating self-examination he had to've undertaken—and undergone—just to be sitting around discoursing as fluidly as he was, to've *transcended* whatever the fuck en route thereto:

"Like I went to a psychoanalyst, one in New York and one in Detroit, for a total of, I dunno, three-and-a-half years. I finally concluded, I mean yeah I'm insane, I've got my problems, my sicknesses are fucking *me*, yeah. I'm sure they both probably helped me, y'know, I know the last guy in New York, it's like everybody I know was totally appalled by my drinking and drugging, well like *you*, right, and everybody else had the same reaction, y'know, except my shrink. He'd say, 'No, that's alright.' I went out to this, he had a country retreat, a whole bunch of us would go out there on weekends. And the first time I went there like I got drunk on Friday night, and Saturday morning I got up and washed down a bottle of Romilar with a bottle of beer while sitting on a slick rock by the stream. I got this great idea for something I wanted to write, I stood up on the rock in boots like these and *whoosh*, went like that and smashed, see it, the scar on my nose? That's how I got it, smashed my face open.

"And he thought my druggin' and drinkin' was great, y'know? He said, in fact he kind of told me I'd be not as great of a writer if I gave all this stuff up. And I said, 'Yeah, but look at all these people, they rot away, they end up like self-parodies like Kerouac and Burroughs and all that sort of shit.' And he said, 'No, no, not everybody's like that.' I said, 'How could I someday be 55 years old and have to take a handful of speed to sit down at the typewriter?' Well he said, 'People do it, heh heh heh!' Well both my shrinks, especially this guy, they had real great humanist compassion and empathy and all that, but I know what both of 'em *did*, and in the long run in essence they were no good for *me*, because *they* were getting off on me being there. It's like they're so bored, one housewife after another, 'I don't love my husband, I don't know why.' Then they get someone like you or I that's actually interesting, that has ideas, and so it's fun time for 'em. I mean if I hadda follow this guy's advice I'd be *dead*, uh, pretty soon."

Hmm: one effing *eery* end-of-quote as, alas, all is now dust—reactively acquired caution or no. Possibly possibly possibly, *any* tonnage of prudence would inevitably have proven insufficient for the auto-pilot courses he was still, evidently, all too capable of flying. Or, reversing horses and carts, maybe his tortured shell was already jus' too beat-to-shit, with even a radical lessening in his scale of abuse being too little—archetypally—too late. And then there's this pharmacological biz about purified cells succumbing to doses they'd have been more than up for when poison was all they knew. (And can we ignore the Wrath of Influenza?)

Even if, to some bitter-enders, his death remains as shrouded in formal "mystery" as those of Robert Johnson and Warren G. Harding, all-of-the-above can't help but provide *a* not-unlikely profile of how Lester came to die. Throw in a few more mainline causalities (cultural: rock-roll glut, esp. coupled w/ too literal an intoxication with Kerouac, Céline, *et al*; primal-psychological: a childhood more woeful than most, his Jehovah's Witness mom—pushing 50 when she had him—mind-setting, almost singlehandedly, a chronic "inability to cope"; geographic: the Apple, even when it wasn't *absolute* Edge Central, affording him, given his makeup, scant opportunity for inner peace) and you'd easily have an *explanation* that'd hold up in a court of his cronies/cohorts/camp followers.

But if Lester was the pawn, victim, and (indeed) fellow traveler of such easy-Aristotelian a-implies-b, he was also, in those last fitful months, a scatterer of all such shit to the winds, a man who showed his true destiny-muscle by throwing *all the elements* out of on-the-head mythopoetic sync just when they threatened, conspiratorially, to reduce him to merely another Jim Morrison, Jimi Hendrix, Mr. Kerouac. Screamingly, courageously, he committed himself, as wholly (really) as possible, to a *counter*-causal gameplan which even if flawed—and accidents, y'know, *happen*—did actually manage to defuse (at least where *I* live & breathe) the mythic oompah of *any* time-delayed rat-trap he may subsequently (or previously) have fallen in. If there's anything almost *pleasing* about the timing, the anti-drama, of Lester's death, it's the monumental Mythic Disjuncture factors he'd set in motion were thereby—implicitly, explicitly—to forever effect.

LESTER'S (WRITERLY) LEGACY—"One of rock's most colorful characters, Bangs made his reputation as a pugnacious, participatory journalist who was not above picking fights with rock stars in pursuit of a good interview." So wrote one voice of prevailing wisdom, Patrick Goldstein, in the May 9/82 *L.A. Times*; nothing—latter part—could be farther from the truth. If Lester (the writer) more than once battled Lou Reed into (and beyond) the wee hours of etc., it was not to *get* a story, it was to *live* a story: to encounter all the rock-related *being* his writerly credentials (as a wedge) were able to afford him (as a person). Nor was he in any way enthralled by the sickening spectacle of stars being stars; artists, *maybe*, but stars, *fug 'em*. When he as mere citizen found himself face-to-face with the pose, pretense, and professional guardedness of such gaudy, extraneous creatures, Lester could not (for the life of him) deal with such crap but to cut right through and speak, directly, to the mere citizen in *them*, or (failing that) force the situation into functional self-destruct—*before* the fact of anything so dispassionate as actually "writing it up."

That his eventual write-ups tended to display utter contempt for the *entire* food chain of music-corporate life, often biting, intentionally, a grimy hand that could not've been more willing—his mighty Credentials & all—to feed him, heck, *fatten* him, was but half the take-no-shit of Lester's essential *statement* as a writer de rock; force-feeding the stuff, *his* stuff, the stuff-as-*writ*, to the only marginally less corporate (or grimy) running dogs of rockwrite publishing was at least as pugnacious a gesture of this-is-what-I-am/this-is-what-I-do/take-it-or-be-fucked. Since the extent of his *success* in shoving it down so many otherwise unyielding editorial throats may have had less to do with *his* willful intent than theirs—camouflage, for inst, for their being life-deep in major-label record company pockets—its significance at this juncture is, at most, merely ironic; the reciprocal *influence*, in any event, of his ease at getting published upon subsequent moments of raw critical-expressive spew was procedurally nil. In fact, what may most enduringly *matter* about Lester's approach to his chosen profession, way ahead of dandy journalistic touchstones— "courage," "integrity," "pride in craft"—that he ate for breakfast like so much broken glass (but which, really, you can still get from Nat Hentoff and Howard Cosell), is the "anti-professional," forcibly non-dehumanized *square-one struggle* he by design submitted to—and could not, with any kernel of his humanity, avoid—in order to pump out critical prose of *any* scale of note. (Pugnacity with form; with ritual creative context; even—especially—with roleplaying writerly/critical *self*.)

That he was ofttimes a *great* writer/critic, so-called, was but icing on the cake. That scant few others, on the hottest days of their lives, have even approached him—or particularly cared to, considering the requisite gravity and passion of the *chore* he'd set—probably says as much about their investment in lesser quals of cake as it does about the relative inadequacy of their writerly follow-through. Rockwriting is, and nearly always has been, the trade of simps, wimps, displaced machos, brats and saps; of, in Lester's own words, "ass-kissers of the ruling class"; of fuddy-duddy archivists with cobwebs on their specs; of pathetic idealizers of a *lost youth* no one has ever (even approximately) experienced or possessed; of sycophantic apologists for chi-chi trends, musical and extramusical alike, without which (so they've always claimed) "rock is dead"; of binary yes/no cheeses with the cognitive wherewithal of vinyl, shrinkwrap, the physical column-inch. Rockwritin' Lester, like anyone else in the trade, was certainly each of these things from time to time, though (probably) none of 'em, singly or in tandem, for longer than the odd *off* review. Sadly, though his untradelike comportment surely *tantalized* mere tradefolk while he lived—at least in terms of Style—and even begat a not-half-bad (early-'70s) clone in "Metal Mike" Saunders, his actual abiding *sway* among such clowns, beyond the occasional liftable riff, was—as it continues to be—infinitesimal.

Finally: the twin silly questions (1) where a still-living Lester might hypothetically 've *taken it* (i.e., beyond the rockwrite fishpond) and (2) what such imaginary newstuff could/would conceivably 've *meant* to his basic audience. Second one first. Okay, that Lester's rockstuff generally read so hot as personal testimony is one thing; for it to have been perceived by so many as being eminently, genuinely *about something*—something rather specific, in fact something "real"—is something else. When you get down to it, the gospel of Lester's radical about-ness rested largely on a big hunk of readerly *illusion*, the illusion of a functional one-on-one between the guy's fertile imaginings and the psychic infrastructure of rock & roll as dealt; there could be harsh discordance, of course, but as long as a firm *relationship* could (for whatever readerly vested interest) be consistently inferred between Lester's mindgames and rock's g-g-games per se, you at least had the stamp of a viable—if totally simulated—one-*on*-one. But, really/truly, while Lester's psychic playground may surely have been one drastically twisted maze, its actual correspondence (sympathetic, hostile, whatever) to rock's own labyrinth, one so airtight and dank as to make his seem like wide open etc., was far too often naught but a matter of *readerly convenience.* Everyone loves a cipher, a living/breathing anagram or two, even some—hey—with flaws more rampant than Lester's, but for the man's writerly *service* to've been gauged (almost solely) vis-à-vis his reliability as a stand-in cipher-of-x, y'-know for readerfolk too lame—or lazy—to suss out x themselves, is the real tragedy of the trip, particularly when the first-&-final glue of most folks' attachment to his writing was never much more than their own desperate attachment to an x they could, and should, have been accessing more independently (and less desperately) to begin with.

So, anyway, here's the rub. Had Lester lived long enough to both sever his own desperate rock connection—*officially,* in sheets read by his fuckheaded fans, simply by writing *other stuff*—and, furthermore, to back it up with an equally official rejection of the Fount of Neurosis from which he'd sung its tune (and they'd listened), it ain't really much of a longshot to imagine him losing a huge percent of the fuckheads—certainly the most gung-ho among 'em—in, well, no time flat. And, c'mon, how much of an immediate, uh, *new* audience was he likely to yank in writing up (as he insisted he would) such transcendently pivotal mere-humanistic trifles as the dearth of love (as we know it) in scene X or Y . . . how this set of new-age culture jerks uses that set of new-age culture jerks as props in regards to bluh . . . New York editors who pull rank (pshaw!) along *collegiate* lines [a hard-hitting exposé] . . . or, I dunno, something about shams and follies in clothes and/or grooming?

Plus, well, though, um—(even *if*)—then again: *Aside* from loss of ad hominem authority due to the fickle scumbait nature of the pop-world Beast, *aside* from the fact that many of his generic partisans would prob'ly now be targeted, topically and even personally, in scathing printed-page rants, *aside* from the limited run such goulash (Sensitive Ties His Laces, w/ Brass Knucks & Footnotes) has *ever* had—hey—*can* ever/*will* ever have . . . aside, aside, aside—the most glaring *fact* fact is how few times, as of his death, he'd as yet even *aspired* to the heights (or whats) of non-rock journalism. Four-five-six, some number like that, in the *Voice* and wherever else, all of 'em still pretty much rockwriterly appendices to the rockwrite "adventure," meaning he had a good ways to go before he'd've got the wings/chops/legs for a total-pulp plunge (or at least a regular shift) at full oldtime capacity (but with newtime thrust and content). Which would've been no fall from grace no matter how you scope it—give the boy time (for fuck sake) to stumble and bumble and *get it right*—but how would any possible Lester have *dealt with* a (previously amenable) shithook book co. like Delilah telling him *not now, sonny* when he handed 'em a ream of copy on (let's imagine) friends who're fuckups? Personal *persona* limelight Lester had learned to live without—but *writeperson* limelight? (It would not've been easy.)

Okay, he's dead. All this new grief and hardship never befell him; never will. But words on pages remain: What is *their* lot? Lester's standard fare was so paradigmatically "of the moment" that he was *the* rockmag shootist. But books of the stuff? Nah; it's kind of nebulous how even his *best* mag outings will wear when inevitably (??) anthologized. For someone so public in his orientation, both as input and output, he was—don't laugh or smirk—one of rock's more precious and fragile "private moments." Private moments you can always *document*—coercively, of course—but try and play 'em back and, well . . . we'll all see, I reckon.

LESTER LEAPS IN—Y'all know by now how Lester leapt *out* of New York; lemme just finish with how he leapt *in*. His first night in town, just a visit, fall '72, he stayed with me and my girlfriend Roni, West Village, 104 Perry St., apt. 4. Arriving semi-direct from JFK, he split pretty quick for the nearest grocer, returning with three six-packs of Colt 45. What he did for the next day and a half—*all* he did—was wade through 18 *big* ones, half quarts, as follows: start can, drink fast, get tired; fall out, dropping remainder; awaken following can's impact with floor; stagger to fridge for fresh one; repeat cycle.

What he mumbled or muttered during any of the 18 *pre*-fallout phases I simply *do not recall.*

•   •   •

So like hey y'know wo hey hey wo-wo *hey,* OLD SPORT: love ya, hope I didn't cramp yer style, g'bye.

84

Stories Dead People
Have Told Me

*I've got hours and hours (and hours) of Lester on tape, all from the last time
I saw him. The fragment used here seemed the most entertaining.*

While still alive; three of them rockwriters.

Whom I know more of dead because I know more of living. Takes one to know one, I was and I did and I do. The only group I know that's deader *per capita* is grandparents.

Gordon Fletcher has been dead, I'm not sure, somewhere between six years and ten. I'm not really even sure when I *heard* he was dead but he is. Last I saw him was '73 or '4. Gordon at the time was one of only three or so black writers reviewing the standard white junk in the usual crappy places. The others, lemme think, well Richard Alan Pinkston was working for *Creem* and Vernon Gibbs was in, I dunno, various New York throwaways. Three, wait there was a fourth, this guy who used to do both rock and classical for the *Village Voice*, can't remember his name, he reviewed *Exile on Main Street*, if I think of it I'll tell you. His last name was two syllables . . . hmm. Anyway Gordon told me this honey of a tale.

Him and his friends, I think this was college, were at a McDonald's. In D.C. Each of them ordered a burger, all in one order, like five quarter-pounders or something, the same exact kind, they get it to go and split for the car. They get settled, everybody eats his except Gordon, he only eats the meat, saves the buns. And the paper, right, he made sure to *carefully* unwrap it and he saves that too. Okay, he's finished with his meat and he goes, he brings his buns and his paper over to the men's room. Where he takes a dump on the—stop me if you've already heard this.

Anyway I'm sure it's true. He takes a shit on the buns, sculpts it around, somehow it's the right amount or he just gets rid of the excess, he wraps it up real neat and he goes back inside. Looks just like a quarter-pounder, same dimensions, same weight, he tells the guy, "We only ordered five quarter-pounders, you gave us six." Honesty is the best policy—the guy thanks him, looks at him like he's some kind of bizarre innocent dipshit, puts the thing back up with all the other burgers. Gordon gets the fuck out of there, they sit in the car and wait, it's like 9:30–10, not too many customers. Finally somebody, this couple arrives, gets something, it's a nice warm night so they're sitting outside. At a table.

Suddenly there's this nightcurdling scream, I forget if it's the boy or the girl; Gordon and company hightail it homewards, laughing (as they sing in the song) *all the way*. I forget how he died. It's a good story.

Lillian Roxon, hers I remember—her death if not her dying. Summer of '73, heart attack brought on by a severe asthma attack, itself brought on by an especially unbreathable two-three days of New York heat and smog. Dunno if New York smog is any worse or better than the L.A. version, *my* sense is it's worse (I was once on a boat on the Hudson where at any one moment, depending on how we were drifting, you could see *either* New York or New Jersey—and sometimes neither—but never both; I can't recall too many days, any season, where you could look up 6th Avenue and *clearly* see 34th Street from 8th), anyway New York I do know is more *honest* about it. I don't mean, well here like people are always noticing, complaining—"Gee I can't see forever from my bran' new Mercedes, life's the shits gosh gosh gosh"—but that's like visual as an end more than an indicator. "Eden is grey today"—as opposed to, um, poison. Or like joggers in Brentwood—cough cough in my $200 New Balance ("This doesn't *sync* with my hard-earned radiant health"). Whereas in New York you get *death stats.*

Every time there's a few days of extra-heinous air they'll tell you, say, eleven hundred people died. In Greater New York, the "Metropolitan Area." On the front page of the paper. Y'know from lung-related stuff. And one of those times the count included Lillian. I've still got her in my rolodex—227 E. 21st St. (P.O. Box 415, NYC 10010). She died alone. And I went up and cried on the Empire State Building. And the next six months, every time I got drunk, I'd get all whimpery. 'Cause she was like the saintliest person I've ever met. Every day she'd call up every person she cared about to *sincerely* en-

courage every fucking hopeless tangent they were on, like uncondi-
tionally. Which doesn't mean she was Mary Worth—more like an actual goddam saint. Which I wanted to get up and, y'know, testify to at
this funeral reception they had, but back then I was too uncouth a
lout (they figured I might wave my weeny) and so her um low-risk
mature survivors elbowed me out of it.

Instead they read a telegram from Helen Reddy who wired something like "No no, I could not have written 'I Am Woman' if not for
Lil"—they were both Australian—and all these well-scrubbed
squaresville types paraded up to say *She was so nice to my 9-year-old son
(daughter)*, and I just felt like they weren't allowing the full *spectrum* of
her saintedness to evidence itself by having at least one token uncouth
get up and say, for inst, *I was her leper.* And it didn't have to be me,
could've been Lester Bangs or Iggy Pop. But they weren't there so I
guess it would've *had* to be me—whatever. And all they played was
some bullshit by Bach (or Handel) when her favorite—everybody
knew—was the Easybeats. Funerals—I don't want one.

Anyway there's this story she never filed, she wrote like eight times
a week for the *Sydney Morning Herald*, pretty much your basic compulsory pop effluvium; I'm sure she never told Down Under her fabulous, incredible Paul & Linda Story. She knew Linda, see, roomed
with her or was like a sister back when Ms. Eastman was rock photog
numero one—and trailblazing "groupie" before they'd even coined
the term. There's a photo you mighta seen, it's famous, of Brian Jones
holding his crotch while blowing a kiss *au camera*. The camera was
Linda. She'd have these um, *weekends* with a band (Blue Cheer, Buffalo Springfield) and her first y'know free moment she'd phone Lillian. Thus was Lil the first on earth to hear, for inst, of Jimmy Page
and the pickle.

And you're the first to hear this one. The first collective audience;
Lil would dig it. She didn't put it in her opus, *Roxon's Rock Encyclopedia*
(Grosset & Dunlap), the first even half-nonworthless grocery listing
of all that shit, which compared to the junk *Rolling Stone* puts out
you'd have to admit reads *extremely* well, so once again it's down to
me (thank you, History!) to spill the . . . oh I just remembered the
black rockguy at the *Voice*: Carman Moore. One syllable. Anyway the
story, Linda, this is well after she's become a rockscene staple, she's
accessed purt near all the superduperstars her photocarnal talents can
handle, and she tells her best friend Lil, who in short order she will
no longer be speaking to, that she's been giving thought, serious
thought, to the notion of finally *acquiring* one. Marrying royalty. And

her list of preferences, of possible targets, is like number one is Mick
Jagger, two is John Lennon, three I'm a little hazy on—I really should
write these things down when I hear 'em—probably George Harrison
unless he was already married, four was somebody like Ray Davies,
and fifth (as far down as it went) was Paul. Paulie. Y'know half of fab
writing duo Lennon & McCartney—and current owner (1985) of half
the world's publishing including the entire Rodgers & Hammerstein
songbook, the Notre Dame Fight Song and the complete Buddy
Holly. Anyway, try as she may the best she can pull off is five, Paulie,
she's got him (plus some great snaps of him on acid) so fuggit, *get
hitched*, why not?

That's it from Linda's end. From Paul's end, said Lil, was Paul was
in love with John; John had gone and hooked up w/ that doggone
Asian; in blind terror (& to really *show* the sonofabitch) he, Paul,
snapped up the first hot blonde to subsequently smile his way. And if
you look at photos (separate story), the photos on his first solo album,
I think it's called *McCartney*, the one anyway that yells (if that's even
the word) *I don't need no Beatles!*, you'll notice there's shots of him,
shots of her, shots of each of them with either their kid or hers from
her previous mirage—but none of P & L together. 'Cause even as a
rock-roll *billionaire* she didn't cotton to her daughter-by-the-previous,
certainly by then of camerable age, fugging with her precious lenses
or tripod. (Or maybe it's the cover of *Ram*.) A separate story.

And a Lester story. I've got lots of Lester stories, him in his own
words on tape. Lester Bangs, dead three, three-and-a-half years, my
pal, my buddy and all that hoohah. People tell me I never let 'em get a
word in edgewise—y'know in the act of dialogue—well maybe in life,
sure, we've all got our little quirks, but in *death*? No way. Deadmen I
do not interrupt. So I won't even put a frame, this was like two
months, three months before he *dropped the body*—verbatim, I'm sure
you will groove & enjoy it:

"Before I moved to New York I flew in one time to see the Ramones and like that weekend the Ramones were playing at Max's and
Television at CBGB's. So Friday night I go to CBGB's and I see Television, right, and I hate 'em. They got a table for me the second set
and I just left. Saturday night I went to see the Ramones and I *loved*
them. Sunday night I went to see Television, I said, 'Oh yeah, I might
be wrong, everybody likes 'em but me'—and I still hated them. When
I saw them everybody had been telling me for three years they're the
new Velvet Underground, y'know? And I go to see them and I said,
'It's the Grateful Dead,' I mean they reminded me so much of the

Grateful Dead, just boring solos, y'know, scales. Like that song 'Little Johnny Jewel,' right, they go into endless, laborious climbing up the scales, then get to the top and there'd be a moment of silence and everybody in the crowd would go berserk applauding, ha! So like on Sunday night I went up to [guitarist Tom] Verlaine outside CBGB's after the last set, we're standin' around, I said, 'Hey man, look'—I'd met him before, I had dinner with him and Patti [Smith], and when I had dinner with him I always wondered why the guy never said anything and had this kinda little *smirk* on his face, I thought maybe he's shy, so, y'know, I looked at him and said, 'Hey man, look, ever since I got here on Friday the first words out of everybody's mouth have not been 'Hey Lester, how ya doin'?' but 'Whaddaya think of Television?' I said, 'Who gives a fuck what I think of your fuckin' band, let's just be friends.' And he gets all weird and cold and fishy, y'know. So then later Peter Laughner calls me, he says that Verlaine said, 'Yeah, I don't think Lester's gonna make it in New York,' all this kinda shit. So after that I'd see him in the street all the time and we'd always like pretend we didn't know each other. And so finally I wrote about this in *NME*, right, and somebody in an interview with him in *New York Rocker* later said, 'Lester Bangs' feelings are hurt because . . . blah blah blah.' My feelings weren't hurt, y'know, they'd be hurt if he recognized me! He said, 'I don't even know what the guy looks like.' And so the next time I saw him in the street I was gonna ask him, say, 'Hey Tom, you know who I am?' And he said, 'Lester,' and we laughed, we went and we had a cup of tea and talked. And I told him the thing about Laughner and all that and he said, 'I never said that, y'know, aw there you go, that's how it is,' right? So we went record shopping together and had a nice little time, 'See you later.' And every time since then I've passed him in the street he won't say hello without stopping him, because he always pretends that he doesn't see me, y'know, he's a weird *snob*!"

Thanx, Lester, but too bad I never taped my cousin Bruce tho, my favorite cousin and legendary *all-time* fuckup who replaced me as black sheep of the Meltzer-Colman extended give-me-a-break and went on to KILL HIMSELF at 30 'cause he couldn't take any longer being "The Kid" (on top of being y'know *thoroughly* miserable), too bad as I cannot recall zip as far as stories go.

About him yeah, but not by him. And ditto for Grandpa Abe who worked as a roofer on Leo Tolstoy's estate. Never taped him and don't remember—sorry!

85

The Pointer Sisters

Dead Man Writing. This isn't from the same acid trip where he insulted Ed Sanders and everybody . . . different one.

Day after last Thanksgiving the famous Lester B-b-bangs came over to my place. He was on el-ess-dee twenty-five and the test pressing of this fine LP was on the machine spinning away. Lester was at the typewriter typing away (and I quote *exactly*):

"Anybody can write. It's like standing outside of yourself on the corner blitzing your own brain. You know, stranded round of nowhere. You look at anything sitting there because they all do and just start describing it. Don't worry if you got the syntax right fore or aft don't make a turd nohow. Speaking of turds the collectors had a bad year. Why? The market don't hold no water. Alright, so much for that, you gotta remember who you talkin to. Tell 'em to take vitamin C some of these limeys say 'Yeah you Mericans alla time poppin them vitamins.' Wal thats just because they don't know about protocols of health. The protocols of healths is what enables you to continue as witers. How do one achieve these protocols you ask. Glad you asked that. You didn anyway but I'm glad you did, cuz I dinot know!

"But look. You say you wanna be a genius. Wal I do too but the main thing is don't work at it. Don't overcommit your attention span. Your viscera you can overcommit. Committ that mother all the way to the supermarket. But jest dont look like you strainin too much or you do be. Zat make sense? Yes, like Miss Francis, or Richard Alpert or one of them other name dropping dog turds, just don't walk it like they talk it and you be okay. Follow me in fact. Take the ball and walk to the side of the bleachers and don't kick none of the fat men in the stomach. Follow me so far? Wait for the Glenda Jackson lookalike to come up and she'll come on to *you* this time and you're home free.

Nice curves round the corners of them lips. She will take care of you. She don't care about no apostrophes. Her face is totally clear and open and she aint bought nothin she read in a magazine since 1966. She probably don't even watch no commercials on TV. Nah she watch TV everybody does but she don't listen to roc an roll.

"Which also makes sense. She don't even think in terms of friends. She's just there. Don't know no zombies. She'll be here sooner or later so I say stick all this bogus nihil jiveass dogwapatit. I get tired of talkin to myself. How many chairs would you break to get where you wanna go? Despere, j'espere, sit in hotel room and wait for blap."

Fortunately for Lestuh it was only the test pressing. No album cover yet. If he'd seen the cover he'd have known he was not possibly in the presence of a Glenda lookalike. Not a single one of the Pointer sisses has Glenda's features. But they sure can sing. Better than Glenda Jackson. Better than Wanda Jackson. Better than four Wanda Jacksons (they're a quartet of siblings) (they're better).

86

Another Superficial Piece about 176 Beatnik Books (excerpt)

Sources, anyone?

I was pushing 50 when I thought, why not?, I'll comb all the used book-stores, the libraries, and read every beatnik book I can find. Read 'em and eventually write about them.

And the more I read the more I came to realize that Lester was as deriva-tive of the beats—whole cloth, whole hog—as H-Bomb Ferguson was of Wynonie Harris. It seemed clear he'd absorbed the stuff early and deep, to the point where it became (way beneath the groundfloor of his consciousness) his method, his language, his, what's the word?, act.

Still, in writing the whole thing up, it didn't seem he quite exactly fit un-til I'd run through capsule takes on folks like Ted Joans . . . Jack Micheline . . . Stuart Perkoff . . . Ray Bremser . . . i.e., the non-household *names of beat.*

Unfortunately—fortunately?—prob'ly just the truth—this is where, I think, he ultimately BELONGS. As a footnote to the dregs *of beat.*

(He also of course found USE for Céline and Bukowski.)

File under beat: Bob Dylan; Ann Waldman; San Diego's own Lester Bangs. Dylan's an easy choice, although the lyrics Ann Charters picked for *Beat Reader* ("Blowin' in the Wind," "The Times They Are A-Changin'") are more Woody Guthrie than Ginsberg-and-beyond (why not "Positively Fourth Street" and "Memphis Blues Again"?). His *Tarantula*, especially in the A.J. Weberman pirate edition, is everything you could want from a beat novel (cameo appearance by Ernest Tubb). Waldman I'll accept although she's the same age I am, if only because everybody else accepts her (based mostly on her con-nection to Ginsberg at Naropa), and if you give me a minute I'll find something to endorse . . . hmm . . . okay, "Queer Heart" ("Kiss pussy, Mother Country") in *Fast Speaking Woman*. Lester is younger than me, much younger—the dead don't age—but he ate all these guys for breakfast, along with the inhalers, and *Big Sur* is as good a blueprint, at least a cipher, for his death at 33, 34, whatever it was, as any you could offer. I thought "Women on Top: Ten Post-Lib Role Models for the Eighties" (in the posthumous *Psychotic Reactions and Carburetor Dung*) was incredible—weirder and weirder misspellings while drinking Romilar—until I read Kerouac's *Old Angel Midnight*. Now I know what he was aiming for.

87

Dead Men Don't Deconstruct

Independent of however Lester's better writing may in fact "hold up" (to whatever audience), any possible Best of Bangs, *cloth or paper, is an insult, an abomination. To be worth a damn it would have to include the worst-of right alongside. With someone as prolific (and as scattered) as Lester was, so open to everything, playing both sides of hell daily if not simultaneously, what's to be gained by avoiding his bad stuff? Bad—speaking both aesthetically and, shucks, morally.*

When Greil Marcus was stacking material for what would later be published as the posthumous Psychotic Reactions, *he asked me, as he asked lotsa people, if I might possibly have something by Lester he hadn't seen. Wow, I told him—indeed I did: the 16-page slab of nonironic racism Lester gave me for the final issue of my '70s 'zine* Ajax, *for which I'd asked contributors for their* worst *unpublished piece. Lester (qua text) at his ugliest: he himself said so. Greil replied that he did* not *wish to see said piece.*

Well, now that Lester is everybody's moral darling, their blue-eyed idealist, I bet YOU wouldn't mind seeing "Drunk Punk Ofay, Pretending He's a Nigger." I've got it stashed, and if I live a bit longer perhaps you will.

Jack Kerouac was a writer. That is, he wrote. Many people who call themselves writers and have their names on books are not writers and can't write, like the bullfighter who makes passes with no bull there. The writer has been there or he can't write about it. And going there, he risks being gored.
—William Burroughs, "Remembering Jack Kerouac"

For whatever it's worth, and it's probably not worth much, a grouchy inner voice assures me I am such a beast: a writer. An absurd, perverse pursuit in the short run as well as long, the activity, the solemn goddam *task*, of writing is not only as arduous, as tedious, as working in a

coal mine—it's as dangerous. Eschew protective gear and you're looking for trouble. Writing can kill. It's killed one out of every three writers—of the true, coal-colored stripe—whom I've known in this life.

Well, yes, all I've really ever *known* have been three: myself and
Nick Tosches, still quite alive (thankyou) and kicking, and the most
woefully self-destructive human I have ever met, Lester Bangs. A
strong case could in fact be made that Lester, an urn of ashes since
'82, was not kilt by "writing"—that rock & roll, presumably as
Lifestyle, or drugs, or a specific drug (said the coroner: Darvon), or
some combination thereof, did the trick.

It has even been contended that his death was strictly, and merely, a
tragic "accident": an aspirin substitute (in a body that had "turned a
corner" on its own disintegration) on top of the flu. "I've always believed," says Greil Marcus in his intro to the newly released *Psychotic
Reactions and Carburetor Dung*, a nearly 400-page collection of some of
Lester's finer work, "that the violence of his attempt to change his life
left his body shaken, vulnerable to even the slightest anomaly, be it a
commonplace bug or an ordinary dose of anyone else's everyday
painkiller; that he had shocked his system toward health and that that
was what killed him."

Among Lester's closer cronies, especially those of us who directly
witnessed those initially promising, yet ultimately fruitless, final
months of the big oaf's gallant attempt to save his own life, this has
indeed, for the past five years, been the prevailing—at least *a* prevailing—view. With minor modifications, I've generally, until now, had
no problem with it. Reading this hefty volume of stuff, however, I
have to reject it as fortuitous Romantic claptrap; as kneejerk revisionism of the sorriest sort. How, *knowing Lester*, we could've even momentarily bought such horseshit is beyond me. After giving him as
thorough a read as I can bear I'm convinced his death was no accident, and that poor Lester's "body" (or its alleged health) was hardly
the culprit. What killed Lester was Lester. Lester wanted, meant, intended to die. No, I take that back. Want or not, it makes no diff.
Lester, writer, fully in control and command of the Lester System,
had exhausted all life options for Lester, sentient being, making it
functionally impossible for any and all Lesters to continue to live.

Lemme see if I can 'splain it.

In 1965–66, when I first started writing about rockroll, it wasn't as
if I could just as easily have been writing "about" something, anything, else. I wrote *from* it as much as about it, it was the first real
writing I ever really did, and whatever it was (or wasn't) it was cer-

tainly far less "writing" than just basically an urgent round of expression/spew re the only thing, in my realm of experience, that *seemed to merit such urgency*. Rockroll was the whole fucking universe. Or a pretty close approximation. (For a heady dose of *exactly* such Rock-as-Universe brouhaha, check the Dennis-Hopper-digs-Roy-Orbison scene in *Blue Velvet*: candy-colored clowns—dicksters of some shitty little *song!*—as All.) By 1969–70, when the young freight-train Lester joined the rockwrite fray, it was barely the state of Rhode Island.

This hardly subtle shrinkage in the damn thing's import and oom-pah—coupled with its simultaneous mega-expansion as "product"—presented problems for Lester, problems for me, problems for the whole dang (ever-expanding) rockwrite crew. What most of the crew, especially its newest recruits—wide-eyed, earnest and employed as they were by mags whose sole source of publishing to-do was a steady supply of record-company adverts—*did* was simply ignore the fact of shrinkage. Get on the mailing lists, listen to everything, write good reviews, bad reviews (though mostly good reviews)—in any event, *reviews*. Affirmations of the ongoing viability of etc.

Neither Lester nor I could hack even a trial run-through of so chickenshit hand-as-dealt a solution. Me first, what I did was (more or less) listen to nothing, sell every promo album that came my way (mentioning this every chance I got), dash off daily/weekly quotas of "reviews" and whatnot on the basis of having eyeballed various LP covers (if even that), always looking for ways to shuffle in fragments of attempted literature from around my apartment, unexpurgated bulk text from the backs of cereal boxes, grocery lists, gratuitous scattergun rants about this, that and the other (only *occasionally* straining for ad hoc topical relevance to the album or issue at hand)—in a word, hoot up my sleeve, broadcast my abject contempt for the food tube of the music industry, and "invent" Dada Rockcrit in the process. What Lester did to voice *his* contempt was climb a horse, climb a tree, a box, a ladder—whatever was available—and yell, scream at the top of his lungs, demanding, insisting that this lame but still sacred fugger, this former Entire Universe by golly, take drastic steps to keep from sinking further (ever further) in the mire.

You could, if inclined, label my act an "abandonment" of the rock-roll monster, and Lester's a not-unconditional "continued embrace" of same. I just couldn't see things getting too much better; Lester wasn't so sure. By the fall of '70 I was doing pieces on such non-rock subjects as boxing and comic books—lucky for me I had other hobbies. Lester was never so lucky. To his dying day, unless you count

rock and drugs as separate—and throw in his final avowed "hobby,"
Humanist Compassion—the man had no interests per se in this here
life but rock rock rock (and roll). None!

Which is sad, *Christ* it's sad; and as you thumb through this collection, sequenced more or less chronologically, you catch stage after
stage, incarnation after incarnation, of Lester's ever-expanding disappointment with a Sole Interest which, try as *he* may, can't manage to
ever quite wise or measure up. I mean geez, first piece in the book
(June '71) and he's already half-laughing, half-crying, 'bout the ultimate *fate* of garage rock: even the *junk* had by then been debased! For
every in-the-flesh Slade there would be eleventen fleshless Bowie albums, and imagine this flesh/blood ne'er-say-die-er actually *listening*
to all 'leventen before discovering something provisionally "good"
(p. 161) on David's *twelve*teenth. (Maybe Marcus, who selected all this
stuff, sees such discovery as "life-affirming"; I see it as tiny compensa-
tion for all the wear and tear to the poor buzzard's finely tuned shit-
detector up to that point.) Imagine, further, this grizzled rock-war
veteran's *astonishment* (p. 252) at a Clash roadie beating on a fan: ya
mean *punk* rock—gulp—'s no different from rock?!?! And imagine,
most excruciatingly of all (p. 267), anyone of one-*tenth* Lester's mettle
using (and being sorrowfully aggrieved by!) Richard Hell as a touchstone for *anything* . . . what a sad fucking joke.

For Lester, more than for any other True Believer covering this
shit, the rock pickings began lean and they got leaner, offering him
progressively far more torture than nurture, as meantime all these
sidelines jerks ("colleagues" as well as readers, goody-two-shoed aca-
demicians as well as one-trick pukesters from hell) awarded him gold
stars, platinum stars, ostensibly for continuing to visit (and thus legit-
imize, even though he progressively loathed it) the same rock
cesspool as they, 'stead of *purple hearts* for his daily doses of shrapnel
to the heart and nuts, his performance of a (hardly essential) service
which *hurt him far, far more than it possibly could them.*

Never one to leave lean enough alone, Lester ultimately couldn't
even let his personal *gods* (Iggy, Lou Reed et al) endure, hounding the
bastards, cracking makeshift whips as they hobbled on assorted cul-
tural/occupational gimps, finally playing themselves out even in *their*
own terms, leaving *him*self with zero means of life-support (he certainly didn't look to *food* for sustenance!) but lingering echoes of the
Myth of Lester. Which he proceeded, as with the Myth of Rock, to
dismantle/destroy/"deconstruct" with supreme-is-not-the-*word* prej-

udice. His days already numbered—and I'm not talking "physically"—he undertook the chore of unwriting his own life.

Not consciously, of course. And not as effectively, perhaps, as in any of his previous missions of note. There was a good deal of sloppiness, tentativeness, indecision; had his focus been clearer, his aim willfully truer, he'd never have made it to 32. But, c'mon, there was more fury and *impetuosity* in Lester's "post"-self-destructive mode than in his non-post at its most arch-brutal, and the semi-unwitting easy target was, whoops, a too-vulnerable, already drastically weakened Lester himself. Bully-boy masochism, Jim! (Heck hath no fury like the wrath of Lester, self-directed, self-contained.)

He no longer let himself get away with *dick*, and double-ditto for "us." Us? Well, hey, I'm not exactly sure—the extended "Lester family"? A contempo-fallen huddled mass of, I dunno, quasi-likeminded unreconstructed scenewarts and sillysillies? In any event, a heap of sufferin' cartoon humanity as absurdly fat-targeted and ill-defined as the unforgettable "them" of pathetic hippie yore. Lester the Great Moralist (who has easily copped the lion's share of *posthumous* Lester awards) (the sickest of posthumous Lester jokes!), the first Lester more right*eous* than right, was an evolutionary development which served no one, least of all Lester.

Lester as Auditioning Saint, for as long as he lived to strut it, was a number, in fact, which never quite managed to ring true. Forget how splashingly the bombastic Young Lester would've *pissed* on it as so much sham 'n' pomposity, ignore what a crummy done-with-mirrors version it was of the *eternally* bitchy/cranky Lester the High-Horse Complainer—the whole thing was simply never as existentially one-to-one with any *actual* Lester-of-the-moment as it was with his role-play de jour. So divorced was it from any experiential "reality," so devoid of concrete "content" (that he could, as needed, pull off an actual shelf), that, like Li Po drowning in the moon's wet reflection, he ultimately couldn't take it to any earthly bank but that of his own non-being. Saints are *dead people*, dig?

Okay, let me can the metaphor. In Lester's Final Act, a frigging *neophyte* was left minding the store. Aside from making for a page or ten of lousy literature (pages whocareswhynamethem) (and I don't think they're lousy, though I bet *he* would), something dying Real Writers are *entitled* to leave around their squalid apts. for the editorially minded to snatch and subsequently print, the real-writer decision (by one whose adult life had theretofore been *animated* by and from some cornball Writing Central) to entrust an untried phantasm (Good Boy Lester) whose experience (or lack of it) placed him/it light years from the center-of-gravity of etc. with the keys to his writerly kingdom, his goddam writerly *persona*, was hardly likely to thereby *illuminate* (or significantly prolong) the remainder of his damn-fool days, to keep him from taking the inevitable handful of 14th Street Darvon for a lousy cold.

And I loved him and sorely miss him and this silly book don't mean SHIT.

WEDDINGS,
BREASTS AND
DIRTY CLOTHES

Introduction

Social living is the best.
—Burning Spear

And how 'bout a taste of the ugliness of *me*?

Some bitchy, brooding chronicles of despicable behavior towards (and with) friends and cohorts. Templates of rock-referenced debauchery. Prima facie evidence of the nihilism of youth: callous and callow.

A cluster of social studies peopled by recurrent faces, manymost of them connected. Candid pix of their outsides and insides, and mine. The great chain of rockroll being.

Including premeditated backstabs and eyegouges: given . . . received (same diff).

You didn't have to know this stuff exists. Why do I feel compelled to share it with you?

Aww, my mother never breastfed me.

And the power of friendship to redeem and heal—or not permanently maim. It'll make you cry.

88

Noted Rock Crit Ties the Knot

At the next press party after this social note appeared, a woman I'd never met came up to me and without ado says, "I'll have you know I passed the audition." Huh whuh? Turned out she's the future Mrs. Christgau, Radcliffe graduate Carola Dibbell. Bobbo must've shown it to impress her on a fucking date or something.

Ah! the power of the word!

Knot-tying is real big in Philadelphia. They're all married. The Tearsons, the Damskers, they're all married. Hooked. Hitched. Fuckin wedded before the eyes of Big Bozo upstairs. New York there's much fewer lefthanded ring fingers with the old metal on it. When was the last one to make it legal, the Richard & Lisa Robinsons? No there was the Bud & Linda Scoppas. And way before that the Ed & Jeanie McCormacks. Christgau's always auditioning somebody for the role of permanent mate but he hasn't turned up anything just yet. Richard Goldstein and his honey-bear have called it "quits." Matrimony in NYC is fuckin shot to shit.

Did I say *is*, I mean *was*. Cause there's a new one now and it's the best so far. Nick & Sunny Tosches. They went down to City Hall and this guy in a lavender shirt and tie did the honors and when she couldn't get the ring on her finger he said "Whatsamatter, eatin too many potatoes?" As a matter of fact she does like the old tuber pretty much whether it's mashed, fried, baked or boiled. Or mashed. She drinks a lotta Almaden white from Californey-ay and speaking of Californ she has fornicated. With Nick. They fucked and fucked and fugged till the cows came home and then once for good measure and this was all before the nuptials had begun.

It all started when he got back from Tampa where he was working as a crab fisherman. Moved into the Alton House on 14th St. & 7th

Ave. where he got a real nice furnished room that included a mattress and a milk crate and a felt curtain and she wouldn't stay there with him so he moved around the corner to her place on 15th & 7th—1/2 a block away from the humble abode of Mr. Mel Lyman. But that was 2 yrs after since he picked her up at St. Adrian's and he knew her for 2 yrs and often brought her to press parties at Max's including the time when everybody went over to Patti Johnson's place and Keith whatsisface tore up her living room and she ain't talked to anyone since.

In fact Patti's apt. was being considered as a potential site for the post-wedding party which was the reason for the wedding to begin with, partyin. Nobody had the balls to call her up tho. And everybody else turned down their house too, especially Daphne Davis. Daphne said her place was okay if she didn't go away for the weekend and she was gonna go away if her car got fixed. So there was this plan for a while but it never got put into effect. It was find her car cause it's always parked near her place at 952 Fifth Ave. and not too many automobiles are permanently parked in that neck of the woods with PENNSYLVANIA PLATES. So it was gonna be find her vehicle and stick some sugar down the gas tank but it never happened and she took to the open road with wheels unharmed.

So it ended up with Nick & Sunny's place getting used for the party and Jerry Flaherty was there in his Sunday best with the Air Raid Kid at his side for when he had to take a wee. And he did. The onion dip was near Jerry so nobody ate any. The guacamole was on one of Sunny's friends' laps and she hogged it till it was gone, complaining all the while about "too much onions and garlic." Speaking of which, Lois Goldberg was present too and for the first time anyone could remember she didn't complain about "you got bad breath." If you remember there was that time at King Street Smith's house when she ended up with a beer on her head for just such a remark but this time all she said was "C'mere dear" to her brand new bearded male companion (looked like a wimp to me). Aforementioned marrieds and exes Mr. & Mrs. McC (their gift was a vintage '66 objet d'art by Ed) and Dick Goldstein were present as was CREEM's own Vince Aletti and Patti (for 5 minutes) Smith. But the following did not attend so fuck em: the Scoppas, Christgau, Paul Nelson, Karin Berg, Mary Jane Geiger. Lillian Roxon had an excuse so she was excused. Sandy Pearlman wasn't invited (he dresses funny). The best present was the snake they got that eats live chameleons. Best shoes were worn by John Dowd. Best wife tits were one of Sunny's friends who smelled pretty good and she pushed your hand away but not too fast.

Sunny's 2nd wedding, Nick's 1st.

89

A Pair of Tim Tales

"Kicked out of Rolling Stone"? Yeah. Jon Landau threw me out of only the review section. Jackson (with the assistance of Asylum head D*a*v*i*d G*e*f*f*e*n) got me axed from the whole thing, which dismayed me some 'cause I'd thought of him as almost an approximate not-too-distant crony. Or chum. Hell, I knew Jackson WHEN, about as when as it gets, both him and his music, and wrote the piece—his first Stone *feature—as a courtesy, a kindness, on the occasion of his first LP. (I know—I say this about all of 'em.) I'd met Jackson through a buddy at Stony Brook named John Wiesenthal, who some years before, when they surfed together, taught him the rudiments of guitar. John was an early member of the first band Pearlman managed, Soft White Underbelly, as for one gig was I. In '68 the Underbelly backed Jackson at an East Coast show or two promoted or arranged by Pearlman, who wanted to manage him. The year before, at Warhol's St. Marks dive, the Dom, Jackson himself had backed (and made whoopee with) the fabulous N*i*c*o, my mention of whom (and which) in the* Stone *story pissed him off no end—that and the surfing. Covering tracks: Jackson was not always Jerry Brown (Sam Shepard?) in singer-songwriter drag, he was the Byron of pre-punk minimalism . . . don't pass it on.*

He was also there (and had input) the night Underbelly drummer Albert Bouchard dropped acid to try and devise a strategy for beating the draft at his physical in the morning (see Aesthetics of Rock, *p. 264).*

Tom Robbins, in 1995, wrote a blurb for my novel, The Night (Alone), *so I'm sure he never saw this.*

Oh, and another connection—conjunction—"convergence": didn't Landau produce a mid-period Jackson album? Two guys getting me tossed from a source of income—independently—and later doing a record together. What's the odds on that?

At this bookstore I once worked, an occasionally fashionable West Hollywood landmark which no longer exists, my first assignment on the first day of my employment was to guard the door for a Tom Robbins whatsis. A gravely serious Tom Robbins booksigning whatsis. Unless he'd just copped a "quickie" from Meryl Streep or Lillian Gish—or planned to later that evening—the Great Author appeared to have left his precious Seattle *solely* for this: to sell and sign hardbacks of his latest piece o' dogshit, something with jitterbug in the title. *Jitterbug Waltz*, no, that's a Fats Waller song, I dunno, jitterbug something. They were selling like hotcakes in Hungerville.

My job was to keep all these idiot yuppies from storming the barricades and also check their carry-in crap. Like if they had any shitty *earlier* novels for His Trendiness's signature, for instance the one with scarecrow in the title or maybe it was woodpecker, or the cowgirl thing, everybody knows that one, I was supposed to attach a sticker indicating "previously purchased." So they wouldn't be faced with the embarrassment of "Have you *paid* for that yet?" This was the storeowner's way of being kind to yuppie scum.

Jitterbug Perfume. That was the title. The line of scum was three times around the block. No, actually it wasn't even once around, not a complete—what's the word?—circumnavigation, it strung out endless to my left but never quite made it 'round to the right. Must've been, dunno, eight hundred? Five hundred? *Lots* of repulsive pus-suckers, lemme tell ya. Outraged jerkos crying, "What?—He's *not* going to read? Why didn't you tell us? I came all the way from Glendale!" People with whining brats begging, "Please, I can't keep my child amused much longer. Can't you let us in *slightly* ahead of our turn?" To which everybody in front of 'em would shout, "NOOOOOOOOOOOOOOOO!" This went on for three-four hours.

At one point suddenly it was Jackson Browne at the door. He'd been on line for maybe two hours with this blonde—I don't go to movies—who it turned out was Daryl Hannah. Everybody went "Ooooooooh." The last time I'd seen Jackson he'd responded to a piece I'd done on him by getting me kicked out of *Rolling Stone* and off the Asylum Records mailing list: oceans under *that* bridge! "I'm here," said he, "because *she* respects the man's work. I've never read him." I put on my very best needs-to-work-in-a-bookstore-'cause-he-can't-make-it-just-from-writing look. It worked—shaming him into buying my ugly buildings book and the first two volumes of my autobiography. It's possible, but I can't remember f'r sure if he had me sign them for Daryl.

Finally—half an hour left—this old wooden pecker sauntered to the door and declared, "I must get in. I must see Tom Robbins. He's a prophet of the New Age." (Oh *boy* was I tired of this job.) I looked in the eyes of this white haired geek, I looked at the muttering throngs, I looked back at the geek and said, "Sure, Tim, if you wanna be an elitist prick go right ahead." He did. The throngs gasped, moaned. "Who the hell was that? Why'd you let him in?" "You didn't recognize the old fart? Why, that was Timothy Leary." *Oooooooooh.*

• • •

I once bought a six-pack of this stuff called Knickerbocker Dark. Only once; never again. Not that I even drank it that time. Tim Leary drank it instead.

I doubt he'd remember it—this was 1966—but if I run into him again in this life I should probably ask him how it tasted. Knicker-bocker, regular Knickerbocker, I guess you would call it their lager, tasted kind of like newsprint. With ink on it. You ever make spitballs out of newspaper? It tasted like that. As opposed to, say, Schaefer, an-other New York beer which may or may not still exist, which always reminded me of rubber bands.

Why, y'might wonder, did I get the dark version of a beer I already knew to be flavor kin to newsprint? I can't recall my motives. I do re-call, though, the cans were sort of rusty. This was before aluminum. Maybe they were all the place I bought 'em at had. The last six-pack in the house.

Anyway, they ended up in Sandy Pearlman's fridge, Smithtown, N.Y. Not far from Stony Brook, N.Y., home of one of *the* great dope schools of the '60s, SUNY-Stony Brook. My alma mater. Pearlman's too. I must've bought the Knicks—as aficionados I'm sure called them (though I have no strong memory of that fact)—from some lo-cal grocer and stashed them at Pearlman's till we got back from Long Island disco-hopping. Or till . . . dunno. As it turned out the till was till Tim got there.

And it happened like this. Pearlman, a one-time best friend who currently owes me between four and six thousand dollars, was out at the Brook for a Leary lecture. One of those "turn on, tune in, drop out" specials. A living's a living. Afterwards, the former student body prexy graciously offered to drive the guy home. But first a thirst stop at the Pearlman manse and—voila!—six Knicker Darks. Which, between Smithtown and Manhattan, fall '66, the Great Dropout downed—unassisted—rust and all.

90

The Blue Öyster Cult:
On Your Feet or on Your Knees

Let's see, what background do you need on THIS?

Bloom became the Underbelly's singer, in the spring of '69, primarily 'cuz he had a van, all paid up, and his predecessor's own van had been repossessed; he also had a PA. His singing, however, didn't guarantee him permanence, and one night a year later, while he slept, the band auditioned me and Pearlman to replace him (neither of us panned out). I'd already sung with them, in a matter of speaking, running around yelling "PISS!" onstage at the Café au Go-Go (fall '67), sticking my head inside the bass drum and unplugging patchcords while people soloed. More importantly, I served as their longtime muse and author (till about '71) of the preponderance of their lyrics.

This has to be my earliest published BÖC piece that Pearlman had no hand in. There'd probably been five or six, pseudonymous or not, where he stood in the room and virtually dictated my copy—to insure I didn't kill the goose that might someday lay whatever. Sure I had an economic interest in their success, but I once had an artistic one too. (By '75 all I wanted was my money.)

Pearlman was big on covering the band's tracks, insisting the world would end if even its former names *were revealed. A classic rock paranoid, he changed 'em from the Underbelly to the Stalk-Forrest Group (the what??) when a West Point dropout, son of one of Patton's generals, didn't so much slag as ignore them—"the less said, the better"—in a* Voice *review of their Fillmore East appearance with Jethro Tull and Jeff Beck. Having never done a rock review before, the guy didn't realize he needn't mention every band, but Pearlman took it hard—"Our name is mud in this town." Oaxaca, my suggestion, was an interim name that didn't stick (they were also briefly the Santos Sisters).*

In 1970 I introduced Patti to Pearlman, who beyond wanting to manage her wanted her, *and who brought her to the session where she met rhythm guitarist/keyboardist Allen Lanier, with whom she would soon shack up.*

"Career of Evil," her contribution to Secret Treaties, *the third BÖC album, was the first forcible fusion of rock and Rimbaud.*

On each of the early Columbia albs I had at least a lyric or two, but on the one after On Your Feet, *the mega-mega* Agents of Fortune *(containing their biggest hit, "Don't Fear the Reaper"), they used NOTHING of mine; I've never known for sure if that was their doing or Pearlman's. I did later get lucky with "Burnin' for You" (their only other hit), but since I never got my full payoff the luck was only relative. Though my best-known lyric, I wouldn't rank it with either "Teen Archer" (on* Tyranny and Mutation*) or "Arthur Comics," one side of the Elektra single which constitutes their total vinyl output from before they went for the faux-nazi sturm und drang, all the heavy-handed laser baloney.*

I'm the dummy, by the way, responsible for the umlaut over the "O" . . . before Motörhead, before Mötley Crüe, before Queensrÿche. Inotherwords, in addition to my many National League batting titles, I also (in all likelihood) introduced GRATUITOUS USE OF THE UMLAUT to U.S. (possibly even Anglo-U.S.) rock and roll. Love me or leave me!

But was David Geffen head of Elektra in '75? And what Dylan was that, Planet Waves?

Anyway, this review didn't run in the high-circulation glossy that assigned it 'cause I fell down with the editor's girlfriend (while he was boogyin' her roommate in Ensenada—oh, life!) and he found out. So I gave it for free to some jerkwater sheet with a circulation of six.

Ran into Eric ("Don't call me Manny") Bloom of the BÖC formerly known as the Stalk-Forrest Group f/k/a Oaxaca f/k/a the Soft White Underbelly the other nite following him and his band's smash 2nd fiddle to the Faces at Madison Square Garden home of the New York (but you can have em Sheboygan) Rangers and the old coozehound (he once got crabs in his beard) tells me I will not be receiving my long-awaited royalty smackola from *Secret Treaties* for the next umpteen sometimes to come. Baaaaaad news in light of the $2500 total I pocketed in '74 for everything I wrote for every magazoon the entire goddam year but seems B. O'Cult Music Publishing Inc. decided this poor struggling beat combo had more pressing need of the songwriting boodle due to heavy travel expenses to Jersey and Pennsylvania and leather hot pants and studded belts and ugly space

bracelets and all the rest-o-things required for projecting the menac-
ing "now" look of today's rock and roll.

Hey I'm not complaining that Patti Smith got *her* royalties from
"Career of Evil" altho she ain't even in the band because Pearlman
thinks if he pays her he can get in her pants even tho she's with Allen
Lanier (when she's not with Tom Verlaine) . . . not at all. Cause
Eric—formerly known as Roy Mucilage—tells me not to worry as
their newie is *bound to go gold* (promises, promises: said the same thing
last time) (Pearlman said it tho, not E. "M." Bloom) and since I got a
song on it ("Harvester of Eyes") I won't hafta be pickin up no varicose
standing on bread lines.

Yeah, swell, goody goody gumdrops, pretty penny's gonna be comin
my way in no time flat, who could axe for anything more? But like I
said I've heard it before so I guess I'll hafta play it safe and encourage
a gold rush with a STRICTLY POSITIVE REVIEW. Don't suppose
these paragraphs're gonna sell or unsell more'n 3 or 4 copies but you
never can tell, people might just suddenly be nutser than squirrels and
the printed rock word—who knows?—may suddenly somehow've
gotten bigger (in Shreveport and Altoona) than the flugging bible, it's
certainly worth the gamble and the effort and what the hell anyway,
this review should net me a solid 2 figures.

Okay, lessee, um well for one thing (my record player's been bust
since April but I did get to hear it off a cassette in a vehicle) Don
Roeser's back in form. Time was ('68-'69-'70) good ole Don was the
goshdamn king of em all, back then you would have to've said out of
the 10 hottest geetar solos live or in studio at least 9 of em had to be
his (I ain't kiddin). In the interim he kind of slipped a couple-three-
four-five notches but who cares cause he wasn't talkin to me no more
anyway. Seems I'm SUPPOSED to've messed up his wedding tho all
I did was fondle his mom around the chest and hind (nice . . . *nice*)
and yell out "Sandi Nazi! Sandi Nazi!" (that's Don's wife altho she
spells it Nasci) and me and Allen each both threw beer bottles thru a
window or something, y'know just havin a good time and in fact I
even already got punished (by KARMA) by arrivin home all sick and
hung over with *shit in my pants* from not wiping thorough enough
(most passengers in Pearlman's car thought the odor was from Manny
but the fact is it was *me*) so you'd think the Roesers woulda forgave
me but no such luck. Well anyway DON'S PLAYING IS NOW
TOP OF THE HEAP ONCE MORE, THE TOPMOST TOP-
MOST TOP AND THAT'S NO LIE.

As great a showcase of pickin as you'd ever wanna hear (c'mon Donny-Boy, time to lift a tall cool one with your old bud Dick again!) and my pal Terry Atkinson listens to it every day while shavin the hairs off his face and even after he's done cause he sez it is *that good*—he oughta know cause he's played it more than me. Rest of the Cult-boys are in ace/primo/A-1 form as well and now that I've complimented all you fuckers how's about usin more of my lyrics next time studio obligations rear their head and I mean two or three or four (such as: "I Live with the Roaches," "A Wrestling Kind of Love" and "Just like Hansel & Gretel" but whichever ones you wanna use is fine by me, I'm tolerant).

Really folks, readers of this sheet, this elpee's their best since the one they cut for Elektra back in '70 (hey David Geffen if you're readin this and all those Cher lawsuits aren't gettin you down, THAT'S THE ONE Y'REALLY OUGHTA RELEASE, IT'LL MAKE YOU MORE THAN BOBBY DYLAN DID, NO SHIT, IT'S IN THE VAULT THERE SOMEWHERE UNDER EI-THER OAXACA OR THE STALK-FORREST GROUP). Nah, this one's even better, 2 records (a "double") so it's *twice* as good, maybe even 2.6 and I'm not talkin Richter scale. Swear to god, I wouldn't lie.

Why would I lie?

91

Handsome Dick Throws the Party of the Century

Another thing that estranged me from Pearlman was my championing (over BÖC) a band I personally brought to his stable, but who never made him a dime, the Dictators. Both the Cult and the Dictators were arguably comedy bands, but the latter were serious about their comedy (and funnier), grounded more in wrestling (and the primeval slime of rock-roll bathos) than "funny Nazi" arcana or mock-metal flummery. In the 'Tators' "Master Race Rock" their master race was fucked up Bronx teenagers.

They also lived funkier lives, and the funkiest of all was their roadie, cook, and eventual singer Richard Blum (a/k/a Handsome Dick Manitoba)—my sometime sidekick and acolyte. Parties with Dick were "Can you top this?" specials—no one-up opp declined (he once bit the head off a stuffed duck)—but at the bash described here he topped everybody.

Essay questions (for extra credit): Is the scene of the party heaven, hell, or merely heck? Is the author beneath, above, or astride contempt? Was AIDS invented principally, or only secondarily, to undermine the "casual" ginch-grope of mid-'70s urban youth (and what are the consequences today of its undermining)? How would you feel if Keanu Reeves were cast to play Handsome Dick? Johnny Depp, ditto?

Co-op City is the f'in end of the world even in the Bronx, it's a goddam real life Alphaville (don't live there). "Handsome" Dick Manitoba's mommy & daddy weren't happy where they were livin in the Bronx part of the Bronx (middle class dimwits) so they packed up Dick and their clothes and furniture and moved em all to Co-op C. No more old neighborhood buddies for Dick (boo hoo) so he figured well he oughta throw em a party the second the folks headed for vacationland.

Look at Dick and you're lookin at a whale cause he's a big'un. Real big and he is also a teen (19). Teens don't f'in do nothin anymore but take downs and Dick is no exception (eats em like candy). He takes em and he's big and clumsy and he falls over on stuff and the other week he woke up in a shower when his buddies dumped him there cause they thought he was OD'ing or something (just to be safe). He's destroyed many a house so all the invited guests figured this was their chance to f his place over in return but they were in for a surprise . . . but first the party.

The party starts out this girl about 17-18 spills a drink on her jeans and starts cryin cause she's wet. Big s so she's wet. Her mouth was wet, her gash was wet but it wasn't okay for her trousers to be wet (very inconsistent). So the idea was replace em with a pair of Dick's sister's pants and since his sis was out-o-town that was e-z to arrange but she wouldn't put em on in front of people (hadda do it in the bathroom). Many of today's teens are shy, they will not stroke themselves in front of otters, scuse me, others.

MUSIC WAS IN THE AIR. Cuts instead of entire sides. "Maggie May." "I'm Waitin for My Man." "Can't Explain." Something by the Flamin Groovies. "When the Music's Over." The usual fare (no Bowie or any of that s was played, not one f'in note, the teenos at this frolic were not the kind you read about in Creem or the Decadence Monthly). SMASH: Dick was smashin records (they were only his sister's). Broken f'in records all over the floor and broken glass in the kitchen which the wet-pants gal was steppin on and screaming some more: an f'in neurotic.

Lots of stray teen gash that no one was touchin at all. That you could reach your hand up, 15, 16, 17, 18, 19. As well as 20. But no one was touchin. F'in deadbeats cause they were f'ed up on quaaludes. Dick was only wearin a jock by now (9 ludes) and pink swastikas in lipstick all over his body. He requested a mouth on his pecker from any gal willing but no go. Maybe it was his party but they weren't about to suck whale meat. But that don't mean they wouldn't suck people meat so I made my move.

I'd been feelin and nuzzlin tit and ass and stealing kisses (including tongues) all night but now was time for some GINCH. Invited a cute short big-tit-and-asser (but don't call her "chubby") into Dick's sister's pissroom (co-op apts have many) and removed her outer and under pants in a flash. Nice f'in bush on the honey, dark and f'in thick with growth. Welcomed her 7teen-year-oldness down on my face on the floor (no glass on this floor til later and no puke yet either) and slurped away. Good f'in stuff containing no FDS (some teens use it cause they don't know no better at their early age). Yum yum yummy, eatin slit, eatin clit, eatin vulva, eatin all the rest of whatever you call it all, tastiest stuff in the house (Dick forgot to buy food and beer and invited 300 people).

Then an f'in knock on the door and it's my old lady (old ladies always get in your hair at teengash parties). Goddam and she knew it was me in there so I hadda zip up and abandon the hanky panky (got more off her later tho and 3 or 5 other ones all let me stick my hand up their moisture cause nobody else was payin attention to em on account of the downers). Told th'old lady (under heavy questioning) all I got was some tit and she fell for it altho not dumb (lucky me). And speaking of her mamms they were swell, ripe f'in melons with a tan line around em from the sun (not too many sunners in New York anymore) and a sore over one nip from a scratched mosquito bite or something.

Music was no longer playing cause by now the record player was broken, Dick fell on it. Also on four lamps including the expensive kind with a vase type thing at the bottom, ugly expensive s (middle classers buy it all the time). An ugly sculpture too which Dick also fell on so bye bye sculpture, you were ugly and deserved to die. Also the couch and the chairs all covered with plastic from the cleaning store cause real plastic covers cost too much and you gotta economize when you're livin the life-o-luxury in Co-op City and Dick stomped on all of em with dirty fat feet and tore several upholsteries in the process.

Also everything, all broken, the whole f'in house. Dick broke it himself so everybody didn't even have to come out of their sopor stupors to get their revenge on him. For having already destroyed their houses or apts. Did it all himself and by now somebody'd hidden his dope in the TV so all he was sayin was "I want some hash and some beer."

Folks out on the veranda or the porch or whatever you call it (great view from there, a great view of nowhere cause nowhere is where it is, millions of miles from anything else so the f'in residents think they're far far away from all the robbin and thieving criminals & delinquents) were droppin stuff over the side and one of em hit a cop car with a torn up cushion (26th floor) so the cops came up and tore what was left of the place apart. But the dope was well hid in the TV so they left Manitobe and the gang alone until they returned to wake him up at 5:30 just to harass his fat ass.

Real good party even tho nobody got laid (I did at home but that's just home, it don't count). In attendance were members of the Dictators, up-and-coming hot rock unit from the Bronx and Queens including Handsome Dick altho sometimes they have second thoughts cause maybe he'll "ruin" it for em. Fine party, very fine and except at the very beginning music DID NOT make it possible. Time was music is what made parties possible. Kids don't f'in need "pop" music no more (any more'n they need soda pop), they get off on life itself: cookin with gas. Pop music is PLOP MUSIC. Nobody needs it.

92

Patti's Pair o' Paps

First of all, a skinmag asked *for this, it was NOT my idea—and I probably* needed the hundred bucks.

My prime motive, however, was to directly address Patti, as if to say: "Pay attention to *me, rockstar/former friend; we were once equals, remember?" I* was also quite certain, in my usual dumb rock-overdrive state, that Patti, in her *rock overdrive, could and would dig it: it was a rock & roll* thing to do *(maybe* Hollywood *celebs would take offense, but at the very cultural least* rockers were cooler—and wasn't Patti the original "tough chick"?). Third: she always wore these loose upperbody garments—the "androgynous" look— and few knew what a bounteous stack she had under there (a Pulitzer-level scoop for the latent reporter in me). But for crying out loud, the lousy piece is* drenched *with irony, parody, satire, send-up, all such broadly painted comedic mirror (i.e., reverse . . . i.e., un-) reality—farce! burlesque!—it's a fucking genre exercise!—not to be taken as depicting my own goddam DIS-POSITION towards women—friends or otherwise, past or present—and their bodies. (And, verily, as with many a malice-filled jester at a celebrity roast, the real "target," the object of "ridicule," if any, is clearly* myself.*) Or was it all just betrayal for betrayal, tit for tat?*

The last time I saw Patti before writing this, backstage at the Roxy, L.A. '76, it was like one of those scenes from Hard Day's Night *with the Beatles in a room full of sycophants, reporters fawning, flashbulbs popping. When the closest I got was to have her tell me, "Richard, would you* move?*—can't you see a photographer wants my picture?"* my blood curdled.

The bit about the "out-of-wedlock crybabe" was just another story SHE used to tell. In no way did I intend it as anything more "scandalous" than any of the bullcrap in my Radio Ethiopia *review: snippets of mythos ear-marked (however briefly) for publication; the ongoing content of her own verbal press release. The problem with Patti was not that she wanted to be all things to all people (she wasn't Madonna), but she did wanna be* lots *of things to lotsa people—and the lotsa changed daily.*

Lemme go on record right now (what's it?, 2/17/2000) and say I am NOT PLEASED WITH MYSELF for having written the accursed thing:

NO! But I can't say I ever really lost any sleep over it, except for the night some 23 years ago, soon after publication, when Allen Lanier called and woke me, threatening to beat me up (an Old South kinda guy, in the last century he'd've challenged me to a duel) before changing gears and using the occasion to re-malebond with me, though I don't know if he and Patti were (in more than theory) still together.

The last time I laid eyes on her, '79 or so, Patti was perched on the sunroof of a yellow Cadillac limo, sipping soda from a paper cup, waving to fans gathered for her in-store appearance at Licorice Pizza on Sunset Strip— waving WELL BEFORE the limo was close enough for anyone to notice. Closer, she tossed the cup and, spotting me, said brusquely, with no trace of a smile, "Could you pick that up? I don't want my fans to see me litter." I just walked away.

In '95, the editor on my novel spoke to her about writing me a cover blurb. She said she'd be proud *to do me one, but I knew she never would. She didn't. Nick Tosches, once tight with her himself, told me recently that he runs into Patti a lot, here and there in the West Village, but she just squints, feigning difficulty in recognition—where's my specs? who you?—and moves on . . .*

Why do I *keep on?*

This scuzzy NYC rag called *Daily Planet* came out this summer with surreptitiously obtained "art pics" of rock songstress Patti Smith's nekkid mamms and bush and the rest of what accompanies em. From when she was livin with artist Robt. Mapplethorpe in the early '70s and all *sorts* of artsyfartsies were being committed left & right. Fact is Pat and the law firm of Delson & Gordon're now suing the *pants* off the *Planet* folks for runnin those shots but in the meantime anybody with one or more eyeballs is in the fortunate position of bein able to 20-20 Ms. Smith's real fine unclothed fleshy goodstuff and even after too cause who's gonna go around confiscating personal property in this man's USA even if the courts throw the scoundrels responsible for revealing PS's outasite twat, hind and suckems in the penitentiary for 99 yrs and a day, right?

No actual dripping beaver is shown however, so all you've got is the shorthaired externals (good hair-pie but, y'know, *big deal*). Ditto on the arse: just a pair of all reet butthalves with nary a trace of rectum (big deal again). TITS THO ARE ANOTHER MATTER EN-

TIRELY. What you see is what she's got. Big-uns for one of so thin a frame (97 lbs). Hangin down to maybe the 3rd rib or so. Squeeze em and your palm and digits will not meet with dissatisfaction (take it from me cause I already *have*—got myself a real good grab that is— and not against the lady's will, goody goody goody for me, somethin that cannot be said for the famous Mr. David Dalton who was once told to lay his fuckin hands *off* brother, this gal is plenty selective).

Nips on em're real fuggin my-t-fine too. Average size with real good definition and by average I don't mean average, I mean, y'know, no smaller than a pair of cantaloupes like hers fully merit. Round (some dames have em elliptical which is fine for geometry fans but rock & roll folks prefer em circular like their latest LP so Patti's right on the money in this regard). A little darker than average, tips a bit darker still when erect (as is often the case during a physical-as-heck Patti performance when she's wearin one of them real swell sweaty t-shirts that can be seen *right thru* but even if they ain't sweated up hard nips'll show thru anyways—in form if not living color) (greatest showtime showbiz nips since Janis's, greater in fact: only Jayne Mansfield's got the edge at this stage of things and she's deader than soot so Patti's got a chance to become *the* all-time nipple queen).

And lest we forget what God *invented* papillae for: yes Patti's have lactated droplets of hot nourishing mom's-milk (had an out-of-wedlock crybabe back around whenever it was).

A "now" woman all the way, Patti Lee rarely adorns her South Jersey knobs in brazeers or any of *that* stuff (bouncy bouncy bouncy). Sometimes she does for heavy dates tho and imagine bein the lucky guy lucky enuff to remove her straps before nuzzlin her knockers and then proceeding south to dig for clam! (Yes dates are most definitely required to get a peek at the actual goldmine beyond her thatch, as Patti has announced that *no squish snaps are likely to be taken in the foreseeable future and printed up for mass distribution surreptitious or otherwise.*)

93

The Blasters: *Over There*

Well, so I wasn't gonna risk messing up another friendship by cogently dis-
cussing somebody's career . . . no thanks.
    The coupling, in the final paragraph, of the Blasters and the Dictators is
anything but gratuitous. Somewhere in the early '80s the two bands, un-
likely compadres de rock—separate coasts, wholly different artistic and social
orientations—hooked up and became actual friends. Handsome Dick stayed
at Dave Alvin's place in L.A. and broke nothing *(but this was nine-ten*
years after the Big Party).

I've been thinking: Friendship is more important than culture. Far as
I can see, the latter hasn't done a heckuva lot of late to save a single
ass from shit, while many of the people I know/like/love are fans or
purveyors of music, visuals, lit-scribble and such I could easily live
without. My best gal Irene, for inst, is big on showtunes (which make
my *skin crawl*) while every time I play the *New York Eye and Ear Con-*
trol LP she takes a long shower. Our relationship has so far survived
the absence of sync for that sort of diddleyscoot, and I'd be a bigger
asshole than I am to want it any other way.
    It's a little tougher (maintaining friendships) when the people you
like are in bands and you won't go see 'em play. Dave and Phil Alvin
of the Blasters are just about the nicest guys I know. I've played poker
with 'em, I've read poems at readings with Dave, we've talked blues
and boxing and math (which Phil used to teach and I once majored
in), they're people I consistently enjoy *hangin' around*. They're such
damn nice guys that the next to last time I was with Lester I brought
him to poker and he and Phil hit it off *without* Lester being drunk.
They're nice, they're swell, but they play music and I won't go.
    I haven't seen them play in over two years and not because I don't
like their stuff. It's 'cause I don't go to live *anything* anymore—can't

stand crowds, can't stand volume, can't stand cigarettes and reefer, can't stand having to get drunk. I'm a fussy old fusser who would rather take his music lying on the floor reading Faulkner and eating a sandwich. Dave used to rub it in, but lately he's been cool enough to just let me wallow in my over-the-hill. Which hasn't (however) been enough to keep me from feeling *guilty,* friendship and guilt (often) running hand in hand.

So in lieu of catching an actual show of theirs in the foreseeable future, I feel like I owe them a review. Which isn't to say it hasn't been (critically) earned, altho with me you never know where one leaves off and the other whatevers. Rock crit and ad hominem rant have always been part of the same basic routine for me; I've never been able to separate music from things like "motives" and objective-correlative hairstyles and shit like that. Simply put, their music (like them) is friendly—it says *welcome* and does not beat you over the head with *statement*—not the stuff of rock-roll hype and legend perhaps (and what a lame way to pay a debt), but whudda ya want, you want me to maybe lie or something?

Having got myself in what looks like a hole let me now worm my way out by putting such biz in a proper *rock-roll context.* When on their last 12-incher they sang about "American music" they were not being xenophobes or chauvinists or even regionalists: they were being genre-ists maybe but certainly what they were was populists. Like Woody Guthrie. On this here EP five of the six tunes are rock-roll/rockabilly/R&B covers, but that doesn't make 'em archive adepts showing off their record collections, nor does it make 'em fifties *fetishists* rubbing your nose in dimensions of nostalgia you could possibly live without. For one thing, their collections include Archie Shepp and Johnny Rot as well as Johnny "Guitar" Watson, and for another all they're really, truly after (as a band) is the goddam *gift* of revival—a generous recap of long-gone etceteras, plural, that happen to ring truer for 'em than anything current or semi-, but which they're not (ever) gonna get messy or sticky about like the Stray Cats or Ray Campi. They go for the proverbial jugular *neither* as revival practitioners (i.e., living, breathing rockbanders like most others—selling kids recycled product from before they were born) nor as posers within the era revived (i.e., campy "kick-assers" hellbent on porking your mom). Latter of which is not to imply they're lacking in musical teeth—they've got twice the chops of purists like Charlie Musselwhite or schlockos like Asleep at the Wheel (for inst) while being a good deal more in tune with the elective affinities of any true rock-era central nervous system . . . they play hard *and* are not full of shit.

For my money, what the Blasters ultimately are (you might like this) is a POST-ADOLESCENT Dictators zen-secure enough in their musical homesickness to finally hone in on x without making a federal case of it, without the need to be sarcastic or ridiculous or even especially *comical* anymore.

Introduction

Enough thematic digression—let's get on with the basic sequence. My gimp-legged march through all the years to HERE. (I'll be fifty fucking FIVE in a week.) Where were we?

The dregs, the last pressing, the final squeezing of my youth.

In my own head, I like to use 1981 as a cutoff point. It's the year I got kicked off the radio, stopped going to shows, drastically cut my intake of rock vinyl, began phasing out rock *once and for all* in favor of jazz and such. It was also a year in which I wrote mounds and mounds of *non*-critical prose (and poetry), where I imagined (and was probably right) that I'd turned a corner in figuring out "how to write," and where, finally, I lucked into the column which enabled me to undertake making it so. Through supreme effort: *bingo*. For *before and after* purposes, I fancy '81 as the year after which my writing undeniably *is* writing. Ha ha.

Ha.

'Cause in the years that followed, along with really Writing, I found myself acknowledging, more and ever more, the twin demands of (ogod) Art and Communication, and paying *their* respective pipers. And writing Better, that is finally writing At All, I earned a lot less (with cost of living, and pipers' fees, factored in) than I did while only faking it.

The column.

For four years I wrote six pages every two weeks for the *L.A. Reader*, and rarely was I asked to please make it be about music. My "specialty," though I wasn't aware of it just yet: anti-L.A. sermons and diatribes (some included in *L.A. Is the Capital of Kansas*). James Vowell, my editor, never messed with my copy, which was something of a respite from the War Years. Now the war went *within*: raging battles (between me and me; 'tween me-and-me and drooling demons) over such folderol as clarity and concision . . . eloquence and accuracy . . . melody and rhythm at the typewriter/keyboard. The unit installment typically took the full two weeks (drafts and drafts and *drafts*) at 40 bucks a throw. 40 dollars in the EIGHTIES? Ha ha ha ha ha.

Through much of that decade I took outside work—bookstore jobs, mainly—my only regular employment, even part time, 'sides writing since I dunno, 1969? '70? Compelling me to contemplate: if it hadn't been for my rockwrite apprenticeship, then what?

I should probably admit I was lucky. Privileged. To have previously been—say it, *say it*—a rockwriter. For it to have been my insidious job but—certainly!—a job. By means of which, and in the course of which, I slowly got the hang of things . . . evolved and matured "in front of an audience" . . . ultimately got the write thing right. There. I never thought I'd say it.

Maybe I'll unsay it tomorrow.

94

Who'll Stop the Wayne?

Is this the 14th piece in which I refer to Marcel Duchamp, or only the 3rd? In any case: the best.

THINGS YOU CAN ONLY LEARN BY TRAVELING—In case you thought L.A. has the monopoly on Raleigh Hills execu-drunk tanks, they also got one in Vegas (so who knows where else) and they even got Gale Storm. Yes I was in L.V. (on business), saw MUCH GOOD TELEVISED SHIT (the business of watching teevee), really fine up-chuck I will share with you in the hope that you'll watch it too (next time you're in Puke City yourself).

CHANNEL 3: Ample Duds commercial featuring STILL PHO-TOS of fatties in the latest up to date blimp attire. "Big, beautiful women, when you're in Vegas come to Ample Duds." (Sizes 36–60.) "You get more of the things you *love* . . . at Pizza Inn." (I LOVE A DONUT, but did not have time to check what flavors they got.)

CHANNEL 5: Every ten minutes they plug EVERY SHOW THAT'S ON SAT. & SUN. ShaNaNaCharliesAngelsLaverne& ShirleyBurns&AllenCrummyCartoonsMoviesYouveSeenSixTimes— 2 seconds of everything. Governor Lisk of Nev. as Smokey the Bear: "Our forests are tinder-dry," he warns.

CHANNEL 8: Jack Concannon (3rd rate QB with the Eagles and Bears, '64–71) does the sports at 11, interviewing the only black faces you'll see in town (besides Redd Foxx and Bill Cosby), those amazing athletes of UNLV.

CHANNEL 10: Crash course in the high cost of entertainment, the making of a "must-see" Vegas show. "You've gotta be a T.V. STAR, lotta television exposure, *maybe* some hit records. Wayne Newton on the other hand is *more than* an enigma, he's a Vegas insti-

tution. He worked his way up thru the boondocks, his feel for an audience is *phenomenal*. But he may be a VANISHING BREED."

CHANNEL 13: "Family Shoes is *going out of business forever*," spoken
with a certain *affirmative joy*, the kind of a.j. you're bound to have with a
great catchy name like Family Shoes. Ben Stepman Dodge (in Henderson): "We're the *other* Dodge dealer." Whoever the *other* other might
be it's no big sweat t' guess why (duller than a CARPET COMMER-
CIAL). 11:30 sign-off editorial: "What percent of auto accidents in
Clark County involve at least one driver who has been drinking?" Ans.:
65. Tho no actual *opinion* is given they welcome your response.

Capsule summary of the sheer greatness of LVTV: Three steps
"down" from L.A. (if that's possible), probably on a par with Fargo or
Sarasota. The town that TV (i.e., Johnny Carson) put on the map has
certainly got its TV "act" together, consistently delivering the Bud-
dhist/Hindu/LSD massage that LIFE IS LOSS—of small-biz staying
power, mind-set tenacity, aesthetic acuity, and the integrity of actual
needs (as well, of course, as wages)—and who're WE to grumble
when it could be "worse"? We could be living in Mormon Penis,
Utah (for inst) or Mumps, Tennessee.

Everything in Vegas feels like (and ultimately *is*) TV and I'm not
talking *Let's Make a Deal* or *Joker's Wild*. The casinos now have slot
machines with *electronic images* of oranges & cherries in lieu of the
customary stamped or painted whatsems. You go to jai alai at the
MGM Grand and the chain-link grid between you and the players,
coupled with the colors and lighting, makes the whole thing look like
TV dots blown up *too many times*—jolting your eyes and making you
"doubt" what you're seeing. There isn't *one* cocktail waitress who
couldn't be a regular on *Three's Company* or *Flamingo Road*. The
whores all resemble Phyllis George. The best food in town is (believe
it) Denny's. IHOP is second.

So after two days of gambling/losing, eating/drinking and digging
the tube-writ-small, I figured it was time for a mega-dose of the
REAL THING, a hefty tune-in on TV per se at its most ersatz,
grandiose and fucked—the sort of BOGO-SIMULATION-OF-
LIFE you can only get LIVE at any of the town's fabulous "rooms."
Quick perusal of the entire Strip offered 16,000,000 TONS of hot
worthless pathetic ugh—Liberace, Mac Davis, Charo w/ David Bren-
ner, Ann-Margret, the Royal Lippizan Stallions (in their worldwide
debut anywhere other 'n turf), Neil Sedaka w/ Fred Travalino, etcet.
But none of these jerks, be they equine or human, had the goods on
y'already know who I'm talkin' about: the one the only mr. entertain-

ment himself WAYNE NEWTON. At the Aladdin which he owns. If TV sez he's the man he's the man.

At 30 bucks a pop (plus 15³/4% "entertainment tax") for 2 drinks and a show, it's got to mean I take my work seriously. Seen the guy on Johnny and a telethon, and already know he's gotta be the biggest no-talent dork ever to simultaneously be the biggest thing in contempo-squaresville make-believe, but still I ain't seen the TOTAL DIMENSION(S) of the thing and fuck if I'm gonna pass up the chance. Besides, Liberace (second choice) is only $17.50 so that must mean the poor bastard's over the hill, and what I'm lookin' for in worthlessness is MR. NOW. The Dadaist in me sez go with Wayne and lemme tell ya DADA NEVER HAD IT SO GOOD.

For starters consider this: *The* first Elvis medley (anywhere ever) comprised SOLELY OF BALLAD SWILL—"Are You Lonesome Tonight?," "Love Me Tender," "Can't Help Falling in Love with You." It's dedicated, naturally, to the man Himself, "a giant of the entertainment industry I had the good fortune to call a close personal friend during his final days on earth"—which is prob'ly even true, and prob'ly says more about CULTURAL ENTROPY than umpteen *This Is Elvis*es. Speaking of which, even after he'd turned to shit himself, Elvis still had the pipes to at least sonically distract you from an obvious retrograde lyric; this was therefore the first time I actually managed to catch the *words* to "Lonesome" and Wayne's TOTAL NON-MASTERY OF SINGERLY NUANCE has gotta be why. Even some demi-quasi-*semi*-pro like let's say Diane Keaton could probably've dredged *something* out of the tune, while this boy comes up empty 'cept for I-miss-you-do-you-miss-me you could cut with a butter knife. Which has gotta be the dandiest OUT-OF-CONTEXT FORCED-ATTENTION TRIP in yrs., the sheer inadvertency of which (not to mention its in-the-cards *inevitability*) hasta put him one up on Marcel Duchamp getting the bumpkins of his day to ogle a urinal.

But don't let ballads fool you, Wayne's a rocker from *way* back, as his hobbling, bobbling renditions of the Elks Lodge R&R Songbook adequately proved to all outpatient "geris" in from Cripple Creek. Average age hadda be somewhere around 67 or 68, and these folks were ALL SMILES as the puffboy in the Slim Whitman 'stache yanked 'em, by the numbers, from "Good Hearted Woman" to "Polk Salad Annie" to that guaranteed showstopper "Johnny B. Goode." And by showstop I ain't kidding, twice the band lurched into "J.B.G." overtime when Wayne insisted on ROCKIN' SOME MORE and each time the show just dead fucking STOPPED. And by smiles I'm saying that's all there was, *the ecstasy was minimal*; was more like these slap-happy sexagenarians were pleased as punch seein' the NICE YOUNG MAN—who could eas'ly be their bouncy beloved GRANDSON—be oh so tasteful & harmless WITH THE MUSIC OF NIGGRAS & REDNECK BEASTS. If he'd done "Midnight Hour" (some sets maybe he does) it wouldn'ta raised a hackle.

Which is not t' say the customers did not at times get *carried away*. They got carried away exactly TWICE. One, a standing ovation for Wayne's stirring (lame & literal) reading of "MacArthur Park"— Tommy Velour could not of read it better—accompanied by frighteningly authentic fake lightning, fake thunder and FAKE RAIN. Two, "God Bless America" (slide show of clouds and a *heap* of unintentional wrong wds.—if they'd been on purpose *somebody* woulda chose 'em a mote less dumb) had 'em on the edge of their seat in silent goo-goo-eyed communion with their LORD (prob'ly ashamed they couldn't kneel), an appropriate response to what had to be the apex— the acme!—of the show; if L.A. is the cultural capital of the republic (for which it stands) then Vegas is the RELIGIOUS CAPITAL, the capital of capital.ism, a truism if there ever was one (and truism is the hick version of irony).

But hicks in Vegas also need DIRT, a passel of smut to give 'em a guilty "thrill" that would only embarrass them and make th'm fear for the social order back in ____ (tired of making up silly hometown names). With his "phenomenal rapport" w/ an audience on the line, Wayne *had the smut*; told this utterly *bizarre* sexist joke that filled their quota and more. "Has anyone out there ever had a COYOTE DATE?" Members of the band say me-me-me. "No, *you* guys don' count. Oh excuse me, you don' know what a coyote date is? Well first lemme assure you this *does not apply* to any ladies in attendance tonight. Let's say you're at a bar . . ." He then goes thru this whole routine of after you've had a few the uggle at the end of the counter is finally not too bad. "So you take her to a motel, I won't even say what the two of you *do* but you wake up in the morning with a head-splitting hangover and this *weight* on your arm. You're afraid to open your eyes and *look*, finally you muster the courage and she's WORSE THAN YOUR WILDEST NIGHTMARE. You've got to get *out of there* before she wakes up, but if you remove your arm that's exactly what she'll do. So you do what coyotes do when caught in a trap . . . YOU CHEW YOUR ARM OFF!" Haw haw hoo as the aforementioned bandboys wave empty sleeves of their tux.

Yes, the rapport is phenom'nal, for a guy with *no discernible charisma* he sure knows how to occasionally get a rise. (Could be he's learned the skill by doing "time" with encounter groups brought in just for him.) At other times tho he falls flat on his nose with self-deprecating INDIAN JOKES (claims now he's part Native-Am., wears feathers on his silver buckle: niftiest way IMAGINABLE to get you t' stop thinking *Mafia*) which expose an itchy inability to even be overtly *insincere*. (He is not your garden-variety "Vegas phony.") Obviously he knows (to some extent) he ain't got nothin' but success (like nobody's *that* stupid), question remains to what extent he maybe fancies himself as a *charlatan* behind it all—how much actually boils down to (what could pass for conscious) "manipulation." In any event, the setup seems to be for everyone (8 million L.V. tourists a year) to see Wayne ONCE—and once is sure as heck sufficient.

But I haven't even mentioned (& I'm sure you'd like to KNOW) the final segment of th' show, the part where he PROVES BEYOND A SHADOW OF A DUCK he is one helluva competent practiced Musician. Earlier, on "Johnny B. Goode," he toyed with a guitar, *possibly* the playing was his, a mere TEASER for his hogwild romp thru the wonderful world of strings-other-than-bass. With malice afore-thought he flaunts his virtuosity on BANJO (bandleader holds up the sagging mike), documents it on amplified VIOLIN. For the rousing grand finale ("Saints Go Marchin'") he even grabs a TRUMPET, hits four-five notes before laying it down, geez this cat can play 'em! . . . nice t' know what it was *about* was MUSIC.

Bravo, bravo, halfassed applause (no encore tonight) and then we're herded out to this stack o' discs. On the Wayneco label—natch—for the bargain price of six bucks (hold the tax) a throw; still plenty time to throw away even more on blackjack, roulette. At this point I can't see ANY WAY I will wager a wooden quoit, not after the total-loss farm of 90 minutes of Wayne. Formula for all this must take into account how much the idiots're likely to bet & lose B.W.—before Wayne—'cause after Wayne it's bound to noticeably diminish . . .

Okay, I did my bit for world TV knowledge, live version of TV has gotta be 50 times more noxious than the basic small-screen gig; please don't 'spect me to do it again—soon or otherwise. Only personal "benefit" from my Vegas stay is after Vegas EVEN MELROSE LOOKS FUNKY. (If you're planning to somehow *vacate* L.A., y'oughta take a quick one to Vegas and L.A.'ll look like San Francisco.)

95

Props

I wrote this after I got home from watching the fights for a Reader *column (Roberto Duran-Pipino Cuevas was the main event).*

A revised version appears in the '99 chapbook Holes: A Book Not Entirely About Golf, *but this is the original, identical to what D. Boon had on his person when*, shit, *read on . . .*

Jazz doesn't have to swing
and rock doesn't have to rock
and religion has next to nothing to do
with God

who what which
is at most just one of the goddam
props
thru which we have
so-called religious experiences.

The beer I mop up w/ a handkerchief
because my new raincoat is in jeopardy
slung over a chair in the east auxiliary press box
of the L.A. Sports Arena during round eight or nine
of Alfredo Escalera-Sergio Medina (1/29/83)
is 'cause:

(he's thinking)

I mop it 'cuz
I am a bourgeois simp
and worse.

96

The Minutemen (Exist)

My final music piece for the Voice.
In the annals of "meta-rock," the significance of the Minutemen—Mike Watt, D. Boon, George Hurley—is incalculable. Last of the great L.A. hardcore bands, they were the *band when it came to making rock-roll safe for text, for all* possible *texts—lyrics—word parcels and sequences. Including: those that don't rhyme, those deemed unsingable, those that look like they could "use more work," those without punchlines or probable interest. After the Minutemen, if they're* words *they can be part of a* hot *piece of music.*
Speaking of which, near the end of when was it, '84? '85?, we were gonna be doing an LP together, with them playing as I read some short bursts of poetry and whatnot. When I called Mike the day before we were supposed to go to the studio, there was this awful silence, then he sputtered: "You haven't heard? D. Boon is DEAD!"
(When the van he was sleeping in turned over, "Props" was among the papers in his pocket.)
One of the terrible disappointments of my life.

Let's face it: I just don't *listen* to th'm anymore. Rock-related discs. Six months go by between spins. I don't play new stuff, I don't play old stuff, I don't even play Byrds albums for old friends sitting around drunk at 4 a.m. What I'm thinking is at long last—maybe—I'm *off the stuff.* Which (if true) would make three loathsome habits I've kicked in less than a year; Copenhagen ("the smokeless tobacco") and TV are the others. What makes it a habit *worth* jettisoning should be obvious (some self-attenuating variation on—for want of a more interesting nutshell—*duh music IS repulsive, has BEEN repulsive, will forevermore BE repulsive, and if not I still ain't gonna stick around t' notice*). All I'm listening to is jazz and some occasional vocal-free dub; I can't hack voices while typing, and I'm ENJOYING typing the most I have since 1970, when I was also trying not to listen to rock (therefore, whatever).

SO ANYWAY—since this is obviously another rock review—somehow this new album slipped through my grid, my rock filter. Which I can't in all honesty (even half) claim as a surprise: I'd been waiting and it came (by mail: yes, still a promo whore). Played it, liked it, played it again (taking notes). May not play it a third time for years to come, but under no circumstances do I expect to sell it, as it is (in all ways still possible) an "important album," as close to same as I'm likely to admit between here and the worms and/or maggots. (And don't tell me there are *many important records* being made all the time, 'cause whether or not I monitor this shit anymore I know a fib when I hear one.)

THIS ALBUM: *What Makes a Man Start Fires?*, the Minutemen, SST Records (and possibly Tapes). Which I waited for because, see, they're my FAVORITE BAND—and favorite bands are exceptions to everything. REASONS they are my fave: (1) they truck mightily in *sound per se*; (2) they've yet to do a lyric that is anything short of AWESOME, whether or not (and "relevantly" or not) its meter-and-pulse as delivered (recited, "sung") has ever particularly meshed with that of its musical accompaniment (which of course is the POINT); (3) their tooth-grip take on structural minimalism has yet to be expressed in anything less than 100% existential/band-experiential terms; (4) after THREE YEARS of recording they have yet to be "seduced by the beast" in a manner even fractionally commensurate with "selling out."

Originally what the Minutemen were *known for* was playing short: everything under a minute, a lot under 30 seconds. Which on one level was "cute"—cute *idea* plus all these actual shortish *gems*—while on another it was the final nail in a coffin which even stalwart coffiners like Black Flag only sidestepped or slept in en route, ultimately, to the same old nerdish "trip": cut duration in a post-Ramones universe (which can get as sticky-conventional as anything likewise/prior; has more or less, even in its *variability*, been firmly parametered by marketplace rote; is a function, finally, of repetition modules as chainlinked to "Hey Jude" as to "Judy Is a Punk" or Black Flag's "Wasted").

The Minutemen, screaming visionaries, may not've been the first band to eschew the use of stacked or leapfrogged rep modules for constructivist-expedient ends, but surely (during their short phase) they were the only one I can name who actually DIALOGUED

WITH THE RIFF AND WON. They told riffs, both unviable and viable, where to get off; used 'em only as suited their fancy, by which I don't mean they were fancyass fashioners, I mean they stripmined their musical souls and picked and chose from a *wider range* of old riffs ('cause there *aren't* new'uns) than, well, anybody (which is not to say they were "eclectic"); within any given songlife-lifetime they made use of such hogwash only as long as they could STAND TO, not however long it took to fill the head of some hypothetical rock-temporal pin.

SO ANYWAY on this new one, their fifth release of whatever size, they've started playing not exactly long but longer. They've evidently gotten *friendly* with some riffs—it's nice to have friends—and in the process have pulled off the first TOTALLY A-HISTORICAL ADD-ON MOVE in all of U.S. postpunk, by which I mean they've actually found the secret/sacred more-is-more button (unused *in context* since—when?—*Beatles '65, Aftermath, Funhouse* or *Metal Box*) and are pressing it with a certain non-parochial, non-simpy glee. If I never play 'em again I salute them for doing what ALL THE OTHERS would, or could, not: "advance rock and roll form" from the inside out, without being card-carrying anti-life shits in the vast army of et cetera, et cetera, et cetera, et cetera.

97

Merde . . . Turd . . . Vomit

When the Minutemen, shortly before the end, made a rock video like every-
body else, even though it wasn't slightly like everybody else's, that disap-
pointed me, too. Videos make me wanna fight.
  You wanna fight?

It's a couple days till Xmas or a week or whatever, an Xmas party at
the home of Paul Cutler and Dinah Cancer of contempo subterranean beat combo 45 Grave. There's eggnog, some my-t-tasty dev-
iled eggs, chips & dips, and cookies shaped like bats—Ms. Cancer's
specialty—but no alcohol and no dope. If there's dope in other rooms
there's dope in other rooms, if there's "lines" and "spikes" (somewhere) that's someone else's biz—'cause none of it's *in evidence*.
What's in ev is guests, guests 'n' more guests—partygoing fun people
of the L.A. undergroun' and so on—sitting aroun' like bumps watching teeeveee. Watching: *MTV*. Official drug of the party is MTV.
  So you get these likable, personable, reasonable swellfolks like Pat
Smear, Rick Van Santen and Michael "Mikey" Ochoa—genuwine
with-it age-bracket muhfuhs beyon' too many shades of a doubt—directing peepers at rock vids of Queen, Men at Work, the fucking Go-
Go's, directing 'em with awe, respect, titillation, hard-ons, rock-roll
pleasure principle stuff, and w/ jerky jealous envy. Pat sees the Go-
Go's and sez: "I remember when they opened for *us* at (somewhere in
the Valley)"—us meaning the Germs who when they existed he gui-
tared for, who were hardcorer than pus on a skid-row piss puddle
(Chris Morris did *not* say that), who were really IT daddy (y'know one
of the greatest goddam all-time goddam bands in *this* word jockey's
band-exposure experience) while meanwhile the Go-Go's who for a
year or two were almost OK, hey they *were* OK, were okay MERELY
as a live & throbbing *parody* of what they subsequently, willingly, *be-*

came: NON-IRONIC DEMOGRAPHIC-SLICK CONSUMER-
FETISH COTTON-CANDY WIND-UP WIMPED-OUT
FETISHES & DEMOGRAPHS—w/ no redeeming anything 'cept
their mass-market store-bought TV SMILES. *Fuck them to hell,* I'm
thinking, *I hope they all die mis'able and alone (except Charlotte who I like
and will hopefully see the error of her ways), as they have helped usher in th'
end o' the world.*

•   •   •

That's me thinkin'; you know me by now, that's just the way I *think.*
Pat meantime is thinking something diff; I ain't no mindreader but
would guess he's WISHING IT WAS HIM. In a nonironic mass-
market ROLE. Making bigbucks playing gratuitous dumbnotes for
grim-smily shits who make vids. At Xmastime you think things like
this; with MTV in your yuletide veins you have not got a chance.
Reason #8 why MTV is WORSE (FOR YOU) THAN HEROIN: It,
uh, panders to prospective *creators* of musical pap as loathsomely as it
does to same's potential kneejerk consumers, thus making the benefits
of one-size-fits-all musical worthlessness functionally seductive (before the fact) to *musicians themselves,* thus (in turn) tightening the
noose a few notches further with yet *another* hand assisting, tightening it (once and for all) beyond the point of fail-safe reckoning:
G'bye, g'night, g'day: It's all o-o-o-over!!!
    That's 8 and here's #3: It totally rejects the PRIMACY OF
SOUND. Once—longlong*long* a-fucking-go but still once—rock &
roll's primary messaging circuits (y'know to the HUMAN NER-
VOUS SYSTEM) were sonic. All that sex and anarchy biz that was
certainly part of the initial package and some later stages too was itself
manifest most CRUCIALLY thru strictly sonic channels. Lyrics,
hairstyles 'n' leather, this trendy grimace & that—even at its most
forefront relevant none of that stuff would ever amount to a hill of
lifeblood beans w/out the goddam sound to serve as its (supportive)
bloodstream, spine and musculo-skeletal whatever. And I ain't just
talking Duh . . . Big . . . Beat or any such rhythm-heavy claptrap
cliche; even goddam ballads and folkshit 're sonic (or they ain't
nothin'): "Dear Prudence," "Back Street Girl" and "All I Really
Wanna Do" (Dylan version), f'r instance, are—insofar as they *work at
all*—as sonically centered and circuited as "Keep A-Knocking," "Land
of a Thousand Dances" or "I Saw Her Standing There."
    You know, arcane music-historical namedrop and that's just part 1
of the background to 3, part 2 is what the Anglo-American musical

MAINSTREAM has done of nascent sonic import in (by my reckoning tho I could be wrong) the last 12 or 13 years: nothing. Nothing, nada, it has not given a good goddarn *hoot* about any such crap; you just plug in & *do it*—"formulas" will keep you from stepping in dangerous doodoo—kinda like putting together a refrigerator. Punk, postpunk, dub, avant (incl. such all-time sonic danger-mongers as PiL, Blurt, Prince Far I, Throbbing Gristle, even 45 Grave f'r that matter): 'Tain't mainline so it don't mainline-compute. U.S./U.K. major-label studio production: a 14-year dead-end street (last entire major LP to actually bother hacking out viably new SONIC SPACE was *The Who Sell Out*, 1968, I mean right?) (while today: Bruce Springsteen cannot be *sonically distinguished* from the theme shit on *Saturday Night Live*; Queen cannot be s.d.'ed from Gilbert & Sullivan; Michael Jackson from Kenny Rogers; etc., etc.). Altho actually there's some exceptions in England, I'd be lying if I didn't cop to 'em, but fuck 'em for now 'cause I ain't got the space or time, MTV's non-Brit anyway so lemme just get to the point which is: Nothing outside the abject status-quo studio mentality itself has been as devastatingly effective in reinforcing R&R's prevailing callousness about sound AS HAS MTV.

Because: Primary rock-roll focus is now audio-VISUAL. Bands signed to CBS, Warner's, etc. now make videos as a matter of course, are so tied to 'em before the fact that they're thinking VISUAL-DRAMATIC PRESENTATION while in the act of conceiving tunes. *Some* total scumboat bands (Devo's the easy target) even carry it so far as to do vocal LP mixes so *intentionally* worthless that SEEING THE VID IS *REQUIRED*, y'know in order to pick up cues enabling you to catch 'n' grasp EVEN THE LYRICS. Mix/shmix—and sonic/shmonic—all LP's having fucking *become* is souvenirs of their various related vids.

So you get: Image is all; guys making formula faces and flexing biceps while pretending to finger guitars (was lipsynching for Dick Clark ever so close-up revolting?); a return to the 1972 basic *look*—yuk!—as well as basic '72 stage staginess (only a *tiny* percent of MTV vids are of mere uninterrupted concert footage 'cause kids don't wanna *know* from that no more; live shows per se gotta meanwhile *measure up* and thus get hokier 'n' hokier w/ all sorts of neo-Alice Cooper, neo-Broadway-for-kids b.s. factored into the stew FOREVER—close yer eyes & all ya get is DECIBELS, mildly REFERENTIAL—open 'em and . . . well ya better close 'em again); all the above filtered thru TV AS THE ULTIMATE GRID* . . .

... *F'r something that was all that saved the fifties from being the '80s to begin with: W/out rock-roll's first incredible gasp TV would've taken over for keeps in its first full decade of access to neurons. Probably ditto for its second gasp and the sixties. Time was (properly) all TV was good for vis-a-vis actual ongoing (musical) culture was *occasionally certifying it as a public fact*: Elvis/Beatles on *Ed Sullivan*; Hendrix on *Dick Cavett*; Doors on *Jonathan Winters*. It was a treat when that stuff was on; it wasn't on much; it wasn't on much 'cause flies in the ointment seldom are. Best way to look at the two is 10–12 years of TV perfecting itself as the ultimate fool-some-of-the-people-all-of-the-time TOOL while out there parallel rock is (for a while at least) keeper of the don't-fool-me FLAME. Time marches on—ain't life funny?—and at last TV and rock are *one*; 'n' meanwhile fewer than 2,000,000 Americans any longer have biologically centered *brains* . . .

REASONS, back to some reasons (w/ numbers): **#4.** *Nobody even knows how to do 'em.* To make rock vids. The last actually decent rock video was the "Memo from Turner" sequence toward the end of *Performance* (Nicholas Roeg, Donald Cammell, 1970). Before that: the "Ticket to Ride" ski stuff in *Help!* (Richard Lester, '65) or *possibly* the "Strawberry Fields" whatsit from slightly later ('67). All told, there have probably been FEWER THAN TEN 100% NOT-SHIT ROCK VIDEOS in the hist'ry of the genre, and my v. own eyes have yet to see ONE on MTV. (Hey, it's a slippery hybrid at best, one mass-possible even as shit only after both halves—musical, cinematic—'ve been sufficiently debauched . . . and drownded like dogs down the generic-equality sewer . . .)

#11: *It accepts the hand as dealt because it* is *the hand as dealt.* Once upon a time you could turn on retrograde pig fodder like *Mod Squad* or *The Partridge Family* and laugh laugh laugh—or snarl snarl snarl—at how totally, utterly out of sync it was with whatever. Like there used to *be* an external mass-existent whatever of no mean substance that TV could only feign some hideous caricature of a "relation" to; today there is not even that. I mean you still get *Quincy* mocking out punks and what-all, but stuff like that is *so* ruling-class chickenshit it feels more like an afterburst of nuke-Iran or anti-abortion (i.e., it doesn't even feel like *approximate* prevailing fiftieth-percentile all-American culture-crime consciousness—30th maybe, but not 50th). Tune in MTV, howev, and you're not dealing with *either side* of any cultural coin (because it is the bank). Far as real/not-real goes, you're seeing something that is a falsification of life BUT NOT A DIS-

TORTION. It simply 'tis what 'tis—and, for at least 11 zillion people, purt-near close to *all* that 'tis: state-of-the-art "reality orientation" thru standard operating food-tube procedures (no choke, no gag; no fuss, no muss).

WHICH IS SO THOROUGHLY FRIGHTENING there ain't too much else short of nuke incineration or herpes of the eyeball that's SCARIER. (No more cultural salvation *ever again* for vuln'able/susceptible young stupid kidpersons—*geez* am I glad I ain't 19!!!)

•   •   •

#1: *It makes the i.d. of rock and the marketplace monolithic and irreversible.* Once, like ten-eleven years ago, I had this literary agent back in New York who also had some agenting or managerial ties to Rocky Graziano and somehow I got invited to pitch TV pilot ideas to Rocky and this gotrocks producer creep. Since the best anything Rocky'd done in recent memory was a string of not-half-bad commercials for all sorts of unrelated items like yogurt and transmissions (automotive), one of my pitches was a show of nothing but wall-to-wall Rocky commercials, like for 30 minutes. Which Mr. Gotrocks thinks is a waste of his time t' hafta listen to. So whuddaya got here but a WHOLE GODDAM NETWORK featuring 24 FUCKING HRS. OF COMMERCIALS, w/ all them zillions of aforementioned lobotoms inextricably in tow, w/ the *primary experience of rock & roll* at last being reduced to one of receiving vectors intended solely for the *promotion* of rock & roll! Like ain't life a scream.

(2), offshoot of (1): *This is (we're told) actually selling records.* Could be a lie but so far MTV's apparently getting sizable nos. of asskids to again start purchasing vinyl garbage in nos. commensurate with what radio used t' be able t' generate. So the music biz gets to mileage its way back to solvency using the same goshdarn TUBE another offshoot of which was nominally causing 'em grief, like video *games* was one of their major alibis for suddenly sucking commercial wind, 's what the asskids were supposedly spending their change on instead of LP's. Home audio taping was another excuse, of course The Depression, nobody in the industry ever went on record for THE MUSIC SUCKS, in any event MTV gets 'em doubly off the hook by it no longer MATTERING that same sucks scrotum poop off a dead rat's mother. (I.e., make a rock vid of scrotum poop pop POO and asskids will consume it f'r breakfast.)

(9) *MTV heightens the* official *disparity between the powered and the powerless—between palace life and the gutter in Calcutta—in* strictly TV terms. (Natch.)

(15) *Racist?* Sure, yeah, for sure, like the only sort of black vids they show're on the order of Prince or *maybe* Stevie Wonder w/ Paul McCartney, plus their only black deejay (J.J. Jackson) is kind of ugg-lee, some say because a *handsome* black vidjock would prob'ly be perceived by too many asskids as a *threat* to their whitebread sense of etc. and that's prob'ly *true*, but I think calling MTV racist is a nearly superfluous *cheap shot* on the order of calling rape unsanitary or accusing Reagan of harboring anti-rent-control sentiments. Of course it's racist, what other news you got?

(4) *More relentlessly "anti-life" digital than radio at even its* hypothetical *worst (or all those* That's Incredible/Entertainment Tonite *prechoreographed piss-fuckers).* Hey!—remove those quotes! Anti-life—wave that banner proud! (Makes *MV3* look like a humanist love feast with beer, pretzels and free contraceptive counseling.)

(6) *It's the hip/teen equivalent of every sickass worthless anti-life* Christian *network.* In every manner, shape & form.

●　　　●　　　●

GOOD THINGS ABOUT MTV—(1) It's not yet compulsory. (2) You c'n occasionally see a rocker or two not thoroughly enjoying his or her self in the production of a vid, sometimes in the case of new bands where just recording the album was homework enough and also old bands who have had enough of EVERYTHING.

98

Another Grammy Year with the Meltzer Clan

Are the Grammies "real"?
  So then I guess I'll have to bring along my "family."

> i have seen the gray flanneled suitors of my generation
> abandon their suits for rock rock rock (and roll)
> i have likewise witnessed rockboys and rockgirls
> smacked out on the jing-jang jegs of mainstream pluralotropism
> furnishing their smelly kitchens and drugrooms with
> flannel wallpaper, gray
> —from "Les Fleurs du Pee" (in progress), Eck Osiris Meltzer, age 15$^1/_2$

Sometimes kids say it all. Sometimes, well let's just leave it at sometimes. At all times, however, some things apply. Is there anything more important in this Life, for instance, than music—and TV—in that order? I think not and neither does that extended herd of Meltzers I am proud to call my family. We would not miss a Grammys for all the sin in Sweden, and '84 was no exception.

On odd numbered years we Meltzes—and related offshoots—plant ourselves firmly in front of the tube: awarding for to view from cushions and couches. As this was an "even," I, not one to shun my patriarchal duties, sprung for tickets: nothing beats live and in person for honoring MUSIC. While my respect for the National Academy of Recording Arts & Sciences may have waned a tad since "Louie Louie" failed to top the '63 voting (an event which caused me to burn my academy card in protest of my colleagues' unwillingness to change with the times and begin recognizing the Now Sound of the sixties), and a tad more since the fateful balloting of '71, when "I Watched You Rhumba" by Hackamore Brick got creamed by James Taylor's

"You've Got a Friend," I still have my memories of the glory years—
ah! fifty-three I remember you well!

And '55 for crying out loud, Haysoose *Christ* what a yr. for winners:
five Grammys for Mantovani, four for the 101 Strings! And the incredible '54 by golly (year Eartha Kitt finally broke the "color line"
by presenting the award for household how-to recording, since
deleted), I'll trade you one '54 for '68, '73, '74, '78, '79 and '83 put together . . . oh but don't forget '52! I won't and I don't, I in fact do a
rather serious "take" on the magical five-two as, brood to the left,
right and rear, I enter the Shrine and (to quote my late—and close—
personalfriend Jimmy Morrison) "walk on down the hall." To the
nearest usher, to get everyone seated and ensconced—and to be excused.

I 'scused myself to visit the press tent, my first trip back since g-d
known when, to check out the "action" and show off selected family:

—grandson Eck, 15, sophomore (and honor student) at Spokane
Jesuit High;

—granddaughter Jujubeena, 17, of "mixed" parentage, recently accepted by the collage department of Vassar University, tho she may
just study art "on my own";

—grandson Bellamy, 12, totally cured of cerebral palsy, thanks in
large measure to the Telethon (so don't knock TV—not to *me*,
buddy!);

—daughter-in-law Woosni, 23, third wife of my youngest son Otto,
a real q.t. who I wouldn't mind . . . only kidding! . . . whose interest
in music is for very good reason (cousin of the late—and great—
Les Baxter).

No sooner were we PRESSED W/ THE PRESS than there they
were (sighted, spied): ole friends and lifers, "industry" hotchas I have
known, terminal critics of the "Big Beat" from coast to coast as well
as abroad. "Why there's that old sodbuster Ed Wallet"—currently
with the Austin *Tex-Dispatch*—"your gramps and him used to *bust sod*
together!" (Covered Bo Diddley's tonsillitis in nineteen forty and
eight—for two papers, long since folded, in Cleveland.) And there
goes Sylvia Sternhurst, metal critic for the French dogmag *Hounds*,
with whom—hup hup—the author was once "unfaithful" to his late
wife Cora. "Hi Syl"—the kids are watching, I can say no more—
"how's tricks?" And great googa mooga if THAT THERE is not
(holy cow!) my *extreme* pal-o-mine Ralph "Bub" Scuba, why Bub
used to work for several *companies* (Hermes, N.M.A., Artista) and I
wonder what he possibly is "doing" now. "I am working for *Record*

Music Magazine" sez the smiling Bub; gosh—time sure flies—me and him used to watch *football* together . . .

Two former cohorts I am not 'zactly pleased to engage however: (1) "true bee-liever" (in ????) Biko Skidmore, whose anti-"factionalism" cooties I will die before I let rub off on ones I love, and (2) the great (she is *great*) Susan Brunette of Chris Columbus Records, who I am *embarrassed* to run into—hi Suze, love ya—on account last time our paths crossed I had officially "dropped out" (i.e., boycotted the Grammys for one year to protest—that's me, mr. protest!—THE CONTINUED, ONGOING, UNINTERRUPTED MARKET-ING OF THE SICK AND FESTERING ROCK & ROLL COR-PUS, MAKE THAT CORPSE). That was a yr. I would rather forget: treatment for ['tween my doctors and myself].

"Grandf-father"—Bellamy tugs at my sportjacket, only the slightest lingering trace of c.p. in his speech—"who is that large-b-b-bosomed young lady over there with the old person?" My lord! can it Be?

"Well, grandchild, that 'old person' as you call him is indeed an-cient. Ever since the collapse of his recording career, and the subse-quent demise of *Hollywood Squares*, he has been searching, rather futilely I might add, for gainful employment. Evidently the 'frail' with the—ahem—protruding *stack* out to here is the 'prop' he aims to utilize in manufacturing a new vocation. She is the one and only Elvira, Queen of Darkness; he, the sadly over-the-hill Alice Cooper." (O! doth weary sadness encircle me: how to 'splain to a youngster the pathos of cultural entropy, the patheticness of rube flesh, late of pig farm, returned to pig *pen* as stool? So I don't even *try* to explain . . .)

From the very old to the very new: Best New Artist. Nominees in-clude: Men Without Hats. "Men Without Hats?" I hear myself ask-ing, the kneejerk voice of incredulity—have they (migod what a cynic I must seem!) slipped us a "fast one"?

"Come on gramps, get with it," sighs Eck with ill-concealed conde-scension towards the "square" who stands before him, "Men Without Hats are *Australian*."

"Whatchoo talkin', you dumb Eck-head"—there's my Jujubeena, I just *love* to see cousins in conflict!—"they be Belgian."

"I think they're from D-d-denmark."

"Quite possibly you're right, Bellamy, but I myself vote for, let me see . . . Uruguay? . . . no, . . . "

"Canada, R., they're Canadian." What?—who? (I *hate* folks who use my old name.) Why if it isn't none other than [bad with names]

English fotogperson. "What brings you back, R.—your gig as a sportswriter never pan out?"

"The name is Richard, mr. shutterbug—Richard. As Ray Charles, and later the Kingston Trio, would say: *If you don't want you don't have to get in trouble*, so I'll trust you to remove your hand from the unprotected hip of my lovely daughter-in-law *toot sweet*."

Which is merely my way of saying I can dig it: lifelong friends have a code of their own. Quickly we are conversing, specifically this yr's Grammys (versus earlier installments). Fotog has a *theory* and, trusting my judgment, tests me of its worth: "This is the year they finally decided to let Rock in on the awards."

"They uh what?" (Am I hearing correctly? Was Men Without Hats merely the setup for something far, far more insidious?)

"Okay let's look at the winners so far: Duran Duran, Culture Club . . . "

"Whoa—" (I am hearing!)

"Performing live: Big Country . . . "

"Nuh—" (Can my heart endure it?)

"Ozzie Osbourne is scheduled to present . . . "

"MY DEAR SIR I have had enough. Is it your intention to imply, nay suggest, that such combos as you mention are of a *different ilk* from, e.g., the Doobie Brothers, winners of quite a stack of cookies in, if memory serves, year of our lord 1979?!?@#$%! Culture Club indeed! Show me a more *antiseptically produced* third-hole version of shall we say the Classics IV—who never received *their* Grammy due if you'll remember correct—and I'll show you . . . something. Duran Duran? Big Country? Fuck 'em, pardon my French, *screw* 'em. No, don't screw 'em, put 'em together, teach [the former's rock-vid] elephants to play [the latter's rock-vid] bagpipes; then, and only then, will mumble mumble tut tut tut. Or like, the uh, these, hum, was for instance Fleetwood Mac a different *order* of b.m. than, y'know, the Eurythmics? Answer me that one—if you dare. It is my contention that, ilkwise, I can pick your face out from the front or behind, you may look pretty but I can't say the same for your mind. Meaning: it is only because . . . homogeneous . . . everything equals everything else . . . I mean Ozzie may have bit the bat's head, but did he swallow it? Billy Joel has bit more heinous things *and* swallowed, for *specific* heinous profit I'll grant you while Ozzie bluh bluh bluh, so what I'm saying, my man, is you are talking illusion, do you read me? The illusion that (a) 'new stuff' is as we speak being welcomed in the door, and (b) its isomorphs in the ilk dept. have not been *previously* rewarded, in spades, for their sick contributions to the final surrender of the human spirit. 'Rock' you say—Paul McCartney but no Minutemen—pshaw!"

The weight of the world thus off my (increasingly arthritic) shoulders, I crane my (equally arthritic) neck for a peek at the nearest monitor, and am (instantly) sorry I left my puke bag on the plane. For there in the seats—this was a seat shot—seated behind my beloved sister Persephone, inotherwords within proximity of the very seat in which my own writerly fundament would be planted should I choose to "use" my ticket, sat, together, not one but TWO faces from the slick and smarmy covers of *People* mag, two REPRESENTATIVES of the "new breed" of entertainer, together, oh my bowels & innards: Michael Jackson & Brooke Shields!!! I know how costly this evening has cost me—a year's supply of Stravinsky lps, roughly—but at times such as etc. there are *higher priorities* than a bleeping record set, I mean to say. "Eck, Juju, etcetera, I *forbid* you to sit near those—yeesh—yuckos. While you may feel like calling me . . ."

"Hey I think he's kinda cute. And I really enjoyed her in *Endless Love*." To think, Woosni—I've loved her like my own flesh & blood—a slut! [Harlot, begone! Exits.]

LIFETIME ACHIEVEMENT AWARDS. Chuck Berry. The Man(!). The Myth(!). The Music(!). In 1984?????? (As opposed to, say, 1961 or—to be charitable in the Fiefdom of Fools—some arbitrary date like let's say seventy . . . *two*.) To think that Chas Chaplin's geezertime invite to the Oscars once seemed a mite, hey, anticlimactic! Chuck!! Hey!! Late (slightly)!! Need men, living, be half *dead* before their times receive *ya* know . . . or, simply, mus' Wayne Newton first "do" their tunes? (Or, likelier still, is yours truly just another crotchety crotch?)

THE SHAME CONTINUES. Herbie Hancock, promising young keyboardist/jass of 19-early-60s, who once had it in his power to be the second coming of Bobby Timmons, or the third or fourth of Junior Mance, up upon a stage not far from where certain Meltzers now stand (the legs they buckle, the head it throbs), functioning muse/ically like the thought (jass) never entered his mind. *Electronic* instruments, yech tho hey we're liberal—8 miles high and when you touch down, you'll find that it's stranger than known—but would ya get a load of those GOD CAN YOU *BELIEVE* IT, BREAKDANCING IS THE CENTERPIECE OF THE ACT!, finally I understand what the Shangri-las *meant* when they said "oh no oh no oh no

RICHARD MELTZER

no no no no" . . . or something, equally chilling, to that effect. (I contain the thought so as not to scare the children; they are entitled to
a—knock knock knock, on wood—trauma-free adolescence.)

"Hey gramps, isn't that whatsisname, *you* know . . . "

"Right you are, Eck, Bob Dylan. Why I've got anywhere from 16 to
18 of his discs in my current collection—none more recent, of course,
than *Blood on the Tracks.* Pitiful—isn't it?—the tragedy of the Formerly In-Touch. The gentleman sure has come a long way from
10,000 miles in the mouth of a graveyard to, ulp, *this.*"

"Y'might say 10,000 *inches* insida this one now!"

"Or at least millimeters, Juju, heh heh—hmm—WHAT TH-?!?
Turn your heads quickly, offspring, avert yon monitor with your
glance—Mike Love is *kissing* . . . the rhinestoned glove of Michael
Jackson . . . and Dennis Wilson not yet cold beneath the ground!!!!!
Tell me that you've heard every sound there is and your bird is green rant
puff" and then it happened: my very first nonfatal stroke.

Past the Caddy limos, black, beige, cerise, they carry me, past the
chauffeurs—was that *marijuana?*—of the very rich due to LP sales
and/or airplay and publishing, crashing, flashing, my life in music
flashcrashing before me: my last moment of recorded consciousness
(could it be?): the Grammys of '49, which one scribe dubbed the
Sammys (Davis Jr. had just copped three, a record at the time); my interview with Sam, the first of many; Cora? where are you Cora?;
Sammy Cora core core your caw caw . . . crows??

donchoo worry Grampa, this Jujubeena, we write it for you. you jus
recover, that your job, we write.

you know you racist what you say bout breakdance, maybe I jus so-
call mulatto but my 'colored' part know you racist. that ok, I realize
you talkin *sound,* Herbie Hancock music be lacking that dee*partment*
you mean to say. and so what all this theatre-rical jivin in the specta-
tor event? that what you mean so jus you lie still in you hospital bed.

one thing you *not* racist Grampa the way you hold back on that
trash Michael Jackson. you too polite—he trash. People's Magazine,
he bigger trash than a Magazine. I of sexual age—maybe you guess?—
but I wouldn take a *shit* on Michael Jackson *face.* but i don know
nothin bout Doorang Doorang or Big In The Country, that stuff in-
ter*changeable* so who care, not me, what I care this Grammy revue say
what special. bout this year Grammys. and that be Michael Jackson
who trash. a embarrassment to the part of me colored.

I won show you this paper cause maybe it kill you. Examining Herald. Biko Skidmore, you know him? 'Michael Jackson Rewrite The Book'. it say. 8 awards, break the record Paul Simon, one them inchangeables, or do I got him confuse the Paul in Michael Jackson video? (tell me when you better). Skidmore say: 'irresistible appeal'. he say: 'half-shy mystique'. that very funny. he say: 'biracial audience'. well *I* biracial, count me out that! he *don* say: sissy boy who sing like a rat cause the whoremones—that a pun—and a operation the skin on his face. so he look like the panther lady Island Of Lost Soul, you know the movie, some say Diana Ross. either way that *sick*. I believe it sick. (don his daddy mommy love him)?

what it cause him is cancer—and cause you cancer jus listen. they give *award* to cancer?? that make no sense, not enough you sell it, gon give you reeward for sellin?? you right Grampa, this world so sad you cry a Pacific ocean. get well or I cry a wet planet Earth.

okay, now it stupid Eck turn, I don know howcum you like him. (guess it because he family).

Hey pops, Eck here. You spelled Ozzie wrong. Should be Ozzy. I'd be bummed if you kicked it, really I would, so take your medicine *lying down*.

I tol you he stupid, Jujubeena back again. in case you spec Bellamy revue Men With A Hat, he have c.p. relapse (cause by traumatic). so nex year maybe we gone the Telethon—it make sense we pass the Grammy.

99

One Commie *Wrong* About Bruce

Invited to participate in a special Springsteen issue of Spin, *I thought jeez, how quaint: s-p alliteration. But when it turned out some hotsos like Amiri Baraka, Tama Janowitz and Rich Stim were also invited, I figured oh, what the fucking hey.*

On my latest reread, I realized that I have more rancor for Bruce now than I did then. In '85 it was more towards the mag, like I couldn't quite figure why a new mag seeking any sort of hip cachet would cash in so quick on the fount of all Nothing. I don't know when the Bruce Thing finally ended—or whether it even has. But at this late date, the archaeologist in my soul (more than my mind) RECOILS at his mixing the '50s and '60s for all the customers who missed, or missed the upshot of, either decade or both.

Hey—the guy is barely younger than me!—so who's he think he's fooling? To slap the decades together as a two-in-one is EITHER mean, nasty, greedy MANIPULATION or irrefutable evidence that the Boss is verrrrrrrry blind, stupid, OBTUSE. (No third possibility.) Maybe Jon Landau could tell us which.

What's particularly offensive is not that Bruce equally weights the '50s and '60s (nothing wrong there) but that he collapses them as if they're the same thing—a twofer as phony, as specifically *phony, as* American Graffiti *or* Happy Days. *The Fonz indeed! Not only were the two decades musically different but they were* separate: *no more continuous (nor contiguous) than Haiti and Australia. Rock 'n' roll didn't "evolve" from its '50s "stage" to a '60s "stage" so much as disappear from the face of the earth and later reappear (with different personnel), fueled by the exhumation of NEW— new to rock—pre-existent sonic meat.*

Look. Utilizing sources your audience doesn't recognize so they'll think you concocted 'em yourself—everybody does it. It's one of the "principles" on which rock has always been based. Even Hendrix in his rock mode got mileage out of sound-forms that had slipped, or were slipping, through the cracks, that would otherwise, without him, have failed to attract rock, i.e., rock audience, attention: Earl Hooker, Guitar Slim, Gatemouth Brown, Albert Collins, et al. He did, however, bring them all to an incredible flash

point where they live, breathe, emanate (oh, what would you call it?) undy-
ing fire.

Bruce, meanwhile, has always just been such a SPONGE, and the dish-
water he soaks up is so stagnant and generic by the time he gets to it, that it
wouldn't even pay to isolate his "influences" (although, again, I'm sure Lan-
dau could tell us something)—they're already so attenuated and diminished.
This is one character who has never appeared to have any sense of the value
of what he's cannibalized, of its socio-sonic reality at source-point zero.

And by not narrowing the gap between rock and its audience—by playing
everybody for an even bigger rube than himself—he only WIDENS it. Ssss.
Grrr.

That's it for Bruce (my middle name, by the way). I'll never mention him
again.

Bruce, uh, Springsteen? The youth-demographic Wayne Newton/
Bette Midler? In THIS mag as opposed to, y'know, that other one? Is
he even an *issue* anymore? (Don't tell me he's on the cover—I'll find
out soon enough.)

I have never liked the youth-demographic Newton/Midler. I have
nearly always loathed him. I've rarely been able to even *look* at the
boring little prick without muttering expressions like "master of ersatz," "the absolute voice of the status quo" or "the emperor's new
jeans & workshirt." Pompous maybe as kneejerk responses go, but
here's this guy, see, the absolute non-irony of whose most prevalent
guise ("earnestness") (a jump ahead of that equivalently unreflected
duo, "sincerity" and "integrity") has always struck me, on sheer scale
alone, as more than a trifle pompous incarnate. But fuck *me* (right?)—
whuddo *I* know?

Basically I've just never gotten the point. Not of his appeal to, well,
consumers of the rampantly consumable, that much is obvious: boogie on DOWN not only without guilt but WITH social conscience—
all bases, or let's just say *both* cases, covered—three hours for the price
of one. Like it makes total sense, for inst, what my ladyfriend Irene
sees in this shit. She's a show fan, see, Broadway and whatnot, a somewhat late (but eager) arrival to the rock-roll shores. She finally takes
to rock and what she takes to is Bruce—and I ain't listening. Eventually she gets her way, sits me down perchance to educate me (lout that
I am), plays me some Bruce and, lout that I am, I jump up (she forgot

to *tie* me down), wave my arms (*to the beat* so she knows, at least, I'm no crackpot), conduct the room to a round of "O!. . . . . . klahoma! where the wind comes sweepin' down the plain!" and dang me if she does not *chuckle* (as opposed, y'know, to sending me home) (lout I forever will be) because (a) she is no fool and (b) I have got the tumult & shout of it not far from purt near *correct*. And I know—and she knows that I know—that Bruce is naught but her long-awaited Conrad Birdie, or whatever their names are from *West Side Story*, made flesh. Or at least made ongoing product.

Which is fucksure cool but, um, note the connection. Just note it.

Or, for further inst, take my pal Scott Kempner. Dictators, Del-Lords (rhythm guitar, etc.). One big hunk of ingenuous mainstream plug-in. Just like a Patti Smith show when she was still stomping the boards, Scott's basic rhythm-of-life shtick has always been The Rock And Roll Fan Club Meets Here. Non-specific and yet specific. Before Bruce was his boss boy it was Peter Townshend. On the non-specific front, ever since that week in '75 when its Face made the covers of *Time*, *Newsweek* and all three trades, the Bruce Gestalt has, for Scott, roleplayed one consistently grand *advertisement* for The Power & Glory Of Rock Rock Rock And Roll, as if by the mere fortuity of its scale 'n' bombast (not to mention its benignity) WE are assured that—this time around—THEY can and will not dare bust "our music." Somehow, in this picture, a seminal (and terminal) wedding of creative lifeblood to marketplace/death-culture death is overlooked (or ignored), but, heck, that's cool too—there's people, I'm told, who actually regard rock videos as *gifts* (cum PRIMARY objects of experience!), and hey, couldn't the y'know FACT of Reagan be regarded as glorious evidence of the persistence of electional demo-. . . what's the word? . . . demogracy?? I.e., *if you want a ring implanted in your cultural nose, someone (by golly) will implant it.*

But, mea culpa, I digress. The *specific* side of the Kempner plug-in to Bruce—sorry, Scott, but use you I must for nefarious purpose—is . . . well I'm not sure about now, but in '75 I asked him flat-out "Whuh?" and he says "If the Fonz had a band it would be Springsteen." Yes!—the Fonz!! This of course was before we knew, or *could* know, that the incredible lovable li'l leather schmuck, the most palatably inaccurate (yet life-affirming) peer group archeTVtype since Maynard G. Krebs, was but an accident on the road to grown-actor oblivion for one Henry Winkler, who in short order would be shown to be not even the equal of fellow (but strictly second-unit) ABC greaser Vinnie Barbarino a/k/a John Travolta. Which, Christ, how

can I knock—actors as pump-primers for purported REAL
THINGERS!—when my own initial plug-in to Elvis Himself ('56, I
was 11) was I'd just seen Kevin McCarthy in the original *Invasion of
the Body Snatchers*, i.e., great moments in psychotic eye movement,
nose movement, lip movement, etc.? Can't knock it in principle, no
sir, but when you've got your Ersatz Quotient up there in *supreme* fal-
sification-of-reality range . . . hey (weepy-eyed stick-in-the-mud humanist that I am), I'm knocking. But not mocking. It is *sad* what folks
sometimes fall for. And *remain* fallen for ten fucking years down the
chute . . . fuggit.

Or for additional inst, 'cause I'm itching to get to what genuinely
pisses me off, back at the dawn of the '80s I had this show on a Pacifica
station that the RCP—Revolutionary Communist Party—was begging me to play their band on. Prairie Fire. I go see 'em and they're,
well, they're no Public Image (or the Fall) (or even the Clash). Just
your basic formally reactionary get-down boogie band with largely
implicit rad/topical "message" superadded—occasionally you'd hear
some reference to whatever through the (earnestly furious) get-down.
Structurally sound reiteraters of an already mega-told tale (American
Music Revisits American Myth); one more entry in—and I don't *really*
mean to insult them—the Springsteen Sweepstakes. Far from being
insulted, their spokeswoman hears the Bruce-word and . . . like wow.
Gee, she reflects, if only the Fire could harness that FAMILIAR
SOUND which People and Workers *already relate to*, and wow like
his songs're so y'know liberating and freeing and and . . . and god am
I one godless stick in the mud.

I hit her with (and she rejects) my whole entire rant re the need to
reject Prevailing Form (the "NO EXCUSE FOR BRUCE After
Punk" routine); she winces at but stands up to my drivel re Bruce as
(a) Hubert Humphrey (if even that much) in contempo-softshoe drag
(b) nose-ring yanker for the palace guard (c) learning-disabled child
of the '60s to whom that decade never even *registered*. All this one-
dimensional quasi-*political* claptrap, then we start talking lyrics, *poetics*.
Bruce's, we're no longer talking Prairie Fire. We bounce "bourgeois"
about, and I ask (pray tell) what the non-bourgeois—shall we say *revolutionary?*—import might be of such Springsteenisms as *wind blows
through my hair (and yours) in my '56 Chevy* and *my wonderful new
sneakers embrace the bright lights of etc.* And she says: "Bourgeois or not,
such lyrics GIVE HOPE to so many." And so be it.

And so be it all. I mean yeah, I certainly can dig how among the
teeming zillions various lames and non-lames alike have plugged into

Bruce. It seems like the sum of the some-of-the-people you can fool all of the time has gotten a little unwieldy, but at heart I'm a pluralist—not all mass delusions make me puke. I just cannot see, really I can't, a single sight, sound or accident WITHIN the delusion which is anything but monochromatic blah.

Is there anything grimmer and greyer than the Myth Of America? I am sick of the Myth Of America. Granted, Bruce's America is at least fractionally different from *Rambo's*—a *good* bad sitcom compared to a *bad* bad one—but since we're talking belief systems and the goddam marketplace, how many billion consumers do you think have bought both? Bruce and *Rambo*. Without missing a beat.

None of which would mean shit to a shithook—and, really, let's not be so ad *mass* hominem—if it weren't for what Bruce, or his shill Dave Marsh, did last October to avoid endangering any *possible* cross-constituency. Of consumers of the left and/or right. A couple weeks left till the election—remember?—and Reagan starts quoting Bruce. Instead of saddling his tumult & shout, riding out and yelling "Vote for Mondale! Our President wants us dead!" (and winning Walt Delaware and possibly Hawaii in the process), the little cocksucker passes it on to his publicist Barbara Carr, who passes it to her wonderful husband Dave. I don't remember the exact words but "rock critic Dave Marsh" did an *outstanding* hem-haw on page one of a respected news sheet I happened to catch. Something to the effect that if the President *would only look at such and such a Springsteen album cut*, he would clearly see that au contraire blah blah bluh. Don't say anything, don't stir anything, don't lose a single potential customer! FUCK THESE PEOPLE!!

And fuck me for getting so steamed. I'm an old grouch alright, but after punk, after Reagan—after everything and anything—why is this transparent dogshit still on the *menu* for crying out loud? Next up, we'll be asked to write about Garfield the Cat.

100

Into the Weird

And now for somebody sorta kinda di   *f*

                    fer

                e

                                             n

                          t:

Early last month, with New Music America about to strut its assortment of New Age sonic wares, KPFK jazz jock John Breckow asked pianist Richard Grossman, a man whose involvement in and commitment to the *truly* new in music goes back a quarter century, if at the dawning of that involvement he could have envisioned such a festival as even a distant possibility. Grossman, who had just finished playing an amazing live set of "free improvisations in and around jazz," responded by saying that sure, no sweat—he indeed could have imagined it. What would've been hard, let's even say impossible, for him to have pictured, he said, was "the scene the way it is now, with so many people *not* taking advantage of the freedom that everybody got to in the early sixties. I mean here you have all these people who were involved in that music and what're they doing now? They're writing elaborate compositions, they're playing straight time, they're playing chord changes, they're making records of standards with bebop rhythm sections. And you hear *very little* in the way of free playing."

The reference was primarily to jazz of course, but the message was a tad more universal: Where anymore in this big fat land where many, many things (sonic at least) are still quite possible are your masses of musicians with a dedication to the *making*, the *spontaneous* making (is there any other way?), of musics that are totally, genuinely NEW—

and totally *renewably* new—solely by virtue of their *continuously* NEVER HAVING EXISTED BEFORE? Well there ain't no masses: there's barely even handfuls. Even within jazz proper, a subuniverse in which "all" music is "always" played new, where (by proud "definition") "every" piece occurs for the "first time ever," there has been precious little temptation of late to man the primordial trenches, to visit and revisit frontiers without name perchance to CROSS-EXAMINE directly and anew first principles that have become articles of but the *remotest* of faiths—articles which otherwise, in their own sweet time, can only become every bit as post-functional as that other sweet article, "American" freedom. Richard Grossman, for the record, is one of those rarities: visitor, revisitor, one hearty breakfaster on the musical unknown.

Yeah, of course, sure, every player, Grossman included, does have his free-associational *habits*, creational modi operandi that are the meat and bone of what he musically *is*, and certainly no one can "play differently"—piece to piece or even, for that matter, gig to gig—literally every time out. But unlike Keith Jarrett, say, whose basic operational *shtick* is that he "doesn't know" precisely what adventure will befall him each time he takes to the keyboard, and who then proceeds to strut out the same old *ur*-familiar posturings all down the line, Grossman is one s.o.b. so forcibly intent on avoiding familiar paths (and where they must even *momentarily* lead) that he has all but dispensed with even the most innoxious of *riffs*. (Certainly neither Anthony Braxton nor Cecil Taylor, for inst, a conspicuous pair with officially solid "free" credentials, play quite as rifflessly as does Richard; nor, in the final analysis, do even such Euro-minimalist stalwarts as Derek Bailey or Paul Rutherford.) His vectors of motion and intent are more open-ended, poly-directional, *abstruse*. Single tones and chords in highly improbable alignment dance and swim headlong into silences so varied in context and duration as to each have their own startling, ineffable *flavor*. Free-floating tensions of a purely sonic order are created, shifted, resolved and/or ignored in collusion with parallel *existential* tensions which rise and fall to accentuate the music's ongoing intimacy with its own non-being. This is hardly an "easy" music—natch—a fact which the man himself has at times underlined by choosing to call it not Jazz, not New Music, but *Weird* Piano.

An L.A. resident since 1978, Grossman scrapped his way through the initial throes of musical maturity in mid-fifties Philadelphia, an aspiring high school bebopper at a time when, from a jazz standpoint, the town was up to its nostrils in a so-called (but quite genuine)

Golden Age. Hank Mobley, Philly Joe Jones, John Coltrane, the Heath brothers, Benny Golson—to name but a few—had already attained extra-regional prominence; trumpeter Lee Morgan reigned as the local high school comer, and a trio of great young bassists (Henry Grimes, Jimmy Garrison, Reggie Workman) were readying their chops in the wings. In the next half-decade Grossman would play with all of the latter, as well as with such variform Philly folk as Rashied Ali, Mickey Roker, Ted Curson, Jimmy Vass, Odean Pope, Randy Brecker, Lew Tabackin and Red Rodney. Then along came Ornette . . . and enter the weirdness.

Me and Richard had a couple-few drinks at The Arsenal on Pico and as happy hour raged we talked about a bunch of this stuff.

Q: There aren't too many people these days who would use the word *weird* in an affectionate, totally non-joke sort of way, let alone in the perfectly, um, *descriptive* way that you do.

A: I like the word! I guess it's a defensive thing. People used to say, "That's weird," y'know, and I would say, "You bet." But I think it's a neat word, and there were so many *bad* ways to describe all that music back when they started to talk about "freedom." The one I really hate is "outside"—outside what?

Q: How about "out"?

A: That's not so bad. But a lot of those terms never appealed to me, and I guess just to adopt "weird" doesn't hurt anybody. Basically it just means playing without regular time, without chord changes and without composition, right? People object to saying "jazz" too now. The thing is those are just words, not the same as music. I guess people used those words politically—the great jazz wars of the sixties. Were you a free guy, or were you a regular mainstream bebop guy or whatever. It's funny to think about it, I guess it's still going on in some ways.

Q: Regardless of what they were calling it, why were there so many guys who actually *played* weird or whatever, like with a vengeance, only to abandon it? Why were they so ripe to do it and then not?

A: I've never really understood that, except that there was an awful lot of pressure to not do it. There was a lot of economic pressure 'cause there was no work for people playing that stuff although I don't know, it always seemed to me that if they had stuck to what they were doing and taken it farther,

eventually there would've been more financial rewards or
whatever they were looking for. But a lot of those guys got
jobs teaching in colleges, which I guess is okay. I was just disappointed that some of them didn't keep the music going forward or doing something different rather than going *back*. I
think a lot of those people were, uh, a little insecure because
they didn't, some of them didn't come up playing in the,
quote, jazz tradition, and they sometimes felt they had done a
shortcut and hadn't paid the dues of playing regular *jazz*. Although some of them played in regular bands, even like in
blues bands and things like that, so they should've felt more
secure about letting that stuff go, but they seemed to want to
go back and recapitulate all the previous tradition. Which I
guess is hardly surprising if you look at today, right, everybody's so worried about *losing* the tradition at the very time
when every damn record has been reissued and the stuff is always there, it's in digital remastering!

Q: It seems though that more horn players have given up playing
functionally free than piano players—people like Archie
Shepp, Pharoah Sanders, Don Cherry. Maybe 'cause with
horns even just your *tone* is this obvious out i.d., so it's just
too, y'know, conspicuous for 'em to . . .

A: Yeah, yeah. It's always been true that piano has been more easily *accepted* doing new stuff, because it's not a loud instrument
and it's not intrusive in the way of a trumpet or a saxophone.
So you can, people just tend to think of the piano sound, uh,
they really don't pay as much *attention*. Maybe if Monk had
been a horn player it would've seemed more radical in some
ways for people at the time—who knows? But as a safe-
sounding sort of instrument, y'know at one point I even got
fed up with the piano. After I did a certain amount of free
stuff with it I got annoyed because you'd have to play this
note or that note, you can't play in between and do all the
things that the horn player can just *do* with his chops, easily. I
always wanted to get past that and I even stopped playing the
piano for a while. I fooled around with electronics and all of
that, it was real hard to get at synthesizers then 'cause they
were so expensive, you had to go to a college or someplace
that had one and get to use it for a few minutes. So I did a little of it, and it seemed interesting at the time, but what I
mostly did was John Cage stuff of using contact mikes and

cheap shit that I could get ahold of and use it inside the piano to make sound things and do tapes and things like that. After that I played cello for a while, because you definitely could play between the notes, it was real satisfying. But I never really got as much satisfaction out of playing the electronic instruments, and I can't imagine the *future* of all that stuff. All this technology, all this stuff that people are so hot for, and what do they do with it? They use it to make drum machines! These people who sell records playing synthesizers are not doing anything that you could only do with synthesizers, they're making something conventional in a new way that's easier, that's all. And I've got to the point with the stuff I'm playing now where I don't even wanna *think* about any of that, I just wanna make music. And the way I make it is on a piano. It's a real old-fashioned thing, it's got levers and hammers and all of that, but you just take it for what it is and try to make something out of it.

Q: As piano players go, well really on any instrument, you probably use more *silence* as an integral part of your music than anybody else in jazz, well maybe you and [trumpeter] Leo Smith.

A: That's funny, I was just reading Leo Smith, he has some elaborate *theories* about silence. Very few people pay much attention to that although the real good improvisers always have used it, I mean look at Miles, look at Armstrong, look at Bird. Monk. The silences and the way they use it with the other stuff for contrast and textures, it's always been part of it, but then I think what happened was during the sixties, the Free Jazz thing, people started with that "energy playing" and it became a value to have high energy all the time. And after a while you'd get a whole bunch of these guys together and they're all playing energy, and whether it's an ego thing or just a natural outcome of when you first discover you can *do* that, sometimes it eventually gets to where it's a bunch of guys blowing their brains out—y'know *that* cliche—and they're just filling up all the space. But you can listen to that stuff, the best stuff is always where people are paying attention and leaving space for each other, and that's when you get to, quote, art. The other stuff you get a lot of *expression*, and I know there's a whole school of thought about that, y'know the whole simple-minded approach of what's inside you has to come out and be expressed and that's good enough—and if you're really a "real person" that'll be it.

Q: Did you ever have a preference for just blowing your brains out?

A: Sure, because when you first find out about it, and you find out it's okay not to play some *tunes* with chord changes, not to play straight 4/4 time, not to play *licks* and all that stuff that you grow up doing, and you find out that you can go past that and cut it loose, and that the sky's not gonna fall and you're not gonna fall into a hole in the earth or something, then you'd naturally wanna do everything at once. So I used to play a lot more notes, I used to play a lot more clusters, a lot more of everything. And I think it's a natural thing, uh, you see a lot of painters do that, when they get older they sort of refine everything and do less and less and the stuff gets better and better. I'm not talking about minimalism either.

Q: What's your beef against Cecil Taylor?

A: There's no *beef*, particularly, I just never really listened to the guy that much. There was a time when it was like "Oh, you play free jazz and you play the piano, well you must play like Cecil Taylor." Well not necessarily, although a lot of people obviously followed that. I mean sure, I think he's a great artist, it's just not my favorite *art*. He doesn't leave space, he fills it all up except in those little parts which are always the most interesting. Aside from that, the harmonic basis that he seems to be working from sounds too much like sort of 19th century European classical music, it's romantic, it's all these diminished chords, that kind of stuff. And the sound of it just doesn't appeal to me. I was always attracted to the Monk kind of voicings with a lot of strange intervals and a lot of space so you can *hear* the relationships. Cecil never, Paul Bley was much more of a direct influence on me. I knew the guy and I talked to him a lot about music and didn't agree with him all the time but I really admired his playing. And one of the things I liked was that he was simply doing something *other* than what Cecil does. He was very interested in space, and I liked the sound of some of his voicings, just the sound he gets from the piano, and the *way* he approached playing I thought was very like *right*. And the things we disagreed about he would, well he was insistent on always having something composed to start with, a little, no matter how slight. He had all these tunes that Carla wrote or he wrote, Annette Peacock, and he would always want something to start with to set the tone of the improvisation that was gonna follow. And I would tend towards having the people that are playing just *do it*—by listening to each other—and try to count on the players and the way it went together to not be, uh, so that everything didn't sound the same. A lot of times when you even just *start* with some composed thing when you're playing free it does tend to start to sound the same on each tune, 'cause people tend to do the same kinds of things.

Q: What was it like first seeing Ornette at the dawn of the sixties?

A: Well there were three people in the club the first night we went and one of 'em was the clubowner, he was walking up and down tearing his hair out. And then the second night a *few* people came. The band was terrific, he had Higgins and Haden, they sounded great. They wore those funny little sweaters that they used to wear, it was wonderful. If you listen to those records now you sort of wonder how they could have stirred up so much hostility and so much misinformation, it seems really straightforward. I'll tell you, when Ornette first came to the East Coast, before he came to Philly, he had already been at the Five Spot in New York for a while, and a friend of mine had gone up to see him. I had heard the records and I asked him what it was like in person, he said, "The guy sounds like Bird," y'know? In a way that's oversimplified but what he meant was they were playing time, they were playing trumpet and saxophone and rhythm, playing solos one after the other and whatnot. The thing of Ornette that was very exciting to me was the way he used the melody to improvise, the way he would take the melody where it was gonna go without reference to a specific set of changes. But I was always wishing that they would do more, they would *stop* playing the time and stop playing those little tunes.

Q: How do you feel about, well Ornette operated an elevator at Bullock's to support himself, Shepp worked at Bloomingdale's and you're working at a record store.

A: So what's it all mean, right? Well you can't be surprised that some people that're trying to make some kind of serious art are not exactly gonna be wildly supported by masses of people. It's nothing new. What's bad is to get into that old, the bohemian thing of how that's *good*, that it's a value to be like all fucked up and starving and everything. I mean it's *not* fun to be a starving artist. And I'm not even sure that it's better what everybody says, "Oh, in Europe the state supports the jazz guys"—well I don't think I *wanna* be supported by the state, you know what I mean? You're just living in some kind of little space that, where nobody's bothering it for the moment. If you don't get into a self-destructive trip like many people do, if you still feel like making art then you're alright. But I don't see that it's gonna improve, I don't see *how* it could improve. It's not the nature of this stuff for it to be a mass art. That's what cracks me up when they call all these people "recording artists," all these people that're on the charts, they're referred to as artists, well that's just the name that they give it.

101

You Can Ask Your House!

The year I turned 40, to see what it was like to actually make music—and I don't mean sing it—I got myself a saxophone.

(For the record, I gave it up after less than a year. The guy yelling out, "You're not getting any better," no matter what hour I practiced, finally got to me.)

This originally ran with blurry photos of all the houses, for which I was paid more than for the piece itself.

Asked: The first seven houses in the L.A. phone book.

Q: *How's your alto sax playing coming along?*

House of John Aab
1040 S. Plymouth Bl.

Well I can't play to save my life, or let's say my mortgage, so far, but give me time, it's only been two, two and a half months. Like I just can't seem to come down from a high octave, y'know D or above, down to say a G or an A without squawking like a sonofagun, can't do it three times running even when I'm concentrating. And low notes in general, bottom B and C, even sometimes low D—they're tough. The main thing, though, is privacy. It's really a *problem* being a house, you're all exposed, it's just you out on the street and all. The other day some joker yelled out, "You're not getting any better!" Well shit, that's not exactly true but who knows it better than me? Heck, if I continue to play as I'm doing, two-three hours a day every day for the *next five years*, I might be as good as the *worst* professional now playing—which'd be fine with me!

House of Mieke Aabca
2260 W. Washington Bl.

It's a total gas. Just being able to string notes together. Songs. Tunes. "I Left My Heart in San Francisco." "September Song." Sappy stuff maybe, but so what? 'S a great feeling. Of, y'know, power. But really I wish . . . see, the main reason I took it up in the first place was here I was such a hardcore *listener* to all this stuff—you should see the size of Mieke's jazz collection—and still I knew nothing about music, not on the level of what music *is*. Like I'd read some liner note and see this biz about "modes," like whatever *they* are, and then I'd listen and assume I'm actually *hearing* that stuff, picking it up by some hokey form of osmosis, in for instance Miles or Coltrane . . . when in fact I haven't a clue exactly *what* I'm hearing, regardless of the genre, even in stuff I really, really like. It's always been a total mystery to me. And still is. I mean I do these exercises with intervals, seconds, fifths—and sure, yeah, I do get a kick out of finally discovering what a flatted fifth *happens to be*—but that's still a far cry, say, from a C-sharp having the same kind of sense-data *sense* that let's say yellow does, or green or whatever. Like to hear a note right out in the ether and have it trigger all sorts of *specific* associations. I got no idea whether single notes can even *do* that—and eight billion other things (I'm such a dumb, innocent one-story klutz!) which maybe somewhere down the line I'll actually begin almost getting to, y'know, know.

House of Karl Aaberg, Jr.
446 S. Ogden Dr.

There's lots of problems being self-taught, and tuning's been one of the bigger ones. How high you have the mouthpiece on the neck, up on the cork, determines how close you are to being in tune. Greg Burk showed me how to monitor that with one of these tone boxes, which I'm not about to buy—he's got it mostly for his guitar—so I just use the phone. Dial tone's supposed to be a D. Usually, though, it only sounds right when the thing's so high up the cork it's almost falling off. So that's gotta be wrong; I could probably use a more steady dose of human assistance. First week I was playing Vinny Golia came over and showed me some tricks, he showed me the breathing and told me practice long tones, whole tones for more than a minute, as long as you can hold it. He also got me on these books, *The Art of Saxophone Playing* by Larry Teal and this one he claims Bird used to use—and him too—*Universal Method for Saxophone*, copyright 1908. Which are fine as far as books go, like I'm up to this section where they make you try runs of sixteenth notes—ha, I can barely handle an eighth!—but inevitably I think I'll have to spring for actual lessons. The problem there is they'd have to come to *me*, 'cause how's a house gonna get to *them*?

House of Aage Aagesen
1941 Silverwood Ln.

Books, yeah, I've got those—I had Vinny come around too. I also got this great, at the time it seemed like ridiculous wishful thinking, the *Charlie Parker Omnibook*, transcriptions of a whole bunch of his solos. The solos themselves, forget it, they're all like endless streams of thirty-second notes—I saw this one bar, I think it was in "Parker's Mood," that had 29 notes *including* a rest—but just the themes, "heads," y'know up front, the theme, chorus, bridge, his tunes are great. And after learning garbage like "Battle Hymn of the Republic" and "Bicycle Built for Two," um, "Sweet Rosy O'Grady," I needed to sink my teeth into something, well, real for a change. So I looked for stuff with lots of quarter notes, the first one I worked on was "Yard-bird Suite." I'm playing it slow, real slow, and even at a snail's pace I couldn't miss this sense of, y'know, the sheer *magic* of the guy's melodic invention, these sharps and flats coming out of nowhere that're just *perfect*, these octave leaps, really amazing transitions. And even in terms of the fingering—well houses don't have "fingers" but you know what I mean—just the motion on the keys . . . his stuff is *very* far out to play. Like take "Steeplechase." Aside from the melody, y'know as sound, going up and down, up and down, he's got this re-ally interesting parallel thing with the physical G-sharp and D-sharp keys—the actual metal—at the far physical reaches, y'know *spatial*, of what he's using of the upper register, one at the highest point he takes you and the other like at a swing point before you circle back down, to serve as touchpoints of *your* actual ride while playing it. I mean the guy was the greatest horn person who ever lived, always my all-time hero, and what he played and wrote for, wrote *on*, was alto—and here I was getting this immediate dose, this info, this introduction to *some* of what his actual genius had to, um . . . why "Scrapple from the Ap-ple" is great music and "Battle Hymn of the Republic" is not. Or even a *clue*, or a clue to a clue to a clue . . . which is certainly more than I'd expected after I dunno, maybe it was a month at the time, five weeks, five weeks of playing a horn . . . wow.

House of Sue Aakerlund
732 S. Mansfield Ave.

Brother, have *you* got the wrong house! I play tenor!

House of Elijah Aaron
922 N. Crescent Heights Bl.

Ha, that's funny, tenor. 'Cause for a while I'd been thinking about getting a tenor instead, y'know myself, rent one first and see. I mean alto was always my favorite horn—Bird, Dolphy, Ornette, like *c'mon*, and then all these guys like Charles Tyler, John Tchicai, y'know Julius Hemphill, Henry Threadgill, guys whose sound, even just their *tone*, could burn a hole eighteen ways through the eye of the universe—except then I got to thinking, I guess from what I happened to be listening to, that the next tier of alto muthas—the Jackie McLeans, Gigi Gryces, the Art fucking Peppers—could sometimes be like a door squeaking in the night. Anthony Braxton. Which I thought I could avoid just by getting the deeper horn. But what happens, I get this alto for my birthday, one month's rental, and there goes *that* solution. So here I am, I'm finally on the playing end of the thing, and I realize *instantly* what a longshot it is, what work, what incredible backbreaking effort, just to have any chops at all. So I start respecting, maybe that's too strong a word but I start buying the notion that Art Pepper, for instance, can really for godsake *play*. And like Braxton, finally I realize that he absolutely *cannot*—zero chops, sorry—but that in the final analysis what he's really essentially *about*, what his genius consists of, is constructing these situations, these various setups for the horn to sort of act like an obstacle course, where *its* natural tendency at certain junctures to make what you might call noise is pushed to the max. So no matter what you try—hard course or easy—if you're coming from a chopless framework it's bound to give you some *great*, great noise. Like if Roscoe Mitchell played the same exact stuff, and I guess sometimes he does, y'know *with* Braxton, plus compositionally he's real similar anyway, probably actually did it first, though maybe not the same sonic *motivation*—okay, when Roscoe, who's a master blower, plays headfirst into even *total* Braxton brick walls he still sounds at worst like a guy playing maybe a *toy*, toy riffs, with lots of bombast and enthusiasm, and dandy shape and articulation like it's anything else he's playing. Which I never realized before, maybe I'm stupid, but all these guys from the sixties and so forth where noise was their middle name, I always assumed *all* of 'em could really play, y'-know create vast monoliths of "conventional beauty" and whatnot, and like they were sticking their nose into noise (per se) just to coura-geously fill in these inevitabilities of the sonic-emotional spectrum—but now I know Anthony isn't one of them. So in a way, insofar as he can't play a lick and neither can I, he's become sort of an inspiration to me. In my hopelessness. And then, ha, as hopeless as I am in terms of tone I'll do something crazy like try and play an actual Parker *solo*—I've got one of those books—and well I tried "Parker's Mood." And believe it or not it sounds okay, right off the sheet, first or second time I played it—yeah, what a cliche, white boy, er, house (better make that *off*-white) plays the blues—as slow as molasses but melodi-cally it's *really* intense . . . so intense I check the record 'cause it doesn't sound remotely familiar. And sure enough the rhythm is so differ-ent—*more* than different 'cause I didn't even *have* a rhythm—that what he's playing is almost you might say conversational, casual, any-way *not* outwardly "intense." So now I know, about as thunderingly as possible, where I'm the lamest: rhythm. Which has got nothing to do with this horn being squeakier than that. I'm just pee-yew . . . the sewer.

House of Dariush Aaryan
1200 S. Hoover St.

Well, I'm doing it; giving it the old household try. Three days it'll go fine, then warmed-over yuck for a week. But you keep on keepin' on, and I honestly can't think of a more . . . uplifting experience at this stage of my life—no lie. Like there's houses my age, people even, who start seeing death all around them, limitations. Not me—all I see is openings. Speaking of which—ahem!—I haven't had so much fun since I fugged whatsername, that slutty condo over in the Marina. Heck it's a chore, sure, but an ecstatic chore, and I'm up for it. So it gives me a headache every time I play it. Well I'll just have to do it 'til I stop getting them. A finite accomplishment. It can be done. Less fi-nite maybe—but bet your sweet chimney I'll give it a shot—are (1) improv and (2) playing *with*. With houses, people, I'd even play with dogs if they could play. Meaning if *I* could. And maybe I will.

102

My Birthday

Basically, the reason I agreed to do the Springsteen thing was I thought it would lead to OTHER THINGS at the "alternative" Rolling Stone. It was my audition for Spin's *ruling narcissist, Bob Guccione, Jr., who would promise the world when you offered something—"I want the piece! I want the piece! Do it! Do it!"—then promptly forget. Except for some reviews (jazz LPs, the Lester book), this whiz-off and "Rock-Crit Blood 'n' Guts (Part 1)" were all that ever made it past his desk.*

Okay. On side two of the Jim Morrison poetry album, *An American Prayer,* right after his only singsong on the disc, "Roadhouse Blues," there's this great exchange between him onstage at some concert and a perky, eager-to-please fan person down in the seats. "Listen, listen," he begins, "I don't know how many of you believe in astrology . . ." At which point she, the fan person, sighs, croons, like an uncoached accomplice at a '67 Zappa gig, "You're a Sagittarius!"

"That's right, baby"—credit where due—"I am a Sagittarius, the most *philosophical* of all the signs."

She, louder this time, honing in on some my-t-good superstar peckermeat: "I know—so am *I*!"

"But anyway"—heh heh heh—"I don't believe in it."

Fuggit (but ne'er say die): "I don't either!"

Which is where *I* chirp in, every time I hear it, *That makes three of us!*—'cause it does.

I don't believe! I don't believe!—and even *if,* for reasons of brain damage, moisture-grope expedience or despair, I were ever to even *voice* belief (in the poetry/causality of birthdate-coded intrastellar b.s.), I trust I would, après cunnilingus, have sufficient non-damage to *reject same* posthaste. "Theism is tyranny"—some Frenchman said that—no exceptions, mono-, poly- or pan-. And if God the Tyrant is

414

to get His regal butt kicked, then how 'bout the frigging planets, moon and stars? Astrology is like going to a shrink to pledge neurotic *allegiance* to your ma and pa. *Free me, oh free me, from the spell of Universe!—offer me not constellations as my chains!—etc., etc., yippity-yay-hey* ... but I don't believe it, not for a sec.

And I think what I buy least about the whole trip is all this twelve-ness crap. Finitude. Although I dunno, maybe twelve is actually kind of a *huge* number when it comes to earth-person taxonomy, to, y'-know, pigeonholing, categorizing "man." You read Rex Stout, f'rin-stance, or Ross Macdonald, Georges Simenon, Ed McBain, and a guy'll crease his brow at *most* this way, that way or the other—that's three. Three creasings, three indicators, three basic types (of persons who crease). Or you can be the sort that prefers to fuck standing, sit-ting, kneeling, crouching, lying, flying or swimming—that's seven. So maybe twelve is like I say, immense. Maybe "too finite" is the wrong, the polar-*opposite* wrong take. Have persons even *got* that much vari-ety—in any dept.?

Dunno.

Nor do I in fact particularly "know" the signs, even just their names, like all twelve of 'em. I mean if you pointed a gun at my head, gave me half an hour, I could probably come up with ten or eleven. But dates, sequence, *nah*, and import—forget it. Libra, for inst, what the fuck is Libra? And Sagittarius, even with the throw-in of it being Jimbo's one and only, I still dunno, is Sagittarius the Goat? All I even half-know is my own whatsit, Taurus ("stubborn"—isn't that the shtick?—"bull-headed"), and the one *everybody* half-knows, the "sex sign," Scorpio.

So, right, all I am is a crackpot, a know-nothing, a good-for-naught mocker and fuddydud. I pee 'n' shit on the zodiac just because it's ... there. All this sound, fury, tinkle, plop, and all I really KNOW is my birthday, May 10, the one I share with:

Fred Astaire
Sid Vicious
Donovan.

The four of us—ain't we neat? Luv that Calendar Dada! Womb-drop according to the laws of chance! Take *that*, astro-fornicators!

Fred, aka Frederick Austerlitz, that subtlest of whitebread hoofers and crooning superstar of *Silk Stockings*, the only Cole Porter–scored pixture worse than *At Long Last Love*, a harmless skinnyboy the gals still love . . . the late Sid, aka who remembers, razor nicks and cuts about the forearm and biceps, a credible interpreter of Frank Sinatra, framed accused slayer of Nancy Spungen, he who did not brush teeth . . . Donovan, aka "The Chameleon," a folkie, then a parody of a folkie, then a psychedelic wagwit and showbiz pickleherring, the original David Bowie, he wore a dress as early as '68 . . . and me, aka "R." Meltzer, aka Borneo Jimmy and Audie Murphy, Jr., pulp scribbler and hepcat from heck, boxing historian, De Niro lookalike, author of this piece and seeker of the end of this paragraph . . . and what have we got, I axe you, *in common*—aside from hot steamy Augusts when our moms went and spread 'em w/out diaphragm, rubbers or an IUD?

Not much.

How much access, in fact, does a hot 'n' random slip-slide in August actually provide *us*, both singular and plural, to any and all Stations of the universal Bull? Could each or any of us, for inst, making uttermost *use* of our personal/universal mettle, with or without guns at our head, even possibly *enter* the bullish lifespace of each of the others, their y'know creative mindset and whatnot, with an eye towards actually remotely *participating* in their Taureated yet highly etceterated "thing"?

Whew—a tough question. Lemme think.

I think not.

To wit: Sid. Could I, in my wildest imaginings, imagine myself playing bass for the Pistols, breathing new life into tired, overrated Eddie Cochran tunes? Yes I could. But Freddy and Donovan, no, I'm afraid not, pardon me as I stifle a chuckle—heh heh—*no*.

Fred's turn. Again *yes*. With practice, lots of practice, I could indeed imagine tripping the light, foxtrotting Ginger from hither to yon. Sid and Don: unlikely.

Donovan? We all, I think, could wear our love like heaven. (But Sid would also wear a swastika.)

Me? No way. None of 'em could, or let's say would, write *The Aesthetics of Rock* (1970) or *Guide to the Ugliest Buildings of Los Angeles* (1984). (The work's too hard, the pay too low.)

So what have we got, we've got inconclusive. You couldn't prove dick from the info at hand. Why this May joker stumbles down this long & winding path and that May joker down that—it beats me, truly. (One of the so-called "mysteries.") If I were a betting person I'd bet my wallet or purse, but not my car, on "E": environment. But such is mere surmise; please don't quote me.

It's always unfortunate when you can't take the back page of *Spin* to the bank, so to speak, to use it to get laid or cuss the establishment. This has been such a time: a time for shallow, peabrained *entertainment*. Trite, pathetic, bathetic *fun*. I've had fun, you've had fun, and if you haven't *fuck you*, it's my birthday. Lots of candles and so much mischief I feel like a kid again. I think I'll go play Jim's record, the part right after "I don't believe it" where he says, "I think it's a bunch of bullshit." Hey, *I'm* a bull!—and bull *shit* is just my kind.

AFTER THAT

Introduction

In the battle of the weekly throwaways, while the *L.A. Reader* was losing its shirt to the crosstown *L.A. Weekly*, the *San Diego Reader*, with no competition, was prospering, and could afford to pay A THOUSAND CLAMS for a cover story (later raised to 2000). They called me now and again, they liked my stuff—why don't I write for 'em? Okay. But feature-length stories took so long to write, because *writing* was by now taking me so long—and then factor in the increase in page count—that it wasn't always cost-effective.

The bigger problem was having to go down there to suck up, and write up, local shit (a week with the Navy, four days with ex-mayor Roger Hedgecock, playing Santa for the kids at an outdoor swap meet). The drive wasn't the problem (they even paid for gas), it was having to actually *be there* a few days, minimum, per visit. If L.A. was the capital of Kansas, San Diego was the county seat of one of its *lesser* counties—what a dump town—and I all but begged 'em to let me do stories I could write without leaving L.A.

In '93 or so, a funny thing happened. Maybe the reprintings of *The Aesthetics* and *Gulcher* had something to do with it, but somebody at the paper, I forget who, happened to discover my old typecast. It was another one of those "Didn't you used to . . . ?" routines. (I was by then—for better *far more* than worse—the forgotten man of music-crit.) What they offered me was ten music features a year, critical whatsems in which I directly *dealt with* music, referring to specific artists, recordings, etcet . . . oh fuck. And not at the cover-story rate, nah, but I wouldn't have to be in San Diego more than *once* a year (which they still required of me). Well . . . okay.

In '95, when I moved to Portland, a thousand miles to the north, I assumed they would waive the once-a-year requirement . . . (please please) . . . wouldn't they?

But other shit was waiting to happen.

103

Of Peep Shows and Piano Bars

When the S.D. Reader *kept putting me up in the same shabby downtown hotel, regardless of where a given assignment was to take me, I started noticing what the area was good for: cocktail lounges and scuzzzz. So the next time down I talked my way into this dream assignment, the first piece I wrote on a computer.*

When it got reprinted in Forced Exposure, *Derek Bailey sent me a fan letter.*

> Romance is mush,
> Stifling those who strive.
> I'll live a lush life
> In some small dive.
> —"Lush Life," Billy Strayhorn

DOWNTOWN INSTANT GRAT—You want it, you got it. You want this, you go here, you want that, you go there. Downtown has got it. Did I want? I don' know. But I went.

Molly's at the Marriott, Sunday night. "Is the piano guy playing?" "Yes he is." A seat, a table, at keyboard right, waitress drops a napkin in my lap. Good aim, safe landing, no touching. Piano guy arrives in a tux, no, tails, black, and yuppie specs. The big round kind with plastic rims—he's the age for 'em. Sits. Ready.

Within seconds, a flaccid rendition of "On the Street Where You Live" from whatsit, *My Fair Lady*. Which when I first heard it in '56, three months before Elvis on *Ed Sullivan*, I liked it, I'll admit it. Kids like stuff. They're programmed to. Tonight, though, this listener, all growed up, this version, keep it. The version, tune, both. The 'sentiment.' "Wouldn't It Be Loverly?" Not tonight, thanks.

Sunday at eight—mostly seniors and baldies and bizfolk and such. An immense noncommodious room, brown monochrome. Mirrored ceiling. One week to Easter: huge bunnies, brown chocolate, white chocolate, on mounds of fake grass, quite green, more like that stringy old-fashioned cellophane kind than any current plastic variety. Not 20 feet away on a screen above the bar, the Mets vs. Cincinnati (exhibition, post-game), great color. Whirr of a blender, subliminal, too sub to drown out the "Laura"-type 'seabreeze' tune: now young mr. piano is in gear. A hip-à-go-go ballad version of "Happy Birthday" (now he's out). Theme from *The Flintstones*.

Waitress, no, now it's a waiter, serves me basket bread and beer. Bread, butter, beer and the theme from *I Love Lucy*. A crackle of hands, he nods—a face only Van Cliburn, or Marvin Hamlisch, or a Marvin Hamlisch-Van Cliburn gene-splice (at a mirror) could love. Solemn. Austere? Somber.

Where's th' waitress? Spittin' image of Shelly Phelan (you don't know), whom I never poked—not in this life—not conceivably in any. Retirees, dowagers, conventioneers, maybe 12 or 13 total in the room. A smattering of claps for the theme from what, *Cheers*?—I've never seen *Cheers*—and for each ensuing TV theme, recognized.

Songs from *M*A*S*H*, *Hawaii 5-0*, *Gilligan's Island*, *Mary Tyler Moore*, *The Beverly Hillbillies* . . . songs without heart, played without mind . . . ciphers for nothing (some things are like that) . . . *I Dream of Jeannie*, *Dennis the Menace*, *Burns and Allen* . . .

Wds. that could easily come to mind: lame; woeful; wretched; pathetic. Too easily.

Another beer and I realize that I, too, am one of the pathetics in this piss-genteel bistro. An old fart like any other, I can cut no more current mustard—of any sort *I* respect—than this tink-tinkler groping for mythosonic whuh?? and a table (two tables) of baldies balding the universe. A 40- to 42-year-old blonde, alone, not unalluring, the vice prez (no doubt) of some petronutrition giant, smiles at me from across the room: I'd rather walk my schnauzer.

A greysuit strides by to request the title theme from *Elvira Madigan*. "I'm sorry, I don't know it." "It's Mozart's thus & such." "Sorry, I don't." Plays instead some generic classical, some nouveau, a nouveau treatment of, could it be?, "My Sweet Lord." Could and is. *Lots* of butter on my bread, not bread, sesame crackers. Most butter I've spread in years—a cholesterol kiss before dying. How pathetic I am that this is my gig ("to write about nuhnuh"). How pathetic that I haven't womanized, wantoned, eaten strange pussy, in half a decade. Give me butter, give me tobacco (I would not now mind—for argument sake—being 'dead').

Different waiter. "Perhaps a little coffee?" "I think that should do it." The protocol of despair.

Piano guy finishes, thud *thunk*, with something like "MacArthur Park"—though there's no substitute *for* "MacArthur Park" (re: composition, not 'interpretation')—he's half a Ferrante & Teicher. No rhythmic, harmonic or melodic 'interest.' Melodies stated, over-stated—as map refs to a network, a cluster, of gridlocked highways. Touch, feel, tune selection—nuthin'. A real plunker. He somberly exits. I also.

According to a lobby poster, Las Cascadas (temporarily closed) is "FRIENDLY." Marina Sea Grill has the "VIEW," YachtClub the "ACTION." Molly's, on the other hand, is "ELEGANT." And elegant it was. Exit and belch, I scare a black tomcat. The night smells— the world smells—like a lubricated rubber.

SAME NIGHT, SAME GALAXY—Pleasureland Adult Video Arcade, 5th and E. "Must be 18 to enter"—'s a good thing I am. Everything arranged so neatly—the vibrator section, the dildo section, the tickler section, the home video section, the smutty magazoons— neat li'l, cute li'l day-glo modules, almost like a many-walled Warhol repetition hoozis, as visually appealing as any of his early stuff (before he got shot, recovered, rediscovered nonironic fashion, and opted for a played-down palette as demographically dealt), much more so than his later pastel-tinged horseshit—*nice*. An inflatable plastic love doll, Candy—"The Bra Buster"—leers down in open-mouthed welcome.

Guy behind the counter is the spittin' im of Larry Mannberg (you don't know) in a Batman T-shirt, yellow on black with the rubberized batsignia peeling off, big not unlikable oafish lout.

Smell: like that of a Woolworth's (or a card shop at a mall). Y'know, benign.

Some fine video titles: *Everything Butt II, The Slutty Professor, Breast Wishes*. Fine mags: *In the Bush, Catfighting Co-Eds, Pussy Power #7, Girls Who Like to Suck Black Cock, 3-Way Ass Fuckers*, and in the gay section, *Head of the Class, Dial-a-Dick, Hand 2 Mouth*—not that buyers/browsers of *Girls Who Suck Black* or *3-Way Ass* are necessarily (of course) heterosexual.

Clientele: nine or ten males, white, black, average age 30–32, all (on appearances) middle middleclass, well dressed, i.e., not unwell, i.e., washed, pressed, moderately in vogue, more night-on-the-town (or fresh-off-the-hanger office gig) than casual, slightly squaresville in the grooming department, all unhurried, unharried, all but one browsing one of the hetero subsections (New Releases, Female, Bondage, etc.) while he who ain't peruses the She-Male—transvestite, transexual—rack: *She-Males Who Eat Cum* (a verygood title).

Two-dollar minimum on tokens. Eight tokens for two bucks. Price hasn't changed since my last visit to a smutstore back room, back in 19 . . . 70. Those days they had drapes out in front of the booths, metal stools, now it's just scoot in, be seated. Vinyl seats. Not uncomfortable. Seeking posted offering #2, "Office Hot Licks," I scurry from booth to booth before I realize you get all channels, many channels, in each, more than VHF (but less than cable). Just hit the knob for a change. Problem is, damn, they're all videotape.

Not film. It used to be film. Video copies of film. Pornmakers used to be filmmakers. Now they're TV producers. Video image is depressing: as cold as the news or a sitcom. You rent new smut these days from vid stores, *mainline* vid stores, it's all video. Must be all they shoot, cut, distribute anymore. Art-supply economics. Sitcom lighting—slimy!—is not for the family of Mammals. Videotaped sex has a feel, a spurious 'glow,' not unlike S.D. sexuality—naked under lights—when lit—but barely ('scuse the pun) the same as Nothing Hid. Not-much in fact is Revealed. Yielded. 'Given.' Videotape-only is the end of the world.

And shaved crotches are no great shakes either. Like shaved armpits, most vid gals seem to have them, which at first keeps my mutton in my pants—keeps things 'journalistic'—but not forever. Two tokens of pudenda, shaved or un-, and it decides on its own, fug it, so I take out the bastard and pump it. Switching, searching, I settle for—settle *on*—channel 10, 'Amateur Lesbians'—no alien peckers to ruin my concentration.

'Amateur' (reviewed). Two marginally attractive white women with tan lines, only one shaved, rub their respective galmeats together. Their galmeats are wet. They rub, they rub, then they pull out a two-headed dildo, each inserts an end up her cunny, they work out, get a herky-jerk rhythm, occasionally touch each other's tits, nipples, not exactly fondle but at least manually *reference*. For as long as I watch them they don't kiss or nibble, but plenty of thrusting, hips, butt, take out the head, stick it back in, etc. Oooh-ahh for soundtrack—there's sound. Facial pleasure gestures, method-act intensity. Certainly better, more 'convincing,' than whatsername in *The Big Easy*. Birkin, Merkin? . . . Ellen Barkin. After about a minute they actually both seem like they're straining to come—more so than any gals, other channels, with their respective meatmen (or Ellen with Dennis Quaid) (was she coming or puking?—purporting to puke or come—only her act instructor knows for sure)—kind of like ('credibly'; willing-suspension-of-disbelieffully) "OK, let's do it—as long as we're at it let's frigging *get off.*"

Though I would not seek the wetness or meatness or bland mammal warmth or embrace of either sweety or both (were she or they to enter my corporeal life)—or of even their 'type'—not actively—I continue to insert coins and stroke it—only medium anxiety over handling both coins and my wiener (microbes & scuzz, y'know?—and cooties)—stroking, pump it, mm, ooff, gg, hnhuh, *gotit.* Four tokens is all it takes, though the gals haven't come yet—all done in veryfew minutes.

No more depressed than I am after shooting my load over some tired, third-rate fantasy during a write break on a Thursday afternoon, I zip up (depressed maybe also that 20 years ago, even 5 or 6—certain hygiene parameters factored in—I'd've *wanted* to sex these gals, that my brief audio-visual encounter with 'em would in any event have fueled at least a couple afternoons' worth of semi-acceptable beatoff, that once upon a not too distant past my tolerance for danger, and I'm not talking viral, went beyond reckless token-handling—i.e., what's BECOME OF ME that I've lost the yen, or is it the zen, for bounce f'r bounce sake with who-cares-whom?—and/but what's the WORLD-as-dealt come down to that they're SHAVING IT?—i.e., what a truly unappetizing world this indeed do be), drop my soiled plaid 40%-cotton hanky and exit.

"Dear Customer," says a hand-lettered sign at the door, "Thank you for shopping at our store. If you have not received a register receipt, you are entitled to a free refund. Please ask for it." Free refund: the best kind. Guess I'll have to come back and buy something.

NOTHING FOR GRANTED—Piano-bar piano as you approach it (in progress) should sound like you just missed the horn player or the singer and you're catching what must in fact be the accompanist's solo, only it lasts longer than a backup's solo could conceivably last, and it doesn't even stop at song's end—ain't life funny?—it goes on all night.

Keyboard sonorities, jazzlike, spill from the lounge off the lobby of the U.S. Grant: so far, so good. Cocktail lounge w/ piano = piano bar.

Piano bar, howev, is not jazz bar. Piano-bar piano is not jazz piano. Sometimes, sure, but hardly necessarily. Rarely but occasionally, and on such occasion count your blessings, but never does it tick-tinkle support of, uh oh, jive muted trumpet.

"That was 'Bourbon Street' by Sting," declares the jiver—oh great. John Lydon, Johnny Rotten, once said that while he didn't personally know what jazz *was*, i.e., *is*, he was deadsure Sting didn't either, although regardless (or because of) this delimiting fact Sting would before he was done believe he'd invented it. Far from done—maybe a fudge truck'll hit him—though it seems like certain third parties may already share such a notion. That if Sting didn't invent it he at least owns it. 'Signifies' it. To make matters worse, tonight's designated third party doubles on vocal, a *dork* of a singer, vocals and posturings . . . drummer a clunker . . . bass okay . . . piano solo.

Cocktail piano calls for a cocktail: I'll have a bloody mary. Happy-hour price, 4 bucks (stiff). Happy-hour import beer: 3 bucks. Happy-hour buffet: brown slop with formerly living animal substance (chicken? fish? mollusk?), some kind of ultralight microstrand pasta, hot fresh deepfried saltsalty tater chips.

Dorko, 35, pallid white, takes a pair of shades from his brown leather sportcoat, models them coyly, slyly, as he sings, blows and *blows* the English-language version of "Meditacão"—"Meditation"—bossa nova mem'ries on this the 29th anniversary of the N. American release of "Desafinado." Jazz as reiterable 'lifestyle': fuck it to hell, no, heck. Switches to flugelhorn, "When I Fall in Love"—Chet Baker slept here . . . zzzzz—but his pianist knows the changes. Navigates tolerable torrents of cliché. No worse than any 200, 300 you could hear in this country in the course of a month. Good bottom to the bass. Piano trio, this or any, would be preferable right now to a dorkster quartet.

Framed oil of U.S. Grant looks down (but doesn't wink) from the far left wall. A trio of happy-hour'ers, 50, 55, in 1000-dollar suits carry on fiercely over scotches and water. "My heart bleeds for his mother, but fuck her." "The Irish, fuck the Irish." "I grew up in Pittsburgh, guineas everywhere." "What we're talking about is *hundreds* of thousands, that kind of shit." "Fuck cheese." "Regulation—believe *me*—or we pay for it up the ass." "They vote, they participate—but they don't know *dick* about real manipulation." "What they don't need is pants." "Scratch the variables, 'cause the natural thrust of any business . . . " "I'm no Communist, but I think Canadians make *much* better farmers."

Plenty o' slop left—come 'n' get it. Upscalers slowly fill the room. Applause, applause—you'd applaud too if you didn't know the 'diff.' Singer is a denatured Bobby Darin, Bryan Ferry. Bones in my slop (fish? chicken? goat?) make real-time chewing iffy . . . salty salt chips—do I wanna die NOW?—so I split.

Peep show is not the Real Thing. Piano bar is not the Real Thing. This isn't even real piano bar. Try again . . .

PEEPLAND BY DAY—New scents at Pleasureland. The stink of disinfectant. The generic reek of modern public place.

Customers a tad more furtive this morning, more desperate (or something), an acuter degree of urgency, whatever. Two fatsos at the register, a bowling proprietor and his CYO handball coach buddy (circa '46). When an antsy guy names them a tape title, they cue it for him and nod knowingly (like having a 'date' with the 1-U-Luv: *nice*): "In booth 3."

Hispanic woman in a Padres T-shirt sticks her head in front: "I left my chemicals back there." Takes along her bucket. 'S a good thing *I'm* not going back this time. Here just to purchase something, anything.

Some fine object. My choice: *Slit Sucking Sweethearts*, $7.95 (reduced from $20—a steal)—shiny—new—excellent ink—two broads pretending to tongue each other, tiptongues not slurps, in three tiptop pics on a saucy glossy cover. I pay and am changed, receipted—damn—but I've got myself a *good'un*.

"F" IS FOR FLOG IT—From its gentrified 4th Avenue storefront to its weave-pattern library-class carpet, the F Street Bookstore is more lush, more plush—in a word: more 'bourgeois'—than Pleasureland. Not a lot more, but more. A healthy potted plant. Tweedy college prof type counterman. Nonsmutty Picasso poster. Ultranormal middleclass consumers (four white, two black) and some groove-groovy product to consume.

Vids: *Bangkok Massage Girls, Lesbo à Go-Go, Splash My Tits, Ambushed, Backdoor to Hollywood.* Smut mags: *Pussy Poking, Bottoms-Up, The Best of Cum #10, The Crotch Connection.* Mags other than smut: *Downbeat, The Ring, Guitar Player, PC Today.* Joy Gel, Anal Eze, women's underwear, novelty condoms (Worlds [*sic*] Smallest Condom—"For that little prick in your life"; Masturbaters [*sic*] Condom—"When you have to take matters in your own hand"). Also for sale: incense, gift wrap, Desert Storm ephemerae, cuddly adorable beartoys.

Smaller tokens than Pleasureland, less coppery looking, same unit price, same nonrefundable minimum. Booths seem less private, uh, more open, wider entry, but they do each have a mini-trashcan for jizz-rag disposal. I find a booth whose can is bare.

A pair of channel changes gives me two gals, both shaved, neither very intense, one on her back, blonde, tits ajiggle, being fucked by this guy off camera (except for his dick) while the second gal, dark, somewhat Judaic looking, sits astride her face facing away, you see her ass (nice), sometimes her asshole (ditto), then number one rolls over ("I'll turn over") to get vagina'ed from behind as the one being et turns to get licked and lapped by her (sporadically) sitting just on bed-sheets, you see her cunt (usually) and number one's asshole and cunt (sometimes) and ass. Seeing her ass, her asshole, a rear p.o.v. of her pud-dilated cunny, and number two's cunny being tongued and her tits (not ajiggle) is a nice touch even *without* simulated passion—even with cruel, severe video lighting. What a difference a day makes!

Which puts me in the mood, après flogging, for some good old-fashioned C&T&A-related pulp. *The Majorette Loved Spreading* . . . what an old-fashioned title . . . with an old-fashioned cover . . . an old-fashioned typeface. (I'm an old-fashioned guy.)

TEA FOR EIGHT—Back again, this time for tea, not me, them. A threesome, a threesome, and a twosome. Afternoon tea at the Grant, High Tea, 4:15 in the lobby. Five 'blue-haired ladies'—they could be D.A.R.—and three 'frosteds'"—post-yuppie, um, neo-middleaged begonia consultants. Teapots with floral cosies, blue and pink.

A betuxed, bowtied dandy the image and likeness of Jeb Stuart or Abe Lincoln, Jesse James—one of *them*—ripples the ivories. A de-cloyed (then recloyed) "Close to You." "I've Got a Crush on You" à la Erroll Garner, limp Erroll Garner, but 'jazz' not 'pop.' Some light classic, not "Liebestraum," not something with "nocturne" in the title. The guy is 'eclectic.' That other Carpenters, not 'We've Only Just Begun'—it'll come to me. Tea lady response: none.

Pillars, posts, potteds, faded landscapes, hundreds (and hundreds) of old living-room 'easychairs.' Where am I? In such a chair, tealess. Drinkless. A group of eye-alive grandmas, grey-haired and white-haired not blue, bounce by and sit tealess in my neighborhood.

"I'm Getting Sentimental Over You"—not bad, okay, left hand comps 'provocatively' for the right. A greyhair bobs her tennis shoe, smiles at me in a grandmotherly (or pre-grandmotherly) postlustful (pre-postlustful?) way. Jeb strings out his ending, more, more, de-

crescendo, *plink*—done. And done for the day, no twitter of applause
from the tea broads, not having played "Tea for Two" or "I'll Remember April."

Speaking of which, "April," there's a great scene in *Bring Me the
Head of Alfredo Garcia*, Sam Peckinpah, '74, where Warren Oates as a
hepcat piano player in Mexico City, this tourist dive where buses stop
and first drink is on the house, is playing "Guantanamera" when Gig
Young and Robert Webber come in smelling of money. A whore
grabs for Webber's dong, he clubs her with an elbow (he's gay, y'see—
and has gangster work to do), then Warren (striped tie, paisley shirt)
tries talking basketball with them ("Bill Russell—1969"), finally they
request "I'll Remember April." The greatest piano-bar scene of all
time? Maybe. Certainly the greatest deconstruction of "I'll Remember April."

Which if I'm not gonna hear here, I might as well try 'n' hear
there . . . across Broadway at the Omni. Where the lobby bar, it
turns out, has ferns the size of mastodons, and the piano sounds un-
tuned (but whuddo *I* know?), and a dignified black guy, thin mustache, red bowtie, is playing cocktail schmaltz (per se) for, or
possibly at, or in the sonic vicinity of, two coveys of drunken Aus-
tralians. Heavy on the arpeggios; long florid lines which ineluctably
lose their continuity; an emotional import which, though of decid-
edly mawkish stripe, defies specification: for taxonomic piano-bar
oompah, this is IT.

The clink of glasses above keys. A table of Aussies in rugby shirts
and another in golf shirts shouting computers? automation? 'systems'? across the brink. Implicit pathos, then a mite more explicit. A
stocky outgoing black guy stops by, work clothes, baseball cap, to
share a laugh with the pianist, who doesn't miss a florid note, and is
soon followed by a tall officious white guy (stinking of Omni) who
speaks briefly to him, after which he, baseball, leaves, leading one to
ponder: does he, baseball, work elsewhere in the hotel, somewhere his
services are currently, perhaps even urgently, 'required'? does he,
dresscodewise, simply 'not fit in'? or/and is he being given the racist-
generic 'bum's rush'? If you can think these things, you think these
things—all part of the Omni Gestalt.

Meanwhile, no break in the music, no change in the music or the
forbearance of its maker, no tunes recognizable as such, but definitely
no "I'll Remember April"—to deconstruct or otherwise. When five
minutes later he stops playing, seemingly in midsong, either because
it actually is (tune unknown) or 'cause the whole set feels unresolved

(musically, emotionally, 'situationally'), he gets up, smiles, not at any-one—another night, another gig.

What a grim, pat Woody Allen world.

LITERATURE: the gift that keeps on giving (reviewed).

Slit Sucking Sweethearts. Two unshaven blasé cuties, blonde (hair in a bun), natural red. Shots of 'em paired on the floor and/or couch in most conceivable one-on-one juxtapositions, but not too many close-ups of Red's right scapula (tattooed). Blondie's labia are nearly always parted in compulsory symmetrical pink, something this writer has always found absurdly artificial (and—yes—sexist); Red's when they're apart have a more genuine asymmetricality and blush. Best pic is that of Red on Blondie's lap, organ above organ, Blondie nuzzling Red's satin nightie, Red licking her own left bicep. Best caption: "Do we ever date men? Are you kidding? Who needs limp, soggy dicks when we have our always-hard, always-ready dildos!" (Blondie's dildo stem is wider than Red's.)

The Majorette Loved Spreading, by Victoria Parker. "NEW BOOK— October 1988," says the football-content cover, players stripping to jockstraps while she spreads 'em (undies still on) at the 40-yard line. No players in the book, howev, just a principal and a chaperone and a janitor and a kid brother and an aunt. Semi-odd in its sexual priorities (handjobs over intercourse), a little overboard on anilingus and panty-sucking, but if lines like "'Ooooh,' she wailed, 'you're tongue-fucking my shitter!'" and "Sue panted, slicking a sticky shoe into her pussy" and "His big cock slapped up in a wobbling hard-on" and "His back was hunched over and he was fucking his prick with a spastic jump-jerk" are not hard litrachoor—the v. real thing!—then what, pray tell, is? And lest you feel "Victoria Parker" a suspect pseudonym, that the *auteur* of this fine prose—to wit—couldn't possibly be female, check this: "Mr. Cavendish sobbed, his prick shooting splats of thick spunk at Sue, spurting thick gobs of jism that flew beautifully, like little puffy clouds, through the air and splashed down on Sue's divine body in simmering pools of jism"—I'd bet my house a woman wrote *that*. Published by Greenleaf Classics, San Diego. Who sez S.D. ain't got no bk. co's?! (Or did have in 10/88.)

TONY ORLANDO'S REVENGE—In the window of Fio's Cucina, northeast corner of 5th & F, can it be? A piano! And at this piano: no person. No player. *No one is at the piano*, not at the moment. Ever? Possibly. Evidence: "Could I Have This Dance"—sheet music—no

question mark—and a roomful of music-starved leisure-class linguini-
eating fuggaducks . . . NO THANKYOU.

Harry's Bar, at the Hotel San Diego. A piano guy is scheduled,
happy-hour beers are a buck, California roll and rumaki are the feed,
but everywhere you look are yellow ribbons, YELLOW RIBBONS,
so I'd better keep my mouth shit, 'scuse me, shut. I'd better say nothing (nothing!) about all-mercenary armies, not to mention navies, not
to mention elephants stepping on snails in behalf of slugs . . . I'd better not . . .

So well okay, why this story? *Because it's there.*

'S the furthest I feel like venturing onto 'sensitive' turf; the deepest
I feel like delving into topical sleaze. Porn . . . poign . . . (get it?).

Do I wack off often watching MTV? *I never watch MTV.* Frequent
'88' haunts for my musical jollies? *I'd rather walk* your *schnauzer.*

No social-redeemment disclaimers: I'm not (this week) an essayist.
Not up for being the Tom Wolfe of Only-the-lonely, or the Tom
Paine of Smut.

SEX, FLIES AND VIDEOTAPE—The principal smell, the only
smell, at Joe's Books, 5th Ave. north of G, is cigar—major-league all-
day cigar—and as I enter Joe (or somebody) is smoking one. Not a
short fat one or a long medium but a long fat one—huff puff *puff,*
Jack. Cigar as ideology, as aggression, as space-defining, earth-befoul-
ing *presence.* In a previous (current?) lifetime Joe or his stand-in was a
bootlegger or a blacksmith or a cockfight promoter or a jukebox re-
pairman or a bookie.

A thoroughly familiar place—like a seedy used record store down
inside a '62 subway stop in the Bronx or Manhattan (but not Brooklyn), only they didn't have cigars there. Old racks, old dust. Mega-
stained, mega-torn, mega-taped carpet. Shabby oldish customers,
y'know *my* age. The old values prevail: cover from the second (first?)
Cars LP, the one with the Vargas (or pseudo-Vargas) painting of the
'forties glamor doll on the hood of a classic whatever the hell it was
. . . nailed to the wall.

All mags, most of them used, seem too manhandled to be worth
even the markdown price. *Cunt Loving Cunts,* #'s 2, 3, and 5 of *Eating
Pussy, Ass Masters Special, Pretty Girls Who Poke for Pleasure*—6 bucks
each. *Australian Erotica,* $12 (down from $40), has several nice shots
of real-looking (as opposed to model-looking) women, some of them
not even blondes, eating (and soaping) each other in showers, as well

as of some *really* nice a-holes of dames being mushpie'd by malemeat from camera south (Down Under), and a generally high quotient of facial lust simulation, but 12 bucks is kind of steep for something likely to disintegrate by the third or fourth beat-through. Which is just as well: why bring more stuff home? The souvenir from places like this should be MEMORY.

Mem'ries of Joe. Videos take quarters in this joint. Guy asks him for change, he snarls, "Don't you ever bring your own?" "But I'm a great customer. I'm here almost every day." "That's what I mean." Guy's wearing a 1973 acrylic boating jacket (and hasn't shaved since Saturday). Joe has a blue woolen 'bopcat' hat (and has).

Booths in back are real beat, chains in front. You enter and hook the chain behind you. Even in 1970 they had lights flashing "occupied" on these things—this is more primitive. In each booth: a plastic trashcan with *liquid* at bottom, splashes and splotches of miracle-of-birth fluid, mostly dry, some wet, on the floor, walls, screen, and—let's assume—seat.

Squalor—I guess the word is squalor—this has gotta be the most squalid viewing room I've ever been in—including scummy *theaters.* Even the tape images are crummy. Tracking, resolution, color—is she Asian? Caucasion? Venusian? They should screen the next Meryl Streep or Richard Dreyfuss movie in a strip of rooms like these. Stick out your glass, some flunky in a tux fills it with warm chablis. All it needs is flies. No flies.

My own fly, though, dunno, should I open it? My dipstick wouldn't feel safe here without a wrapper, so I wrap it. Last of my allotted sacrificial hankies. A nipple, a bush, I hardly know what I'm seeing—I pull it in record time. (Whatever the *next* sex-transmitted lab-created multi-year-incubation blight after AIDS turns out to be—if I ain't caught it here I ain't gonna get it.)

Joe's: one of this town's enduring cultural treasures, worthy of landmark preservation status. A towering/festering monument to et cetera.

A CIGAR MAY BE THE TICKET—Palace Bar, Horton Grand, 8:10 PM. "Someday My Prince Will Come"—keyboard and bass: *good.*

A virtual full house, white, 28–65, mixed levels of hip (though only the younger ones bop their heads). Several odd couples; a disproportionate number of fatties. I grab the furthest seat in the place, distant rear view of the pianist's head, and light up. Waitress: "This is the busiest Wednesday I've seen." Looks like an art teacher from a jr. high in Iowa (whatever that means).

"Taking a Chance on Love," played at quarter-tempo with dark chordings that almost work. Mostly almost work. What doesn't work is when he finally ups the tempo as if finally, decisively, "taking a chance"—hoky, no? But he's far from awful, far from even bad. Quotes Bud Powell twice—"Parisian Thoroughfare" and that krazy end section from the 1950 Clef version of "Hallelujah"—and Charlie Parker's "Au Privave." Not quite the same as playing his life, his revealable 'essence,' but he's not playing *New Yorker* cartoons either. "Embraceable You" gets lost in too much slow, too much introspect, noodles around in cocktail spheres per se, and pulls in loud claps accordingly.

The Palace doesn't have waitresses in Old West drag anymore, they don't even seem to have waitress*es*—only the one—but still plenty-o-decor: chandelier, marble tables, antique lamps, precariously hung oldshit, brass electric-candle fixtures. Century-old wood, ten-year-old whiskey.

Idle thoughts on cigars. A good buzz, a very good buzz, but as far as 'this' cigar or 'that' cigar, you can smoke all day, all night, search the wide world over, and still not find the perfect cigar. Cigars are at best just approximations. Like good beers, good cigars can only hint at the possibly better, find such a one if you can, and then in turn the . . . and . . . but . . . (With "Body and Soul"—the usual, 'historically correct' reading—and "But Not for Me," with interpolations from "Mean to Me" and "Now's the Time," as backdrop.)

"There Is No Greater Love"—fast—OK—but I've never liked the song (or the not dissimilar "Be My Love" either). After which I catch sight of the pianist in profile: black (well, well), specs. No tux, sportjacket. Bass guy white, specs, no jacket, shirt—a semi-wellknown West Coast session man. Hey, I could give you literal *names* f'rchrissakes, but since I didn't for the porn players . . . Anonymous is better.

A comparatively youngish woman (38–40) with a bawdy Liz Taylor look (or Liz Taylor fixation) sways by and joins an old goat lighting his pipe. A table of bald geezers with fat geezer wives eye the pair longingly: ah! youth.

Piano guy himself is, I dunno, 30, early 30s—th' music's from before he was born. On the outside, 33, 34—an idiom whose first and final true head of steam (if not its ongoing nocturnal usefulness) dead-ended nearly 35 years ago—how'd he (why'd he?) access it? This rather than anything else. As a mode of expression, an operational 'sensibility.' Which is not to say he's actually some kind of 'flawed jazz player,' that sort of deal—this seems his *level* of choice as well as his musical ballpark. His preferred niche. It's just simply not-about his life, not-specifically, not-from it, any more than pseudo-'fifties rock (revived) is about Springsteen's (i.e.: not, nohow).

Tonight, fortuitously, the not-about that such music fundamentally is (or ideally can be) is the same not-about that skewers the space-time protocols of two-thirds the call-it-a-lifes in the room—or quite similar. Not-about *his* life, not-about *theirs*: a benignly not-unpleasant (and not-unpleasantly almost-shared) not-unmutual not-aboutness.

An ostensively bluesy original (?) reminiscent of Miles Davis's "So What" doesn't go very far, doubles back on its own not-much, and is louder, suddenly, jarringly, than anything so far, but fine, swell, 's bearable. An arco solo by B-, oops, the bass guy, big sound, interesting in intent if not delivery—too rounded, not enough mammal accident (he's no Charlie Haden). Segues into, or possibly always was, a funky "Have You Met Miss Jones?" Cheers, cheers—like they're Tommy Flanagan and George Mraz or something.

I meet and greet an old sometime chum in the men's rm. mirror—the dazed 40-year-old this time, not his crony the tired 45'er—and return to my beer, my life, and a *very* old reading of "Cherokee"—totally pre-Bird, pre-bop—over really quick, more like a linear sneeze fit than a tune, prompting everyone to laugh, musicmakers included.

An okay set—when they're like that, you can't be *too* disgusted with all-that-much—but was it the music or was it my Don Diego Monarch?

STILL ONE PLACE TO GO—Oh they go ring ting tingle-y, ring ting jingle-y jing. Three tokens in my pocket—and no quarters—should I use?

104

All the Tired Geezers in the Sun

Not quite a literal geezer, I was only 46, 47—but getting ready.

Half the appeal of this one was a shorter drive—the Lawrence Welk Resort is in the north end of San Diego County—but rain and traffic nullified that pretty quick. Lawrence himself died while I was writing it . . . see how I cover for that at the end (without having to go back and rewrite). One of the best pieces (any subject) I've ever written.

. . . duh ♫ duh ♫ . . . when I'm 64. Well I am. One old fart and a half. But I still ain't got the hang of it. Being a geezer. An old fuck. A senior "citizen." Citizen of what, I ask—the land of universal cancer?

In the last ten months, aside from getting my back adjusted, my blood pressure modified, my specs upgraded and my hemorrhoids scraped, I've had my first surgical stroll with Mister "C." Basal cell carcinoma. Skin cancer. Well, sure, it wurn't no *melanoma*—but fuh. Getting cancer *avoiding* the sun, meeting (but never greeting) the fucker only en route to the shade, marinating my façade in sunblock, wearing high-collar longsleeves (in summer) and wide-brim hats— and then this pal of mine gets lung "C" never having smoked a cigareet: if AIDS don't get us first, "C" is our Destiny.

Although, okay, maybe it *was* only Little "C," this pearly molelike whatsit the size of a couple-three pinheads, one small hatpin, but to off it they hadda cut a three-inch slice above it, below it and especially to the sides, and when they stitched me up I looked like Raymond Massey in *Arsenic and Old Lace*, and eight months later it's a red three-inch worm crawling down my neck which I tell people I got in a knife fight with an editor. I don't mind fictions but gee, to have to write 'em . . . you write 'em.

And if I got it once, never going near the sun, I will damn sure get it again—a worm for the other side of my neck, or a centipede for my chin, a lizard for my cheek . . . my earlobe, they'll just clip it all off. And if I can get *that* kinda cancer, not having willfully or knowingly contributed to *it* causally, how can I miss getting cancers of the pancreas, liver, tongue, sinus and scrotum? Incisions, excavations, tissue down the dumper, tubes in my veins, chemotheraphy, emotherapy . . . and I'm not talking fear of death, or even fear, I'm just talking normal wear and tear . . .

I can see it all coming: young whippersnaps cussing me out for slowing things down on the goddam escalator . . . falling down nightly en route to the pisser and breaking my weasel . . . wearing a helmet to bed so I don't smash my etc. on the etc.; a goddam diaper . . . prostate pills and constipation pills and Parkinson's pills . . . what a dismal such-is-life, Jim.

Which, like I said, I just can't seem to get the hang of . . . the orientation, the "attitude"—adequate "prep" for the fugging Inevitable. No shirker of duty, of unwanted chores—if I wanna see how it's done, I might as well go where they do it in spades (and I don't mean clubs): a wonderful weekend at the Lawrence Welk Hotel and Resort, Escondido.

Horse-Ass Realism

Established in 1964 by famed orchestra leader Lawrence Welk, the resort began as a four-room motel with a modest restaurant and clubhouse bordering a nine-hole golf course. Lawrence Welk's "little bit of heaven on earth" has since developed into a beautiful 1,000 acre self-contained destination resort located at the gateway to San Diego's wine country.

According to the Resort Property Owners Association, a national consumer information bureau, the Lawrence Welk Resort is one of only six resorts in the Southwest to have earned a top rating of "10" based on guest experience and positive consumer feedback, and it is the *only* resort in California to receive this top rating. In addition, the Welk property is named 14th in the "Top 400" properties nationwide by *Lodging Hospitality* magazine.

The Resort Restaurant serves breakfast, lunch and dinner daily, and guests may dine in casual elegance overlooking the golf course fairway. The best in Southern California cuisine may be ordered from the menu, or one may prefer the tempting luncheon or dinner buffet featuring carved meats.

—Lawrence Welk Resort press release

Rain, rain, rain, rain, rain, rain, rain, rain. A multi-hour boatride—from 5 to 78 to 15 to Mountain Meadow exit to Champagne Blvd. to . . . where the hell's the road?—before me and the missus finally arrive, hungry as fuckshit, at 9:05 PM . . . all right, let's eat. The desk broad, an overly cheery 18-to-30-year-old, regrets to inform us of the restaurant's closing at 9. "*The* restaurant?" "Yes, we only have one. The closest thing open is in Escondido." Rain, rain, rain, rain . . . enough to float the moon . . . I have drove my last mile of the night. In a painting behind the desk, a dozen horse butts stare out of frame as a dozen riders and 48 hooves make dusty tracks for sunset and food.

On another wall: a large canvas portrait, no, photo of the bandleader himself with grin and golf bag. Uneven brush strokes (acrylic gel? linseed oil?) give shine to the surface of an actual untextured photograph (rather than an image, photo or 4-color, printed on stroke-textured paper), producing, though inadequately at best, not so much the illusion of photo-realism, i.e., that what it "looks like" is a photo, as the illusion of its being a photo-realist *painting*. Art contriving—and failing—to appear *more* ersatz rather than less . . . far out. From beneath his coat of strokes the leader seems to say: "Heaven on earth, suckers! Heaven on earth!"

"You sure you got nothing *here*?" I ask. "Oh well, there's a vending machine outside the pro shop—candy bars and cookies." "That's it?" "And peanuts or something, or chips, in the lounge—as long as it's open." Now you're talkin'.

Dance of the Infidels

And not simply peanuts: glucose-coated peanut matter. And sodium-rich pretzel bits, Pepperidge Farm Goldfish, Pepperidge Farm Butterflies, salty toasty crouton things. Mike the bartender can appreciate our plight, and he refills our bowl with commendable dispatch . . . a fucking prince.

Three brands of crème de menthe, that geezer holiday treat, and two of crème de cacao. Wild Turkey 101, Stolichnaya, Bushmill's, but no Carstairs, no Imperial—only high-booty hooch in this cozy den. Akvavit? Hmm . . . I don't see Akvavit. "What kind of beer you got?" "What kind do you want?" "Oh, something like Bass Ale." "Well, our imports are Heineken and Corona." "What's on tap?" "Michelob." "Uh . . . okay, two."

Ceiling: black plastic w/ flashing "stars." Are they in actual constellation configurations? Dunno. 8 X 10 glossies of Lawrence on the wall. I ask Mike if he ever actually comes in, y'know this very room. "Not lately, because of his health. He used to come maybe once a month. Sometimes even brought his accordion." "And played?" "Played."

In the alcove behind the bar an unWelkish, not unjazzy amplified guitarist drowns out the rain playing/singing "New York, New York," then a Willie Nelson song, then a Bette Midler, injecting a lick from (of all things) Thelonious Monk's "Straight No Chaser." A short, plump senior in a red V-neck yells out for six Black Russians. No response, he yells again. Mike, sensing provocation: "Okay—we'll get to it."

THE VARIETIES OF THE FATSO EXPERIENCE—Fewer than ten porkers, male, not all of them bald, most remaining hairs grey, in V-necks, cardigans, crew necks (red, beige, white, green), no conspicuous jewelry; an equal number of fatties, female, with 2-1b. earrings, hair recently in rollers, lightly teased and sprayed, some golden blonde, some silver-blue (but no pink), primary-color sweaters, decorated w/ embroidery and doodads. Underneath sweaters, both sexes, a shitload of Ban-Lon (does that still exist?) in lieu of current synthetics. No visible cancer scars. Everyone *impeccably* groomed.

On the silent huge-screen TV—an accident but dig it: a rerun of *The Golden Girls.* Featuring more, but not radically more, made-up versions of babes in the rm. "Pregnancy & alcohol do not mix" warning over the bar: nobody here has been pregnant in the last 40 years.

A feisty couple in sopping golf duds, 65ish, saunter in. All the way from Petaluma . . . two days on the road . . . reservations six months back. "We were thinking, hey, maybe we'd play *thirty-six* holes today . . . think again." "Didn't even bring an umbrella." "Shoot." "Double shoot."

I WON'T DANCE—DON'T ASK ME. Michael Ventura—what a goofus—once wrote: "Our generation will never get old, because we dance." He was talking about *his* generation, of course, but well here's oldies dancing and they're *old.* I myself, through every phase my gen has been through, have pretty much danced for one reason only—courtship. Strutting feathers for nookie, and right now I've got nookie—Gopi—Mrs. M. Three couples slow-dance the "old-fash-

ioned" way, spinning and dipping and shit. The dames seem to be enjoying themselves, can't really tell with the men. Fast dance, a dame
dances with a dame, they giggle like KR-R-RAZY, the husband of
one urges 'em: "All the way, all the way!" Gopi (I could see it coming): "You wanna?" "Uh . . . *later.*"

Beer and pretzels, pretzels and beer—nummy nums!

In All Languages

Welk is German for *faded, withered; (of the skin) flabby, flaccid. Welk* in
English is an alternate spelling for *whelk*, not the one defined as *any of
numerous large marine snails (as of the genus* Buccinum*), esp. one* (B. un-
datum*) much used as food in Europe*, but that which serves as synonym
for *papule, pustule; welt, wheal.* Withered Lawrence Pus.

Geezers in the Rain Without Remote

> Reading Popeye comics with those
> funny looking hag people on an island.
> His sister was home but he didn't
> fug her.
> A bath and a shower they did not
> take.
> Green & purple motherfucking *shit*
> in the house.
> Then it rained.
> —W. H. Auden, "Nice Day if It Doesn't Rain"

Gloomy Saturday. An under-50 couple across the way—youngsters—
wave from *their* rainwet window to ours . . . nice friendly folks.

Rain rain go 'way, but in the meantime let's play Got . . . Don't Got
with the contents of our luxury suite. Kingsize bed . . . got. Pillows
. . . got. Pastel coloration . . . got. Legless cylindical table . . . got.
Twin night tables . . . got. Desk . . . got. Phone . . . got. Mirror . . .
got. Mirrored closet . . . got. Hookless anti-theft hangers . . . got. Un-
comfy chair . . . don't got. Comfy chair . . . got three of 'em. Trash can
w/ Hefty bag liner . . . got two. Table lamp . . . got. Floor lamp . . .
got. Wall lamp . . . got. Ceiling light above entrance . . . got. Stucco
ceiling . . . got. Patio with lawn chairs . . . got. Carpet w/out burn
holes . . . got. Rudimentary coffee machine . . . got. Complimentary
coffee . . . got. Heat and A/C . . . got. Heat lamp in the crapper . . .

got. "Santa Fe" bathroom wallpaper . . . got. Shower cap . . . got. Soap . . . got. Conditioning shampoo . . . got. Hand & body lotion . . . got. Tissues . . . got. Toilet paper . . . got two full rolls.

Framed triptych of shiny pebble photos . . . got. Pseudo-Paul Klee watercolor of palms and boots . . . got. "Abstract" painting of spread legs and lady's genitalia . . . got. Individually wrapped deluxe condom . . . don't got. Looks like, but it's only a sewing kit. Safety pin, needle, buttons, black, brown, blue, pink, white, grey treads, make that threads . . . got. Writing paper . . . got. Writing implement . . . don't got. Complimentary postcard . . . don't got. *The Lawrence Welk Show Musical Family News* . . . got. *Temecula Valley Magazine* . . . got. Restaurant menu . . . got. Cable TV . . . got. TV listings . . . don't got. Remote control . . . don't got. Holy Bible . . . don't got.

No bible, no listings, no remote, so we hand-crank the set and take what we get. *Some Came Running* on superstation WWOR, New York. Frank Sinatra, Dean Martin, Martha Hyer, Shirley MacLaine. Vincente Minnelli's third or fourth best (or is it his third or fourth worst?) film, an interesting sociological curio. Class struggle in Terre Haute '58 ('46?) but not much struggle . . . "sluts" and poker . . . slumming . . . Frank finds his center of class gravity. Commercial: "If your wife says you're a drunk . . . and your kids say you're a drunk . . . and your boss says . . . friends say . . . dog says you're a drunk . . . you're a drunk. Call 1-800 . . . "—a *great* New York commercial.

Speaking of which, or of what, the first and only time I ever in fact watched Lawrence Welk's Saturday night whatsis was in New York. Wait, I take that back, there was a second, but the first was like late '56, early '57, winter, my family had just been getting *TV Guide* on a regular basis for a couple months. I was 10 or 11, and this one week I got sent out to get it, a candy store four blocks away, this was Friday, we needed it for Saturday, a v. urgent mission, Friday night in a snowstorm. It was 15 cents then, and I remember dropping a nickel and having to pull off a glove to dig it out of the snow, hadn't brought any extra change of my own. Last *Guide* in the place. The cover was tan or orange.

I didn't usually read the TV "news items" then, text without pictures, but my mother did, and that week they had a bit about the "surprise hit of the season"—*The Lawrence Welk Show*. 'S always nice to spice up yer dreary life, family doldrums can always use dynamite, at least change, so she talks us into watching it—"It won't kill us." I remember it went on at 9, I can tell you also what we watched it instead of (*Gale Storm* and *Hey Jeannie*), I can even recall what we ate that night (English muffin pizzas), but I can't remember *dick* about the show. No recollection, nuthin'. No, that's wrong, "Champagne Music"—I remember the phrase and remember thinking (not having drunk the stuff yet) that champagne must be like lemon-lime soda left in the sun for a week. Enough experimental t-viewing. We never as a family watched the sumbitch again.

In '67 and '8, deep in the heart of Psychedelia, I watched TV, when I watched it at all, for one purpose alone: to accompany the taking of drugs. Sound on or off, no matter; when it was on, it was usually to supply an occasion for frontally "goofing" on things. This was, after all, when TV had momentarily lost its power and expertise to suck you in, plant a ring in your nose, connected by long invisible chain to . . . gotcha. (Drugs were a great, great liberator!) In the wake of which they sat down and decided—"think tanks" and such—that TV should and would never again relinquish its heart-mind-soul control over all us saps at sea . . . it hasn't . . . (even drugs today have been totally stripped of their liberating function) . . . it only gets nastier all the time. So anyway, one Saturday, probably '68, nothing better to do, I turn on Lawrence. He's by now got a black tapdancer . . . a rock combo that looked like something out of *The Gene Krupa Story* (*that* drug era!) . . . a light show. I dunno, maybe the rock band did "Last Train to Clarksville." The look and feel of the whole thing I remember being no *more* fraudulent, no more anti-life unwatchable, than anything else on TV at the time—*Mod Squad, Star Trek, Ironside* . . . you've seen reruns, you know what of I'm talkin'. Nixon was running for prez again then, and all these people, the musicians, the geezers, looked like they'd be voting for him—all except the tapdancer—20–30 votes guaranteed. I'd like to be able to say I took acid to watch it, at least mescaline, but my girlfriend and I only smoked a small piece of hash.

Wait, oops—did I say 64? I must have got the digits reversed. (A natural mistake.) I'm 46. Which is old anyway. Hemorrhoids, skin cancer—the whole bit. I can't tell a 19-year-old anymore from a 32. No diff, and no jealousy, I hate today's "kids" anyway—talk about rings through the nose! (An old cuss.) Ain't been old for long, though. Like the first 17 years were what you call it, Infancy. Diaper time all the way. 25 years, a quarter century of active Youth, and I was finally a Grown-up at 42. Right on time, glad to be growed, but wouldn't ya know?—at 45 I was already Old. From maturity to dotage in a snap! And it don't come easy. Takes me FORTY TIMES AS LONG to write a paragraph—I figured this out—as when I was 30. I only beat off *every other* day. Need near-lethal doses of caffeine to start the engine . . . mid-day naps . . . lower back pain . . . upper back . . . sensitive to cold . . . hangovers get worse . . . can't see my hand in fronna my face . . .

I'm certainly closer to the End than even the Middle . . . or maybe my arithmetic is wrong. Dunno. In any event, I can say whatever I want about geezers. Call it self-hate. I'm allowed to hate myself. (Am I right or am I right?)

Color me Old but not my hair. 46 and I ain't grey yet—what's wrong with me? Should I maybe use talcum?

Postcards of Welkville (1)

A road. A football-shaped green, green lawn. Distant and not-so-distant green hills or mountains. Boring garden plants and stairs leading up to shingles or fake bricks or whatchacallems, light brown, crowned by four pointy roofs against a blue, blue sky. Sparse clouds. "Lawrence Welk Village Center Welcomes You to the Welk Theater Museum and Newly Opened Village Shops." For inst the shop wherein this very card was purchased, along with beer and sunscreen, and those in which golf tees, golf clubs, Welk-logo geezer hats and sweaters, ceramic ducks and eagles, and miniature souvenir accordions were displayed, seen, touched and in some instances gently mocked during our not much of a shopping spree between downpours, along with a card touting the Resort Restaurant's "atmosphere of relaxed comfort" and "fine food," before proceeding to said grubbery for Saturday lunch.

Excellent Affordable Grease

Most handicap parking spaces ever seen in one lot (although none in use today).

DECOR: an interesting cross between "fine restaurant" and coffee shop. Vinyl-upholstered booths with "Rousseauian exotic" motif outlined in black Rapidograph. Pseudo-silver tableware—stainless steel in "classy" patterns just like "heirloom" silver in Your Own Home—but no cloth napkins. Different species of cloth and plastic flowers at every table. A real palm in a pot, reaching almost to the ceiling, an umbrella dangling from one of its lower spiky juts. Shamrocks on pinecones at the window—All Holidays Celebrated Here? The real Holiday Inn?

The joint is *clean*—similar in pervasiveness to Disneyland's cleanliness-*is*-godliness number. A menial *carefully* spruces the metal outside a currently inactive fireplace.

FOOD (cheap): chicken burger—not a burger but a broiled breast w/ ham and Jack cheese—spiciest non-ethnic, non-barbecue chicken item I can remember eating—on a seeded kaiser roll (very fresh);

Primavera Omelette—fresh vegetables, cheese and spice—nutmeg? cumin? cayenne pepper?—interesting mix;

deep fried battered artichoke hearts—like great big bull's balls—ultra-greasy w/ sour cream inside—*excellent* grease;

fries—crisp to the max—same fine grease.

CLIENTELE: party of ten including a couple in their 50s (others: 70–75)—guy and his wife look and act like a congressman & spouse from Missouri stumping for the Senior vote;

a disgruntled golf couple about 40—colorful non-generic youth-wear;

one golden ager with the same shoes as I got;

an old codger with red-white-blue suspenders, pale blue bowling shirt, gaudy green cardigan—estimated age, 75–80—one great hepcat 'cept for his "born dead" 1930s look;

hardly anyone with a tan—either they're from northerner climes or sunscreen use is now pandemic—these busters knew something 'fore I did (less "C" than me!);

just as last night, everyone spiffed to the nines—no "vacation casual" for these folks—as fastidious (or more) about their time off as their time on.

EXCITEMENT witnessed: two women, 25 and 75—grandchild, presumably, and grandma. "But Mom says you *love* patty melts"—no go, she then suggests potato skins, no, soup—well, okay—"Low on the clams, please." Older woman is *stern*, upturned-nose-y—or possibly just troubled by indigestion.

The Knower and the Known

Only between the common logic and my work there is this difference, that my question is,—what can we hope to achieve with reason, when all the material and assistance of experience is taken away?

—Immanuel Kant, *Critique of Pure Reason*

Spicy food aside, this place is *bland*, daddy. So bland that it's difficult to really see much—"pay attention"—long enough to get a firm, functional read of any depth or import, especially re the particulars of explicit Human etcetera: a journalistic Black Hole. To adequately suss this biz out would require a real inclination to gawk and snoop, some genuine interest in all the faces and whatnot—both before the fact and by virtue of their fortuitous proximity—which is kind of hard to muster when the quarry truly *is*—on the surface of the surface of the surface—so bland. To peg these jackjills as *retired smalltown bankers (and their sewing-circle wives)*, or *neutered Republicans*, or *mega-squares w/out bite*, is patently unfair not because such characterizations might be subjectively "biased"—which of course they *are*—but because even insofar as they might in fact contain kernels of "objective" truth they're still only chickenshit "approximations": as lame and hoky as the projected bottom line on any real-or-metaphoric hicks from the sticks (rubes from the cubes), as shallow and no-dimensional as can't-think-of-the-metaphor. Hey, I'm lame, lazy, fuck me. But to actually poke beneath the surface, or even infiltrate prominent hatchmarks *of* surface, to "get real" about any of this . . . hey, Margaret Mead I'm not—sorry!

FORCE ME to look, however, to guess, and I'll come up with SOMETHING: These are (by and large) a generally *robust* lot of old'uns we got here. Geographically, culturally, none among them could pass for the seed or the spawn of the Dust Bowl—except maybe foreclosing Dust Bowl bankers. Even if their having been bankers, and thus exercised power as an end in itself, is the reason/root/source/cause, most males do seem to behave as if still empowered (unlike some their age you might encounter who appear w/out enablement or decisiveness). In at least one crucial area, these people are not Disneyites—there's alcohol everywhere. (So they're not, arguably, anti-pleasure.) *When the music's over, turn on the tap . . .*

The Three Hills of Welkville

Harmony Hill . . . Melody Hill . . . Broadway Hill. Two of Music, one of Bigtime.

The sun at last emerging, we treat ourselves to a hike, a stroll, making use of our one-color complimentary map. Where to start . . . what to see . . . hmm . . . got it: the 9th Hole Snack Shop. 'S always fun to see golfers get loaded. OK, that's north, let's see, take Lawrence Welk Drive to Camille to . . .

What th-? After not quite forty paces a guard gate halts our progress. Not the gate, the guard: a smiling bejowled grandfatherly type like a town father on *The Andy Griffith Show*, someone who'd've offered Opie an apple for the answer to a tricky math problem, then withheld the goods, cackling, "Trust no one, my son, trust no one!"; different from the guests only in magnitude of jowls and the fact that for him there is no vacation, no moment's respite, from the job of smile-driven intimidation. "This is time shares."

"Okay. Yeah."

"*Time* shares."

"Right. And we can't look?"

"No—this is *private*."

Oh. The divine right of their class. Why not just mark the map with skulls & bones?

"You could walk over to the sales center and arrange a tour. They have them every—" Thanks—I'd rather walk my rat.

A last look at the map before tossing it in the wildflowers. On Broadway Hill: Brigadoon Villa . . . Oz Villa . . . Gigi Villa. On Melody Hill: Moonglow Villa . . . Tangerine Villa. On Harmony Hill: Memories Villa . . . Volare Villa. *This* is what they want from the rest of their lives???

Shakespeare Farts

The L.W. Resort Theatre presents: *Kiss Me Kate*, Cole Porter's immortal adaptation of the also immortal *Taming of the Shrew*. Former greats who have played here: Dorothy Lamour (*Barefoot in the Park*), Forrest Tucker (*Captain's Outrageous*). Lucky for me—lucky for us—I'll be attending with actress Gopi Montenegro (credits include: *On Golden Pond, Star Trek III, Driller Killer*), whose critique will be invaluable you can be sure.

But first, dinner—in Champagne Room #1. A full house, very full, lots of San Diego Rotarians. At our table, a father-daughter combo from Point Loma discuss plays (*Phantom, Les Miz*) . . . belly dancing . . . the Unknown Eater . . . noise from Lindbergh Field. Dad's seen the *Kiss Me Kate* movie with Kathryn Grayson and he can't recall the actor . . . was it Gordon MacRae?

ALL YOU CAN EAT, ". . . but the law requires you take a fresh plate each time": roast beef, lasagna, baked ham, mashed potatoes, rice, broccoli, cauliflower, rolls, champagne sherbet.

The 45th anniversary of Mr. and Mrs. Peterson is announced, scattered applause, where are they? They don't stand, everybody looks around, wonders—maybe they're too old to stand. In the men's room, at adjacent urinals, one Rotarian to another: "There are some things *not* for public performance" . . . pause . . . he farts.

In the lobby before curtain: the fabulous exhibits of the Lawrence Welk Museum. Band photos like R. Crumb cartoons of fictional slicked-down bozos of yore; a band bus that looks more like a mobile beertruck home. The Champagne Ladies—Lois Best, 1938 (a hot one, didn't last long, did Mrs. Welk insist he bounce her?)—her successor (Jayne Walton) not nearly as hot. Repro of a poster for a show at Lake Okoboji, May '45—"Look, Lois—Lake Okoboji!" A pair from Sioux City know the place. Actual poster from Ruthven, Iowa— Lawrence Welk and His Honolulu Fruit Orchestra. The Farm Years—"Born March 11, 1903 in a sod farmhouse near Strasburg, North Dakota" . . . the Welks taught their 8 children "to work, to share, to love God—and to honor this country" . . . in 1920, his father bought him a $400 accordion, which to pay off he hadda work the farm till he was 21, meanwhile forking over all earnings from barn dances and weddings: a $400 accordion?!! Which is like what—a $10,000 ukelele today?

Curtain up, I'm game, but the play is just a blur, like a junior college version of Pirandello, a Neil Simon caught outdoors where every distant motorboat sound, every mosquito, is not only distracting but *more interesting*. I try to focus, to stay focused, but all I pick up is the snappy line "Brush up your Shakespeare, and the women you will wow." The pit band consists of four pieces including synthesizer— Lawrence always had a *thing* about unions.

Gopi Evaluates

Saturday night—why not?—neither of us has got AIDS that we know of, let's have sex. Okay. And then . . .

"That was *okay*, but there wasn't much ebb and flow. The sand and the sea is a good example—of the sea reaching out and licking the sand, *pulling* it into the sea, and the sand being part of the, as the wave retreats, okay, what happens is the sand is lying there, the wave gets *ready*, and as it's getting ready it pulls back, and when it pulls back it takes the sand with it as the wave builds its arc—this big arc. And then as it's pulling back it goes forward in this huge *licking* of the sea, well, splashing over into, this huge—I mean of the sand—this huge licking into the sand. This arc. And the sand is part of its ident—if it didn't have the sand it wouldn't have the pliability. It couldn't do this very well on rocks."

"What does the sand do?"

"If the sand wasn't doing something, it wouldn't be there. What-ever it's doing—it's *there*. It's part of, it's all one. No, it's *not* passive. Did you ever feel the sand? Maybe it lies dormant until the sea comes along. When the sea comes, it lives with life, it vibrates with life—all the little particles, it *contributes*—the sea is doing it for the sand. The sand motivates the sea."

"Didn't you ever see ocean hit rocks?"

"Yeah, it just goes off and goes away. It's nothing. It doesn't, the ocean does not have as good a time with the rocks, I'm telling you. Have *you* seen it? It just goes and beats against it and goes back. I'm talking about the *communication* between the sand and the sea. The communication between the sand and the sea is *much* more special than the communication between the ocean and rocks—it is! The rocks just are immovable, they're not pliable. To have pliable sand is a *great* gift. If you could pull sand—just think of this as an analogy some time—if you were capable of taking sand and pulling it with that kind of power and then building at the same time and then splashing it—I mean that's quite a wonderful thing to be able to experience. I would think. Whereas if you're just splashing on rocks . . . "

"How about slamming in a pot of stew?"

"That's *nothing*. Richard, I'm talking about the beauty and the power of this kind of communication as opposed to just splashing pudding. I'm talking about a, you know, *heightened* experience."

"You seem to be talking about depths."

"No, I'm talking about the height of that wave. The higher the wave goes, the deeper the girl, uh, the experience."

"Girl is sand?"

"I would think, even though I think traditionally ocean is . . . "

"I think that's not politically correct."

"I don't know, because traditionally they've always said water is sex-ual, but I don't know if water is woman sexual. I don't know if it's po-litically correct or not, I'm just talking about *primal sexual feelings*."

"Oh, it goes beyond politics?"

"No, I mean—yes, it does! In a way it's like the play if it had been done well. Y'know that's really, you could look at, the production we saw was really so horrible that you could see how bad the politics of the play were, are. But if that male character had been cast correctly and had sexual charisma and stuff, where you *wanted* it, then it would be a different story. I mean people would have all sorts of different feelings."

"But what you call sexual charisma might be what others would consider unacceptable male posturing."

"No, they *might* at the same time, but if it was cast, like for instance when they did *Taming of the Shrew* with Richard Burton—"

"What, you're saying everybody wants to fuck Richard Burton?"

"Well, I'm saying there are universals."

"There *aren't* variants of macho behavior that are universally acceptable."

"I'm saying you can *only* get away with that if the person has got that kind, if there's that kind of *chemistry* involved."

"But it still has to be *acceptable*. It's not just that it's there."

"What do you mean by 'acceptable'?"

"The sand has to *want* it."

"Yes yes yes! Well that was the element—"

"The sand might just say, 'Leave me alone.'"

"Or beyond that, 'Leave me alone, I'm not at all attracted to you, I've got no need to be with you in any kind of way.'"

"'I'd rather be sand in a pond with salamanders crawling around.'"

"Yeah, 'than be with you,' which is the case that it was in the play. But what I'm saying, if it was cast with a character that *did* have a complicated sense of, you know, that was, there *was* an attraction there, then it's a difficult issue. I guess what I mean, not politically acceptable but understandable, palatable."

"And by 'universal' you probably mean something like conventional, um, conventional variables."

"Yes."

"Okay, and what if *still*, you're just sand on the bottom of a pond and you're used to it being quiet there, and you don't want storms stirring it up?"

"Well, you have that *right*."

"You have the right as *sand*?!"

"Yes! I'm talking about passion, though—passionate, passionate energy."

"Passionate sand!"

"Richard, I'm just using this analogy. I don't want you to use this in the piece."

"What piece?"

"Ha ha. Oh, I didn't *tell* you about this woman I met in the ladies' room after the play. She must've been 75, brown hair, 5'1" or 5'2", round but not exactly fat, fake eyelashes, very long and curled, she's putting on lipstick and she says, 'Colorful costumes, weren't they?' 'I guess so'—trying not to sound too enthusiastic. 'Did you like the show?' I tell her, 'I liked the *music*.' She tells me she saw it once before in Philadelphia, 'Oh, who with?' 'Alfred Drake.' 'Well, it *needs* an Alfred Drake. Somebody with some passion'—she doesn't know what I'm talking about. 'Well, he's a good actor.'"

"That was the third or fourth worst play I've ever seen."

"Well I don't think *Kiss Me Kate* is a bad play—I mean traditionally it's a bad play, it's from an era that, well—personally I was looking forward to seeing it, okay, because I knew exactly what it would be, and never in my wildest dreams did I expect it to have every ounce of fun drained out of it."

"What fun?"

"You see, that's the point, if it was cast well, if it was done well, you could enjoy these characters, there's the sexual thing, the songs, the stupid jokes, just for whatever it, as a relic from another—but you can only get away with that if it's cast well. It wouldn't have even been bad in terms of direction if everybody didn't suck, especially what's his, Petruchio. I suppose the acting is the director's responsibility, but these actors were so beyond it—nobody in this production had a clue. I suppose for a high school production it was okay, but even as that it was Ham City. While we were watching the play it felt like you had to imagine which members of the cast were related to the management, like of the theater, you know, the niece of some-one—nobody could sing or dance except on the most mediocre of levels, they were all doing only what they were told to do. Like the lead woman did everything like 'Look at me, I'm doing it—I make this funny face, they laugh'—they were all very prideful that they were 'doing it right,' being prideful about the mediocrity. They manipulated with pride, that's what putting on a show is for them. As a professional, and I never look to see anything bad about fellow actors, say anything, I'm sure they felt they did a good job—so their *standard* is wrong. Their idea of what is good is an extension of high school—actually children's—performance. It doesn't have to have reality, but it has to have some sort of truth to it. I mean these people could've been puppets. What made me feel sad was I don't think they know the difference."

"Was it all just *sand*?"

"Yeah, I guess, if you want, but you have to have both. I suppose if you only have one—sand . . . you know what aspect was missing in the analogy? The moon. You know how the moon pulls the tide?"

"Yeah."

"And there's a force that is bigger than the sea or the sand, so the sand, the tide, the moon makes the force—there was no moon in this play. I guess you could call the director the moon. He wasn't very much of a moon."

Fear of Music

Lawrence and Fern are bursting with pride these days and well they might! Their beautiful little great-granddaughter Kate Elizabeth is giving indications that she might turn out to be a musician! Says Lawrence, "I just love this picture of her sitting at the piano. She's about 7 months old here, all dressed up to go to a costume party. None of our other children or grandchildren showed much interest in music, but judging by this picture, perhaps our little Katie will carry on the musical tradition. And wouldn't that be nice!"

—*The Lawrence Welk Show Musical Family News*, spring quarter '92

Where one culture uses as a main thread the vulnerable ego, quick to take insult or perish of shame, another selects uncompromising bravery and, so that there may be no admitted cowards, may like the Cheyenne Indians invent a specially complicated social position for the overfearful.

—Margaret Mead, *Sex and Temperament in Three Primitive Societies*

What's *this*—"POPULAR TV BANDLEADER DIES AT 89"?!?— fuh. Shit. It takes weeks, sometimes months, to write these things, you know. (Spend too much time selecting epigraphs, and next thing you know you're writing epitaphs.) I'm not gonna go back and revise, though, I'm almost done. You want tenses changed, you want a less mocking tone (out of respect for etc.)—*you* change it. You be the author, it's okay with me.

I'll just come to terms, right here, right now, with the dead man's music. None of which was in the air during my two nights and a day at his resort.

Like there were big absurd bronzes of him conducting, silly shrines with quarter notes and G-clefs, an entire bandstand—with instruments—reconstructed in the museum . . . so many references to music: why no music? The only sounds at all were in the lounge, the play—all non-Lawrence. No music on the grounds, at the check-in, none in the museum, the shops . . . hardly an ambient peep . . . the whole place was *really quiet*. Hmm.

Theories? Perhaps, as God's was for Meister Eckhart, the Welk oeuvre's presence may in fact have been in its absence. I.e., the quiet somehow *was* Lawrence. To wit: the man's music, by acclamation sonically "harmless"—non-assaultive—was as hazardous and compelling as vanilla pudding. Anything therefore *less* assaultive, i.e., tending functionally towards silence, would be at least as acceptable—and possibly more so. (Theory #1: *Turn it down.*)

While at the resort, however, I picked up a copy of *Lawrence Welk Live at Lake Tahoe* (Ranwood RC-10001), which having since played I find *not* harmless—far from it—my life feels at serious jeopardy as I listen and take notes. Guy & Rona's cloying version of "You Light Up My Life" is like a duet between Linda Ronstadt and the partner she's no doubt been waiting (if not praying) for, the one and only Pat Boone. Joe Feeney's "Who Can I Turn To?" has all the spine-tingling excitement of a performance by, say, Dennis Day. Emotionally, sexually neutered, as a singer he makes Sting—Jerry Vale—Doublemint commercials—seem expressive and mammalian by comparison. Semantically neutered: Kathie Sullivan's read on "The Way We Were" as a—no joke—"happy" song. Arthur Duncan tapdancing to "Wait 'til the Sun Shines, Nellie" . . . the frog-voice bathos of Larry Hooper . . . Basically, this is music by and for people who don't even *shit.*

Which doesn't maybe assault *some* people who do, maybe some indeed are "comforted" by it, but sheez—I find it excruciating. (Vanilla pudding with razor blades.) Look, I'm not claiming "universality" for my own squalid taste, but if *I* respond that way, others can and may as well. (Anything's possible.)

Giving rise to Theory #2: a certain percentage of the Welk audience finds the music as troubling as I do—a minority, let's say, of husbands, wives, family members otherwise along for the extended Welk "trip." The Welk organization knows this—that while some may harbor Welk values in general, they can't hack the music *nohow*—so to avoid taking any chances, to be demographically safest, there is simply *no* Welk music at the resort. (Theory #2: *Turn it off.*)

Although maybe, a further listen tells me, it isn't even *music.* It evinces nothing, after all, re the physics of feeling and sound, it *aspires* to evince nothing, and by nothing I mean less than Wayne Newton's does, than Liberace's did . . . *that* kinda nothing: nothing without even the resonance of nothinghood. It isn't "bad" music—it's simply not music.

So many genres are namedropped—"Hawaiian music," "Irish music," "Latin," "Dixieland," "disco," "country music," "film music," even "nostalgia"—but none're actually delivered, *performed*, with a commitment, a vigor, that might—even as concept—differentiate one from another. Everything, by design, is attenuated, weakened, to the point of being but a neutral component in what . . . "One Music" . . . "World Music"? No: Homeopathic Music! (Microdilution with ground-zero overkill.)

Heck, the motherlode of this is Amateur Night at the O.K. Corral—Joe Blow trumpeting the legs out from under "You Made Me Love You"; Jacques Bag o' Donuts frothing up "La Vie en Rose"; the Jill St. Cardboard Singers whining a soggy path through "Cottonfields"—which might (with luck) be its only saving grace, its one true shot at being Music at all, of being about Accident even if *by* accident—but it's polished and *perfected* amateur night, amateur drained of its innocence and working for scale, amateur cut to size, mounted, and nailed to the wall, which all but eviscerates that possibility.

At its most arch, its most "successful," this is produce hand-crafted as if for doting grandparents by favored grandchildren ("Ooh . . . how beauty-ful!"), as if no element or aspect could matter beyond its being by-the-numbers dealt and done with. The polar opposite of something created and lived like "your life"—or anything—"depended on it," it's over before it's over, long before it's even begun: no present-tense being, no musical *now*, no *potential* musical now—or musical ever.

PLUS: for that segment of the audience (and, who knows, maybe the band itself) for whom virtually *all* music qua music is the devil's handiwork—naughty stuff!—smart demographics would again dictate playing it safe, deftly subjecting all parties concerned to No Music.

And the closest space-time counterpart to this non-music, this nothing, is the non-music, the nothing, of the Lawrence Welk Hotel/Resort itself—natch—independent of all external sonic considerations. Already the bleeping EPITOME of non-music, it surely needs no sonic non-music, no *musical* non-music, to bolster its "case." The foundations of Welkhood require no such gratuitous reinforcement. (Theory #3: *Don't bother—no need—to even in the first place turn it* on.)

Anyone's death leaves a wake—no pun intended—of silence. Lawrence of Strasburg's death leaves us with 10,000,000,000,000,000,000,000,000,000,000,000,000 units of SILENCE. . . . SILENCE MUFFLED. . . . NOTHING (NOT EVEN SILENCE OR MUFFL

Postcards of Welkville (2)

Lawrence (in close-up) between two tree trunks in a bright red synthetic-fabric shortsleeve shirt, white lace-up front, white trim on collar and cuffs, wide white belt holding up what look like red and blue floral-pattern pants, a 5-iron sticking into frame like a bent metallic dick, inane "can't keep it down" smile not quite snappy or complacent enough to be labeled fatuous, photo posed in (a good guess) early '70s.

In the course of my now concluding search, I have learned nothing new from this gentleman about growing old, or being dead. I'm a slow learner . . . but *c'mon.*

Once cardboard-in-flesh, now a thinner paper product minus all corporeal intimation, this dozo's graceless bub-strut is NO MORE.

105

From Schubert to Hitler

If major labels with classical divisions (like Columbia, Mercury and London) had sent rockwriters of my era an occasional dose of classical releases, they would probably have hooked enough of us that we'd have actually BOUGHT the stuff once in a while, thus enhancing their profits. That they never thought of it is mind-boggling.

(Oh yes: dig the turnaround from "Meltzer at the Met," written 19 years before.)

"My friend the jazz piano guy"—that's Richard Grossman, who died of lung cancer in '92.

For I dunno, three reasons I can think of, this is the year I started listening to classical music. First it was like here I was, a guy on the rockroll dole for almost 25 years, these companies sending me their shit—fewer all the time but still maybe 20–30 promos a year (in '75 I averaged 50 a week)—mostly current rock but once in a while they'll send me jazz, blues, R&B, folk, whatever; but never ever have they sent me classical. Which if they'd sent me over the years I probably wouldn't have sold everything, I'd've occasionally broke the shrinkwrap, played it once in a blue moon and picked up, got a token sense of at least some of it. Instead I knew nothing about it—*nothing.* Well, no, some I must've known from soundtracks, but I didn't really know I knew it, enough to do an i.d.—"That's . . . um . . . Mahler." So I figured finally I'm old enough, I'm 48, right? To check the whole thing out like looking through books of 19th century landscape paintings. To get familiar with—because it's there. By the time I thought this I was already borrowing CDs from the widow of my friend the jazz piano guy—keyboard stuff he'd listened to: Schoenberg, Cage, Stockhausen, Morton Feldman and the like. Conlon Nancarrow.

Which got me kind of hooked on the modern end of the beast . . .
now to go back and survey it back to the egg.

Plus I felt like, in my own writing, the evolution of this and that—I
used to be a jazz player, an improviser, everything bang bang, in real
time, and now here I was, look at me, writing notes on cluttered note
paper, slow, what a drag, an old *composer*, ha—ain't life funny? A weird
turn of etc. but okay, I'll live with it; now gimme the music.

So I started trading all this junk I had—recent promos, rock LPs I
hadn't played in ten years—for used classical CDs, just lots of bulk at
first so I could take in a big wide uneducated swath of it. Like Bach,
Beethoven, Mozart—for inst—whatever I could find in the used bins.
And after hearing, well, not too many pieces by each, my preliminary
take, which I haven't yet budged from, was Bach isn't even music so
much as mathematics, with music (per se) (experienced as such) as
only the occasional *occasion* of the math, like in the first movement of
the sixth and last *Brandenburg Concerto* (which sounds like, I dunno,
bluegrass? folk rock?—good folk rock) but few moments, to that extent, in any of the five others; Mozart is *music*, a little sweet and generally nonironic about it (though his third string quintet, K. 516,
seems loaded with sarcasm—or something) but still, y'know, some
sort of highwater mark for aurally pleasant organized sonic ado;
Beethoven, meantime, is an urgent mammal presence, his belly sticking out over his belt, his underwear showing, stains on his shirt, his
nose dripping.

If I hadda be pinned to just these three options, I'd take Beethoven,
natch, but his symphonies (and piano concertos) all seem like so many
hunks and clunks of ponderous kitsch. *This* big hunk and THIS
hunk—can't reduce 'em, gotta remain hunk-size—let's see how we
can slap 'em together this time . . . helps you see what Albert Ayler
could've had in mind. Actually, I kind of don't mind the 4th Symphony, but maybe that's only 'cause it's not one of the main ones.
What the hell do *I* know, but in classical as in jazz the heart & soul
seems (so far) to be in the small combos, the chamber pieces, piano
pieces—and Beethoven's first cello sonata and his last piano sonata
are like Charles Mingus, Bud Powell . . . straight from the
heart/mind/gut, no showy detours, no insulation. (Strong shit without the requisite bombast.)

Things I picked up early that I liked at least enough not to trade
back: Liszt's *Les Préludes* (hey: music from the Flash Gordon serials!)
. . . Mendelssohn's *Italian* Symphony (starts the way most of these
things try to end) . . . Chopin's Sonata no. 2, op. 35 (more Bud Pow-

ell, and a touchstone or something for Duke Ellington's *Black and Tan Fantasy*) . . . Ravel's *Daphnis and Chloe*, the complete ballet (talk about kitsch: theme from *The Honeymooners* meets Nino Rota) . . . Prokofiev's *Lt. Kije* Suite (which I recognized from a bank commercial and, what was it, some British film . . . *The Horse's Mouth*) . . . Haydn's 94th and 95th Symphonies (Mozart without the depth maybe, but also without all the sweet) . . . Mussorgsky's *Pictures at an Exhibition*, piano version (a lot like my tribute to Lester Bangs) . . . Webern's Six Bagatelles for String Quartet (miniature what? . . . pitchforks in your coffee or beer) . . . some Wagner overtures (still can't hack listening to actual opera, tho—to the classically trained *voice*-as-weapon) . . . Messiaen's *Des canyons aux étoiles* (Eric Dolphy sometimes got ideas listening to birds; this guy gets actual piano parts from specific species: the oriole, the mockingbird, the white-browed robin) . . . Scriabin's Piano Sonata no. 8 (a slowed-down early Cecil Taylor) . . . Ives's 4th Symphony (*great* controlled cacophony).

The first one I bought new, Stravinsky's *Rite of Spring* (Deutsche Grammophon, Cleveland Orchestra, Pierre Boulez conducting), was fine for a few listens, swell, but I couldn't really figure what all the fuss was—still can't. It's no more wild and nuts than *West Side Story*. I ain't making jokes, or playing dumb or anything, 'cause obviously there's no *West Side Story* without Stravinsky—he's its fount—but that's not what I mean. I mean there's something a little overly . . . what's it . . . Apollonian about the allegedly Dionysian *Rite of Spring* that keeps me from, well, surrendering to it. Even its much-vaunted "primitivism" isn't a tenth as rhythmically interesting—let alone exciting—as the first three bars of *West End Blues* by Louis Armstrong. And the rest of what I've heard by him, this neo-classical biz—*Dumbarton Oaks*, Octet for Wind Instruments—some of it has its charm, sure—if charm is what you want—but Mr. 20th Century? I don't get the hype. Whereas Bartok's 4th String Quartet or *The Miraculous Mandarin*—the latter, dig, is the shower scene from *Psycho* for 30 minutes—or virtually anything I've heard by Schoenberg (before, during and after 12-tone) is willfully, functionally, viably *out there*, daddy. Where I—fuck me—would prefer it be (if it can't be Beethoven).

But again, whuddo *I* know?

I know finally, for one thing, what CD players are good for. For isolating individual movements of these muthas. Very little, even *great* great pieces—any genre—is all that great all the way through. It's like cuts on jazz or rock albums, no big deal: pick and choose. You don't need to hear wholes if parts'll do: the 3rd movements of Beethoven's

9th, Brahms's 4th, and Schubert's Quintet in C; the 3rd and 4th of Mendelssohn's Octet; the 1st and 4th of Berlioz's *Harold in Italy;* etc . . . why force dead men to deliver beyond what's poss?

What's not (I don't think) poss. for *me* at this point is to gauge with any accuracy what a good performance of a given piece *is*—what it might consist of—or rather to know whether something I don't care for is merely lacking for better musicians, conductor, recording engineer, and/or studio/venue acoustics. (Haven't a clue!) (And am still only guessing as to whether I truly enjoy the music—or do I just like being able to identify pieces on the radio that so many million Euro-descended squares have in their blood? Dunno.)

A couple of out-on-a-limb parting comments: 1. Jazz is what classical half-knowingly wishes it was (tho too rarely aspires to be); maybe not its actual sonorities or historically driven formalisms, but its basic generatrix for a music totally there—here—NOW. (A 30-year familiarity with jazz is what I imagine gives me an affinity for this hokum in the first place.) 2. You don't need Wagner to get to Hitler. Beethoven (the 6th! the 6th!) or even Schubert would do.

106

F**k My Childhood

More geezer-think, and the beginning of the New Perk Order: getting re-imbursed for opera boxes; using the gig to assist my hearing (in due time) as much as I want from the classical syllabus.

Liszt, *Les Préludes,* New York Philharmonic, conducted by Leonard Bernstein, Sony SMK 47572

Wagner, *Der fliegende Holländer,* with Simon Estes, Lisbeth Balslev, Matti Salminen, Robert Schunk, Bayreuther Festspiele, conducted by Woldemar Nelsson, Phillips 416 399-2

Verdi, *Aida,* with Maria Callas, Richard Tucker, Fedora Barbieri, Tito Gobbi, Orchestra del teatro alla Scala di Milano, conducted by Tullio Serafin, EMI CDCC 7 49030 2

Two approaches.

One.

Six-seven years ago, taking notes for a piece I was planning on why I wasn't a parent, I jotted down the following:

"To recall fondly their own childhood as a trigger for generating kids of their own verges on the oxymoronic: viewing a time when they knew better, when their unbridled intellect and imagination ruled the world, viewing it well after (and from the context/vantage point of) having had it all beat out of them: absurdly believing they will not beat it out of their own potential offspring, and not simply because they believe they are not beaters, but because in having been beat they have also lost their elemental smarts, their purity of perception (not to mention any genuine, operative, more than ad hoc compassion): losses which preclude their leaving another's purity/etc. intact even if they were God.

"To be socialized at all is to have been beat out of much: ironically the principal much they now so tenaciously cleave to."

The dynamics of which still ring true to me, basically, though my own romance with the part that's been beat is pretty much gone in the ether. I feel no great gush anymore for the "purity"—for my own or anyone's—real or hypothetical. Squalor is more like it. I say FUCK my childhood (all our childhoods). What a chump-change touchstone of nothing.

Childhood as magic? No. Childhood is belief in magic. A bigger diff than the diff between 4000 tulips and a pack of Luckies. (Between *War and Peace* and a pizza.)

Hey. Basically I feel like I'm somewhere in a life, certainly closer to its end than beginning, and while I have little nostalgia for the early parts (other than once in a while, not always, for the limitless time it seemed I had left then), I do have a memory, too much memory, for such hokum; I forget nothing . . .

Basketball games with a trashcan and my dirty socks . . . discovering a mound of maggots and, taking them for caterpillar eggs about to hatch, putting them in a jar with dirt and enough grass and leaves to serve as a week's caterpillar food . . . the time I cut my hand on a razor blade I picked up in the alley behind my house to fend off a twisted strand of cloth-covered wire I thought was a snake, my mother insisting the cut had been caused by a rusty nail though I swore and swore it hadn't (I didn't tell her it was a rusty razor blade), good thing I was up to date in tetanus shots . . . in the mirror after a fight, seeing a glob of pink gummy candy stuck to my face and believing it was a piece of my ear fallen off . . . thinking of Roy Rogers every time I had tuna, Gene Autry whenever it was salmon . . . the month I couldn't score the current issue of *Superboy*, finally finding a beat-up copy in an old drugstore where I had a burger that tasted like liver and a warm oversweet Coke . . . visiting a classmate who was drinking milk and puking on strips of cardboard . . . fuggit . . . and this was the good stuff.

And I'm not even talking 'bout the horrors of adolescence, nor does this have anything much to do with what I think of actual children, today, although, yes, I think they're entitled to NO special (moral, political, aesthetic) consideration, in fact the proper consideration—the best consideration (i.e., with respect for more than their cuteness and presumed "innocence")—is to treat them as SMALL PEOPLE. Small people who haven't had the goods beat out of them yet, or who have and, well—I already said that.

(Entitled to no special treatment, but if I had one, like every other I who has one, I would of course treat the little darling as a precious prize and all such blah blah blooey: MINE: how nazi! Or see *all* of 'em as darling simply because *I* own and operate one, i.e., am a member of the parent class and all *that* misdirection, sick sociology—but that's another piece; I still haven't written it.)

And obviously—big fucking truism—there's a child (at least one child) in everyone. We're all still, some more, some less, in daily communion with our childhood unconscious. The circuits may be askew, but old triggers remain in place, or some place. Big shit.

Anyway, anyway . . . this stuff makes me dizzy . . . let's see . . . something about how giving kids special status only demographically isolates them for the slimy likes of Ronald McDonald, Barney, the Little Mermaid, etc., etc.—the stuff grownups (esp. those that control the marketplace) would love to have 'em like, love, eat, piss and shit . . . exploitation . . . the susceptibility of targeted unmolded dough . . . (I mean fuck, even rock and roll as such is kid music, it too was once and forever isolated to that dead-end street—kid music that has once in a blue moon GOTTEN AWAY—the ticket that exploded—though I suspect most, if not all, of its explosions are safely in the past) . . . hack, clear . . . sort through . . . till we come at last to the foreground of the piece, its ostensible "subject matter," which is:

Music encountered during the miasma of childhood, of MY weary childhood, which I find I can now retrieve/recycle without (somehow) the cloying taint of that cheezy Gestalt. Stuff I can bear to listen to that I first heard then.

My favorite TV show in the early '50s was this ongoing dinnertime replay on a local N.Y. channel of about a dozen '30s/'40s serials, half of 'em starring Buster Crabbe, with such protagonists as Buck Rogers, Flash Gordon (three separate serials), Red Barry, Don Winslow (in the Coast Guard; in the Navy), Tim Tyler, Ace Drummond. You'd get a chapter a day till they ran through each one, 12 to 14 chapters, then on to the next; repeat in sequence when finished with the lot. The best of the Flash Gordons, and the best of the whole set, was the first of that series, *Space Soldiers* (1936), which in addition to giant standing lobsters, lion-men, a flying palace kept airborne by prisoners stoking the dread Atom Furnace, and Ming (the Merciless) had snippets of the first music I ever felt compelled to call "exciting." Last year I was able to i.d. the snippets as having been lifted from *Les Préludes*, the 1854 tone poem by Liszt.

Close behind was *Captain Video* (a/k/a: *Captain Video and His Video Rangers*), which, broadcast live, had no music to punctuate the action, but it did have a great opening theme—more of that Exciting shit—

15–20 seconds of what I recently figured out was the overture to *The Flying Dutchman* (1840, revised on and off until 1860).

Not in quite the same category—not as Exciting—but still functionally, I dunno, "moving" or something, is the Triumphal March from *Aida*, which got played at assemblies by the crummy school band at P.S. 44, which I was in for about a month on clarinet (they gave us plastic reeds 'cause we went through the normal ones too quick). We also played, or tried to play, the phony spiritual from Dvorak's *New World Symphony* and something called *March Marionette* (not Gounod's *Funeral March of the Marionette*) by I've got no idea who. Only the march from *Aida* stuck with me.

From snippet to whole cloth, microcosm to macrocosm . . .

Les Préludes is 17 minutes of mostly filler, lots of lulls. The "exciting part" doesn't come till about 2:30 or so, suddenly it wells up and THERE IT IS—as "gratuitous" an occurrence, a payoff for the wait, as in the serial itself. Not as staccato as I remember, heck ('cause staccato would be better); is this Leonard Bernstein's fault? Wait—the second appearance of the theme (at 15:30) is much more percussive, bombastic, so maybe this is the one they used.

Flying Dutchman, heard now, the whole opera, not just the overture, I can get into right away, it's "infectious," a pieca cake. It's conceivable I could've ridden with it for a few minutes at a stretch even then (although much of both music and text is about gonads and madness, which probably would've been as beyond me as *Duel in the Sun* had been when I saw it at 5 or 6 with nothing to prep me but TV Westerns); the *Steuermann, lass die Wacht!* routine in the third act would've made me sweat no more than a typical number for chorus from a '50s Broadway musical. Anyway, now, there's enough quick-turnover tension/release from beginning to end to make the whole thing as emotionally easy as falling off a log.

Aida is a different story, the march is way in the middle, so you gotta wait and wait for it, all the way in the second scene of the second act (middle of the second disc), a haul I couldn't possibly have held up for as a kid, even the "heroic" parts earlier on wouldn't've held me. But generally it's okay, and at times (for inst the aria *Su! del Nilo al sacro lido*) is kind of rousing like the *Internationale* (which for whatever it's worth breathed its first breath the same year, 1871), or a cross between the *Internationale* and *Onward, Christian Soldiers* (same diff if you're a kid). The second act, ending with a reprise of the march, plays well enough. All in all, I'd have to say I prefer the parts which—like the best of Nino Rota—sound like they could easily devolve into barrel-organ music, or *Finiculi, Finicula*—i.e., those that totter on the brink of not so much kitsch, certainly not grand kitsch, as populist kitsch (folk kitsch?). But even with a shitload of such biz, it's still in all a little, yes, assembly-hallish (or Italian boy scouts). The ending—the opera's plot solution—burial alive—would likely have appealed to the kid in me who saw mummy movies, but I didn't actually see those till they started running them on TV, when I was at least 12 or 13.

Aida needs to be played loud to work, while *Flying Dutchman* feels good and loud (at any volume) to begin with.

Second take.

I saw Bo Diddley and Chuck Berry at the Brooklyn Paramount; Elvis on the *Ed Sullivan Show*; the Beatles at Shea Stadium (twice); the Doors something like FORTY times, more than half before Jim even wore leathers (no: jeans and a surfer shirt); Sonny Rollins at the Five Spot after he got down off the Williamsburg Bridge to start gigging again (he had a Mohawk); Ornette Coleman at the Village Vanguard after *his* woodshed time-out to add trumpet and violin to his arsenal. The first time I heard the Troggs was on a jukebox as I peed in a urinal trying to make cigarette filters stand on end while my blind date not exactly waited for me at the bar, a total washout.

I could go on for paragraphs, pages, volumes 'bout all the rock and jazz things I experienced not only in real time but in *their* real time— their only time (before history got them—as it gets everyone and everything—wrong, before they got nailed to some idiot conception of the great chain of being, or the Time-Life lie-lie-lie-lie, or worse) and certainly mine (and double certainly theirs and mine in even proximate relevant conjunction); maybe someday I will.

The point for now being simply THIS: I have *no* context, *no* history (other than remote; remoter than remote; wholly, utterly incidental) to plug into when I listen to classical music, no *environment* in which to meet and greet it even halfway—none in which I really *wish* to participate (the concert scene, hanging out at Tower Classical, subscribing to archivist/discophile mags) (it's just too, what's the word, yes, too *fussy*) (too Euro, too creepy): no nexus of any sort, any import, OTHER THAN the shoddy Gestalt of childhood, or (and here's the kicker) some icky yucky structural equivalent: stamp collecting, model airplanes, by-the-numbers kid chemistry: a socially redeeming "hobby."

Or a—heaven help me—school project (for "extra credit")—I'm still a fucking overachiever. I diligently sift through exemplars of "baroque," "classical," "romantic," "modern," "avant garde" as I would through the airmail imperforates of Belgium, New Zealand and Estonia; I wiggle my toe in the vast ocean of opera, using my encounter with easy/early Wagner to give me entree to difficult/late, I go from *Aida* to *Rigoletto*, from *Les Préludes* to *A Faust Symphony* to *Mephisto Waltz #1*. I'm, as they say, "learning." I probably don't have enough years left to actually ever come up to speed with it, but I'm also likewise at a stage of mammal froth where such a fact don't faze me. Or do I have it backwards? Is this in fact an *apt* preoccupation for my coming dotage—pipe and slippers—geezertime, daddy-o?

In any event, it feels somewhat absurd at age 50 or age anything, given the downscale biases of my music-critical past, that I'm sort of reviewing—that I've lived to review—make semi-reasonable non-pejorative allusion to—in a single piece—two operas and a tone poem, but, y'know, hey: fuck *me*.

107

Real Time, Real Demons:
Bouncing with Bud '64

And my childhood qua jazz *was even more limited (maybe I saw Louis Armstrong on the* Colgate Comedy Hour*). Late adolescence was my jazz childhood.*

The "Hallelujah" discussed here is the same one cited in "Peep Shows and Piano Bars."

More box sets for Richard . . .

Bud Powell, *The Complete Blue Note and Roost Recordings*, Blue Note
 CDP 7243 8 30083 2 2
The Complete Bud Powell on Verve, Verve 314 521 669-2
The Return of Bud Powell, Fresh Sounds FSR-CD 27
Earl Bud Powell, vol. 7: Tribute to Thelonious '64, Mythic Sound MS
 6007-2

It was Rebecca Rosen's fault I never saw Bud Powell live. Or D. Gerber's. Or maybe Roy Lichtenstein's. Lots of things were stacked against it. But mostly Rebecca. By then I didn't feel like doing anything she wanted, or much of anything with her, period, even things I instigated. I pretty much couldn't stand her.

Late summer of '64. Bud was at Birdland. After he'd come back to New York (from Paris) to die. It was to be our last major date—thankgod—before returning to college for the fall semester. An obligatory wallet buster. I was just finishing a tour at this crummy seasonal job, collecting tolls on a bridge in Rock Rock Rockaway Beach. Irregular shifts, lousy days off, one day I'd go 6 AM to 2 PM and next day 7 PM to 3, so I might get to see her for a couple hours Tuesday after she finished her job at the hospital doing some clerical bullshit. Saturday or Sunday off meant major expenditure: World's Fair, first-run movies and meal, Peter, Paul and Mary at the Westbury Music Fair. This week I had both Friday and Saturday off, but as it worked out, even with the Lichtenstein print, even with the flowers, it was probably cheaper than Birdland Friday and whatever we might've done Saturday would've been.

Rebecca was my first completely sexual relationship as such things were defined in those days. In six-seven months of physical whoopee I never came in her without a rubber, and had to hold the thing up under a lamp to prove to her each time that nothing had leaked. In spite of this, or because of it, every month was a pregnancy scare for the ages (a prisoner of stress, she was never less than five days late). She never sucked me, never let me near her ass and, most regrettably, I never ate her. If I had, I'd probably have fonder memories than I do, at least a bit more grist for recollective beatoff.

From mid-July on, after her friend Sandi got pregnant, all that was allowable, orgaz-wise, was my hand on (and/or in) her snapper and me then stroking the salami *elsewhere*—after she gave it a few arm's-length tugs—preferably at the other end of the room. As I wasn't a complete insensitive, such was of course understandable. I knew her patterns. A master hypochondriac—one of the greats—she'd come home from the hospital imagining herself with a variety of ailments and afflictions: gonorrhea, syphilis, TB, cataracts, leukemia, diabetes, multiple sclerosis. Once, in the movies after a pizza, she blurted out, "I have cancer of the esophagus!"—people turned around to look— when all it was was heartburn. She was the second or third worst girlfriend I ever had.

In the best of circumstances, though I told her I loved her and all that shit, and sometimes probably meant it, I would have to say I essentially didn't even like her. She hated most of the music I cared for (jazz, Dylan, the Stones) and the visual art I was then partial to (the 20th century). If they put whipped cream on her chocolate pudding, she scooped it off and wrapped it in a napkin—many napkins—and had me signal the waiter toot *sweet* to take it away. She was always asking if I thought her thighs were too fat, and I generally told her yes, which always angered her—what kind of "bastard" was I to tell the truth? Young love: a horror then as now.

So anyway, Bud. Finally she conceded me jazz. Though Birdland was a dump, Manhattan—the City—made it a class dump. And though Bud meant nothing to her, he'd mean something to her hip-ster classmates. A class date—why the hell'd I bring it up?—there seemed no way out.

So what happened was this. Friday afternoon, I'm at Legs Forbes's house, D. Gerber calls, says there's a pop art show out in Southampton, some gallery, last day, let's go. A photo in *Newsday*—he brings it over—billboard-size painting of Joan Crawford by Jim Rosenquist: "I smoke Chesterfield because . . ." Great pic. Also some Lichtenstein, Segal, Wesselman, I forget, maybe Warhol. I tell him fuck, I would love to go, damn, but I got this Rebecca thing—we'll never get back in time. Says c'mon let's just *go*, the three of us, we'll figure out en route what lies to tell her.

We come up with a dumb one. *Real* dumb. Passing through Quogue, just before the Hamptons, or East Quogue, whatever, a great name, there's this curve we decide is the perfect place to set an accident. Skid and hit something. Avoiding a squirrel, no, a possum. Gerber's driving. He's okay, I'm okay, but Forbes is—change it to *was*, he's conscious now (but still bedrid')—in a coma. At such and such hospital. The car's not drivable, it's being worked on—an axle—we won't be back till tomorrow.

When I call and recite this to Rebecca, it's already like 6:30, 7:00, she's taken a bath, done her hair, all dressed and ready—the "big night"—she starts crying. Tells me I'm a bastard for doing this to her. "But your dear friend Legs Forbes"—he once took her bowling—"is in the goddam *hospital*." "You shouldn't have gone *anywhere* today . . . sob . . . bastard . . . you have absolutely *no sense of priorities!*" "Hey, you're right, I'm sorry . . ." ". . . bastard, *bastard* . . ." ". . . well, I'll see you tomorrow"—click. Then we got drunk and had a great time running along the beach yelling obscenities.

Maybe it was the possum that made her suspicious, but next day I brought flowers and she made me tell the whole stupid story all over again. Okay—Quogue, the curve, swerve, bang, Forbes in a coma. "You're lying." Huh? "I was *worried* about Legs so I called every hospital in Suffolk County and every one in Nassau County and then I called his place in Merrick and his mother didn't know what I was talking about. You lying bastard. We're finished." Oh . . . grief. The heartbreak of heartbreak. Grief for a week and then . . . hey, I'm rid of her.

So did I go see Bud without her? I did not. Not then, not any time subsequent. He even shared a bill—Judson Hall, I think—with Albert Ayler. (He died in '66.) And every time I've played him since, or maybe not every but three out of four, and not immediately but eventually—and today more than ever—I think: I never ate Rebecca Rosen. My cross to bear in hearing Bud—but I can take it.

What's harder to take is when it reminds me not only of my sexual youth but my writerly youth. I used to sit writing for hours—typing—to his music, I'd put on whole sides and just . . . go. This was before I used a computer—before they were compulsory—back when mags still paid people to typeset your copy, which you handed in on paper (so it got edited *on* paper, and you'd end up with fewer typos than you get when they edit on screen). Computer keyboards are *not* percussion instruments, the impacts are a joke, a bad dream—the sound of plastic *clicking*, or not even clicking. No feeling of contact, no feeling of movement. With typewriters—manual, electric, it didn't matter which—it was like you were this runaway freight train, or at full tilt could *imagine* being one (unless you're a child you've used one—remember?)—in my heyday I wrote pretty fast. And could think fast. This was also of course before I lost my improv skills to *composition* (i.e., moving words and commas around the page, endlessly), but really, I wouldn't lie, I was once capable of full-speed, full-throttle creation in real time, every time. G'bye to all that.

With Bud at the height of his powers, it wasn't a matter of playing/thinking/creating in real time, but in real double time. Take a cut like "Un Poco Loco"—the fast parts—or, better yet, the entirety of "Hallelujah." Maybe Art Tatum played this fast, but most of what he played was gratuitous filigree. Cecil Taylor (the only pianist, for what it's worth, to make full use of Bud's speed module) can play about as fast, but only occasionally at Bud's level of novelty and precision. On any instrument, only Charlie Parker ever played as fast with rhyme, reason, absolute musical relevance.

"Hallelujah": a continuous whirl of ideas, sub-ideas and tangents—cascades of all sorts of shit—rivulets to streams to raging rivers to floods, dammed and released—redirected—"March of the Wooden Soldiers" (or some such) quoted, "Go in and out the window" (wherever that's from), but not in kitchen-sink fashion, not like Sonny Rollins, auteur, saying anything equals anything else (musical objects in musical stasis), more like you can get *anywhere* from here (motion!) in real-time context—real in time, alive in time—new in time—Bud the MAMMAL auteur flailing, dervishing his way to a fake ending, make that two fake endings, two and a half—depending on how you count these things—the biggest fake factored in in heart-stop micro-time, not preconceived, or if preconceived, reconceived—re-preconceived—in real different time, a sudden rethink (hey, I've got more left to say!), resurge to the fore for another jubilant half-minute then . . . bingo.

I'm eight years older than Bud when he died, almost twice the age he was when he cut "Hallelujah," and what does it sound like right now as I'm hearing it? What does it in fact seem to be "about"? IM-MORTALITY.

And for mortality and *slow* real time, there's the '54 Verve reading of "It Never Entered My Mind." A pillar-to-post type of guy, a heart-on-his-sleeve/no-insulation type of player, Bud covered the gamut in life, in art, and all stations between. Here, at a dirge-like clip, he visits and surveys the far horizons of a multiplex of worst-case spiritual/emotional scenarios, what's left of the soul (his, everyone's) after the realest of demons have devastated it—nothing left—the to-tality of his vision a full step (at least) beyond Kerouac's in *Big Sur.* Possibly the darkest, bleakest traipse through a major-repertoire bal-lad ever, bleaker than anything by Little Jimmy Scott. (Bleaker than "Various Times" by the Fall.) Hear it and gasp.

You want abstraction? Bud could abstract it with the best of 'em. In his three takes of "Tea for Two" from June 1950, he pulls off a more re-lentlessly, handsomely "conceptual" unravel of the tune than even his pal Thelonious Monk's deconstruction/appropriation for Riverside; as explosive a de-struction—well, almost—as Ornette Coleman's blowup of "Embraceable You" or Sunny Murray's "This Nearly Was Mine."

Which reminds me, I didn't finish the story 'bout the print. When we got there, the gallery still had some signed Lichtensteins left at 15 bucks a pop. Nothing with speech balloons—they'd just sold their last copy of this one with a guy in a beret with a machine gun ("And now, mes amis—pour la France!")—but I got myself a good'un of a boot stepping on a hand no longer holding a handgun, yellow, red, black (signed, dated, 61/300), which I kept in a closet for another couple years, at which point I hacked it up into smaller rectangles and pasted the rectangles inside an issue of the crummiest comic I had on hand— *The Fightin' Five,* a Charlton Comic (from Derby, Connecticut). Dada inspirations are like that. About ten years ago, when the comic fell apart, I rescued all the pieces of Lichtenstein, matched and mounted them—as sloppily as I could—on a board now hanging on a wall of the room where I write.

If I hadn't hacked it, it'd now be worth what?—a few hundred bucks? Big deal. Just as well it's hacked and hung—a visual reminder, though it only works once in let's say 80 peeks—every couple weeks— of the fact that I never saw Bud or ate Rebecca.

Didn't see but can now hear, more or less. The Bud I would've seen—perhaps—the time frame is right—is hearable on a pair of CDs, one fairly awful, one sort of okay.

The Return of Bud Powell is the reissue of a '64 Roulette LP that hyped itself as "his first new recording since 1958," which is bull-shit—he'd made a whole bunch in Paris in the interim. While not quite as dire as assholes at the time (Leonard Feather et al.) made it out to be, his playing is often lumbering and clunky—changing tem-pos like shifting in traffic, marking time to get his bearings, circling back to fill gaps he'd once have leaped (or ignored). Whole stretches sound like run-throughs of bop cocktail conventions, a rehash of rou-tines he'd been laying on hordes of lesser (and less discerning) talents since the mid '40s. Instead of directing mighty rivers, basically he's wading in puddles.

Half the selections on *Tribute to Thelonious* are from the Birdland gig. Though the diminished capacities in evidence on *Return* are still a factor, on the cuts chosen for inclusion he seems generally more sure of himself. In the booklet, Francis Paudras talks about "the calm and serene message of an artist who has found his bearings and com-municates only the essential. Beauty in its pure state, art without pre-tense." Well, there are moments. The level of feeling is high. If fewer emotional details are given than would've been Bud's wont in the '50s, what's given is given in stark clarity, with crisply outlined shadows—crisp enough. Even if only in microcosm, the VOICE is still there—the *sound*—the atom of utterance, loud and proud—long may it live, or wave, or whatever the fuck dead voices can do.

No, I didn't see him, he wasn't as great as he had been, but it would've been nice to be in the same room with him.

108

Ten Cage Reviews

All the John Cage you can eat: my most elaborate classical spin-off. And most rock and rollish.
Last in a line of uses/misuses of the reimbursement perquisite.
The one that got me canned.
Less than a month after this ran, just in time for Christmas, San Diego "rethought" the arrangement and deemed me expendable. Thirteen other people were "released" that week—the cost of newsprint had risen (y'know how it is).
Using my flimsy setup to acquire CDs had not been a brilliant idea. I got greedy (what can I say?), if not quite as greedy as Springsteen (or Landau) (or any thousand/million others). Writing and fretting in my 50th year, no decent promos—no keepers—in over a decade, I got carried away.
May I never write (or fret) about this music shit again.

If John Cage can roll dice, I can roll dice. Well, actually, no, he didn't roll—he threw the I Ching. The I Ching is for simps. You want me to do this, I'm gonna roll. Rolls will "determine" the reviews—give us our parameters. We won't do shit unless the dice say it's cool. Absolutely no cheating will be permitted.

Quartets I-VIII (San Francisco Contemporary Music Players, Newport Classic NPD 85547), a piece written for the U.S. Bicentennial, consisting of old American hymns fragmented by chance operations, to be performed by anywhere from 24 to 93 players, no more than four of whom play simultaneously.

Let's roll it. First roll will tell us how much the reviewer may talk about the actual music at hand, from *not at all* to *not very much* to *some* to *very much* to *almost entirely* to *nothing but.* A two it is—*not very much*—so roll again to choose source of text. This time it's a five:

469

combination of *hymn buzz words* and *1962 boxing record book data.*
Okay:

The Lord is Gene Fullmer stopped Carmen Basilio in the twelfth
round at Salt Lake hallelujah Tokyo, Japan, May 23. Becerra then announced his down by the river when he stopped Paul Pender after
nine whole world in His vacant N.B.A. title by kayoing Jesse Bowdry
in the angels on Thailand, April 16. Pone Kingpetch retained his my
shepherd-round draw in Bozeman, Montana, with Satan's fifteen
rounds, at the Metropolitan Gym, in the sheaves unanimously over
Ray Robinson at the Garden in Boston, Mass.

Atlas Eclipticalis for Three Flutes (Eberhard Blum, piccolo, flute and
alto flute, Hat Art 6111), produced by superimposing music sheets
over astronomical charts—or is it the other way around?—with stars
thus becoming notes requiring further chance operations to determine their musical relations to each other.

Three rolls this time—six, two, four—restricting us to *63 words or
less* in a *benign* critical mode, *all uppercase*:

AS SPARSE AS THE SKY, SPARSER BY FAR THAN COUN-
TRY SKY: CITY SKY—WHERE YOU MIGHT SEE THREE
STARS A NIGHT. *LONG* SILENCES WHERE YOU THINK
IT'S OVER AND THERE'S 50 MINUTES LEFT. ONCE IN A
GREAT WHILE IT SUDDENLY GETS SHRILL LIKE A
STEAM WHISTLE—THAT'S NICE. GOOD ACOUSTIC NOT-
MUCH, LIKE AN EMPTIER VERSION OF JAZZ MINIMAL-
ISM. A VERY SATISFYING ZERO, ACTUALLY.

Fontana Mix & Solo for Voice 2 (Blum, flute and voice, Hat Art 6125),
i.e., the tape overlay of three separate realizations of *Fontana Mix* and
one of *Solo for Voice 2*, each of which is variously determined by the in-
tersection of points on transparent sheets containing such biz as
curved lines, broken straight lines, graph grids, vowels and conso-
nants.

A three, a four, a three again, which translates to: *slightly longer* than
previous critique, *variably neutral and mocking*, with unit words *ran-
domly upper or lower case*:

Even with ALL the OVERDUBBING, this whatsit IS AS empty
AS an atom, with SOME RATHER ABRUPT slips INTO echoless
silence MADE possible by very LITTLE ROOM sustain. BLUM
gets his FLUTE TO sound AT times like SANDPAPER, OTHER
times HE'S Roland KIRK mumbling INSIDE THE fucker. On

THE WHOLE, SORT OF like KIRK doing ROSCOE Mitchell (OR VICE versa). THE vocal TRACK is just a BUNCHA NON-SENSE syllables, BUT at ONE point he seems TO BE saying "No COOZE."

Indeterminacy (Cage, reading, David Tudor, music, Smithsonian/Folk-ways SF 40804/5), consisting of 60 pieces of linear text ("stories") read either fast, slow, or at normal speed to precisely fit one-minute slots over which are also dubbed various unrelated nonverbal acoustic/electronic excretions.

One and a three—well, how 'bout this: my rejected *Christmas-wishes-'95* piece for *Los Angeles* magazine sight-typed in *one-minute bursts with resultant typos left uncorrected*:

My wish this XCmas is simple: that L.A, blight of the planet, of all-possible plantes, get what ity ha so richly deserved for the last, oj, 130 yearsm tp wit: that an earthquaks of lety's say 11.4 magnityde finally level eberyu cancerous atom from (1:00)

Santa Momica to San bernardino, form Exnard to OceansideL done. My second choice wold be for soemething in the 7.9 range, one at least suficenet to so disruopt film prduction that the mobie industry wold ve forced tyo relocvate ne mazse top (2:00)

Phoenix or Bermida, and all mechamisn would this be romoved for yje town to any longer lie to itself, certainly not with its cuirrent ob-scene effciency. anmd a; l direct tioes to the world of "glamor:" would be severed forover, and the socallled "city" (ha ha ha ha ha (3:00)

haha) would stand nakjed beside Detroit and Cleve;land, for inst, opn the short lsitf o tiopical civic trivia joikes, and the most melavo-lent (and least credinle) pyramid scehmne in the annals of te knOwn unievrse would at last, well, . . . you get tje pictrue. (4:00)

4'33" (acoustic realization by Frank Zappa, on *A Chance Operation: The John Cage Tribute*, Koch International 3-7238-2 Y6x2; electronic realization by Peter Pfister, on *Music for Five*, Hat Art 2-6070), to be performed by a solitary musician (any instrument) sitting motionless and playing nothing for 4 minutes and 33 seconds, during which (in theory) all sorts of ambient sonic shit will get to be noticed.

Hard to believe it, but dice don't lie: six and one, compelling me to *sit (but not write) at the computer keyboard* while allowing *my cat* to con-tribute an ambient review:

. . . . hjhjuhn0—ppoooooooo0——-
vcxc

```
op            dfcfd
  9p0;;;.
  kl, . . . . . . . . . . . . . . yt766455666909-----------8iiiiiiiiiuuuu
uuu=_lool9*+0. . . .
  dp;'nmgftrvw b   b   b   sx
```

A Flower (Joan La Barbara, voice, on *Singing Through*, New Albion NA 035), for voice and closed piano, to be sung wordlessly without pitch change, at indicated points "like a pigeon" and "like a wild duck."

Hey—this should be something—five, three, two: *topically inappropriate generic speculation* in the manner of a *crabby Kant scholar* often bordering on *sheer flummery*:

Re (Kant's) synthetic a priori: why does Cage accept only the most *accidental* of synthetics, and not very many (if any) levels of *active* synthetic (e.g., "human participation" *within* the experiential Gestalt)? Why must the hand as dealt be so clean, so antiseptic for both dealer and dealee—white gloves f'r godsakes? Possibly the sickest aspect of the whole thing: he doesn't seem to allow for "faking it"—shortcuts, feigned compliance w/ too stringent rule modules, saying you do when you don't (when who the hell would know the diff?)—as even a sometime factor, a goddam *variable*, in the move from "concept" to "actualization."

Freeman Etudes, Books One and Two (Irvine Arditti, violin, Mode 32), a chance-generated but calculatedly difficult series of notated studies for violin, calling for tricky speeds, "impossible" fingerings, and instantaneous changes in volume and playing style.

A tough piece o' music demanding tough analysis—six rolls: two, one, one, four, six, three—saddling us with *"prepared" criticism* composed of *forward, backward, and alphabetized* versions of a *letter received from conductor James DePreist in response to my having sent him a Richard Grossman CD*, this text to run with *no punctuation* and *thirteen words* replaced by others dealing with *urination*:

belated weewee for the compact piss and article about wetpants Grossman I piddle your thoughtfulness

peed your appreciate I yellow Dick about urinal and disc diaper the pisspot thanks belated

dogpiss and appreciate number-one belated compact Dick leak for Grossman I whiz the thoughtfulness your

Europeras 3 & 4 (Long Beach Opera, Mode 38/39), each of which has people playing opera 78s, singers singing arias of their choice, pianists playing excerpts from Liszt's opera transcriptions, etc.

A simple one this time—two rolls: five, one—giving us: *175 words of unedited notes followed by an out-of-context guest comment (reviewer's choice):*

Why the hell does he leave opera—of all things—functionally untouched? Does he want everybody to be repulsed once and for all by its "excesses"? Or is it simply for the already addicted, or at least initiated? And/or is it truly a deconstruction—a literal disembodiment—albeit a failed one—of a mega-slice of the operatic repertoire? None of the materials used are post-Puccini, which would be akin to Duchamp limiting his readymades to the artifacts of pre-impressionism: a more "conventional" opera audience is thus (intentionally?) factored in. In any event, isolating the aria and the orchestral swell (in the final minute of *Europera 3* alone, snippets of the piano versions of *Parsifal* and *The Flying Dutchman* strut their stuff) is kind of the opposite of Cage's usual approach, making foreground more foreground, spotlighting the dominance of already primary focal points. Close to mere camp and kitsch; as hoky, if less meanderingly "personal," as most sound-things by Yoko Ono.

Says Ned Rorem ("A Conversation with Ned Rorem," Lawrence D. Mass, in *Queering the Pitch: The New Gay and Lesbian Musicology*): "Look at the operas in this country that work. They aren't by Elliott Carter or John Cage. They're by Philip Glass and John Adams, and it's all nonmodulatory, super-simple music."

Works for Percussion (Quatuor Hélias, Wergo WER 6203-2), seven early works for drums, bells, gongs, wastebaskets, conch shells, coils of wire and the like.

Four rolls, okay—four, three, six, five—oops—this could be painful: *extremely negative idiot rant*, written *drunk*, many years *before I'd heard a single actual work by Cage*, which it *embarrasses me* not to have destroyed now that I have:

Shake a glass that has a small amt. of water in it. Shake it 90 degrees so the water goes flying. It flies to the sink, careens against the drain and sounds like sttut. Shake it again it sounds like sttoot. Once more and you're hearing sttizzt. Three more times and 's all over, Jack (th' water is GONE). Stop me if it's too obvious but I jus' wanna *know*: How come glasses of water (& the music they make) are nowhere to be found in the works of the mighty Mr. Cage??? Or if they are I haven't heard and maybe THAT is the pt. Not hearing. Never hearing. Silence of nevernot? Could it?

Ans.: resounding NO. This is "classical" music—composer controls it. So only if thee COMPOSER SEZ SO. No free agents in Johnny's music! (Booooooo!!!)

Alt. ans.: only while he is alive. He is dead! Fug him! YOU call it. WE call it. Liberate the muhfuh's muse-ic. Credit HIM with stuff he never wrote. Stick him with your LEAST INTERESTING SONIC TRASH. He fugging deserves it.

Bunny Berigan, *The Pied Piper 1934–40* (Bluebird 07863 66615-2), selected by dice roll (one: let a stranger, female, under 5'3" pick it for you) to stand in for a Cage recording.

One more roll: two, *say something—anything—about a single cut*:

In the original release print of *Chinatown* there's an early scene, before Jack Nicholson gets his nose cut, where he's combing his hair while Bunny Berigan plays and sings "I Can't Get Started." It's just about the greatest scene in the movie, a pic-perfect evocation of late-'30s white sensitive-male etcetera: "The North Pole I have charted, still I can't get started with you." Could it be the same version of "Started" that's on this CD (recorded 8/7/37)? Dunno—he cut at least three versions that I'm aware of, and there's no way to check it against a video of the film: the scene has been removed. Removed? Removed. But the song is still mentioned in the credits.

HOUSEKEYS TO
THE KINGDOM

Introduction

A pair of powerful items which make only minor allusion to music . . . but which have everything to do with it. Everything!

Each dealing with a matter vital to an understanding of *American* music:

Racism.

Wrestling.

The latter composed at the time of the first WrestleMania (1985), the former during the '92 L.A. Riots. The term "self-evident" appears in both. This is capital-t Truth Time, readers! More than virtually anything else I've writ in the last 15 years, these just about "wrote themselves" (were drafted in a state of agitated *compulsion*).

DEAR EDITPERSON: I *need* to have these glory-ous write-ings in here. Need to! Whoever's at the other end of the corporate ding-dong—"marketing," "demographic yuppification," "anti-author subterfuge," or whatever the prevailing euphemism is—tell 'em to *fuck off*, these pieces STAY in the goddam book, okay?

Lookit. I've suffered ENOUGH frustration already in being branded a reviewer of babymusic; in having the best thing I ever wrote, my fucking novel, go over the falls when my editor in that case didn't consider me youth-demographic *enough* . . . phoo and fie and fuggaduck.

This stuff *stays*, goddammmit!

109

The Last Wrestling Piece

In much the same way that existentialism is the metaphysics of pragmatism (or is it vice versa?), wrestling is the metaphysics of rockandroll. If it isn't, what is?

In the cultural chain of late-century being, if wrestling was in crisis, what wasn't?

There is no more a problem of truth in wrestling than in the theatre.
—Roland Barthes, *Mythologies*

I threw the paper into the corner and turned on the TV set. After the society page dog vomit even the wrestlers looked good.
—Raymond Chandler, *The Long Goodbye*

What is portrayed by wrestling is therefore an ideal understanding of things; it is the euphoria of men raised for a while above the constitutive ambiguity of everyday situations and placed before the panoramic view of a univocal Nature, in which signs at last correspond to causes, without obstacle, without evasion, without contradiction.
—Barthes, *Mythologies*

I can beat anyone up. And I can walk and talk too.
—Hulk Hogan

Okay, get out your notebooks. This here is lecture time. Wrestling Goes Mainstream. An outcome that is vile, it's loathsome, it may even cause cancer—don't laugh, this is *serious*. Somebody help me wheel out the blackboard ... where the hell's my chalk? Okay, pens and pencils ready: I HOLD THESE TRUTHS TO BE SELF-EVIDENT.

1. By plugging right smack into the Master Program, wrestling has gone from being something *uniquely* fake, *archetypally* fake, para-digmatically *fake for real*, to something nonironically fake per se, stan-dardly fake like Everything is fake: movies, TV, "real" sports, fashion trends, heart transplants, national elections.

2. An all-too-willing conspirator in the Ruse Writ Large, it is no longer the needle-threading, universe-belching master of its own per-sona, ceding (in all ways crucial, for a mess of pottage) the Grand Generatrix of its own awesome face to the cloning yuck—for shame! for shame!—of *demographics*.

3. Where once upon a not so distant past wrestling proudly mucked and traded in all that was Low—as in geeks, carnies and bathos—its current sense of market is defined wholly and simply by that lowest of common Denoms: children, hipsters and morons (prin-cipally Caucasian).

4. Formerly (same time frame) the incarnation of Bombast/Pure/No Limit, it has reeled in its oompah, chiseled its swagger, to coalesce with the twin towers of topical cowpoop strut, Get!Down! and U!S!A!

5. Not in the wrestling lifetime of any of us under 50 have even the *most* impressive of good guys exhibited the consistently com-manding Presence, or been ultimately as Interesting, as your average bad guy, 50th percentile and up. And while roleplay flexibility, includ-ing the option of 180° reversals on a dime, has always been a vital part of the trip, bad-to-good transitions have become an all-too-prevalent fact of life, as witnessed by the surrender-of-self of far too many Sig-nificant Malevolents in the last couple annums: Hulk Hogan, Sgt. Slaughter, Superfly Snuka and—saddest of all—Lou Albano. (Reagan Era culture death at its most chilling.)

6. With its own entertainment I.D. no longer that of the bad guy—or even *a* bad guy—wrestling hooks up with *the* perennial bas-tion of choreographed insincerity (a.k.a. telegraphed sincerity), it-self once Quite Bad but recently born again Good ("We Are the World"; Cyndi Lauper for Cystic Fibrosis), the festering mega-corpse of mainstream rock. Underlining even more than the preem-inence of Product over Art, this alliance made in Suburban Hell officially certifies our current megadistance from a world in which, massively, minutely or otherwise, art (or daring) ever really, truly *functioned*.

7. A TV staple since virtually the medium's birthing, wrestling for 35 years had the firmness of mission to ignore the insidious beseechings of any and all cathode Style Sheets, serving up the rawest and (possibly) most steadfastly life-affirming of broadcast gestalts: seamed and seamy—but such (ah!) is Life. Today, TV-ized to the gills and snout, it is seamless, sanitized, canned-featured, digitally animated, color-commentated, slo-mo'ed and SLICK—as suffocatingly awful as *Wide World of Sports* (or the bloody Super Bowl).

8. With the WWF running, basically, the whole entire show, and the NWA, AWA, etc. reduced *collectively* to less than a sliver of the pie, wrestling's once mighty Pluralism—its infrastructural one-up on all-American athleto-monistic hooey—has been sent the way of the horse, the buggy, the Bill of Rights.

9. More a geo-conceptual problem than an econo-monopolistic one, today's centralized national setup all but banishes Geographic Mystery from the stew. To wit (for example), where in New York '73 it was announced that Stan "The Man" Stasiak had wrested from Pedro Morales the then-WWWF championship *off camera* in Philadelphia, and it was debated by bemused cognoscenti whether in fact Philadelphia *existed* (i.e., as a WWWF outpost), it would be downright *fruitless* to any longer doubt your Phillies, your Boises, your Buzzard Creeks—the WWF blankets us all. To wit number two, "Parts Unknown," the hearth and home of Mr. Wrestling II, The Spoiler, Spot Moondog et al, is (as any kid up on the "new math" will tell you) finally *inside* the bubble!

10. As the breakdown/abandonment of regional promotion becomes more or less complete, local *non*-televised wrestling cards, once the quasi-lifeblood of the whole dang whatsis, tend to suffer most (proportionally) of all, especially with the goddam Hulk so unassailably entrenched as the Big Cheese-Designate and coast-to-coast hogger of hype. The Hulkster and his immediate foes can only fight so many nights a year, see, and with no local *first* units to draw from—such folk having either been absorbed nationally, shipped to jurisdictions unknown or locked out to rot—towns large and small are too often stuck with national second units that essentially *stink*, so great is the disparity of urgency (at Choreography Central) between Hulk-level horseshit and everything else. And without loser-leaves-town matches to occasionally fall back on (as there's no longer a "town" to leave) . . . *gosh*.

11. Okay. Here's one for laughs. Time was muscles, make that muscles *without* accompanying fat, were the exclusive domain of "narcissists," sissyboys—in any event, *some* kind of weirdos—and bullies. Muscle creeps were hideous monsters, good guys never had them, certainly not the swollen fibrous crap you'd see in muscle mags, and even *strong* good guys, those to whom strength was their *thing*, had about as much flab sticking out their trunks as your average beer slob.* Nor was there ever the faintest need for flabless abs, pecs or delts to even *alternately* serve as any sort of mat-tempered Fitness Metaphor, for what was fitness but the sick joke of joggers? Okay, fine, great, amazing: a wrestling iconographically fair to the natural slob in Everyman. So what happens but Fitness Chic erupts like a case of the hives, in-shape Olympic dipshits, *hundreds* of 'em, grab the national scrotum without subtlety or mercy, Schwarzenegger makes a couple pics with and without his shirt—so what's wrestling go do but ruthlessly pander-to-trend. Possibly the sickest hallmark of the New Wrestling is rippling goddam fibers across the board: from bad guys as always (Paul Orndorff, Brutus Beefcake) to principal good guys (Hogan, Snuka) to peripheral stiffs (Ricky Steamboat) to even— wouldja believe it?—*announcers* (Jesse "The Body" Ventura). Add to this all those hokey ersatz training tapes (". . . pumping iron with Dick Wazoo in his Gym") and what we're faced with is Slob Disenfranchisement of the most nefarious ilk. Pshaw!

12. By shilling for itself on priorly occupied turf (Letterman, *Saturday Night Live*, the sports sections of major metropolitan dailies), wrestling actually finds itself in a position to catalytically undermine an incredibly stupid and docile nation's belief structure re Everything, to effect the removal of the Master Program ring from a people's collective nose as it were. À NOUS LA LIBERTÉ—wrestling style!! But such is far, *far* from its bag of intentions—and it sure don't want snot on its hands.

Let's be fair. Not *everything* stinks about today's wrestling, not even that practiced by the essentially repugnant World Wrestling Federa-

---

* Only exceptions: those rare bozos whose not-half-bad overall physiques were really no more than corny general echoes of acceptably overdeveloped anatomical trademarks—Antonino Rocca and his "educated" bare *feet*; Pepper Gomez and his *stomach* that could withstand Killer Kowalski's claw hold; etc.

tion, formerly the World *Wide* Wrestling Federation, which according to a recent *Village Voice* cover story has penetration rights to a whopping 87 per cent of U.S. TV homes—and climbing—and is so Johnny-on-the-nosering it even puts out its own wrestling *mag*, kind of the equivalent of a hit sitcom marketing its own *TV Guide*; Freddie Blassie (for instance) does not stink at all. In fact he is coming up roses.

During the hype hoedown which preceded MTV's "Rock & Wrestling Connection" whizoff between Roddy Piper and Hulk Hogan, for inst, while everyone from Little Richard to Gloria Steinem was delivering cheesy well-rehearsed cliché in support (mostly) of Ms. Lauper's cultural sugardad Hogan, Classy Fred, nonpartisan to a fault, went straight for the corporate jugular, bellowing a mothereffing *gem* of from-the-hip truth & concision: "WHAT GOOD IS MTV???!!! THEY NEVER PLAY 'STARDUST' OR THE RUSSIAN NATIONAL ANTHEM!!!" Indeed, indeed, and howzabout a couple months back when, prodded to explain how as a loyal American he could give succor to "Communists and Iranians," namely his tagteam charges Nikolai Volkoff and the Iron Sheik, this top-five all-time *master* interviewee (the others being the *pre*-sold-out Lou Albano, the late Grand Wizard, and the long-gone John Tolos and Killer Kowalski) exclaimed simply, "I support WINNERS!!!"— inspirational or what? (Up there, in the author's opinion, with Ron Dellums' voice-in-the-wilderness characterization of Jimmy Carter's '80 Olympic boycott, which he was one of only like maybe two-three members of Congress to refuse to endorse, as "hysterical"—Great Moments in Keeping the Faith.)

Then there's master interview*er* Roddy Piper, he of WWF insert *Piper's Pit*, one talkshow host who really knows How. Former house villain at (L.A.'s own) Olympic Auditorium, a likable hack whose principal shtick never amounted to much more than aggressive *cowardice*, Roddy has finally graduated to a task that suits him, beating out-of-ring good guys (qua naive, unsuspecting talkshow guests) with chairs, smashing bananas in their face. "Sympathy," he's been quoted as saying, "comes after stupidity and suicide in the dictionary." Talkshow hostility carried to its logical, inevitable conclusion (and the only leap in either tenor or scale—from Old Wrestling to New, from local dungeon to national slick—which seems to have been worth the effort, the gamble, whatever the hey).

Actually, though, to be *really* fair, Vince McMahon's macro-talk-show *TNT*, formerly *Tuesday Night Titans*, has also had its moments, including probably *the* big world-is-watching (hundreds of thousands? over USA Cable) moment of 'em all: the Butcher Vachon wedding. While the WWF kingpin's sense of Manifest Bombast has too often of late been that of a golfing banker or nonironic (barely even cynical) pesticide lobbyist, those rare occasions when he's let the empire's hair down, and trusted the thing to communal autopilot, have been purt near transcendent. The Wedding: collaborative improv/sequential pluralism on a par with some of your better Battle Royals, or Ornette Coleman's *Free Jazz* (for instance).

And Kamala, the three-hundred-some-odd-pound Ugandan Giant, he of few teeth and fewer traditional holds, a true innovator, he just kind of knocks 'em over, falls on 'em and eventually gets up, too *pure* for the WWF so now he's out in the boonies of something called the Mid-South—anyway *he's* okay.

And King Kong Bundy, 458 lbs. of monster metaphor/mixed (radiation-sick colossus meets shaved-head vampire meets world's largest amoeba meets lab animal that fucks-your-mom), wrestling's ultimate genetic accident (in the hands, no less, of the mad, post-scientific WWF) and master of the 5-count pin (3 is for simps, wimps and earlier phases of the beast): as okay as it gets.

And someone I've never actually seen wrestle, just his photo in the "Mat Mania!" issue of *Sports Illustrated*, this guy (?) with stupid hair and face paint called the Missing Link, no idea where he wrestles but I'd *bet* he's alright. I would bet ten bucks.

Otherwise—suddenly I'm feeling generous, I don't know why, but let's give some points to Big John Studd, Ken Patera and Bobby Heenan for clipping Andre the Giant's healthy head o' sheep hair—otherwise, and I've been watching this junk since 1956 (so I know), otherwise *nada*, 's an average lame era at best, the EMPEROR'S NEW YUPPIE THREADS—and I'm being fair. I am.

I've been watching the shit since 1956, actually earlier; have *followed* it since around '56—more or less continuously. Some multi-year gaps here & there, sure, but also some great big hunks of uninterrupted focus, bigger than for 2/3 the things in my life. I've been to it live at least 200 times in various cities, or let's say 175–180. I've seen 8 or 9 battle royals. Wrestling was the first sport (by any definition) that *meant* anything to me, like I'd catch the world series or a bowl game most every year but so what. Discovered and learned the whole sporting pot pourri in sequence to *it*, first bought *The Ring* 'cause they had maybe 2–3 pages of wrestling in back, eventually read the boxing up front and started watching, hadda then buy *Sports Illustrated* and *Sport* to widen my boxing horizon, in the process managing to additionally notice (in sequence) football, hockey, basketball, baseball, etc. *[Where the author is "coming from."]*

Around '53 or '54 I remember my grandfather watching on a tiny black & white, sweat dripping, seegar jutting/jerking in his twisted mouth. In turn-of-the-20th Russia he himself had wrestled, or so he claimed, taking on smalltown bullies (Greco-Roman style) for a bottle of vodka. As half a century later wrestling could not help *remaining* a matter of honor, this almost-an-anarchist nobody's-fool would yell at the screen, "Use your hammerlock!"—affairs of honor can scarcely be faked. *[Germplasmic source of a cultural postulate.]*

Independent of gramps I hooked into the whatsis somewhere during my first semester of junior high—a couple months after hooking into rock & roll fifteen years before it was pan-corporate slime by catching Elvis on the *Ed Sullivan Show*. Krazy music (from then on) I could always catch—the home radio'd all but been abandoned in the wake of TV—but krazy ringside hi-jinx I had to (appropriately) fight for. All they had on in New York back then was Thursday night wrestling from D.C., promoted, interestingly enough, by McMahon's old man Vince Sr., which since it shared the slot of bran'new goddam *Playhouse 90* meant I hadda fight the folks to even catch five minutes. (A compromise was eventually reached: alternating weeks. Which meant, in one typical stretch, them missing part one of the *Playhouse 90* "For Whom the Bell Tolls" and me missing Mark Lewin & Don Curtis losing the U.S. Tag Team Championship to the Graham Brothers, Eddie & Dr. Jerry, while they lucked into catching part two.) By the time I was in the 9th grade I was so gaga for wrestlin' I wormed my way into a car with ten or eleven relatives I couldn't stand 'cause they were headed down D.C. for Easter where they had this 6-man whoosis they weren't gonna televise—Lewin, Curtis and 601-lb. Haystacks Calhoun vs. the Grahams and Johnny Valentine—and jesus was it a *lulu*. In the second fall the Grahams refused Valentine's tag, he wasn't their brother so they let him get his ass beat. He got pinned and some stretcher guys carried him out but then midway through the third fall he came running back out with a bandage around his head swinging this long fucking pipe at all five of the rest of 'em, eventually *pinning* Haystacks (kayoed by a chair) while the others were busy swinging stuff at each other, the only time (though I could be wrong) the big fatso was actually counted out, shoulders to the mat 1-2-3—and I was there. And I was there, 1974, seventh row ringside, Madison Square Garden, when Freddie Blassie actually punched Bruno Sammartino *in the balls*—without (hey hey?) a script?—and I'm such a sap I've even gone to, and sat through, midgets in Texas. *[Evidence of abiding affection.]*

And I've seen Blassie, '71 at the Olympic Aud., biting John Tolos's head for must've been 10–15 minutes of *just biting*—nothing else!—until he just kind of relinquished his grip and the bit-up Tolos fell over flat 'n' inert like so much dead meat, ONLY TO COME BACK STRONG AND COP THE THIRD AND DECIDING FALL—so I know comebacks. And this current whatever it is Wrestling Writ Large is supposed to be undergoing is not (not) a comeback. 'Cause, writ large, it's never been "away." Or particularly "down." I mean yeah, some regional promotions *had* dried up 'n' out from their own flaming ineptitude (the Olympic's LeBells for inst), and the mass consumption of Hulkamania t-shirts does represent *some* kind of "advance," but truly, writ Large, with or without the glitz, the thing has been superpopular for *decades.* Or some such duration.

Like I've got this page clipped from a mid-'73 *Wrestling News.* It says: "Professional Wrestling Is Our Number One Sport!—we have statistics to back this up!" And the stats have Pro Wrestling at 35,000,000, ahead of College Football at 33,000,000, Major League Baseball at 30,000,000, College Basketball at 25,000,000 and so on, down to Pro Boxing at a crummy 5,000,000. This is "1972 U.S. Sports Attendance" they're giving, not as profit-ledger significant as *paid* attendance maybe—and certainly no bottom-line plurality without concurrent sales of caps, headbands, bumper stickers and bobbing-head dolls—but significant nonetheless. "Amazing But True!" exclaims author Norman H. Kietzer but I'm neither amazed nor incredulous: I wasn't then and I am not now.

'Cause what's the 35 million ultimately represent? Let's say you've got a hardcore of 10 million wrestling fans, or had one in '72, a low estimate either way but all you need to pack in 35 is each of 'em hauls ass and goes live 3.5 times a year—a reasonable assumption. I mean even marginal fans go *at least* once per average year (to a battle royal, for instance), more than has gotta be the case for baseball, football, tennis or whatever. Factor in all the *occasionally* gungho azzholes like myself (I went, for inst, to *every* Island Garden card in West Hempstead, N.Y., from '57 to '59, *every* Madison Sq. Garden show from '72 to '75, every *weekly* Olympic bash from late '75 to early '77, and though I currently watch maybe 80 football games a year I've *attended* but one since '78) and 3.5/per is a no-sweat cinch—and we're not even talkin' those hundreds of thousands of weird fucks who're so beyond cycles of interest they (and their families) go *every* time. And you want availability of product? These guys still rassle 300 times a year; draw a circle around *any* major burg and there's gotta be (even *post*-dryout) 5–10 shows a month within 100 miles; probably more. Multiply dah dah dum by dah dah dee . . . you get the picture. '72, '85, whenever: demonstrably superpopular.

All that's going on is Vince Jr. performing insidious thus-&-such with this legitimate mass popularity at its base, structurally redistributing the remaining world's access to its variables & whatnot 'til he gets to have it All and Then Some—conspicuously. VHF, UHF, cable, closed circuit. Ads for jeans and Valvoline. Headbands, sweatbands and posters that fit *exactly* on the bedroom doors of suburban New Age 12-year-olds. Aesthetically coequal competitors—many of whom his dad even played quasi-friendly ball with—cringing, sighing, crying in his New Age mega-capitalist wake. Which, apropos of comebacks, is akin to Columbia Records buying out WEA, MCA and Polygram (or undermining their promotion, distribution, etc. 'til they're down 'round the scale of India Navigation and SST), prodding Springsteen, Michael Jackson and whoever-the-fuck to record five albums/each a year and listing them at $22.50 (everything else, $18.95) . . . and hailing *that* as a glorious comeback for American Music.

Palm Sunday, guys! And gals and gimps and toddlers. The L.A. Sports Arena—hot outside, cool within. WrestleMania. You've seen the hype, now here's et cetera. On a big fucking SCREEN from Mad. Square Garden.

8,257 (announced attendance)—a sellout. Mean age: 14 (not a minute over). Whole *gaggles* of kiddies w/ daddies or guardians or uncles. More whiny, noisy, screamy, stand-in-your-way little bastards than at a baseball game; at least they're not dressed like cubscouts. You know how at baseball they think every fly ball is a home run and they scream and prance accordingly? Well this is worse—and the triggers are endless.

Clusters of hippies, punkers, yuppies, guppies, unaffiliated sports dodos, less than half of one percent blacks (even with Junk Yard Dog on the bill) and almost no Hispanics (even with Tito Santana). Blacks have always been too hip for this shit; Hispanics, who used to make up 99.999 percent of the local wrestlegoing public, and always seemed *incredibly* patient wading through all the Chavo Guerrero/Raul Mata/El Azteca blandness the Olympic would sometimes feed 'em, are too hip—finally—for anyone even *named* Tito Santana. Especially at 12 bucks a pop.

Twelve here, and a whopping plopping HUNDRED at the Garden. For ringside. Here it's 12 everywhere—all seats, all sections, up in the corners where the screen's this narrow slit at like 20 degrees, down behind the projector on this scaffold where the thing's straight on at 90, only 40 tons of metal are in the way—all marked at 12, all *un*numbered for seating. As if a computer couldn't just, y'know, number 'em and then everybody wouldn't hafta show up two hours ahead just to scramble (if the doors're even open) (they're not), otherwise line up in the frigging heat, stand stand stand for an hour, get the kids ready to *scramble* . . . then *be happy* with wherever you've got. EVERYBODY'S happy (so I am blue).

I'm sitting at 50° next to this guy from Orange County who keeps telling his boychild, 10, not to lean on him so much, to (even though it's his birthday) lay off the male-male affection. "Johnny!—we're NOT at home!" Nope, you, him, me and another million-point-two (WWF figure) 're out TV-ing in public at some 200 locations nationwide—minimum of a million (Associated Press). The sound stinks, the picture's none too bright, light streams in through a curtain every time a wee one runs out to buy a wiener or take a whiz, but, still, there really kind of sure/maybe/almost has never quite been ANYTHING—in the annals of wrestledom (as opposed to boxing) (or Evel Knievel)—quite like THIS. This big, this bigness-y, this pompous/ponderous, this TV-plays-itself-quite-so-BIG-ish, this definitively ONCE-and-probably-never-ever-AGAIN. Or something.

Back in '76, for inst, the Muhammad Ali-Antonio Inoki *mixed* boxing-wrestling hoop-dee-doo (for the World Martial Arts Something or Other) managed to get closed-circuited from Tokyo into venues like the Olympic as the first half of an all-nighter topped off locally with live (unmixed) wrestling, but it sold for shit, most of the customers were boxing fans anyway (so they split in a huff before the wrestling even got started), and mainly the damn thing was just a big boring anticlimax, 'cause for some reason they opted *not* to pre-orchestrate it, figuring the great Ali (who once claimed Gorgeous George as a major thematic influence) and this Asian superduperstar could wing it themselves—no such luck. So that don't count, and at the scale we're talkin' it's the only precursor.

TV—of any size screen—and wrestling have had a constant if herky-jerk relationship since the late '40s. Steve Allen's first TV gig was announcing it; gameshow buzzard Dennis James did same, on the Dumont Network (one of the original Big Four), for something like six years. Also on Dumont was Jack Brickhouse, a "legit" sportscaster before, during & afterwards, play-by-playing it from Chicago's Marigold Garden; CBS and NBC both ran it—in PRIME TIME—as did ABC as late as September '54. Now you've got all this syndication and cable, and there's always been, whether live, tape or kinescope, plenty of you-name-it from mass- and multi-regional down to micro-dot in-studio local/nonexistent, but at ALL times the *function* of tele-vised wrestling—other, of course, than (ad-inducing) entertainment *now*—has been the setting up and telegraphing of grudges between designated combatants so's to spur live gates (here, there, everywhere) at shows featuring *un*televisied contests between 'em; no other sport has sold itself so well by means of the airwaves, or rather so *exclusively* via same. (The Dodgers and their greed-ilk, sure, but never with such synchronous wit or transparent downhome malfeasance.)

Anyway: the Payoff. Snake bites tail—untelevised is televised—heavens gape wider than pussy as one-million-plus prepare to bear witness. The Absolute unfolds Itself. The gift of fire (it's a *drug*, y'dig?) to Man. Which'd probably be as exciting as hell if you gave half a fuck.

The "Woodstock of Wrestling" is what our bigscreen guide Mean Gene Okerlund is instantly calling it. (Better they should pitch a ring on Yasgur's Farm.)

Anyway, underway. Some Wrestle to go with the Mania. Transmis-sion's on time—roar roar ROAR—1 p.m. Pacific Standard. Like clockwork ticktock-work the prelims just *go*, whatsis following whoosis in an unbroken string of interview/pre . . . match . . . inter-view/post . . . bang bang bang bang bang. And the kids're just as re-lentless, hoopla-ing way out of proportion for so early on a card, *any* card, like it's an NBA championship (or something) with every basket, every rebound and dribble additively *counting* even in the first two minutes. What do these kids know that wrestling *ain't* additive?—the least additive (or numerically logical) of sports.

Only surprises before intermission—6 matches total—are the an-nounced time of King Kong Bundy's demolition of Special Delivery

Jones (9 seconds, when clearly it was anywhere from 45 to a minute-
30, like why not call it *8* seconds or maybe a nice round 5?) and Nikolai Volkoff & the Iron Shiek's tagteam triumph over goody-goody
champeens Barry Wyndham & Mike Rotundo (could it be Vince's
plan to work these sickening purehearts—their theme song, "Born in
the U.S.A."—as *underdogs* for a while?) with a vital assist from manager Blassie's rhinestoned cane. Two out of six is prob'ly okay—I'd be
a dickbrain to expect more—so I get a beer to ease me through the
Total Descent (down, y'know, the Toilet) which once they rewind the
clock is sure as fuck to follow.

And does. First, Andre the Giant's body-slam outing with Big John
Studd. For weeks or months or years Studd and manager Bobby "The
Brain" Heenan have been waving this wad of lucre—a *big* wad—some
or possibly all of the 15 thousand big ones to be given the man who is
Man enough to body-slam the Big one. For weeks or possibly months
one or the other of 'em has also been toting the famous bag-o-hair,
Andre's hair, from the time they knocked him cold and snipped him, a
somewhat *necessary* backup prop as what's a mere $15,000 anymore?
Two weeks ago at the Sports Arena they had *neither* in hand for Studd
& Ken Patera's Texas Tornado Match (two tagteams, no tagging, all
four in the ring simultaneous) versus Andre & Junk Yard Dog, must've
mislaid 'em at the hotel or on the plane or somewhere; this keeping
track of details *bicoastally* is a bit above the bean of even whizzes like
The Brain (apparently). With the very reputation of the WWF at
stake, however, both sets of objects (or reasonable facsimiles) are this
time *on* hand, *in* hand and waved at camera. After which: the anticlimax of the decade—if not the afternoon. Andre and Studd face off,
make contact, puff, pant, retain grips, sweat, grunt, waddle slightly—
an unmatched pair of vertical sofas—and after *many* minutes of no fan-
fare, no calling of shots, Andre finally just lifts his sofa and slams him
. . . big fugging deal. Interviewed, the victor (*worst* interview in the
WWF—mumble mumble w/ a French accent) (but kids loooove him
so promote him from Quasimodo to quasi-main-eventer) almost *cries*
he is so sincerely touched—mumblemumble/sincerely—touched and
tickled that kids and grownups have gotten off on his sofa toss, gotten
off/dancing prancing and 'scuse me while I puke.

Next: Wendi Richter-Leilani Kai. For the WWF—yawn, hum—
women's crown. Not an *a priori* bummer or any of that, wimmen's
wrestling is a perennial drag mainly 'cause there've never been
enough of 'em at any one time to make it halfway interesting. Right
now there's like three-four females on the whole entire WWF circuit.

Kai's manager, the recently (and perhaps only temporarily) retired Fabulous Moolah, was gender champ when I started watching in the '50s. By pre-Big Lie standards this is a match of minor import at best; even in earlier incarnations of wrestling à la Vince it would never have figured higher than a third or fourth prelim on some shithook off-month bill. Yet here it is semi-main on the Bill of Bills, and Cyndi is to blame. Granted you might not've had an actual concrete rock-wrestling Connection—so-called—at least not the *official* horror the thing is currently saddled with, had not Lou Albano made a guest appearance in one of Lauper's videos (and History proceeded from there), but to reward her by letting her "manage" a WRESTLER, any wrestler, is a bit flugging much. And since Vince's vision is still too, um, symmetrical to allow her a role in the ongoing career of some simpy unmanaged *male* like say Ricky Steamboat (let's see her tie her 1943-version "New York accent" around him!), we're stuck with the spectre of a WWF Women's Title that won't, despite severely limited battle drama (and even more limited personnel), GO AWAY. Women's wrestling at its try-hardest self-exceeding *best* is never really a whole lot more than dance (*non*-ironic choreography) per se, and these folks—present company—are basically ersatz models cum aerobics-class'ers anyway, so 'scuse me this time if I don't even WATCH as Lauper's Richter beats Moolah's Kai, though no way can I avoid HEARING, postfight, the voice of '43 (makeup of '78) sound off blah-blah whine-whine bluh-bluh/TRIUMPHANT.

Okay, *one* more.

Main is not the word for this event.

Which probably—easily—could have carried the whole doggone shebang by itself.

Which everyone's been adrenaline-rush WAITING FOR all day including *my*self—'cause (once complete) it just might put X months of sorry, weary bullcrap in the fridge.

Roddy Piper . . . and . . . Paul "Mr. Wonderful" Orndorff . . . versus . . . Hulk Hogan . . . and . . . Mr. T.

Which . . . You Saw The Hype—bit the ballyhoo—read the reading—but in case not 'tis just the damndang OUTGROWTH of MTV's "War to Settle the Score" (during which T, a ringside *bystander*, rescued both Lauper and his old pal Hulk from Piper, Orndorff and their "bodyguard" Cowboy Bob Orton), itself a growth of when Piper kicked both ass & insult, during Dick Clark's presentation of some stupid AWARD to the raven-haired ditz, on not only Cyndi and her stooge Albano but her four-eyed *music* manager David Wolff.

Wolff (if memory serves) wore a neck brace for awhile; Hulk met T on the set of *Rocky III*: collaboration in one acting milieu—and now another.

WILL SLY STALLONE COME CHARGING THE RING TO RESCUE T AND UP THE ANTE ANOTHER NOTCH??

Christopher Reeve as Superman?

Adam West as Batman?!

Lou Ferrigno as the Hulk per se?!!!

Fat chance—don't mind me dreamin'!—the thing's got anticlimax writ all over it. At least from a mixed-medium standpoint. Vince certainly hasn't scrimped on celebs (Billy Martin, ring announcer; Muhammad Ali, guest referee; Liberace, timekeeper—though not for King Kong Bundy), but delivering 'em so heavy, gummy, gooey up front pretty much forecloses the likelihood of *additional* onslaught by outsiders. All the better: simpler, easier for his designated insiders (plus one) to get their date w/ destiny quickly the f over with.

And quick it does in fact go. WrestleMania's already into its third hour—the things we've got to ENDURE to write the last wrestling piece—and kids by now're *jumping* so you gotta stand t' see, but truly it's quick and almost painless. Except for the sight of Ali swinging combos at not only air but air in WHOSE vicinity?—has he been coached?—he who not only paid wrestling its ultimate COMPLI-MENT (Gorgeous George made me who/what I am), not only supplied it with 14 lifetimes of viable if misreadable INFLUENCE (creative integrity, *absolute* creative integrity, qua bombast—personal expression being screamed even when whispered, therefore SCREEEEEEAM!!!!) (read by Nouveau Wrestling as: "How to Use Television") ("... and Count the Bucks"), not only belongs *enstatued* in any and all Wrestling Halls of Fame aside from being, all things considered, the *least* gratuitous cipher of all-things-wrestling (for Nick Tosches in *his* last wrestling piece), not only was Mr. T once HIS bejeweled bodyguard, not only not only ... Ali should NOT be dealt with in such superficial, non-thread-the-needle fashion. Otherwise no pain.

T has been taught some tricks—headlock, snapmare, airplane spin—other TV actors should be so lucky. Hulk and Roddy do their usual dance, hack/cornball and topically familiar, Grenada/Nicaragua as fabulous *accidents* of me-you hostility (which *Reagan* the actor could pick up some functional cues from: kick ass, eat shit—one & the SAME!) (so let's fucking eat it). Standard wanton tagteam jollies—how to police four guys goin' wild?—until finally Piper hireling Cowboy Bob Orton, cast on his forearm, bangs cast with full force on the head of *whoops*, ALMOST Hogan but not quite: Orndorff! The Hulkster, hammerlocked by Orndorff, MOVES, ever so slightly, as Orton bops his v. own man—ouch! out! party's over!—whom someone (or other) pins for the win, the V, the end of WrestleMania.

While Piper and Orton split—toot sweet—to let him regain "consh" in the presence (sole) of his ENEMIES. What a rude, modern awakening! What a beyond-the-scope stripmine of the trans-WWF subsconscious!

More to the point—consciousnesswise—NO! BLOOD! has been spilt the whole entire goshdamn day: a wrestle/rassle first. Never before so sanitary, so ultra-considerate of suburban rugs & linoleum.

And I may be a *putz* but I'd rather 've seen 2¹/₂ hours of great interviews.

THE FUTURE OF AN ILL 'LUSION—more of Same at least until winter. *Saturday Night's Main Event*, subbing monthly for *Saturday Night Live* reruns, spring/summer, NBC; a Hulk Hogan *cartoon* (isn't he one already?), Saturday mornings come fall, CBS.

But a backlash may be brewing. The entertainment-industrial complex is not, as a unit, all that firmly behind its new partner-in-schlock's center stage aspirations. David Letterman seemed ten times as snotty with Mr. T the "wrestler," guest-promoting WrestleMania, as he'd conceivably have been—at his existentially *most* ill-tempered—with T the "actor," promoting some shitty movie or a new season of *A Team*. Even on *Saturday Night Live*, guest hosts T and Hogan served as little more than token-trendy walk-ons, showing up in no skits except as themselves, even though Hogan in particular, in spite of all the bug-eyed grandiosity, is a *far* better comic actor than any current *SNL* regular. Like he well may be (from certain angles, in certain lights) an overinflated, hyperventilating Martin Mull doll, but he's still got it all over your Martin Shorts and Billy Crystals—therefore use him but *subdue* him.

And then, the topper so far, the belated foofaraw of Richard Belzer (rhymes with Meltzer) after Hogan, in the process of demonstrating a sleeper hold, dropped the fatuous comic, host of cable dogshit *Hot Properties*, on his head. Speaking by phone the following day over Stanley Siegel's *America Talks Back*, Belzer presumably stumped for All Entertainers when he said: "Our only weapons are our wit and our minds, and we never physically impose ourselves on others." Yeah, but didn't his ma ever teach him not to trust his person to monsters?

What soon may make for problems, however—Real Problems—is the glaring fact that *in* the ring, one-on-one with the biggest and baddest of *professional* opponents, the Hulkster is no less imposing. With the possible exception of King Kong Bundy, who's either being groomed as his Rival Apparent or merely being readied for a round of pattycake with Andre the Giant, he really hasn't got *dick* to square off with. Even Piper, as delightful a fuckface as one could demand in a foe, is just too puny—231 lbs. to the Hulk's official 305—to continue commanding Hulkoid credibility without the Orndorffs, Ortons, whoevers forever woven into the plot. And let's say, for argument sake, you take the search *outside* the cozy confines of the WWF to peruse, for a Hypothetical Contender of suitable dimension, the register of the nearest promotional rival, Verne Gagne and White Sox owner Eddie Einhorn's Pro Wrestling USA. Okay: WWF bailout Sgt. Slaughter, 310, physical enormity plus sado-military oompah—perfect. Only he's a good guy now, and will be as long as soldiers of the red/white/blue are regarded by schooltots as he-ros. He'd *never* pull a First Strike on the Hulker, and how else could the thinning blond Come Back in all his bug-eyed, calorie-scorching awesomeness? Okay: Ric Flair, Jerry Lawler. Baaad guys, fine—at least the last time I looked—vainglorious muhfuhs to the frickin' *gills* . . . but not much bigger than Piper. 243 and 234, respectively. So I dunno, even on imaginary drawing boards it's a Problem. Bigger Lies will hafta be concocted. (Or maybe I've watched too much boxing.)

Which is why I prefer wrestling INTERVIEWS: all voice boxes are anatomically equal. Or close enough.

PHONY OR FAKE?—John Stossel still can't know the half of it. Goes up to David "Doctor D" Schultz in the waning moments of an embarrassingly deadpan wrestling-is-fake segment on ABC's *20/20* and coyly solicits the 6-6, 270-lb. on-off switch (always locked *on*): "I have to ask you the *conventional question* . . . "—as if the guy reads Derrida or subscribes to the *New Yorker*—"is wrestling fake?" For which, not surprisingly, he gets whapped in one ear, then the other, after which he claims "loud buses" make his head ring; Babwa Walters commiserates. Poor John.

JUST IMAGINE, on the other hand, if he'd slithered up instead to some windup stooge from *Dynasty* or *Matt Houston*, or some ABC movie of the week about teen pregnancy or white-collar alcohol abuse, and axed 'em, right after they'd shot some typical maimer of the human fudnugget (on the income from which they could wine, dine and toot far, far better than the king & queen of Belgium), "Lemme just *hit you* with this one: How do you um uh *relate* to the possibility that you have, just now, willingly participated in the complete, utter, wanton and systematic falsification of Reality as even a cactus would understand the term?" I mean not *every* recipient of the query would punch the dork's lights out (or even snarl menacingly), but automatons do have their pride, and after this one not even Babwa would be around to commiserate.

How role-playing robots behave under sudden fire is hardly the issue, though. Nor is the "veracity" of newsman Stossel's presentation (fixed! fixed!) before getting whapped. As umpteen-year wrestling partisan Bill Liebowitz puts it: "Why doesn't he do an exposé of Doug Henning? So it's done with wires and mirrors! So he's not really a sorcerer! I mean come on."

Come on, indeed; some targets are too fat even for a laugh. The nightly news, for instance—show me a more *malignant* forcible orchestration of metarealities. Wrestling's 200 worst Reality crimes are benignly pale in comparison. But fat is fat, and I won't touch it. What it *does* behoove me to touch, howev, and get all testy about is Letterman's treatment of T in sequence with the *rest* of that night's show. Right after T they had this newcomey actress person, some raving loon I have still not seen in her fucky-wucky film with Madonna so who am I to comment, but she sure seemed like e-z fodder for Dave to mock the living *fluid* out of minutes after doing same to T, Rosanna Arquette. I mean maybe in fact she's a veritable *bee's knee* of the big wide silver screen—anything's poss—although nothing like that ever stopped him from lickety splitting for obvious jugulars, never stopped him before and here he had all these cues *flying in his face* and all he did was act POLITE, CHARMING and APOLOGETIC (for a joke he *rescinded*). Like maybe she was just his week's quota of gals to be nice to, but it seemed purt near obvious, what with her and T juxtaposed like that, that when the chips were down, with personal squaresville "image" on the line, Letterman the Not-So-Nihilistic can always be counted upon to ally himself—on a dime—with one convenient strain of showbiz sham, one fly-by-night manufactured reality, over a slightly more topically disposable other. Contempo cinema over ringside pus!

At which point T if he was any sort of *real* wrestler would've surged back onto the set & split massive hairs for the viewing world to see. Realer wrestler (and realer actor!) Andy Kaufman would've done it automatic.

ANDY KAUFMAN: the Rosebud in rassling's attic. Who, you may recall, once got himself a late-night "busted neck" (courtesy of Jerry Lawler) the so-called *authenticity* of which we may never truly know—'cause now he's dead. Everybody's got a theory; mine stems from when Allan Arkush set me up with the guy while directing him in *Heart Beeps*. I had this treatment I'd done years before with my pal Nick for a blaxploitation wrestling pic called *Soul Stomper*, and Arkush thought Andy'd be interested. Would've been—maybe—only the thing (7 sketchy pages) didn't stress, quite to his satisfaction, didn't *underline* enough that wrestling was f-fixed. A structural purist, he wanted things right-on correct from the gitgo, nothing a neophyte could read as ambiguous. So my own initial read on his getting piledrived by Lawler was he'd either (a) misread the extent to which Lawler's "knowing that *he* knew the code" would make things functionally palsywalsy (wrestling-as-*dealt* being to Andy the selfsame matter of Honor that wrestling as primal grope had been for my gramps), affable enough on a co-insiders' plane for his brother-in-spirit not to betray him (a slight variation on Stossel/Belzer) or (b) he'd already opted to *become* wrestling.

When, in the last year or so of his life, he began appearing regularly *as* a wrestler on Memphis TV, occasionally as a sap bad guy who could not do zilch to save his pipsqueak butt, but more importantly as a *great* interview ("You're all rednecks! I'm from Beverly Hills!"—i.e., carpetbag archetype city), the half-guess of (a) became more and more a vanity of cranky Empiricism. With the neck-grudge against Lawler fully in context as a rite of wrestling passage, and King Kong Bundy's present manager Jimmy Hart as his squeaky-intense "advisor," Kaufman tossed off some all-time *wonders* of squared-circle shtick. Like I've seen this tape of what's gotta be his greatest public moment, something so amazing that Richard Foos at Rhino, who's already got distribution on the great-enough (despite crummy sound) *My Breakfast with Blassie*, oughta waste no time in securing home-cassette (if not theatrical) rights to, a testament to Hope—and Glory!—which our world of pain could surely use a dose of.

What happens is this. Kaufman, in street clothes and a silly rhinestoned crown, paces aimlessly outside the ring during a tagteam match involving Hart-managed bozos when suddenly Lawler emerges from the wings to hurl "fire" in the face of our carpetbag anti-hero. He writhes on the ground. Hart's boys leave the ring—and are instantly disqualified—to selflessly come to his assistance. He writhes some more, hands covering his face; (first rule of First Aid) they strategically restrain him. After much delay a stretcher arrives to bear him away. Hospital reports are flashed over subsequent matches. Finally at card's end the hospital-treated Kaufman appears, "burn marks" on his never-exactly-handsome mug, conventionally bound "scripts" in his mitts. "DeNiro . . . Pacino . . . Robert Redford"—he bitterly lets 'em drop—"*all of them* wanted me in their movies"—gasp, pant—"but because of YOU, Lawler, I will never work in Hollywood again!!" Followed by an obligatory "I'm gonna GET YOU!" and who knows, maybe he never did get to make another pitcher.

Anyway the *real* Rosebud in this monkey farm is did he or did he not already know he had cancer? Because clearly, absolutely, Wrestling was hardly just another warmup for him, another cold-reading class, a craft-honing actperson workshop—or even a more radically advanced waiter gig at the Bagel Nosh. That sort of hooey might have had meaning for the Andy Kaufman of *Breakfast with Blassie*, a journeyman bloke (with a strong sense of irony) role-priming his licks as Stanislavskian setups for rants by the Great One. Taking the plunge, committing to Wrestling as IT, he *became* Blassie—or a screamingly brilliant facsimile. So what we need to know, vis-à-vis possible death-knowledge, is was this (by choice) his literal Final Stand?

Someone must know.

HOLD THE PRESSES—Orndorff too. Has just fired Bobby Heenan & become a good guy. Abandon all hope—the show is *over.*

110

One White Man's Opinion

Yeah, this is the article alluded to in the intro to the opening section. I've thought about it and thought about it, and I don't feel like waiting for it to fit "better" in some other collection—it fits fine here.

This is one I didn't have to go to San Diego for.

Keeping up to date with the, um, opinion, and tryin' to give it a little musical specificity, the older I get the clearer it seems, for whatever it's worth, that the white SIXTIES more directly stole from black musical sources than even the fifties (when in large part what was lifted was basically just some rockin' attitude and temperament, a lusty mammal orientation, y'know a certain body freedom, with an identifying dose of musical hyperbole attached, and the bulk of what music qua MUSIC was stolen was simply plagiarized, and poorly at that), if only because white musicians had in the interim gained the chops to more thoroughly filch, purloin, appropriate stuff.

And ditto for the '70s and '80s, especially among arena-rockers—every mega-rehearsed guitar asshole—Mark Farner, Ted Nugent, Eddie Van fucking Halen—whether the appropriation is first- or secondhand at this stage hardly matters—until the black reservoir just gets so submerged, by being so on the surface, who's to comment on it anymore? Unless, of course, you're Stevie Ray Vaughan and reveling in it.

In more recent times even, oh, let's say Sonic Youth, insofar as it's at heart just another guitar band, is skeletally indebted to blues licks that predate its existence by 70 years. Couldn't exist without 'em. It exists verywell, meanwhile, w/out a lingering TRACE of that other avowed wellspring of rock, C&W. (As plain as day.)

Without the black "contribution," there really ain't much meat on the bone. (Wrestling would be the metaphysics of something pretty bloodless.)

What would be left, Billy Joel?

L.A., May 4

What it's all about—pure and simple—is *white* man's inhumanity to man.

All I see is a noose tightening tightening tightening on the neck of Black Underclass America . . . of Black America, period.

I've lived here, in this idiot airless town, for 17 years and have never for a moment felt the slightest stirring of anything you might call civic pride. Through the goddam Olympics, through winning Laker and Dodger seasons, through all these superimposed film and arts festivals: nothing, never, far from it. Not until, that is, the second day of the uprising, the "riot," when suddenly like lightning it hit me: this was its finest hour! The heroes, the martyrs, trashing and torching the town!—taking their wrath beyond the ghetto, from Bullock's Wilshire to the Farmer's Market to Beverly Center to Frederick's of fucking Hollywood, saying loudly, clearly not even just No (which itself would have been a monumental achievement), but a very unambiguous Something: the system doesn't work . . . even the system of oppression doesn't—can't—always do it. Against super-daunting odds: their finest hour. If I had photos of every black and Latino martyr killed by cops, by feds, I would put 'em on a T-shirt and wear it every day of my life.

We've heard quite enough, thank you, about "our courageous police officers"—these bastards who (even if on orders, and even if the orders arose from a collective fear of death) (why do you think they get such incredible pensions, huh?—if they don't risk death, if that's not what they're in fact THERE FOR, who *needs* their bullyswagger shit?) did nothing for the first two—the first 24—hours. It wasn't till it all came north and west to the white neighborhoods that the response was worth a hill of beans. Even just judging from TV, every channel zooming hither and yon to get the latest-greatest helicopter shot, you couldn't miss *nohow* the LAPD's abject refusal to come and "aid" the ghetto the first night, and its piss-in-pants rush to secure white districts throughout the second.

On Normandie near Florence, what a sight: 30 armed cops fleeing 50 civilians in the opening moments of the rebellion. Any shrink'll tell you: bullies are cowards.

Somewhere during the second night, Thursday, the torch came within a block of my apartment house in a rare integrated neighborhood considerably north of South-Central. I'm not sure when it happened—the view out my window is just another building, and the shriek of sirens, the ratty whirr of copters, the thick pinch of smoke, from blazes far as well as near, were constant round the clock. (Four days later, the sirens and the copters haven't really stopped yet.) Sure I felt fear—hey, I don't wanna die, I don't even want all my silly stacks of paper especially messed with—but the fear was overwhelmed by a total sense of rage, so throbbing in my gut, my face, my chest, that if they'd gotten my street I'd've felt no additional anger, certainly none directed at THEM: if their ass, as the Simi Valley verdicts proclaimed, wasn't worth a dime, then nobody's ass was worth a dime. My rage was their rage.

Their grief, their rage *is* my grief, my rage.

L.A. TV's vilest hour (every channel, every newsperson, no exceptions): from naked live to edited fake in no time flat . . . from realtime interviews with anyone and everyone (an enraged Hispanic woman calling for the head of "that motherfucker," Daryl Gates . . . Ice-T before a monitor image of a burning warehouse: "What they really wanna be venting their anger on is cops") to canned Q-&-A's with acceptable "voices of reason" . . . running bullshit graphics like "The L.A. Riots" and "Violence in the Streets"—instead of "Travesty of Justice" or "Racism '92" or "Gates's Grim Harvest" . . . airing *The Cosby Show* for ratings and social control.

The racism continues—how nasty can these news cretins get?: insulting without letup the ongoing casualties of injustice . . . characterizing the participants as thugs, hooligans, hoodlums, anarchists, animals, bad people—not even, y'know, "suspected bad people"— purveyors of ugliness . . . calling the rebellion "senseless," i.e., lacking sense (when what could make more sense?), pretending not to understand Why, not even copping to the fact that if you treat people like dogs they eventually BITE—this from the medium, the industry, that gave the world *Lifestyles of the Rich and Famous.*

The mind reels: that they could designate as a hero a black guy who rescued a white guy, then another who rescued an Asian—which is fine, dandy, swell of course (credits to their, um, race)—but at no time, not even for the sake of symmetry, a black (or even a white!) who rescued a black! Black life still not apparently being life that officially counts . . . infuckingcredible. (How *dare* they insult people so!) Hey: in *my* experience at least, blacks have *always* been the likeliest Samaritans.

And reels: edited shots of the South-Central cleanup, early, before some whites joined in to "help speed the healing process." Over images of black men and women sweeping up, performing a *historically familiar* menial task, a white voice speaks approvingly of the "good people of South-Central" . . . time for a rerun of *Beulah.*

And reels: barely a mention of Latasha Harlins, whose unredeemed death could easily itself have been the straw that etc. but wasn't (how supremely *patient* these people really are) (and how 'bout Eulia Love, for chrissakes?), dealing with racial persecution solely in terms of Rodney King (i.e., something isolated, something *new*), playing timorous voice-overs by Simi Valley jurors and concluding: "See, it wasn't racist, it wasn't w/out, well, deliberation." *If they say it, it's so.*

A really sick line from channel 9: "At this point, thousands of arsonists are clogging up the criminal courts system"—get fucked.

But maybe toughest to swallow was this: that none of these jackjills, opportunity knocking like a migraine from hell, expressed a dust mote of outrage that a document from their own merry medium, an 81-second *un*funniest home video—and one unedited at that—I'm talking Rodney and the cops—could have been so discredited as to evidentiary oompah, self-evidence, Truth . . . that, this video's brutality forever logged in their crania, they could then show a white trucker getting stomped and not utter—scream—the phrase *déjà vu.*

Consider: the thoroughly OBSCENE prospect of TV footage being used to identify and convict looters, trashers, bashers, bystanders, etc. (and thus once again underscore whom—and at penalty to whom else—the system truly "protects and serves").

RODNEY KING THE MAN: the vulnerability, the humanity, of this person . . . as seemingly overwhelmed by events of the previous two days as by his own beating . . . what courage in appearing at all— Jesus! . . . prob'ly the first guy on TV to that point to evince genuine unrehearsed *pain* for the dead. Young, shy (which I can relate to, being shy—and once young—myself): shy 25-year-olds have *reason* to occasionally take drink. Switching channels Friday afternoon, I missed the intro the first time he was on and didn't even know it was HIM, and yet everything about him, his words, face, bearing, BE-ING, turned my eyes to fucking oceans. The destruction, the dismantlement, of a human life: Jesus god . . .

And to then trivialize and exploit even *this* footage of the man by playing it every hour in a cheap appeal to "cool tensions" . . . what ruthless fucking shit.

The force the swine used on Rodney King would have been excessive if he'd killed their mothers with them as witnesses. Denial of due process is denial of due process—even criminals are protected by the Constitution. Most of the framers had been designated criminals themselves, remember?

I've seen the LAPD bust rock bands for the crime of plugging in, harass white *seniors* for slumping on a bench in 100-degree heat. Every couple years they shoot and kill a *naked* person—no weapons, dig— for "striking a martial arts pose." Given sufficient time, cops in this city would kill anybody (everybody!) for spitting on the sidewalk. But in the short run they're fifty times, a hundred times, likelier to do it if you're African-American, Hispanic, Samoan, anybody dark-skinned, whatever.

Don't know 'bout you, but one thing *amazing* to me is that in the immediate wake of the verdicts they couldn't—in the name of "public safety"; as a token of mercy to an afflicted community—sacrifice even this one wretched piece of pus, Daryl Gates. At a cocktail fund raiser against Charter Amendment F (which, gee, would put *one civilian* on a police misconduct review board), he skipped the first couple hours of action, BY DESIGN letting the ghetto burn, then showed up in uniform like Ollie fugging North to hurl insults at its inhabitants, babbling about their "agenda of ten fires an hour," blaming a "Mexican criminal element." Mayor Bradley, the City Council, the Police Commission—why couldn't they just corner him and say: "Resign, you evil beast, or we'll rip the nose off your face"? Not even this small *crumb* (qua crumb) tossed to people of color . . .

All that is likely to follow on the "police reform" front is more mean, ill-tempered cops, more repression.
   "More crime" too (after the "recovery")? Sure, since the poor will have only gotten poorer, the angry angrier, the desperate desperater—and with it a police state to end all police states (but "American style," natch—with its predictable mini-quota of *permissible freedom, allowable dissent*).

And even if they did (by some miracle) reform the LAPD, you'd still have Sheriff Block to contend with, and all the various local Southern Cal PDs . . . fat chance.

The notion some share that "good will come of this" in the form of "increased sensitivity to racial issues" is hogwash: somewhere else, maybe, but in L.A. it can't and won't last more than five minutes. No memory and no mercy, L.A. is, and for a long, long time now has been—in terms of implementation and influence—the most rightwing major town in America—the goddam Bible Belt has nothing on this place. Not only does it rob from the poor and give to the rich for *breakfast*, zone, segregate, and isolate its minority neighborhoods like South African townships, preach money-worship like you wouldn't find even in Vegas, treat labor like so many underfoot insects, aerial-bugspray its own urban residents, little things like that: its most widely disseminated homegrown product—film—has been churning up and *exporting* racial intolerance, revising racial history, creating and perpetuating noxious stereotypes for over three-quarters of a century.

This is where the biz made Griffith's tribute to the Klan, *Birth of a Nation*, '30s blaxploitation forerunner *Harlem on the Prairie*, and *Charlie Chan in Egypt* (in which Stepin Fetchit plays three castes down, at least, from a Chinese and an Egyptian—both caricatured by whites), and this is where they make 'em still. Though these days Hollywood seems to be picking more on Asians and gays, and though some black directors like Spike Lee, John Singleton *et al* have been getting budgets, some control and whatnot, it hasn't stopped pumping out loathsome claptrap like *Mississippi Burning* (wherein a gallant FBI—in what world was this?—takes up the proud sword of Civil Rights), *Driving Miss Daisy* (once again: the slavish fidelity of an honorable black man to White Destiny) (and yet another "meaningful role" for an underworked black actor—black actors gotta work, and most Hollywood roles, for anyone, are demeaning, but *c'mon*), *Weird Science* (for non-ironic comedic purpose, surly white kids mock out the patrons of a black bar).

Do I even need to mention all the GOOD COP movies released annually? War enlistment adverts like *Top Gun*? Smarmy hokum like *Pacific Heights* (tenants as criminals, landlords as saints)? When was the last *love story* made here that kindled and stoked the cold fires of "truth"? Blah blah blah—what was I getting at?—oh, right: Hollywood rules the hearts and minds of locals at least as severely (and cavalierly) as it does those of hicks from some theoretical sticks. And after the *de rigueur* five minutes of topical "race-sensitive," "poverty-sensitive" films, I can't see it giving a duck's ass on Mars about the fate of the black man, the poor man, any man (qua man). When a major studio funds a black L.A.-based *Battle of Algiers*, then I'll stand corrected. The only conceivable role for Hollywood through the coming "renewal process" will be to help L.A. LIE ANEW TO ITSELF.

And that lie will be next year's (next Tuesday's) breakfast food.

Racism at large (example 552): white drivers in L.A. are a good deal less likely to stop at crosswalks for black pedestrians, Latino, virtually anyone of color. My own observation is they *usually don't*.

Exacerbating the divisiveness: the LAPD letting Koreatown get hit without even the illusion of a response.

Although: dunno if standing by as Korean businesses got torched was the result of an actual divisiveness *strategy* or of a police mindset which perceives Koreans as less-than-white too. Two-thirds the latter, one-third the former? Dunno.

Violence? Violence as an *issue*? After Bush blows the breath out of 200,000 Iraqis? The entire history of this country is built on violence—we erect statues to killers, we put 'em on stamps—starting with George fucking Washington, that slave-owning, potsmoking "thug." The language of this country is BLOOD. In the last five years, more blacks have been killed by American authorities than the total of *all Americans killed in Indochina*.

"Looting"? Our Euro predecessors looted this land from the Indians, plundered human lives from African soil to work it . . . when, I ask (I might've missed it), did they or their descendants ever settle either of *those* accounts?

Robin Hood (and I don't mean Kevin Costner) was a "good" looter—remember?

We're talking about people who with whips to their back, guns to their head, have built this country, clothed and fed it, cleaned its toilets, raised its children, suffered its directed sadism and degradation, given it the only indigenous (post-pre-Columbian) arts it's ever had, jazz and rock (only to see others reap the lion's share of profits and

praise), bestowed upon every sport they've touched its essence-flaunt-
ing power chord and grace note, its utter crowning *Americanness*
(ditto), given us "hot," "cool," taught us more about "style" than a billion Parisians, been the republic's moral barometer through all
weathers, all seasons, its only true pillar of even *conventional* virtue . . .
these are generous people, Jack! . . . to have, for the past 400 years,
endured slavery, wage-slavery, rape, pillage, lynching and myriad
baroque forms of abasement and discrimination, to have expended so
many unrewarded lifetimes, so much perpetual energy, in the service
of those who would in turn characterize them as "shiftless," "lazy"—
building the Pyramids was easier than what they've had to endure . . .
and after how many times? how many times? how many endless cycles of frustration, despair, waiting for payback, never a payback,
never a break-even, economic injustice, social injustice, political injustice, judicial injustice, they're lucky if they've got an asshole left to
shit with . . . after all THIS, and more, this event you call a "riot" is
hard to comprehend???

Violence "against one's own community"? When there's no way out!
no way out!, what the bloody deuce do you do? Haven't you ever,
when emotionally cornered, dug your nails into your wrist, slapped
yourself in the ear, smashed a favorite cup against the wall, lashed out
at those you truly love? Y'know: spontaneously done "something self-
destructive"? Never, you say? Well, you're lying. (Or have so submerged the role of feeling in your life that you're ice on ice—in a
vault—at the bottom of the sea.)

This is a city so culturally without a clue that even *graffiti* is considered an act of violence.

"American family values"? 70% of all violent crime, 80%, some such
number, is committed in the family. The American family—the *white*
American family—is a nest of coiled serpents, a den of rabid wolverines.

From the White House, from the corporate board rooms on down,
this country cares about NO ONE: racial minorities, religious minorities, women, children, gay people, old people, poor people, working people, the unemployed, the uneducated, the educated, the
handicapped, the incarcerated, the formerly incarcerated, the artisti-
cally creative, veterans of its own goddam wars—anyone without a

white face, a home in the suburbs, $75,000-plus a year, and a job that brings death to the planet.

A class war in general; a race war in particular. MANY of us are leaves in the American wind; those of us with melanin to boot are dry leaves in the fury of Hurricane Georgie. Come boom, bust, heck or high water, blacks as a group will always be the first ones inched, urged, shoved off the raft.

A recent study shows black college graduates as having roughly ONE-SEVENTH the chance of *equally skilled* white applicants of being hired for a cross-section of given vocations . . . so what chance for the underskilled, the systematically underschooled?

Job market for L.A. blacks: soldier, cop ("trades" that seek to tap—and encourage—their alleged violent tendencies), guy who has to take three buses twice a day to change the grease at McDonald's.

From a tenuous spot on the lowest rungs of "the ladder" to suddenly finding the rungs're underground . . . black and homeless, forget it, who at this point's even gonna spit on you? As karmically deserving as white society at large certainly is of another Great Depression, an Earthquake (the Big One!), then again, all such a scenario would summarily mean would be fewer scraps still for an expanding *under*underclass.

In this country right now, the top 1% have 65% of the wealth: grab them by the heels and shake them. How can those who own America see any other writing on the wall?: redistribute the wealth, the power, the opportunity, or rot in everlasting hells beyond imagining. Anyone who has been a billionaire—a millionaire—a minute has been one long enough. No one is chronically rich without exploiting unto death the chronically less-so. Tapping the "private sector": take the first 30 billionaires in the phone book and pick every pocket in their closet of 10,000 suits. Tax their dicks, their eyes, their livers, their shit. Trade their Rembrandts, their Rollses, their wine cellars for ten million units of quality low-income housing. When Ross Perot liquidates *everything*, gives every penny to the inner city, and dresses like Gandhi—*then* maybe he can run for dogcatcher.

Tapping the public: scrap the fucking space shuttle . . . the White House Christmas tree . . . let the prez and his missus make their own beds . . . call Super Bowl winners at their own expense . . . pay for their own security . . . no more genocidal wars against Third World countries (the last of which cost us 42 billion) . . . *eat* the B-2 . . . stop underwriting the Army-Navy Game . . . REINSTITUTE GRADU-ATED INCOME TAX . . . REPEAL PROPOSITION 13 . . . no more scenic gardening for Southern Cal freeways . . .

Every winter we're tube-fed our annual dose of *A Christams Carol.* This film version and that. If the Ruling Class can't face *its* ghost of Christmas past/present/future and cop at last to being Scrooge incarnate, it's time they shelved all versions right along with *Ishtar* and the made-for-TV Karen Carpenter film.

When was the last movie *these* cocksuckers "took to heart," *Patton?*

Pete Wilson comes to town quoting Martin Luther King and leaves saying, "Oh, let's cut welfare by 25%." Can't he even as a mere good-will *gesture* drop such bone-nasty bullshit, announce: "Oh—my mistake. Bad idea. What ever could I have been thinking? So sorry. Never again."

Too little, too late, but not even *that.* What scum!

The Reagan-Bush feeding frenzy—greed greed greed!—the rich get richer, the poor get even poorer, lock the vault and throw away the key—never in a million repeats of this sordid dance will anything worth mentioning "trickle down"—so what's a little *petty* greed (looters getting, say, a non-essential couch in addition to quite essential groceries and Pampers and shoes) compared to that? I am sick of all this compassionless tripe about people on welfare. Where the hell do you think welfare dollars ultimately go if not deep within the coffers of American business—agribusiness, petrobusiness, the jean and sneaker business, etc.? Food, rent, utilities, clothing, transportation, medicine—"recipients" don't get to keep it!

A PIECE OF THE PIE . . . to look in store windows, to every time you turn on TV, be shown gaudily, garishly what you CAN'T HAVE . . . let's hope some people scored big. Even if a few who hit Fedco and such places were actual, y'know, "thieves"—professionals—thieves deserve a break sometimes too, thievery's as tough (and dreary) a job as any high-risk other . . . did anyone score an ATM?

Some looters as "opportunists"? Okay, sure, but none like *these* jerks and their riot-centric career moves: Edward James Olmos, Geraldo,

Arsenio Hall, Tom Petty, Jerry Brown . . . even Sonny Bono drove around w/ Jesse Jackson!

Pepsi and Sparkletts getting millions in free publicity outside a South-Central post office where hundreds waited to pick up checks when mail service got canceled . . . do it *every* Friday for the next 20 years, then you're talking. Not talking much, but talking.

Bush's War On Drugs. *What* war on drugs? All it is is a war on the poor, a war on civil liberties. By no stretch of the imagination can the federal government, can the collective governments of this country, even *hypothetically* want drugs out of the ghetto. A drug-free ghetto means open rebellion every day, an ongoing War Against Oppression.

Besides: people take drugs because life *needs to be altered.* Do you know anybody who hasn't taken drugs? *I* sure don't.

There is no drug as harmful—as lethal—as television. Betcha California's next scheduled execution of a *black man* gets televised. Or if not very next, soon, eventually.

Capital punishment as cruel & unusual punishment? For America's young black men, a quarter of whom live life-as-dealt behind actual bars, whose tax for being is being confined, IMPRISONMENT is cruel & unusual punishment.

In 1974, in the aftermath of Rockefeller's Attica massacre, Charles Mingus recorded "Free Cell Block F, 'Tis Nazi U.S.A.": well it certainly does right now seem to be. And I don't even mean metaphorically. I'm talking real, total, no-joke capital-F fascism. *Genocidal* fascism. There are differences of course, just as there are differences between our current state and the one coloring-booked in *1984.* Big Brother, for inst, doesn't always watch *you.* Instead, you servilely watch *him* on a monitor *you* pay for—more cost-effective, and ultimately more effective. Likewise, without even constructing ovens, African-Americans do appear earmarked for extermination. Without government spending an additional cent—and isn't that the point?— black life is being systematically—acceleratedly—marginalized, cheapened, removed from the drawing board, starved to extinction. A disposable underclass, more disposable than ever, access denied to all viable means of survival. As the profit margin from capitalism-as-usual goes down, eliminate the minimum wage. New jails an extrava-

gance? Just pack 'em with a shoehorn in existing dungeons. They
want justice? Give them Clarence Thomas, who can help overturn
Brown vs. the Board of Education—how many weeks away is that?
Separate but equal . . . then separate and unequal . . . finally separate
and *nothing*: why expect the continuation of free public schools? Or of
nominally free two-steps-up-from-a-butcher (and lucky-if-you-can-
get-it) emergency medical care? Or of any form of public assistance
whatsoever—'cept for defense contractors and savings & loans? Ac-
knowledgeable problems will soon have *only* law and order solutions.
The only affirmative action will be more black police—beat on your
brother or perish. The physical ghetto will be further ghettoized,
turned into reservations—until the developers need new turf to gen-
trify, and then . . .

Is this Germany 1933—the stage we're up to? '38? Dunno. But if
Bush isn't Hitler, if Reagan wasn't Hitler, then Hitler wasn't Hitler.
(Unlike the setup with Hitler, however, Reagan/Bush's Court lackeys
will carry on an American Reich *program* long after its authors are
dust.)

To American whites: either identify and withdraw your complicity,
refuse with every sinew to cooperate, DO SOMETHING ABOUT
IT FOR CRYING OUT LOUD, or go down with Hitler.

This piece is *for* white people, obviously. Black people have known all
this garbage for years—and don't need to hear *my* whining anyway.

"White fear"?: then how 'bout some white remorse? If Germany
can apologize for the Holocaust—little or nothing that it means—
white America can confess, concede, acknowledge, repent, and make
nonstop restitution—economic, social, political, you name it—its priority for the *next* 400 years . . . short of that, fuck white fear.

And oh yeah—what to immediately "do about it," the fear. Simple:
give THEM, those you fear, everything they want, everything they
currently need, desire, ask for—on *their* terms—everything. HELP
them with fervor to squeeze the rich dry. If you're rich, you know *easy*
all you haven't done—do it. Get the scum who represent you in government to dismantle the system—all systems—that create, shape,
condone, maintain any and all forms of inequity; vote out the scum
who don't or won't. Boycott, divest from all businesses and organiza-
tions unwilling to voluntarily facilitate a reversal of ghetto fortunes
NOW. And by all means, stop watching television. Could anything be
simpler?

And what about *black* people's fear? The fear (for starters) that in the wake of The Verdict individual cops, *all* individual cops—independent of any "game plan"—have now been given a warrant to murder, maul, or at the very least humiliate them with absolute impunity.

A few nights of curfew? *Every* night, in too many white L.A. 'hoods, is curfew time for blacks (of any class). Drive too groovy a car, behave as freely as an extroverted white person, and the protect-&-serve boys will find an excuse and occasion to draw guns, instill abject terror, slap the cuffs on.

Arresting the HOMELESS for curfew violations: what hath God frigging wrought?? (There are now 50,000 homeless in L.A.)

Friday, outside a bank near my street, I saw an uppermiddleclass white woman make a four-year-old middleclass black child cry. The woman, maybe 50, well dressed, got so lathered over the bank being unexpectedly closed she threw a *fit*. Even without racial content, her craziness was upsetting. To the little girl, after two days of race-specific horror, she must've seemed a white monster. At the bus stop where they both stood, her mother hugged and shielded her from the sight.

White people wanting sympathy, pissed about any inconvenience: aw, *gee*.

One thing all too clear is that the cretins, 'scuse me, "public servants" whose policies, whose pathological indifference, whose continuing deeds most conspicuously fueled, kindled and further enflamed this thing—and will inevitably (if they're still around) fuel/etc. the next—don't even mind being hated. Powerful and privileged the OLD-FASHIONED WAY, they don't care *dick* if they're loathed: Gates, Block, Wilson, Bush (and standing in the wings cheerleading, Patrick Buchanan).

After Grenada, Libya, Panama, Iraq, how many years can it be before the entire non-U.S. world returns the favor?

Marines in the streets of L.A.: where have I seen this before? I wasn't here for Watts: the monster movie *Them*. (Giant ants in the sewer.)

"L.A. under martial law"—what redundancy. L.A. is never *not* under martial law (of one flavor or another).

Look: maybe I'm just a silly, fatuous (and ultimately presumptuous) whiteboy like all the rest, but my shame as a white man, my shame at *being* a white person, knows no bounds right now. I realize I'm prob'ly no better, no worse, for all that, than a "well-intentioned" white in South Africa: an outsider looking in, even if with a shitload of "compassion"—my commiseration, my pain, can't mean squat to anyone experiencing—directly—the full-throttle malignity of white-supremacist barbarity. If you're black and reading this and I'm talking nuts, please tell me and I'll shut the fuck up, never say so much stupid stuff again, but I don't feel right now it'd be a significant loss if, at the finger-snap of some suddenly vengeful or impatient (or merely whimsical) god, the white race and its entire history were erased from the human record. Homer along with Mussolini, Jackson Pollock along with Margaret Thatcher, Shakespeare along with Daryl Gates—there is simply, all told, not enough approximate Good to outweigh the Evil; all the alleged former put together will no longer outweigh the single massive white cleated boot in current dominance of our land: to erase the whole damn slate as if it had never been a shimmer, a glimmer—*poof!*—a longshot solution if ever there was one.

By which I'm not talking, not suggesting—oh, wipe 'em out, wipe *us* out, any of that . . . I'm merely thinking/saying on my feet that I've had enough pain even *thinking* about white plunder and blunder. For half a millennium now, the "white menace" has lain waste to entire continents, cultures, systems and icons of wisdom and belief, animal, vegetable and human totalities, you know the story, and it's just simply time someone else ran the show. Let 'em even run it wrong, let 'em do the *wrong* thing from here to eternity, and that would be just fine with me. It's simply THEIR TURN . . . their turn for everything . . . their turn to have *their* self-interest dominate, to never again have to talk like, dress like, act like their oppressors . . . their turn, even, to have *their* lies (should there be lies) believed, or if not believed, then to have their lies *rule*. Hey—I'm no utopian: when black lies are as cogent as white lies, *that* I'd be willing to accept as justice.

It is their turn, if that be the number, to have absolute power, and be absolutely corrupted by it. The damage inflicted could be no worse than ours.

In the meantime, and in any event, African-Americans have retained far more of the courage, far more of the goodness and wisdom, of *their* ancestors than we as Euro-Americans have retained of ours (if they ever had it). Let's grant that maybe Socrates had it (y'know, *maybe*) and if so follow his opening tack (in The Apology) after being tried and convicted of thought crimes against the Athenian state. Given the option of selecting his own punishment, he says, "Okay, give me a pension"—or maybe it was a new school, whatever—to which they shake their heads, come back with: "How 'bout ostracism?" (No go, he finally chooses hemlock.) Anyway, my proposal is this: Give those citizens and subjects of L.A. who actually Did This, rose up bravely on April 29, 30, May 1 and beyond, those still living, should they be caught, come to trial and get nailed; give them as their punishment (and directly to them, not to some handpicked coalition of uppermiddleclass black and Chicano Republicans) at least the following: Beverly Hills, Bank of America, two of the four TV networks, controlling interest in CNN, chancellorship of the UC system, complete control of the L.A. Unified School District . . . that's just for *instance*. That would be a penalty to fit the crime.

WHORING AGAIN?

Introduction

But the *S.D. Reader* wasn't through with me. Less than a year after terminating me from doing what I didn't want to anyway—write about muse-ic, too often, though as far-rangingly as I wished—they phoned with the offer of a job even less appealing, for less money, one calling for me to write about it as *narrowly* as it gets, and more often—an offer I resisted with every sinew for at least a minute before relenting ('cuz god I was BROKE).

The pitch: every week I would author a blurb, a preview—hype!—for a rock concert in San Diego. Oh, the torment. Not only had they punished me already for the sin of billing 'em for CDs, but here they were back again, as if in cahoots with ALL theys, bum's-rushing me back into rockwrite servitiude. As a last futile gasp, I explained that I no longer knew the fucking bands, even by osmosis—the "20–30 promos a year" mentioned a little ways back had dwindled to zero—but they tol' me *not to worry.*

Oh? Won't it matter, I asked, if I haven't even HEARD of an artist, a band? *It won't matter.* Are you saying I can make it all up? *You can make it all up.* May I froth with contempt for superduperstars? *You certainly may.* Is it a problem, not living there, that I don't know any of the clubs and such? *No problem.* Is it okay to piss off the ones that advertise? *'S okay.* Can I say *nothing* when I've got nothing to say? *Sure.* So what's the hitch? *You gotta be entertaining.*

Well, I guess I could do that. But how 'bout if I use a pseudonym? *Y'can't.* Not even Borneo Jimmy? *Nope.* Audie Murphy, Junior? *We want you for your name value.* Ha ha ha.

I, blurbwriter!

And all I gotta do is mention the band by name, at least once, so they can highlight it in boldface. About a month in advance I get to see the list of who's upcoming and pick from that. The choices are mine, solely. (I try to avoid San Diego bands, but just looking at names you can never be sure.) Though all I'm required to produce is

100 words, I've gone as high as 300. Some weeks I put a lot of work into it (the "craft," y'know). It's not *too* different from things I did in the early '70s, but WITHOUT FREEBIES. (On those rare occasions when they send me a CD—for "reference"—they always demand it back—for their "files.")

In a perverse way, there are times it's almost, well, fun . . . amusement . . . like I'm walking through the whole thing again, only in a dream (one not *usually* a nightmare). Or like I'm not really doing anything present-tense at all, just recycling—like any rock-roll scoundrel—some of my better hotlicks from before most readers were born . . . "playing" a rockwriter, or more precisely: an atypical rockwriter, the sort of rockwriter I *used to be.*

Sometimes I reuse copy from the '70s—verbatim, except for the name change—who's to check up on me? Or I'll find some old note on a card that I can't recall ever using, but which is so good I can't believe I didn't, so maybe I did ("Coin toss in a binary universe. Heads: they're good. Tails: they ain't. Heads it is")—either way, use it NOW.

And it's always a kick bringing my "sister" Koko and my "late wife" Cora back to help me.

But why am I speaking in the present tense? Because, dear reader, it's my CURRENT GIG. They haven't bounced me yet. Must be 'cause I come so cheap this time. (Wanna know what I'm paid? It's the cube root of 421,875 . . . in dollars.)

Am I a whore—or just the world's biggest mark?

All things being equal, unequal, unfair, never fair, though fairer perhaps than most people get anymore, do you know how it MADDENS me to still be writing such dogsucking @*&%$#?+=! thirty-plus years down the road?

Don McLean, 10/12/96

Don McLean was born October 2, 1945, which means he's been around for MORE THAN HALF A CENTURY. If you think it also means you'd better go see him while you can, y'know before he croaks or something, my guess is there's really no hurry—you've got another 20 years to think about it. This is one rock-roll jackjoe who is not fond of danger—doesn't sky-dive, doesn't shoot opiates, doesn't even smoke them—and his music is safer than he is. (Makes Stephen Bishop look like Iggy Pop.) Yet he makes more in a week from the air-play of "American Pie" on oldies stations in Utah than you or I make in a good year at the pus factory—and he needs US to sit and wiggle for his road-show folly? If he wants our approval let HIM pay for it . . . fuh.

Railroad Jerk, 11/22/96

In his musical prime, blind jazzman **Railroad Jerk** often played two, and sometimes three, reed instruments at the same time—usually tenor sax, manzello (something like a curved soprano sax), and stritch (something like a straight alto). While certain tightass critics labeled this a gimmick or worse, it not only made sonic sense but as an "over-lay" of instrumental textures seemed (in 1962) quite comparable to what Jasper Johns was doing with overlaid canvases. In retrospect, it would probably not be too farfetched to identify Jerk's work as an early example of topical Postmodernism.

An overblower of the first rank, his tenor solos were quirky master classes in circular breathing. Also one of the great flutists in jazz, its only nose-flutist, and a pretty good judge of personnel, he assembled groups responsible for such fine recordings as *We Free Kings*, *Rip, Rig and Panic*, and *The Inflated Tear*.

Even after a stroke paralyzed one side of his body, Jerk, by then billing himself as Rahsaan Railroad Jerk, courageously carried on. Continuing to perform until his death in . . . oh wait a second—all bets off—I was thinking of *Roland Kirk*.

Geggy Tah, 1/4/97

A a a also and answers, appeared Are are Asking away! band, be best better birthplace blue? boat but by certain combo desire. did Diego, dispute Does don't e entry ever excel eyes forget, from, from? Furthermore, **Geggy** get greatest have have help I (I in in Into is is is It just know). last left like many matter may me mega Merry musical never never New night! not of of of off on one ones or or otherwise, out Pennsylvania, people person? places. played pluribus presumably pure questions repeat: run San say Scranton, several shake showtime single some some speaking speculation, Stratford-on-Avon, strictly **Tah** talented that that, the the the the the the the their them. there they they they they things This this those though thousand time to to turned unsaid unum. visited well, were were where whether whiteskinned who will Windsor. Without Wives woods? wrote you you You'll your you're Zealand

Guttermouth, 2/7/97

Without exception, rock bands whose names form complete sentences have a leg up on the competition: They Might Be Giants, Dead Can Dance, Bill Wears Mary's Kotex, Kick My Mother, There Goes George Hamilton, Take Off Your Pants (I'm Interested), And Your Goat Can Sing, Blow Me, Vodka Comes to Cyberspace, Keep It!, Let Them Eat Plums, Let's Go Bowling, Donnez-moi Syphilis, Shoot the Polo Player, This *Can't* Be Snot, Whaddaya Mean? Whaddaya Mean?, That's a Fact, Fuck Thanksgiving, Stravinsky Influenced Nirvana, We're Having a Baby, Heroin Cures Cancer, Orrin Hatch's Puke Stinks Worse than Nixon's, A Tattoo of Christ and I'm Happy, Please Love Me Forever, Donuts Is Why, Sleepless in Seattle Meets Pulp Fiction, Glaucoma Is No Guarantee of Federal Funding, You Don't Know Poop from Chef Boy-ar-dee Macaroni-O's . . . all esteemed combos, all musically outstanding, and **Guttermouth** is no exception.

115

Ventures, 3/1/97

Mrs. Geoffrey Bagadoogian of Mission Hills writes: "I was appalled to read in last week's *Reader* the tasteless assertion that your sister is no longer living. I know Koko very well, bump into her frequently at Fashion Valley, and let me assure you she is not only alive but kicking. Your claim that the Demolition Dollrods are her favorite band is equally groundless; she told me herself she has never seen—or heard of!—these bozos. Of all the nerve!"

Well, Mrs. B., thanx for the info. I haven't actually seen my sis in, oh, it must be 10-12-15 years now. Naturally I *assumed* she was dead—I stand corrected. As to the Dollrods, well, that was just a wild guess on my part—sorry—a deadline was approaching and heck, anything's possible (she always did like dolls). I *know*, however, with complete certainty that her favorite band of all time is the **Ventures**. (Shoot, they're everybody's.) Get Koko to show you her "Walk Don't Run" tattoo—right above her left buttock.

Idiot Flesh, 3/8/97

For voting, to a man, for Ed Fitzhenry, the Socialist candidate for mayor of Akron (his slogan: "Redistribute wealth—that's what it's there for"), **Idiot Flesh** deserves our continued support. You may, howev, believe that art and politics don't mix, and prefer an alternate means of gauging this band's ultimate worth.

ANAGRAMS can tell you all you need to know about anything—at least as much as a Ouija board or a blurb in this sheet—more than you may indeed want to know. Some gnarly 'grams for appraising Idiot Flesh:

I shot, I fled . . . idol fetish . . . I.O. the IFDS (haven't paid my dues to the Int'l Federation of Dong Surgeons) . . . "To idle fish" (Voltaire's dedication to the Paris edition of *Never Enough Leg*) . . . i.e., shit flo'd (in torrents) . . . le fish do it (Cole Porter said so) . . . Idol fites h. (Billy battles humanity!) . . . id shoe lift (Freud's advice to shorties) . . . hot Elfis I.D. (his actual drifer's license) . . . he toils, I f.d. (he works, I fuck ducks) . . . she'd "O" if lit (get her drunk and she'll come) . . . I.F.'s "D" hotel (Stone's *last choice* in lodging) . . . the I.I. of LSD (its "intrinsic inevitability") . . . Idi to Lesh: F (Amin to Phil: an F-chord, please) . . . Lesh to Di: "If . . . " (when you get rid of that mama's-boy prince of yours, *maybe*) . . . life is d., tho (it's death—no way around it) . . . dies o' filth (worst way t' go).

117

Ruben Blades, 9/26/97

The cover of John Tesh's *Avalon*—have you seen it? The one where he's sitting/leaning on a railing looking down, way down—100's of feet up—at the rich bastards' yachts below? Actually, he's looking away—if he looked down it'd freak him more. And he *is* freaked—note the tension on his face, his silly beard caught in a frown, the avoidance of weight on his right outside hand, the left hand balled in a fist. Thoroughly uncomfortable, he isn't even *fake* comfortable, and this is one jerk who does fake very well. Seems only a tad less nervous than Klaus Kinski in *Aguirre: The Wrath of God*, the shots where he's on the raft wearing all that armor—one false tilt and ker-plash, he ain't coming up.

So tell me—who would YOU like to see push John Tesh over the edge? President Clinton? Sheryl Crow? Robert Rauschenberg? Porter Waggoner? The ghost of John Fitzgerald Kennedy? There are many good choices, but after careful consideration I nominate **Ruben Blades** to do the honors.

What—you think he's too nice? He *is* nice, very nice—we would all, I think, enjoy a pizza and Cokes with the Panamanian charmer. But did you see him in the worst jazz movie ever made, *Mo' Better Blues*? Plays a baaadass, real bad, orders a hit on poor Spike Lee and Denzel Washington's trumpet hand gets in the way. Ouch. (Almost redeems the film all by himself.) *That* Ruben Blades is just the man to send Tesh to his—ahem—reward. Could and would—and in some alternate universe most assuredly WILL, God bless him!

Pat Benatar, 11/28/97

ROCK DEATHS THIS WEEK: Art Garfunkel (stroke), Van Morrison (smallpox), Doug Sahm (suffocation), Sid Vicious (cirrhosis), John Densmore (exploding TV), Rod Stewart (multiple stab wounds), Jimmy Page (kidney failure), Bernie Taupin (OD), Nick Lowe (tongue cancer), Mark Mothersbaugh (crushed by falling safe), Donovan (pleurisy), Howard Devoto (bladder cysts), Marie Osmond (allergic reaction to margarine), Bob Seger (ulcerated spleen), Roger McGuinn (ritual torture death), Wild Man Fischer (Lou Gehrig's disease), Phil Collins (suicide by ingesting ammonia), Olivia Newton-John (drowned in bathtub), Ian Dury (esophageal hemorrhage), Belinda Carlisle (contract killing), Suzanne Vega (complications of routine appendectomy), Richard Hell ("natural causes"), Meatloaf (AIDS), Johnny Cash (eye illness), Jim Carroll (syphilis), Phoebe Snow (drank raw sewage), Toni Tennille (rabid owl bite), Bill Laswell (ax accident), Jello Biafra (murdered by nurse while being treated for prostate ailment), Keith Moon (lung cancer—never smoked!), Diana Ross (tainted tetanus shot following fishhook removal), Lulu (heart attack while attending porn film), Cat Stevens (don't ask), Steven Tyler (deviated face).

STILL LIVING (but don't bet the mortgage on it): Roky Erickson, Chubby Checker, Ellen Foley, Mimi Fariña, Alex Chilton, Dallas Taylor, Shaun Cassidy, Elvin Bishop, Flea, Eek-A-Mouse, Linda McCartney, Mars Bonfire, **Pat Benatar**.

Life of Agony, 12/30/97

Open letter to Mark Casta, who didn't dig my review of his band some months back, and recently cussed my ass in a letter to this sheet:

Hey, dumbo, if you don't know a RAVE when you see one, I can't fucking help you. What I did was try and get "into your head" and expound upon its glorious et cetera. If you haven't *got* a head, sorry I gave you one.

If making a fucking record—in nineteen NINETY seven—isn't its own reward, you're in the wrong business—not to mention the wrong life—and have an endless haul of bitterness to look forward to. Treasure the fact of getting anything done at all, and don't wait for the likes of me to validate your achievements. You say you've got airplay on 105.3—well, lucky fucking you. I haven't got airplay on dick—do you see me crying to *you*?

As to your claim that I didn't *listen* to your CD, I certainly did—it's fine. (As fine as any 200 or 300 others that come out every year.) If you don't care for my "abstract" manner in expressing same, tough turkey, asshole.

Nobody owes you anything, especially not on *your* dotted line, and as far as "windows of opportunity for getting reviewed" go, gee, I can sympathize. I write books, great books, I've worked for this sheet for 12 years, and never once has anyone here reviewed one. The fact that nobody, in fact, READS ANYMORE hasn't deterred me from continuing to write . . . it's my choice, Jack, and similar choices remain yours.

Do your fucking job and don't complain. Be a real band—like the Agony of Life, excuse me, **Life of Agony**—and in 50 years, if you're lucky, you'll be DONE with this wretched waste of cosmic malice some fools call a gift.

Total, 1/23/98

Get your tickets early!! Of all acts worldwide in 1997, **Total** finished 12th in concert box office, with the highest overall percentage of sell-outs.

Heading the list is Garth Brooks, who last year sold out 270 of 273 shows, grossing $600,312,265, with a paid attendance of 11,061,321, followed by the Clash (115 of 118, $365,765,330, 10,117,015); Frank Sinatra, Jr. (106 of 108, $341,244,976, 12,433,281); Paul McCartney & Wings (79 of 81, $335,846,237, 9,238,296); Neil Young (240 of 248, $263,086,931, 8,476,553); Foreigner (75 of 118, $252,660,889, 7,999,495); Burning Spear (100 of 120, $230,782,525, 8,350,422); the Cowsills (98 of 213, $215,809,652, 5,738,551); Gloria Estefan (57 of 60, $195,217,270, 7,679,160); Michael Bolton (15 of 350, $183,800,000, 1,140,258); and Steppenwolf (43 of 70, $176,620,914, 6,725,939).

Total, the hardest-working bank—make that band—in showbizness, performed 370 times in '97 and sold out 368 (99.46 percent), with 17,109,038 fans shelling out a respectable b.o. of $151,569,850. One of those sellouts (June 31st—Captain Cook Day—at the Brisbane Metropole) produced the fourth largest single-day body count in arena-rock history: 310,540. Like I said, shop early.

Irish Rovers, 3/16/98

Did you know that since 1985 there have been 317 deaths from black lung directly attributable to toil in East California coal mines?

To underscore this grim fact, the **Irish Rovers** recently played a miners benefit in Danby, where their set consisted of "Blue Suede Shoes," "High School U.S.A.," "My Way" (Sid Vicious version), "Cop Killer," "The Blues in the Night," "To Know Him Is to Love Him," "Ubangi Stomp," "Volare," "Quiet Village," "Mashed Potato Time," "Mia Farrow Took A Dump in the House Where I Was Born," "A Fistful of Budweiser," "Your Wild Irish Arse," "Gemini Rising, Aquarius Slumming," "Li'l Bro's Abuse Rag" (a/k/a "The Pull-It Concerto"), "Yipes! Mr. Ipes," "(I Am) Queen of Uranus," "Testosterone and Toothpaste," "The Love Generation Conquers Fear," "Electric Donut," and the anti-heightist anthem "Hold the Mustard, I'd Rather Fuck a Dwarf," the last 11 of which were written—words and music—by my late wife Cora, who succumbed last June to lung-related maladies of her own.

As the benefit was a huge success, a percentage of the take has been set aside as the Cora Clark Meltzer Memorial Mining Scholarship, cosponsored by the AMW—Associated Mine Women—of East California, which she for many years served as assistant mine secretary. The initial recipient will be named between sets of the Rovers' first local appearance since 1966. Be there!

Anne Murray, 5/17/98

BLUES LECTURE WITHOUT SLIDES!!
As no photos are known to exist of Little Hat Jones, Buddy Boy Hawkins, King Solomon Hill, Geeshie Wiley, Henry Thomas, Bullet Williams, Six Cylinder Smith, Otto Virgial, Hi Henry Brown, or the Mississippi Moaner, the subjects of her latest pre-concert country blues lecture, **Anne Murray** will this time be spinning sides and discoursing without her usual slide accompaniment.

"It was bound to happen sooner or later," says Anne, referring to the finite pool from which she has drawn her previous principals, such stalwarts of '20s/'30s lore and legend as Robert Johnson, Charlie Patton, Blind Blake, Peg Leg Howell, and Funny Paper Smith, each of whose features fortuitously endure in black & white likenesses. But even without pics, her commitment to "roots" music is to be commended.

"Where it all comes from is the B-L-U-E-S," says she who gave the world the classic 12-bar "Snow Bird." (How true, how true.)

My only suggestion: Ms. Murray's lecture voice can at times be monotonous, so bring along a walkman if you don't feel like listening.

Fourplay, 6/15/98

Oh boy oh boy oh boy: Tantamonny Souczek is coming!!

That's right—Tantamonny Souczek, "Society Maestro of the Finger Lakes," whose inimitable big-band stylings have been synonymous with "music" for half a century. Star of seven Inaugural Balls, most recently that of George Bush, where he "wowed" them with his tasty rendition of "Sink the Bismark," Souczek is not one to rest on his laurels, ceaselessly changing with changing times. Due to the current popularity of the "twist," whose fame has filtered down (and up) to all levels of American society, he has added arrangements of "Peppermint Twist" and "Twistin' Six-Guns" to his already colossal repertoire. This will be a good opportunity as well for us to check out the virtuoso theremin of Waldo Wasserman, soon to retire after 37 years with the Souczek organization.

What?—Oh no! Tantamonny Souczek has been hit by a beer truck in Saskatchewan! Intensive care at Saskatoon General, IV's in his arm . . . will he pull thru?? . . . let us pray.

Music at such a time is only secondary, but one question must be asked: can **Fourplay** fill the maestro's mighty boots? Unfamiliar with their music, I couldn't even hazard a guess. (My apologies.)

124

Cigar Store Indians, 9/5/98

Just got back from Biloxi, where I had the pleasure of attending the opening of the National Soup Museum, and lemme tell you it is a *lulu*. Featuring more than 80,000 soups, the pride of such acclaimed purveyors of canned potage as Campbell's, Stouffer's, Heinz, Progresso, Eat-Rite, Soupco, and Ethel Merman's Gourmet Kitchen, this thousand-acre edifice is a marvel of exhibitional enterprise.

Most fascinating, perhaps, are the displays in the Extinct Wing, devoted to flavors which for various reasons have through the years been removed from company rosters. These include:

Olive and Watercress, Homemade Gull Chunk, Dawg, Maraschino Kidney, Wax, Cream of Pupa, Turkey Glutton, Olde Fashioned Gruel, Black Putty, Chicken with Starch, Pond Salamander, Blowfish Noodle, Sow Butt, Airedale Tenderloin, Badger Biproduct, Scrod Gill, Striated Mutton Pulp, Sour Barnacle, Sparrow Cauliflower, Cootie Broth, Puff Ball, Phlox, Spaghetti and Mole, Inkblot, Slithering Skink, Horse Nuts (yes—it's what you think), Rat Specks & Gouda, Cole Slaw with Bubble Gum, Creamy Prune, Stove Top Marigold, Imitation Penguin, Dutch Lipo, Pepper with Eel Guts, Lentil Banana, Gizzards with Talc, Bagel & Pizza, Marshmallow Owl, Tomato Coelenterate, Curried Slopwater, Montana Style Clam Chowder (not based on a dairy or tomato stock but—wouldja believe?—turpentine), Prenatal Chimp, Mock Roadkill, Puppy Eyes, Udder and Donut, Weasel Plop, Szechuan Pigeon Foot, Parsnip & Cricket, Steroid and Gluten, Whale Vulva, Aerated Mucus, Styptic with Toenail Bits, Toad Scum, Tartar Control Moth, Jogsweat Lite, and Fat-Free Pantyhose.

Of particular interest are the soups of the Wood and Paper Room: Oak Bisque, Mahoganny Puree, Balsa Barley, Redwood with Lard,

Sawdust & Pelican, Pencil Shaving, Spicy Spitball, Playing Card Gumbo (made from an actual "French" deck), and not one, not two, but three **Cigar Store Indians**: Painted, Unfinished, and Kaw-Liga (with a full-color likeness of Hank Williams on the label).

Great museum!

Joe Cocker, 9/24/98

Response to my report on the National Soup Museum has been immense. Of 41 letters received to date, the following is especially gratifying:

"As a fellow fancier of defunct soups, I too was pleased to see the category finally given its due. After further research, however, I have been disheartened to learn of many fine and excellent flavours of the past which did not make the museum's final cut:

"Plaster, Greasy Tulip, Gazpacho with Crud, A Fistful of Tabby, Bunny Clone, Ants in the Pan, Trichina and Rose Hips, Shellac, Alphabet Peacock, Creole Style Smack, Vitamin Enriched Wool, Make-Believe Strychnine, Football Leather, Baseball Lace with Ham, Spam & Eggplant, Absinthe Cuke, Centipede Camembert, Third Generation Denim, Skunk from the Crypt, Tiparillos 'n' Cream, Imported Sea Bubble, Pachy Strips in Vino, California Phlegm, Louisiana Snot Pot, Non-Endangered Koala, Murky Lemon, Trooper Ed's Bat Sausage, Jowl Time U.S.A., Goat & Oat, Irradiated Vinegar, Cup-o-Sand, Petting Zoo Stew, Meatballs and Bologna, Menudo and Creosote, Smallpox and Wolf Jizz, Purple Crayola, and the highly prized Borscht with Bunion Bits. Let us hope that in the future they will *all* be given their rightful place among the elites of defunct. Yours truly, **Joe Cocker**."

Joe Cocker? Joe Cocker? Could it be *the* Joe Cocker? The spelling of "flavour" is a giveaway—must be a Brit. *The* Joe Cocker! Gosh, I'm flattered.

126

Edna's Goldfish, 10/17/98

Contrary to popular belief, the 24 hours in a day are not divided neatly and evenly into 12-hour AM/PM segments, but into an AM of 11 and a PM of 13 hours, respectively. You would have to stay up on a lot of caffeine or controlled substances to notice, so personal demonstration of this fact is not advised. (For further information, see *Studies in the Adventure of Time* by Walter Walloo, Random House, 1926.)

In any event, every band worth its salt has an hour that is theirs, no one else's, and the hour of **Edna's Goldfish** is 4:13 AM: the hour to be *blue and troo and new (on cue)*. Few have been as blue, or as troo, or as new (on or off cue). You owe it to your "self" to check 'em out. Do.

Unfortunately, their Belly Up set will be over well before that time.

CURTAINS

Introduction

Is this it? This is it.
All things end and all things die and stuff like that.

Aren't you glad I've at no time tried to seduce or entrap you with an oboy-ogosh-rock-n-roll-come-and-get-it-yum-yum-yum! type come-on? What I've done instead is lure you into taking an interest in ME. Thank you kindly for putting up with my breath and my metaphors. For being so nice, these last two pieces are my gift to YOU. (Next time you're in town let's have a drink.)

But I haven't said a word about the wear and tear. The physical-emotional wage of the, ummm, addiction. Of what it's taken just to write my way this far. There are days when it feels like throwing a 300-pound basketball through hoops 70 feet in the air. On some mornings they get raised to 90 feet. Whether you have the muscle for it or not, the bones don't quite hold their form for such an endeavor.

A few more crumbs to get out of the way:

Everything has its moment, but over the long haul I'm really not sure: is rock my PRIMARY MUSIC, or is it jazz?

I haven't played anything classical in a couple years, I listen a lot to old blues, and think NOTHING in rock has the purity of Garfield Akers' 1929 "Cottonfield Blues (Parts 1 & 2)," by which I mean nothing but: its eerie pared down beauty and *fearsome* efficiency.

But I gotta say, if only because I can't keep my big mouth shut, that there've been x many times in my life where I've felt like I was about to TAKE OFF—like a rocket. Where I had this feeling of not only impending flight but vertical acceleration. (A breakneck break on UP not through.) Either I've been the rocket or just a passenger—it's the same rush either way. And every time I've felt this it's had some connection to rock & roll. Like maybe while it was playing I was in the throes of an escalatingly intense experience, or I was listening and suddenly found myself surging through a startling progression of thoughts that had never in any form crossed my mind before. So anyway, recently, for the first time since I started compiling this book, it happened AGAIN.

I was driving somewhere and this song comes on, dunno by whom, female, bang!, she goes into this torrid amazing stutter-riff, "my my my my *right hand*"—how fucking wanton!—20 times as wanton as "Peach" by Prince. Wanton and feisty and *desperate*. Except for the jive ending, the greatest rock song in 15-18 years: "Right Hand Man" by Joan Osborne, whom I never heard of ('cause I never heard of anybody). I'm driving as it echoes and *pounds* in my head, feeling: got to, got to—gotta buy a record? (how crazy). It was like thinking about sex, wanting it wanting it (minus only the hard-on, y'know, and the ejac)—gimme gimme. So I scrap all plans and zoom home, grab some shit to trade (four John Cage CDs) and head straight for the store . . . here 'tis . . . yippee. For two days it was the foreground in my dreams.

The rest of the disc was so awful I asked around, who's Joan Osborne? "She's not very good." "A 10th-rate update of *bad* Joni Mitchell" . . . I'd say more like 11th. Totally worthless, but on one cut, just by PLAY-ACTING WANTON, she pulls it off; accidents still happen.

Even if I no longer pay much attention to the music being issued in its name, I still verymuch operate from some convoluted variant of rockroll as a system of thought. *A* system!—the ultimate system—the one that eats its own guts out.

Rock (the system) has in too many ways been my means of using up philosophy. Of thoroughly exhausting thoroughness. ("I can't be thorough no more, honey, 'cause the world gone wrong.")

Well, that's it. Gonna try and get back to my new novel now.

Keep your powder dry, y'hear? (And doncha take no wooden nickels.)

127

Vinyl Reckoning

And now . . . my valedictory address. Or is it my resignation speech? (Flag of surrender?)

Deathbed blather, anyone?

Enjoy your summer vacation.

Things we've saved and saved and SAVED. For all the stupid reasons you or I or anybody saves things. You can't take them "with you," not all, not any, but chances are what's left is but a microfraction of the total heap o' shit that in the course of a life has passed through your prehensile puppy-paws. Gone is that copy of *Zap Comix* number three, and gone is the radium-dial Howdy Doody watch, and the actual puck Frank Mahovlich scored goal number 489 with against Toronto; and gone gone GONE are all the silly goddam STAMPS you once fervidly "collected," only a fool would hold onto *that* shit, and you're no fool, neither am I.

But you've kept the tattered squirrel hanky, right?, that old snotrag your mom hand-painted for your sixth (or was it seventh?) birthday, and the yellow plastic space helmet from 1953, *excellent* plastic like they don't make anymore—hard, not very flexible, like you think would be brittle, but 'tain't brittle—with a brim like on baseball caps—this is one dizzy helmet!—or if YOU haven't kept 'em, I know I have.

And oh, speaking of plastic: records.

As they always had previously, the last time I played the eponymously titled *Revolutionary Ensemble* (Inner City 3016), somewhere in the early '80s, the sparrows nesting in the vent above my living room gas heater responded to it. In the notes to that album is a poem about symmetries in music and nature ("The trees joyously wave their branches in rhythm with the wind"), and here was evidence in my own frigging home: birds don't just sing, sometimes they listen. As I was obsessed with cacophonous post-'60s jazz at the time—following the death of punk-rock, it's what I played even to wake up in the morning—it was nice to see the birdies share my preference, and for this particular alb they chirped like banshees. Chirping *with*, not against—although y'never know . . . this was four or five homes ago.

Dunno how they'd've felt about *Swift Are the Winds of Life* (Survival SR–112), an earlier recording by the Ensemble's violinist, Leroy Jenkins, with Rashied Ali—I never played it for them. All I know is Justine Carr didn't like it, and neither, not really, did I. Certain installments of Leroy's playing have struck me as shrill and toothy without real bite, neither shark nor bulldog teeth (like you get with Ornette Coleman's fiddling, for inst, or Billy Bang's), at most maybe greyhound teeth—and "romantic" in the annoying sense of hot & bothered yet austere—and this outing was one of them.

In 1976 or '7, to persuade Robert Christgau, my bag-o-wind editor at the *Village Voice*, to let me write about jazz (he considered me a "rock-identified critic"), I did a non-rock "think piece" in which I claimed, among other things, that increasing the aural input of jazz around the house will enliven (for example) your dreams and sex acts. With the latter in mind, just to test the premise with album X, I fucked and ate Justine—my number three or four all-time love object—with a side of *Swift Are the Winds* spinning . . . which *probably* didn't prolong my tenure.

(The piece never ran.)

At the absolute height of my collectional zeal, bloated by too many years on the promo-album dole, my LP stash numbered in the THOUSANDS. Three? Four? Five? I now own, well, hundreds— many, most, almost all of which I never play, probably *will* never play. True—many or most are scratched, warped, caked with beer, wine and fingerprints. But even among those eminently playable, there isn't that much turntable action. (I also have, oh, at least a thousand CDs—so what's new? My acquisitiveness appears undiminished.)

Thousands down to hundreds—for all the fine and stupid reasons I or you or anyone periodically tosses stuff. Every time it seems like I've hit rock-bottom, nothing left to toss, it turns out there's another item or five to weed out. In any case, it feels *mandatory* to regularly check the stack, and rarely if ever is playability, alone, a criterion. (It's far more neurotic than that.)

Hundreds; how 'bout we go for *fewer* hundreds?

Retaining . . . tossing . . . merely FUSSING WITH. Even with a drastically shortened stack, an unending chore.

In the fall of '66, I embarked on a simple mission: to expand the palette—the text—of philosophy as dealt at American institutes of higher et cetera by slipping massive references to rock-roll, psychedelic drugs, pop art, biker films, and other contempo-cultural wigouts into term papers, classroom discussions, and the Q&A's which followed lectures by celebrity academics—a reasonable goal, no? My mistake was in believing such a hoot would play the hallowed dungeons of the grad school at Yale, where the Mayflower fucks who ran the show would've shit in a teacup before letting my atheistjew contagion defile their ivied walls.

I didn't fare much better with my fellow philo students. In the waning weeks before my expulsion became final—already on probation, I could smell it coming—I'd invite these dullards up to my room, offer them pot (they'd decline), and put on some sides. Though I had everything by the Beatles, Stones, Dylan, Byrds, Love, most of the Kinks, the first Doors—it was the spring, by now, before the SUMMER OF LOVE—all they would sit for was "I Feel like Homemade Shit," on *The Fugs First Album* (ESP 1018). Those who had heard it before would tell newcomers, "Listen—here!—he's saying 'shit'!!"—underneath all the mock country harmonies and copious yodeling—then the newies would grill me, "Is this illegal? Could we all go to *jail* for this?" What a pack of cheesepuffs!—these jackjills who today teach our kids, or yours (I don't own, excuse me, have any).

In his *Metaphysics*, or was it *Physics*?—'s been so long since I read this crap—Aristotle speaks of four causes, none of which're all that close to how we think of cause these days, something on the order of *that which produces an effect, result, or consequence*—they're more like parameters of responsibility or even (in an old-fashioned legal sense) *liability*. Actually, one isn't too far off: efficient cause, i.e., whatever the hell brings a thing or event into being (for ex.: a maker or parent). He's also got formal cause (the form, shape, structure of the whatsit), final cause (the use or goal it embodies), and the most seemingly nobig-deal of the bunch, material cause (simply its matter).

Apply this bullticky to records, to the recorded-music EXPERIENCE, pre CD, and the material component—grooved, sculpted vinyl—more than holds its own. So supremely vulnerable is this whatzostuff, so susceptible to further onslaughts of form—resculptings, regroovings, smirchings and encrustings—that a whole hot WAD of variations on theme is table-set and served from the getgo:

Stations of sonic show & tell, shown/told . . . all the skips, sticks, jumps, hisses, cracklepops which document devotion, confirm get-off . . . "To love a record is to kill it" (the CD lobby speaking), but love or loathe, it's abuse either way . . . flat black plastic: as "interactive" as silly putty (or a slice of pizza) . . . wear-and-tear as index of both age and youth—the record's age and the object-management blunders of YOUR youth . . . ditches-cum-glitches fractionalizing, obliterating, rendering inaccessible even quasi-original sound, grave-marking its exit from this auditory life . . . (hey, I once got a used Sun Ra elpee, took it home and found a hole in it, not the spindle hole—a CRATER at the start of one track clear through to the other side) . . . books, by comparison, don't suffer such wear/tear in finite time, or rather, their wear/tear doesn't *normally* preclude continued full-bore interaction, doesn't annihilate lines, pages, whole chapters (or render them especially unreadable) . . . even in their DISPOSABILITY, a residuum of sonic potential: records as frisbees—the adventitious sounds of flight and smackup . . .

All penultimate to the final outpost of vinyl irony: the unit record, *irrespective* of its health or welfare, DECOMMISSIONED . . . freed of sonic obligation . . . serving no ongoing material function but to give body to a cover and sleeve . . . silenter than a Cage silence piece . . .

SOUNDLESS MERE MATTER.

The question is this: Have I saved the LP version of the Germs' *(GI)* (Slash SR–103) as an "investment," or as the one Los Angeles punk-era thingy I might wanna ogle and caress someday: my designated L.A. Punk keepsake? To make the rent, sure, I'd probably sell it for 50 bucks, no, it would hafta be at least 100—75?—but for now it's a keeper, even though the CD reissue, *Germs (MIA)* (Slash/London 422–828 808–2), sounds pretty good, pretty close. Which is something you gotta consider with digitalized analog rock—if you're thinking *replacement*—'cause all hype to the contrary, CDs do NOT sound better, and rarely anywhere as good. Even recordings not butchered in remix (eat shit, Paul McCartney!) tend to lose more in mere remastering (intangibles like "presence" and "warmth," in addition to simple aural *data*—the forest *and* the trees) than decades of surface destruction can ever take away. The fact is: pre-digital rock ALWAYS sounds superior, even with all the destruction factored in—

for moments anyway—enough to supply GLIMPSES, at least, of not only an *imaginably* better sonic world, but an actual preexistent one . . .

Anyway, PUNK as once upon a time actual . . . more than a metaphor . . . '79: a verrry good year. L.A., a worthless sucktown for just about everything else, had somehow become the locus for prob'ly the vitalest, most interesting assortment of punk groups in the country . . . a small miracle. Three-four nights a week I went and saw 'em play, and on Saturdays I hosted an all-night FM punk hoot where one week, from the sweaty palm of my guest, *Slash* mag editor Kickboy Face, I received a copy of the first 12-incher pressed by Slash Records. It was also Darby and company's first (and, as it turned out, last): a *perfectly* executed knee to the groin of life-is-a-gift precept and practice which today, nearly 20 years later, appears to have been the highwater mark of L.A.—U.S.—Anglo-U.S.—make that WORLD punk recording . . . this is it.

I haven't let the cover—shiny black w/ the famous Germs blue circle—go to seed, and even the taint of the woman then managing them, my v. worst ex-gal to that point of my life, worst as gal and just as bad as ex, one of the few exes I've never jerked off thinking about, whom in the wake of Justine Carr's ignobling departure I'd on several occasions lain with, has been insufficient to indelibly sully this sacred object.

There 're possessions I've housed (if not quite clothed and fed) longer, like I mentioned the space helmet, and once in a great while I'll stumble into my birth certificate at the bottom of some drawer—though I couldn't say which drawer it's currently in—so in a sense that's the oldest scrap of matter from my own lifetime, the oldest unit of CONTEMPORANEOUS matter, still lying around, as opposed to items whose actuality predates my first breath—boxing cards from the turn of the century, say—hoozits acquired more or less as curios, antiques. My skaty-eight hundred boxing magazines, which I began amassing in junior high, are under shoes in the closet, in cupboards over the sink, in cartons I haven't opened (or directly thought about) since 1980.

If that seems a longgg time—like excessive deadtime—I've got albums that haven't kissed stylus SINCE BEFORE KENNEDY—the first Kennedy!—got shot. Played or perennially un-, when something lingers that long, just eyeballing the damn thing oughta be good (if it's good f'r anything) f'r triggering the occasional ancient memory.

Because music has been so central to my, um, being, records are the only collective heap-o-stuff I've maintained continuous hands-on control of, and since played and un are stacked together—what would be the point of not?—a goodly percentage of even the uns have been, and remain, the material *and* efficient cause of towering mountains—avalanches—gravel pits—of recollective blah blah blooey.

They would seem in some cases the only dependable, the only *conceivable* generatrices of such biz (certainly not letters, photos, books, toys or rusty license plates). Notmuch otherwise, short of dreams, happenstance, or the memory bank itself spitting out interest I wasn't expecting nohow, could serve as so efficient a provoker.

Reminder. Prompt. Intimater. Mnemonicon.

Cipher.

Axis: Bold as Love (Reprise RS 6281). I peek and it says to me, smiling, *Ah, shit, man.* Nice artwork. I'll admit it's nice artwork: Hendrix as a Hindu god with many arms, surrounded by cobras and elephants and little Keystone Kop types with angry demons on their tongues. But not so terrific an album—his second—a big letdown after the first. Didja know I did the first American feature on Jimi Hendrix? For *Crawddaddy* (*Rolling Stone* didn't exist yet), which I'd started writing for while at Yale, but which a year-plus later still didn't pay anything. Yes: having by then INVENTED rock criticism as we know it, I sought not only recognition but a mess of pottage . . . a couple bucks.

Out of academia almost a year, I had no job but was writing lyrics for, and sometimes living with, the Soft White Underbelly, a not-bad psychedelic combo who would eventually surface as the 2nd-rate pseudo-metal (though some would say *metal*) Blue Öyster Cult. Don the guitarist had a girlfriend named either Cindy or Debby who behind her back everybody called Ah Shit Man (rarely did she go ten words without saying it). A fond mem'ry: the time I went to piss and there she was on the floor, naked, hugging the toilet, trying to vomit—she was on mescaline. She turned her head just enough to recognize me—"Oh, *hi*," then "Ah, shit, man, I sure do love Donald"—three days later, they split. She had a *great* ass.

It turned out her father was the classical editor for the Sunday *N.Y. Times*, possibly music editor overall, this guy who'd been there 20 years. She set it up and we met at his office—grey hair, grey tie, immaculate, polite, an upper-middleclass square, a CUBE, who'd probably seen *Tosca* and *Tannhäuser* 13 times each; I think I was wearing purple bell-bottoms, hair as long as, oh, George Harrison's. We shook hands, exchanged nothings; yes he knew who Hendrix was. Was anyone scheduled to review *Axis*? (Back then, before they realized the killing to be made in record ads, newspapers ran the *occasional* rock review—it wasn't compulsory.) Nobody was, but he wouldn't assign it, it would have to be on spec. No kill fee. Whuddo I know, I'm 22, a dumbass neophyte. I buy the record, play it a week, never quite get "into" it, but write the fucker anyway, waxing arcane for 300, 400 words which of course they pass on . . . like *shit*, man.

Before a set by his quartet at the Village Vanguard, summer of 1970, Ornette Coleman declared: "Music is a way of remembering." It probably is—but how so?

Once, in '73, '74, when my stereo was on the blink for three months, my inability to scare up a soundtrack to my life, especially with all the *modules* of soundtrack heaped all around—my burgeoning stack—was tangling me in knots. When I finally got it working, the first thing I played (Moby Grape's first album) affected me so deeply I *cried*: dig: music COUPLED WITH the instant recall of its healing/nurturing/bliss-o-genic payoff . . . the whole damn ear-to-heart trip, *as ever* . . . ear-to-head-to-heart . . . ear-direct-to-body . . . music as both accompaniment for the memory of its own eternal etc. and a ritual releasing—into the room, back into your blood—of something already internalized, absorbed, at a level deeper than the cell . . . internal/external/eternal . . . an often shattering experience. Or some such. (But *how so?*)

Likewise, what's it, the contrary?—the converse?—the corollary?—should be equally true: REMEMBERING IS MUSIC.

When the cops arrived, the live version of "Means to an End" was spinning on the turntable, which I'd reconnected, and the footprint made for odd little chitters more like wheezes than pops or clicks. Don't know why I bothered calling them—they were such abusive shits—it wasn't "cost effective," they said, to waste their time on so meager a burglary; they bummed me worse than the burgle itself, which I'd walked in on, but less than Kathleen's betrayal. As I was entering my apartment this big wide muther was standing there about to walk out. Dropping my equipment, he swung the door at me and jumped out the window he'd used to break in. There was hardly any new damage to the turntable, which was already pretty shot, but a big athletic shoeprint graced the disc, which had flopped off in the drop.

Joy Division's *Still* (Factory FACT 40) was one of the last punktime waxings I actually bought, as opposed to scamming a promo of, which would've been tough since I no longer had a radio show, having been tossed for too much on-the-air obscenity (profanity?) (whatever). By the time it came out, Ian Curtis had suicided. The punch line to "Means"—"I put my *trust in you*"—gravely addressed, one assumes, to she over whom he would shortly hang himself—took on special meaning when my current amour wouldn't come over, or even exactly talk to me (except to say she was, well, unavailable . . . *preoccupied*), while I was waiting for the fucking cops to show.

Which was indeed to be expected. Kathleen and I had barely *been* speaking since she caught me, or maybe didn't catch but found out about me fucking so-and-so on the radio station floor, after which we'd split for a couple months, though technically we were again "together." And this time: break in . . . break up?

Among items taken: TV, cassette player, car keys, binoculars, trench coat—but no records.

(1) Loss of objects. (2) Objects which themselves testify, specify, petrify loss. (Of anything and everything.) Losing the latter equals loss of loss? No, you dope: *double* the loss.

Loss of the past—that's given—but throw in loss of *sightlines* to the past, to the interconnections of things past, to causalities (both mighty and mighty slim) governing present predicaments . . . *that* smarts.

"ACCEPT LOSS FOREVER"—Jack Kerouac said that. Re both life/lived and its moldy oldy souvenirs. (Take out the trash.)

Between now and the grave: *increments* of loss. Okay, but is it like sand in the hourglass simply drip dropping away, a haphazard real-time (regularly irregular time) "letting go"—or the goosestep of effective (too effective) potty training to the last bittersweet gasp of rudely and crudely allotted time?

Bitter sweat.

Back to Justine: her '77 abortion.

Everything was fallin' apart, fallin' apart . . . dwinking, dwinking: dwunk! . . . biggest lush I'd ever known and/or loved. She wrecked my car and was bit by bit wrecking my life, yet I woulda done 'most anything to keep her around. Including: give up my own drinking ("set an example"); have a baby with her (a prospect she often raved about)—two things that ran violently against my grain, 'specially babying. When she got pregnant (drunk, she could never get her cycle right), a golden opp presented itself, but *her* choice was to terminate. Femmes fatales are nothing if not capricious.

I dropped her off at the clinic, then hit a record store and browsed the used bins. When I picked her up, she was a bit shaky but said she was starving, so I took her for steaks and, when she couldn't finish, ate both myself. Everything was cordial enough till we got to my place, where, wary of exposure to microbes so soon after surgery, she refused to sleep in the same bed with me, insisting I was "coming down with something"—I sounded congested from all the meat—so I dragged the couch a discreet distance from the bed and occupied it.

For our sleepytime kicks, I put on the day's purchase, pianist Jaki Byard's *Freedom Together!* (Prestige PR 7463), which I immediately felt pleased about having got—first album by Jaki as leader that measured up to those he did backing Eric Dolphy. I hadn't cared for a couple of others, but lying on the couch I didn't mind this one, and we both really dug Jr. Parker's vocal on "Getting to Know You" (at a moment—no irony—where we knew each other too well), though when I play it today it sounds like the mannered labor of a 50th-percentile '40s big-band singer, a few pegs up from Earl Coleman, yeah, but a few down from Johnny Hartman just as sure—and I don't think it's my retroview of the day-o-purchase which alone drives the rating so low.

In any event, there was no drinking that night. And not the faintest threat of sex of any sort—then or ever—as they'd told her to abstain for two, or was it three, weeks (could the romance *last* that long?).

So take out the trash.

Kokomo, *Asia Minor* (Felsted FS 17513). Bought for 99 cents, brand new, at Billy Blake's, Smithtown, Long Island, 1962 or '63. Possibly my first cut-out LP.

Title cut ("based on Grieg's Piano Concerto") made the top 40 in 1960 or so. Other cuts are lifted from Chopin, Bizet, Liszt, etc.: synthetically hopped up transcriptions of the classics for "rockin'" piano w/ strings.

No photo. "For personal reasons, Kokomo dislikes being photographed. Being eccentric and very moody, if his recording brings him sufficient fame and fortune, he is likely to desert it all for some far off island such as Majorca . . . and spend his time in the simplicities of life." Which led me to believe "he" was in reality a piano roll.

Saved solely for bathetic purposes.

Acceptable loss . . . memory of loss . . . loss of memory. Of the faculty of memory. "Memory chops."
(select one)
1. *The Persistence of Memory*, a painting by Dali. I don't remember it. How it looked. Just the name.
2. Dali's *Persistence of Memory* is a truly (truly) shitty painting. Yet I remember once liking it.

If there is a "Rosebud" to my collection, Ray Charles/*Modern Sounds in Country and Western Music* (ABC-Paramount ABC 410) may be it.

The first time I heard "I Can't Stop Loving You"—wait a sec, we could look up the date. It was on the radio when I got home from watching Benny "Kid" Paret get killed by Emile Griffith, well he didn't die for 10 days, but the fight took place March 24, 1962—Griffith knocked him out in the 12th and he never got up. I was in high school, it was the first boxing I saw live, and a few weeks later I bought my first LP, the one from which "Can't Stop" was taken.

Which in its own way transformed family life as much as the Elvis "Hound Dog"/"Don't Be Cruel" single, which six years earlier had given me the upper hand vis-à-vis my parents and their Bing Crosby and *South Pacific* 78s. Rock-roll singles went a long way towards offsetting the muse-ical squalor chez Meltz, but having the means to command 20 minutes of turntable time—consecutive—ultimately proved a lot more EMPOWERING than unit bursts of $2^1/_2$ to 3. Thank you, Ray.

Empowerment . . . musical wisdom . . . not to mention: one of my most applicable all-time musical conceits: the Unknown Tongue (see pp. 113–127 of *The Aesthetics of Rock*).

After *Modern Sounds* I got *Genius Hits the Road* and a couple more ABC-Paramounts, then moved on to his earlier albs on Atlantic, which alongside goodies familiar from the radio—"Yes Indeed!," "Swanee River Rock"—featured some archetypal outpours of the blues, real hardcore blues, not just blues-*y*: the tension-release, catharsis/transcendence, headlong dives into the abyss, the whole torrential gamut of FEELING, intensity *as* musical form, the technology of grief reduction, of its transformation to joy—umpteen varieties. As a bonus, Atlantic inner sleeves then had these neat little repros of album covers from other acts in the stable—the best artwork of the era—the lure of which led me instantly, inexorably on-ward to JAZZ: Ornette, Coltrane, Mingus, Monk with Art Blakey, Lennie Tristano.

Plus those sunglasses with the wide black plastic frame: "Genius shades." My freshman year of college, I wore them at night—to those in the know, they signified *abandon*. (Just as Ray's music still linger-ingly defined hip for a certain subclass of white teenagers only a tad or three behind things.)

The problem is, I haven't been able to STAND the ABC stuff since I weaned myself off it in favor of the blues, no later than fall-winter of '62. Play it now and the tempos feel slow as molasses, the string arrangements gloppy as raspberry mouthwash, and the omnipresent whitebread chorus . . . keep it.

Sequence *is* critical.

Did the Kinks release *Arthur* between *Village Green* and *Lola*, or was it before *Village Green*? I can't remember, that is I have no clarity about it, and don't possess a reference work that could be consulted on such an ish. (If I had all three albums, which I don't anymore, even though this was before they listed release dates, catalog numbers would tell us in a second.) Every time any kind of rock source book has happened my way I've quickly chucked it, figuring my recollective muscle—especially regarding the late '60s—would always get me through: wrong!

Does it trouble me that I've forgotten (and have no backup to help me fake it), making me less of an "authority"?

NO, NOT AT ALL.

(He asserted.)

Then one of those classic dead ends (and I don't mean classical): *Rhapsody in Blue/An American in Paris*, Hamburg Pro Musica Orches-tra, conducted by George Byrd (Forum F 9044).

Through my freshman year, jazz, Ray, and hits-o-the-day—"Big Girls Don't Cry," "Do You Love Me?"—were in competition with lotsa hokey hogwash in the dormitory ether: Doris Day, the Mormon Tabernacle Choir, barbershop quartets, Enoch Light and his Light Brigade, Sergio Franchi, the soundtrack from *Mr. Lucky*. Somehow nobody had classical, but in its place: plenty o' what wouldja call it, classy?—or just "grownup" (for our ever "maturing" taste)? Simula-tions of adultness: a dead-end street of the heart-mind-body-soul if ever there wuz one.

My personal contribution to this socio-sonic miasma was a 69-cent Gershwin LP, so shabby the cover was coming apart, which I played the heck out of for at most a week, by which time I was bored silly— sick of it—'s kinda lightweight, eh?—for this and ALL possible life-times. As to what it meant to me, y'know for as long as I could bear to have it on, dunno f'r sure what the phenomenology of the deal mighta been—how & why it hit me—but I'll speculate: a dose of jazz-iness if not jazz (could the clarinet solo in *Rhapsody* have briefly im-pressed me?), a dose of "night music" à la *Mr. Lucky*—those two things meeting AHRT on a pedestal just as I was beginning to check out cubism, futurism, and so forth—a nascent curiosity 'bout things Euro—while entertaining very dumb "theories" on this & that (an ahrtist myself, I conjured up bogue genres with names like "monocu-bism" and "statio-kineticism": what a dipshit). I wouldn't listen in earnest, or at all, howev, to actual high-booty Euro *music*—classical per se—till 1993, at no time since which have I played (or considered playing) this alb. When I hear this pap in Woody Allen movies, I wince.

So how come I continue to keep such bosh? I keep it as a souvenir of non-redemptive folly; as not only kitsch—contentwise—per se, but the kitsch of youth it-self per se, or let's call it late adolescence. But most of all I keep it for the groovy liner notes:

"George Byrd, the celebrated coloured American conductor renowned for his interpretations of the music of George Gershwin . . . in 1947 formed in Harlem his own orchestra . . . consisting of ap-proximately fifty per cent each of white and coloured people" . . . wow, coloured!

Sentimental surplus value.

From the Radio Ranch . . .

Ernest Tubb's Greatest Hits (Decca DL7–5006). Early 1980: a good three years since I'd been even semi-earnest about country music— *ancient* sounds in country/western—which in the backwash of punk seemed an even goofier joke than mainstream rock. On the cover, Ernest in his big white Stetson flashes the world's biggest, and fourth or fifth phoniest, smile, but my hunch at the time was he'd comple-ment whatever music X were likely to bring along. Every week, after the first hour, musicians would show up and I'd spin anything they handed me, which in John Doe's case turned out to be Al Green and Jimmie Rodgers. And sure enough, when I played "Waltz Across

Texas," he and Exene got up and waltzed around the booth: a touching moment (when in marital sync, they were very impressive).
    The Beatles/1967–1970 (Capitol SKBO 3404). The double album
with the blue cover, one of but two Beatle releases I got as promos,
and the only one later than the White Album that I still own—and
only for one cut: "Across the Universe." (I never bought the loathsome *Let It Be*, on which it originally appeared, so this was my one
lucky shot at it.) By the ass end of '80—the week John Lennon died in
New York—it was a dozen years since the Beatles had in any way been
musically viable, so the news he was dead didn't immediately distress
me, especially since I and my friends in L.A. were in deep-shit
mourning for Darby Crash, who had overdosed (intentionally) a couple days previous. Tears for Johnny took me a few days to activate,
and amounted to little more than a short gush for my own younger
days, but Darby's musicmaking was present-tense all the way, and his
death for many of us was sheer misery—revealing (as if we hadn't
known) the essence and pigment of local frontline punk: not anarchy
but a terrible unhappiness.
    The Saturday after both deaths, this kid named Bosco whom Darby
had been in love with, but who was too straight to reciprocate, arrived
at my show while "Across the Universe" (following the Germs' "We
Must Bleed") was spinning. At its conclusion, Bosco announced that
it was Darby's favorite Beatle song—(and who'd've thunk he was even
aware of the Beatles?)—ain't life funny?

Promo albums. Pennies (not even nickels) from corporate food-tube
heaven.

The Very Best of Gene McDaniels (United Artists UA–LA447–E), a late-
'70s compilation for someone who hadn't had a hit (or much of a
miss) since the early '60s, is a singularly unappealing package: the
singer against rose/pink/lavender horizontal stripes; no liner notes
like U.A. had done with their Fats Domino, Jan & Dean, and even
their Ricky Nelson collections. The tunes, while pleasant in a pre-
British Invasion pop sort of way, are hardly even middleweight (wel-
terweight?); the vocals, a whiff-and-a-half too clean in their
articulation.
    What keeps me hangingonto it is during my sophomore year I had
a jazz show on the campus station, knew my way around dials, and
somebody got the bright idea to preempt regular programing and let
me do commentary 'tween rounds of the first Sonny Liston-Cassius

Clay fight—he wasn't Ali just yet—pirating the blow-by-blow signal from the national broadcast, delivered locally by WABC. (A station unafeared of risking FCC wrath, we had a range about as far as the parking lot.)

I said things like "Hey, that was some hook," but anyway, before *their* fight coverage began, the last thing ABC played was "A Hundred Pounds of Clay," McDaniels' two-year-old hit—nobody gave Clay much chance of winning. If you've never heard it, and it can't still be in oldies rotation, 's about God creating gendered woman (weighing in at one-oh-oh) and the upshot for gendered man . . . oh, how—what's word?—catchy.

Some year I'll take off the shrinkwrap and play it.

No, that's a lie—actually, I do have a rock book or two. Though maybe not the kind that'll do us factually any good. Right now I'm reading *Please Kill Me*, the Legs McNeil/Gillian McCain oral punk thing, where on p. 159 somebody mentions the Academy of Music show, New Year's Eve '73—well I was there, wasn't I? The list of bands seems wrong—New York Dolls, Kiss, the Stooges. No: the Stooges did play, and Kiss opened (billed fourth, behind Teenage Lust, and nobody knew them, they got booed off the stage), but Blue Öyster Cult headlined, and the Dolls weren't on the bill.

But lemme really be sure about this—*was* I there? Was it that year or '74? Thinking . . . thinking . . . hmm . . . GOT IT: '75 was my last year living in New York, so '74 was the New Year's Eve I wanted to be dead and went to a party hoping somebody had a gun I could use. Some things I would remember if you cut away two-thirds of my brain: it was the LAST SHOW I saw the BÖC do before I realized they were cheating me. Or maybe I'm all wet; maybe 2.5 thirds are already gone.

That's what "rock history" is: collective bad memory.

Remembrances of dope days past: *Hums of the Lovin' Spoonful* (Kama Sutra KLPS–8054); Jefferson Airplane, *Surrealistic Pillow* (RCA LSP–3766).

On a greygrim weekday in the final stretch of my crawl to the finish at Yale, my pot stash exhausted, knowing no dealer any closer than Brooklyn, I downed almost a full tin of nutmeg—pirates did it, right?—perchance to get looped. Nothing happened at first, so I ingested more (bitter!), more (vile!), till in two-three hours: *bingo.* High as a blimp, I wandered the streets of New Haven, reading the minds of passersby, stumbling over subatomic sidewalk particles. Although I wasn't hungry, it occurred to me that I should eat, so I got a sandwich and fries at a George & Harry's, only to discover that I couldn't taste a thing. This was somewhat unnerving, so to test my 'bility to perceive *anything* ('fore chucking it all, throwing in the epistemological towel, and accepting the "flow"), I went to the juke and selected "Full Measure," a single off the third Lovin' Spoonful album. The summer before, stoned on hash, I'd thought "It's All Over Now" by the Rolling Stones, a song which couldn't've been more familiar to me, was actually being sung by Ray Stevens—that's how I *heard it*—but this sounded like nothing. And I don't mean it sounded "unlike anything else"—unusual, unique—I mean like nothing. Which maybe in hindsight it was, and the Spoonful were: NOTHING.

One of a handful of groups to submit whole-hog to the transidiomatic shuck known as folk-rock, the Spoonful in retrospect lacked the balls, the rigor, or the mischief to parent as provocative a folkfringe hybrid as the Holy Modal Rounders (or for that matter the Fugs), opting for a music devoid of danger or true sass. Somewhere that spring, to worm their way out of a bust, they ratted out their pot connection, an act of heinous careerism (oh, they were *worried* Zal the guitarist, a Canadian, might lose his work permit) that effectively (and ironically) ended their run as credentialed exponents of contempooogabooga.

Back at my room, I cast my fate to the Airplane. I had both of their albums and hadn't got much out of the first, except a sense that they were kinda what—*post*-folk-rock? (Or something.) The second, which in short order would play a foreground role in sonically redefining the late '60s—the Psychedelic Era qua music—I hadn't yet listened to. First spin, soon as I put the needle down, huge ugly blotches of dark green algae sprung up *everywhere*. Needle up, they vanished. Noticing a track called "My Best Friend" and feeling gee, I could *use* a friend, wondering if in fact these folks whose sounds I barely knew could be *surrogate* friends like the Beatles had for so long seemed (wouldn't THAT be nice?), I tried again—whoops—more algae.

Dying for some human contact—music wurn't contact enough—I ended up at the Yale Library, a stone-cold old-stone repository of the pompous and dead, laughing uncontrollably. People glared at me (though no one had the pep to shut me up), and then suddenly, whoopee!, a FOX HUNT—redcoats on horses jumping over tree stumps—I'm not making this up—the most vivid hallucination of my life.

New fugging Haven: where George Bush and William Buckley (Oliver Stone and Jodie Foster) learned HOW.

The last time I thought about it, my favorite philosopher was Heraclitus. "You can't step in the same river twice"—I'm sure you know that one. "The way up and the way down are one and the same." A bunch of fragments, aphorisms. "Nature loves to hide." One that I've always got a kick out of, and a shitload of writerly mileage from, is "Consult thyself," translated also as "I consulted myself." I don' know Greek, it's oke either way, but meaning what: "Empiricism starts here"? Spotlight on the subject (before Western philosophy even *had* a subject-object split)?

In the intro to *Rock She Wrote*, a 1995 collection of female-authored rockcrit, Evelyn McDonnell argues that, hey, it's COOL that women acknowledge their subjectivity. She concedes that *some* gendered males have also walked this path, "not just in a gonzo, macho style (Lester Bangs, Richard Meltzer)"—hey, that's *me*—"but with heart-baring sensitivity (Bangs, Tom Smucker)." Gosh—I must be the part of gonzo (whatever th' fuck it is—I've never known!) (even as sound, the word makes me gag) Lester threw away.

Way back at the dawn of the '70s, Robert ("Bob") Christgau, whom I've already griped about, a bust-ass (and I don't mean kick-ass) editor who later pulled rank on Lester by advising him that he'd graduated Dartmouth (while Lester'd graduated nuthin'), actually voiced a not-so-begrudging respect for *Rolling Stone*, a truly horrible sheet I occasionally wrote for (Bob didn't) but never EVER read, which he hailed as at least fulfilling our need for "rock journalism"—reportage—"investigative" or otherwise. I now realize what he had in mind was simply topical news of the "trade," of a scene writ LARGE (but still of questionable existence) for which he relentlessly shilled, shills, will always shill (when you review *everything*, or pretend you do, without an external guarantor of the "fact" of such supposed mega-reality—even one as lame and noxious as the *Stone*—you would pretty much seem a freakin' FOOOOOOOOL, eh?). Whenever he spit the notion of journalism at me, I shot back with "Consult yourself," which he in turn poo-pooed as "bourgeois individualism" or whatev—'twasn't "universal" enough for the bastard . . . fuck *me*.

Then as now, on the street as at motherfucking Yale, my fundamental concern was with truth, THE truth (hee *haw*), i.e., for starters: what you can be surest of. If we're talking records and bands and whatnot, all you c'n be anywhere NEAR sure of is the shadow of this shit in your own playpen. Which is no easy ride—mercy! To confront and interrogate your merry ass, you've gotta be objective, impersonal, you've gotta go straight at your own jugular—mix a metaphor—and take furious notes while the blood is still fresh. If the initial calculus ain't perfect, you're nowhere, and anywhere you proceed is triple nowhere.

And of course certain fuckheads will ask: Where are you *then?*—y'-know, anyway. They'd say you're in autobio land. Well, fuggit. If such procedure smacks of diary keeping, if the text thus generated is MERE autobio, so be it. Christgau's own autobiographical slip, for the record, has been as visible as anybody's. Terror of aging—of the possibility of *appearing* old—has always been a dominant theme. When Chuck Berry's "My Dingaling" came out, Bob had just turned 30 and was taking it hard. Rather than call Chuck's first hit in some time what it was—cynical toss-off; play-down to a pack of children—he aligned himself with the children and lauded "Dingaling" as evidence of ageless Chuck's neverending oompah. ("The kids are alright" *my* dingaling.)

Which Bobbo would certainly never admit, or admit the relevance of (the personal he'd allow to be political—hell, he'd insist on it—or even historical, but that's just everyone else's personal: the third-person personal). Truck extensively or extendedly with the first-person personal (except briefly for "parable" sake) and you run the risk of having this jerk and his ilk accuse you, as he has me, of "narcissism." LISTEN GOOD.

What I write, on music or anything, is *not* narcissism—NEVER!—any more than bodybuilding—if you do it *right*—is narcissism. (Sayeth Mr. Schwarzenegger: you've gotta *judge* your delts—y'can't love 'em!) Nor is it "solipsism"—hey now, I'm talking to you, YOU!, why would I waste my time scribbling this bullcrap for myself? Or masturbation—"self-indulgence"—geez, I'm getting defensive, don't wanna be defensive, NO MORE DEFENSIVE.

Go ahead. Call me a philosopher/poet, that's OK, or an archaeologist of the real-time micro-moment, even (I'll grant) a phenomenologist, but *please*. I am not now, have never been, and have never had any interest in being a "journalist" (good or bad).

From the night in '79 he was on my radio fandango to somewhere in the '80s, when our correspondence dwindled to nothingness, Mark Smith of the Fall and I were something like friends. When he played L.A. we hung out, preferably in bars where he didn't expect to meet members of his band ("It's a bad idea to socialize with your musicians"). On one occasion, he berated me for going home with a woman he'd introduced me to, a rockwriter who when I kissed and fondled her had no panties and a dangling tampon string, oo wee ("Sex is not a good motivating factor"). Before my VCR got stolen, I ran him a tape of *Plan Nine from Outer Space*, and he played me a cassette of songs about trucks by some actual trucker trying hard to sound like Dylan ("It's not the Dylan part that matters—it's the truck part"). He decried London as "too French," unlike Manchester, his home ("The Norman Conquest didn't make it that far north"). Back there during the Falkland Islands thing, he feigned a rooting interest in the U.K., contending it was "much too easy to side with Argentina." Mark *E.* Smith: a man of pith and whimsy.

As a band, as a musical realization of something, the Fall were more intelligent, more after-the-end-of-the-world (a/k/a "post-rock"), AND more sonically compelling than Sonic Youth (if less nerd-empowering). The last of their albums he sent me was *Grotesque (After the Gramme)* (Rough Trade 18), which I must've played but don't remember; I'm sure it's a good'un. The cover is an old Dick Tracy-type guy gritting teeth like the likeness of Phil Alvin on the cover of the second Blasters LP. Speaking of which, of whom, the last time I saw the Fall play I was standing with Dave Alvin, who after a couple songs said, perplexed, "There's no hooks." "Well," said I, "that's the *point.*"

Do I namedrop too much? Here's a name y'don't know: Ed Abramson. 53–35 Hollis Ct. Blvd., Flushing, N.Y. Rubber-stamped on the back of Bobby Darin's *That's All* (Atco 33–104), containing both "Mack the Knife" (though different from the '59 single version) and "Beyond the Sea," plus sixteen tons of hotcha-style pop filler. I haven't seen Ed since '66, but we lived in the same wing of the dorm, and somehow the alb ended up in my stack (I didn't steal it).

In November '63, he and I drove to Philly for a double date with high school cheerleaders. The big homecoming game, however, was canceled when the, uh, President got shot, as was the date itself when I didn't behave aggrievedly enough. On the ride back, all you could hear on the radio was dirges and stuff, except for Canadian stations, fading in and out, on one of which we heard (for the first time) the Beatles, who would soon supply the accompaniment for post-JFK Ameri-teen whoop-de-doo, them and—that's right—the fabulous TRASHMEN, givers to the world of punk 13 years before the fact: "Surfin' Bird." I can't think of those weeks up till Christmas without feeling an equal rush of Beatles and Trashmen, who together, where *I* lived and breathed, kind of reinvented rock & roll, dead as a donut (as full-field hell-&-gone you-name-it) since, well, before Bobby Darin. Hey, believe it: that was the Gestalt, the context, the nexus, the TEXT. The literal HAND AS DEALT.

You take Sally and I'll take Sue . . .
   It isn't so much that rock history is or must be revisionist (it gener-ally is, but so what?) but simply, and more to the point, that it is and can't help but be visionist. Historical hands, insofar as they're dealt at all, are dealt to persons—to singles and multiples of 'em. Persons are touchstones of the *efficacy* of chronology: how history *did its thing.* What exactly happened? Everything. But sequence, hierarchy, syn-chronicity—scratch that—the *assertion* of all such meat 'n' taters, of a calculus and phenomenology of micro-moment progression, scale, nuance, and tangent, is at least two-thirds the *statement,* voiced or un-voiced, of each and every rockcritperson. His/her stab, strut, and (in a nutshell) *oeuvre.*
   Or let's do it this way. Every rockwriter (sportswriter) (geekwriter) has his/her own book of genesis. Has? *Exudes.* An Old Testament con-catenated fable. Gospel according to fill-in-the-blank. Every critic a "witness," a zealot and crackpot, and everyone's testament different, heck, it had *better* be. A fragment from MY glorious goddam scrip-ture—the Absolute unfolds itself, thusly (take it or take it):

   Re: anything besides punk that has had mainstream play since 1970.
   Things either get filed with the '70s (Alex Chilton, Steely Dan, the Re-
   placements, R.E.M., Nirvana, Metallica) or the '80s (Sonic Youth and its
   partisans). There's no room left in the '60s, they're completely full (were
   full by late '67); the '70s and '80s are still very sparse. Rap files perfectly
   with the black '60s—a separate warehouse finally almost full. Madonna
   goes with the pre-rock '50s, alongside Eddie Fisher. Springsteen is on the
   plane with Ritchie Valens and the Big Bopper (Buddy Holly took the bus)
   (or rather: never quite fully existed). Did I say the rock '50s were over be-
   fore Bobby Darin? They were over before Elvis entered the army (true).
   Hardcore Metal fits in with 19th century classical—the intervals, the bom-
   bast, the ponderousness—nothing later than Bruckner. The '90s are an
   empty room.

It would appear there's a lotta Lavender Hill Mobs around. Perhaps you've seen *Lavender Hill Mob* the film, but I bet you've never seen Lavender Hill Mob the band or heard either of their TWO eponymous longplayers released within a year of each other, by the same label yet. And isn't there also a Lavender Hill Mob turkey breast, and a Lavender Hill Mob deodorant stick?

Wow and hey and fuckaduck, but I was actually AT the session that produced the first of the *L.H. Mob* elpees (United Artists UA–LA719–G), late '76, the only time I got flown somewhere by a record company, as opposed to already being in the vicinity, just to attend a recording session. Snowy blowy Quebec, an hour from Montreal, wonderf'ly scenic, great food, nice kids in the band, incredibly civil for rock-n-rollers. A company gladhander gave me percodans. The Parti Québecois won a big election that week: dancing in the streets. A goodtime all around. As a quid pro quo, I was all set to call this wholesome, some would prob'ly say innocuous, 6-piece combo, I dunno, "genuinely innocent," "vanguard of the anti-punk backlash"—whew—I can fling it with the best of 'em—but when *Creem* deemed 'em too marginal to bother with (unless, of course, U.A. advertised), I didn't have to.

These were also days of goodtimes with Justine, you remember *her*—before her alcoholin' got the final better o' things. A song on the album, "No One Compares," inspired me to compare her, all too favorably, to my previous galpersons. Clearly, I was asking for it. But for a brief twinkling even she would acknowledge that we were, yes, in RAPPORT—ref'rence to a line in *Creation of the Humanoids* where the sister of Don Megowan, head of the robot-bashing Order of Flesh and Blood, boasts that she herself is in an advanced relational state with a robot, a "clicker": "Pax and I are in rapport." Justine was gonna print up announcements—"Justine and Richard are in rapport"—but never got around to it.

Fast forward to her abortion, to the day some weeks after it when, she was told, a penis would again be fine, dandy, at least physiologically permissible. This could be the night I got lucky. She hadn't, far as I knew or believed, had a drink in the interim. Ring ring, door unlocked, there she was on the floor, an empty liter bottle at her feet. Couldn't shake her awake, she scowled and pushed me away. On a coffee table, a water glass with two inches of wine sat on my copy of *Lavender Hill Mob*, a red ring at its base. She probably hadn't played it (Abba was on the turntable), only used it as a coaster—how fastidious.

I split and returned with some objects she'd left at my place, dumping them beside her still comatose figure, which this time I made no attempt to disturb ('cept to paw and sniff the enormous dark spot on her crotch and find it, yup, cold wee-wee), arranging them in a pile:

her unread copy of my second book, a sneaker she'd once aimed at my TV, various undergarments, a cotton blanket, her vegetable steamer and cosmetics case, a jar of French-import strawberry jam, half a box of Kotex nappies.

To the pile I added my wine-stained album, on the jacket of which I scrawled, "J.—Thanx for the rapport. R.," then changed my mind, snatched it back, and have toted it with the rest of my lifeless belongings ever since.

Exhumable but rarely exhumed, my fifties/sixties singles pass time in a carton. Last one played: "Whispering Bells" by the Dell-Vikings, 'round 1986. It was *totally* beat to shit. By and large, they all are.

When you get down to it, the very idea of the single is rather amazing, and in retrospect almost preposterous. Two sides, one song per. One!—what forcible focus on the unit sonic offering! Not the pot luck of a many-unit album, but a treat acquired 'cause you've already heard it and *like* it. Too bad, 'cause we're also talking vinyl at its thinnest, frailest, most destructible: the "love is to kill" theme directed at unit *targets*. They may be jewels, gems—but for permanence they're fucking rhinestones.

Interesting, at this crossroad, that CDs have meant an end to two-sidedness; that 102 percent (approx.) of viable releases in the format have so far been REISSUES of analog vinyl (and shellac). Which is to say what?—that it's somewhat ridiculous for the CD to present us with the metaphor/illusion of indestructibility—"immortality"—which ballyhoo for the "unbreakable" LP once heralded too, y'-know?—when the bulk of current sonic fodder is (dare it be said?) more ephemeral than ever?

But back to th' singles: yes, they're maimed, mutilated, on a terminal gimp—*way* more than my average semi-retired LP—but that's hardly reason for leaving them ALL in the effing box. For exhuming NONE of them. Well, it ain't fear of disappointment—that I won't "enjoy" hearing some once-favored tune for the first time in so many moons, or that it won't "satisfy" on some whacked-out, esoteric dotted line. 'S more like an eerie suspicion, a tingle on the back o' my neck which tells me that ONE MORE PLAY of anything might well use it up, play it OUT, for the remainder of my days; and that using up has gotta be a shoddier dance of loss/forever, a crummier outcome than merely losing access . . . losing track . . . um, uh, forgetting . . . LOSING YOUR WAY.

Two trains running—two MORTALITIES—the music's and my own. Music that (I postulate) helped *form me*: to see a single component DRY UP, lapse, is to feel my life dismantled one more notch—like Jeff Goldblum and his vanishing body parts in the remake of *The Fly.*

"Fear of loss of being"—that Heidegger hokum from where was it, *Being and Time*? Finally, in 1998, I find an application that doesn't seem gratuitous. (Middle age can do that.)

A friend g-g-g-gone!—and I don't mean dead. Written off; written out. (I wouldn't piss on his grave.)

No names, no names, but he was a goodfriend, he was a bes' friend—then once he wasn't he was NO FRIEND. Somewhere in the middle, when he was just a mid-friend, he helped originate rockwriting. Wait—didn't *I* originate it? Give him an assist. He had a hand, was at least a catalyst, the person I tried some of this crap out on. A lot of my riffs came in dialogue with him. Which is something, considering how little he knew 'bout rock & roll—it was virtually all bluff. Like here was a guy whose prior exemplar of musical ecstasy was *Carmina Burana*, whose first try-on-for-size of what he took for rock/roll was *Trini Lopez Live at PJ's* (which you'll probably miss the humor of if you're under 45). *Meet the Searchers* (Kapp KL-1363) was his second.

Did ya know that the Brit Invasion, stage one, consisted solely of the Beatles, the Dave Clark Five, and the Searchers?—then maybe Peter and Gordon, possibly Gerry and the Pacemakers—it was six months (or more) before the first real U.S. impact of the Stones. Well, this pal, this buddy, championed the Searchers over the Beatles (his favorite Beatle—what a card!—was Stu Sutcliffe, the dead one), imagining a song or two of theirs more overtly "sexual" than either the known works of the Fab Four or his subnovice's inkling of the rock norm. Putting his money where his mouth was, he bought *Meet the Searchers* (a/k/a *Needles & Pins*), then I did. From the condition of my copy, I prob'ly spent more time perusing the cover (for Merseybeaters, they dressed and greased themselves like Joey Dee and the Starliters) than playing it. I've got no clear sense no more of what they ever could've meant to me, other than to look in the index to *Aesthetics of Rock* and see there's SEVEN entries for 'em . . . well that's *his* doing.

My buddy! my pal! who in the late '60s forwent a "career" in rock-crit (jus' kidding!: 'twurn't such thing) for a career in rock commerce,

a career of rock evil?, that's putting it too poetically; who as manager
of I won't even name *them* owed me much I never saw for band ser-
vices/rendered, who fucked my royalties *royally* at a time, a longtime,
bloody *years* over which I could never consistently pay the rent (and
was never out of debt); oh! the image of him in his $50 cowboy hat
with his four new cars and his roll of hundreds every time I'd ask him,
beg him, for my fucking money. I wouldn't puke . . .

And wasn't there more?, didn't he try to "steal" my gal-of-the-
time?, one of 'em anyway; oh and he never invited me on a tour (although he took I won't name her either—to Europe yet), even just as
a friend goddammit; and as a final insult sent me a gold record, so
suitable for framing it was already framed, in lieu of any recent payment—whatsofuckingever—'gainst the five figures by then legitimately if so improbably due . . . hoo! . . . a good deal of which can
easily be writ off as just, well, ROCK AND ROLL, its wage, its consequence, its everyday walk-the-streets surface and substance, durn
near everything but its music, ha ha ha ha ha, but more of which was
plain basic treachery, perfidy, b?d faith, non-generic interpersonal
DOUBLECROSS.

I wouldn't puke on his mother.

Meanwhile, yonder in loss-of-beingville, the situation gets grimmer.
It's *all* a house of cards, see, the whole setup, not just crapshoots with
individual fuckin' oldies—'cause that's what they are, ha ha—there's
more to be concerned with than exhausting some tunes. I dread, well
I no longer dread, I *know*: that prolonged listening to this old shit—
shoot: prolonged thinking about!—will just as surely burn out ancient CONSTRUCTS, entire sputtering SYSTEMS, the very
MINDSETS in which the mix-&-match of any of this shit CO-
HERES. The "natural process" of rock, insofar as it *is* rock, involves
a systematic real-world/real-time/communal/personal playing out.
All culture, certainly all of it built around the sequential offering of
product—TV, movies, mags and books, cars, sports, clothing—is
about turnover—a truism—but only rock foregrounds and RITU-
ALIZES it in extremis. (Roll over, Beethoven . . . roll over, Plastic
Bertrand.) And if that's the deal with IT, why should it be a different
deal with *reflecting* on it, reflecting *truly* on it? Right? (Wrong?) (Another truism?)

Another approach. Regardless of the whatzis under scrutiny, there's
always a basic fatuity, if not outright dishonesty, behind the tacit insistence that the true will f'rever *play*—that its vectors of *interest* are as

perpetual as its rightness. *Existential* perpetuity is a pisser. Even with superficial taters like narrative structure—the warp and woof of the scrutinizer's "voice"—how many times do you wanna read Sir Joe Bag-o-Donuts' definitive take on Late Renaissance painting, say? How many times could you possibly wanna read *me*? How many times do *I* wanna read (or even think) me?

The text-partaking self—yours, mine, everyfucker's—is not only historical (yawn yawn) but eschatological. It's also a *very* effective agent in the nullification (cum disintegration) (and I don't mean the ending) of history: its relegation to terminal irrelevance. Wake up one morning and old pet "hypotheses" are suddenly a little unwieldy—inapplicable—useless—the self can't use 'em (they give it the *creeps*)—to the point, ultimately, where NO specific retroview is any longer "worth advancing," even between one and oneself, any longer "tenable," and not so much 'cuz it can no longer be "tested"—it's just that further *to-do* would only render everything all the more trite—banal—"meaningless."

Which'll jar your bones, Jim! . . . sap your breath . . . distort your hearing for your own concrete thoughts 'til they screak like the muddled static of distant homily.

Tutti frutti perpetooty . . . And if it's ROCK qua meaning (qua "art") we're wasting brain cells on, there ain't too many ways you can trick it up, bolster it, to insure it'll play even short perpetuity. Everything that rock rock rock and roll "is," it also isn't—and I'm not quoting general semantics—and when things start rolling down the hill (and you're rolling with 'em) the ISN'T, believe me, is what will predominate.

The "sixties"? The "fifties"? One house of cards built upon another. Rock in its "primordial" form? Oh, you must mean *before* Rock-Surround—back when rock-roll was a bona fide *antidote* to the ills of the world, and not so central (or conspicuous) a source of them. Well, okay, if that's the case, yes—for that it would pay to look to the "sixties," the "fifties," or even the actual '60s and '50s. The actual '60s are grounded, actually, in the actual '50s, and the '50s as groundwork are a basement, a groundfloor, whose support time, strictly limited, has EXPIRED. People who think they know the '50s or the '60s but have only seen cartoon versions haven't a clue of the *fragility* of the whole damn thing; nor can they guess how long ago the mess came crashing down (during the '60s?—most of it) (after punk fell?—the rest of it), crashed *silently*. (Unless you're really listening, and why would you be?, silence doesn't announce itself.)

And here's the kicker: With or without your cooperation, your complicity, your personal suspension of systematic disbelief, NO VERSION of the fifties, real or imagined, can prop the mess up anymore, any more than can YOU on your own, in your most strenuous imaginings, your wildest, most neo-adolescent games of "pretend."

Oh, and furthermore, even if it could and you could: It can't SAVE you, any better than Jesus—Godzilla—the tooth fairy—can.

(Up the hill . . . down the hill. You would have to be a Buddhist, or a flaming masochist, to feel that *this* way/down is as groovy as its predecessor/up.)

"All is but knowing so," wrote Marcus Aurelius. Sounds about right, sure, maybe. But severe chronic knowing can lead to some *nasty* un-knowing . . .

Hey, remember flunk-rock? *Now* that *was something.* Held together with the spit, and warmed over by the belch, of history? *I don't doubt it.* David Byrne? *Oooh, he was an* x-tremely *big cheese.* Father of post-longshoremanism, wasn't he? *I thought it was postmormonism.* Tell me, *is* there some way outta here? *It starts with* D.

The disposable, too long undisposed of.

All dust in the wind.

What—another Searchers album? Uh . . . yeah: *Take Me for What I'm Worth* (Kapp KS–3477), their fourth, fifth, or maybe even last LP. Note the older-type shrinkwrap—that rubbery, stretchy kind of thick plastic—with "stereo" and "our price" in big letters, and a little map of the U.S. The wrap is broken, so I probably played it, though I wouldn't bet on every cut. Arguably *the* wretched excess of my collection, but conditions did make its purchase my-t-appealing.

Technically, Yale had finally expelled me—it was official—but by some crazy accident they forgot to cancel my last fellowship check, a big chunk of which I decided had to be spent on albums. Had to. I used to claim I blew the entire 600 bucks—there's a nice ring to that—or 400, but it was more like only 100 or 200 bucks.

In addition to the Searchers, I got the first Grateful Dead, the first Country Joe, *Over, Under, Sideways, Down* by the Yardbirds, everything I didn't have by the Kinks, at least a couple of Donovans, *Ascension* and *A Love Supreme*, the first Pharoah Sanders and the first Albert Ayler on ESP, and a slew of items I must've got rid of 10–15–20 years ago—the second Troggs (containing "With a Girl like You"), Los Bravos (w/ "Black Is Black"), the Fortunes ("You've Got Your Troubles"), the Mindbenders without Wayne Fontana, the first solo alb by

Gene Clark—all bought, presumably, *simply because they were there.* After what the yalemonsters had put me through, how could I not take my reasonable share of frivolous war trophies?

Why I didn't sell the Searchers 10–15–20 years ago is one thing. Some records are old friends, and old friendship, like new, isn't exclusively about good or bad, or even real affinity. Others are people you *feel sorry for;* and if the Searchers, in spring '67, were already obsolete, by the '80s even their dust was obsolete. Today, they're the last remaining piece of fellowship booty that never became an integral part of my master stack; the most purely meretricious of trophies (not even a belt buckle—or an ear—of the enemy: more like its lint), one as valueless as the graduate degree I never got.

MEANWHILE, an actual war was going on, y'know? No matter what I said about enriching the palette of philosophy, my real mission at Yale, the reason I became a grad school schmuck in the first place, was to delay getting drafted as long as possible. So dig the picture: I've been pummeled and poleaxed—rejected, daddy!—I don't have a job, a girlfriend, fucking 'Nam is in full swing, but records'll redeem the day! Ah! the sixties: the blithering optimism of it all.

And six mints, make that six months later, Jacques Derrida came to Yale as a visiting professor. MISTER deconstruction or whatever— shit, he mighta been my thesis adviser (at least an ally). Good thing I missed him or I'd still be rotting in academia.

Christ am I glad to be DONE with academia.

But who sez I'm done with it?

Having fled the academic gauntlet, escaped by the skin of my shoes, I walked smack into a new gauntlet about as depressing, and almost as draining, one with—what? not again?!—distinct academic coloration. Neo-academic? Crypto-academic? Pseudo-nonacademic?

Like femmes fatales who "don't know it," academes who don't know it, or feign ignorance of the fact, can be—as they used to say—bad medicine. Bad enough. But wave the academy flag as if to disclaim it— "Only funning!"—while meantime masquerading as a practicing populist, and you're fucking RAT POISON. A pair of parties-I-have-known fit this bill, have fit it hand-in-glove for the last quarter century, behaving for all the world not merely like entrenched (and *very* constipated) academes but petty administrators . . . self-tenured department heads . . . deans, by golly—well one of 'em anyway.

Did I tell you that Christgau, good old Bob, once dubbed himself The Dean of American Rock Critics? He had a T-shirt made up with his name above that title, and a likeness of Little Richard. What, you might wonder, could possess someone to adopt a handle so aridly pretentious, so dauntingly . . . insipid? Part was just ill-conceived hoax, as obtuse a sham as Springsteen's in bearing a nickname with zero proletarian reverb—The Boss!—but in larger part, it did accurately convey the man's aura of swaggerless dogmatism. Both personally and professionally, he is one drably imperious prick.

The Dean!—who to this day (in his syndicated "Consumer Guide") gives LETTER GRADES to albums and has a routine enabling him to monitor, or simulate monitoring, the complete "curriculum"— every current release. Years ago, more than once, I saw him in action. He'd put six LPs on the changer, stack all the covers in the same sequence, go about his bizness. If he suddenly heard something to catch his fancy, he would count discs and check the covers—"Three, four— oh, isn't that something?—Tom Paxton." Nowadays, I would assume he's got a multi-CD unit with a digital display so he needn't even count: technology favors the lame. (Dean of what *branch*, though? Admissions? Paper clips? Alphabetic studies?)

For us rock-crit underlings, The Dean in his incarnation as bigwig editor tried his darnedest to affect a supervisorly demeanor with an almost schoolmarmish (hit-you-with-a-ruler) facade. Looking back, it was sorta laughable, but every time I turned in an article, a review, sooner or later he'd phone, "Get your thesaurus—it's word choice time," and for two hours try and argue me out of certain key adjectives. Laughable but exasperating, and in hindsight maybe mostly laughable.

It was more in his "intellectual oversight" capacity—as surveillance pilot at large, unpaid and unassigned, far above the rockwrite fray— that this joker did me any lasting damage. In tandem with copilot/tag-team partner Greil Marcus, he at a crucial juncture blocked my progress to wider (um) recognition, effectively consigning me to marginality, and in the long run has denied me any significant role in official—"authorized"—"accredited" rockwrite (as opposed to rock) history. The annals—the archive—the fugsucking "pantheon"! Oh yes—another pathetic house-o-cards for sure, but these two clowns act like they fucking OWN it.

And why do I care? Why do I care? I CARE.

It irks the hell out of me that while Marcus doesn't grade albums, he does grade people's CONDUCT, and conduct—alone!—is what kept me out of this high-bounty, high-visibility anthology he edited, oh, probably 18–20 years ago—yup, another *old* grudge. *Stranded* he called it, and he asked purt near every living, breathing rockwriter or rockwrite pretender of even quasi-note to contribute an essay on his/her favorite album—the one you'd bring to a so-called desert island. I know, I know: cor-*nee*. But each contributor got $750, a whole lot more than I'd ever made off a single piece.

And what kept me out, he told me three years later, was my rude behavior at the final Sex Pistols show, the last of the Sid Vicious era, at Winterland. My job that night, well it wasn't a job, it was a labor of love, had been to go out and insult the audience before and after each band. Some guy from the Pistols' crew thought it all seemed too placid, too pat—"like a Grateful Dead show"—and asked me to give the ticketholders a jolt. All the invective in my arsenal I dispensed—in spades—I was one uncouth lout—until Bill Graham physically picked me up and threw me out of the building—"You can't insult my city!" Although what, precisely, was/is rocka rocka roll—or punk—or any kind of youth-twitch—supposed to entail "if not that"? If not the high risk of behaving like a FLYING FUCKING ASSHOLE?

Marcus, who had been there, and been offended, never expressed regret for the slight, the exclusion, but later in the '80s he averred that, knowing what he knew *now*, now that he "understood punk," he would NOT have excluded me. Oh goody.

What I heard on the grapevine at the time the book came out was that he'd also disapproved of what I might *write*. The buzz was that Christgau, who "knew" me better than Greil did, told him, "Oh, he'd probably pick a *Doors* album anyway"—an odious no-no to Bob and Greil both—but that's just rumor. In his foreword to the '95 reprint of *Stranded*, Christgau, in a curious negative namedrop, draws attention to the lack of anything by "the irrepressible Richard Meltzer" . . . irrepressible? Is that like being a *bon vivant*? And if I couldn't be repressed, why the fuck did they have to repress me? (Like that of Meister Eckhart's cold germanic God, my presence remained in my absence.)

A more persistent rumble back thereabouts was that these bozos found my rockwriting "politically incorrect" (ostensibly: I wasn't as keen as they on helping rock-roll find, adjust, and micro-tune its moral/humanistic compass, or in lieu of its willingness to accept same, SUPERIMPOSING suchever upon it)—the first time I actually heard the now all-too-familiar aspersion. Basically, this signified only a slight upping of the transgressional ante, as I had already been deemed of dubious *intellectual* grounding. As far back as '73, Christgau was branding me "anti-intellectual": in a saner universe (in his purview), I'd have been tarred, feathered, run out of town.

What's daffy about *this* pair coming on so hoity-toity in their exercise of sovereignty is these're guys who need a telescope to reach—approach—make out the general outline of whatever it is they purport to be confronting, so mega-removed are they from any tangible earthly what-the-hey. Like most culture wags laureate, what they are—all they are!—is pious OUTSIDERS. (Like Sam and Ann Charters.) Breast-beating squares. (Like George Will and Norman Podhoretz.) Stuffed-shirt know-it-alls. (Like John Updike and Leonard Feather.)

As point-to-point-to-point-to-point arbiters of the socio-culturally valid, they're as embarrassing as the Medved Brothers.

They don't have the existential oo-poo-pa-doo to be trucking in anything so both high and low (and so alien to their alleged lives) as standard-issue rock and roll. In their frigging fifties, they haven't caught on yet that one thing rock does *rather well*, too well to ignore or dismiss—one of its stocks-in-trade—is SECOND-PERSON HOSTILITY. The many stations of I-dislike-*you*. Which isn't "good" or any such easy-moral A-equals-A, certainly isn't "nice," but it's the goddam rock-roll terrain, it's fucking *given*. Might I add "universal"? Such itchy biz rubs Bob and Greil the wrong way, especially when the targeting is, well, non-rational, irrational, and above all "unjust." Taxonomically prejudiced (and prejudicial). They insist, for inst, that ANY TIME a male gender-specific voice expresses antipathy to a non-male gender-specific other, UGLY SEXISM has reared its head—ring the alarm!—the voice forfeiting any claim to even *antipathetic* universality. It doesn't matter, say, that the gender voicings could be reversed, that with minimal change a female subject could be cussing out, shitting all over, a male object . . . that ill will is as central to rock as it is to boxing . . . it doesn't matter!

So meticulous have they been as rock watchdogs that they've troubled 'emselves over what Randy Newman might really 've MEANT by "Short People" (yes—of course!, Randy's being ironic—but should anyone even *say* these things?) . . . how poignant.

They try so-o-o hard to be good, caring New Deal Democrats, and good Boy Scouts, and far more telling: good boys, they've never been bad boys, never even tried it on for size. They wouldn't dare commit adultery. Never farted in the subway. They don't know danger from the inside looking out, locked away from any relief, asylum, any exterior safety net. Fuh, do they even know mischief? They've never tasted their own bile, never looked death in the eye in a mirror.

When I wrote somewhere that one of the things which helped kill Lester Bangs was WRITING, each of them accused me of romanticism—how can writing *kill?*, they questioned. Well, guys, it doesn't always kill, but it certainly comes closest when you're doing it right. Only when it makes active use of your blood, your heart, your nerves, glands, sex fluids, vertebrae and whatall, and don't forget your stink, in a word: your body. In a word: your life. They were more annoyed, I would guess, that I considered it a pity *rock*writing was the genre that gored Lester, that a diet of rock and nothing but had rendered him too dumb to get out of the way.

At the risk of overextending my own 2nd-person animus and getting downright ad hominem about all o' this, I'm gonna introduce a new term to the proceedings: COOTIES. I don't give a ding dang doodle if these blockheads ever stumble on some remote semblance of the True, or accurately peg the Good and/or the Beautiful—the smutch of their imperialist intentions will contaminate anything they touch, their seal of approval rendering LESS ACCEPTABLE the goods of its unfortunate recipients. In *my* idea of a saner universe, the sight and sound of such card-carrying outsiders fattening up, even commentarily, on the goodies of the culturally/intellectually aboriginal would release fucking ANTIBODIES in the world. Imperialist cooties: nothing to sneeze at.

Or if "imperialist" sounds too vigorous and resourceful—too vibrantly alive—like Teddy Roosevelt or Cortez or somebody—let's just call it "proprietary." Ideational as opposed to material proprietorship . . . dominion . . . superintendence of turf and sightlines. No matter how you slice it, the reigning King of Proprietary Cooties—let's print *that* on a shirt—is Greil Marcus.

It's hard to go very long without seeing this man's maiming-by-NOT-damning commentary on something. No other recent celebrity outsider—not George Plimpton, not Nat Hentoff, not Dr. Joyce Brothers—has functioned so relentlessly, so adamantly, as proponent, evaluator, certifier of relevance both passing and eternal, chalkboard huckster for so turgid a line of see-Spot-run. Michael Cuscuna? Well, that's only on jazz reissues.

So unremitting has he been in affixing his byline to so much NOT requiring his collusion, his stultifying illumination, and certainly not HIS italics, that every juxtaposition of it and *anything* has come to feel as WRONG (i.e., as corrupt) as the mating of basketball footage to "The Revolution Will Not Be Televised" on a Nike commercial.

A couple months ago, an article in the *New York Observer* complained about Marcus's liner notes for the reissue of the Harry Smith Folkways anthology. Author Mark Schone's beef was that in gushing all over Harry there was an implied denigration of rival folklorist Alan Lomax, who Schone felt deserved a better fate.

What irritated *me* about Greil's presence in the package was simply that—his presence—although I could nitpick and say his lyric/historical spinout on Clarence Ashley's "The Coo Coo Bird," for one thing, bore traces of a METHODOLOGY of song dissection (and archaeology) I introduced to rock-crit (and yes, was better at) in my first published pieces 30 years ago . . . but fuck, I'm too much the folkie and populist myself to ever invoke an intellectual "copyright"—ownership isn't my game. (I don't own things in the air, I don't even own names I've given them.)

Anyway, it would've been preferable, I think, for Schone to have been more patient: chances are, left up to his proprietary avarice (the pipe dream: champion something and you'll forever be associated with it), that Greil would eventually have carved his name on Lomax's legacy too . . . and still may. Who/what *won't* he put his name on?

Hey: this is a man who accepted payment to report nightly on a MICHAEL JACKSON TOUR for Ted Koppel's *Nightline*.

He even put his grimy stamp on one of *my* books, the '87 reprint of *Aesthetics of Rock*—which he didn't even like. And I didn't ask for (I wanted Billy Altman), but *he* insisted and the publisher acquiesced. Wittingly or un-, his intro did little more than bracket the work, trivialize it (first paragraph: "I'm most of all convinced that the book is not a joke"; key word: "convinced"—thanks MUCH, you fucker), make it small (while lauding its hefty page count), *finite*, bounded, glibly sum-up-able, socially agreeable (". . . the coolest book to be seen carrying"), no longer autonomous: a Greil-endorsed hunk-o-pulp.

The endorsement didn't even improve my case with the endorser. So shallow had been his display of regard for me, so much did he not deem me even a colleague, that I didn't make it onto the mailing list for his own next book, *Lipstick Traces*, and he balked at first when I asked for a copy (how much humiliation did I think I needed?), telling me to go bother his publicist . . . he was in no mood to do so himself.

It wasn't mere protocol that prompted me to ask him, as this was the tome in which Greil reputedly "came to terms" with the events of Pistols night at Winterland. When I finally saw a copy, I wasn't in the index, or on stage at *his* Winterland, or anywhere else. Once an apparent eyesore, I was now beneath his notice (both forward and back).

It was a book which struck me also as, yes, derivative—secondary—
and which M.T. Kinney would later proclaim a "broken-leg try at duplicating the Everest climb R. Meltzer pulled off in *The Aesthetics of
Rock*. On an insight level it's the pits"—he said it, not me.

So what the hell am I after?

My due.

Don't think I want credit for having "influenced" Greil, or Bob, or
the pen-pushers of their cardboard academy, for trailblazing an activity which inevitably *leads to them*. I didn't (and if I had, I would rather
I hadn't) and I don't.

But if they didn't actually "get it from" me, plenty of it, it didn't
hurt 'em to have me as forerunner. To have my trial-and-error, naked
as it was, ease the path and prime the pump.

Credit? I want credit for being Copernicus—Magellan—goddam
Socrates to their coffee-table Thoreau—and Thoreau to their
Michael Medved. (Do you have any idea how degrading it is at this
stage of my life to have to beat my own drum? What such a dance
does to my "dignity"? They can kiss my fucking feet.)

Lester Young once said of Stan Getz, who profited mightily from a
saxophone way-of-being Lester had pioneered: "There he goes driving *my* pink Cadillac." I don't want no Cadillac (though a middle-
class income, after all these years, would be o.k.); I want to terminate
the academy.

And what, *precisely*, is it that gives me the willies about the ascen-
dancy of their shit and not mine—other than the obvious?

The reality of their ultimate message. Everything they write testi-
fies: THERE IS NO JOY. NOTHING IS POSSIBLE. Regardless of
what *they* imagine or wish it to be saying.

Seeing this travesty and obsessing on its repercussions forces me to
redouble my efforts. I'm tired and tired and thinkin' I might maybe
resign from this sorriest of "callings," and here I am stuck with a bran'
new mission.

Needed (first things first): a countercootie to their cooties on
everything. On things I still love.

Shit.

Come one, come all, come onna my house! Come alooka my c'lection.

Hardly nobody comes t' see me no more—I bore their ear off
with "war stories," heh heh. The shameless EXHIBITIONIST in
me is left holdin' the bag—oh woe—but in an alternate lifetime in
the weeks preceding my death, visitors galore will come & pay their

"respects," and with whatever sumthin' I have got left I'll lead 'em to my *special albs*—ones I've retained mainly so strangers will ooh and ahh. People, I've found, are impressionable—sometimes you c'n impress them. (I so much want th'm to love me—doesn't ev'rybody?)

Those that're lucky and "suck up" to me enuff—just jukin', 'scuse me, jokin'!—or can prove they have read at least FOUR of my books, I'll give a fistful of albums to . . . my patrimony. Ain't got no offspring—childless—and the broad I'm livin' with, my final surviving womanperson, she don't care about this stuff—she'd jus' go & sell it. Besides, she's an old y'know, an oldperson—old as me anyway—how much time's *she* got? Y'can't take it w/ you—*I* can't—and neither can she, but THEY can take it HOME.

Watch out for spiders, don't mind the dust 'n' dinge—follow me, single file. Jazz upstairs, step lively . . . then the cellar.

Lookit: Thelonious Monk's signachoor on Five by Monk by Five, *source of the title—that's all—of the Stones'* 12 X 5, *a big sweeping hand; the LATE RICHARD GROSSMAN'S copy of Jimmy Giuffre's* Western Suite, *nice cactus, doncha think?*

Duke Ellington, Second Sacred Concert—*a stinker, t' put it mildly. Even with "A" personnel—Johnny Hodges ain't dead yet, Harry Carney, Paul Gonsalves, Lawrence Brown—'s almost as lousy as that one he did with Teresa Brewer, pee-yew. Check out the cover, tho: Salvation Army sticker. And inside: tickets to th'actual concert, row 1, signed by the Duke. The owner musta died and some dumbbell relative junked it.*

Claude Nougaro, Femmes et famines—*what an ugly Zappa-ripoff cover. He's got stigmata, what's the singular, a stigmatum? stigma? There's only, just on one cut, "Gloria"—not the "Gloria"—Ornette backs him up— a 14th-rate sweaty French chantoozer.*

Billy Harper, Black Saint, *first release on Black Saint the label, where's it, shit, I musta sold it. No—could I 've sold it?—I'm losin' my marbles. Or has the old lady been sellin'? Or stoleden by some "caller" . . . sheee. C'mon downstairs . . .*

Hackamore Brick, One Kiss Leads to Another. *One o' the great bands y'never heard, proto-punk. "Zip Gun Woman," "I Watched You Rhumba"—before the punk nut got cracked, it seemed like t' get there you hadda throw in a stiff dose o' the '50s. Urban proto-punk—this is New York—wasn't "garage music"—city kids don't have garages. Urban shabbiness, y'know, was a major early rock-roll ingredient. Look at this guy, Tommy Moonlight—and this was before Tom Verlaine, speaking of jive names, who the world coulda done without anyway.*

Flamin' Groovies, 'nother quirky (tho not too quirky) '70s chip-off-the-'50s. Less obscure than, more like an overrated pseudo-pre-punk—or pre-pseudo-punk—cult band. Their last halfway decent, Teenage Head. *The "Flame-Ettes," that's me, I was drunk in the studio, they needed handclaps. Me, Karin Berg, ah Karin—she and I were once . . . I won't say—and Jean-Charles Costa, my editor I b'lieve, can't remem'—a late installment of* Crawdad? *Boones Farm—was that* apple *wine?—and I couldn' keep th' beat, couldn't feel the timing, hadda watch them t' keep it up.*

Lester Bangs, Jook Savages on the Brazos, *only one that came out while he was alive. 'S kinda awful, he was doin' GALLONS of Romilar then, but he was my frien'—ya didn't know that?—I wouldn't sell it. (You got twunny-fi' bucks?)*

Velvets w/ the banana, a piece of the peel's missing but see, it was paper—not plastic . . . Satanic Majesties w/ the plastic "optical" thing—you're s'-posed to be able to see Hendrix somewhere—I've never seen him . . . Metamorphosis—*I doubt* this *is on CD—buncha gay stuff they put out after the Stones went to Atlantic—"I'd Much Rather Be with the Boys"—wanna hear it?*

More recent *Brit shit?—okay. Scritti Politti, 12-inch 45—what's this even called? 4 A Sides? Pre-Langue Release? How postmodrin. One "side," which?, I'm never sure, makes ref to Mussolini.*

Bow Wow Wow, See Jungle! See Jungle! *One o' the seven or eight greatest rocksongs, make that popsongs, of all time: "Chihuahua." A strange, almost a '50s kinda feel—do I overstate my "thing" for the '50s?*

WAIT—where's my Blurt in Berlin *. . . first two Mekons . . . Pindrop by the Passage . . . Prag Vec . . . the Australian pressing of the first Public Image??? There is something VERY WRONG 'round here, somebody's been, can't they wait for me to "go"? The greedy wheezers . . . 50 years of compulsive etcet'ra gone to naught . . . I can't bear it . . .*

THUMP THUMP THUNK . . . *my ticker . . . this is IT.*

Okay—each of you take 11 records—my fav'rite number—and leave the rest f'r Jimmy McDonough, 1040 Willow Ave., Hoboken, NJ 07030. I'll give yer regards to Tommy Bolin . . . Gene Krupa . . . Charlie Watts . . . oh th' pain, th' pain, th' . . .

So what was that brouhaha about "calling"?

Am I a goddam teacher—is that it? An "imparter of wisdom"? "Entertainer with a lesson plan"?

Or am I he who distances you from all teachers: "Think for yourself or perish"? (Rock itself, when it was a full-service enterprise, once fulfilled this function.)

Or just another overreacher struggling in vain to have the verbal side of life catch up, aloud, with the experiential? A head full of too many ideas, leaking, spilling—where to begin *directing* them? (It would seem that I'm the only man/alive whose writing is informed EQUALLY by boxing and wrestling, by jazz and rock . . . that's a lotta mental baggage!) The printed page as recycle bin: pass it on, reassign responsibility for babysitting hotstuff with no ongoing use even as ballast—I'm already topheavy—yet too valuable to treat as mere trash, to relegate to some nameless ideative landfill.

Or am I nothing but a blowhard in neurotic need of an audience— as brazen as any attention seeker with a lampshade on his head? (Character in a comic book . . . light bulb above his hairline flashes ON . . . next frame, a balloon: "Yes! I'll wear that 'shade awhile!")

If I jest, it's to deflect your judgment and mine re my state of denial 'bout this teacher b.s. In the final analysis, I'm as culpably, reprehensibly didactic (pedantic!) as anybody. To properly do my job, I have not only to hold *my* act together—keep it coherent—but also the world's. While no snooping academic, I mind the world's business— in the WORST way—and I don't mean I read the morning paper. (Or *The Nation.*) But you're in this too. Should we both accept the assignment, we get to meet in the middle, in *a* middle. You need to read it, I need to write it . . . ain't life a scream?

Psst! Mesdames et messieurs! The lowdown on . . . received cultural dandruff. I was a kid when rocka-roll was a kid—before the controls were set—and kidhood is half the story . . . regrettably. Before MTV? I was around before teevee! Eight years before Elvis was on, and that's not long at all, er, the *young* Elvis, not the old fat one they declared a saint in the name of crowd control, you had Hopalong Cass—hey, don't go to sleep, I'll get to the *good part* soon enough. Cut me some slack, okay? I feel like the misfit in *Pebble in the Sky*, time-traveling to straighten out, rectify mis—oh, you don't know that one, Isaac Asimov?, also before?, well that's alright, I'll just blah blah blah blah blah blah blah blah blah.

Off with his hat.

Which still leaves my, uh, custodial duties . . . Curator and Prop-master, Vinyl Division. RECORDS: the burden, the commitment. Even as props behind dark, gloomy curtains in airless subbasements, they're essential the way all designated essentials are: the universe would topple without them (but it all depends how strongly you designate). Like yellowed maps and extinct textbooks from everybody's squalid grade-school prison stay, without 'em the student-teacher charade just can't be "authentic." Besides, they're more for me than for you. Like a fat, over-the-hill Jake LaMotta, clinging to the mantra of Brando's "contender" speech at the end of *Raging Bull*, I need the ritual *fact* of my records (in all their balmy uselessness) in order to DEEM MYSELF armed and dangerous. So I can go to another room, as revved up as I'll ever be, for a FOR-MERLY EASY task. (With the "whole world," in a microcosm, watching.)

I wish my fetishes on no one.

Now let's get REALLY ponderous. Everything gets tougher. Nothing gets easier in this doghump of a life. While my powers ebb, THE BOULDER GETS BIGGER . . . the Sisyphus benchpress. My freaking task and welcome to it: to maintain the delicate filigree of my infrastructure for data retrieval, y'know from old hibernating LPs, maintain it by any means nec.; to coddle the collection, personally relating to each and every disc, that they might rest in readiness to someday (should it be required) yield their secrets, thus aiding me in not only putting my finger on but demonstrating to others what it wuz *that* it wuz, and in the process make prehistory "live again," as bizarre and implausible an eventuality as all the souls of all the departed being reconnected to bodies *some fine day*; to midwife a flame, long extinguished, which no match, no Bic, no collision with a comet can rekindle. This is some jolly gold-from-lead, square-the-circle, angels-on-pinheads type horseshit, folks!

But. All demons being equal, I think I'd rather be propmaster, worrying about decrepit matter, than propwriter, having to articulate its import. (Demons're encountered either way.) Of the two cheezy endgames, only one of which can KILL—as this piece, now 10 months old, is within a hair's breadth of doing—I would much rather fret over my shitty records than write about them.

Off with his face.

In *The Western Lands*, for all intents and porpoises William Burroughs' last important fictional work, the narrator (an old writer identical to the author himself) sets before himself the chore of *writing himself out of death*. Out of ever having to die. At book's end, so near/so far, he gazes upon a literal river of shit, uncrossable—the final image of finality, of mission failure. "The old writer couldn't write anymore because he had reached the end of words, the end of what can be done with words."

All I'm trying to do—while failing just as miserably—is write myself out of the rockwrite equation.

Look. Some days, possibly most, it occurs to me (in no uncertain terms) that rock, and all writing about it, has NOTHING TO DO WITH ANYTHING. Y'know: "anymore." Imagine a world where manymany, toomany people wrote about . . . meatless lasagna. (And thought they were hip—and "on to something"—for doing it.)

Do I really really really really *really* want originator's credit, or do I disown it? "I just think it should be *my* option, *my* call. (I'll keep you posted.)"

Off with his head.

I am the prophet of, of . . . oh, it'll come to me. It's, it . . . was . . . well,

um,

I FORGET.

I need to hear, I need to hear . . . "Where Have All the Good Times Gone." Kinks. One of the great mid-'60s masterpieces. On *The Kink Kontroversy* (Reprise RS 6197). Let 'er rip . . .

"Time was on my side" . . . "easy ride" . . . "yesterday" . . . "feet back on the ground"—well, it certainly is "the densest reference-tongue field known to man" (Borneo Jimmy was right).

Nice riff: dum . . . dum . . . *dum.* But it's, phoo, it's very tinny sounding . . . mushy . . . is that fake stereo? I'm not complaining, but soundwise it isn't all that . . . tumultuous. You'da thought . . . huh.

And again. Hmm.

Three times? Well . . . for the road. For the good times. Where the piss-shitty HELL did they go?

Great song, g'bye.

It will never come back to me.

"How rilly and truely cosmic this li'l 'treatise' would be," l'auteur dit (and I translate), "if only I could recall what it was I was on the VERGE of getting at."

Writing about music is *not* like dancing about architecture. Writing tends to be *about.* Writing about music is not very different from writing about trees. (Writing about *writing,* on the other hand, might be *something* like architecture about architecture—if only architecture could itself be about things: structure sussing out structure, self-consciousness of self-consciousness.) My objections to writing about music are not about untangling metaphors.

The vast ocean that separates any particular piece of music (as one order of things) from its impact on humans of the species (as another) is *unbridgeable*. They occupy different dimensions, they're apples and oranges, vastly different beasts. ("Correlate" them at your own risk.) Lester Bangs told me about some mental patient he met who claimed to've been "helped" by such and such a Black Sabbath album, as if, well, that was Sabbath's *value*. That they were IN TOUCH WITH various "disturbed states," and delivered an unsettling (yet right-on) mix of associated highs and lows . . . and maybe so. But isn't it likely that twice, three times, 40 times as many have been helped through the occasional horror by Carole King or the Captain & fucking Tennille? Merle Haggard? Alvin & the Chipmunks? The Monkees? Who are or aren't any more/any less genuinely in touch with . . . whatever. The POWER OF MUSIC—it's everything, and nothing. Like love to Colette, it's *the* great commonplace. Somewhat suspect when applied too globally, too generally. (Second opinion from Lou Reed? Art Schopenhauer? John Sebastian?)

A tougher question than Am I a rockwriter?: Was I ever a rockwriter? (Do I even really qualify?) (Am I "overqualified"?)

Three trains running, four trains, five and more. "There's the Soul Train, and the Coltrane, but gimme that good ol', dumb ol' Rock & Roll Train." IS THERE ALSO a rockwrite train? WHERE might it go? NOT the Land of Oo-bla-dee. NOT Old Cape Cod. No longer stops at Ilikeitlikethat. The local but not the express. I have rid' the train—I think I'm sure I believe I know. But I don't know I don't know I don't know (I cannot be certain): maybe it's just my train, not their train. No: I am not the only rider—I see multitudes of others—but I wonder: am I the only one paying FULL VERBAL FARE? Or is this a dream? (Is it Buddhism yet?) From a crackling loudspeaker: "Flaunt signature verbiage or die." OK, OK . . . I'll pay . . .

I changed my mind.
I lied.
All I have is yours.
I'm too, too generous.
Don't take me seriously.
No more serious than your life.
Don't tread on me.
Correct me if I'm wrong.
School is out.

Clothing optional.
Fast 'n' loose.
C'mon, pick a fight with me.
Write me a letter, drop me a line (if you're female and under 50, enclose a
pic). (And if, by chance, it's 1972: a pubic hair.)
I begin with truth.
Truth, that whore.
You're better off without her/him/it.
Can't you take a fucking joke?
Forget it.
If you can read this, you can write this.
You couldn't write this with a gun (knife) (crossbow) at your head.
Hey, d'I ever tell you the one about . . . ?
Too solemn for words.
(As your, ahem, teacher, it is my obligation to inform you that) it's OVER
. . . so turn out the light.

Or did I catch the WRONG rockwrite train?

128

As I Lay Dead

A chapter from my novel-in-progress.
   Like a terminal twit in a dreary Beckett play, I still cling to certain point-less rituals—some in fact w/ rock content.
   Is it "good" or "bad" that rock is part of my endgame spiel?
   "Reviews of wrestling and lubricated condoms": yes, this is how I fill my novels—like Gulcher *all over again. When I told you I wrote novels, what'd you think I meant,* The Great Gatsby? *It's publishers who force you to call something a "novel"—I'd just as soon call it a* book.
   Usually, no matter what size and scale whatsit I'm working on, I have a title in mind from the beginning. It's the doorway *to the whatsit; you can't start until you've turned the knob. With this one it's been hell trying to de-cide. Among the titles I've considered so far:* A Dust; Continued; Compul-sory Third-Person Sequel; An Unrequited Throb of Stiff Meat; Jerk a Little Off; The Graves of My Enemies.
   Right now, Graves *looks pretty good. Apropos of which, it is my wish on this dark, rainy Wednesday that my own tombstone read:*

IT WAS NOT ENTIRELY UNBEARABLE

Thanks again! Here's where I sign off.

Richard Meltzer
Portland, 2000

It's 2035. I've been dead 30 years. Welcome to my treasure trove. My hand-chiseled mausoleum. You and eight or nine others have stum-bled in here: *lots* of goodies, take 'em and enjoy! And take your merry time, they ain't going anywhere. Where the hell were you when I was alive?

Ah! the thudding frustration of "slipping through the cracks"—
"dying invisible"—or even worse: being branded a "cult writer"
(whatever *that* is. Sounds like caves and dungeons. Moonlight); the
bitter exhaustion of having to cheerlead my own act, my so-called career (why do we strive? why do we strive?)—fuck *me*. Luck was never
mine. Whatever could go wrong, did. You don't need a sob story. Not
the complete one. Now that it's over, what's the diff? What ever was
the diff?

But anyway, come in, take your shoes off, probe and grope me.
While I was alive I didn't care much for the notion of scoring—being
"discovered"—after I died. It means nothing to me now. "Me" doesn't
exist, not anymore, "I" don't either, and "we" never did.

Don't wanna sound like a frigging solipsist (*I die . . . it's over . . . I
take it all with me*), it has nothing to do with such biz. Obviously life
goes on—the last reader isn't dead yet—so here's how we maybe
should play it: I was generous then (i.e., now: *my* now), always gave
the whole wad away, squandered my fluids on writerly whims with but
the most esoteric of payoffs, spent 5-6-7 years on books that didn't
get me laid, didn't earn me a can of clams, and the bounty of that generosity lingers on. If I can have a corpse, if I can *be* a corpse, so can my
work . . . consider it dead. Bountifully. Does death fascinate you?

(While we're on the subject, I sort of doubt my corpse wishes were
heeded: to be left naked in the street for the flies to feed on. Please be
sure my grave is kept clean.)

Anyway, here 'tis: a gen'rous helping of smut, rant, provocative grocery lists, reviews of wrestling and lubricated condoms, bon mots,
lively filler, evidence galore of the author's having ripped the eyes off
his face, ripped the skin from his bones and poked it with an icepick,
hammered the bones with a claw hammer, lopped them with poultry
shears . . . a shitload of fine "stuff" from a deadman who knew how!

Hey, I *was* a contender—almost—in the final uneasy days of writing
as we the still-living know, er, knew it. Or am I lucky I ever got published at all?

None of which exactly *matters*, y'understand, but it can still be a
pisser, still living, to live with it. The taint of "failure." Non-recogni-
tion. Something almost like "shame." A cheesy burden on waking
consciousness. (Fuck me fatuous.)

And why *do* we strive? Why in the face of setbacks and etc. there
aren't sticks (bats) (clubs) enough to shake at, do we persist in *believing*
it matters? Damned if *I* know. (Don't give me any hogwash 'bout the
"indomitability of the human spirit.")

Listen, I grew up at a time when TV was new . . . none in my home till I was five years old. Imagine such a world (a world also without rock-n-roll). Now you're probably six steps beyond laser discs—I'm talking *your* now. Do "novels" exist anymore? Books as such (without compulsory audio/video/smellorama)? Is "text" just something you at your *option* download off a CD-ROM, database X or the Internet, or whatever's replaced them? (Do eyes exist anymore? Do teeth?) This is *not* a science-fiction novel. Or maybe it is. I don't care if you don't.

In any event, behold the document: a "kitchen sink" (as we might once have called it) of life-wish and death-wish and grandiloquent nullity . . . a swag chest knee-deep in glowing all-for-naught . . . a rich accumulation of aromatic dust.

Early in the final decade of the last century, I got interviewed for a French documentary about a 1960s band called the Doors. Their singer was hot shit for a while. "How," I was asked, "would you describe the sexuality they projected?" Well, I told the guy, making it up as I went along, it wasn't basic rock whiteboy sex of either the '50s or '60s, it wasn't black, y'know, R&B sex, the blues, and it wasn't British-style androgyny or anything especially kinky or even all that topically macho. It wasn't specifically *any* of that so much as—well—it seemed from *this* end, seeing them in this crummy little club every night, like nothing less than a musical evocation of MY OWN dick.

May this heap-o-pulp likewise serve as the ur-expression of YOUR vanity. A foretaste of your own aftertaste, of your own extinction. Don't be shy: use me. I don't mind at all being useful. Let my legacy be your legacy. Fuck legacy. Fuck fuck—I'm a duck.

INDEX